CHURCHILL–ROOSEVELT–STALIN

The Road to Pearl Harbor
The China Tangle
Between War and Peace: The Potsdam Conference
Japan Subdued: The Atomic Bomb and the End of World War II
(Revised Edition, 1966)

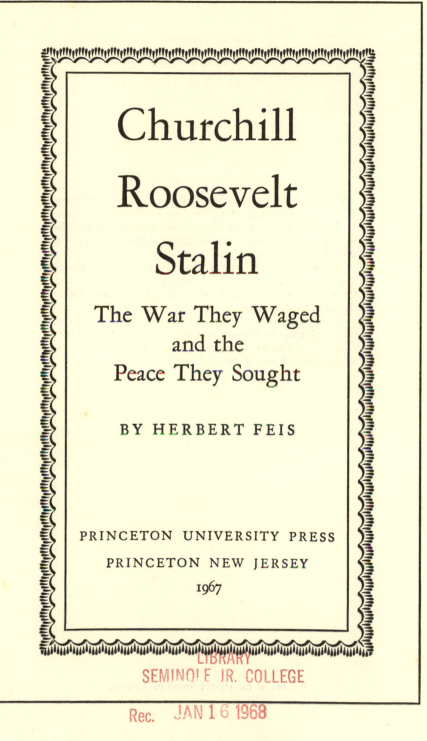

Churchill
Roosevelt
Stalin

The War They Waged
and the
Peace They Sought

BY HERBERT FEIS

PRINCETON UNIVERSITY PRESS

PRINCETON NEW JERSEY

1967

The passages quoted from the following works of Winston S. Churchill, *Closing the Ring, The Grand Alliance, The Hinge of Fate, and Triumph and Tragedy,* are reprinted by permission of an arrangement with Houghton Mifflin Company, the authorized publishers.

The short extracts quoted from John Ehrman's *Grand Strategy,* volumes v and vi, are reprinted by permission of the Controller of Her Britannic Majesty's Stationery Office, the authorized publisher.

Appendix II, entitled "The Three Who Led," was originally published by Herbert Feis as an article in the January, 1959 issue of *Foreign Affairs,* and is reprinted, by permission, in the 1967 edition of this volume.

Printed in the United States of America

FOREWORD
AND ACKNOWLEDGMENTS

THE will to write this book came from a desire to find out for myself what happened and why. In the telling of what I learned there is little invention and much care. I have favored consecutiveness over concentration on a few main dramatic occasions or acts. Since the fulness of reality—or truth, if you will—resides in the continuity of influences and behavior, it is to be perceived only by slow travel along the whole stream of eventful detail.

I have been much aided by others—to whom I want to make acknowledgment here.

The Honorable W. Averell Harriman encouraged and aided the effort throughout, sharing, in fact, in its origination. He has allowed me to use the records of, and connected with, his many assignments during the war, particularly as Ambassador to the Soviet Union beginning October 1943.

The State Department permitted me to utilize its records for the earlier period. Many members of the Historical Division assisted me— among them the Head, Dr. G. Bernard Noble, Dr. E. Taylor Parks, Chief of the Advisory and Review Branch, particularly in locating and evaluating material, and Miss Doris E. Austin, his assistant, for cheerful responses to many requests; also Mr. Charles A. Patterson of the Division of Records Management, who guided me with his incomparable knowledge of the files, and Miss Mary Ellen Milar of the Reference room. Similarly, Dr. Roberts Kent Greenfield, Chief Historian of the Department of the Army, responded to my queries whenever he properly could, and made it possible for me to read the draft of several chapters of a study in preparation by Dr. Howard McGaw Smyth: *The Sicilian Campaign; the Surrender of Italy,* one of the volumes of the History of the U.S. Army in World War II.

I am indebted to the Library of Congress for study room facilities and research assistance, particularly to Mr. Willard Webb, Chief of the Stack and Reader Division, and his assistants; and similarly to the

Council on Foreign Relations for full use of their library, particularly to Miss Ruth Savord, the Librarian, and her assistants.

I am obliged to Former President Harry S. Truman for permitting me to examine the collection of his correspondence with Churchill and Stalin during the spring of 1945, and to Professor H. F. Heller of the University of Kansas for helping me in so doing. Also to the Honorable Allen W. Dulles, Head of Central Intelligence Agency, for the loan of the manuscript of an unfinished narrative telling of the secret attempt to arrange for the surrender of German forces in Italy in March–April 1945. To the Honorable George Kennan, for papers written while he was Counsellor of the American Embassy in Moscow during the war, and for interpretative comment on some episodes of importance; and to Dr. Philip E. Mosely, for information which added to the significant papers he has published on matters dealt with by the European Advisory Commission while he was serving as Deputy to the American member; and to Professor Arthur F. Funk of the University of Florida, for the privilege of reading the manuscript of his study on our relations with the dissident French.

Others who have aided me in one way or another in the research for this book or arrangements for its writing and publication, are the Honorable Dean G. Acheson, Professor Philip C. Jessup, Professor Elting Morison, Professor John Hazard, Dr. Rudolph Winnacker, Dean Mc-George Bundy, Mr. Arthur Page and Mr. Harold P. Whiteman.

Then there are those who shared the labor and fatigue: especially Mrs. Arline Van B. Pratt, veteran of *The China Tangle,* for essential and comprehensive help far beyond the call of duty in research and critical examination of manuscript and proof; Miss Florence E. Thompson, for the patient and reliable work on the manuscript through its many revisions, and custody of the records; Miss Catherine F. Oleson, Miss R. Miriam Brokaw of the Princeton University Press, and Miss Ruth Forbesner of Columbia University; and for sustaining aid in all ways and parts, to my wife, Ruth Stanley-Brown Feis, who after editing and proof-reading prepared the index.

I am grateful to the Rockefeller Foundation for assisting me with a grant, and appreciative to the Columbia University Council for Research in the Social Sciences for lending its auspices to the project.

The aid given by persons in the government should not be construed as an indication of official sponsorship or approval, nor should that given by persons outside the government be taken to mean that they share responsibility for the contents of the pages that follow.

York, Maine   HERBERT FEIS

CONTENTS

PERIOD FOUR

The Summer and Autumn of 1943; the Collapse of Italy and the Problems that Ensued

PERIOD FIVE

To the Conference of Foreign Ministers in Moscow, October 1943; the First Coherent Consultation about Political Matters

PERIOD SIX

The Convocation of the Heads of State at Cairo and Teheran, November 1943; When the Three Wills Came Nearest Concordance

PERIOD SEVEN

Teheran to the Cross-Channel Invasion, June–July 1944: Despite Grave Contention over Poland Military Cooperation Proceeds

PERIOD EIGHT

Summer and Autumn of 1944; the Channel Crossing Achieved, while Political Issues along the Circumference of Combat Engage the Coalition

PERIOD NINE

From the Second Quebec Conference in September 1944 to the Conference at Dumbarton Oaks; Plans to Conclude the War and Efforts to Conceive for Peace after the War

PERIOD TEN

From the Churchill Visit to Moscow in October 1944 to the Yalta Conference; Wartime Political Accords and Coordination of Strategic Programs

PERIOD ELEVEN

The Conferences at Malta and Yalta, February 1945; Constant Military Understandings and Inconstant Diplomatic Compromises

PERIOD TWELVE

After Yalta; Corrosion within the Coalition as the Soviet Union Extends Its Realm of Control

PERIOD THIRTEEN

The Spring of 1945; Victory Close but the Common Cause Cut by Mistrust between the West and the Soviet Union

PERIOD FOURTEEN

May 1945; the Combat Won; the Three Wills at Odds, and the Oncoming Time Clouded

MAPS

PERIOD ONE

To January 1942: The Compulsory
Coming Together

---

1. The Start of the War Coalition

THERE is a continuity in the way in which the conditions of peace turn into war and affect the conduct of war. And a further continuity in the way in which the demands of war affect the conditions of peacemaking. This flow is unbroken. The student of peace and war gets the sense of being on a boat going downstream along a bank on which past history stands eternal, as it was, and then on from the present into the future.

The coalition against the Axis may be deemed to have come into full formal being when the Declaration of United Nations was signed in Washington on New Year's Day of 1942. But our glance back along the bank of history must comprehend what led to that event.

Great Britain and France had gone to war in September 1939 against National Socialist Germany after a humiliating effort to avoid that ordeal. They had been appalled by Hitler's brutal words and violent actions. But the British had been slow to judge German conduct because of an uneasy notion that as parties to the Versailles Treaty, they might be in some measure responsible. The French had been haunted by the suffering of the last war and distracted by internal divisions. Thus both had long hoped that their diplomacy either could make terms with Hitler, outwit him, or, toward the end, form a combination that might restrain him. This diplomacy had been streaked at times with the further thought that even if Hitler's aggression went further it would be directed toward the East, and that the Soviet Union, not themselves, would be the first to be beset.

The Nazi forces had moved east into Poland but in conjunction with the Soviet government. Britain and France had been shaken by this payment for their past compliance. Defense of their historic position, of their power to take care of themselves, at last had caused them, in standing by Poland, to go to war. National pride, touched with disdain, had supported that decision. But the one acclaimed reason for it was that Germany and its partners were making the peace intolerable. The only clear resolution at the start had been to bring Germany down, and Italy too if it joined Germany. All that had been asked of any available ally was that it should share faithfully this one major purpose.

Other war aims came after. Some were adopted to lead peoples—depressed by memories of the results of the First World War—to fight this one. Others came out of a wish for greater security against possible future attacks, or for the elevation of power and position, or for economic gain. Still others were conceived as a means for preventing future wars, of blessing the world with an enduring peace. All these were war-born. They emerged during the struggle of war. And so, on the one hand, they were subject to military needs, real or fancied; on the other, they were used at times for military ends.

The Soviet Union had been brought into the war even more unwillingly than Britain and France. Soviet diplomacy had at some previous intervals professed the wish to share in collective action for the restraint of Germany and Italy. But the western European governments had not been eager for this companionship. As expressed in an entry made by British Prime Minister Chamberlain, March 26, 1939, "I must confess to the most profound distrust of Russia. I have no belief whatever in her ability to maintain an effective offensive, even if she wanted to. And I distrust her motives, which seem to me to have little connection with our ideas of liberty, and to be concerned only with getting everyone else by the ears." [1] They were also afraid of the consequences if the Communist forces should thereby be admitted to the West.

By that time the Munich agreement had allowed Hitler to tear Czechoslovakia apart, leaving Poland and the Soviet Union exposed to German assault. And even after the seizure of Prague, Chamberlain had continued to try to keep at peace with Germany. Any qualms or fears that the Soviet authorities may have had about a deal with Hitler gave way before the chance to escape the conflict and profit from a war in the West. The deal was made in August 1939—a non-aggression pact, with a secret protocol partitioning control of much of eastern and central Europe and a trade agreement.[2] The Soviet government had hustled to claim the premiums. Soon Eastern Poland had been in-

---

[1] Keith Feiling, *The Life of Neville Chamberlain,* page 403.

[2] The main line of partition that was agreed on ran from the Baltic Sea to the Black Sea. In the north, Lithuania was left outside the Soviet sphere. In the south, the dividing line ended where the northern arm of the Danube Delta reached the Black Sea, forming the southern boundary of Bessarabia (which had been part of Russia from 1812 to 1917, when it was occupied by Romania). The two governments did not agree on the division of influence or control south or southwest of that line, and this area became soon afterwards one of the primary causes of friction between them.

By agreed on amendments to the Protocol made on September 28, 1939, Lithuania was awarded to the Soviet Union and the partitioning line for Poland was changed. The provision regarding the division of Poland will be found in our later account of Soviet-Polish relations. See page 30.

corporated in the Soviet Union; the Baltic States, Estonia, Latvia, and Lithuania had been gradually brought under Russian military control; the independence of the only other Baltic State, Finland, had been threatened; the Province of Bessarabia had been taken back from Romania, and Bucovina and the islands of the Danube, and international control of the Delta of the Danube had been ended.

In after years Stalin was wont to say that even when he entered this pact with Hitler he knew that some time or other the Soviet Union would have to fight Germany; that in fact the main purpose of his patience was to get the protection of buffer areas to the West, and time to build up Soviet forces. But it is clear that at the time neither he nor his colleagues had anticipated the swift and decisive German victory over France in June 1940, and the looming danger that the British Commonwealth would also founder. We may be sure the Soviet rulers did not foresee that within a year Germany would be in a position to turn against them. Certainly they did much to keep Hitler well disposed. They had tried hard to please him and had favored the Nazi war effort. Their propaganda had supported it before the whole world. They had seen to it that Germany got food and raw materials although the Russian people were forced to stint, despite the fact that Germany did not live up to its part of the bargain.

Weeks before the German armored cars began to roll across the Russian frontiers, both the American and British governments had warned Moscow that Germany was planning to invade. The Soviet government had ignored these unsought predictions. The wish to avoid war with Germany, or at least defer it, had been strong to the last, as marked by the way in which Molotov, the Soviet Foreign Minister, addressed himself to the German Ambassador in Moscow in their interview on the very eve of the attack (as recorded by the German Ambassador):

"There were a number of indications," Molotov began with suave understatement, "that the German government was dissatisfied with the Soviet government. Rumors were even current that a war was impending between Germany and the Soviet Union. They found sustenance in the fact that there was no reaction whatsoever on the part of Germany to the Tass report of June 13; that it was not even published in Germany. The Soviet government was unable to understand the reasons for Germany's dissatisfaction. If the Yugoslav question had at the time given rise to such dissatisfaction, he—Molotov—believed that, by means of his earlier communications, he had cleared up this question, which, moreover, was a thing of the past. He would appreciate it if I

5

could tell him what had brought about the present situation in German-Soviet Russian relations." [3]

Molotov could grovel as well as growl. But still the blow had fallen. The Soviet Union had found itself in a struggle to survive.

2. British and American Support for the Soviet Union

The British and American governments had decided to let bygones be bygones and had gone to the rescue. To Britain this had been an act of self-preservation. To the United States it had been a straight development of its current policy of aiding any country fighting the Axis, by all means short of war.

Churchill, by the beginning of April 1941, had become fairly sure that Germany was going to threaten if not attack the Soviet Union. So he had resumed his effort to effect some kind of working connection with the Kremlin. Eden had sounded out Maisky, the Soviet Ambassador in London. Maisky's response slid away, being merely that the Soviet government was not discussing any new agreement with the German government and that it was not worried about Nazi army concentrations. Churchill had overborne this answer. He had told Maisky that in case of a German attack Britain would be ready to help the Soviet defense in various ways. Maisky had then replied that such help would be the more welcome if Britain first recognized Soviet absorption of the Baltic States.

Despite this indifferent rejection Churchill had gotten set to offer support as soon as the Russians saw the Germans coming. He had sent a personal appeal to Roosevelt for parallel action on June 15, 1941. From every source of information, he had said to the President, it seemed to him that a great attack on Russia was imminent. "Should this new war break out, we shall, of course, give all encouragement and any help we can spare to the Russians, following the principle that Hitler is the foe we have to beat. I do not expect any class political reactions here, and trust a German-Russian conflict will not cause you any embarrassment." [4]

[3] *Nazi-Soviet Relations 1939–1941*, Publication of Department of State, page 355.
[4] Winston S. Churchill, *The Grand Alliance*, Boston: Houghton Mifflin Co., 1950, page 369.

Within the State Department the impulse to come to Russia's aid had been checked by resentment. The brusque way in which Russia, while working with Germany, had been demanding vital war material of us, as its due, had given offense; and its greed for territory had caused alarm. Thus, left to itself, the State Department, even after the German attack, would have done little more than relax restrictions on American exports for the Soviet Union. However, the President, eager to do more, had edged forward to line up with Churchill.[5] Winant, our Ambassador to Great Britain who was in Washington, had been asked to tell this to the Prime Minister. He had hastened back to England in time to join Churchill, Eden, and Sir Stafford Cripps, the British Ambassador to the Soviet Union, at Chequers on June 20th. Churchill, sure that the attack was just about to start, was engaged in writing the statement that he would make over the radio. As later told by him, "The American Ambassador, who was my guest at the weekend, brought me the President's answer to my message. He promised that if the Germans struck at Russia he would immediately support publicly 'any announcement that the Prime Minister might make welcoming Russia as an ally.'"[6]

Churchill has since commented that he had not the slightest doubt where British duty and policy lay. When his private secretary, Colville, asked him whether by joining up with the Russians he was not "bowing down in the House of Rimmon," he had replied, "Not at all. I have only one purpose, the destruction of Hitler, and my life is much simplified thereby. If Hitler invaded Hell I would make at least a favourable reference to the Devil in the House of Commons."[7]

In Churchill's broadcast made on the night of June 22nd, he said, in part, "We have but one aim and one single, irrevocable purpose. We are resolved to destroy Hitler and every vestige of the Nazi regime. From this nothing will turn us—nothing. We will never parley, we will never negotiate with Hitler or any of his gang. . . . Any man or state who fights on against Nazidom will have our aid. . . . It follows, therefore, that we shall give whatever help we can to Russia and the

[5] The Secretary of State, Cordell Hull, had been equally ready to do so. As recalled in his *Memoirs* (Chapter 70), he was ill at home when the news came of the German invasion of the Soviet Union; but he at once telephoned the President and Welles and said, in effect, "We must give Russia all aid to the hilt." And then, in the following days when he was recuperating in White Sulphur Springs, he recounts, ". . . I was in constant touch with the President and Welles, urging that we give Russia the most vigorous assurances of all the help we could extend." Pages 967 and 973. This and subsequent quotations from *The Memoirs of Cordell Hull*, edited by Walter Johnson, New York: The Macmillan Company, 1942, are used with the permission of the publishers.

[6] *The Grand Alliance*, page 369.

[7] *Ibid.*, page 370.

Russian people. We shall appeal to all our friends and allies in every part of the world to take the same course and pursue it, as we shall faithfully and steadfastly to the end. . . ." [8]

This is how the nature of the enemy influences not only the conduct of the war but what comes after. The peace gets fitted to their faults and the fears they have aroused. So the evil effect of men like Hitler and Mussolini lives far longer than they.

Parts of Churchill's broadcast were printed in *Pravda*. But the Soviet government did not hasten to respond. So on July 7th the Prime Minister had taken the initiative again. He sent a message to Stalin saying that Britain would do everything to help Russia that time, geography, and British resources allowed. And he held out a welcome for the military mission which the Russians had been wanting to send, in order to concert future plans. Stalin had proceeded to talk with Cripps about the terms of two possible Anglo-Soviet accords. One was to be a joint pledge for mutual aid and against a separate armistice or treaty of peace; that was completed and signed by Molotov and Cripps on July 12th. The other was to deal with political matters; that was left pending.

One week after this extension of the coalition, Churchill, old opponent of Bolshevism, had received his first direct personal message from Stalin. Wanted most of all was that the British should create a second fighting front in Europe—in Northern France and in the Arctic. Stalin argued that this was a good time for these ventures because Hitler's forces were all busy in the East. Churchill had answered quickly that Britain would try any and all military operations that it sensibly could. But he had then explained the problems created by limited means and geography: these, he said, in the view of the British Chiefs of Staff, made any thought of a large-scale successful undertaking in the West impossible at that time. He had reminded Stalin that Britain had been fighting alone for more than a year, that the battles at home and in the Middle East took all available land and air resources; and that the battle of the Atlantic and the movement of convoys took all British naval resources. Thus he had concluded that the only immediate new operation that the British could take was in the north by air and sea against German shipping.

They were, at the same time, doing their utmost to get planes to the Soviet Union, giving up some of their own and diverting others provided by the United States. They were also beginning to make special exertions to supply various products needed at once in the Soviet Union: boots and raw materials such as rubber, tin, wool.

Military necessity was uppermost in the situation. If Russia gave up,

[8] *Ibid.*, page 372.

while the United States was still wavering, the British Empire could hardly hope to hold out. In London this did not seem a time to ask questions or make terms. No matter what later troubles Soviet victory might bring, these were dim compared with the greater dangers that still hung low over Britain—death from the air, starvation, invasion, and the possible disruption of its whole empire.

The United States was not facing any such dire prospects. Thus the American government had taken more time to consider in what measure and on what conditions to make good the President's promise to contribute to Soviet resistance. Even granted the wish and the will to defy domestic opposition, the question was not a simple one.

By then—June–July 1941—the United States had adopted Britain's fighting cause (and that of the smaller opponents of the Axis—the Fighting French, Dutch, Belgians, Greeks, Yugoslavs, and Poles). It had engaged itself to stand behind their effort not only in the United Kingdom and on the seas, but on distant battle areas such as the Middle East. For this purpose, the weapons we were producing had to be gotten to wherever they were needed. To do that the American government was patrolling the delivery routes, at the daily risk of becoming engaged in fighting action. American troops were taking over from the British that control post in the North Atlantic, Iceland. Plans were being made further to extend our convoy operations, and to ask Congress to allow American merchant ships to enter combat areas. But Roosevelt at the time had been undecided about such further measures even though his military advisers were telling him they were necessary to save Britain. Popular opposition to steps still more likely to bring us into actual conflict was strong.

Concurrently, the American government was trying by persuasion and pressure to discourage any further Japanese military advances. Secretary of State Hull and the Japanese Ambassador in Washington, Nomura, had in April–May begun their talks about ways to ease the growing tension; Hull without much faith yet with a wish at least to postpone the showdown as long as possible. But the negotiating effort up to then had not progressed, and in July there were important new warning signals that Japan was about to start its next thrust southward. This danger in the Pacific was very much in the thoughts of the President and his advisers as they considered how fast and how steeply to enter the Anglo-Soviet coalition.

Despite these threats from the Pacific, one grim thought had ruled the American decision: that if Russia were defeated quickly and thoroughly, Great Britain, and soon the United States, would be faced with stronger and more confident assailants. The first official acts to which this thought had led were based on the expectation that Russian resistance would probably be brief, and that the short term allowed should be used to the utmost to get ready for the struggle to come.[9]

The President had moved cautiously and obliquely. He had allowed Acting Secretary Welles (on June 23rd, the day after the German invasion of Russia) to clear the way. The press was told: "In the opinion of this government, consequently, any defense against Hitlerism, any rallying of the forces opposing Hitlerism, from whatever source these forces may spring, will hasten the eventual downfall of the present German leaders, and will therefore redound to the benefit of our own defense and security." On the next day the President had been a little bit more definite both in act and speech, but only a little bit more. Soviet dollar funds in the United States were unfrozen and so made available to the Soviet government for buying weapons. The President at his press conference, while saying that he was ready to aid Russia, added that he did not know what the Russians needed—which was in effect an invitation to the Soviet government to tell what it wanted most. When reporters tried to lead him into discussion of his reasons or details of what we intended to do, he had dodged their curiosity. Thus when asked, "Is the defense of Russia the defense of the United States?" the President had suggested that the inquirer ask another sort of question such as "How old is Ann?" [10] Then two days after that, on the 26th, the White House announced through Welles that the Neutrality Law would not be invoked against the Soviet Union. This meant we would be able to provide it with war materials and American shipping would be able to continue to enter Russian ports, particularly Vladivostok.

During the next fortnight the Soviet government had submitted lists,

[9] This line of advice is well exemplified in the memos which the President received from his Secretaries of War and Navy who, in turn, listened to their professional military colleagues. Thus take Stimson's first memo of June 23rd which said in substance:

1. That Germany's action seemed almost like a providential occurrence.

2. That the Germans would be thoroughly occupied in beating the Soviet Union for a minimum of one month and a possible maximum of three months.

3. That the time should be used to push our movements in the Atlantic Theater of Operations with the utmost vigor.

"By this final demonstration of Nazi ambition and perfidy, the door is opened wide for you [the President] to lead directly towards the winning of the battle of the North Atlantic and the protection of our hemisphere in the South Atlantic. . . ."

Secretary of the Navy Knox in a letter to the President the same day said, "The best opinion I can get is that it will take anywhere from six weeks to two months for Hitler to clean up on Russia. It seems to me that we must not let that three months go by without striking hard—the sooner the better."

[10] *The New York Times,* June 25, 1941.

to us as well as the British, of its most urgent needs. These were immense.[11] While they were being studied, on July 12th, as already told, the British and Soviet governments had signed a joint pledge to help each other and stick together to the end. On the next day, the 13th, as the fighting on the Eastern Front went into its third week, Harry Hopkins had left for England to discuss matters of supply and strategy with Churchill and his advisers.

In London Hopkins had found a glimmer of hope that the Soviet forces would be able to hold out until winter. Churchill had been struck by the fact that Stalin, while urging Britain to make greater military effort, did not show any sense of desperate dependence on help; that, in fact, he had seemed more intent on talking about frontiers and spheres of influence after the war than anything else. Of this more will be told presently.

Roosevelt, during these same days, had taken vigorous steps to try to get weapons for the fighting Russians. He issued unusual orders to his administrators; as when on July 21st he directed that the Russian requests be reviewed at once, and that he be given, within forty-eight hours, a list of what could and ought to be shipped at once. He saw to it that these orders were heeded. Despite opposition in the Army and Navy and hesitation within the State Department, he got the first list through the mill by notes to his defense assistants that were straight commands. The Soviet and British governments were kept advised of this special effort—and Hopkins, in London, could count upon its continuation.

Because of the uncertainty about what was going to happen on the Eastern Front, Hopkins had found it hard to bring his talks with the British about plans for operations in the Atlantic and Middle East to a firm conclusion. So he had abruptly decided that he ought to hurry on from London to Moscow to try to find out more about the Russian prospects and the Russian needs. On July 25th he had sent word to the President, "I have a feeling that everything possible should be done to make certain the Russians maintain a permanent front even though they be defeated in this immediate battle. If Stalin could in any way be influenced at this critical time, I think it would be worth doing by a direct communication from you through a personal envoy." [12] The President had at once authorized him to go on to Moscow. He would

[11] On July 8th the Soviet Ambassador in Washington, Oumansky, had submitted a program of requirements which the various departments of the American government found staggeringly great, running to almost two billions of dollars, and including such items as 3,000 pursuit planes and 3,000 bombers.

[12] Robert E. Sherwood, *Roosevelt and Hopkins: an Intimate History*, New York: Harper & Brothers, 1950, p. 318.

be the bearer of a personal message to Stalin which would confirm our willingness to come to Russia's aid. No more than Churchill had Roosevelt at this time thought of asking anything in return except that the Russians should keep up the fight.

Hopkins had gotten to Moscow on July 30th, the same day that the Soviet and Polish government-in-exile signed an agreement, another act of alliance. In his first talk with Stalin, Hopkins had marked the nature of his approach. "I expressed to him [Stalin] the President's belief that the most important thing to be done in the world today was to defeat Hitler and Hitlerism. I impressed upon him the determination of the President and our government to extend all possible aid to the Soviet Union at the earliest possible time." [13] Stalin of course had been pleased by this statement, whereupon Hopkins had invited him to state what Russia needed most from the United States at once and then for the long war.

In their second talk (on July 31st) Stalin, responding to Hopkins' remark that the President was anxious to have his personal appreciation and analysis of the war between Germany and Russia, had described the whole military situation and outlook. As Hopkins informed the President, Stalin repeatedly said that he did not underrate the German army—their organization was of the very best and they had large reserves of food, men, supplies, and fuel enough for a winter campaign. But "he [Stalin] expressed great confidence that during the winter months the line would be in front of Moscow, Kiev and Leningrad—probably not more than 100 kilometers from where it is now." Stalin was all but sure that the Soviet forces could withstand the Germans until winter set in. But how the battle would go beyond that "would largely depend," he said, "on the ability to enter the spring campaign with adequate equipment, particularly in aircraft, tanks and anti-aircraft guns." And before the talk was over he had told Hopkins, as reported to the President,

". . . that he believed it was inevitable that we [the United States] should finally come to grips with Hitler on some battlefield. The might of Germany was so great that, even though Russia might defend herself, it would be very difficult for Britain and Russia combined to crush the German military machine. He said that the one thing that could defeat Hitler, and perhaps without ever firing a shot, would be the announcement that the United States was going to war with Germany.

"Stalin said that he believed, however, that the war would be bitter and perhaps long; that if we did get into the war he believed the Amer-

[13] *Ibid.*, pages 327–30.

ican people would insist on their armies coming to grips with German soldiers; and he wanted me to tell the President that he would welcome the American troops on any part of the Russian front under the complete command of the American Army " [14]

Hopkins had told Stalin both the American and British governments were willing to do everything they possibly could during the following critical weeks to send supplies to Russia. But he pointed out that only supplies already made could be sent in that period, and Stalin must understand that probably even this could not reach his battle lines before the bad weather began. He urged that talks be started of plans for the longer stretch of the war since it would be necessary for the American and British governments to take all requirements into account; and that thus they would not be willing to send heavy weapons "until a conference had been held between our three governments, at which the relative strategic interests of each front, as well as the interests of our several countries, was fully and jointly explored." Stalin had said he would welcome such a conference.

Hopkins had been elated over these talks. He was pleased by Stalin's sturdy, capable directness and firmness of decision. He was impressed by the note of assurance that the Russians would fight on, as shown by the nature of the Soviet requests. Thus he briefly reported to the President on August 1st: "I feel ever so confident about this front. . . . There is unbounded determination to win." Writing later of Hopkins' visit to Moscow, Robert Sherwood called it ". . . the turning point in the wartime relations of Britain and the United States with the Soviet Union." It marked rather, I think, the "point of no return." Hopkins' reports reflecting Stalin's stable confidence and transmitting Stalin's warm tributes to Roosevelt and the Americans had given a firm basis for an already strong inclination. The American government, which up to then had responded to Soviet requests without taking any obligation, on August 2nd accepted an official engagement. It had entered into an exchange of notes with the Soviet government which stated ". . . that the Government of the United States had decided to give all economic assistance practicable for the purpose of strengthening the Soviet Union in its struggle against armed aggression."

Hopkins had hurried away from Moscow, back to England, so that he might go along with Churchill on the warship that was to take him to meet with Roosevelt off the Newfoundland Coast. By the time they talked (August 9th–12th, 1941) Soviet resistance had lasted six weeks. The two men had before them Hopkins' convinced report that it would

[14] *Ibid.*, pages 339, 342–43.

endure until winter, and that season would give the Soviet Union the chance to rebuild its armies, improve its defensive positions, complete the relocation of war industries, increase its production of weapons, and better the equipment of its fighting forces. Stalin had already named the hope that the British would make a landing in Western Europe at once. Churchill had told him that could not be done. This had probably increased a sense of need to make plain to the Soviet government that British and American support was for the duration, not merely for the crisis. Roosevelt and Churchill, meeting at Argentia Bay, had decided (following up an idea of Hopkins) to send a joint mission to Moscow, thoroughly to discuss a continuing program of allocation and supply for the Soviet forces. They sent off a message to Stalin proposing this.

Stalin had welcomed the proposal. Churchill told Roosevelt he would send Lord Beaverbrook. It would have been natural for Hopkins (who had begun by then to assume control over the allocation of war supplies) to have gone back to Moscow, but his health would not stand it. The President had decided to send W. Averell Harriman, who was then in charge of war assistance affairs in London. By that time Harriman had a warm relationship with Churchill, and with many of the senior members of the British military and supply organizations, and much experience in working out methods of aid.

Upon his return to Washington from Argentia the President had at once set about trying to put the supply mission which was to go to Moscow in a position to meet Soviet requirements. His attitude is to be seen from the letter he sent to Secretary Stimson on August 30th: "I deem it to be of paramount importance for the safety and security of America that all reasonable munitions help be provided for Russia, not only immediately but as long as she continues to fight the Axis powers effectively. I am convinced that substantial and comprehensive commitments of such character must be made to Russia by Great Britain and the United States at the proposed conference." [15] At the same time the President asked for estimates as to the overall production effort of important items that would be needed for victory; the Victory Program of production in which Russian needs were to figure on a priority basis.

By this time the American military men were changing their opinion about Russian resistance and the advantages of sustaining it. For example, the Joint Army and Navy Board report, sent by the Secretaries of War and Navy to the White House on September 25th, said, "The maintenance of an active front in Russia offers by far the best

[15] W. L. Langer and S. Everett Gleason, *The Undeclared War,* page 792.

14

opportunity for a successful land offensive against Germany, because only Russia possesses adequate manpower, situated in favorable proximity to the center of German military power. For Russia, ground and aviation forces are most important. Predictions as to the result of the present conflict in Russia are premature." [16]

Still the President had taken care not to provoke argument about coming to the aid of Communist Russia. He put off from day to day what he knew he would have to do to carry out his policy—to be sure that before qualifying Russia for Lend-Lease Congress would not deny the necessary appropriation. In an attempt to clear the way he had tried to get Stalin to say something in approval of freedom of religion which might avert Catholic opposition.

The British government meanwhile was continuing work on measures to produce and provide the weapons that would enable Russia to fight on. It did so despite the fact that during this interval the back-and-forth talk between the British and Soviet governments was unpleasant—Stalin being, in Churchill's words, "surly, snarly, grasping, and so lately indifferent to our survival." [17] Churchill's messages, telling with zest what the British government was trying to do to help Russia, had drawn only dissatisfied responses from Stalin. The cheerfulness with which Stalin had talked to Hopkins had ebbed as the German assault grew harder to bear. His comments had virtually scoffed at what the British were doing in the struggle against Germany, and ignored the Japanese menace in the Far East. As bluntly put by him to Churchill in a message of September 4th: The Germans were not being prevented from moving forces to the Eastern Front with impunity; they ought and had to be; and the only way in which the situation could be saved was by creating during 1941 a second land front in France or the Balkans. Stalin wanted the British to draw thirty to forty German divisions away from the East. This demand was to be heard again and again; it was a constant dissonance in the theme of coalition.

When Maisky presented this message to Churchill he spoke so woundingly that Churchill—as he has told in *The Grand Alliance*—called him down. [18] To Roosevelt Churchill had confided the next day that although nothing in Maisky's language during this interview warranted the assumption, he could not exclude the impression that the Russians might be thinking of separate terms. This possibility had not caused the American and British governments to modify their mili-

[16] *Roosevelt and Hopkins*, page 417. See also Mark S. Watson, *Chief of Staff: Prewar Plans and Preparations*, pages 349–52.
[17] *The Grand Alliance*, page 452.
[18] Pages 455–58.

tary plans. But it had impelled them to hasten the dispatch of their joint mission to Moscow.

The British and American visitors had arrived in Moscow on September 28th. Both Beaverbrook and Harriman in their first words to the Russians tried to convey the eagerness of their countries to bring help. Yet at first the mission's reception had been, to use Churchill's word, "bleak." The subordinate Soviet officials had shown themselves skeptical, if not mistrustful, and swayed by the sense that Great Britain ought to start a second front at once and could do so if it wanted to. Then, at the first meeting with Stalin on September 29th, the mistrust had seemed to give way to good feeling. But at the second, ill will had been evident anew; Stalin had been rude to the point of insult, again seeming to treat the help being offered as of little importance compared to the burden the Soviet armies were carrying, and imputing that Britain was allowing the Soviet Union to suffer all the loss and agony. At the third meeting, still another change of mood and demeanor had been experienced. Stalin and Molotov had been receptive and enthusiastic. Since they stopped trying to exact more than could be given, an agreement had been reached with little trouble.

Beaverbrook, who was seldom displeased by his own performances, thought this turnabout due to his own clever plan of campaign. Harriman had found it more puzzling, especially Stalin's rudeness at the second meeting. Still he, also, had been glad of the "sunshine after rain," as Beaverbrook called it. The Russians, too, at the end had seemed fairly well content. Stalin had said he was. Litvinov, who was acting as interpreter, bounced out of his seat and said loudly, "Now we shall win the war." Molotov, in a speech that he made at the final meeting on October 1st, spoke of "our profound gratitude to the initiators of the conference" and said that the work of the conference "predetermined" victory over Hitler. At the dinner given by Stalin that evening joviality had reigned. Stalin showed his pleasure by the number of courses served, by the number of toasts proposed—some forty—and by the number of times he, Stalin, left his seat to clink his glass against that of the author of a toast—the whole macabre routine that was to become so familiar during the war conferences.

At Stalin's request the program of prospective supply was put in the form of a written Protocol signed at the Kremlin on October 1st. This set out the quantities of each item to be supplied for shipment to the Soviet Union from October 1, 1941 to July 1, 1942. These included 400 planes a month, among them 100 bombers; 500 tanks a month; a substantial number of scout cars and trucks; antiaircraft and antitank guns;

telephone equipment of all kinds; aluminum (of which, because of the German advance, the Soviet Union was desperately short); tin, lead, nickel, copper, magnesium, steel, oil, chemicals, rubber, leather, shoes, wool, army cloth, wheat, and medical supplies. All these goods and more were promised without requiring full information about total Soviet needs or Soviet stocks—information of the sort that was asked of every other country seeking Lend-Lease aid. The American and British authorities did not obligate themselves to deliver these products to the Soviet Union but merely to make them available "at British and U.S.A. centers of production for the Soviet Union." But it was specified that "Great Britain and the U.S.A. will give aid to the transportation of these materials to the Soviet Union and will help with the delivery." Later on, the Soviet authorities were to argue that this was equivalent to an obligation to see that the goods got to the Soviet Union, and to reproach the British government with a breach of faith when it suspended convoys to the North Russian ports.

Serious delays had ensued in providing and shipping many of the products promised the Soviet Union before and in this Protocol. But what was sent had been of real, perhaps vital, use to the Russians during the following winter. The planes and weapons made up in part for great deficiencies; the trucks increased the mobility of the army. The materials and machinery lessened the effects of the isolation of Petrograd and of the German capture and destruction of factories and power plants.

But more important in the immediate crisis had been the assurance given the valiant resisters that they had strong allies who would not let them go under. This they had needed sorely. For the autumn weather over the Russian plains had lingered late that year, and the Germans had been able to keep on attacking longer than had been expected. One great crisis had come in the middle of October soon after the agreement was signed. The Germans had broken the Russian defense at Kalinin and had come within thirty or forty miles of Moscow. The Soviet government had evacuated many of its departments and the diplomatic corps five hundred miles east to Kuibyshev. But Stalin and his chief military colleagues had stayed in Moscow and ordained that the besieged capital should be defended to the last. It is probable that the American and British support helped to make the defense so unyielding. The defenders were told to be of good heart because they were not fighting alone. Thus the Moscow radio (on October 14th) had broadcast to them:

"Our people calmly look into the face of truth. The enemy is trying to break through to Moscow. . . . Snow is falling on fields covered with blood. . . . Hitler cannot go through our winter. We are beating the Germans at Melitopol and at Murmansk, and at the same time powerful reserves are streaming to the battle front. Never will the Germans conquer Russia. While thousands of Germans are dying in the forests of Briansk hundreds of British aeroplanes were setting Nuremburg on fire . . . military supplies are being shipped to us and to Britain across the oceans. America is building 5,000 aeroplanes a month. Time is our ally. . . ."

Time, space, stout hearts and strong bodies, the freezing cold, the Western enemies of Hitler—these had prevailed. And around the bend, as events flowed along the banks of time, the United States was about to be pitched headlong in the war. This had happened on December 7th when Japan, embittered by our obstruction of its efforts to make itself supreme in Asia, bombed our base at Pearl Harbor and sank most of our Pacific fleet.

3. With American Entry into the War, the Coalition Is Completed

Japan, by entering the Tripartite Pact in September 1940, had joined its fortunes with those of Germany and Italy. It had chosen to become a member of that sinister combination which the American people were determining must not be allowed to prevail. Contrary to the hope with which this accord was conceived by its sponsors, we had not desisted in our support of China and Great Britain. To the contrary, from that time on the attitude of the United States toward Japan had hardened.

The final opposed measures which led to the climax had been taken in the following July. They are so well remembered that there is no need to review them here.

By November the talks between the Japanese and the American government (acting for the British Commonwealth, Chinese and Dutch governments as well) about a possible understanding were in a state of dismal dissension. In an agony of inner division Japan had tried to postpone the necessity of decision by offering a truce. It had proposed an agreement of brief duration during which the Japanese army in

Indochina was to take a first step backward and the United States and its associates were to resume their shipments of oil to Japan and suspend their support of China. The terms had been judged unclear and inadequate. After a week of tortured deliberation, the American government had rejected them. It had resolved against trying to make any accord of this sort. One basic reason had been fear that such an agreement would break up the coalition against the Axis. The Chinese government might feel justified in making a deal with Japan following our own. The Soviet Union, which was just barely managing to stand up against the Germans, might choose to compromise with Hitler rather than fight on. In sum, even if by then Japan had been ready for reform, the repentance had come too late. The conflict could no longer be eased by minor adjustments; its momentum was too great. Germany-Italy-Japan had forced the creation of a defensive coalition more vast than the empire of the Pacific for which Japan plotted; this was not now to be satisfied, perhaps endangered, by a pause along the fringe of the Japanese advance.

Thus the last American answer of November 26th had been to offer Japan not a bargain but a chance to join with the United States in the acceptance of a set of general principles of national behavior.[19] This was uncompromising. No space was left for the responsible Japanese leaders to pose before the Japanese people as successful statesmen. No remnant of reward for past aggressions was allowed.

The Japanese government, faced with this choice and driven on by its military elements, had chosen war. On the morning of December 7th (our time) they struck at the nations—and the principles—which were frustrating them.

Thus the American government had chosen in this crisis of war and peace to make a defiant contradiction of the whole Axis adventure. In the final hour the record it made was aimed to guide the future rather than to justify the past. It had grasped the dramatic chance of defining broad common aims for the whole cause to which it was proving its loyalty.

[19] As advanced by Hull early in the talks and reaffirmed in that final statement of the American position presented to the Japanese government on November 26th, 1941, they were:

a. Respect for the territorial integrity and sovereignty of each and all nations;

b. Support of the principle of noninterference in the internal affairs of other countries;

c. Support of the principle of equality, including equality of commercial opportunity;

d. Nondisturbance of the *status quo* in the Pacific except as the *status quo* may be altered by peaceful means.

This was the full resort to a practice to which the American government—particularly Secretary of State Hull—was addicted. At almost every dark turn in the past he had appealed anew to the brawling nations to heed the rules of good conduct. This had been helpful in drawing the states of the Western Hemisphere together in peace, and for their common defense. The principles propounded had varied in number and meaning. For a time they had been made to serve as a reason for neutrality, a substitute for taking sides in either the struggles in Asia or Europe. Hull could never quite grasp why other countries did not conform to them, and never lost hope that they would. For to him they were not vague or static or dreamlike. "They were solid, living, all-essential rules. If the world followed them, the world could live at peace forever. If the world ignored them, war would be eternal." [20]

In the same spirit as Argentia Bay the previous August Roosevelt had conceived with Churchill a declaration of principles and war aims which became known as the Atlantic Charter. As we were merging our fortunes with those of Great Britain and the Soviet Union, it had therefore seemed natural for us to seek to bless the common effort by a definition of the common aims for which we would be striving. Practical advantages may also have figured in the issuance of such a statement. It might elevate our association with foreign powers into something more than a military alliance. It would stand in the way of selfish and secret wartime deals that might cause the United States to recoil from the association, as had the secret treaties made during World War I. Then also, by providing a vista of a good and just future after the war was won, it could sustain the spirit of the peoples suffering under Axis rule. To Churchill, such a project must have seemed good for one other reason: the mere issuance of a joint statement on common principles for war and the peace would cement and dramatize the working unity of the United States and the British Commonwealth.

At dinner on August 9th—following a preliminary talk between Welles and Cadogan (British Undersecretary of State for Foreign Affairs)—Roosevelt had proposed to Churchill that they should issue a joint statement "laying down certain broad principles which should guide our policies along the same road." Churchill took the idea back to the "Prince of Wales." As usual with him, the span between idea and action was short. By the next day he had a draft ready for examination.

This draft had contained three of the four momentous affirmations made in the Atlantic Charter. These were:

[20] *Memoirs*, page 536.

First, their countries seek no aggrandizement, territorial or other;

Second, they desire to see no territorial changes that do not accord with the freely expressed wishes of the peoples concerned;

Third, they respect the right of all peoples to choose the form of government under which they will live.

To this third point in Churchill's text, Roosevelt had roughly pencilled in an added clause: ". . . and they hope that self-government may be restored to those from whom it has been forcibly removed."

Churchill approved the extension, and asked that it be made to read ". . . and they hope that sovereign rights and self-government. . . ."

Churchill's draft, in addition, had looked toward some form of international organization to provide security. The pertinent sentence read: "They [the United States and Britain] seek a peace which will not only cast down forever the Nazi tyranny but by effective international organization will afford to all states the means of dwelling in safety within their own boundaries. . . ." The President had struck out the phrase "by effective international organization." Churchill had urged him to restore it. Roosevelt had not wanted to, since he was afraid of the mistrust and suspicion that might be caused in the United States. Besides, as he explained to Churchill, he would not be in favor of creating a new assembly of the League of Nations. His thoughts about a future international organization were at this time cruising. He was sincerely convinced that a collective organization akin to the League of Nations could not work, and was restlessly searching for some other way to assure future political and moral order. At this time—August 1941—he was taken with the idea that the United States and Great Britain might be able to bring this about simply because they would be able to dominate the peace settlements, and have the power to suppress aggression; they were to act as the two policemen (who were soon to recruit a third, the USSR, and later a fourth, China).

But Churchill had been bothered by probable criticism in Britain of a statement of war aims which dealt solely with the transition period when some sort of joint police power would have to be exercised, and which omitted all reference to the need of some effective international organization after this period ended. So later that same day he asked the President to consider the introduction of a new clause into the final article in which they declared themselves in favor of disarming all nations who might threaten the peace ". . . *pending the establishment of a wider and permanent system of general security . . .*" [21] [author's italics]. The President, urged by Hopkins and Welles, had accepted. He had decided that it was all right since the whole para-

[21] *The Grand Alliance,* page 442.

graph made clear that there was to be a transitional period after the war, and that the permanent international organization would only be set up afterward. It will be seen how Roosevelt came later on to revise his schedule of purpose.

The American people in the main had responded to the Atlantic Charter with the same uncritical ardor which marked what Hull, on August 14th, said about it: "It is a statement of basic principles and fundamental ideas and policies that are universal in their practical application." [22] It was hailed not solely as a moral code by which nations ought to try to live but as a definite guide for settling the numberless questions that the war would bring forward. During the years ahead, as the narrative will tell, the American government tried very hard to have the coalition employ these (and confluent) principles as a basis for their combined decisions. When there was no sharp cleavage of purpose or conflict of interest, the effort succeeded. But where desires sharply clashed, principle was bent.

Principle, in other words, proved vulnerable to circumstance. Within a war coalition it must be so. Each member must give in to the others. Each must respect any of their wishes even though it be out of accord with its own interpretation of principle, and each must yield to any lasting fear or antagonism of the others. A coalition, in other words, is heir to the suppressed desires and maimed feelings of each of its members.

Then, too, situations arise as the fighting goes on in which some military advantage can be won only by compromising principle, and this is done. Furthermore, in every war the idea develops that a country has a valid right to keep what it has conquered by death and suffering, that this ought to be regarded as a principle. And lastly, nations may have at one and the same time conflicting desires, and thus favor conflicting principles. Such are some of the ways in which doctrine is battered.

But all this was realized only later on. For the time being in 1941 the principles of the Charter expressed prospects which made it easier to induce the American people to take measures nearer war. And as soon as we were at war, the American government had sought to bring a far larger group of countries within their fold—by the Declaration of United Nations signed on New Year's Day of 1942. This, while binding all governments at war against the Axis together in a full war alliance, pledged them to support the principles of the Charter.

The power of principle was in fact being subjected to a severe test

[22] *Memoirs*, page 975.

even as this Declaration was being signed. It appeared particularly that the Soviet government was going to insist on acceptance of territorial claims not easily reconciled in Western eyes with the avowals of the Atlantic Charter and the United Nations Declaration. Of this the story ought to be told before we turn to an account of the great strategic decisions which the coalition began to make as soon as the United States was in the war.

4. Principles to Govern the Coalition and Soviet Desires

During the period of association with Germany, the Soviet Union had greatly extended its frontiers. It had taken over the three Baltic States, the eastern part of Poland, an adjacent segment of Finland, and from Romania the Province of Bessarabia, formerly a part of Russia, and Bucovina and the islands of the Danube. Ever since, it had longed to have other governments recognize its control of these areas as legitimate. As soon as the question of a war alliance with Great Britain and Poland arose, this wish had been brought to the fore, without apology and in the belief that it was justified by history and current experience.

The Americans and British had been cognizant of this Soviet aim as early as June-July 1941 when they had first decided to come to Russia's support. They had merely allowed the issue to rest. So had Roosevelt and Churchill when, at Argentia on August 9th–12th, they had confirmed their intention of standing by this unthanking ally. The Atlantic Charter had put its sponsors on record (1) as wanting no new territory and (2) as opposed to territorial changes not agreeable to the peoples concerned. But there had been little time, even if there had been a wish, to consider the rough questions that lurked under the smooth surface of these statements. That was not the hour for the dissection of difficulties. So Roosevelt had been free to hail these provisions of the Charter as universally acceptable. So Churchill also had been able, in good faith, to join in praising these general vows, though resolved that they should not be construed as applying to the existing British Empire.[23] The Soviet government too had soon thereafter subscribed to

[23] In a speech in the House of Commons on September 9th, 1941, he explained: "At the Atlantic Meeting we had in mind, primarily, the restoration of the sovereignty, self-government, and national life of the states and nations of Europe now under the Nazi yoke, and the principles governing any alterations in their territorial boundaries

them (on September 24th through Maisky, its Ambassador in London) though in a qualified way.[24]

When Beaverbrook and Harriman had been in Moscow, working on the program of supply aid, Stalin had shown himself curious about the war aims of their governments. He had given a hint of skepticism as to whether they would be satisfied with the eight points of the Charter, and of the opinion that these would not cover the purposes he had at heart—such as compelling Germany to pay for the war. And he had again shown the wish to convert the war accord with Great Britain that had been signed in July into an alliance for after the war which presumably would deal with their political aspirations and intentions.

Soon afterward, the two countries had sharply differed as to whether or not Britain should declare war on Finland, Romania, and Hungary—who had joined Germany in the attack on the Soviet Union. Stalin had felt intensely that Britain should do so. Churchill had been doubtful whether that was wise, whether it might not mean the loss of a chance to separate these countries from Germany. This had led Stalin to say that he did not think there could be the mutual trust or clarity in the relations between the British and Soviet governments without an explicit agreement on war aims and plans for postwar organization.

Churchill had concluded that it would not be possible to have really good military cooperation unless the state of mind of the Russian leaders was improved and made more trustful. On November 21st, therefore, he had proposed to Stalin that Eden might accompany British military experts who were being sent to Moscow. His instructions, Churchill had explained, would allow Eden to discuss every question relating to the war, but his primary purpose would be to talk over war aims and peace settlements. Stalin had welcomed this advance.

The British had turned to the task of deciding what might be put up to the Soviet government. During this same momentous week of November 1941 (the 20th to the 26th) the American government had been engaged in writing out that statement of principles which was given Japan as a proposed basis for their future relations. No connection had been made at the time between the two efforts. But Churchill

which may have to be made." Churchill, *The Unrelenting Struggle,* page 248. Roosevelt had in mind a wider geographical application.

[24] Maisky's statement made to an inter-Allied meeting in London was characteristically ponderous. "Considering that the practical application of these principles will necessarily adapt itself to the circumstances, needs, and historic peculiarities of particular countries, the Soviet government can state that a consistent application of these principles will secure the most energetic support on the part of the government and peoples of the Soviet Union."

and the British Cabinet had known, as they were considering how far they might go to satisfy Russia, that war might come in the Pacific any day. It may be surmised that they guessed that if and when this occurred, it could not make any quick difference on the Soviet-German fighting front, and that Russia and Japan would not go to war against each other.[25]

It was only on December 4th, by which time Eden's instructions were pretty well set, that the American government seems to have been informed of the purpose of his trip to Moscow. Eden had then advised Winant, our Ambassador in Great Britain, that the purpose of his visit ". . . would be to dispel Soviet distrust and, without entering upon definite commitments, to give Stalin maximum satisfaction. Among other things he would try to secure a reaffirmation of Soviet acceptance of the Atlantic Charter and an official restatement of the assurances in Stalin's speech of November 6, as well as Soviet approval of the eventual disarmament of Germany and of federative agreements among the weaker European states." [26]

Hull had been worried lest Eden, to ensure Soviet war cooperation, might be led into an accord about Soviet territorial demands—at the very time when we were risking war with Japan because of our refusal to grant similar claims to frontiers formed by force. So on December 5th, with the approval of the President, he had hurried a message to Winant to be passed on to Eden before he got away to Moscow. The Foreign Secretary was to be told that American postwar policies had been outlined in the Atlantic Charter; that we thought it would be a great mistake for the Soviet, British, or American governments to enter into any agreements in regard to the specific terms of postwar settlements, or to take obligations as regards individual countries which would jeopardize the common aim of enduring peace; and that, above all, there must be no secret agreements. Winant had given this message to Eden on December 6th. This positive warning flared out of Hull's memory of the great trouble which the secret treaties, made

[25] These conclusions turned out to be correct due to Hitler's stubbornness. The unauthorized publication in the *Chicago Tribune* on December 4th of the text of ABC-1 Staff Agreements with the British of March 1941, the Joint Army-Navy War Plan, Rainbow No. 5, and Joint Board Strategic Estimate that had been signed by Stark and Marshall on September 11, 1941, caused the German military advisers to submit a revised strategic plan to him. This contemplated a suspension of German offensive effort on the Eastern Front, and the transfer and concentration of German forces for naval and air offensive against Britain and to secure control of the Western Mediterranean. But Hitler rejected the plan, in one of the most momentous military decisions of the war. See "A Military Danger," an illuminating article by Captain Tracy B. Kittredge in *United States Naval Institute Proceedings,* July 1955.
[26] As summarized in *The Undeclared War,* pages 824-25.

by our European associates in World War I, had caused President Wilson.

After the Japanese broke loose the next morning, the British government had hesitated about having Eden set off as scheduled for Moscow. But Churchill had concluded that the great new event did not lessen the need of a firmer basis for cooperation with Moscow, nor necessitate any change in Eden's instructions. So off he had gone, while Churchill was eagerly starting to plan for his first wartime visit to Washington; and while there, at intervals between military discussions, to complete with Roosevelt the United Nations Declaration.

While Eden was in Moscow, December 16th–28th, 1941, he and his colleagues in London had made a point of keeping the American authorities well informed. Members of his mission told Walter Thurston, Counsellor of our Embassy in Moscow, who had stayed behind in Moscow when the rest of the staff had moved to Kuibyshev, the general drift of the discussions. Then also, Eden's reports to the Foreign Office about his talks with Molotov and Stalin had been shown to Winant.

Eden had found out that he was expected by his hosts not only to confirm a friendly alliance but to pay immediate tribute to it. The pledge of alliance and of mutual good conduct based on familiar principles had not satisfied the Soviet rulers. What they sought was a definition of what the Soviet Union was to have at the end of the war. Stalin had proposed a written understanding regarding (a) the western frontiers of the Soviet Union after the war; and (b) the settlement of most other European political and territorial questions that would emerge from the war. These, Stalin had suggested in his first talk with Eden on December 16th, might be put in a secret protocol to the Treaty.

He and his colleagues were peering past the present frozen battlelines far into a victorious future. Their wishes had been definite, large, and firm. Stalin asked first of all recognition of Soviet boundaries as they were roughly before the German attack in June 1941. The Baltic States, the detached part of Finland, and the province of Bessarabia were to be kept within the Soviet Union. The boundary between Poland and the Soviet Union was to be based on the so-called Curzon Line, which meant in effect retention of almost all of Eastern Poland that the Soviet Union had occupied in 1939.[27] Romania was to grant special facilities for Soviet air bases. Additionally, Molotov had hinted that the Soviet government would also ask that its frontiers be carried into East Prussia, and that it wanted additional air and naval bases in Finland.

[27] An account of the derivation and status of this boundary line and a definition of it will be found in the Appendix.

In return for British assent to Soviet wishes about frontiers and territories, Stalin told Eden that the Soviet government would be glad to accede to British wishes. He said that he was ready to support any arrangements whereby the United Kingdom might secure bases and similar facilities in other Western countries—for example, in France, Belgium, the Netherlands, Norway, Denmark.

Churchill, on shipboard en route to Washington, had read somberly Eden's reports of these proposals. The brightest of his thoughts were absorbed in the making of war plans which were to be discussed with his great new ally. Certainly it was no moment to disturb the welcoming party by entering into an accord with Stalin so out of line with its fond precepts. Thus, he had sent back to Attlee from shipboard (on December 20th) a message on the subject for the War Cabinet. This had read firmly: "Stalin's demand about Finland, Baltic States, and Rumania are directly contrary to the first, second and third articles of the Atlantic Charter to which Stalin has subscribed. There can be no question whatever of our making such an agreement, secret or public, direct or implied, without prior agreement with the United States. The time has not yet come to settle frontier questions, which can be only resolved at the Peace Conference when we have won the war." [28]

Eden had held to this line though leaving open the way toward later acceptance of the Soviet terms. He had explained to Stalin that he could not sign an agreement guaranteeing recognition of Soviet frontiers or containing other territorial provisions. One of the reasons he gave was that the British government had promised the American government not to do so.[29]

Stalin had been gruff. He had said that he thought it axiomatic that the Soviet Union, in view of its losses in the war and its need for security, would regain all the territories it had. When Eden had referred to the principles of the Atlantic Charter, Stalin had remarked that he had thought that that Charter was directed against those who were trying to get world domination, but it was beginning to look as though it were directed against the Soviet Union. He had gone further, saying that if the British refused to recognize the established Soviet frontiers, it would look as though they were creating a chance to dismember the Soviet Union. Eden had soothingly denied these statements. He had assured Stalin that his government's refusal to validate Soviet territorial wishes in the Treaty did not mean that it thought these to be in conflict with the Atlantic Charter. He had not entered into dispute about the justice of any of them. But he had stood fast on the position

[28] *The Grand Alliance*, page 630.
[29] *Ibid.*, page 629.

that the British government, because of its promise to the American government, could not do what Stalin asked. Time was needed, he had said, to discuss the Soviet proposal not only with the American government but with those of the Dominions. Stalin had concluded that rather than sign a treaty which did not contain the desired provisions, he would wait and allow the British government to carry on these consultations. Eden had promised that they would be conducted promptly, and on this understanding the matter had been left in suspense when Eden left Moscow. Suspended but not forgotten. What happened next will be told in connection with the account of the visits which Molotov, a few months later, paid to London and Washington to discuss this subject along with that of the second front.

Even while these talks with Eden had been going on, the Soviet authorities had also been discussing a treaty with the Poles. Their country had been despoiled. But after the German invasion the Russians had grown inclined to restore it and treat it as an ally. In the course of these talks the Soviet authorities had advanced the same proposals about future Soviet-Polish frontiers as they had made to the British. In view of the crucial importance of this subject in the relations between members of the coalition—past, present, and future—its background and earlier history ought to be clearly recalled.

The reason why issues concerning Poland figured so vitally were various and deep. First was its geographical position between Germany and Russia. This made the matter of its frontiers and its diplomatic and military connections of great moment in any struggle for power. The tragic record of three centuries attested that fact. Both the Russians and the Germans thus viewed Polish questions through the vista of past conflicts with one another, and fear of future ones. The Poles had sustained themselves with pride and valor—which caused all compromise with their dreams to seem to them only another injustice added to the many past ones.

The Poland which had been restored as an independent state after World War I had been a disappointment to the statesmen and patriotic idealists who had striven for its creation. In the course of that miserable relay of intrigue that went on in Europe in the following years, Poland had touched hands with every possible partner.

The hostility between the Soviet Union and Poland had remained unabated during the interval between the wars while the German threat had become more ominous. The Poles had done nothing while Germany took over Austria. Then after Munich, when Hitler broke up

Czechoslovakia, they had seized the Province of Teschen (October 1938). This act had deplorable consequences; it had hurt Poland's cause and standing in the West and affected its title for sympathy.

In the spring of 1939 the Chamberlain Cabinet had been finally convinced that Hitler planned to make National Socialist Germany master in Europe, and it had determined that it must defend Poland. On March 31st the Prime Minister had stated in the House of Commons that ". . . in the event of any action which clearly threatened Polish independence and which the Polish government accordingly considered it vital to resist with their national forces, His Majesty's government would feel themselves bound at once to lend the Polish government all support in their power. They have given the Polish government an assurance to this effect." The French government had done the same.

The Soviet government had insisted that if any similar pledge on its part were to be genuinely effective the Soviet Army must, in the event of a crisis, have the right to march into Poland and Romania. But the Poles had been afraid of opening their frontiers to the Red Army even if it were coming to their defense.[30] They had refused their assent despite the fact that the British and French offered to get absolute guarantees of the eventual withdrawal of any Soviet troops that might enter Poland, and even to give "absolute guarantees of those guarantees." The Soviet government had taken the perverted view that the stubbornness of the Polish government meant that it was conniving with Germany, or was ready to do so.

What happened next has been told. In the notorious pact of August 23, 1939 the Soviet and German governments had again divided Poland up between them.[31] Having waited to be sure it would not encounter any British or French troops in Poland, the Red Army had crossed the frontier on September 17th. A sentence from the note which Potemkin,

[30] When on August 15th, 1939, the French Foreign Minister, Bonnet, raised the issue with the Polish Ambassador, warning him that in the event of a refusal anything was to be feared, including a German-Russian understanding directed against Warsaw, M. Lukasiewicz answered "M. Beck [the Polish Foreign Minister] will never agree to letting the Russians occupy the territory which we took from them in 1921. As a Frenchman, would you consent to entrust Alsace-Lorraine to the protection of the Germans?" *Defense de la paix:* II, Fin d'une Europe, pp. 277–78.

[31] A secret supplement provided that "In the event of a territorial and political rearrangement of the areas belonging to the Polish state the spheres of influence of Germany and the USSR shall be bounded approximately by the line of the rivers Narew, Vistula, and San.

"The question of whether the interests of both parties make desirable the maintenance of an independent Polish state and how such a state should be bounded can only be definitely determined in the course of further political developments." *Nazi-Soviet Relations 1939–1941,* page 78.

Molotov's aide, had handed the Polish Ambassador in Moscow, just a few hours before the invasion started, is notable as an effort to make an act of enmity appear as an act of kindness.[31a] ". . . the Soviet government proposes to take all steps to extricate the Polish people from the unfortunate war into which they were dragged by their unwise leaders, and to enable them to live a peaceful life."

The German advance had been more rapid than foreseen and the Germans had marched far east of the Vistula into that part of Poland which had been assigned to the Soviet Union under the secret accord. So Hitler had asked to have the dividing line changed. Ribbentrop had gone to Moscow again and an amended secret treaty had been signed. This allotted to Germany Lublin province and part of Warsaw province—thus pushing its frontier some seventy to one hundred miles farther east than the first accord. In return Germany had waived its claim for the greater part of Lithuania. At the time the British government estimated that almost five million Poles were living in the territory then annexed by Russia.[32] But the Russians denied this, and solidly asserted that the territory acquired had been and properly ought to be regarded as part of the Ukraine and Byelorussia.

The Polish state had been liquidated, but members of the Polish government and some senior Polish military commanders had escaped both invaders and found their way to France and England. They had set up a government-in-exile which presently located in London. The British government had recognized it, and accepted it as a full ally. It had provided the means for organizing important Polish air groups that played a valiant part in the defense of Britain and ground divisions who fought well in Italy and France.

The American government had likewise recognized this government-in-exile (October 2nd, 1939) and maintained diplomatic relations with it. But the Soviet government had scorned it, and had tried to wish it out of existence—until Germany in June 1941 had turned east and marched on through those parts of former Poland which the Soviet Union had absorbed. At once the question had come up, could the two

[31a] The reader may well be reminded of the utterances of a leading character in the fable of Red Riding Hood.

[32] On the basis of the 1931 census and without taking into account any subsequent increase. See statement Butler, Undersecretary of State, in House of Commons, October 18, 1939. An American study prepared by an Interdepartmental Committee estimated that on the basis of the Polish census of 1931, the territory occupied by the Soviet Union in 1939 had an approximate population of 11.8 millions, of which 4.7 (39 per cent) were Poles, 4.0 (34.2 per cent) Ukranians, 1.0 (8.3 per cent) White Russians, 1.0 (8.7 per cent) Jews, and the rest of diverse national origin or affiliation. See Appendix 16, page 492, *Post-War Foreign Policy Preparation 1939-1945*, Department of State Publication.

countries be reconciled? Could the Poles be asked to work with the Russians unless promised in advance that Poland would be restored at the end of the war, and with what frontiers?

General Sikorski, Prime Minister of the Polish government-in-exile, had wanted a reconciliation with the Russians. After talking with Churchill and Eden he had announced this wish on the radio as early as June 23rd—the day after the German invasion of Russia started. But he had added, "We are entitled to assume that Russia will cancel the [Soviet-Nazi] Pact of 1939 and bring us back to the Treaty of Riga of March 1921." The British government had avoided judgment on this issue as it strove to bring the two former enemies together in talk. So had the American government.

On the 4th of July Maisky had informed Eden of Soviet ideas about a renewal of relations with Poland. The Soviet government, he had said, was ready to deal with the London group as the government of Poland. It would give them facilities to form a Polish National Committee in the Soviet Union. This would be allowed to form a Polish National military force out of former Polish soldiers in the Soviet Union, for which the Soviet government would provide the arms and equipment. And it favored the establishment of an independent national Polish state—with boundaries "corresponding to ethnographical Poland." If, Maisky had gone on to say, General Sikorski and his government found this offer acceptable, the Soviet government was prepared to make a treaty with him to form a common front against aggression.

On this basis in early July 1941 the British had managed to bring Sikorski and Maisky together to discuss whether and how they might heal their quarrel. Their first encounter had been, as Churchill has recalled, "frigid." The Soviet government had shown itself disposed to accede to most of the Polish suggestions. But it would not agree to return to the restored Polish state those sections of former Poland which had been annexed to the Soviet Union. Maisky had argued, first, that ethnographically they belonged to Russia; second, that the British government had in July 1920 sponsored a frontier line (the Curzon Line) that was almost the same. Of this tracing on the map much more will be heard.[33] And third, that the experience then being undergone proved how essential these areas were to the defense of the Soviet Union, a point which Stalin had tried to drive home in his first wartime message to Churchill (on July 18th), remarking that, "It is easy to imagine that the position of the German forces would have been many times more favourable had the Soviet troops had to face the attack of the German

[33] See Appendix.

31

forces, not in the region of Kishenev, Lwow, Brest, Kaunas and Viborg, but in the region of Odessa, Kamenets Podolski, Minsk, and the environs of Leningrad." [34]

On these grounds, throughout the talks with the Poles, the Russians had stood firm: that Russia's western frontiers (and hence Poland's eastern frontiers) had been settled once and for all. This pronounced and unadjustable demand meant that the war would not bring a mutually pleasing settlement of the historic question which had devastated three centuries: how to divide the land area of this central part of Europe between Russians, Poles, and Germans.

Neither the British nor American government had seen an immediate way of removing this preventative of Soviet-Polish agreement. But the quarrel could be adjourned. That had been done despite the reproaches of the Russians and the doubts of the Poles. On July 30th, an agreement along the lines already described had been signed. The only provision which bore on the issue of Polish frontiers was a statement that the Soviet-German treaties of 1939 concerning the partition of Poland ". . . have lost their validity."

The same day this treaty was signed, the British government had given the Polish government an official note putting on record the fact ". . . that His Majesty's government do not recognize any territorial changes which have been effected in Poland since August 1939." Eden had given emphasis to this assurance by quoting it in a speech in the House of Commons on the same day. But in answer to a question as to whether this note meant that the British government *guaranteed* the 1939 frontiers of Poland, Eden had said it did not. Later, as the narrative will show, the British government came to adopt the view that the new frontiers which the Soviet government proposed for Poland were suitable.

The American government had similarly refused to promise to help Poland regain its former frontiers. It had taken refuge in a vague statement (July 31) which left ample room for wishful interpretation.

The Poles had tried to imprint their own views on their agreement with Moscow. Sikorski, in a public statement, had intimated that the frontiers should be restored as they were before the invasion from West and East. He had gotten his answer on August 3rd in *Izvestia* to the effect that the Soviet Union had promised nothing in that regard.

The resumption of official relations between the Russians and Poles had not led to easy cooperation in the common cause. They had proceeded to sign, on August 14th, a military accord stipulating the way in which the Polish army in Russia should be formed. But the Poles had met trouble after trouble in trying to carry out this plan. They thought

[34] *The Grand Alliance,* page 383 .

the Soviet default on some of its promises was willful. But also the complaining Poles may not have appreciated the extreme suffering and strain within the Soviet Union during this first autumn and winter of the German invasion, nor the Russian need for Polish labor for war work. Despite the obstacles and deficiencies, a small Polish army had been brought together. But one circumstance of which the Poles had become aware was that far fewer former Polish officers—out of the prisoner-of-war camps—came to join them than had been anticipated. The Soviet authorities had no explanation. The mystery had imprinted itself deeply in Polish thoughts and was to be the immediate cause of the later break in Polish-Soviet relations. But that still lay in the disappointing future.

In the meanwhile, after American and British mediation, General Sikorski in December 1941 had gone to Moscow again, just before the Eden visit. There he and Stalin had signed a Polish-Soviet Declaration of Friendship and Mutual Aid. The Polish Prime Minister had won some of the concessions he wanted but far from all. Stalin had promised again that all Polish citizens in the Soviet Union would be released without delay; but he meant, it turned out, only those whom he regarded as being of true Polish nationality and no others (Jews, Ukranians, and White Ruthenians). He had agreed that six or seven Polish military divisions were to be formed in Russia, to be equipped mainly by Great Britain and the United States.

Sikorski had been almost content with these promises, the best to be had. Stalin had also seemed pleased. But their talk had left the toughest of their differences, that of frontiers, unsoftened. Stalin had wanted to talk about it. He would have liked to get it settled before Eden came so that the issue would no longer hinder the completion of the desired treaty with Great Britain. In a span of amiability in their talk, Stalin had suddenly said, "Should we not now talk about the frontier between Poland and Russia?" But Sikorski knew that the frontier line was barbed wire and electrified. He said that he could not discuss it; more than that, he saw no need to do so since the boundary had been settled in 1921.[35] It may be that at this time the Polish government missed its

[35] Ciechanowski, who was Polish Ambassador to the United States at the time, has written in his book, *Defeat in Victory*, pp. 78–79, that Stalin tried to induce Sikorski to discuss frontiers by saying that the changes wanted were very slight, and would not seriously affect Poland.

According to W. W. Kulski, *Foreign Affairs*, July 1947, in an article called "The Lost Opportunity for Russian-Polish Friendship," Stalin said that he wanted the prewar Soviet-Polish frontier changed a little (Tchout-Tchout), adding that he would not, in any case, claim the town of Lwow, which was ethnographically Polish. The article seemed based on original information, but regrettably the author does not identify the record on which this statement is based, or even its source—and there seems no way now of judging its authenticity.

33

best chance to win some measure of compromise from the Soviet government. Russian powers of resistance were being most exhaustingly tried. Friendship and support in war probably meant more to the Soviet rulers just then than ever again.

Such revealed differences in political desires and ideas among the members of the coalition did not prevent progress in the discussion of main military plans. They were not forgotten nor ignored, as will be seen. But they were not allowed to stand in the way of the development of war plans and actions in the period ahead.

PERIOD TWO

1942: The Year of Main Strategic Decisions
and the Containment of Germany
(North Africa and Stalingrad)

5. Basic Strategy Determined: Europe or the Pacific First

THIS consecration to the war effort served the men who were doing the fighting. Under its influence the American military organization in particular felt free to proceed on three constant premises: that all members of the coalition were fighting the same war, not separate ones with different purposes; that decisions about military actions could be based on military grounds, and need not reckon with their political bearings; and that the war was to end only on complete surrender of the enemies.

However, the postponement, for military reasons, of decisions about political issues exposed the ultimate results of victory to the hazards of war. And while the fighting went on it left the field of action the more open to suspicion and maneuver within the coalition. For it provided a temptation for each member to pursue its own political aims through its military strategy. And each—as the narrative will tell— did so in some measure: the Soviet Union on the continent of Europe, engrossingly; Great Britain in the Mediterranean, preservatively, and the United States in the Pacific Ocean, waveringly.

But in the making of total American strategy, political purposes were in general subordinated. In no respect was this more evidenced than by our agreement that American combat effort should be directed first and foremost to the defeat of the Axis in Europe.

Since the military historians have so thoroughly traced the trail of this decision, here we will merely mark its main phases and features. The basic strategy had been delineated while the American government was still limiting itself to measures "short of war." The controlling principle had been stated in a memo by the Chief of Naval Operations, Admiral Stark (November 12, 1940). This had recommended that, after providing for the defense of the United States and the Western Hemisphere, American efforts should be directed "toward an eventual strong offensive in the Atlantic as an ally of the British, and a defensive in the Pacific." This general precept had guided the consequential staff conferences which were held with the British soon after (in Washington from January 29th to March 29th, 1941), and shaped the combined plan (called the ABC-1 plan) which had been adopted.[1]

American war plans had been revised to be in harmony with ABC-1.

[1] A convenient account of these conversations and of the resultant Report is to be found in *Chief of Staff: Prewar Plans and Preparations*.

Successive reviews had confirmed them—as marked in that joint memo which General Marshall and Admiral Stark sent to President Roosevelt on November 5, 1941, in the face of Chinese pleas for urgent American military help and the knowledge that Japan was about to take some further action that was likely to bring us into the war. The memo solemnly stated that:

"The Chief of Naval Operations and the Chief of Staff are in accord in the following conclusions:

a. The basic military policies and strategy agreed to in the United States-British staff conversations remain sound. The primary objective of the two nations is the defeat of Germany. If Japan be defeated and Germany remain undefeated, decision will still not have been reached. In any case, an unlimited offensive war should not be undertaken against Japan, since such a war would greatly weaken the combined effort in the Atlantic against Germany, the most dangerous enemy."

The loss of so large a part of our Pacific Fleet at Pearl Harbor and the swift Japanese landings in Southeast Asia had upset the execution of our prepared war plans. A thorough new look was taken not only at their details but at the principles which had shaped them. Churchill and his military advisers on their way to Washington a fortnight after Pearl Harbor (for the talks called the Arcadia Conference) were greatly worried lest we might reverse our policy and direct our combat resources first and mainly to the Pacific. As recounted by him, he was afraid that the American people might fail to understand "the true proportion of the war as a whole." He has written: "We are conscious of a serious danger that the United States might pursue the war against Japan in the Pacific and leave us to fight Germany and Italy in Europe, Africa, and in the Middle East." [2]

Thoughts about Russia's part in the wars in Europe and the Far East were also a possible cause of a leaning toward a reversal of strategy. We had tried right after Pearl Harbor to convince the Soviet government that the Japanese had dangerously dispersed their strength in their first southern thrusts; and so if Russia should join the United States, Great Britain, and China in concerted resistance, the Japanese could be severely handled. The answer had been a sustained refusal. But still American Chiefs of Staff worried over the chance that Japan should capture the Maritime Provinces of Siberia. This fear also stimulated the impulse to make our main war effort in the Pacific. Opposed to this, the Soviet government was urging the creation of another fighting front in Europe.

[2] *The Grand Alliance*, page 641.

The American Chiefs of Staff had again concluded that, with some intermediate adjustments, the accepted essentials of combined strategy still held good. The reasoned estimate which governed the conclusions reached at this first great U.S.-British war conference was well summarized by Churchill in a paper written for the British Chiefs of Staff and the War Cabinet on January 10, 1942:

"It is generally agreed that the defeat of Germany, entailing a collapse, will leave Japan exposed to overwhelming force, whereas the defeat of Japan would not by any means bring the World War to an end. Moreover, the vast distances in the Pacific and the advantageous forward key points already seized or likely to be seized by the Japanese will make the serious invasion of the homelands of Japan a very lengthy business. Not less lengthy will be the piecemeal recovery, by armies based mainly on Australia and India, of the islands, airfields, and naval bases in the Southwest Pacific area. . . .

"While therefore it is right to assign primacy to the war against Germany, it would be wrong to speak of our 'standing on the defensive' against Japan; on the contrary, the only way in which we can live through the intervening period in the Far East before Germany is defeated is by regaining the initiative, albeit on a minor scale."[3]

In their formal agreement of January 12, 1942, the American and British Chiefs of Staff hinged the balance between these two main areas of war on this provision that, "only the minimum of forces necessary for the safeguarding of vital interests in other theatres should be diverted from operations against Germany." Churchill has let us know that, "No one had more to do with obtaining this cardinal decision than General Marshall."[4]

In the Far East, it was stipulated, the enemy was to be prevented from capturing Hawaii and Alaska, Singapore, the East Indies Barrier, the Philippines, Rangoon and the route to China, and the Maritime Provinces of Siberia. The minimum forces to be used in these tasks was to be settled later on. Roosevelt had told Churchill that he would, if necessary, send 50,000 American troops to Australia and 25,000 more to occupy New Caledonia and other places on the route between the United States and Australia.

These January decisions, it was to turn out, did not closely regulate the deviation from earlier plans, nor even settle once and for all the argument over this element of basic strategy.

The assaults on the Dutch East Indies, on Malaya and the base at

[3] *Ibid.*, page 703.
[4] *Ibid.*, page 705.

Singapore, on the Philippines and on Rangoon (the great port of Burma)—all these induced a demand and need to divert more and more American forces to the Southwest Pacific. The Navy first, its pride struck and will fired, and under its new Commander-in-Chief, Admiral King, who was not associated with earlier strategic plans, pressed for emergency changes.[5] It advocated the use not only of our naval forces but also of our army and air strength first to protect remaining Allied areas in the Pacific and then to seize bases from which to hit back against the scattered Japanese. The excited appeals affected the allocation of our combat resources. Of the 132,000 army troops which were sent overseas during the first two and one-half months of 1942, only 20,000 were sent to Iceland and Northern Ireland, in accordance with previous plans, while about 90,000 were sent to stations along the line between Hawaii and Australia.

The clamor to do even more became disturbing to the top strategists in the Army and White House. Of all the pleas and analyses during this period in favor of clinging to the challenged plans, none were more vigorous and persuasive than those written by one of the Assistant Chiefs of Staff, Brigadier-General Dwight D. Eisenhower. The tone of his thought is suggested by a personal note which he made on January 22nd: "We've got to go to Europe and fight—and we've got to quit wasting resources all over the world—and still worse—wasting time. If we're to keep Russia in, save the Middle East, India and Burma; we've got to begin slugging with air at West Europe; to be followed up by a land attack as soon as possible." [6]

The nature of Eisenhower's reasoning is illustrated by the systematic statement which he presented to his colleagues on February 28th. Therein he argued that although Germany and its satellites had the greater combat power, Japan was, for the time being, in a stronger position since it was not at war with the Soviet Union. Furthermore, he went on to stress the point that while the combined effort of Britain, the United States, and the Soviet Union could be brought against German and Italian forces, this could not be done against Japan. And, lastly, that as a matter of decisive practical import, it took three or four times as many ships to transport and maintain a given American force

[5] Admiral Stark had actively supported the view that the Atlantic took precedence over the Pacific, and that the Navy should play a supporting role to a land war in Europe. Admiral King disagreed thoroughly with this policy. Thus his appointment as Commander-in-Chief of U.S. Fleet (a new title), because of his assertive personality as well as his opinions, was one of the important factors in turning strategy toward the Pacific after Arcadia.

[6] Maurice Matloff and Edwin M. Snell, *Strategic Planning for Coalition Warfare 1941–1942*, Washington, D.C.: Office of the Chief of Military History, Department of the Army, 1953, page 156.

in the Pacific as in the Atlantic. Therefore he concluded that strategic and supply considerations both substantiated the soundness of the decision to concentrate first against the European Axis. Along that line he advocated the development of a plan of operations against Northwest Europe in conjunction with the British on a scale sufficiently great to engage from the middle of May onward, an increasing portion of the German Air Force, and by late summer an increasing amount of his ground forces. The Joint Chiefs of Staff endorsed these conclusions on March 16th.

The President and the American military authorities began at once to try to translate this strategic design into a precise program and schedule.[7] For that purpose Hopkins and Marshall went over to London to talk with the British Chiefs of Staff and the British War Cabinet. On April 14th a provisional agreement was reached on a plan proposed by Marshall. Of this more will be told in the following section; within its broad span, prime effort was to be directed toward building up a great force in England for an invasion of the continent on April 1, 1943; and there was a secondary project for an emergency landing in 1942, if required to avert Soviet collapse on the Eastern Front.

The principle of the war in Europe first was thus preserved, but not without payment of a fee to those who were eager to push the fight in the Pacific. The London accords did not absolutely debar enlarging movements toward the Far East. Indeed the British, despite their wish to put the battle for Europe first, made their consent to the cross-Channel invasion project conditional on there being enough combat strength left in the east to defend India and protect Australia, New Zealand, and the line of communications and islands leading thereto. In response to the clamorous operational demands espoused by the Navy, by the Southwest Pacific Command under MacArthur, by the Australian and Chinese governments during the following months of

[7] The President felt called upon to explain and justify this decision to the Dutch government. The letter he sent to Queen Wilhelmina of the Netherlands on April 6th doing so was imbued with a curious optimism no doubt intended to cheer:

"Unfortunately we have to recognize the major conduct of a world encompassing war and I think we realize that the principal danger in the next six months is German success against Russia—for if Russia is driven to her knees this Summer Germany will be able to release very large forces against the Near East and the Middle East and seek to join hands with Japan.

"In other words, we are forced to come to the conclusion that our major strategy must be the defeat of Germany this Summer in her Russian effort, for the very simple fact that if this can be accomplished the probability is that Germany cannot survive another year. When and if that happens the combined power of the United Nations will not take long to drive the Japanese back into their own Islands. The Netherlands Indies must be restored—and something within me tells me that they will be. . . ."

1942, there were substantial diversions of combat resources to these areas. Early in May the President wavered under this combination of pressures and became disposed to send still more planes and men to Australia. But Marshall argued with effectiveness that this would destroy the cross-Channel project and the President withdrew in writing the approval he had hastily granted. The root of his answer to the dissatisfied, as may be traced in his message to MacArthur of May 6th, was,

"In the matter of grand strategy I find it difficult this Spring and Summer to get away from the simple fact that the Russian armies are killing more Axis personnel and destroying more Axis materiel than all other twenty-five United Nations put together. Therefore, it has seemed wholly logical to support the great Russian effort in 1942 by seeking to get all the munitions to them that we possibly can, and also to develop plans aimed at diverting German land and air forces from the Russian front." [8]

But the advocates of greater action in the Pacific were probably no more persuaded than was MacArthur, who argued—as in the message he sent Marshall on the 8th—that besides its other advantages this would be the best and quickest way to provide maximum support to the Russians. Still the President stuck stubbornly by his opinion. In his firmness during the following weeks there may well have figured the affirmation he made to Molotov (on May 30th) when the Soviet Foreign Minister was in Washington (about which visit much more will soon be told) that he might inform Stalin "that we expect the formation of a second front this year"; and he meant a second front in the Atlantic. If this was not borne out, it would not be because of his default.

The contest between sponsors of Pacific and Atlantic areas of action was stirred up again when in July the British War Cabinet drew back from the cross-Channel invasion and began to revive a project for landing in North Africa. This turn in judgment, of which the account must also wait, distressed Marshall. He switched about and briefly joined King and others who were continuing to urge a basic change in the distribution of our combat effort. At a meeting of the Joint Chiefs on July 10th, Marshall—Stimson being his buttress—proposed that there be a showdown; that the British authorities be told that since they would not go through with the plan which they had accepted in April, we would turn our backs on them and face to the Pacific for decisive action against Japan. And in a joint memo which King and Marshall sent to the President that same day they concluded: "If the United States is to

[8] *Strategic Planning for Coalition Warfare, 1941–1942*, page 214.

engage in any other operation than forceful, unswerving adherence to full BOLERO plans, we are definitely of the opinion that we should turn to the Pacific and strike decisively against Japan. . . ." [9]

Respectful as the President was of the authors of this memo, and inclined as he was to persuade them rather than command them, his answer, sent down to Marshall from Hyde Park on July 14th, laid down the law. "I have definitely decided to send you, King and Harry [Hopkins] to London . . . I want you to know that I do not approve the Pacific proposal." On getting back from Hyde Park to Washington on the next day he told Stimson that he did not like the tone of the Marshall-King memo in regard to the Pacific; that it seemed to him a little like "taking up your dishes and going away."

In the memo of instruction which the President gave the mission on the 16th, just before they left for London, he made clear that whether or not the British continued to refuse to commit themselves to an effort to cross the Channel in 1942 or the spring of 1943, Germany was still in his mind the enemy to be downed first.

"I am," he wrote, "opposed to an American all-out effort in the Pacific against Japan with the view to her defeat as quickly as possible. It is of the utmost importance that we appreciate that defeat of Japan does not defeat Germany and that American concentration against Japan this year or in 1943 increases the chance of complete German domination of Europe and Africa. On the other hand, it is obvious that defeat of Germany, or the holding of Germany in 1942 or in 1943 means probable, eventual defeat of Germany in the European and African theatres and in the Near East." [10]

The following sentence is of ironical interest. "Defeat of Germany means the defeat of Japan, probably without firing a shot or losing a life." [11]

Hopkins, Marshall, and King, in London, found the British adamant.

[9] *Ibid.*, page 269. During this period there was confusion in the use of the code name BOLERO, it sometimes being taken to indicate the build-up for the cross-Channel operation, and sometimes the operation itself.

[10] *Roosevelt and Hopkins*, page 605.

[11] It is of interest that this memo of the 16th was very different from the draft instruction for Marshall and King which the War Department on the 15th had prepared and submitted to the President. It is also of interest that Churchill, in *The Hinge of Fate*, says that he regards this instruction of the 16th as the ablest statement of war strategy which President Roosevelt ever presented to him.

Another cogent reason adduced by the President was that it would not be possible to conduct a decisive offensive in the Pacific until our Navy was much enlarged. Many more aircraft carriers and landing craft were needed. The President made this point in talking to Hopkins about his trip to London, saying that in the Pacific, "Troops and air alone will not be decisive at once—it requires the increasing strength of our Navy—which takes time."

Hopkins stressed this when reporting to the President. But rather than reverse basic strategy as between Europe and the Pacific, the President proceeded, as later pages will tell, to agree to TORCH, the North African operation, as a way of getting American ground troops in action against Germany in 1942. This major decision, as expressed in operational orders, gave the North African expedition priority over other American military activities in all other parts of the world. But it was not an absolute or all-absorbing priority.

In the months that followed, some new defensive operations in the Pacific, and even a limited tactical offensive there, were approved. The Navy and MacArthur found War Department resistance to their requests weaker than it would have been if the cross-Channel operation had been underway. Most of our Navy was already in the Pacific. The flow of troops and equipment to the Far East went on; until August at least it was actually greater than across the Atlantic. The balance changed only when the North African operation got actively underway. To glance ahead, a year after Pearl Harbor—with the fighting ranging along the whole North African Coast, with preparations for a cross-Channel operation in 1943 being resumed—the number of American Army forces employed in the Pacific against the Japanese was still roughly equal to the number deployed in the United Kingdom and North Africa. There were about 350,000 men in each of the two areas. Of the Army aircraft outside of the United States, about one-third was in action in the Pacific.[12]

To carry the story of allocation of resources a little further: from this time on the preponderant movement of both ground and air forces was toward Europe. But enough more were sent to the Pacific to make possible a vigorous start on the offensive. The principle which allowed this expansion in the Pacific to occur, while the war in Germany was far from won, was not stated explicitly in any planning memo or decision of the Joint Chiefs. But the idea seems to have been accepted that any increase in the forces we devoted to Mediterranean operations should be roughly matched by additions to our Pacific forces. The War De-

[12] The chief diversion from BOLERO was of bombing planes—in accord with a memo of Roosevelt's to the Joint Chiefs of Staff on October 24, 1942, in which he declared it to be necessary at all costs to hold Guadalcanal, and added, "We will soon find ourselves engaged on two active fronts and we must have adequate air support in both places even though it means delay in our other commitments, particularly to England. . . ." This memo gave temporary priority to urgent needs in the Pacific but did not alter basic strategy. See W. F. Craven and J. L. Cate, *The Army Air Forces in World War II,* Vol. II, pages 280–82.

partment used this equation in dealing with Admiral King and General MacArthur, and also with the British, as a discouragement of their efforts to get the American Army to make greater forces available in the Mediterranean. Thus, as an offset to the consent given at Casablanca in January 1943 to the advance from North Africa to Sicily, the Americans required approval for enlarged excursions in the South and Southwest Pacific. This utilized an increasing portion of American naval forces and consequently a disproportionate number of American landing craft. So strongly maintained was the claim upon these indispensable boats for active service in the Pacific that more were engaged there than were made available for the landing operations in northwestern and southern France. This was one of the main reasons—as will be noted at later points—for the postponement of both these ventures; the Allies waited for shipyards to build more rather than deplete the great assembly in the Pacific.

In review, while in every formal statement of basic strategy it was reaffirmed that Germany was to be defeated first—and while this was in the end effected—an effort of growing size and impetus was maintained in the Pacific until the climactic period of the cross-Channel invasion.

Continuing briefly to look ahead: it may be noted that the one place where the roll of priorities was allowed to unfold detrimentally was in the China-Burma-India Theater. We did as much as seemed necessary to keep China in the war, and little more than that. Of the 700,000 American Army men who had been sent out of the United States by the end of 1942, only 16,000 were in that theater, and most of those in India.[13]

The subordination of China to the combat demands of other theaters was in a degree one of the fees paid to the other members of the war coalition, Britain and the Soviet Union. The British and Russians were both unwilling to have scarce combat resources absorbed by the war in that country. It should be remembered that we thought we were only deferring greater assistance to the Chinese government—deferring it until victory over Germany would enable us and our allies, without dangerous strain, to beat a way into China, and along with the Chinese to expel the Japanese.

The tendency to devote American resources first to defeat Germany had, of course, many consequences. Had we taken the contrary course,

[13] *Strategic Planning for Coalition Warfare, 1941–1942*, page 228.

45

the state of the world and the relative position of the United States, Britain, the Soviet Union, and China at the end of the war would have been different.

It is hard, perhaps to the point of futility, to figure out what the ultimate consequences of such other decision might have been. But some conjectures may be let loose on these pages. They are intended merely to identify some points in this boggy land of the might-have-been.

1. If the operations in the Mediterranean and Italy and the cross-Channel invasion had been restrained or retarded, the recovery of the Soviet forces might have been slower; and at the end of the war the Soviet Union might have been weaker.

2. The American position in the Pacific at the end of the war might have been more dominant. We might have had substantial forces in China and possibly in Manchuria and Korea. The later settlements reached about these areas might, as a result, have been more satisfactory.

3. Hitler might have brought France more completely under his control, and perhaps have been able to devote enough strength to the Middle Eastern battle to defeat the British there. The Nazis would have remained dominant longer in Western Europe, breaking down more thoroughly the stamina and health of the people under their rule, and smashing their political institutions. These conquered people might have thought us indifferent, and more of them than did might have come to regard the Soviet Union as their one great liberating friend. This is in itself, I think, the basic political justification for our strategy.

4. The German assault on Britain by rockets and guided missiles might have been far more destructive; it might have become so deadly that the Allies would have had to invade France before their preparations were complete.

5. Had the defeat of Japan been accomplished while Germany was still fighting on, the end of the war in Europe might have been brought about not by the closing in of armies but by the first fall of the atom bomb on Germany. Then the course of surrender and the arrangements for occupation might have been different—for better or for worse?

Even these leashed conjectures indicate how great, how various, and hard to trace the consequences would have been of a strategic policy by which the foremost American fighting effort was directed to the defeat of Japan.

In tracing the line that was taken, I have skimmed past the strenuous argument which occurred between the Americans and British as to whether, assuming that the first great effort would be in Europe, their forces should try to cross the English Channel in 1942 or the spring of 1943 or rather attempt to land in North Africa and on the shores of the Mediterranean. To this issue the narrative will next turn.

∞-∞-∞-∞-∞-∞-∞

6. The Second Front in 1942: Cross-Channel Invasion or North Africa

∞-∞-∞-∞-∞-∞-∞

Concerning this issue there was among the makers of strategy a marked difference of judgment and contest of wills. The argument that took place may have had unrecorded political overtones; the Americans thought so. It had ups and downs; the plans were changed several times and the strain of discussion once or twice all but tore apart the combined war planning.

Churchill and his military group had brought to Washington in December 1941 a lively idea that the first combined military measure which the United States and Great Britain should take was a landing in North Africa. They had visualized this as an exciting initial step in closing the ring about the territory under German control. Churchill had brought up the project at the first informal discussion of this Arcadia Conference, on the night of December 22nd. He was afraid, he said, that if we did not do this quickly Hitler might foreclose the chance —by moving through Spain and Portugal down to the African shore. He was enthusiastic over the vision that British forces might soon gain a decisive victory in Libya and be pushing westward to the Tunisian frontier at the same time that an Allied expedition would be moving along the Mediterranean coast from the opposite direction. Roosevelt, to whom the project was not new, had agreed that this might be the thing to do. One reason was that this operation would give the American people a feeling of being in the war. Churchill probably had valid ground for reporting to the War Cabinet after this first session that "The discussion was not *whether*, but *how*" (Churchill's italics).[14]

In the report made at the end of the conference (December 31st) the military staffs had agreed, as stated in the official record:

"In 1942, the methods of wearing down Germany's resistance will be . . . ever increasing air bombardment by British and American forces . . . assistance to Russia's offensive by all available means . . .

[14] *The Grand Alliance*, page 664.

47

[and operations] the main object [of which] will be gaining possession of the whole North African coast. . . . It does not seem likely that in 1942 any large scale land offensive against Germany, except on the Russian front, will be possible . . . [but] in 1943, the way may be clear for a return to the continent across the Mediterranean, from Turkey into the Balkans, or by landings in Western Europe. Such operations will be the prelude to the final assault on Germany itself." [15]

But during the next fortnight adverse events both in the Pacific and in the Middle East had cut off the possibility that an adequate expedition to North Africa could be gotten ready in short order. As already told, the Japanese advances in the Southwest Pacific had forced the Americans and British to hurry out to that region many more ships, planes, and men than they had intended. At the same time German forces had managed to create a strong defensive position in the Eastern Mediterranean; and Hitler, halted by winter on the Russian front, had begun to send new divisions to the Middle East. Thus on January 13th, in response to the President's request for further analysis, the Chiefs of Staff had advised him that a substantial North African operation would have to await the return of troop and cargo ships from the Southwest Pacific—at any rate until after the middle of May. Churchill, greatly disappointed at the setbacks which British forces in Africa and Southwest Asia were suffering, had reconciled himself to this conclusion. He has put down his reflections on leaving the United States in the middle of January: "My hopes of a victory in the Western Desert, in which Rommel would be destroyed, had faded. Rommel had escaped. The results of Auchinleck's successes . . . had not been decisive. The prestige which these had given us in the making of all our plans for the Anglo-American descent on French North Africa was definitely weakened, and this operation was obviously set back for months." [16]

During the following period of waiting, American military judgment had come to the belief that the North African operation would be a wasteful use of combat resources, and a dangerous one.[17] The selection of a better course had been urgently argued in a series of discussions at the White House during March. Vigorous Stimson, backed by impressive Marshall, in accord with the staff planners headed by persuasive Eisenhower, explained over and over why it was essential to avoid "dispersion" and to concentrate on the build-up of forces in the United Kingdom for a cross-Channel assault. The supporting

[15] Gordon A. Harrison, *Cross-Channel Attack*, page 9.
[16] *The Grand Alliance*, page 706.
[17] *Strategic Planning for Coalition Warfare, 1941–1942*, page 177.

reasons were impressive. As summed up in another memo which Eisenhower had submitted to his colleagues: that since our lines of communication to Britain had to be kept open anyhow, there would be no diversion of American forces; that this operation would use the shortest sea route and so make the most of available shipping; that it would be enough of a threat to prevent Germany from concentrating against the Soviet Union in an effort to finish it off before the next winter; that the land approaches to Germany from this route were easier and better than any other; that it would be possible to get air superiority over the battle area from Britain; and that within this operation most British combat power could be used without endangering the British home defenses. These were to remain the standard arguments in favor of the cross-Channel invasion of Germany.

Toward the end of a tense meeting on March 25th, when the President, who had shown signs of wavering again, suggested that the subject be turned over to the Combined Chiefs, Hopkins made a strong plea against taking that risk of delay and devitalization, and urged that as soon as the Joint Chiefs had perfected the plan "someone" (Marshall) should take it directly over to Churchill and the highest British authorities. Marshall and Stimson had left the meeting with what they conceived to be an order to hurry the completion of the plan on which their staff had been working. They had done so. On April 1st, after listening to Marshall's report of the staff studies, the President had approved the plan and forthwith asked Marshall and Hopkins to proceed to London.

The plan as then roughly conceived, in what came to be known as the Marshall Memorandum, looked toward the start of an actual entry in France on April 1, 1943 (Operation BOLERO). The United States was to furnish about 30 divisions and over 3,000 combat aircraft, the British, 18 divisions and over 2,500 combat aircraft. The preparations for this ultimate action, however, were to be so arranged that it would be possible to attempt a much smaller assault (Operation SLEDGE-HAMMER) earlier in the fall of 1942, in either of two contingencies: to come to the rescue of the Russians if they should weaken; or to take advantage of any unexpectedly fine chance of victory arising from events in Germany.

This vision of a vast American force of men and planes coming to carry the main brunt of the invasion had stirred and impressed the British. Thus after a few days of consideration, on April 12th, Churchill informed the President that the British Chiefs of Staff were in entire agreement *in principle* with the U.S. proposals. Two days later the British Chiefs of Staff stated that they were acceptable. On that same evening of the 14th, at a meeting of the War Cabinet Defense Committee, attended by Marshall and Hopkins, Churchill cordially and formally endorsed them, properly calling them "momentous." But in reality British assent was tentative.[17a]

It is hard to tell whether Marshall and Hopkins had failed to assess, or chose to minimize, the streaks of uncertainty in British attitude. They had left London with a belief that a firm decision had been made. Marshall's report to Stimson and his colleagues in the War Department was to the effect that the mission had been accomplished in the face of very serious trouble and anxiety in Great Britain over the current dangers on all sides; and that the American project had been adopted with little change and light restrictions. But hardly were the American advocates out of sight of Whitehall than Churchill and his military advisers had become downcast by doubts. Their brief enthusiasm had passed.[17b] The more thoroughly they considered the proposed operations, the greater the risk of disaster seemed if it were begun before German strength was much reduced; or, short of that, the greater the chance that the battle might settle down into a prolonged agony like the trench warfare of the First World War.

The revulsion against the American proposals had been strong, stronger than Churchill let Roosevelt and Marshall know at the instant. He and the British Chiefs of Staff had virtually dismissed from their minds any thought of trying to make a lodgment on the Continent in 1942—even as an emergency measure. Anything that could be done that soon, they had concluded, would be only a dangerous and futile gesture that could not relieve the Russians in any serious measure. They reckoned that even if Allied forces managed to get into Cherbourg or Brest they would be penned in there and have to be defended all the next winter and spring; that this would be a serious strain on shipping and on resources and retard all other operations; and that moreover it would not compel the Germans to transfer important forces from the Eastern Front in 1942.

[17a] Field Marshal Alan Brooke, Chief of the Imperial Staff, who had played so able a part in saving the British army at Dunkirk, recorded in his Diary for April 14th: "A momentous meeting [of the Defense Committee] at which we accepted their proposals for offensive action in Europe in 1942 perhaps, and in 1943 for certain." But according to his interpretation, "What, in effect, the British Chiefs of Staff had agreed to was to start preparing plans, in conjunction with the U.S., for an invasion of Europe whenever it became a practical operation, and to welcome in the meantime the maximum concentration of American military strength in England. . . ." Arthur Bryant, *The Turn of the Tide, 1939–1943*, London: Collins, 1957, pages 355–57.

[17b] They estimated that the number of landing craft available would be so few—enough to land only four thousand men at a time—as to make the plan a "mere pipedream." *Ibid.*, page 373.

Churchill, in his own later account of his sway of judgment, implies that what most concerned him was the question of what was to be done before the invasion was attempted in 1943.[18] He did not wish, because of a devotion to unrealizable invasion plans for this earlier period, to let other great military opportunities slip away, especially the possibility he had discussed with Roosevelt in December of an expedition to North Africa in conjunction with a British thrust from the east. But I think that the swing of his opinion was wider. Clearly he had become disturbed over the whole prospect of invasion in 1943—or perhaps even in 1944. The Americans seemed to him to regard this operation as the decisive effort, the one in which Germany's main strength was to be met and smashed. The British, remembering 1914–1918, did not want victory to be won that way. They wished to postpone the stern encounter until Germany had been much worn down, deprived of its Italian ally, and then threatened from the Mediterranean side. Then the invasion from the west would be the closing act.

Whether or not the change in British inclination at this time went that far and that deep, it was real and definite. Harriman, who was then in London in charge of Lend-Lease and related activities, and in intimate working touch with Churchill, had noted this trend with worry. The divergence between what he understood Marshall and Hopkins were reporting to the President, and what the Prime Minister was saying to him, seemed great enough to cause serious later dissension. Anxious over this, he was about to make a special trip to Washington but fell ill.

The difference in willingness to venture upon a cross-Channel invasion had been revealed when Molotov visited London and Washington and raised the question of the "second front." For a comprehensive account of what happened then, the reader will have to turn over a few more pages. In this connection it is enough to note that during Molotov's first stop in London (May 21st–26th), before he went on to Washington, Churchill was cautiously indefinite. He refrained from direct and positive answers to Molotov's urgent inquiries as to whether and when the United States and Britain would start an operation against Germany in the west. But when Molotov got to Washington, the President was less guarded, and told Molotov several times that he hoped and expected to open a second front in 1942. Then when Molotov returned to London after his Washington visit, Churchill, while allowing him to retain the impression that it was probable that a cross-Channel operation would be started—possibly even in 1942—gave him

---

[18] See the illuminating statement of his views and tactics in Winston S. Churchill's *The Hinge of Fate*, Boston: Houghton Mifflin Co., 1950, pages 322–25.

a memo which stated that it must be understood that the British government was not giving a promise to that effect.[19] And on May 28th, in informing Roosevelt of the way in which his discussions with Molotov on military matters had ranged, he significantly said, "We must never let 'Gymnast' [landing in French North Africa] pass from our minds. All other preparations would help, if need be, towards that."[20]

By the time Molotov left London for home, the British government had defined the conditions which it thought ought to be satisfied before any cross-Channel operation was undertaken. In a meeting of the War Cabinet on June 11th Churchill proposed, and the War Cabinet agreed, that any such attempt in 1942 was to be subject to two principles: that there should be no substantial landing in France unless the intention was to remain; and that it should not be tried unless the Germans were demoralized by failure in their fight against Russia. Churchill, aware of the fact that Marshall and others were still set on the idea of trying a landing of some sort on the Continent in 1942, as immediate relief for Soviet forces and prelude to a main invasion in 1943, had felt it necessary to travel again to Washington to make his objections plain and effective. He knew that if he failed to persuade the Americans, the whole structure of Anglo-American military cooperation would come loose. He knew also that to prevail he would have to present some other project in which American and British forces could be used against Germany in 1942. The operation he had in mind was the North African one.

Churchill had made the days of talk (June 19th–25th) at Hyde Park and Washington resound with a skill of expression that made most of his command of fact. He exerted himself to convince Roosevelt that it was not excessive fear, or prejudice, or national calculation but careful military measurement that led him and his colleagues to their conclusion. He had not been able to find, he bluntly asserted, a single responsible member of his staff who thought a landing in the northwest could be achieved in 1942; the Germans had made themselves impregnable for the time being; and he shrank from sending troops to another Dunkirk.

Marshall, with Stimson thundering bolts of logic behind him, argued back stubbornly. He was less confident than Churchill that the Russian resistance could continue without emergency relief in 1942. The German offensive in the Crimea was rolling along; another great assault in

[19] *Ibid.*, pages 341–42.
[20] *Ibid.*, page 340.

the Kharkov region headed for the Caucasus was getting underway; and farther north in the Kursk region still another great German army was being massed for a sweep east, ultimately to Stalingrad. Even if the Soviet forces managed to hold some line of defense, he was afraid that the Germans might still be able to establish themselves so firmly and so far toward the east that they could spare greater forces to contest a later landing in the west. About the alternative proposed, that an expedition be sent to North Africa in 1942, he was wary; he feared that it would absorb what would be needed for a later invasion of France.

But, and despite the threat already related that the Americans would turn to the Pacific, the British stood fast against any cross-Channel venture in 1942 under the conditions then in prospect, and they reserved their freedom of decision in regard to making the attempt in 1943 until they could measure more definitely the opposition to be met. Toward the end of a very emotional all-day-long tussle at the White House (on the 21st) it was agreed that the American military organization should go ahead with full vigor with preparations for BOLERO until the first of September; at that time there would be a review of the situation, to see whether a real attack might be ventured.

This was a week of calamity in Libya. While these talks were going on, the grave news was received that Tobruk had surrendered, leaving the way open, it was feared, to an easy German capture of the whole Suez Canal region. Then the Germans might be able to move on with such speed and strength that the rest of the British forces in the Middle East might either be destroyed or have to be withdrawn, and the whole region up to India be exposed. This possibility had an impact on actual movement of combat forces and equipment which affected the prospect for any invasion attempt in 1942. Before the fall of Tobruk the Americans had offered to send the Second Armored Division to take part in the defense of Libya, if the British would provide the shipping. After the fall of Tobruk the British sought to have that division sent there as soon as possible and so asked the release of ships that were to have carried American troops to Britain—particularly the *Queen Mary* and *Queen Elizabeth*. In order to avoid that disruption of BOLERO the Americans urged the British to send a division of their own to Libya instead of an inexperienced American one; and in order to get them to do so, promised to provide the British forces in the Middle East a very large number of tanks, self-propelled artillery mounts, and other weapons. The emergency diversion of this equipment saved that situation, but hurt the chance of being ready for any attempt to land on the Continent. This the Americans had regarded with gloom.

On July 2nd, a week after Churchill left for home with the issue still unsettled, the American and British Chiefs of Staff took actions which marked their separate wills. The American group decided to go on the offensive in the Southwest Pacific, beginning with an assault on Guadalcanal. The British group sent a gloomy report to Churchill; they did not expect it was going to be possible to attain those conditions which the War Cabinet had specified ought to exist before launching a second front in 1942. Four days later Churchill presided over a meeting of the British Chiefs of Staff at which "it was unanimously agreed that operation 'SLEDGEHAMMER' [an emergency landing in 1942] offered no hope of success, and would merely ruin all prospects of 'ROUNDUP' in 1943." [21]

Churchill determined that the dissension and indecision must end; that, in words which he used later to describe his thought, "The moment had come to bury 'Sledgehammer,' which had been dead for some time." [22] Once again he put the reasons for his stand before the President in the plainest of terms. The essence of his statement, made in a personal message sent to Roosevelt on July 8th, was that "No responsible British general, admiral, or air marshal is prepared to recommend 'Sledgehammer' as a practicable operation in 1942." And then, later on in his exposition, "I am sure myself that French North Africa ['Gymnast'] is by far the best chance for effecting relief to the Russian front in 1942. . . . Here is the true second front of 1942." [23] Two days later, on July 8th, the British War Cabinet backed up Churchill's personal message by one which it sent to the British Military Mission in Washington for the information of the U.S. Chiefs of Staff.

Marshall still insisted that this would mean giving up major chances for a minor one. But the President had become really disturbed by the vigor of the differences which had emerged between his military advisers and the British, and impatient because this was preventing any forward action. Thus, on the 14th and 15th he told Marshall that he had decided to send him, along with Hopkins and King, to London immediately. There they were to reach *some* decision which would bring American ground forces in action against the enemy in 1942. There was to be no ultimatum to the British (the threat of the Pacific alternative). And if the British continued to refuse to participate in any cross-Channel invasion in 1942, some operation in Africa before

[21] *Cross-Channel Attack,* page 27. ROUNDUP was the newly adopted name for the later invasion operation.
[22] *The Hinge of Fate,* page 433.
[23] *Ibid.,* page 434.

the end of the year was to be determined upon. He then proceeded to rewrite the instructions for the mission. His drastic revision ended with two brief paragraphs of imperative tone such as he seldom employed:

"Please remember three cardinal principles—speed of decision on plans, unity of plans, attack combined with defense but not defense alone. This affects the immediate objective of U.S. ground forces fighting against Germans in 1942.

"I hope for total agreement within one week of your arrival." [24]

Without denying that some of the risks and disadvantages stressed by the Americans were probably weighty and correct, Churchill and the British Chiefs remained convinced that the North African operation was still the most promising of any that could be attempted in 1942. Thus they were unyielding in their talks with Marshall and his colleagues.[24a] This was grimly reported to the President. He accepted the conclusion and directed Marshall, King, and Hopkins to settle with the British on any one of several possible alternatives.

Thus, being compelled by higher command to give up what they wanted most to do, they chose the North African operation. However, they did this in a spirit of pessimism and resentment. This was reflected in the inverted form in which, at the final meeting with the British Chiefs of Staff on July 24th, Marshall wanted the decision to be recorded. He wished it to be stated that it was to be understood that ". . . a commitment to this operation renders ROUND-UP, in all probability impracticable of successful execution in 1943 and therefore that we have definitely accepted a defensive, encircling line of action for the CONTINENTAL EUROPEAN THEATER, except as to air operation." [25] And he sought to have it stipulated that the final decision as to whether or not to abandon the cross-Channel operation in 1943 (and therefore whether or not to go ahead in North Africa) was to be postponed until September 15th, and then to be made on the basis of the probable course of the war in Russia. The British Chiefs of Staff would not subscribe to this way of expressing the plans adopted. But the text that emerged from the meeting allowed Marshall to argue even after his return to Washington that the issue had not been really settled.

The President, however, had made up his mind. On the same day,

---

[24] Memo President for Hopkins, Marshall, and King, July 16, 1942, "Instructions for London Conference," *Roosevelt and Hopkins*, pages 602–05.

[24a] An hour by hour account of the consultations may be found in Brooke's Diary entries, July 22, 23 and 24, 1942, *Turn of the Tide*, pages 425–29.

[25] *Strategic Planning for Coalition Warfare*, 1941–1942, page 280.

July 24th, and probably before he had seen the final report which the British and American Chiefs of Staff developed, he sent word to Hopkins that he was in favor of landing in North Africa as soon as possible. Then he proceeded to ignore the contingent implications that might be found in its text. On the very next day, the 25th, he sent further word to London that he thought the North African operation should start not later than October 30th, and asked Hopkins to tell Churchill that he was delighted that the decision had been made and that orders were "full speed ahead." The President read this message to Secretary Stimson, Admiral Leahy, Generals Arnold and McNarney, but did not invite their comment.[26]

When Marshall, after getting back to Washington, continued to maintain the argument, the President was not perturbed and did not waver. On the 30th of July he told the Joint Chiefs that, as Commander-in-Chief, he had decided that the North African operation (under the new name of TORCH) was to be begun as soon as possible; that it was our principal immediate objective; and that the assembly of means to carry it out should take precedence over other measures, such as, for example, the concentration, training, and equipment in Great Britain of the forces for the future cross-Channel invasion. But in so ruling the President defied Marshall's and Stimson's prophecy that if the American-British forces became engaged in North Africa, there could be no attempted invasion of France in 1943. As General McNarney reported to Marshall after seeing the President, ". . . he could see no reason why the withdrawal of a few troops in 1942 would prevent BOLERO in 1943." [27]

Roosevelt did not foresee how great a retardation would be caused in both the preparation for a cross-Channel attack in 1943 and in Pacific operations. The long campaign in Tunis in which the American-British divisions were to find themselves enmeshed was to prove him wrong. But even if he had foreknown that this would happen it is likely that he would still have decided that the most important aim should be to get American forces in action against Germany and Italy without a further long wait. When interferences with the invasion

[26] Of all the American proponents of the invasion, Stimson was the most downcast about the decision, fearing it meant that the United States would have large portions of its combat forces scattered and isolated in North Africa, Great Britain, and Australia at the very time when, having defeated the Russians the Germans would be free to turn all their forces to the west. He put these views before the President by telephone, memo, and letter, up to and even after the President had made his decision. On looking back later upon the failure of his pessimistic prophecies to come true, he identified three reasons: The unexpected victory of the Russians at Stalingrad, enormous good fortune in the North African landing, the spirit of success over the German submarines.

[27] *Ibid.*, page 282.

happened, there was the consolation that Hitler, reacting to the North African venture, lost a quarter of a million troops and irreplaceable equipment, and took away air support from the Russian front. Lastly, it remains open to surmise whether, even if all the effort and resources used in North Africa had been directed toward the preparation of the cross-Channel attack in 1943, it would have been adjudged—by the British if not by us—advisable to attempt it while the Germans were still so strong.

As for Churchill, he was not too greatly concerned as to whether the North African operation might cause an indefinite suspension of the cross-Channel plan. The capacious record which he has made of his thought reveals the hope that successful extension of combat action to the south and north of Germany, along with the exhausting struggle in the east and the air assault, would have such impact on Germany that no invasion from the west would be needed, or only when Germany was almost prostrate and open to the final blow.

Further, he deemed the North African venture not an avoidance of any obligation which he and the President had assumed—to bring relief to the Russians in 1942—but the most practicable and reliable way of fulfilling this obligation. With this conviction Churchill took up, with his usual hearty courage, the task of reconciling Stalin and the Soviet military authorities to the fact that the Americans and British were not going to make a main assault on the Continent in 1942. To understand how and why this decision entered into later relations with the Soviet Union, it is necessary to look back carefully at what had been said to the Russians on the subject.

7. The Soviet Connection: The Second Front and Soviet Frontiers

As soon as the first German tank charged into the Soviet Union, Stalin had begun to clamor for action by its allies which would cause the Germans to divide their forces, and thus lessen the weight of their eastern assault. Both the Americans and British, despite their differences over how this should be done, were determined to accomplish it during 1942. How much this was to the fore in Roosevelt's thoughts is indicated in the message which he had sent Churchill on April 2nd, telling him that he was sending Marshall and Hopkins to London to

57

explain the salient points of the plan for the cross-Channel operation. "It is," Roosevelt had said, "a plan which I hope Russia will greet with enthusiasm, and, on word from you when you have seen Harry [Hopkins] and Marshall, I propose to ask Stalin to send two special representatives [Molotov and a senior military officer] to see me at once." And he said again in a letter which he sent the next day (April 3rd) to Churchill: "What Harry and Geo. Marshall will tell you all about has my heart and *mind* in it. Your people and mine demand the establishment of a front to draw off pressure on the Russians, and these peoples are wise enough to see that the Russians are today killing more Germans and destroying more equipment than you and I put together. Even if full success is not attained, the *big* objective will be."

Roosevelt had not waited for a thorough analysis of the military practicability of a cross-Channel operation before letting Stalin know that he had something of the sort in mind. As soon as the British had agreed to discuss the project he had let Stalin know. For this haste he had another major reason. He had hoped that by giving the Soviet government satisfaction in this vital military matter, he could cause it to desist in its efforts to have Soviet frontiers dealt with in the Treaty of Alliance with Britain which had been begun when Eden was in Moscow the past December and which was again being actively discussed.

It will be recalled that Eden had promised Stalin that he would consult the American and Dominion governments about the Soviet proposal that the frontiers which it claimed should be acknowledged in the treaty. Molotov had not allowed Eden to sleep over this. Hardly had Eden gotten back from Moscow to London when Molotov had sent him a reminder. Churchill was still in the United States, resting in Florida. From there he wrote Eden (on January 8th, 1942):

"The transfer of peoples of the Baltic States to Soviet Russia against their will would be contrary to all the principles for which we are fighting this war and would dishonour our cause. This also applies to Bessarabia and to Northern Bukhovina, and in a lesser degree to Finland, which I gather it is not intended wholly to subjugate and absorb. . . . In any case there can be no question of settling frontiers until the Peace Conference. I know President Roosevelt holds this view as strongly as I do, and he has several times expressed his pleasure to me at the firm line we took at Moscow." [28]

But Hull had continued to worry and fret. He knew how strong the impulse might become to grant any wish of the Soviet government in order to ensure the Russian will to fight on to the end. In any case,

[28] *The Grand Alliance*, page 695.

he had thought it necessary to keep pressure upon Churchill and the British Cabinet counter to that being exerted from Moscow. Thus on February 4th he had sent another memo to the President in which he again set forth the reasons why he regarded any and all wartime agreements about territories as bad practice: as contrary to the Atlantic Charter, as a reversal of the American refusal to recognize areas annexed by force, and as a device of power politics.[29]

But he also made clear that he was resisting the concrete Soviet claims in themselves, that there was a real underlying clash in ideas as to where the range of Soviet power ought properly to stop. Or in other words that our wish to defer decision, while a matter of principle, was also a device of diplomacy. Hull hoped later on to be able to persuade or induce Stalin to moderate his claims; to persuade him to put his trust in a postwar peace organization rather than in land boundaries; to induce him to do this by offering mutual pledges for the suppression of future attempts at aggression.

Prodded by Hull, the President on March 2nd had appealed directly to Stalin to omit territorial matters from the prospective treaty.[30] Stalin had answered that he was taking note of Roosevelt's views—nothing more. Maisky, the Soviet Ambassador in London, had explained later to the Foreign Office that the Soviet government had sent so curt an answer because it had not asked for American opinion. The Soviet government had urged the British similarly to disregard what it called "American interference." The British could not do that. But as Hull had feared, they had begun to doubt whether it was wise to continue to reject this pertinacious Soviet demand. They had become more worried about what might happen if they continued to deny the Russian wish, and dubious about what could be gained in the end by doing so. Their veer in judgment had been marked by the message of March 7th in which Churchill had told Roosevelt:

[29] The text of the memo is paraphrased in full on pages 1167–69 of his *Memoirs*.
[30] Roosevelt might have been touched by the same dread of disrupting the military coalition as swayed President Wilson during World War I to evade the issues presented by the secret treaties about territorial questions. As glaringly expressed by Colonel House in April 1917, àpropos the visit to Washington of Arthur Balfour, British Secretary of State for Foreign Affairs, "I hope you will agree with me," he wrote President Wilson, "that the best policy is now to avoid a discussion of peace settlements. . . . If the Allies begin to discuss terms among themselves, they will soon hate one another worse than they do Germany and a situation will arise similar to that in the Balkan States after the Turkish War. . . ." *Intimate Papers of Colonel House,* Vol. III, page 37.
The Poles were also protesting against the possibility. For example, on March 9th Sikorski warned Eden that recognition of Soviet claims would smash the foundations for future victory since it would end the faith and trust of "those countries which are inflexibly resisting the Third Reich and her satellites," and have a bad effect on the attitude of the neutrals, including Turkey, and of Catholics everywhere.

"The increasing gravity of the war has led me to feel that the principles of the Atlantic Charter ought not to be construed so as to deny Russia the frontiers she occupied when Germany attacked her. This was the basis on which Russia acceded to the Charter. . . . I hope therefore that you will be able to give us a free hand to sign the treaty which Stalin desires as soon as possible. Everything portends an immense renewal of the German invasion of Russia in the spring, and there is very little we can do to help the only country that is heavily engaged with the German armies." [31]

The Prime Minister's opinions about the Baltic States had not changed. But he had come to believe it imprudent to imperil Britain's cause in their behalf. As he wrote when reflecting on this episode, "In a deadly struggle it is not right to assume more burdens than those who are fighting for a great cause can bear." [32]

Churchill's fear was probably unjustified but easily appreciated. It would have been natural for him to remember keenly that British and French reluctance to accord Russian control of the Baltic States was one of the matters that had stood in the way of an agreement with the Soviet Union in 1939, and left the way open for the Ribbentrop-Molotov Pact. Be that as it may, two days later (March 9th), the Prime Minister had informed Stalin that he was urging Roosevelt to approve the inclusion in the treaty under negotiation of a pledge regarding the Soviet frontiers after the end of the war. Stalin had sent thanks. Churchill had kept up Stalin's interest by telling him that Lord Beaverbrook would soon be going to Washington, where he would help smooth the way to Presidential assent.

For the sake of the war, Churchill's request for acquiescence was hard to resist. But Roosevelt still disliked this payment in advance to the Soviet Union and Hull was still dead against it. [33] Various vocal minority groups in the United States were sure to be unhappy about it. So the President had scurried about in search of a compromise—or he called it that. This was to the effect that the Finns, the Lithuanians, the Latvians, and the Estonians who did not wish to be incorporated in the Soviet Union should have the right to leave these territories with their properties. Hull was ill and absent, and Welles, who was Acting Secretary of State, on April 1st had passed on this suggestion to Halifax. Eden had tried it out on the Russians. They had not been willing to have it included in the draft.

[31] *The Hinge of Fate*, page 327.
[32] *Ibid.*
[33] According to Sumner Welles's *Seven Decisions That Shaped History*, pages 134–35, the Joint Chiefs of Staff were also opposed.

Such had been the much ruffled situation within the coalition when Hopkins and Marshall arrived in London on April 8th to discuss the cross-Channel invasion project. Hopkins, as instructed, had first of all made it clear that the American government was still much against formal recognition of Soviet frontier claims. As recorded in the memo which he made on April 9th, after talking with Churchill and Eden:

"I also told Eden the President's position about signing the treaty with Russia, making it perfectly clear that the President did not approve of this action. I told Eden the President could not, of course, prevent them from signing it but in the last analysis it was a decision the British must make and that no useful purpose could be served by exploring it further with the Russians. I impressed on Eden as strongly as I could the President's belief that our main proposal here [the second front] should take the heat off Russia's diplomatic demands upon England." [34]

Here is the clue to the hurried, premature invitation to Molotov to visit Washington. The Soviet government was to be lured away from one boon by a choicer one, away from its absorption in frontiers by the attraction of quick military relief.

Two days later (on the 11th) Roosevelt had proceeded with the step which he had told Churchill he was going to take. He sent a message to Stalin which, after expressing regrets that he and Stalin could not themselves arrange to meet soon, said he thought that it was of the utmost military importance that they have, as soon as might be, the nearest possible approach to an exchange of views. "I have in mind," the President went on, "a very important military proposal involving the utilization of our armed forces in a manner to relieve your critical western front. This objective carries great weight with me." [35] Thus he asked Stalin if he could send Molotov and a general on whom he could rely to Washington in the immediate future since "Time is of the essence if we are to help in an important way." He offered to provide an American transport plane for the round trip.

But Stalin was not to be turned aside by such vague intimations. He took his time deciding whether and when to let Molotov go to Washington. And in the meanwhile he continued to press Britain for assent to the treaty provisions he wanted; in fact, he was making acceptance of these a test of trust in Britain as a true ally. The British government tried to find a way out of the impasse by treaty language that would appease if not satisfy. But Stalin would not have it. Either impatient or worried, while still leaving Roosevelt's invitation un-

[34] *Roosevelt and Hopkins*, page 526.
[35] *Ibid.*, page 528.

answered, on April 23rd he told Churchill that he proposed to send Molotov to London at once to see whether he could not at long last settle the differences. Stalin added that he thought this visit to England all the more necessary since Roosevelt had raised the question of the second front in a message which invited Molotov to come to the United States; and he, Stalin, thought that before sending Molotov there for this purpose, an exchange of views with the British was required. In sum, Stalin had two reasons for having Molotov go to London before he went to Washington. He recognized that although the American government was taking the lead in the cross-Channel invasion project, the British would have to bear the brunt of any such operation in 1942, and their consent had still to be gotten. And, second, if Molotov could reach an accord on the treaty provisions with the British before going on to Washington, it would be harder for the American government to sustain its veto.

Churchill of course answered that he would be glad to see Molotov in London, and Roosevelt fell in with the idea that Molotov should go to London first.

In the next interval, before Molotov turned up in London, Winant, as instructed by Hull, urged the Foreign Office not to give in. It did not. The Soviet government was resentful. Because of this, Molotov, who had been expected in London a fortnight before, did not get there until May 20th.

The Soviet Foreign Minister in his first talks that day had maintained all the Russian pretensions, most particularly the wish to keep the eastern part of Poland which had been occupied in 1939, and the claim on Romania. Eden once again refused to accede. On getting from Eden (on May 21st) a report on these talks, Hull seemed to spin with agitation. In a memo to the President, he averred that if the British and Soviet governments signed an agreement which included territorial clauses it would be a terrible blow to the whole United Nations. He hinted that if they did so despite its protest the American government might have to disassociate itself publicly from the Anglo-Soviet agreement and thus make the dissension plain. The President approved this memo and told Hull to send it on to Winant for transmission to Eden. This was done at once.

Evidently it made its mark. For at his very next meeting (on the 23rd) with Molotov, Eden had ended his effort to find a compromise arrangement. He went on directly to propose that they should put aside the territorial agreement, and sign merely a general and public treaty of alliance containing no reference to frontiers and good for twenty years. In this talk Molotov for the first time showed signs of giving in.

Who can be sure why at long last Molotov renounced the demand? Perhaps because he was impressed by Anglo-American solidarity. Perhaps because of other events that were taking place. During the previous two days the Germans had broken through in the Eastern Crimea and had stopped the Russian counteroffensive in the Eastern Ukraine. Molotov, in discussing with Churchill the possible ways of drawing off forty German divisions from the Eastern Front, had asked what the British attitude would be if the Soviet Army failed to hold out during 1942. In short, there are signs that the adverse turn along much of the length of the Eastern Front made the Russians even more eager than ever for a second front in the west in 1942; and they may have realized that the impulse in Washington to do the utmost to bring this about might be affected by continued Soviet insistence on securing their territorial claims after the war.

Winant saw Molotov on the evening of the 24th. After referring to the relief program for Russia which the American government had in mind and to the second front, Winant had emphasized how strongly Roosevelt and Hull were opposed to introducing frontier problems at this time. Molotov listened attentively. In March Stalin had let it be known that he regarded the President's attempt to influence the outcome of the negotiations with the British as unjustified interference. Now Molotov told Winant that he thought the President's view warranted serious attention. He said he would consider Eden's proposals further, and might delay decision until he had seen the President.

But the Soviet government apparently decided that nothing was to be gained by waiting and that immediate accord might cause the Western allies to come to the aid of the Red armies. So on May 26th it had signed a treaty from which all provisions regarding territories were omitted. Churchill felt that a perilous passage had been safely achieved, one which would have reduced the vitality of the coalition, perhaps even broken its unity. On May 27th he informed Roosevelt: ". . . we have completely transformed the treaty proposals. They are now, in my judgment, free from the objections we both entertained, and are entirely compatible with our Atlantic Charter. The treaty was signed yesterday afternoon, with great cordiality on both sides." [36]

Stalin had seemed to be quite as well satisfied. According to Churchill he "was almost purring." [37] His message to the Prime Minister certainly evidenced appreciation of having a reliable ally in the grave crisis through which the Soviet Union was passing: "I am sure this

[36] *The Hinge of Fate*, page 339.
[37] *Ibid.*, page 341.

treaty will be of the greatest importance for the future strengthening of friendly relations between the Soviet Union and Great Britain, as well as between our countries and the United States of America, and will secure the close collaboration of our countries after the victorious end of the war." [38]

Hull had spoken as though he thought the world had been saved— for a better fate. Roosevelt was pleased and showed it in his expansive comments to Molotov on political matters when the Soviet Foreign Minister turned up in Washington four days later. With the trouble about the treaty disposed of in accord with the American wishes, Molotov had the more reason to expect a cordial reception and favorable consideration for Soviet longing to see a battle line in the west.

8. The Soviet Connection Continued: The Second Front and Soviet Frontiers

While Molotov was on his way from London to Washington, Roosevelt (on May 27th) had told Churchill that he would be glad to know what had been said to him about the project for a cross-Channel operation. Churchill answered by transmitting a copy of a memo which he had made of his formal talks with Molotov on the morning of May 22nd. In this he had expanded upon the plans and preparations which the Americans and British had underway without giving any definite indication when they might eventuate into action. Then he had proceeded to stress two points which he thought Molotov ought to bear in mind. One was that with the best will and effort it was unlikely that any move could be made in 1942 which would draw off large numbers of enemy land forces from the Eastern Front. The other was that the Western Allies were already confronting forty-four German divisions in other theatres of war. However, he had concluded, they were not satisfied; and if any other sound and sensible plan could be devised they would not hesitate to put it into action. The Prime Minister also let the President know that he had broached other military actions to Molotov as well—a landing in the north of Norway, northern convoys to the Soviet Union on the northern route, and possible extension of the campaign in Libya.

Molotov had left London perplexed as to what this talk portended.

[38] *Ibid.*

Rather than try to grope his way through the fog of uncertainty, he tried to dispel it by asking the President a direct question. As first put to Roosevelt at dinner on the 29th: would the Americans and British create a new main fighting front soon, a front which would draw away as many as forty divisions from the east? At no time did Molotov suggest that, even if this were not done, Soviet resistance was likely to collapse. But without such relief, he warned, if Hitler should decide to use all the power under his command to deal a crushing blow, the Russian lines might be shattered. Moscow and Rostov might be lost, and the Russians might be compelled to retreat to the Volga, leaving all of Central Russia to the Germans. The food and raw materials of the Ukraine, perhaps the oil of the Caucasus, would be gone. If that should happen, the whole brunt of the war would fall upon Great Britain and the United States. And if, after waiting, they then tried to form a second front, the Germans would have to be met in immense strength in the west. Therefore, he tried to convince the President it was in the interest of the United States to do its utmost while Soviet battle lines were still holding and the Soviet Army was still strong to draw away substantial forces from the Russian war front, and so enable the Red Army to deliver a smashing attack. Thirty U.S.-British ground divisions and five armored divisions landed in France, he reckoned, would be enough to bring this about.

In short, Molotov had not come to beseech help, but to get the West to recognize its own best chance. His presentation made a strong impression on Roosevelt. But he was compelled to heed the difficulties of organizing and conducting such a great and dangerous operation in haste. The President explained that the great problem was to find means of transport, especially landing craft, rather than to find soldiers. He asked Molotov if he thought it would be enough if ten divisions were landed in France—as a diversion without intention of keeping them on the Continent. Both he and Hopkins said they thought the United States would support such a more quickly manageable enterprise. But Molotov was doubtful whether this would serve much purpose.

In the course of a following talk, which took place on the morning of May 30th, the President had asked Marshall in Molotov's presence whether developments were clear enough so we could say to Mr. Stalin that we were preparing "a second front." "Yes," replied the General. The President then authorized Mr. Molotov to inform Mr. Stalin that we expected the formation of a second front in 1942. He did not state where that second front would be—whether in Northwest Europe, which Molotov had in mind, or somewhere else. General Marshall spoke up to indicate that this should be regarded as a forecast, not a promise. He remarked that "we were making every effort to build up a situation in which the creation of a second front would be possible." [39]

The President had thought that the dangerous situation on the Russian Front required of him a more conclusive answer than that. He consulted with Marshall and King again in regard to what more might be said to Molotov before his departure. Roosevelt read to these military advisers a message which he was sending to Churchill, saying that he was more anxious than ever that a cross-Channel operation be started in August to continue as long as the weather permitted. Marshall told him that he thought the stipulation of so near a date would arouse British resistance. Roosevelt said he would try it anyhow. So the message, slightly revised, went off.

On the next morning (June 1st) the President told Molotov again that he expected to set up a second front in 1942, without, however, making mention of the possibility that it might be started as early as August. Instead he said merely that if the Soviet government would reduce the volume of Lend-Lease supplies for which it was asking under the Second Protocol (from 4.1 to 2.5 million tons) the shipping saved could be used to increase the movement to England for the cross-Channel operation. The second front would thus be brought nearer to realization. The Soviet Union, he remarked, could not eat their cake and have it too. Molotov thereupon retorted that the second front would be stronger if the first front still stood fast. He asked what would happen if the Soviet government cut down its requirements and then no second front eventuated. Then, before allowing the talk to end, he pressed again for a more conclusive answer. The memo made of the reply records:

"To this direct question the President answered that Mr. Molotov could say in London that, after all, the British were even now in personal consultation with our staff-officers on questions of landing craft, food, etc. We expected to establish a second front. General Arnold would arrive next day (Tuesday, June 2nd) from London, and with him Lord Mountbatten, Marshal Portal, and General Little, with whom it was planned to arrive at an agreement on the creation of a second front. Mr. Molotov should also say in London that we could proceed toward its creation with the more speed if the Soviet government would make it possible for us to put more ships into the English service." [40]

This was as definite an answer as could be given him then. But it was

[39] *Roosevelt and Hopkins,* page 563.
[40] *Ibid.,* page 575.

one that put the possibilities to the fore and left the hindering facts to the rear.

There is one more element in the story. While the talks with Molotov went on, thought was being given to the text of a public statement to be issued concurrently in Washington and Moscow when Molotov got back home. Although the State Department had played almost no part in the talks about military plans, it was given the task of preparing this statement. Molotov had not liked what was turned out. So he submitted one of his own. This used language which, without saying so, could be construed to mean that the American government had virtually agreed to start a second front in 1942. The clinching paragraphs read:

"In the course of the conversations, full understanding was reached with regard to the urgent tasks of creating a second front in Europe in 1942. In addition, the measures for increasing and speeding up the supplies of planes, tanks, and other kinds of war materials from the United States to the Soviet Union were discussed. . . .

"Both sides state with satisfaction the unity of their views on all these questions."

Marshall had thought the sentence about the second front too strong, and he urged that there be no reference to the year 1942. But in it stayed, at the President's wish. As a prod, or a prospect, or a promise— neither the American nor Russian nor British sponsors were quite sure.

Before we travel with Molotov back to London and Moscow and pursue the further discussion about the second front, brief note ought to be taken of some of the political areas covered in talk between the President and Molotov while he was in Washington. For they also were seriously weighed and remembered in Moscow as the war went on.

About the issue of Soviet frontiers, which had long stood in the way of the treaty with Great Britain, little was directly said. Molotov before dinner on May 29th asked the President, who had kept away from the topic, whether he was familiar with that treaty. The President said he was; that he thought it all to the good that it did not comprehend frontiers; that this question would present itself eventually, but he did not believe the present was a good time to deal with it. Molotov remarked quietly that his government had thought otherwise, but had deferred to the British views and what he understood the President's wishes to have been.

It may be that Molotov was somewhat consoled at having had to yield in this matter by what he learned of the President's ideas about postwar settlements. These were expansively outlined in span of their several talks. Roosevelt reviewed his theory of why the League of Nations did not work. He attributed the failure to two main defects. One was too great diffusion of responsibility for decision; too many nations had to be satisfied. The other was the lack of concentrated police power. He had gone on to mention to Molotov some ways in which the task of maintaining peace and security might be more successfully managed. Present enemies were to be disarmed and kept disarmed. Smaller countries who had shown themselves disturbers of the peace in the past—and possibly even France—might be subjected to similar control. The three great members of the war coalition, plus China perhaps, would together see that this was done, and act jointly to suppress future trouble. Thereby, he had remarked, there would be twenty-five years of peace at least—"peace in our time." Molotov had asked some questions. Would not many countries resent such measures, would not Turkey and Poland, and surely France? Roosevelt had acknowledged that they might, and had then gone on to say that he thought France might be reestablished as an important power in ten or twenty years. Molotov also wondered whether China was qualified for a main part. But at the end of the talk he had remarked that he thought the President's ideas about disarmament, inspection, and policing quite realistic; that Stalin knew of them; and the Soviet government would support them fully.[41]

Roosevelt had then gone on to say that he wanted to acquaint Molotov and Stalin with another point in his thought: ". . . that there were, all over the world, many islands and colonial possessions which ought, for our own safety, to be taken away from weak nations. He suggested that Mr. Stalin might profitably consider the establishment of some form of international trusteeship over these islands and possessions."[42] Molotov said he had no doubt that the President's principle of trusteeship would be equally well received in Moscow.

There is every reason to believe that these intimations of American policy were genuinely meant. But it may be surmised that by spreading them before Molotov at this time the President was trying to moderate looming Soviet territorial claims. Was he not offering a permanent postwar alliance to keep Germany and Japan weak and safely under control? Would this not provide Russia with a better form of security than the extension of its frontiers beyond the point of friction? Did not his loose trustee proposal open up for the Soviet Union a chance of getting centers of activity in various parts of the world outside its own frontiers?

In the medley of ideas which he threw off the President had a sound

[41] *Ibid.*, page 573.
[42] *Ibid.*, page 572.

purpose. But there was a prematurity and carelessness about all this which must have puzzled the Russians then and later. We are led again to reflect on the political costs of coalition.

Roosevelt, according to a note which Hopkins sent to Winant, thought that Molotov's visit went "extremely well." When Molotov reached London on his way to Moscow, Churchill found him animated over the cross-Channel operation in 1942. As previously told, the project was then still under study in conjunction with the American staff and in the British view "nothing but difficulties had as yet emerged." Still, Churchill has since told that he thought no harm would be done by issuing the public statement that had been discussed with Molotov in Washington; and that it might worry the Germans. It was published on June 11th, containing the portentous ambiguity, "In the course of the conversations, full understanding was reached with regard to the urgent tasks of creating a second front in Europe in 1942." [43]

It was on this day that the British War Cabinet resolved that the cross-Channel operation would be undertaken only if and when certain defined conditions were attained. Probably with this in mind Churchill made a special effort to guard against the chance that the words of the public statement would be taken as an irrevocable promise. Privately he gave Molotov a memo for the Soviet government which read:

"We are making preparations for a landing on the Continent in August or September, 1942. As already explained, the main limiting factor to the size of the landing-force is the availability of special landing-craft. Clearly however it would not further either the Russian cause or that of the Allies as a whole if, for the sake of action at any price, we embarked on some operation which ended in disaster and gave the enemy an opportunity for glorification at our discomfiture. It is impossible to say in advance whether the situation will be such as to make this operation feasible when the time comes. *We can therefore give no promise in the matter* [Churchill's italics], but provided that it appears sound and sensible we shall not hesitate to put our plans into effect." [44]

Molotov, moreover, had heard enough talk of the British and American military men to have known that many had deep doubts as to

[43] This communiqué was issued by the White House June 11, 1942. On the same day, after Eden announced the treaty with the Soviet Union, the Foreign Office gave out a communique covering not only the treaty but other subjects discussed. In regard to the second front, the same language was used as that in the American statement, "Full understanding was reached, etc." The Soviet government gave out two statements on June 12th. One dealt with the London talks, especially the treaty, the other with the talks in Washington about the second front.

[44] *The Hinge of Fate,* page 342.

whether any cross-Channel invasion could be tried with reasonable hope of success in 1942. Yet, both in public and private, he went on to talk as though the matter was all but settled. Thus, in speaking to an Extraordinary Session of the Supreme Soviet on June 18th called to welcome him home from London and Washington and to ratify the alliance with Great Britain, he chose as his theme words that had been used by Eden in signing the treaty: "Never before in the history of our two countries has our association been so close or our mutual pledge for the future so complete." Then he continued:

"Serious attention was naturally paid in our negotiations both in London and Washington to problems of a second front. The results of these negotiations are dealt with in similar words both in Anglo-Soviet and Soviet-American communiqués. Both communiqués declare that in the negotiations 'complete understanding was reached with regard to the urgent tasks of creating a second front in Europe in 1942.' . . . Let us hope that our common enemy will soon experience to his cost the results of the ever growing military cooperation of the three great powers." [45]

The American Ambassador to the Soviet Union, Admiral Standley, had found Molotov on the next day "openly jubilant" and emphasizing the statement on the second front. "This *could*," he was saying as he had in Washington, "mean winning the war in 1942, certainly in 1943." The Soviet press and radio led the Russian people to believe that this great action was near.

At this juncture a diversion took place that is not easy to interpret. It probably originated in reports, which were half-credited in Washington, that the Japanese were preparing to attack Russia. That may be the whole story; the President may just have acted hastily on wrong military intelligence. Or perhaps he saw a chance to make a gesture which would prove to Stalin that the United States was a devoted ally even though it had not yet come to the relief of the Red Army by landing in France.

Whatever the prompting cause, on June 17th (six days after the issuance of the statement about the second front) Roosevelt sent a message to Stalin saying that there was tangible evidence that the Japanese were probably about to conduct operations against the Soviet Maritime Provinces. "We are ready," he said, "in case of such an attack to assist you with our air power, providing there are available suitable landing fields which are adequate." He was glad to learn from Litvinov, he went on, that Stalin liked the idea of moving American planes from Alaska to the western battlefront via Northern Russia. In view of the urgency

[45] Embassy of the USSR, *Information Bulletin,* June 20, 1942, pages 3 and 4.

of these matters, the President suggested that secret combined staff talks be started at once.

Having no information that the Japanese were about to attack the Soviet Union, Stalin may well have thought that the President was trying to turn his interest away from France. He waited a fortnight before answering. In the meantime, on June 22nd, Ambassador Standley sent a warning message to the President: "In view of the manner in which the Soviet government and people have accepted what would appear here to be a solemn obligation on the part of the United States and Great Britain to create a second front in 1942, I feel convinced that if such a front does not materialize quickly and on a large scale, these people will be so deluded in their belief in our sincerity of purpose and will for concerted action that inestimable harm will be done to the cause of the United Nations."

During the next week Molotov spoke even more freely than before about the impending second front, saying at one luncheon among the diplomats that it was the test of the value of the treaty with Britain, and that great disillusionment would follow any failure to redeem "Anglo-Saxon promises." When (on July 1st or 2nd) Stalin answered Roosevelt's messages about coming to Soviet aid in the Far East, he ignored the President's reference to a possible Japanese attack on the Maritime Provinces. While adopting the plan for an Alaska-Siberia ferry route, he made it clear that he wanted Russian, not American, pilots to fly the planes from Alaska to or over Soviet territory. Whether or not he got his second front in France, he was going to continue to take every care not to provoke Japan.

Actually there is reason to believe that both Stalin and Molotov appreciated that no firm pledge had been given of a second front in the west in 1942. On July 2nd Stalin, talking with Standley about other military matters, remarked dryly that "wanting" and "having" a second front were two different things. Molotov also retreated. Churchill and Eden were not willing, as Roosevelt seemed to be, to let the pressure of undue expectation rise freely. So they asked Clark-Kerr to let Molotov know that the British government was upset at the way in which he was spreading the impression that a definite promise had been made about the second front. Clark-Kerr did so on July 14th. In friendly tone, Molotov remarked that much of what he had said at the disturbing luncheon was "subjective." He admitted that when he was in London the problems of a second front had been made clear to him, and that it had been foreseen rather than forecast. By way of extenuation, he pointed out that in his speech to the Supreme Soviet he had not spoken of any promises; he had merely stressed the eagerness of the Soviet people and army for a second front and, not unnaturally, they had gotten a feeling of assurance from the statements issued in London and Washington.

In fact, as we have seen, by the middle of July hope of achieving any landing on the Continent in 1942 was almost an empty one and soon thereafter it was renounced in favor of the North African landing. The greater venture was put off to·the future, although not without anxiety by the Americans that the decision might bring our good faith and our motives into question in Moscow. The two Western war leaders were also gloomily coming to the conclusion, of which more will be told later on, that the convoys carrying war supplies for Russia around the tip of Norway to Murmansk would have to be suspended during the summer days of prolonged daylight.

With explanations to be given of why the measure most wanted by Russia could not be carried out, and with the news of the prospective North African campaign to communicate, Churchill determined that he himself ought to go to Moscow. He could best uphold these decisions in the fresh arguments that had already begun.

The words exchanged between Churchill and Stalin had turned cold. On July 17th the Prime Minister sent his explanation of the decision to suspend the northern convoys. This had revealed that his visions of the next battle were roving to the south, not across the Channel. Stalin quite probably knew of the argument then going on between the American and British staffs; and he also learned or guessed its outcome quickly. In any case, his answer to Churchill (of the 23rd) reflected knowledge that the proposed cross-Channel operation in 1942 was being set aside. He told Churchill that he inferred this from Churchill's message to him, and then went on to say, "With regard to . . . the question of creating a second front in Europe, I am afraid it is not being treated with the seriousness it deserves. Taking fully into account the present position on the Soviet-German front, I must state in the most emphatic manner that the Soviet government cannot acquiesce in the postponement of a second front in Europe until 1943." [46]

Roosevelt had agreed (message of July 29th) with Churchill that the answer should be soft—that they must always, "bear in mind the personality of our Ally and the very difficult and dangerous situation that confronts him. . . . I think he should be told, in the first place, quite specifically that we have determined upon a course of action in 1942 [TORCH]. I think that, without advising him of the precise

[46] *The Hinge of Fate*, page 271.

nature of our proposed operations, the fact that they are going to be made should be told him without any qualifications." [47]

Churchill accordingly made no direct rejoinder to Stalin's recrimination. But he saw the need to acquaint Stalin more fully with the British military position and resources, to state the compelling reasons why it had been decided that the cross-Channel invasion could not be begun in 1942, and to explain the value of the TORCH operation. By thus improving Soviet understanding, he hoped to end Soviet suspicion that Great Britain and the United States were not fully cooperative, and so improve the future basis for the conduct of the war.

Churchill, displeased by the conduct of the campaign in the Middle East, had already planned to go as far as Cairo to set straight the British military command in that area. He made up his mind to go on to Moscow, taking along chief members of his military staff. This was arranged—Stalin inviting him to come "to consider jointly the urgent questions of war against Hitler." [48]

When Churchill set off on this Moscow mission he did not count on having American company in his talks with Stalin. Roosevelt was ready to let him make the explanations, take the blame, and get the clouded credit. Harriman, in London, thought that the visitors from England might find it very rough going in Moscow without some indication of American support. When Molotov had been in Washington the previous April, the Americans had spoken to him quite freely about the difference in attitude between the British and themselves toward the conduct of the war in Europe, and Harriman feared that Stalin might well have inferred that the American and British governments were not in genuine accord about the most recent military decisions. So it occurred to him that if some American official could be present when Churchill talked with Stalin, to confirm the Prime Minister's exposition, the Soviet response might be better. Therefore he proposed to the President that he be sent along with Churchill. The President hesitated, saying that he feared that Harriman would be regarded as "an observer," by which presumably he meant someone present to keep watch on Churchill and Stalin both. But then Churchill sent word to the President, "I should greatly like to have your aid and countenance in my talks with Joe. Would you be able to let Averell come with me? I feel that things would be easier if we all seemed to be together. I have a somewhat raw job." The President answered at once: "I am asking Harriman to leave at earliest possible moment for Moscow. I think

[47] *Ibid.*, pages 271–72.
[48] *Ibid.*, page 454.

your idea is sound, and I am telling Stalin Harriman will be at his and your disposal to help in any way." [49]

Churchill and Stalin had not met before. As his plane flew toward Moscow, Churchill thought his errand to be "like carrying a large lump of ice to the North Pole." To do well the job that was taking him there, he was going to have to repress the memory that before the Germans attacked the Soviet Union the leaders of that country, in his own words, ". . . would have watched us being swept out of existence with indifference and gleefully divided with Hitler our Empire in the East." [50] He was also going to have to control his gift for retort. In the talks ahead there would be sharp differences in memories of the past, and of judgment about what was fair for each to expect of the other in the future. Without great care his mission might smash against these crags.

His anxiety, to foretell, was justified. Several times Stalin's rough insults and Churchill's animated anger almost broke the talk to pieces. Harriman's presence added weight to what Churchill said and his calm support eased the way over some rough passages.

The first two hours of their first talk (on August 12th) Churchill remembers to have been "bleak and sombre." Stalin's sketch of the situation on the Eastern Front was grave. He explained how tremendous an effort the Germans were making to get to Baku and Stalingrad, saying he thought they were draining the whole of Europe for troops; and he indicated that he was not sure whether the Russian forces would be able to stop them. Even around Moscow, where the position seemed sound, he said he could not guarantee in advance that the German attack would be repulsed. But in the subsequent conversations Stalin's view of the military prospects and the ability of the Soviet forces to prevent the Germans from gaining any main victory seemed to become more assured and brighter. This allows room for speculation as to whether the first estimate was not darkened on purpose. What advocate for a cause just and dear does not select from his palette of possibilities?

Stalin's description of the combat situation did not make it easier for Churchill to impart what he had come to tell. But he determined that it was best to do so at once. Thus, after listening to Stalin, he bluntly stated that: "The British and American governments did not feel themselves able to undertake a major operation in September, which was the latest month in which the weather was to be counted upon. But, as

[49] *Ibid.*, page 473.
[50] *Ibid.*, page 475.

M. Stalin knew, they were preparing for a very great operation in 1943." [51]

Stalin was grim and unconvinced. He gave way to his evident feeling that the British were afraid of the Germans, and were avoiding the payment of what he regarded as the natural price of war. When Churchill dwelt on the difficulties and the great and futile losses which he thought would result from a premature attempt to cross the Channel, Stalin said, "After all, this was a war." Churchill answered, "War was war but not folly, and it would be folly to invite a disaster. . . ." An oppressive silence followed. Stalin broke it at last by saying that if the British and Americans could not make a landing in France this year, he was not entitled to demand or insist upon it, but he was bound to say that he did not agree with Churchill's arguments.

Whereupon Churchill, having braved the harsh wind, went on to describe with vivid enthusiasm what he thought his country and the United States would be able to do in 1942 in aid of and relief to the Soviet Union. Of these he mentioned first the plan for the extension— until it became formidable—of the great bombing assault of Germany. Churchill's anticipatory sketch of the shattering damage that would be done had a stimulating effect upon the gathering, and from then on the atmosphere became more cordial. Harriman, noting this in his report to the President, remarked that "Between the two of them they soon had destroyed most of the important industrial cities of Germany."

Next Churchill told of the great projected expedition to North Africa, so large and so threatening that Germany would have to devote much attention to it. Egypt was to be won by the British forces in September; the landings in the Western Mediterranean were to be made soon after; all of North Africa was to be brought under American and British military command by the end of the year; and then they could threaten Hitler's Europe from there—in conjunction with the 1943 cross-Channel invasion. The better to explain why he thought this North African operation could be a vital blow against Germany, Churchill drew the famous picture of the crocodile, and compared the Mediterranean operation to a stroke at the "soft under-belly," delivered as the hard snout was also attacked.

As Churchill worked up his vision of the results of this strategy, Stalin seemed to catch on to all that might be done through TORCH. The American records contain a summary made by Stalin that night of its conceived strategic advantages, more glowing than any made by its British-American planners. But he was puzzled about what he called

[51] *Ibid.,* page 478.

the political basis of the operation—being concerned lest French resistance or Spanish interference defeat it.

Churchill went on to decorate the feast of possibilities. He said that the British, or the British and Americans, might send combat air forces to fight on the southern end of the Soviet Eastern Front. Stalin said he would accept that help "gratefully."

Both Churchill and Harriman left this first meeting with a sense of relief because the hard news had been told, and apparently it was not going to harm relations with the Soviet Union and the conduct of the war. As Churchill later wrote of the occasion, "He [Stalin] now knew the worst and yet we parted in an atmosphere of good will." [52] Harriman's report that night to the President told him:

"I came away with the conviction that although Stalin had been much disappointed in our inability to be of greater military assistance to him and although he was critical of us, particularly the British, he gave me the feeling throughout the evening that he had considered he was dealing with two nations with whom he had binding ties and that with you and the Prime Minister he could personally interchange views in the frankest of manner without fear of breaking the relationship. At no time did he show any indication that some action or lack of action on either of our parts might fundamentally affect this understanding."

But this impression was roughly upset by the talks on the next afternoon with Molotov, and on the next night with Stalin. Molotov reminded Churchill of what had been said to him in Washington and London about the second front and of the statements issued after these visits. As Churchill was about to leave alone for his second talk with Stalin, word came that Stalin wished to have Harriman again present at their talk. He confronted the two callers with copies of a formal aide-memoire signed by himself. This memoire forcibly recorded Soviet dissatisfaction with the decisions which the night before he had seemed to accept as a good second best. The Soviet government, it said in summary, had been led to think that the organization of a second front in Europe had been predecided while Molotov was in London; that the Soviet High Command had planned its own summer and autumn military actions on this supposition; and that the refusal to carry out this program offended Soviet public opinion, complicated the situation of the Red Army at the front, and prejudiced its plans. It restated the opinion that the conditions of 1942 would be most favorable for the second front since almost all the German forces were engaged on the Eastern Front, leaving only small and poor remnants elsewhere. It ended by

[52] *Ibid.,* page 483.

expressing Stalin's regrets that he had not been able to convince Church-ill and Harriman.

Both auditors wondered then and later about the reasons for the abrupt change. Guesses varied. Was Stalin merely making a record for defense against opponents at home, and for possible use in future nego-tiations? Or was he paying tribute to the views of other members of the Politburo or of his military staff? Or did he think that a protest of this sort might still cause the British and Americans to change their plans? There was no way of knowing.

After the memo was read, Stalin went on to sharpen its edges on the grindstone of his tongue. The British, he said, need not be afraid of the Germans; if the British infantry fought as the Russian soldiers had and, he interjected, as had the Royal Air Force, they would find out that the Germans could be licked; soldiers had to become used to blood. Churchill quietly said that he would allow this particular re-mark to pass only because of the bravery of the Russian Army. It may be observed that Stalin's comment made no allowance for the difference between fighting invaders on home soil and leaping across seas into foreign territory. Nor did it show recognition that the Soviet Union could bear the loss of millions of men while Britain, still short of young vitality because of the First World War, could not.

Churchill was not silent under Stalin's continued barrage. About his response he later wrote, "I repulsed all his contentions squarely, but without taunts of any kind." [53] So he did, at times not even allowing the translator of Stalin's remarks to finish, snapping back fast after each sentence. Harriman, called on by Churchill to say what he thought, made it plain that the decision about the invasion had been made after the most careful study, and had been approved by the President—who thought it was also in the interest of the Soviet Union.[54]

About the lag that was occurring in the arrival of promised war sup-plies to the Soviet Union, Stalin also had harsh things to say that night. The Soviet government was, he said, grateful for what had already been received and for what was promised. But, he continued, of the many plans and programs of supply that had been prepared, some had had to be abandoned; and so, as a matter of fact, the Soviet Union had received little as yet from either the United States or Great

[53] *Ibid.*, page 486.

[54] Both Churchill and Harriman gave Stalin the next day written replies to this memo. Harriman's answer said that, having seen the one that Churchill was making, he thought no useful purpose would be served by adding to it, and went on, "I feel, however, that I must reaffirm his [Churchill's] statement that no promise has been broken regarding the second front."

Britain. This complaint had a valid basis. The volume of supplies that had actually reached the Soviet Union had been much less than scheduled.[55] But Stalin's reproaches were excessive and unfair: what supplies had been received had been of enormous use to the Soviet armies in their winter and spring campaigns.[56] Churchill's rebuttal was that the Americans and British had promised only to make the supplies for the Soviet Union available in British ports; that the British government had done its utmost to deliver them to the Soviet Union, but that the northern convoys had met such destructive attacks that only part of what had been sent had arrived; that, in fact, out of the most recent northern convoy, the 17th, only one-third of the ships had reached their destination, and yet it was proposed to send another convoy in September. Stalin refused to accept this as sufficient reason for not getting all that had been scheduled. He hinted that the British and Americans could have delivered much more if they had tried hard enough and had been willing to accept the losses; but that they would not do it because they did not appreciate the importance of the Soviet front, and so had sent only what they could spare. Churchill and Harriman denied this with justified indignation.

But the anger seeped out of the argument as the talk went on. Stalin calmly repeated what he had said the evening before—that he had no choice but to accept the British and American refusals and denials. Then abruptly, almost in the same sentence, he asked Churchill to dinner the next night. Churchill accepted, and said he would be leaving at dawn the following day. Stalin, with expression unchanged, asked, "You do not have to be in such a hurry. Have you done all you came to do?" Churchill's answer showed his hurt. He told Stalin that he could find no ring of comradeship in his attitude. Stalin relaxed into friendly admiration for the spirit of the man speaking—or so the others present thought. Thus this rough session, probing as it did both the question of good faith and obligation to sacrifice, ended without rupture. Mutual need prevailed over grievances.

Churchill, reporting to the War Cabinet about this white-capped

[55] As broadly summarized by E. R. Stettinius, Jr., Lend-Lease Administrator, in *Lend-Lease Weapon for Victory*, pages 207–08.

[56] By the middle of 1942 we had shipped more than 2,000 light and medium tanks and 1,300 planes; the British had sent even more—over 2,400 tanks and over 1,800 planes. The trucks and jeeps which we provided were of the greatest use in meeting the German summer offensive. Without the telephone equipment and wire sent from the United States, the Soviet armies would not have been able to maintain communication along their 2,000-mile front. The tons of shoe leather and the several million pairs of American-made army boots had enabled the Russian soldiers to withstand the heavy snow and extreme cold of the previous winter campaign and the deep mud of the spring campaign.

talk, said he thought that Stalin, knowing at heart the decision was right, may have been compelled to speak as he had spoken and might later make amends. But it was the British and Americans who tried the harder in that way, seeking to get their Soviet associates to appreciate how much they were doing and proposed to do to take the burden of war away from the Russians and unto themselves. The military men of the three countries again thrashed out the question of the cross-Channel invasion—with no admitted change of opinion on either side.

On the night of the 15th Churchill had a final talk with Stalin which, taking an intimate turn, went on till almost daybreak. For the first and last time he was taken into the family, served at table by the daughter, answered with gay banter, and given solid military information. This convivial night did not induce any new decisions nor lasting trust, as time was soon to show. But it extracted the thorns of argument and made the associates in the same cause comfortable with each other again. The issuance of a joint statement became easier and more natural, a statement which reaffirmed that close friendship existed between the Soviet Union, Great Britain, and the United States.

Roosevelt had been and remained eager for a similar personal meeting with Stalin as soon as the American elections were over and it could be managed. Stalin had assured him that he shared the desire and the sense that good would come of it. Referring to the previous exchange of messages on this project, Harriman told Stalin that the President wished to say again that he would very much like to find the chance to meet with him. Then Stalin repeated that he was in accord, commenting, "It is of great importance." They went on to talk briefly about where and when the encounter might take place. Stalin said perhaps the Far East, perhaps Western Europe, and observed that he was not as busy with military matters in the winter as at other times. Harriman remarked that the President did not fly; that he had considered the Aleutian Islands as a meeting place but now the Japanese were making that difficult. Stalin then suggested Iceland in December. Harriman indicated that might be possible for the President but too dangerous for Stalin. But this did not seem to worry Stalin, who remarked that he had good planes for the trip.

Churchill, in his dinner talk on the 15th, alluded to this proposed meeting between Stalin and Roosevelt. If it were to be in the winter, the Prime Minister observed, Stalin should consider the difficulties of flying; and Stalin again showed his inclination by saying that, nevertheless, a meeting must take place. Churchill then revealed his thought by saying that he hoped he, too, could be present. Stalin remarked that would be the best combination—if the three of them were to meet together. The subject was dropped for the time being. Harriman seemed amply justified in reporting to the President that there was no doubt that Stalin would make every effort to meet him at any time or place. But, as the later narrative will tell, when it came down to actual plans soon after, Stalin would not leave Russia to join the other two at Casablanca.

ᴓᴓᴓᴓᴓᴓ

9. The Coalition Gets Along: Before and After TORCH

ᴓᴓᴓᴓᴓᴓ

On hearing cheerily from Churchill about the outcome of his visit to Moscow, Roosevelt hurried off a message to Stalin. Once again he said that he was sorry not to have been present. Next he told of our island operations underway in the Western Pacific, and then:

"I well realize on the other hand that the real enemy of both our countries is Germany and that at the earliest possible moment it will be necessary for both our countries to bring our power and forces to bear against Hitler. Just as soon as it is humanly possible to assemble the transportation you may be sure that this will be done. . . . The fact that the Soviet Union is bearing the brunt of the fighting and losses during the year 1942 is well understood. . . . We are coming as quickly and as strongly to your assistance as we possibly can and I hope that you will believe me when I tell you this."

Stalin's response (of August 22nd) did not reveal whether he was convinced. After all, acts would tell. He and his associates followed intently what the Allies did about each and every one of the main items in the varied panorama of action which Churchill at Moscow had spread before them. To list them systematically these were, in addition to the operations in North Africa:

The bombing assault over Germany.

The introduction of a British-American combat air force on the Soviet southern front.

The maintenance of the northern convoys to the Soviet Union.

The improvement in the southern supply route running from the Persian Gulf to the Soviet border.

The increase and expedition of the flow of Lend-Lease supplies.

Possible assault against the German positions in Norway.

80

The Russians took what was done about each of these activities as a measure of the wish and will of the West to help the Soviet Union rather than allow it to become exhausted in the struggle.

The British expanded the weight and ferocity of their night bombing assaults on Germany. For the Royal Air Force this was a period of learning to use new devices, especially radar, which later added so greatly to the effectiveness of their mass attacks. For the American Strategic Air Force it was an interval of chores. Somewhat to its chagrin, it was compelled to postpone daylight attempts against Germany because of other urgent assignments.[57] Much of its strength was spent in clearing the way for TORCH by attacking German submarine pens along the Bay of Biscay, aircraft factories, and repair depots in France, and by hampering German air attacks against the sea routes to North Africa. This still young organization was learning, preparing, and testing. Its recognition of the need for more time is reflected in the easy attitude which it took toward the possible deferment of the cross-Channel operation.

The idea of sending British and American combat and transport air forces to fight with and for the Red Army on its Southern Front, to hold the line of the Caucasus Mountains and the Black Sea coast, had been in Churchill's mind before he left for Moscow. He had broached it to Stalin as early as July as an offset to the prospective suspension of the northern convoys. The President had favored the project. Churchill had put it forward in his talks with Stalin—with Harriman's approving knowledge. He had explained that it was of vital importance to Britain as well as to the Soviet Union that the German assault in the south should not succeed, because it would open the way to control of the Persian Gulf, endanger the British forces in the Middle East, and create a possible route for a joint Japanese and German advance upon India. But despite Roosevelt's attempt to dissuade him from doing so, Churchill had made the offer contingent upon the course of the battle in Egypt; that the air squadrons could be provided only when and if the British had beaten back Rommel. Stalin had not complained because British battle needs were kept first. He had said that he would be glad to get

[57] Churchill was skeptical of the practicability of the daylight bombing operations on which the American Air Force stationed in England was intent, and he and his colleagues argued forcefully against their methods. This opinion makes more understandable his rather unappreciative comment (made in *The Hinge of Fate,* page 679): "It was certainly a terrible thing that in the whole of the last six months of 1942 nothing had come of this immense deployment and effort, absolutely nothing, not a single bomb had been dropped on Germany."

this help, subject to agreement upon a definite plan as to what it would be and how it would be used. He had added that he would be glad to have either fighters or bombers and that he would do what was needed to enable them to take part in the battle.

Not long after his return from Moscow Churchill had submitted to Roosevelt (on August 30th) a plan for establishing this U.S.-British air force. The American share was to include one heavy bombardment group, then in the Middle East, and an air transport group of at least fifty planes to come from the United States. According to the schedule then in mind, the planes and men were to be moved from Egypt as soon as the situation in the Western Desert allowed, and Churchill thought it could be brought together in the Baku-Batum area about two months thence, early in November. This would be, it was expected, time enough to enable these forces to take part in a winter campaign in front of or in the mountains. Roosevelt informed Churchill that he thought this program satisfactory and that he would try to fit it in with other operations. Both General Marshall and General Arnold, Commanding General of the Army Air Forces, were in fact doubtful about the value of this effort compared to its requirements and possible accomplishments.

While this air expedition for the Caucasus was still under study in Washington (late August and early September), and with TORCH looming up, the question of whether the northern convoys to Russia would have to be suspended again, came to the fore.

Before we recount what was done, a brief review of that inspiring effort will put the decision in perspective. In all the previous months of war, the German submarine attacks on the sea lanes to Britain and Russia had been most threatening. Each naval vessel was desperately needed to protect these Atlantic routes or to arrest the Japanese advance. Each merchant ship sunk meant a reduction of combat strength. Each cargo of weapons or supplies lost meant that soldiers or workers suffered.

The northern route to the Soviet Union was around the North Cape of Norway and through the Arctic Seas to Murmansk. About three-fourths of the vessels used along this route were British and American. Many of the seamen were Norwegian volunteers; they never shirked a voyage. The trouble had become serious in March 1942, the Germans attacking both by aircraft based in Norway and by submarines; there was also a constant threat that the force of naval surface vessels which the Germans had collected in the region—including the *Tirpitz*—would descend on these merchant ships.

The convoy that had been sent at the end of March 1942 (PQ-13) had lost five of its nineteen cargo ships. Of the next (PQ-14), most of the ships had been forced by ice to turn back before they reached the danger area; only eight of the twenty-three ships arrived in Murmansk. The next two convoys (PQ-15 and 16) sent in April and May had been, despite heavy naval protection, hard hit. Substantial damage had also been done to the escorting naval vessels. Still, urged on by Roosevelt to devote all the shipping and naval resources that could possibly be risked, the British had made an even greater effort during May and June to get the badly needed war supplies through. Churchill had impressed upon all branches of the British services that not only Stalin but Roosevelt would be greatly upset if they did not continue the convoys and had remarked, "The operation is justified if a half gets through. Failure on our part to make the attempt would weaken our influence with both our major Allies." [58]

But then convoy PQ-17, an assembly of thirty-four merchant ships, of which twenty-two were American, with large naval escort, which had sailed from Iceland for Archangel on June 27th, had been badly hurt. Naval orders had been misunderstood; the convoy had been scattered and twenty-three of the thirty-four ships had been sunk; and only 70,000 of the 200,000 tons of cargo sent had reached the Soviet port. Thereupon, the British Admiralty had proposed to disband the convoys until the ice blocks melted and the days shortened. In a message he had sent on July 17th, to which reference has been made, Churchill had informed Stalin that, much as he regretted it, the northern convoys would have to be suspended during the period of perpetual daylight. He had gone on to say that, to make up in part, the British government was planning to send some of the ships and cargo that were to have gone by the northern route by the southern route instead.

Stalin's response of July 23rd had been, as Churchill later described it, "rough and surly." He was aggrieved not only about the notice of suspension of the convoys, but also by his guess, or secret intelligence, that the cross-Channel operation was to be postponed. That decision had been made the day before. In any case, he had bluntly said in this acknowledgment that "Our naval experts consider the reasons put forward by the British naval experts to justify the cessation of convoys to the northern ports of the U.S.S.R. wholly unconvincing." [59]

Roosevelt had agreed with Churchill that it was best not to answer this blunt criticism in kind. They had let it pass. In August the U.S. Navy had run a special convoy mission of its own. In response to an urgent plea by Stalin, the heavy cruiser *Tuscaloosa* and two destroyers

[58] *The Hinge of Fate*, page 261.
[59] *Ibid.*, page 270.

had loaded up in Scotland with ammunition, radar equipment, medical and other supplies, and had dashed across to north Russia.

Then in September—to come abreast in our narrative with the account of other elements of military cooperation with the Soviet Union—Convoy PQ-18 had been sent off. It had an unusually large naval and air escort. Even so, only about two-thirds of the merchant vessels in this convoy got through. At the same time that this heavy toll of shipping on the northern route was being paid, losses of vessels in the Atlantic were also great. So the British Admiralty was reaching the conclusion that it would not be possible to bear this double burden while the North African expedition was being assembled and sent on its way. Churchill, although unhappy about it, concurred.

The Russians, Churchill recognized, were entitled to quick notice of this, since it might affect their battle plans. So on September 22nd he sought the President's opinion of a message he was about to send to Stalin to tell him of the forced curtailment. The President, in his answer of the 27th, accepted the fact that "the realities of the situation require us to give up P.Q.19." [60] But he suggested that since a final conclusion regarding the Caucasus air force could be reached in ten days (as was then expected) it would be best to wait a little before telling Stalin and then inform him of both matters at the same time. Churchill agreed to tarry.

Some days later (on October 5th) Roosevelt, obviously worried, followed this up by another message urging Churchill to forebear serving the disheartening notice to Stalin. He advised the Prime Minister that instead of doing so, he should send on their way to Murmansk the ships which were already loaded and waiting for the voyage, not as a large, closely-convoyed unit, but in small dispersed groups of two or three. He also asked Churchill to join with him in telling Stalin at once, and without conditions, that an Anglo-American air force would be sent to fight on the Caucasus front. To enable the British to do so, he offered to replace all the planes which they might transfer from the Middle East for this purpose. The United States Air Force, he said, would provide the heavy bombers.

The reasons for Roosevelt's rather sudden surge of anxiety can be identified. The situation around Stalingrad had grown poorer during the previous weeks. Stalin was complaining (as he did this same day, October 5th, to Churchill) that this was largely due to the fact that the Germans had air superiority, and that the Soviet Army was short of planes, most of all fighters, to protect the troops. The Soviet government, as will be described more fully in another connection, was ex-

[60] *Ibid.*, page 573.

plaining to its people that their plight was largely due to the failure of their allies to give all the aid and support they might, and was maintaining a clamor for the second front. About the primacy and urgency of Soviet needs Stalin left no doubt when talking with Ambassador Standley the next day, October 6th. The occasion for this interview was the presence in Moscow of General Follett Bradley, of the Army Air Forces, who had been sent there in accordance with an agreement reached by Roosevelt with Stalin, to make surveys of facilities in Siberia for a ferry-route from Alaska to be used for sending planes being delivered to Russia under Lend-Lease. Stalin soon turned from this subject to those of more urgent interest to him. He asked Bradley what was being done about providing American-British air support in the Caucasus. Bradley was vague, offering to present the matter sympathetically to the War Department if Stalin wished. Stalin remarked that this had been under discussion since August, that he had said then he would make airfields available. But there had been "talk, talk, but no action."

Despite Stalin's plaints and Roosevelt's worries, Churchill was remaining firm in his view of what could or could not be done with just measurement of risks, means, and benefits. So on October 7th he told the President that he saw no chance of a PQ convoy either as a unit or in successive groups, but was preparing to send ten merchant ships individually during dark of moon in October despite terrible danger. And he continued, "I believe that the blunt truth is best with Stalin. . . . I feel strongly that he should be told now." [61] He further said that no planes could be moved out of Egypt until that battle was won, since Germany's air force might be swung away from Russia to Egypt or against TORCH. With more assurance than was felt in Washington, he summed up "If therefore we offer 'Velvet' [the Caucasian air operation] as now defined, plus increased aircraft deliveries and the individual ships on the P.Q. route, I trust this will be sufficient to bridge the gap before 'Torch' opens." [62]

The answer which Churchill sent to Stalin (October 9th) rested on this hope. He dwelt on the expected effect of the new British offensive in Egypt, to be begun at the end of October, and of TORCH, to be begun in early November. He said also (1) orders had been issued by the President and himself to assemble the air force for the Caucasus so that it would be available for combat early in 1943; (2) that Great Britain and the United States would send him by the Persian Gulf route substantially greater numbers of fighter aircraft; (3) that, alas,

[61] *Ibid.*, page 578.
[62] *Ibid.*

85

large convoys to the northern route would have to be suspended as naval escorts would have to be withdrawn for TORCH, but individual ships would, during this hard period, sail singly.[63]

The President escorted Churchill's message to Stalin with one of his own, confirming the plans and intentions which the Prime Minister had set forth. And then a few days later (on October 12th), having received from Admiral Standley a restatement of Stalin's priorities, in another message he made these promises more positive and exact.

Stalin's answers to these messages from Churchill and Roosevelt were laconic. The one which reached Churchill said merely: "I received your message of October 9. Thank you." [64] The other, delivered by Litvinov, the Soviet Ambassador in Washington, to Hopkins for Roosevelt, said only that.

Now it was Churchill's turn to feel upset by the unfair suspicion in Moscow and rude refusal to appreciate the war effort which the British and Americans had underway. Hearing nothing more from Stalin about the several projects described to him, on the 24th Churchill told Roosevelt that he was perplexed and baffled by the correspondence from Moscow—or rather the almost complete lack of it. Roosevelt, assuming an air of calm, replied on the 27th: "I am not unduly disturbed about our respective responses or lack of responses from Moscow. . . . I feel very sure the Russians are going to hold this winter, and that we should proceed vigorously with our plans both to supply them and set up an air force to fight with them. I want us to be able to say to Mr. Stalin that we have carried out our obligations one hundred per cent." [65]

Churchill had braced up also, beginning a Minute which he wrote to Eden on this same day with the statement that, "I am sure it would be a great mistake to run after the Russians in their present mood; and still less to run around with them chasing a chimera." And then he went on to aver, "I assure you the only thing that will do any good is fighting hard and winning victories. . . . Should success crown our efforts you will find that we shall be in a very different position. Meanwhile, I should treat the Russians coolly, not getting excited about the lies they tell, but going on steadily with our task." [66]

In this spirit the northern convoys were suspended while the forces for TORCH were being brought into position, and the formation of

[63] It might be noted that about the same time Churchill—on the advice of his naval people—felt compelled to put off an urgent American appeal made through Admiral Nimitz for the temporary assignment of British aircraft carriers for operations in the Central Pacific.

[64] *The Hinge of Fate,* page 580.

[65] *Ibid.,* page 582.

[66] *Ibid.,* page 581.

the air force for the Caucasus remained uncompleted. However, during these same autumn weeks, larger assignments were made of planes, trucks, and other items vitally wanted by the Russians. Special efforts were planned to get them to Russia by every available route: part were to go across the Pacific; part by the northern route over which convoys were soon to start again; and the rest, in growing volume and safety, by the southern route via Iran, which was being enlarged and improved.

Of this last undertaking a brief account belongs in the story before it travels farther along its main path.

The trans-Iranian railway runs north over mountains and deserts from Persian Gulf ports to Teheran, and on to the Caspian Sea and the Soviet border. The Allied armies in Iran and Iraq were dependent on it. But the British had not had the means to spare to build up the capacity of the ports, or the needed railroad and road construction equipment, or the railroad engines and cars, or the trucks. Even before we entered the war, in 1941, the American government had tried to help to increase the capacity of this route. American engineers, railroad men, railroad shop construction men, and others had been made available under the Lend-Lease program. They had done most useful work.

Then in July 1942 several events which have already figured in this record had combined to spur the effort to improve this passage: the reverses of the British forces in Libya, creating emergency needs; the advance of the German troops toward the south in Russia; the brief suspension during the longest summer days of the northern convoys. On the 16th of July, when telling Churchill that he regretfully agreed with the need for this last action, Roosevelt had gone on to say that nothing which might increase the capacity of the trans-Iranian railway should be overlooked. He had then asked Churchill what he thought of the idea of turning its operation over to American railroad men. Casually he had remarked, "They are first class at this sort of thing."

Harriman, who had striven so hard to get supplies allocated for the Soviet Union, had made up his mind that some better way than any of those in use had to be found to deliver them where they were needed. The route through Iran seemed to him clearly the most attractive; and out of his railroad experience he had been sure it could be greatly developed. With flashing vigor he had set about to get this accomplished. Before going on to Moscow with Churchill in August, he had stopped off in Iran and had surveyed the situation with American railroad men, getting an idea of what needed doing and what could be done. He arranged to have these American railroad men and their British associates meet with Churchill, in order that the Prime Minister might hear for himself their opinion that the plan was feasible. Churchill had been sufficiently persuaded to let Stalin know, in the course of their August talks in Moscow, that a program of betterment was being studied. But he had put off definite approval because of the opposition of the British theater commanders. They wanted to be sure that if the Americans took over the operation of this railroad, the needs of the British forces in the region would be well met.

After his visit to Moscow, Harriman had made another tour of inspection in Iran. When at Cairo he had rejoined Churchill, who was en route to other places, he had spoken still more confidently about the soundness of the idea. Having in the interval consulted the President again, he had won Churchill's assent by proposing that British representatives should retain the right to allocate the traffic facilities of the railroad, thereby assuring that British needs would not be overlooked. Churchill had agreed to ask Roosevelt to take over the job. The Prime Minister, after all, was sharing influence and activity in a region over which for many decades Britain had kept jealous guard.

Generals Marshall and Somervell (Chief, Army Services of Supply) had favored acceptance of the assignment. The President had approved it. The War Department had agreed to manage the enterprise; an operating organization headed by General Donald H. Connolly, an army engineer, had been recruited and flown to Iran. Diesel engines built for American railways had been requisitioned. Ships to transport construction materials and railway supplies had been found despite the competing demands of TORCH. The immediate results were only scantily praised by the Soviet authorities, but they no doubt counted closely the enlarging volume of supplies that began during the autumn to reach the Soviet Union over this route.

Progress was well underway in November. By that time, to return to the main scene, the Allies were no longer being compelled carefully to divide the bare means of staving off disaster. They were beginning to accumulate the greater means of pressing forward on the offensive.

For during November, success—dramatic and multiple—was about to reward the efforts of all members of the coalition. The British forces under Alexander were winning their first great desert victory, flinging Rommel into retreat from Alamein. The German armies on the Soviet Eastern Front were stopped, the large one before Stalingrad near exhaustion. TORCH was getting underway.

Before TORCH was effected, some stubborn differences between the Americans and British as to how it should be conducted had to be adjusted. These had clustered about three connected questions: How many landings should be made? Where? And by what forces?

The Americans had been fearful of risking large operations inside the Mediterranean past the Straits of Gibraltar. They were afraid of being cut off either by the Spaniards or the Germans coming down through Spain. But Churchill and his military advisers thought that the shadow of this peril ought not to rule. They were convinced that the whole operation would turn out to be of small importance unless it reached into Algiers—in Churchill's words "the softest and most paying spot." In supplementing the reasons that he gave the President for so venturing, the Prime Minister had reminded him that "supported by Harriman with your full approval," he had told Stalin that TORCH would be of large dimensions and reach well into the Mediterranean. The plan of campaign that had been adopted was a compromise between American perplexities (which Stalin in Moscow had seemed to share) and British assurance. One landing was to be made on the Atlantic coast of Africa outside the Straits of Gibraltar, at Casablanca; the other two were to be inside the Mediterranean, one as far east as Algiers.

The other point of difference had turned out to be somewhat unreal. The American government had maintained diplomatic relations with the Vichy regime. Neither the British nor Soviet government had done so; each had shared the uses of this unpleasant association without its onus. The Americans also had made an elaborate secret effort to get the help for their entry of top French commanders and governors holding posts in North Africa. Because of this, and the tradition of mutual Franco-American aid in the cause of freedom, Roosevelt had the buoyant belief that all the French in North Africa except the fervid Vichy devotees would welcome the Americans, while they might well oppose the British. So he proposed that the initial assaults should be made only by an American ground force, supported by British naval, transport, and air units; and that the British landings, which were to be farther to the east, should follow after French compliance was assured. Churchill had said he would not oppose this plan if the President insisted on it. But he had presented such pointed reasons to the contrary that in the end it was decided that the landings should be simultaneous —with American troops in the van. The local French defenders, it developed, behaved much the same toward both sets of oncoming liberators.

Before the decision-makers as they pored over the prospectus of their huge military plan there had beckoned the chance that the whole

African coast might be swiftly captured. This large aim was expressed in the directive which the Combined Chiefs of Staff had prepared on August 13th for General Eisenhower, who had been selected to be Commander-in-Chief of the Allied Expeditionary Force. Its first sentence read, "The President and the Prime Minister have agreed that combined military operations be directed against Africa, as early as practicable, with a view to gaining, in conjunction with Allied Forces in the Middle East, complete control of North Africa from the Atlantic to the Red Sea." [67]

The assault from the east started first. The British in Libya moved upon the Italian and German lines on October 23rd and within ten days the defenders were in prison camps or fast retreat. In this victory, known as the battle of El Alamein, Churchill detected the turning of the hinge of fate. He has written "It may almost be said, 'Before Alamein we never had a victory. After Alamein we never had a defeat.'" [68]

A few days later (November 8th) in the west the landing craft, crammed with soldiers who had come from the United States, pushed through the surf and put down on the strange African beaches at Casablanca, Oran, and Algiers. To the immense relief of Eisenhower, waiting for word in his cramped headquarters at Gibraltar, the landings were made without Spanish or German intervention—but not, it is true, exactly at the points intended, nor with orderly flow. It was a daring and instructive amphibious operation rather than a model one. [69]

Within two days, Eisenhower as Commander-in-Chief, assuming responsibility for an act which his advisers told him was necessary to cut short local French resistance, made a deal with Admiral Darlan (who had been Vice Premier, Foreign Minister, and Minister of the Interior in the Vichy government). This surprised and disquieted the American and British people. Roosevelt and Churchill stood behind this arrangement as an expedient justified by military stress and purpose. [70] War

[67] *Strategic Planning for Coalition Warfare 1941–42*, page 291.

[68] *The Hinge of Fate*, page 603.

[69] Both plans and events are lucidly explained in *Operations in North African Waters, October, 1942–June, 1943* by Samuel Eliot Morison.

American official anticipations and fears about TORCH were more or less wrong in a variety of respects, notably: (1) the fear that Spain would intervene; (2) the belief that the previous preparation which our secret agents had made would avert all or almost all local French resistance; (3) the notion that the French would receive the American forces quite differently from the British forces; (4) the hope that the Frenchman we had selected to head French forces in North Africa, General Giraud, would be able to influence local military officials. These faults of judgment were small compared with the German failure to grasp in advance what was going to be attempted. The signs that they might have read were many, early, and obvious.

[70] See statement by President on temporary political arrangement in North and West Africa, Nov. 18, 1942. *State Department Bulletin,* issue of November 21, 1942.

was having its own upsetting way, imposing its own demeaning terms.

Darlan's influence brought French resistance in North Africa to a quicker end and saved some lives. The capture of French Morocco was eased; control of West Africa, with the port of Dakar safe, was secured without a fight. It also lightened the task and worries of the expeditionary force in connection with the local government of the areas entered. But greater chances had lured on the sponsors of this unwholesome working accord with one associated with the elements we were fighting. It had been hoped that the landing forces would be able to advance swiftly into Tunisia, there to make junction with the British forces advancing from the east. This expectation did not lapse at once. Two weeks after the landings, General Marshall was still advising the President that the Americans would be in control of Tunis within two or three weeks unless the Axis developed unforeseen strength. But Hitler sent strong, fresh forces into Tunisia so that the battle went on there months longer.

What the intangible costs of this dealing with Darlan were no one can feel sure of knowing. But, to draw upon my own impression of the event and its contemporary reception, it shook hard the faith of many in the durability of the principles for which we professed to be fighting, or in our devotion to them. However, the recoil from it may well have deterred other similar war bargains later on.

In the first days after the acceptance of Darlan, the Soviet press gave space to many stories from abroad reporting foreign criticism. Stalin at this very time was letting the British know that he was suspicious of the meaning of the Hess flight to Scotland and the silence that had followed his internment; he did not bar out the possibility that some sort of secret arrangement with Germany might be in the making. Molotov told the American and British Ambassadors in Moscow that he had qualms about what was going on in North Africa, that he and his colleagues were confused over the meaning of the rapport with Darlan. The American and British governments sought to allay these suspicions. They explained in terms of military necessity their use of men who had served Vichy and had appeared willing to serve Hitler. The President's public statement of November 18th, calling the Darlan deal one of temporary expediency and again repudiating Vichy policies, was cited as proof. It was effective. On November 20th Molotov asked Loy Henderson, then in charge of the American Embassy in Moscow, to let Washington know that he understood the transaction. He also served a reminder that the Soviet government was deeply interested in French Africa, and hoped that the American government would not set up any sort of administration there without advance consultation.

Stalin next made it plain that he thought it would have been foolish to have allowed taste or principle to have deprived the Allies of advantage in their war. On December 13th, when writing Roosevelt to tell him again that he would not be able to join him and the Prime Minister at Casablanca (about which soon more will be told), he went on to say, "In view of all sorts of rumours about the attitude of the Union of Soviet Socialist Republics towards the use made of Darlan or other men like him, it may not be unnecessary for me to tell you that, in my opinion, as well as in that of my colleagues, Eisenhower's policy with regard to Darlan, Boisson, Giraud and others is perfectly correct. I think it is a great achievement that you succeeded in bringing Darlan and others into the orbit of the Allies fighting Hitler." What counted most with him at the moment was that the deal might enable the Red Army to get help more quickly than if French resistance in North Africa was prolonged.

The assassination of Darlan on December 24th blanched but did not wholly wash away the association with men formerly attached to Vichy. The American and British governments kept Moscow informed of their guiding thoughts in dealing with the succeeding French authorities in North Africa. We would not, it was explained to Molotov, set up a French government in North Africa. In dealings with General Giraud and all other French factions we would welcome all elements of French resistance and deal with them on a basis of the support they promised in the fight against Germany. We would support and maintain French administrations and French territories on the basis of their contribution to the war effort. Civil representatives were to be appointed to relieve military commanders of political problems, acting as agents of the United Nations and working side by side with military authorities. The Soviet government did not object to this program.

However, there was another and unruly French movement with which to reckon. General de Gaulle and his Free French associates and supporters were determined to displace General Giraud and all other French groups as speaking for France and its empire. For that purpose they did not always scruple to play upon the differences of judgment or purpose between the three main Allies. It was not going to be easy to fit a liberated France back into the concert of democratic powers. But the story of how this problem emerged comes later. For here, at the end of 1942, the coalition was discussing what it should do when it left North Africa safely behind the line of battle.

10. What Was to Follow TORCH—The Second Front in 1943?

All the while that TORCH was being organized, the planners had been looking beyond it. They were trying to decide how next to direct their combat effort as between the multiple points of possible action. The strain between the Americans and British which had marked the decision for TORCH in July had not entirely yielded to the momentum of their association in this venture. It had lingered on, especially in the minds of the Americans who had lost out.

When planning talks had been resumed in September, the U.S. Joint Chiefs had entered into them with a seeming wish to vindicate their original view that TORCH would not be worth what it would cost; that it was likely to absorb so much vital combat resources, including shipping, that any attempt to invade the Continent in force would have to be indefinitely postponed. They had noted with a kind of grim satisfaction the belated English recognition of this fact. As put by Eisenhower in a message to Marshall on September 21st: he had the impression that the Prime Minister and certain of his close advisers were at long last becoming actively conscious of the "inescapable" cost of TORCH; and astonished "to find out that TORCH practically eliminates any opportunity for a 1943 Roundup [cross-Channel invasion of France]." [71]

Whether or not in reality that fact was a surprise for Churchill is hard to tell. In his backward-looking account of the matter, he has since implied that it was and that he accepted the conclusion only regretfully. "I," he wrote later in *The Hinge of Fate*, "had not yet brought myself to accept this view. I still hoped that French Northwest Africa, including the Tunisian tip, might fall into our hands after a few months' fighting. In this case the main invasion of Occupied France from England would still be possible in July or August, 1943." [72] Accordingly he had continued to argue that while conducting TORCH and other sanctioned operations, Great Britain and the United States ought still to be able to find the needed means for an invasion in 1943. In this spirit, on September 22nd, the day after Eisenhower had reported to Marshall that Churchill was learning better, the buoyant

[71] *Strategic Planning for Coalition Warfare 1941–1942*, page 325.
[72] *The Hinge of Fate*, page 648.

controversialist had sent a message to the President saying that he was troubled by the view that Eisenhower and other Americans were taking in this matter. He had then gone on to remark, in regard to the apparent American disposition to renounce the invasion project in 1943: "This will be another tremendous blow for Stalin. Already Maisky is asking questions about the spring offensive." [73] Churchill was finding it hard to decide what could, what had best be done.[74]

September to early October, to note the fact again, would not have been a good time to tell Stalin that a cross-Channel invasion in 1943 was out of the question, for this had been the period when Stalingrad stood in greatest peril. Both Maisky and Litvinov were openly expressing fears that the city was doomed, that the Caucasus would be taken, and that the Germans would then push on to the Urals, placing Moscow in a state of siege similar to that of Leningrad the year before. The Soviet propaganda agencies were keeping up their agitation for the second front. The Russian government was proving to its people that it was doing all it could to get help for them; it was providing this vent for the suffering being endured; and it was keeping the Allies reminded of what Russia expected of them.

The way in which the situation was portrayed to the Russian people is exemplified by a cartoon to which *Pravda* (on October 6th) gave front-page space. Its title was "A Meeting of Military Experts: The Question of a Second Front." The cartoon depicted two vigorous young Red Army officers, whose tunics bore the identification General "Determination" and General "Courage." One was pointing to a map while appealing to a group of fat, elderly officers seated around the table. Each of these also was labelled, to wit: General "They Will Beat Us," General "Is It Worth the Risk," General "No Need to Hurry," General "Let's Wait," and General "Something Might Go Wrong." There was a calendar against the wall lettered largely "October 1942" and a clock with hands standing at 11:30.

Nor had the Soviet government eased up on the theme when in November the situation on the Eastern Front changed decisively and

[73] *Strategic Planning for Coalition Warfare, 1941–1942*, page 326.

[74] Field Marshal Alan Brooke's Diary and notes reveal that during the autumn of 1942 Churchill's attitude swung back and forth. Thus Brooke's comment for December 3rd, 1942, reads: "Up to now I had been able to carry Winston and the other two Chiefs of Staff with me, but now Winston was suddenly swinging away and wanting to establish a Western Front in 1943. At that afternoon meeting . . . he said, 'You must not think that you can get off with your "Sardines" (referring to Sicily and Sardinia) in 1943; no—we must establish a Western Front, and what is more, we promised Stalin we should do so when we were in Moscow.' To which I replied: 'No, *we* did not promise.' " *The Turn of the Tide*, page 530.

Stalingrad and the Caucasus were saved. As showing the panorama of thoughts which Stalin continued to keep before the Russian people, two extracts from his Twenty-Fifth Anniversary Report as People's Commissar of Defense (on November 6th, two days before the landings in North Africa) are worth scanning.

In explanation of why it had been possible for the German forces to advance during the past few months:

"How are we to explain the fact that the Germans were nevertheless able to take the initiative in military operations this year and achieve substantial tactical successes on our front? It is to be explained by the fact that the Germans and their allies were able to muster all their available reserves, transfer them to the Eastern Front and create a big superiority of forces in one of the directions. . . . But why were they able to muster all their reserves and transfer them to the Eastern Front? Because the absence of a second front in Europe enabled them to carry out this operation without any risk." [75]

To assure the Soviet people that the war coalition was solid and a guarantee of ultimate victory:

"It would be ridiculous to deny the existence of different ideologies and social systems of the various countries that constitute the Anglo-Soviet-American coalition. But does this preclude the possibility, and the expediency, of joint action on the part of the members of this coalition against the common enemy . . . ? Certainly not. More than that. The very existence of this threat imperatively dictates the necessity of joint action among the members of the coalition. . . . Is not the program of action of the Anglo-Soviet-American coalition a sufficient basis upon which to organize a joint struggle against Hitler tyranny . . . ? I think it is quite sufficient. . . . The only conclusion to be drawn is that the Anglo-Soviet-American coalition has every chance of vanquishing the Italo-German coalition, and that it certainly will do so." [76]

This continuous Soviet pressure for the second front was one side of the triangle in the arguments between the American and British staffs that had continued as TORCH-Day (November 8th) had arrived. The second side was the inclination of the U.S. Joint Chiefs of Staff, if the invasion of the Continent was not to be possible in 1943, to devote resources to the Pacific rather than to the Mediterranean. The third side was the desire, at its peak in Churchill but shared by Roosevelt, to develop operations in the Mediterranean Sea across from the North African shores.

[75] Stalin, Joseph, *The Great Patriotic War of the Soviet Union*, page 61.
[76] *Ibid.*, pages 67–68.

No sooner had the expedition landed than Churchill gave way to his longing to roam far down this third side. He counted the advantages to be gained by securing control of, or at least safe military passage over, that sea, and then on to Sicily or Sardinia, Italy or France, Greece and Turkey—where else? His visions, as recorded in the memo he sent to the British Chiefs of Staff on November 9th, were prancing: first, the capture of Sicily or Sardinia; and then, while pinning down the enemy in Northern France and the Low Countries by continuous preparations, to invade, to make "a decisive attack on Italy, or, better still, Southern France, together with operations not involving serious shipping expense and other forms of pressure to bring in Turkey and operate overland with the Russians into the Balkans." [77]

Roosevelt, as he too read the early bulletins from North Africa, was carried along this same route. Thus in the message he sent to Churchill on November 12th, to tell him how pleased he was with the way affairs were going in North Africa and Egypt, he went on to remark:

"This brings up the additional steps that should be taken when and if the south shore of the Mediterranean is cleared and under our control. It is hoped that you with your Chiefs of Staff in London and I with the Combined Staff here may make a survey of the possibilities, including a forward movement directed against Sardinia, Sicily, Italy, Greece, and other Balkan areas, and including the possibility of obtaining Turkish support for an attack through the Black Sea against Germany's flank." [78]

Who encouraged the President to look that way? Certainly not the War Department. But Churchill was cheered. He was bent on pursuing this "peripheral" strategy. But perhaps the better to smooth the way toward its acceptance at his prospective meeting with Roosevelt (which took place at Casablanca in the coming January), he seemed to seek to give the impression that his Service Chiefs were imposing their views on him rather than the other way about.

Stalin spoke out admiringly about the Allied campaign in Africa.[79] But he continued to regard that action only as a prelude to more decisive operations in the west, not as an equivalent or good alternative. Despite sunnier diplomatic weather, at every chance he repeated the

[77] *The Hinge of Fate,* page 649.

[78] *Ibid.,* page 630.

[79] As in his reply to questions presented by Henry Cassidy, Moscow Representative of the Associated Press, on November 13th: "The African campaign refutes again the skeptics who affirm that the Anglo-American leaders cannot organize a serious war campaign. No one but first rate organizers could carry on such serious war operations as the successful landings in North Africa across the ocean, as the quick occupation of harbors and wide territories and as smashing of the Italo-German armies being effected so masterfully."

same question to the Americans and British: When may we expect you to fling yourselves across the Channel, and thus cause the Germans to divide their armies?

To glance to one side and slightly forward for a moment, at this time Operation VELVET (the U.S.-British combat air operation in the Caucasus front) was being allowed to expire. When it had first been proposed in July–August, Stalin had thought that the force was ready enough so that it would be able to engage quickly to hold the line of the Caucasus. But the British contingent, as has been told, was held back until the battle for Egypt had been decided; and other critical demands delayed the coming of the American contingent. While these were still being brought together, the crisis in the Caucasus had passed its worst period. So on learning how much accommodation they would have to provide for these foreign air squadrons, and how much of the tonnage of supplies coming over the southern route they would consume, the Russians decided that this help would not be worth the draft on their own resources and energies.[80] Thus when Roosevelt renewed the offer in December, Stalin said in effect: Thank you very much, but we no longer need your airmen on the Eastern Front; we would greatly like to have the planes, but we can pilot and take care of them ourselves. What we need from you is battle action in the west that will take or keep away from us forty German divisions or so.

Pelted from above and afar by the hailstorm of plans, the British and American Chiefs of Staff continued their separate examination of the problem of what to do next. And in December the weather of decision was harsher as the fighting in North Africa took a disappointing turn; the advance from the west lagged, then came to a halt.

In the last presentation of their views which they made (on January 3rd) to their American colleagues before the meeting at Casablanca, the British Chiefs of Staff restated their reasons for patience in preparation for the time when the cross-Channel operation could result in a great victory. If, they reckoned, we first forced Italy out of the war and the Germans tried to maintain their line in Russia at its current length, they would be some 54 divisions and 2,200 aircraft short of what they would need on all fronts. They recommended as the next step the in-

[80] The British government renewed the offer in the spring of 1943 when the Tunisian situation was cleared up. Then Stalin again let it lapse. Churchill asked Maisky, the Soviet Ambassador in London, why; and Maisky said that the Soviet High Command thought that about 25,000 men would be needed to maintain these air squadrons on the ordinary American and British scale; and that so great a drain on Soviet combat forces was not likely to be justified by the combat value of this foreign air force. Note from Churchill to the Chief of Air Staff, May 1, 1943, *The Hinge of Fate*, page 955.

vasion of either Sardinia or Sicily. While the advance in the Mediterranean was carried forward they conceived that the Americans could build up a huge air force based on England and continue to send ground divisions, so that by the fall of 1943 the force assembled might be great enough for an attempt to cross the Channel. But they visualized only a shrunken operation, one for which less resources would have to be accumulated, and to be ventured only if German combat power was by then much reduced. They thought this dual program practicable if only the U.S. Joint Chiefs did not insist on going ahead fast with the war in the Far East.[81]

Churchill did not set his face against this advice. He was still alert not to give the impression that he was renouncing the cross-Channel invasion project for 1943.

The U.S. Joint Chiefs of Staff were divided and frustrated. Military historians will tell more fully than I can here of the doubts in the planning groups; of the controlled differences in opinion between four strong-willed men—Marshall, King, Arnold and Leahy; of the compromises and changes of mind in this time after TORCH. Many of the studies and memos written within this responsible circle had a brooding tone. They were pessimistic about the rate at which the resources needed for a large cross-Channel invasion could be gathered if the campaign in the Mediterranean was carried further. All dismissed the proposals for a smaller invasion as wasteful and futile. Some, particularly those produced by the Navy, urged greater offensives in the Far East, no matter what was done elsewhere.

Admiral King and General Arnold were drawn by what might be quickly achieved in the Mediterranean. The American Air Force was pleased by the chance to get more time to build up bombing squadrons for use against Germany. But General Marshall remained firmly of the opinion that primary effort must be devoted toward getting ready for a cross-Channel operation in 1943. He thought this measure would be more effective than advancing on Sicily or Sardinia, since it would cost less shipping, give more satisfaction to the Russians, and engage German air forces more fully. But the Joint Chiefs did not adopt this as a common conclusion. When on January 7th the President asked them whether it was agreed that they should meet the British at Casablanca "united in advocating a cross-Channel operation," Marshall replied, "that there was not a united front on that subject, particularly among the planners."[82] The President seems to have been ready to go along either course.

[81] *Cross-Channel Attack,* pages 36 and 37. *Strategic Planning for Coalition Warfare 1941–1942,* pages 377–78.
[82] *Cross-Channel Attack,* page 38.

Roosevelt and Churchill were going to meet at Casablanca, along with their Chiefs of Staff, in order to transmute these stacked-up differences into a joint policy. For months a personal meeting of this sort had been in prospect. But the efforts to arrange it had at times gotten as criss-crossed as the discussions about strategic plans. Here I shall tell only of the main items in the last segment of a three-cornered correspondence that had been protracted, and at times disorderly.

On November 21st, the landings in North Africa having been accomplished, Roosevelt had sent Stalin a message saying that he and Churchill thought the time had come to talk with him and the Soviet military staff. Such a conference, the President had explained, seemed most advisable before they took the next steps in the Mediterranean, since these would bear definitely on the Soviet battle situation and Stalin's winter campaign plans. Before Roosevelt got Stalin's answer to this bid, Churchill (November 24th) had renewed earlier proposals that the Americans and British meet without further ado or without waiting for the Russians. His urgency is to be understood by reference to the fact that he knew at this time there was another brief impulse within the U.S. Joint Chiefs of Staff to turn to the Pacific. But Roosevelt had been bent on having the Russians present at any military-strategical conference, and said so in his answer to Churchill (November 26th). He thought this triple conference should be held as soon as the Germans were knocked out of Tunis, which he hoped might be within a month or six weeks. "I feel very strongly," he had remarked, "that we have got to sit down at the table with the Russians." [83]

Churchill had sent his answer that same day. He agreed, he said, in principle that there should be a conference with the Russians. But he thought that it should take place only after the Americans and British had first talked their problems out and arrived at a joint and agreed view. One of his reasons was that the Russians' main demand would be a heavy invasion of the Continent either from the west or the south, or both, in 1943; and this could be dealt with effectively only by Roosevelt and himself with the help of their expert colleagues.

In his answers to Roosevelt and Churchill (of the 27th) Stalin had not grasped the chance for a personal meeting. He suggested instead that the three military staffs might confer, and submit recommendations which the three of them might then consider by correspondence. This did not promise effective results. But the President would not admit he was stumped. He had still clung to the chance that Stalin could be made to see that he ought, both for the sake of Soviet interests and the

[83] *The Hinge of Fate,* page 662.

common war effort, to meet with Churchill and himself. So he had sent another appeal to Stalin (on December 2nd), saying, "My most compelling reason is that I am very anxious to have a talk with you. My suggestion would be that we meet secretly in some secure place in Africa that is convenient to all three of us. The time, about January 15 or 20." Nor had he become willing to hazard the chances or outcome of the triple conference he was seeking by conferring separately with the British in advance; he told Churchill the next day: "I would question the advisability of Marshall and the others going to England prior to the conference, because I do not want to give Stalin the impression that we are settling everything between ourselves before we meet him." [84] Churchill, resilient, had ranged himself along with the President in a cordial bid to Stalin: "I earnestly hope you will agree. We must decide at the earliest moment the best way of attacking Germany in Europe with all possible force in 1943." [85]

Stalin was not to be persuaded to leave his post of command. He had answered both suggestions on the 6th that he favored the idea of a meeting to fix the general line of military strategy. But then he had gone on to say, "To my great regret however I will not be in a position to leave the Soviet Union. Things are so hot now, it would be impossible for me to be absent even for a single day. . . ." And then [to Churchill], "I am waiting your reply to the paragraph of my preceding letter dealing with the establishment of the second front in Western Europe in the spring of 1943." [86] He had attached to these replies the latest news about the further course of battle in the Stalingrad area, saying that he hoped to annihilate the German armies there. By then the German attempt to relieve the encircled Sixth Army in Stalingrad had failed; the whole of the Army Group Don had been pushed so far back that it would no longer be able to intervene against the final Russian assaults on the surrounded force; and even Hitler had at last been compelled to consent to the withdrawal of German armies from the Caucasus in the south.[87]

The President, though still wanting some Soviet representatives in on the next bout of talk on strategy even if he could not get Stalin, had come part way round. He was probably becoming impatient with the persistent differences between the American and British Chiefs of Staff, for the time left for decision was getting short. He had agreed that he

[84] *Ibid.,* page 664.
[85] *Ibid.,* page 665.
[86] *Ibid.,* page 666.
[87] See the lucid account of the Stalingrad campaign by Colonel General Kurt Zeitzler, Chief of the Army General Staff, in the collection of narratives brought together in the book, *The Fatal Decisions,* edited by Seymour Freidin and William Richardson.

and Churchill should get together even if Stalin did not join them. But he still thought that second best. So he had suggested to Churchill as well that if "Uncle Joe" should say that he would meet with them later, say March 1st, then the military staffs of the three countries might meet first somewhere in Africa and make preliminary recommendations. As a matter of fact Roosevelt had already (in a message sent off on the 8th and delivered on the 10th) asked Stalin whether he could not look ahead and set a tentative forward date for a meeting in North Africa at the start of March. Once again Stalin had replied that military reasons would make it impossible for him to leave the Soviet Union either at once or at the beginning of March. The rest of his answer had implied that anyhow he did not understand what there was to talk about—all the British and Americans had to do was to keep their promise and open a second front in Europe in the spring.

This third refusal had settled the matter. Arrangements had been quickly completed for the American-British assembly. It is quite possible that by staying away Stalin avoided a serious quarrel. It is doubtful whether he would have assented to anything less than an unconditional promise of a cross-Channel operation in 1943, and most doubtful if Churchill would have given one. The Americans would have been under pressure to suspend offensive operations in the Pacific. Roosevelt did not seem to be worried by such possibilities, though while en route to Casablanca he did suggest to Stalin that he would like to send General Marshall to Moscow in the very near future, presumably to guard against Stalin's possible displeasure at decisions that would be made in his absence.

Would the President and Prime Minister be more successful in coming to an accord as to what should best be done, and in what order, than their service staffs had been after four months of work? What program for the invasion could be fitted in satisfactorily with projects in the Mediterranean and prospects in the Far East?

All such problems had been up to then determined solely by reckoning of military chances and costs, advantages and risks. But records of Churchill's thought since made public tell how actively his foreseeing mind was already engaged with the many political questions that would press as the American, British, and Russian forces moved on. Accordingly, he wished to have Foreign Secretary Eden along with him at Casablanca. But this intention was snagged by the President. Roosevelt had been conducting his correspondence about the prospective meeting personally through the White House. He did not consult Hull or the State Department about the matters which were to come under review at Casablanca. He did not wish to have the Secretary of State or any representative of the State Department at this meeting. He planned to have Hopkins along to deal with any questions outside the military sphere that might require attention. Thus he asked Churchill to leave Eden at home. Against his own wishes, Churchill agreed that he would.

There is no record of the President's reasons for excluding his Secretary of State. So one is left to choose between surmises. Perhaps it did not seem out of the way because the primary purpose of the meeting was to decide military matters. Or perhaps he mistrusted the ability or wish of the State Department to maintain secrecy. Or perhaps, since he had in mind to see de Gaulle, he feared Hull's petulance in that connection. Or perhaps—the final perhaps—the two men at this time were getting along poorly and the President felt a lack of concordance in spirit and idea.

Whatever the reason, one is left to wonder whether, if Eden and Hull had been present, the conference would not have paid more and earlier attention to the political issues that were to emerge before the year 1943 was out—especially those that were going to arise when the attack moved against Italy. And also whether, if they had been present, the momentous statement regarding unconditional surrender which was made at Casablanca would have been made, or made in the way it was made.

PERIOD THREE

From the Casablanca Conference, January 1943, to the Assault on Sicily in July; the Coalition Carries On Despite Cacophony over the Cross-Channel Invasion

11. Casablanca Conference: Military Decisions and Unconditional Surrender

DURING the Conference at Casablanca, which started on the 12th of January 1943, the British Army in the desert was moving well through Tripoli toward the Mareth Line. General Alexander, Commander-in-Chief in the Middle East, by his spirited reports swayed decision in favor of going on to complete control of the Mediterranean. The Russians at Stalingrad by then had General Paulus, Commander-in-Chief of the Sixth German Army, and his quarter of a million men shut up in the shattered city, and were engaged in two forward actions in the Don Basin. There was no longer a need to reckon with a possible emergency on the Eastern Front that would require a sudden rescue effort from the West.

Aided by these improvements in circumstance, the Americans and British at Casablanca managed to adjust their ideas sufficiently to arrive at an accord upon their combat plans for some time ahead. But they left open the basic strategic dilemmas which had compelled them to meet.

The essentials of the military decisions made there need only be briefly summarized:

1. The security of sea communications to Britain was to remain the first charge upon combined resources. The loss of shipping up to the end of 1942 had exceeded new construction by about a million tons. Field Marshal Brooke called the shipping shortage "a stranglehold on all offensive operations."

2. The effort to supply Soviet forces was to be sustained. But no important new measures to do so were authorized.

3. The battle for the whole North African coast was to be carried on to complete victory.

4. Concurrently, preparations for taking Sicily (Operation HUSKY) were to be started at once, with a view to beginning this action at the earliest possible moment. The American Chiefs of Staff were reluctant to agree to this movement. Marshall particularly was afraid that it would deter and delay the contemplated landing in France without achieving any decisive result. He was met with the argument that no other good use could be made during 1943 of the forces already in the Mediterranean. The facts adduced by the British Chiefs of Staff proved that any possible cross-Channel invasion effort that could be tried in

the summer of 1943 would at best be too small to make much difference in the course of the land battle in Europe, and at worst could be such a ruinous failure as to make another attempt impossible. In contrast, the reasons given for advancing against Sicily were strong. Beyond the accountable ones but well fixed in Churchill's mind was the hope that this passage across the Mediterranean might knock Italy out of the war, and cause the Germans to use many divisions to defend Italy and take over the control of the Balkans from the Italians. Marshall yielded, saying however as he did so that "he was most anxious not to become committed to interminable operations in the Mediterranean. He wished Northern France to be the scene of the main effort against Germany— that had always been his conception." [1]

5. The combined strategic bombing offensive against Germany was to be increased. The American program of day bombing was to be added to the British program of night bombing. This extending assault was needed to keep wearing down the German air force and reducing German ability and will to resist the cross-Channel invasion.

6. The principle that the United States and Britain must continue to concentrate forces in Great Britain for the defeat of Germany was reaffirmed. Preparations for invasion were to be as great and as rapid as other projects would permit and the invasion was to be started as soon as judged feasible. More conclusive than this vague direction of resources for the invasion build-up was the accompanying agreement to set up at once a combined command and planning organization in London (COSSAC). This group was asked to work out a program for reentry into Western Europe—in 1943 if Germany neared collapse, or possibly a first small wedge that year, to be developed into an invasion in force in 1944. This was the start of the planning that produced OVERLORD, the prelude to the appointment of Eisenhower as Supreme Commander and the establishment in February 1944 of a combined command headquarters (SHAEF).

7. The way was left open for such further operations in the Pacific as the U.S. Joint Chiefs might decide on. But this authorization was subject to an indistinct caution to the effect that the combat means to be used there should not be so great as to prevent the Allies from grasping any good chance that might come along to defeat Germany in 1943. In consenting even to this guarded authorization, the British Chiefs of Staff went against their judgment and wishes. They did not see any essential military reason for taking the initiative against Japan that spring. They feared that to attempt to do so might use up resources needed to go on with the fight in Europe; and they did not

[1] *Cross-Channel Attack*, page 43.

think the Philippines, which the Americans were already eyeing, could be taken until after Germany was defeated. The Americans, however, were convinced that the Japanese ought not to be allowed to settle themselves more solidly in their Pacific positions, and from there start new offensives. Admiral King tried to face down the British with an estimate that of the total war effort against the Axis only fifteen per cent of Allied resources was then being used in the Pacific (including the Indian Ocean and Burma). He and Marshall wanted that proportion doubled.[2] They went so far as to threaten once again that unless enough resources were kept in the Pacific to establish what they regarded as a sound position there, the United States might regrettably have to restrain her commitments in the European theater. But to settle the argument they agreed that the various Pacific operations should be spaced out over the year, and also that they would be carried out "with the resources available in the theatre"—which included most of the American fleet and much of our shipping and landing craft.

This was the accord which in 1943 sent American and Australian forces on their way from Guadalcanal and New Guinea to capture (or isolate) the Japanese base at Rabaul and to break through the barrier of the Bismarck Sea; and to go northwestward toward Truk and Guam.

8. An effort to recapture Burma in 1943 and thus open a land route into China was provisionally approved. Subject to later confirmation, there was to be a land offensive in the north part of Burma and an amphibious operation in the south to recapture the port of Rangoon. But not long after the Conference it became evident that Churchill was stubbornly opposed to this last venture, and later he fought it to a standstill.

9. The American combat air force in China was to be strengthened at once. The air transport fleet flying the dangerous route over the Himalayas from India to China was also to be substantially enlarged. These measures were thought necessary to keep China in the war. Roosevelt would have liked to have done more. Chiang Kai-shek thought them too little.

This compromise program of many elements was left loose at the joints to allow flexibility in execution. As carried into effect the military decisions made at Casablanca were to mean:

that the future destiny of the countries at both ends of the Mediterranean was going to be in American-British hands;

that Italy was to be exposed to so great a weight of war that it would collapse and be the first member of the Axis to surrender;

[2] Admiral Ernest J. King and W. M. Whitehill, *Fleet Admiral King*, pages 416–17.

that the Soviet forces—though substantially relieved by the combination of Allied operations—were going to have to continue to bear the main brunt of the land fighting in Europe during 1943;

that the U.S. Joint Chiefs would retain their right to control military decisions for the southwest and central Pacific. They used this leeway freely and boldly.

If this planning for the flow of military operations had been all that was said and done at Casablanca, the assembly there would not have a spectacular place in the history of the war or the coalition. It would, and properly, be regarded in retrospect merely as an interim determination of military measures. What has made it so memorable is that, at a press conference, the policy of "unconditional surrender" was announced. The members of the Axis were told that the United States and Great Britain would not negotiate or bargain with them about the terms for ending the war they had begun; that they would have to give themselves over to the sense of justice and kindness of the peoples whom they had sought to crush. This they were told, and later on would be told most plainly, not in a spirit of retribution, but so that it should be clear that their surrender was as complete and unqualified as their defeat.

Contrary to the impression current until more ample records had become available, Roosevelt's announcement of this policy was preceded by discussion. Nor was the fact that he was considering the policy unknown to his military advisers. To the contrary, representatives of the Army and Navy played a part in the adoption of the doctrine.

As early as April–May 1942 one of the subcommittees organized under the aegis of the State Department had begun to consider the problems that would be presented when and if enemy states showed a wish to end the fight. This was the Subcommittee on Security Problems. Norman Davis, former Ambassador-at-Large and intimate colleague of Secretary of State Hull, was its chairman. General George V. Strong and Admiral A. J. Hepburn (with Admiral R. E. Train as alternate) were its Army and Navy members. The prevalent opinion in this group had been that the United States was at war again only because Germany had not been compelled to submit unconditionally at the end of the First World War; that its people were therefore easily convinced that they had been betrayed. This had led to the recommendation (approved on May 21st) that "On the assumption that the victory of the United Nations will be conclusive, unconditional surrender rather than an armistice should be sought from the principal enemy states except perhaps Italy."

Just what was meant by this is hard to tell from the ambiguities in the scanty record. It is unclear in particular whether the subcommittee visualized that the political authorities should be required to surrender the whole nation on this basis or merely an unconditional surrender of the armed forces arranged by their commanders.[2a] There are indications that this latter course was favored by most of the subcommittee, impressed by General Strong's prognosis that since there would be twenty-odd allies wanting a share in the determination of surrender terms, they would be hard to settle through a political process and the resultant military terms might well be weakened.

Subsequent events suggest that Roosevelt found the views of the subcommittee, as reported to him by Norman Davis, sound. But the question remained dormant until shortly before Roosevelt left for Casablanca. Then (on January 7, 1943) he informed the Joint Chiefs that he intended to support the "unconditional surrender" concept as the basic Allied war aim. It is likely that he also told them that he would discuss with Churchill possible joint assurances to Stalin that the United States and Great Britain would continue on until they reached Berlin, and that their only terms would be unconditional surrender. I do not know of any contemporary protest by the Joint Chiefs, or even of any staff study of the military value or consequences of this policy.

In any case, at the famous joint press conference of January 24th at Casablanca, after reference to the military program that had been adopted, Roosevelt went on to say:

". . . Peace can come to the world only by the total elimination of German and Japanese war power. . . . The elimination of German, Japanese, and Italian war power means the unconditional surrender by Germany, Italy, and Japan. That means a reasonable assurance of future world peace. It does not mean the destruction of the population of Germany, Italy, or Japan, but it does mean the destruction of the philosophies in those countries which are based on conquest and the subjugation of other people."[3]

According to a memo (presumably by Hopkins) printed by Sherwood, Roosevelt pretended that he had not thought of stating this policy

[2a] In a paper delivered to the American Political Science Association in September 1956 entitled "A Comparative Analysis of Problems and Methods of Coalition Action in Two World Wars," Captain Tracy B. Kittredge, USNR (ret.) former historian of Joint Chiefs of Staff, stated, "It has been recommended by representatives of the Joint Chiefs of Staff that no armistice be granted Germany, Japan, Italy and the satellites until they offered the 'unconditional surrender' of their armed forces. These recommendations were submitted to the President at the end of December [1942]."

[3] Rosenman, *The Public Papers and Addresses of Franklin D. Roosevelt,* 1943 vol., page 39.

that day, until he found himself doing so. This reports him as telling the memo-maker that:

"We had so much trouble getting those two French generals together [de Gaulle and Giraud had been brought to Casablanca] that I thought to myself that this was as difficult as arranging the meeting of Grant and Lee—and then suddenly the press conference was on, and Winston and I had had no time to prepare for it, and the thought popped into my mind that they had called Grant 'Old Unconditional Surrender' and the next thing I knew, I had said it." [4]

Roosevelt's final action in making the announcement may have been such a flash impulse. But the record shows plainly that the idea of doing so had been in his mind for some time. And it is not improbable that when he went into the press conference he thought that he might get round to doing so that day. For, according to Hopkins, he spoke from notes which contained the substance of what he said. [5]

Whether his announcement at Casablanca was sudden or premeditated, some of the reasons why the President made it can be guessed at with confidence. It could serve to offset the mistrust created by the deal with Darlan, one of the worst of the Vichy crew, by inferring that no other deals of the kind would be considered. It could help to reassure the Soviet government that the United States and Great Britain were in the war to the end. And it would tend to ward off such troubles as beset Woodrow Wilson after the First World War as a result of discussing conditions of peace with enemy political authorities *before* surrender—his sad experience of alienation from his associates in the war and the righteous German cries of deception.

Churchill was taken aback by the President's utterance. This is puzzling because he had been forewarned by Roosevelt that he favored this policy and was thinking of acquainting the world with it. [6] This is evidenced by the radio he sent to Attlee and the War Cabinet on the 20th of January from Casablanca: "We propose to draw up a statement of the work of the conference for communication to the press at the

---

[4] *Roosevelt and Hopkins,* page 696.

[5] *Ibid.*

[6] Just when is still not clear. Elliot Roosevelt, in his book *As He Saw It,* page 117, tells of being at a lunch at which, according to him, the phrase "unconditional surrender" was born. "For what it is worth," this passage in his book reads, "it can be recorded that it was Father's phrase, that Harry Hopkins took an immediate and strong liking to it, and that Churchill, while he slowly munched a mouthful of food, thought, frowned, thought, finally grinned, and at length announced 'Perfect! And I can just see how Goebbels and the rest of 'em 'll squeal.' "

For what it is worth! Can others hear the Prime Minister say "the rest of 'em 'll squeal"?

proper time. I should be glad to know what the War Cabinet would think of our including in this statement a declaration of the firm intention of the United States and the British Empire to continue the war relentlessly until we have brought about the 'unconditional surrender' of Germany and Japan. The omission of Italy would be to encourage a break-up there." [7] The War Cabinet did not call the policy into question. To the contrary, it answered that it thought it would be better to include Italy, because of the misgivings that would otherwise be caused in Turkey, the Balkans, and elsewhere.

But despite this preceding consideration of the subject, the Prime Minister was, as has been said, surprised and upset when the President, without more ado, burst forth with the announcement at their joint press conference. Possibly this was just because no explicit understanding had been reached that this momentous step would be taken. Apparently the two had not reviewed the question since the talk which prompted Churchill's message to the War Cabinet, and in the interval they had examined the text of a joint public statement to be issued at the end of the Conference, in which there was no reference to "unconditional surrender."

Howsoever, the Prime Minister did not allow his surprise to appear. He lined up with the President at once, telling the assembled press that design, purpose, and unconquerable will would be applied to enforce "unconditional surrender" upon the criminals who had plunged the world into the war.[8] After all, at the time of signing the first accord with the Soviet Union in July 1941, providing that there should be no separate peace with Germany, Eden had declared that Britain was ". . . not in any circumstances prepared to negotiate with Hitler on any subject."

Here a brief incidental comment may be indulged. When Roosevelt was called on to explain what was meant by the demand for unconditional surrender he usually answered by recalling the surrender of the Army of Northern Virginia by General Lee to General Grant at Appomattox Court House. In using this historical instance, the President's

[7] *The Hinge of Fate,* page 684.
[8] *New York Times,* January 27, 1942. According to the account of the press conference in the *London Times* of the same day, after the President had explained what the policy of unconditional surrender did or did not mean, "it was then that the President suggested, as if it were a happy thought that had just entered his mind, that we might call this the 'unconditional Surrender' Meeting. As if in appreciation of Mr. Churchill's ready 'Hear, Hear,' the President remarked that he and Mr. Churchill both had great confidence in the results of the meeting for they had the same purposes and objectives."

association of detail was slipshod, but the example was appropriate to what—his later course showed—was in his mind.

His remembrance of the final scene of surrender at Appomattox Court House, as summed up in later talk with Harriman, was roughly as follows: "General Lee stated that before surrendering it was necessary to have certain things settled, such as the right of officers to their horses which were their own property. Grant stated that his terms were 'unconditional surrender.' Lee accepted. Lee then asked about the horses. Grant replied that the decision was that the officers should retain their horses for they needed them for spring plowing."

In actuality General Grant had used the phrase and earned the sobriquet in an earlier episode in the Civil War, in 1863 when his former classmate and friend at West Point, General Simon Buckner, then Confederate General in command of Fort Donelson, asked for terms. Grant's answer had been, "No terms except an unconditional and immediate surrender can be accepted. I propose to move immediately upon your works."

Grant, however, never made so absolute a demand upon Lee at Appomattox Court House. The surrender there was preceded by, and safeguarded by, letters between the two. In these Grant promised that, having given up their arms and given their parole ". . . each officer and man [of the Army of Northern Virginia] will be allowed to return to his home, not to be disturbed by the United States authority as long as they observe their paroles and the laws in force where they may reside" (Letter Grant to Lee, April 9, 1865).

The correspondence dealt only with what was to be done by and to the Confederate Army surrendering. There was no discussion of or understanding about the treatment which the North might accord the helpless people of the rebel states after the end of the fighting; there was neither an explicit admission of the right of the victors to impose any terms they wished nor any explicit condition restricting their freedom to do so. In short, the surrender at Appomattox Court House was handled as a military matter, and set only the terms on which military action was to be ended. In that regard it was a conditional not an unconditional surrender, as Roosevelt conceived it to have been. But in reference to political authority it was in effect an "unconditional surrender," since it left the Northern authorities bound only by tradition, their consciences, and the rules of humanity. This was, I think the method and basis of surrender which Roosevelt aimed to effect. The later narrative will show how stubbornly he maintained the opinion that this was the most satisfactory way to deal with any and all possibilities of surrender by the main Axis powers.

Both Roosevelt and Churchill soon made an effort to see that the reasons for this policy and the policy itself were understood—and not taken to mean severity without limit. Thus Roosevelt, upon his return, spoke to the White House Press Correspondents Association (on February 12th) of the efforts of the Axis to

"create the idea that if we win the war, Russia, and England, and China and the United States are going to get into a cat-and-dog fight. [This was in the vain hope] . . . that any of us may be gullible and forgetful as to be duped into making deals at the expense of the Allies. To these panicky attempts we say that the only terms on which we shall deal with any Axis government or any Axis factions are the terms proclaimed at Casablanca: unconditional surrender. In our uncompromising policy we mean no harm to the common people of the Axis nations. But we do mean to impose punishment and retribution in full upon their guilty, barbaric leaders."

So Churchill also, in his Guildhall Speech of June 30th:

"We, the United Nations, demand from the Nazi, Fascist, and Japanese tyrannies unconditional surrender. By this we mean that their will power to resist must be completely broken, and that they must yield themselves absolutely to our justice and mercy. . . . It does not mean, and it never can mean, that we are to stain our victorious arms by inhumanity or by a mere lust of vengeance, or that we do not plan a world in which all branches of the human family may look forward to what the American Constitution finely calls 'life, liberty, and the pursuit of happiness.' " [9]

The subject may be left for the present with two brief comments. First, even after the Casablanca announcement, the Allies remained free in practice to indicate in advance to any enemy considering surrender, what treatment they might expect. Second, the adoption of this formula of surrender did not *in itself* determine the terms later imposed on Italy, Germany, and Japan. It did not, for example, dictate the actual terms of the Cairo Declaration ending the Japanese Empire; nor, for further example, did it necessarily lead to Soviet demands on Poland and Germany for territory. Such decisions followed their own determinative causes in each instance. They were not, as is so often argued, the inescapable wake of a policy that required the enemy to submit with no recourse.

In its proper chronological place, more will be told of how the formula of unconditional surrender was in practice interpreted and applied, and more note will be taken of its significance.

[9] *Onward to Victory,* War Speeches by the Right Honorable Winston S. Churchill, pages 169–70.

12. After Casablanca; Again the Soviet Side

After their formal work at Casablanca was over, the President and Prime Minister (on January 25th) sent reports of their decisions to Stalin and Chiang Kai-shek. The one for Stalin was the more informative, but still rather general. As requested, Ambassador Standley and the British Chargé delivered it together at midnight (of the 26th). As he did so, Standley congratulated Stalin on the encircling operation before Stalingrad which had been announced just a few minutes before he had entered the Kremlin. Stalin remarked that he was not satisfied, that he wanted greater progress. The important thing, he said twice over, was not to be afraid of the Germans; as soon as the Russians ceased to fear them, they began to beat them.

After brief summaries of the other intended operations, this is what the message to Stalin said about the prospective cross-Channel invasion:

"In addition, we shall concentrate in the United Kingdom a strong American land and air force. These, combined with the British forces in the United Kingdom, will prepare themselves to re-enter the Continent of Europe as soon as practicable. All this will certainly be known to our enemies, but they will not know where or when, or on what scale, we propose striking. They will therefore be compelled to divert both land and air forces to all the shores of France, the Low Countries, Corsica, Sardinia, Sicily, the heel of Italy, Yugoslavia, Greece, Crete and the Dodecanese." [10]

Having listened to a translation of Standley's summary of the message, Stalin handed the Russian version to Molotov, and spoke briefly to him. Molotov answered him with two short, sharp exclamations. What Stalin had wanted so urgently to know was whether Churchill and Roosevelt were sending him a definite promise to start the Second Front, and Molotov had told him—no, not yet, not yet. Stalin did not change expression.

But Stalin did not allow whatever resentment he felt to enter his acknowledgment of February 1st. This was in the nature of a more definite test of the prospect. He said in regard to ". . . the decisions adopted by you [Roosevelt and Churchill] in relation to Germany as

<hr />

[10] *The Hinge of Fate,* page 743. The message was sent from Casablanca to the War Cabinet in London, thence to the British Embassy in Moscow for joint presentation by the U.S. and British diplomatic representatives in Moscow.

an undertaking to defeat Germany by way of opening a second front in Europe in 1943, I would appreciate receiving information regarding the operations planned in this respect and the times which have been selected for their realization." He repeated his assurances that the Red Army would continue to do its full part.

On getting back to London, Churchill sent a fuller account (on February 12th) as a joint message from himself and Roosevelt. Stalin had been asking why operations in North Africa had been slowing down. He was told that it was now hoped that the battle in Tunis would be won in April. And then by July, or earlier if possible, it was intended to seize Italy. Next, possible action across the Channel in August or September. "We are," the message said about this, "also pushing preparations to the limit of our resources for a cross-Channel operation in August, in which both British and United States units would participate. Here again shipping and assault landing-craft will be limiting factors. If the operation is delayed by weather or other reasons it will be prepared with stronger forces for September. The timing of this attack must of course be dependent upon the condition of German defensive possibilities across the Channel at that time." [11] This could be read, perhaps was meant to be read, as a confirmation rather than a repudiation of what Stalin had said he assumed about Allied intentions. But the reserved right to review in the light of future conditions in effect left everything open.

The two Western Allies could hardly have given a more conclusive answer even if they had been in full agreement, which they were not. The decisions made at Casablanca, stretching over all battle areas of the world, made it unlikely that an attempt could wisely be made to cross the Channel in 1943 unless German resistance suddenly broke somewhere. The war in Tunis was dragging out, and thwarting plans for the move to Sicily; it would cause deferment of preparations for the cross-Channel operation.

There was compensation in the fact that each day the Tunisian battle was consuming German combat strength. But this was almost sure to seem too meager to Stalin and his military advisers. The Russians at this time (mid-February) were engaged on the Eastern Front against about 185 divisions, including able Italian ones. Their advance was reaching its limit for the winter with the capture of Kharkov. The weight of the struggle bore down on Stalin's next communications. He said on February 16th that he knew that since the end of December the Germans had transferred 27 divisions from the west to the Soviet Front, due to the slack in operations in Tunis. He stressed the advan-

[11] The text of this message is printed in *ibid.*, pages 743-44.

tages of utmost exertion in North Africa and France so that the Soviet armies could maintain their offensive. And then, coming around to the intermitted cross-Channel operation, he wrote, "It is evident from your message also that the establishment of the second front, in particular in France, is envisaged only in August–September. It seems to me that the present situation demands the greatest possible speeding up of the action contemplated. . . . In order not to give enemy any respite it is extremely important to deliver the blow from the West in the spring or in the early summer and not to postpone it until the second half of the year." [12]

Stalin's main point was strategically valid. But he was asking the impossible—unless the Allies not only abandoned their plan to go across the Mediterranean after the capture of Tunis but also suspended their war in the Pacific and the Far East. This is evident from what happened as the program approved at Casablanca was developed during the months ahead; the crunch of competing demands was going to get harder, not easier. Even without making the change in the allocation of combat resources that would have been required to meet Stalin's wishes, Eisenhower was forced during the coming summer to delay his landing in Italy; and all theaters of operation in the Pacific and the Far East were skimped.

Roosevelt, in his next message to Stalin (February 22nd), after reviewing the circumstances governing our strategic policies, went on to say: ". . . you may be sure that the American war effort will be projected on to the continent of Europe at as early a date, subsequent to success in North Africa, as transportation facilities can be provided by our maximum effort." [13] Churchill, battling hard against a virus infection, was struck down with pneumonia. As soon as he was well enough he concurred in Roosevelt's confirmation; but he also made it plain to both Roosevelt and Stalin that he was not going to be rushed into the cross-Channel action until he thought chances of success warranted it, that he would not court "a bloody repulse." His message to this effect, sent to Stalin on March 11th, ended, "The Channel situation can only be judged nearer the time, and in making this declaration of our intentions there for your own personal information I must not be understood to limit our freedom of decision." [14]

Stalin thought he had a just grievance. He was not convinced by the expositions of the difficulties. He was impatient with the caution of his allies over great loss of life. So bluntly in his next answer (March 15th)

[12] *Ibid.,* page 745.
[13] *Ibid.,* page 747.
[14] *Ibid.,* pages 749–50.

he flung out, in a way to hold them responsible, the fact that while Allied effort in North Africa was at a standstill, the Germans had moved 36 divisions, including 6 armored, to the Soviet Front. The attack on Sicily could not, he went on, be regarded as replacing the second front. Then, after referring to past admissions that it might be possible to enter France in 1942, or in any case not later than 1943, he concluded, "I recognize the presence of the many difficulties resulting from the lack of transport facilities. . . . Nevertheless I consider it necessary with all urgency to warn you, from the point of view of the interests of our common cause, of the serious danger in any further delay in the opening of a second front in France. Therefore the vagueness of your [Roosevelt's] reply, as well as that of Mr. Churchill, in regard to the opening of a second front in France, provokes alarm which I cannot suppress."

It was hard to tell just what danger Stalin had in mind. Was he merely warning that unless the Soviet armies in the east were much helped during the coming summer battles they might give way to the Germans? And if this happened, that the Germans would be able to place much greater forces in the west to resist the invasion while the Soviet armies might be too weak to enter into a concerted offensive? Or was he suggesting that the Soviet government might feel compelled to enter into a truce, perhaps an armistice, with Germany?

Perhaps this is as good a place as any to point out that during the whole of this same period in which Stalin was protesting the delay in invading the continent of Europe, he was repelling repeated American requests for cooperation in the war against Japan. Time and again, on the advice of the Joint Chiefs, Roosevelt tried to get him to agree at least to start preliminary staff talks looking toward combined operations in the Far Eastern theaters of war. These applications to Stalin were made on the ground that Japan might attack Siberia. But it is safe to surmise that they were construed as an attempt to incite Japan into an attack. Thus it may be said that the Americans were trying to get the Russians at least to take the risk of having to fight on a second front—in the Far East. Stalin never felt called upon to give any justification for his refusals other than the fact that his armed forces were so greatly pressed in Europe to defend Russia. The Americans recognized the Soviet difficulties but the Pacific enthusiasts among them were disappointed by his caution.

And now there came along in this latter part of March the need for still another unwelcome notice to Stalin. The report adopted at Casablanca had stated, "The Soviet forces must be sustained by the greatest volume of supplies that can be transported to Russia." And Stalin had been told, "We shall spare no exertion to send you material assistance by every available route." [15]

German planes and submarines were again making the northern transit perilous even under strong convoy. Furthermore, the Germans had assembled a formidable surface fleet at Narvik, in position to move against the protecting naval force. British escort convoys all over the world were slim and the American Navy was refusing to lend Britain any more destroyers. It appeared foolhardy to send another group of merchant ships on the northern route without adequate naval protection, and that could not be provided without risking the British battle fleet and command of the Atlantic. There was worry also over possible great losses of merchant shipping; stocks of food and raw materials in Britain itself were low; prospective assaults on Sicily and movements in the Pacific were going to absorb more shipping than was being built.

Thus with great regret Churchill and his advisers concluded that it would again be necessary to suspend the northern convoys till September. The Prime Minister told the President of this (on March 19th) while Eden was in Washington. Only four days before, they had both received Stalin's accusatory message about the postponement of the cross-Channel invasion. Roosevelt did not dispute the decision about the March convoy, but he suggested to Churchill (on the 20th) that it might be sensible to wait a bit before telling Stalin, and to pause and watch awhile longer before deciding about the later convoys.

Churchill waited about ten days. Then having heard amicably from Stalin in the interval, on the 30th he told Stalin of the decision about the March convoy. He explained the reasons. And he forecast great increases in the transport of supplies by the southern route and across the Pacific. Stalin sent a grave but not ungracious answer—stressing that the decision was certain to hurt the Soviet armies. Churchill's response was firm but appreciative—based on a view of Russian war effort, unpinched by memory. "I am deeply conscious of the giant burden borne by the Russian armies and their unequalled contribution to the common cause." [16]

Toward the end of the month the American and British blows against Germany were really beginning to tell. British night bombing attacks on the Ruhr were doing immense damage; American day bombing was developing better system and beginning to be effective. Fine progress was being made from the east and west in Tunis; Montgomery's

[15] *Ibid.*, pages 692 and 742.
[16] *Ibid.*, page 755.

troops were in possession of all the Mareth defenses, and the Americans under General Patton were hurrying on. The ships carrying equipment, supplies, and men for Rommel's army were being dangerously exposed to air bombing and torpedo attacks. In these circumstances it was not thought likely that Hitler would continue to expend still more valuable combat forces in an attempt to hold the tip of Tunis, and thus prolong the battle till May. In sum, the prospect was improving that the West might soon be able to undertake large-scale direct operations against the enemy which would ease the Soviet struggle. This, along with the calm way in which Churchill and Roosevelt treated his complaints, was probably why Stalin remained affable even after being told about the northern convoys. He sent messages blessing and applauding the Allied effort in Tunis and the air assaults on Germany. On thanking Churchill for a film on the campaign along the eastern shores of the Mediterranean called "Desert Victory," he praised it as depicting how magnificently Britain was fighting.

Stalin's state of feeling toward his Western Allies varied as they knew, and was subject to change for reasons not understood. But following upon the stormy March passage, the wind from Moscow continued to be relaxing—until, to foretell, Stalin learned definitely in May that there was to be no cross-Channel invasion in 1943.

<hr>

13. The First Review of War Aims: Eden in Washington, March 1943

The American government had been inclined to put off discussion of the political issues to be met when and as the Axis nations were defeated. It wished them to stay behind the armies, but they could not be kept there. They crept forward; as they had when the Anglo-Soviet treaty of alliance was being made, and as soon as Allied troops landed in North Africa. They came in for attention whenever, in fact, British and Soviet diplomats looked at any part of the European land area between them. They appeared on the horizon whenever military planners mapped campaigns in the Pacific and Far East.

So the American government was compelled to heed and discuss them sooner than it wished. The worst of the military perils having passed, the British government began to look ahead. It wanted to do so in company with the American government since our assent would be necessary to any major decision. Thus in March, Eden travelled to Washington.

In reflecting upon Eden's talks with American officials we should bear in mind that at this time both Roosevelt and Churchill thought it would be possible to get along with the Soviet Union after the war. Roosevelt had not allowed himself to be harried out of this opinion, either by the overbearing ways of the Russians or by the warnings of those who thought otherwise. And this was one of the periods in which Churchill was also hopeful about the future of relationships with the Soviet Union. He had been openly saying so, as, for example, in his talk with the President of Turkey some six weeks before, aimed to get that country to enter the war. Churchill minimized the need to fear how the Soviet Union would act at the end of the war, saying that he had seen Molotov and Stalin and his impression was ". . . that both desired a peaceful and friendly association with the United Kingdom and the United States." He had stressed the fact that although he could not see twenty years ahead, Britain, nevertheless, had a twenty-year treaty with the Soviet Union.[17]

Both Hull and Eden at this time were similarly hopeful about being able to live and work satisfactorily with the Soviet Union after the war.

The most important of Eden's talks (March 12th–30th) were in the White House with Roosevelt and Harry Hopkins, Welles being the liaison with the State Department. Once or twice Hull was present. But he received Eden separately in his office.

There, to tell first of his part in the consultations, Hull used his chance mainly to try to bring the British government into line on a few matters close to his heart. After reviewing his grievances against de Gaulle to the verge of being querulous, he besought Eden to assert the power of the British government to compel that Frenchman to be more pliant. He also tried to persuade the British Foreign Minister to go along with measures which he had in mind for converting colonies into "trusteeships" on the way to independence. His aim in this field was to place all dependent peoples under international supervision; colonial relationships were to be allowed to continue, subject however to inspection by international agencies which would be authorized to publish all pertinent facts regarding their administration. This was one of the two great transformations which Hull sought to bring about as an outcome of the war—the other being the formation of a universal collective security system.

[17] *Ibid.,* page 710.

The numerous talks in the White House touched many subjects in a lively though inconclusive way. In brief the main ones were:

1. *Concerning the Form of the Permanent Organization for Peace and Security.* During the year that had elapsed since he had expounded them to Molotov, the President's conceptions in this field had evolved, probably due to the tuition of State Department committees guided by Hull and Davis. In his talks with Eden he visualized three connected parts within the new organization which was to be world-wide; a general assembly in which all nations were to have a place; an advisory council of representatives of the great powers and some six to eight other countries; and an executive council made up of the United States, Great Britain, the Soviet Union, and China, to which he hoped the advisory council would entrust pretty wide powers. In essence as expressed by the President, ". . . finally, that the real decisions should be made by the United States, Great Britain, Russia, and China, who would be the powers for many years to come that would have to police the world." [18]

Eden said that his government was thinking along similar lines. But he doubted whether it would be possible or practicable to entrust so great authority to an executive group of the Great Powers alone. And he, as had been Molotov before him, was skeptical as to whether China ought to be treated as one of them. About this time Churchill was publicly showing favorable interest in a variant scheme of international organization—one which visualized regional bodies, a council of Europe, and a council of Asia under the world institution. This confused the discussions in Washington somewhat.

Roosevelt tried out on Eden another idea for assuring that the new organization would be able to prevent aggression. He suggested that it should secure and keep permanent control over strategic points and bases ("strong points") in different parts of the world. Some of these might be in Germany or Japan or Italy. Others might be located in other countries. As examples of the latter he mentioned Bizerte in Tunis, Dakar in French West Africa, and the harbor of Formosa. All of these, his idea seems to have been, should be formally under collective direction, but each was to have been garrisoned by the forces of some one member to whom the assignment was given. It is hard to tell from the talks just what Roosevelt had in mind on this point—whether he conceived that these garrisons would all be part of one international armed military force or separate national units provided by the "Four Policemen."

[18] *Roosevelt and Hopkins*, page 717.

In any case, as will be seen, this improvisation did not weather well. Even if it had been judged desirable and practicable, one very hard fact would have stood in the way of its realization; the strategic points in mind could have been detached from national control only by compulsion.

2. *Some Prospective Soviet Territorial Claims.* The President asked Eden whether he thought there was anything in the view that the Soviet government was determined to dominate the whole of Europe by armed force or propaganda. Eden answered that he did not believe so. But in any case he thought it wise to cultivate Soviet confidence and friendship—to pave the way toward cooperation and avoid rigid Soviet hostility. That, he added, was not always easy to do since the Soviet government was difficult and so very mistrustful. Some further light on Eden's thought is cast by a comment he made in the course of another talk about the future of Germany. As recorded by Hopkins, "Eden said he believed one of the reasons Stalin wanted a second front in Europe was political; that if Germany collapsed, he had no desire, in Germany, to take full responsibility for what would happen in Germany and the rest of Europe, and he believed it was a fixed matter of Russian foreign policy to have both British and U.S. troops heavily in Europe when the collapse comes." [19]

Eden summed up for Roosevelt what he thought Soviet territorial demands would be. He could be definite since Maisky, the Soviet Ambassador in London, had called on him just before he left for Washington and had described freely what the Soviet government wanted.

a. The Baltic States. Eden thought that the Soviet government would insist on absorbing these, and that it would reject the proposal which Roosevelt thought ought to be made—that a second plebiscite should be held in these countries before any such action was taken. Roosevelt remarked that we might have to agree to this absorption but, if so, it ought to be used as a bargaining counter with Russia.

b. Poland. Eden thought that the Soviet government would claim for itself some of the territory that had been part of Poland in 1939—possibly up to the Curzon Line. He observed, however, that the extent of Soviet claims in this region might depend somewhat on the way in which it regarded the group who might be controlling Poland at the time of the peace conference.

The discussion also touched, though only loosely, on Poland's western frontiers. The President and Eden agreed that Poland might have East Prussia after the war. Eden thought the Russians would agree to that, but were not yet ready to say so to the Polish government in London.

[19] *Ibid.,* pages 711–12.

Stalin also was disposed, he thought, to change the Silesian frontier in favor of Poland. With these accessions in the west, Poland would have a satisfactory living space, and Stalin, Eden thought, wanted Poland to be strong.

In general, in his talks with Eden, the President's comments on frontier questions were reserved. But he did remark, apropos of the pretensions of the Polish government in London, that the big powers would have to decide what Poland should have, and that he did not intend to bargain with the Poles or other small countries at the peace conference.

This comment was stimulated by Eden's account of how assertive the Polish government-in-exile was being; how utterly unreal in its notions of the place and power of Poland after the war; and how stubborn in its wish to keep the eastern frontiers which it had between the two world wars. Eden thought that the Soviet government would not insist on having a Communist government in Poland, but he was sure that it would demand that any and all future Polish governments be representative of the popular will. Therefore it would not be disposed to allow the existing exiled group in London to retain power, though not unfriendly to some of its individual members.

This whole patch of discussion with Eden about Polish matters was tinged with worry as to what Russia might do. But no special ways were seen to guard against a possible bad outcome.

c. Bessarabia. The President agreed with Eden that the Soviets were entitled to regain this province—on the Romanian frontier—as it had been Russian throughout most of its history.

d. Finland. The President and Eden agreed that the Soviets would insist on the boundary line that had been drawn at the end of its war with Finland in March 1940. They both thought this reasonable. But Eden forecast that the Soviet government would also demand Hangoe as necessary for the security and defense of Petrograd. They both also seemed to think that it would be hard to dispute this claim since the war had shown how dangerously exposed the city was to capture.

e. Yugoslavia. The President thought it would be absurd to force the Croats and the Serbs to continue to live together as a nation. But Eden thought otherwise; he felt that they could and should live together.

f. Czechoslovakia, Romania, Bulgaria, Turkey, and Greece. The President and Eden agreed that the future determination of the frontiers of these countries should not cause serious trouble.

g. Austria and Hungary. The President and Eden agreed that these should be established as independent states. Austria was presumably to regain its former frontiers. Eden thought Stalin would want to punish Hungary and have it yield territory to Romania.

h. Germany. The President seems to have left it mainly to Welles and Hull to talk with Eden about the future of Germany. Eden told Welles that the thoughts of his government, and his own thoughts in particular, were turning toward dismemberment. It would of course be best, he added, if this came about spontaneously. Welles, saying that he was talking for himself alone, thought nothing short of partition would end the German menace. He sketched four steps—including the transfer of East Prussia, the separation of Prussia, and the formation, out of the rest of Germany, of two or three other independent states. But Hull, talking with Eden that same day, said that he had not made up his mind whether anything of the sort should be done. The talk recorded agreement that it would be well for the world if Germany were partitioned, but did not decide whether partition ought, if necessary, to be imposed by force. Obviously the subject would have to wait upon consultation with the Russians.

i. China. The President and Hull told Eden they were sorry that Churchill, in a speech which he had made the day before, had not mentioned China as among the great powers. The President said that he thought that since China might be of use in policing Japan, he wanted to strengthen it in every possible way. But Eden said he was doubtful whether China could stabilize itself and thought it might have to go through a revolution after the war. Moreover, he remarked, "he did not much like the idea of the Chinese running up and down the Pacific." [20]

j. Other Far Eastern Questions. The President suggested that Manchuria and Formosa be returned to China; that Indochina be placed in trusteeship; that Korea also be put under a trusteeship to be directed jointly by China, the United States, and one or two other powers; and that the Japanese mandated islands be internationalized. The inconclusive discussion that followed left Roosevelt free to develop them later on, as he did in the momentous Cairo Declaration—which pronounced the end of the Japanese Empire.

All early talks about postwar arrangements, such as these with Eden, had to be a forced exercise in imagination, a drill guided by surmise about facts that only the future would define. This is one reason why the record of these discussions leaves the impression that they were conducted in a vacuum. But there was, I think another reason as well. The contingencies of war were not allowed to complicate the exchange of opinions of what ought to be done after the war was won. Not enough

[20] Ibid., page 716.

heed was paid to the way in which military developments could affect political possibilities. Only once, at dinner on the 14th, did the talk straggle onto this subject. As recorded by Hopkins, "We then discussed at some length, the political effect of our troops being in Italy as against France at the time of the collapse of Germany and, while both Eden and the President thought it would not be as advantageous, it was far better than not being there (on the Continent) at all." [21] No one suggested that military strategy be adjusted to serve the political purposes and settlements in mind.

Roosevelt was trying to fight a coalition war without coalition politics, lest these hinder the conduct of the war. The State Department was intently engaged in studying the politics of peace. Hull was content not to be called on so soon to deal with the barbed issues in this field of moving events.

As soon as the talks with Eden were over (on March 31st) Hull summarized for Litvinov what had been said. In doing so he stressed that Eden had shared our desire to work with Russia after the war, and the opinion that the Americans, Russians, and British must together try to restrain agitation and troublemakers in their own as well as other countries. He also took pains to tell of the formula which had been explained to the British about the policy toward "dependent peoples," based on our hope of seeing a general forward movement around the world relating to an awakening of these peoples. On the same day the State Department sent a similar account of the Eden talks to Ambassador Standley for Molotov. This more definitely called attention to the fact that no attempt had been made to formulate agreements or decisions. Molotov did not say whether or not he believed this statement. It will be seen how anxious Roosevelt and Hull continued to be right up to the end of the war to give the Russians no ground for believing we were in a secret combination with the British, or in a separate camp with them.

A brief after-note should be added to this account of the Eden talks. When some weeks afterward Churchill again came to Washington, he added to what Eden had said about some of the points discussed. He spoke warmly of the possibility of the United States and the British Commonwealth making joint use of common bases in the territories of both countries; whether or not as part of a more general plan for "strong points" was not clear. He remarked that he thought it important that France be strong again ". . . for the prospect of having no

[21] *Ibid.,* page 712.

strong country on the map between England and Russia was not attractive." [22] But he did not relinquish the idea of partitioning Germany; he visualized at least the separation of Prussia from the rest of Germany.

However, these comments on political matters were only incidental to the primary purpose which brought Churchill to Washington: to thresh out anew the troubling questions of military strategy both in Europe and the Far East.

∰∰∰∰∰∰∰

14. Spring 1943: Trident Conference Decisions

∰∰∰∰∰∰∰

The Prime Minister proposed to the President on April 29th that he and the British Chiefs of Staff should come to Washington for another general review. Roosevelt welcomed the idea. On May 8th Churchill explained to Stalin the purpose of his mission: ". . . to settle further exploitation in Europe after Sicily, and also to discourage undue bias towards the Pacific, and further to deal with the problem of the Indian Ocean and the offensive against Japan there." [23]

Churchill, as recorded in his notes and memos, by this time had fixed on two conclusions: one, that the best objective, after the capture of Sicily, was Italy; two, that a cross-Channel operation in 1943 was not going to be possible, because of the comparative strength of German forces in Western Europe. But he was being careful not to challenge the Americans and Russians by being downright in so saying.

On May 12th, the first day of the Conference (known as Trident), news came from Eisenhower that all resistance in Tunis had ended, that 160,000 prisoners had been captured, and that the control of nearby sea and air was complete. These events brought closer the greater rewards that might be won by continuing on with the campaign in the Mediterranean. Churchill gathered up all the gleaming possibilities in his opening presentation. The British and Americans, it was his thesis, must set about at once to knock Italy out of the war. The potential results of doing so he thought tremendous: (1) total Axis strength and ability to protect their many exposed fronts would be reduced; (2) Italian troops would have to withdraw from the Balkans, and this would make it necessary for the Germans either to give up control of that region or greatly increase their forces there; (3) the demobiliza-

[22] *The Hinge of Fate*, page 803.
[23] *Ibid.*, page 789.

126

tion or surrender of the Italian fleet would release British naval strength to the Pacific or the Bay of Bengal, and thus make possible quicker action toward Japan, or in Burma or the Dutch East Indies; (4) Sardinia and the Dodecanese Islands would be extremely useful bases; (5) these developments might cause the Turkish government to agree to enter the war.

The excellent chance of achieving these gains he thought more than adequate reason for pursuing this objective. But, arguing from the situation which had followed from the original decision to enter North Africa, he now pointed out that this was the best if not the only way in which the vast British-United States armies, navies, and air forces then in the Mediterranean area, and which would be freed after the capture of Sicily, could be used during the rest of 1943. Otherwise, much of this combat force would remain idle, since scarcity of shipping would limit the portion of it that could be moved to Britain for any cross-Channel assault in 1943; and there would be great problems of deployment, reorganization, and reequipment. Furthermore, he contended that by advancing into Italy the western allies would best take the weight of combat off Russia. For he reckoned that the Germans could be compelled by this initiative to transfer to Italy and the Balkans so many divisions that they would be more weakened on the Eastern Front than by any cross-Channel attack that the Allies could make in 1943.

This was the forceful reasoning with which Churchill bucked the inclination of the United States Chiefs of Staff to halt operations in the Mediterranean after Sicily was captured. Roosevelt agreed that the large force of twenty divisions which had been assembled in the Mediterranean must not be allowed to remain idle until the cross-Channel invasion could be started. But he hesitated over the proposal to go beyond Sicily and Sardinia—into Italy. He said that he was afraid that the Allies might find themselves in a long and hard struggle on the Italian peninsula which would use up more and more men and shipping. He did not want to allow that to occur. His judgment was, therefore, that all surplus resources had better be set aside in preparation for a cross-Channel operation on the largest scale in the spring of 1944.

Churchill did not deny that the Germans could or might conduct a sustained and major struggle for Italy. But that did not seem to worry him. He was optimistic that the Italian venture would not require combat resources needed for the cross-Channel operation a year away. He tried to assure the Americans that their concern on this score was unjustified, particularly since he thought it would be possible to conduct the campaign in such a way as to leave the Allies free and able to decide, no matter what the Germans did, the rough limits of the means which they would devote to operations in Italy.

After days of talk (May 12th–25th), the Americans and British managed again to adjust their desires and fears in a mutually acceptable program. The Report of the Combined Chiefs of Staff, approved by Roosevelt and Churchill loosely embraced three strategies:

1. *Operations in the Mediterranean against Italy.* Eisenhower was to be directed to get ready to start offensives against Italy as soon as Sicily was captured, to force Italy's collapse; and in so doing to facilitate the air offensive against Eastern and Southern Germany, wear down the German fighter plane force, and develop a heavy threat against German control in the Balkans.

However, operations in and against Italy were to be undertaken only to the extent they could be carried on without jeopardizing a cross-Channel invasion in 1944. It was stipulated that seven of the divisions then in the Mediterranean were to be held in readiness after November 1st for transfer to England as part of the force that was to invade Northwestern Europe. Against this provision Churchill was later to strain in vain; it turned out to be the crucial later deterrent to the extension of Mediterranean operations.

2. *The Cross-Channel Operation.* It was decided that "forces and equipment" should be established in the United Kingdom "with the object of mounting an operation with target date 1 May 1944 to secure a lodgement on the Continent from which further offensive operations can be carried out." [24] The size of the forces to be allotted at various stages of preparation and attack was also settled. The air assault to reduce German capacity to resist the invasion and to overcome the German Air Force was to be sustained and vastly expanded.

The British had wished to regard the target date as tentative. They wanted it understood that it need not be met unless by that time the German Air Force had been mastered, and the size of the German Army to be confronted in France was not greater than a stated maximum. But the Americans—particularly Marshall and King—would not agree to any such provisional plan. They wanted a firm date. They were not willing to proceed to concentrate a great part of American combat resources in Britain during the next year if the invasion might be indefinitely postponed.

The Americans believed that they got their way. And it is true that in the report no conditions or qualifications were attached to the authorized preparations for the enterprise. But, to foretell, the British

[24] *Cross-Channel Attack,* page 69.

continued to regard not only the program of preparation approved by Roosevelt and Churchill, but also the target date and the ultimate decision to invade, as within the realm of discussion. They felt within the bounds of their understanding when they pleaded for measures elsewhere which could cause delay in preparation or execution of the Channel crossing. The issue was reintroduced as soon as the British-American Planning Group (COSSAC), to whom the Trident Conference turned over the task of converting its general intent into an actual plan, started work.

3. *The Offensive against Japan*. The pace of advance from the Southwest Pacific was stepped up and a rapid movement across the Central Pacific was envisaged (Marshall and Caroline Islands). The American authorities were left free to decide what combat resources were to be devoted to these actions, but subject to the provision that "the effort of any such extension . . . to be given consideration by the Combined Chiefs of Staff before action is taken."

Additionally, it was resolved to provide substantially greater resources of planes, airmen, and organization for the air route over the Hump from India into China, for air activities in China, and for Chinese ground forces, particularly those units which were to resume the effort to clear a land route through Burma to China. But these modest provisions were left vulnerable to imperative demands from other fighting centers.

The Trident accord did not specify just what measures should be taken toward the objective to drive Italy out of the war. It stated merely that ". . . the Allied Commander-in-Chief North Africa will be instructed, as a matter of urgency, to plan such operations in exploitation of 'Husky' [Sicily] as are best calculated to eliminate Italy from the war and to contain the maximum number of German forces. Which of the various specific operations should be adopted, and thereafter mounted, is a decision which will be reserved to the Combined Chiefs of Staff." [25]

Was the effort to be cautious, perhaps restricted at this time to the capture of Sardinia? That would have satisfied the Americans. Or was the first move to be a major one and planned to gain a position on the Italian peninsula? Nothing less seemed to the British good use of great chances. Churchill was in a hurry for a decision which would assure uninterrupted pressure against the Italians. So he proposed to Roosevelt that Marshall go with him at once to Algiers, there to confer with Eisenhower and the other commanders. Marshall was agreeable. Then

[25] *The Hinge of Fate*, page 810.

or later he remarked ruefully to Stimson apropos of this trip that he ". . . seemed to be merely a piece of luggage useful as a trading point."

They flew off together from Washington, arriving at Eisenhower's headquarters on May 29th. There they were joined by General Brooke, Chief of the Imperial General Staff, and the British Commanders in the Mediterranean—Generals Alexander and Montgomery, Air Marshal Tedder, and Admiral Cunningham. All the British military group were of the opinion that an assault on Sardinia would be an inadequate way of using the forces that were available for action in the Mediterranean. Their view had the more weight because, by this time, the British had almost three times as many troops, four times as many warships, and almost as many airplanes as the Americans for use in the area. Churchill's brief for moving on to the Italian mainland was substantially the same as the one he had made in Washington, and was capped by the assertion that "No other action of the first magnitude is open to us this year in Europe."[26] He was careful not to give the impression that he had in mind at this time any major campaign in the Balkans, or even in Northern Italy.[27]

Eisenhower, though in favor of continuing at some time into South Italy, was reserved. Marshall was cryptic. He did not quarrel with Churchill's presentation. But he still was against commitment to any plan of campaign in Italy which might absorb ever greater forces, either for the assault or to hold a defense line, and so set back prepara-

[26] *Ibid.*, page 825.
[27] At his opening exposition at the Trident Conference on May 12th the Prime Minister had revealed a marked interest in possibilities of action in other points of the Mediterranean area besides Italy. But it is unclear as to whether he had in mind large organized expeditions or merely small commando operations in cooperation with local guerrillas, bombing attacks, and the like; and his own later account of his thought and words—in *The Hinge of Fate*, pages 790–93—leaves it unclear. Admiral Leahy, who was present, got the impression that Churchill was strongly urging an invasion of the Balkans: see *I Was There*, page 159. But if Churchill as much as glanced in that direction, the U.S. Joint Chiefs were apt to see ten divisions diverted there. They were suspicious of the subtleties and variations in his subtle approach to Mediterranean strategy —"as the cat jumps." This he has explained in Winston S. Churchill, *Closing the Ring*, Boston: Houghton Mifflin Company, 1951, page 162. "The best method of acquiring flexibility is to have three or four plans for all the probable contingencies, all worked out with the utmost detail. Then it is much easier to switch from one to the other as and where the cat jumps."

Here again at the conference at Algiers some of the American military men were convinced, however, that the Prime Minister, despite his guarded utterances, was bent on bringing about a major campaign in the Balkans. H. C. Butcher, *My Three Years with Eisenhower*, page 316.

It may be noted that in this month of May 1943 the British sent their first missions to work with Tito. Churchill at a conference with his Chiefs of Staff emphasized the very great importance of giving all possible support to the Yugoslav anti-Axis movement, since it was containing 33 Axis divisions in that area.

tions for the cross-Channel invasion. Thus, he wished to wait to see how the attack on Sicily fared, how the Germans reacted to it, and how the fighting on the Eastern Front was going, before making an irrevocable decision. Churchill could only cultivate, not compel, assent and so agreed to leave the ultimate decision to Eisenhower. However, Churchill had solid ground for his feeling that he had made great progress toward his object, because he found "that everyone wanted to go for Italy." [28]

The talks in Algiers ended on June 3rd. Churchill and Eden flew to England and Marshall went back to Washington.

15. Following Trident, a Season of Strain and Recrimination

Now once again, mainly due to the decision made at Trident to defer the attempt to create the second front for which the Russians were waiting, relations with the Soviet government were harshly strained. The turn from the affability of the spring to resentment by early summer was marked. To trace its course and causes, the narrative must retrace several trails of concurrent events during the months of June and July.

Before the start of the Trident talks the President had decided to change our Ambassador in Moscow. He wanted an alert and zealous proponent of cooperation in the post. Whether or not with the thought of offering him the Ambassadorship, the President asked Joseph E. Davies to leave at once on a special trip to Moscow. He had served there as Ambassador before, in the thirties, and ever since had portrayed Russia as a land of friendly people and the Soviet rulers as sincere men of good will.

Davies had carried with him a letter (dated May 5th) from the President to Stalin. This explained that Davies was going to Moscow for one purpose and one purpose only—to bring about a personal meeting between Roosevelt and Stalin. The President wanted to avoid the problems of large staff conferences and diplomatic talks. He proposed there "an informal and completely simple visit for a few days between you and me," at which he conceived that the two of them could get "a meeting of minds." He did not think official agreements or declarations

[28] *The Hinge of Fate,* page 829.

in the least necessary. As for time, he suggested the coming summer, since there was a chance that the Soviet offensive might cause a German crack-up during the coming winter for which they ought to be prepared. As for place, various locations such as Iceland would be unsuitable, since both he and Stalin would have to make long flights, and there Churchill's absence might seem peculiar; he suggested either the American or Russian side of the Bering Straits. This was to be diplomacy of the most personal sort. The President would come only with Hopkins, an interpreter, and a stenographer. Only the seals and the gulls could overhear.

Roosevelt's wish to talk with Stalin without Churchill seems to have been born of several thoughts. These are in the realm of surmise, but in easy reach, I think. Churchill had met with Stalin alone the previous August in Moscow and in that way had gotten to know him as an individual; Roosevelt probably felt the lack of similar personal knowledge of and contact with the man. Possibly he was also tantalized by the mystery and isolation surrounding Stalin. Reasons of policy fitted in with the hankering to break through the zone of remoteness. There was a tendency in the United States to think that Roosevelt was too much influenced by Churchill; and that at any conference of the three, Churchill would shape the decisions. A meeting alone with Stalin might dispel that idea and could be politically helpful in the United States. Then too, at this time and for some time longer, the President was confident that he could get along with Stalin better than did Churchill; that Stalin would not regard him with the same mistrustful memories; and there would be a better chance of getting a friendly understanding if Churchill were not there. Such a meeting of the two of them, he thought, ought not to give just offense to Churchill or arouse his anxieties. The President had proved his steadfast devotion to Britain's cause. And yet some matters to be settled with the Soviet government were of more direct interest to the United States than to Great Britain, and so might first be examined by the two of them, just as Great Britain and the Soviet Union had worked out their Treaty of Alliance.

Hull had shared Roosevelt's purpose. This is shown by the way in which, when Churchill was in Washington for Trident in May, he went out of his way to impress the Prime Minister—during one of his gusts of pessimism about Soviet affairs—that he thought it most important that ". . . our two countries should proceed systematically through carefully selected persons to talk Mr. Stalin out of his shell, so to speak, away from his aloofness, secretiveness and suspiciousness until he broadens his views, visualizes a more practical international cooperation in the future, and indicates Russia's intentions both in the East and in the

West." [29] In short, Stalin was to be wooed with proofs of good will and ideals. If the Secretary of State recognized that Stalin was master and devotee of a system that combined another vision of social justice with hate, he did not think this doomed the effort to futility.

The Davies mission was marked by mishaps from start to finish. It hurt Ambassador Standley, who was made to feel unwanted at Davies' talks with Stalin and Molotov. It led to a row with the American press correspondents in Moscow. For Davies chastised them for their criticisms of the Soviet government, as verging on treason, and as serving Hitler by making much of every minor trouble.

The dinner which Stalin gave Davies on the 23rd seemed to members of our Embassy both dull and comic. The Russians showed friendliness but seemed bored. Davies orated long on the greatness of the Soviet armies, leaders, and peoples, and proposed that Stalingrad be left in ruins as a monument to German atrocities, and a new city be built five or ten miles up the river. After dinner he gave a showing of the movie that had been made, a fictionalized record of his former experience as Ambassador, "Mission to Moscow." The other American guests thought it was watched with "glum curiosity" by their hosts.

But, for all that, the Davies mission must have seemed at the time to have usefully advanced the particular purpose which the President had in mind. On May 22nd the Soviet government announced that the Communist International organization (the Comintern) would be dissolved. It is probable that this step had been decided on some time before, but, coming while Davies was in Moscow, it brought him credit.

The answer which Stalin had given Davies (on May 26th or 27th) to carry back to Roosevelt said in substance that he shared the wish for a meeting but was not sure when he could manage it. He explained that he expected that the Germans would start another all-out offensive on the Eastern Front during the coming summer; and that the Soviet armies were preparing for it, but were short of aircraft and aircraft fuel. It was, he continued, impossible to foresee what measures of resistance Russia would have to take; that, in part, would depend on how fast and active Anglo-American military operations in Europe were. Thus, though he agreed with the President that the two of them ought to meet soon, he could not give a definite answer. He would not, in view of imminent battle crisis, be able to leave Moscow in June, but perhaps a meeting could be arranged for July and August. A simple, personal meeting with only a few advisers, as suggested by the President, suited him also.

[29] *Memoirs*, page 1248.

All this Davies reported to the President on his return to Washington early in June, and on June 5th the President thanked Stalin for his cordial reception of Davies and expressed his pleasure at finding Stalin so closely in accord with his ideas.

But the good will expressed in these exchanges of sentiment was about to be severely tested by the joint message which Stalin—that very day or the day after—got from Roosevelt and Churchill, informing him of the military plans which had been adopted at their recent conference at Washington.

They had found it very hard to compose this message. One probable reason was that, as already observed, the main Trident decisions were a contingent combination of strategies, and difficult to restate. Another may well have been that they foresaw that Stalin was not going to be pleased with the report and so thought it necessary to find a form of statement which would show it to best advantage. Moreover, it is possible that Churchill and Roosevelt had slightly different intentions about the execution of the loose military accord they had approved, and each wanted the message to Stalin to lean his way.

Churchill has told how in Washington he and Roosevelt had kept rewriting the draft of the message until their scribble made it almost impossible to read.[30] But still at midnight, after the conference had ended, they were not satisfied by the text they had. Churchill had then offered to keep on trying on the plane on his way to Algiers the next day, and to send back the result of his further efforts to the President. The President, Churchill thought, took up the idea with relief. General Marshall, it had been arranged, was to join Churchill at Eisenhower's headquarters. The President, as the much-written-over papers were being collected, asked why Marshall should not go from Washington on the same plane so that they could continue their consideration of what was to be said to Stalin. Churchill at once invited Marshall to come with him. While over the Atlantic they had completed the message. Churchill has given Marshall credit for putting it in shape from "the bundle of drafts." [31] After the British Chiefs of Staff added their approval, it had been sent back from London to the President. He had made only one minor change. Then it had been sent on to Stalin by special courier. It told truly of the military program that had been adopted.

Stalin's response was sent on June 11th. The decision to act quickly to

[30] *The Hinge of Fate*, page 811.
[31] *Ibid.*, page 812.

knock Italy out of the war, while leaving the cross-Channel operation until 1944 and so still in the cradle of circumstance, deeply dissatisfied him. In his biased measurement of what the United States and Britain could do if they were willing to bear the cost, the plan seemed akin to defection. He had tried every mode and means of persuasion, and none had overcome the stolid determination of his Allies to wait until *they* were ready to attempt the invasion. Thus his comment was stern, and impressed some of its readers as a most able argument for flinging forces across the Channel in 1943. This was the first of a series of messages between himself and Churchill during June in which each, with firm conviction of the right, upheld his views.[32] Regrettably efforts to locate copies of the unpublished texts of these later messages came to nought. So the student must rely for his impressions of their tenor and tone on the skimming summaries of them based by Sherwood on the Hopkins' papers and Ambassador Standley's confirming descriptions.[33] But it is to be gathered that in one or other of them Stalin reviewed at length the assurances which, in his interpretation, had been given him about the opening of a second front, concluding with words that, according to Sherwood, "could be interpreted only as charges of deliberate bad faith by the Western Allies." [34] Past and forgotten was the appreciation expressed in April of the damage done to Germany by the North African campaign, the bombing raids on Germany, the forced diffusion of German armies to guard against unmapped Allied action. One of Churchill's answers—sent off without consulting Roosevelt—was, again according to Sherwood, "scorching," and according to Standley "superheated." [35]

While this exchange of salvos with Stalin was going on, the Prime Minister revealed to Harriman when they dined together on June 25th that he was disturbed by the President's efforts to arrange a meeting with Stalin alone. No doubt he was truly convinced that the presence of all three was required for satisfactory formulation of common purposes in and after the war. But it may well have been that with Stalin's combative charges so current, he feared that Roosevelt and Stalin would encourage wrong ideas in each other—especially about the cross-Channel operation; that they might agree on projects which would harm

[32] Churchill to Stalin June 20th; Stalin to Churchill June 24th; Churchill to Stalin June 26th.
[33] *Roosevelt and Hopkins*, page 734, and William H. Stanley and Arthur A. Ageton, *Admiral Ambassador to Russia*, pages 380–81 and 465–66.
[34] *Roosevelt and Hopkins, ibid.*
[35] *Ibid.,* and *Admiral Ambassador to Russia*, page 381.

Britain.[36] Perhaps also he was upset a little by the thought that his position at home might be harmed. But despite his anxiety he made it clear to Harriman that if the President was bent on meeting alone with Stalin he would accept the wish in good part.

But by the next morning that vital spirit began to seek a better way. He wrote a dissuading message to Roosevelt, talked it over with Eden, showed it to Harriman, who said merely that it seemed to him to express Churchill's views very well, and sent it on its way.[37] In this he proposed that Eden, Molotov, and Hull (the Foreign Ministers) meet first to discuss the issues over which there were possible differences, before Roosevelt met with Stalin or the three of them met together.[38] And then a few days later, reviewing the quarrel into which the Allies had fallen, Churchill decided it would serve no good purpose to continue this "rough" argument with Stalin. With a touch of rue, he explained that he had felt compelled to make his blunt rebuttal because Stalin had implied bad faith. He had always made it clear that military operations from the West must depend on combat estimates, and not be sacrificial.

Concurrently with its abrasive comment about the deferment of the second front, the Soviet government was expressing dissatisfaction over Allied policy in North Africa. The Soviet authorities were suffering from the sense that they were not being well enough informed, and certainly not being consulted about what was being done there. In order to appreciate this further cause of discord among the main members of the coalition, it is necessary to review—if only summarily—first, the changes in the organization and status of the French groups who were continuing the war against Germany, and becoming able validly to claim attention for their views in the name of a reemergent France; and, second, the involuted past association between the Soviet government and the Free French movement, led by General de Gaulle.

The earlier relations of the various French groups with the American and British governments—winding and troublesome—others have written about fully. So I shall touch on them only to link them with what followed.

[36] He might have been anxious over this possibility, though as far as available record shows Roosevelt stood steadfastly with Churchill in the presentations to Stalin. Thus on June 20th he informed Stalin in connection with the defensive exposition which Churchill was sending that same day "What the Prime Minister cabled you has my full accord."

[37] I do not know the exact date—presumably June 26th, 27th, or 28th—and have not seen the original text.

[38] Roosevelt and Hopkins, pages 738–39.

In North Africa the American authorities had sustained General Giraud as Civil and Military Chief, in accord with the secret agreements which Roosevelt had made with him at Casablanca (the so-called Anfa accords), and in which the British had concurred after revision. They had rebuffed and checked efforts of the Free French movement led by de Gaulle to gain control over French armed forces and civil administration in the Mediterranean. While providing weapons for the Free French combatant groups that were fighting in the heart of Africa, the American government had stubbornly resisted their climb toward sovereign power. De Gaulle's pretensions had been thought false, his contribution to the war small, and his ambitions dangerous. Moreover, Roosevelt and Hull had been cool to the idea of any central French authority. Their attitude, as summed up by Hull for Eden during the Foreign Secretary's visit to Washington in March 1943, had been ". . . that no supreme political power should be set up now to exercise control over the French people. No provisional Government should be created or recognized, and any political activities should be kept to the minimum dictated by necessity." [39] There is little reason to wonder that de Gaulle had construed American policy as being opposed to French unity and a strong France, and as being aimed to alienate part of the Empire that used to be.[40]

[39] *Memoirs,* page 1215.

[40] The British and Soviet governments—while refusing an explicit pledge to restore its territories—in their 1940 and 1941 agreements with the Free French committee had both promised ". . . the integral restoration of the independence and greatness of France."

The American government had made no agreement or understanding at all with de Gaulle on this subject. But Robert Murphy, then American Consul-General in Algiers, and in charge of activities aimed to secure French cooperation with the United States–British forces who were to land in North Africa, in the letter which he wrote Giraud on November 2nd, 1942, defining the basis on which Giraud was to take the lead in bringing French forces to the Allied side, wrote:

"Referring to the declarations made on various occasions by President Roosevelt and to the engagements already entered upon by the American Government as well as by the British Government, I am in a position to assure you that the restoration of France, in all her independence, in all her grandeur, and in all the area which she possessed before the war, in Europe as well as overseas, is one of the war aims of the United Nations.

"It is well understood that French sovereignty should be reestablished as soon as possible over all territories, metropolitan as well as colonial, over which the French flag waved in 1939.

"The Government of the United States considers the French nation as an ally and will treat it as such."

This letter had been approved by General Eisenhower. See Langer, *Our Vichy Gamble,* page 332. Whether or not it was also submitted in advance to the Combined Chiefs of Staff and the President, I am not sure. Eisenhower in his report to the Combined Chiefs on November 8th, after his first frustrating talk with Giraud, reported

The British government, on the contrary, had continued to lean toward de Gaulle, and had regarded with favor his conception of a unified French authority that could represent French interests and direct French activities all over the world. This had not debarred it, however, from opposing or ignoring him when it was deemed essential.

Then early in June the two main resistant groups announced that they were combining in a new French Committee of National Liberation. De Gaulle and Giraud were to be co-chairmen. The colleagues of each, who included such excellent men as Monnet, Massigli, and Catroux, were given important responsibilities. The committee announced itself as "the central French power." Its claim of authority was all-inclusive. "The Committee," their statement read, "directs the French war effort in all its forms and in all places. Consequently it exercises French sovereignty on all territories not subject to the power of the enemy; it undertakes the administration and the defense of all French interests in the world, it assumes authority over the territories and the land, sea and air forces which, up to the present, have been under the authority of the French National Committee and the Commander-in-Chief, civil and military." But care was taken to state definitely that the committee would ". . . relinquish its powers to the provisional government which will be constituted in conformity with the laws of the republic as soon as the liberation of metropolitan territory permits, and at the latest upon the total liberation of France."

Roosevelt and Hull, after consulting Churchill, decided to accept this arrangement and made that fact known. Churchill, in his explanatory statement to the House of Commons (on June 8th), combined welcome and reserve. The British government, he declared, would deal henceforth with this committee. But, he added, "There is a further and larger question, namely the degree of recognition of this Committee as representative of France. This question requires consideration from the British and United States Governments, but if things go well, I should hope that a solution satisfactory to all parties may shortly be reached."

---

that both he and General Clark had ". . . urged Giraud to go along with us temporarily on the basis previously outlined and under assurances that the President had already made respecting French sovereignty and territorial integrity. . . ." *Ibid.*, page 339.

Among the points of agreement between Roosevelt, Churchill, and Giraud set down in the Anfa accord (as revised) was the statement that "The form of relations between France and the United States of America, the postwar consequences of the association of France and the United States in the fight against Germany . . . have all been defined in letters exchanged between the Consul, R. Murphy, in the name of President Roosevelt and General Giraud before the landing."

De Gaulle does not seem to have used these affirmations made to Giraud in his arguments with the United States government.

The accord had brought about a real measure of unity among the French factions toward other countries and for military purposes. But as between themselves, it meant only that they could continue their contest for control around a table rather than at longer range. The first critical test was whether Giraud as Commander-in-Chief was to be allowed to continue to exercise decisive authority over French armed forces, or whether he was to be subject to the orders of the committee. The real meaning of the dispute was whether or not de Gaulle (the Free French group) was going to be able to get control of the French armed forces, as a first main step toward combination of both military and civil affairs. To have his way, de Gaulle resorted to his well-worn but also well-meant threat to resign.

At this very time the Allied plans for landings in Sicily were being completed and the campaign in Italy was in near prospect. For these operations Eisenhower felt it essential to be sure of friendly and dependable order in the North African base area, and he was counting on the aid of the French forces, under Giraud's command, which we had been arming. Thus the American government made it plain to de Gaulle that we would not allow the displacement of Giraud as Commander of all French military forces in North Africa. As stated in a message of June 17th from President Roosevelt to Eisenhower for the direct cognizance of de Gaulle, Giraud, and the other members of the committee:

"The position of this Government is that during our military occupation of North Africa we will not tolerate the control of the French Army by any agency which is not subject to the Allied Supreme Commander's direction. We must have someone whom we completely and wholly trust. We would under no circumstances continue the arming of a force without being completely confident of their willingness to co-operate in our military operations; we are not interested moreover in the formation of any Government or Committee which presumes in any way to indicate that, until such time as the French people select a Government for themselves, it will govern in France. When we get into France, the Allies will have a civil Government plan that is completely in consonance with French sovereignty. . . ." [41]

A second Presidential requirement was that control of Dakar and West Africa should be retained by elements independent of de Gaulle, because of the importance of these places to operations in the South Atlantic and South America.

Churchill and his British military and civil colleagues stood with Roosevelt on the essentials of these stipulations, although they were

[41] *Closing the Ring*, pages 175–76.

not ready, as Roosevelt was, at this time to break with the French leader who in June 1940 had stood with Britain against the German menace.

Eisenhower on June 19th, braving de Gaulle's proud resentment and his gesture of repudiation, laid down these joint American-British requirements. The fortnight of maneuver among the French ended (June 22nd) in a wickerwork arrangement. Giraud was to retain command of French forces in North and West Africa, de Gaulle over those elsewhere in the Empire. The sudden resignation of Boisson, Governor General of West Africa, upon whose retention Roosevelt had been insisting, threw that command post into the sphere of de Gaulle's influence.

Macmillan and Murphy, the British and American political advisers in North Africa, concluded that this new arrangement complied with the President's directive to Eisenhower, and that the results provided as good a temporary solution as could be hoped for under the circumstances. Thus they recommended that it be accepted as such. But they stressed that the episode showed that real unity had not been achieved, and that there should be no illusion about the continuing determination of de Gaulle to dominate the situation. After Eisenhower confirmed the fact that the accord meant that French forces in the area would still be subject to his ultimate command and direction while the battle for Italy went on, the American and British governments followed this advice. They allowed the French antagonists to continue their contest for control over the High Command and for political supremacy without direct interference. And they resumed their exchange of formulas in regard to the reception to be given the new committee and the nature of the relationship to be maintained with it.

On these developments the Soviet government had kept an interested watch. In the past it had maintained an active connection of convenience with de Gaulle, at which memory ought to glance. As soon as the Germans (in June 1941) had attacked Russia, de Gaulle had held out his hand to the Soviet government on the ground that ". . . before philosophizing, one must live—that is to say win. Russia offered the chance of doing so. At the same time her presence in the Allied camp brought Fighting France a balancing element against the Anglo-Saxons, of which I was determined to make use." [42] Though it had denounced the Free French movement up to then, the Soviet government had cordially grasped the connection. Letters had been exchanged in Sep-

[42] General Charles de Gaulle, *The Call to Honour*, page 225.

tember 1941 which recognized de Gaulle's leadership and promised aid to the Free French in the common struggle.[43]

Talks between de Gaulle and Molotov when the Soviet Foreign Minister had been in London (May–June 1942, negotiating a treaty of alliance with Great Britain) had led to a diplomatic combination. As recounted by de Gaulle in his Memoirs:

"The Soviet Minister for Foreign Affairs reached agreement with me on what his government and the National Committee should do for each other in the immediate future. Free France would urge the American and British allies to open a second front in Europe as soon as possible. At the same time she would aid, by her diplomatic and public attitude, in doing away with the isolation to which Soviet Russia had long been relegated. The latter, on her side, would support us in Washington and London in our effort to reestablish the unity of the Empire and national unity by fighting. . . . As for the future, it was agreed that France and Russia should work together over the shaping of the peace."[44]

The way having been thus prepared, the Soviet government had publicly accorded de Gaulle's committee the role of representing France which the American and British governments were still refusing. On August 27th it had issued a statement recognizing the French National Committee ". . . as the representative of the national interests of the French Republic, and the leader of all French patriots struggling against Hitler tyranny, and to exchange with it plenipotentiary representatives." Not long afterward members of the Communist resistance movement in France (Front National) had swung their support to de Gaulle.

These ties with de Gaulle had not deterred Stalin from endorsing the subsequent deal with Darlan in North Africa, nor from supporting the decision to use General Giraud thereafter to command and develop French armed forces. But the connection with the Free French had still been used as a switch to enliven Allied efforts in the west. Neither Stalin nor de Gaulle had seemed embarrassed by the tinge of duplicity in their association.

All through the early months of 1943, while the contest between the two French factions had gone on, the Free French representatives in

[43] Following upon the de Gaulle-Soviet accord of September 1941, the Soviet government had withdrawn Bogomolov, its Ambassador to the Vichy government, and designated him as representative with the Free French Committee in London. De Gaulle had first sent a military liaison officer to Moscow, General Petit, and then in February 1942 had sent a political delegate of the French committee, Garreau, to conduct dealings with the Soviet Foreign Office.

[44] *The Call to Honour*, pages 229–230.

Moscow had poured into the ears of Soviet officials their grievances and suspicions. The Americans and British had taken no special pains to keep Moscow informed of the ins and outs of the quarrelsome bout between the French factions. But when accord between them came into sight the British government (on June 15th) began to consult with the Soviet government, as with the American, about the possibility that the three might assume a common attitude toward the new fused French authority. The Soviet government favored prompt recognition. The American and British governments, in accordance with views that have been explained, urged delay—until Eisenhower made sure that Giraud would retain effective command of French armed forces in North Africa. And, on June 22nd, while Churchill was defending the Trident decisions against Stalin's reprovals, he sent him a firm message on this subject also. In rough paraphrase: "De Gaulle has been struggling to get effective control of the French Army since his arrival in Algiers. One cannot be sure of what de Gaulle will do or whether he will be friendly with us if he should get mastery. Both Roosevelt and I are agreed that de Gaulle might endanger bases and communications for the Sicilian operation. That risk cannot be run."

Stalin in his answer (June 26th) rejected, as unsubstantiated, the case for delaying recognition. Still, he said that since the British government was requesting it, and was giving assurance that no measures would be taken without consultation, ". . . the Soviet government is prepared to meet the wishes of the British government." This polite answer ended by hoping that Churchill would "take into consideration the interest of the Soviet Union in French affairs, and will not withhold from the Soviet government current information indispensable for the taking of appropriate decisions."

On the same day (June 26th) the Soviet Ambassador in London, Maisky, told Winant and the British Foreign Office that his government wished to send Bogomolov (Soviet Ambassador to the Fighting French and Exiled Governments in London) to Algiers at once for about ten days to report on the situation there. The British Foreign Office hinted to Maisky that this was a matter for the French Committee of National Liberation and Eisenhower to decide. But it confided to the American Embassy that it thought the proposed visit might inject a new and perhaps mischievous element into an already delicate situation. Eden told Winant that he and Churchill both thought the Soviet request should be treated as one of military security, and that they would accept joint responsibility with the Americans for whatever answer was given. Winant was instructed (on the 29th) to tell Eden that the American government looked at the question the same way;

and to tell Maisky that although Eisenhower would be glad to provide any information which was wanted, it was thought that a postponement of Bogomolov's visit would be in the best common military interest. A few days later (on July 2nd) Molotov railed at Ambassador Standley about being warded off in this fashion. The Soviet government, he again averred, did not know what was going on in North Africa, and could not find out unless it was allowed to send a representative there. The Soviet Chargé d'Affaires in Washington quizzed Hull. The Secretary of State told him frankly that the American and British governments were afraid that the sudden presence of a Soviet diplomatic representative in North Africa at this crucial time might stir up the French political situation and interfere with the impending assault on Italy. The Soviet government, to foretell, permitted its request to rest—while the campaign for Sicily was being fought.

At this juncture all three members of the coalition sensed the need to cease quarreling, and lapsed into healing silence. When Sherwood, afterward, read the Hopkins papers telling of the dissensions during this June-July period, he was reminded of the atmosphere before Molotov and Ribbentrop signed their pact in August 1939, with revival of the fears of a separate Russo-German armistice.[45] Who is to know for sure, unless and until the Soviet archivists tell us, whether or not Stalin and his advisers weighed such an alternative to a continuation of the alliance with the West? Scattered in journalistic articles there are allegations of some secret initiatives from Moscow, some indirect attempts to see what might be possible. But those which I have seen contain only whiffs of thin and suspect detail, not evidenced enough to warrant historical examination. The weight of circumstance was against any such act or even impulse of separation. Soviet resentment at the West, though genuine, was not deep enough, and the outlook for ultimate victory in association with the West was commanding. By then, I believe, the war coalition was welded together, for worse as for better, till victory might come between them.

[45] *Roosevelt and Hopkins,* page 734.

PERIOD FOUR

The Summer and Autumn of 1943; the Collapse of Italy and the Problems that Ensued

16. After Sicily: The Quebec (QUADRANT) Decisions, August 1943

THE invasion of Sicily began on July 9th. The question of what should be done next was still pending. Due to a wish to guard the means assigned for OVERLORD, Eisenhower's first recommendation after the consultations at Algiers had been circumspect: that his forces should next seek to capture Sardinia or to land in Calabria, the nearby toe of Italy. This was not vigorous enough to satisfy Churchill, even before the battle in Sicily proved that the Italians were a quarter-hearted foe though on their own soil. He lunged at what seemed to him the opening chance to knock Italy out of the war with one good hard blow and then to close in on Germany from the Mediterranean side. He did not propose to allow the Russians to browbeat him nor the Americans to thwart him into giving up what he considered this brilliant opportunity. He made it known that he would not be content in 1943 with anything short of the capture of Rome. As expressed in a message which he sent to General Smuts on July 16th, "Not only must we take Rome and march as far North as possible in Italy, but our right hand must give succour to the Balkan patriots. . . . I am confident of a good result, and I shall go all lengths to procure the agreement of our Allies. If not, we have ample forces to act by ourselves." [1]

Stimson was in London at this time (July 15th–19th). Churchill tried very hard to get him to share his vision of the main military results that might be achieved in Italy and to convince him that the next move should be bold and powerful. He challenged the military sense of merely crossing over to the tip or heel of Italy.[2] But he professed that he was not thinking of going beyond Rome unless a particularly good chance presented itself. Eden, however, argued for carrying the war into the Balkans and Greece. Stimson drew the definite conclusion that the program they were proposing could thwart the cross-Channel operation. But the Prime Minister avowed simultaneously that he remained faithful to the idea of a cross-Channel operation unless his military advisers could present him with some better opportunity. But only, he emphasized, when the British and Americans thought time and

[1] *Closing the Ring*, page 36.
[2] His thought was expressed in a question, "Why crawl up the leg like a harvest bug from the ankle upward? Let us rather strike at the knee." *The Turn of the Tide*, page 671.

circumstance right, not when gruff Russians told them to, for he was really afraid the operation might be a disaster—that the Channel might be full of the corpses of our men.[3]

But Eisenhower had meanwhile surprised the British by recommending as additional operation—that a landing be effected in Salerno Bay, two hundred miles up the coast near Naples. The President and Joint Chiefs approved the proposal. They also agreed to increase Eisenhower's armies by 66,000 men for this assault. But that was to be the whole of the force which they were willing to devote to the Mediterranean; they refused to go along with the British wish to assign 50,000 more. And they stood fast on the stipulation that had been laid down at the Trident Conference that after the capture of Sicily some air and naval units should be moved out of the Mediterranean, and that after November 1st seven divisions also should be transferred from the Mediterranean to England to train for OVERLORD. Churchill did his best to get more flexibility, but the Americans were adamant. It is not hard to understand why. At this time, the end of July, there was only a single American division in the United Kingdom and most of our transatlantic shipping effort was being exerted to supply the requirements for the Mediterranean operations.

The campaign in Sicily progressed well while these questions were being talked back and forth. On July 25th Mussolini was dismissed as head of government. This event, bringing into office men who were freer to quit the war and more disposed and likely to do so rather than compel the Italian people to endure great suffering, seemed to the British to make the case for a major landing in Italy incontestably strong. Discussion from then on took place with anticipation of Italian surrender, but with uncertainty as to what Germany might do to maintain her military position on Italian soil if that happened.[4]

And all this while the Soviet authorities were keeping the Americans and British constantly reminded of what was expected of them. Current

---

[3] Stimson Report to the President, August 4.

[4] The British, however, hoped that if Italy was invaded with sufficient force, and suitable ports and airfields for large operations were secured, the Germans would not try to fight south of Rome, but would retreat to the Lombardy Plains. This hope was based on the belief that poor transport facilities through mountain territory, in the face of United States and British command of the air, would make the Germans unable to hold in the south.

Actually on July 26th, the very next day, a new German army group of eight divisions, placed under Rommel's command, had begun to move into northern Italy from France, the Tyrol, and Carinthia. It was sent to prevent loss of that territory and stand behind the German forces that were farther south. As will be seen, despite extensive and concentrated Allied bombing of their communication lines, the Germans managed to maintain a strong defensive line south of Rome well into 1944.

press and radio campaigns blended reproaches that Roosevelt and Churchill had not kept solemn promises with statements that there was no longer any acceptable reason for further delay in the cross-Channel invasion. The American Embassy in Moscow was inclined to believe that this clamor might have political as well as military purposes: to shake American-British solidarity, and possibly to prepare the way for a more demanding foreign policy.

At Churchill's initiative it had been agreed that he and Roosevelt and their Chiefs of Staff should meet soon again to determine anew the progression of their world-wide strategic program. The Conference (code name QUADRANT) took place in Quebec from August 14th to 24th.

While Churchill and his group were on their way across the Atlantic, the President and the Joint Chiefs had resolved to insist that the cross-Channel invasion plan be carried out. Only thus, they were as convinced as ever, could Germany be decisively defeated. They had concluded also that the United States would have to assume leadership in this operation and propose that it be put under an American commander. Logically they decided to oppose any plan to advance in Italy beyond Rome. Such was the line of purpose with which the United States Chiefs of Staff proceeded to Quebec, where the talks among the military men started on August 14th, and where Roosevelt later joined Churchill.

During the period of the formal conference and in the three following weeks while Churchill remained in Canada and the United States, events in Italy took other dramatic turns. The Badoglio government, which had taken over from Mussolini, sent word to the Allies that it wanted to change sides. Surrender talks were started. The capture of Sicily was completed. These events of course affected the course of discussion of strategic matters. But since they had larger and more permanent influence on the course of the war and peace-making, the tale of their occurrence is best told separately later on.

The Service Chiefs at Quebec took measurement of all Allied combat situations and resources throughout the world, and the position of the several members of the Axis. The branched, connected decisions made there determined the future distribution and range of combat effort in and as between the many fields of action—catching up in their sweep Italy and the Mediterranean.

The Conference, consonant with the Trident resolution, adopted a plan for a 29-division cross-Channel operation with the target date of May 1st, 1944. The planners were instructed to develop its dimensions.

But Churchill's assent to this operation was given subject to a warning that the decision could be considered again if, when the time came, the military outlook was poorer than anticipated. Specifically his approval was contingent on (1) a substantial reduction in the strength of the German fighter aircraft force in Northwest Europe before the assault began; (2) the supposition that there would not be more than twelve mobile German divisions in North France at that time; and (3) that the problem of beach maintenance of large forces in the tidal waters of the English Channel was overcome.

Furthermore, he and his military advisers resisted the American wish to accord preparations for invasion conclusive and complete priority over all intermediate activities in the European-Mediterranean Theater. But after three days of constant staff conferences they did agree that OVERLORD was to get whatever might be needed to assure its success, even though operations in the Mediterranean went short. In Stimson's phrase, "from this time onward OVERLORD held the inside track." [5] As gradually construed, these contemplated landings in Sicily —the main one near Naples—with the idea of advancing to the capture of Rome; then the seizure of Sardinia and Corsica, and if possible the Dodecanese; and then later in connection with OVERLORD, a landing in Southern France in the region between Toulon and Marseilles.[5a]

The Conference also—for the first time—gave major attention to the war against Japan. In fact more of the effort and heat of the formal dis cussions were devoted to this than to European military questions. In their final report the Combined Chiefs declared that, "From every point of view operations should be framed to force the defeat of Japan as soon as possible after the defeat of Germany. Planning should be on the basis of accomplishing this within twelve months of that event."

Important amphibious, air, and naval operations in the Central and Southwest Pacific were approved and scheduled. MacArthur was enabled to continue his thrusts toward the Philippines. The Navy was authorized to operate against the Gilbert, Marshall, and Marianna Islands with the hope of reaching the Ryukus Islands, the threshold of Japan, by the spring of 1945. The means for these operations, especially those granted to the Navy, were accorded top priority. To this the

[5] Henry L. Stimson and McGeorge Bundy, *On Active Service in Peace and War,* page 439.

[5a] The development of these operations in the Mediterranean was, however, confined and retarded by constant scarcity of shipping, particularly of landing craft. This the British Chiefs of Staff resented, since they attributed it to the excessive demands of the American Navy and Gen. MacArthur for their ventures in the Pacific—which they regarded as an unjustified distraction at this time.

British gave reluctant and somewhat forced consent, thinking that these actions might be restrained and the means better used in Europe.

Provision was made for the offensive, sketched out earlier at Trident, in Northern Burma to start in February 1944 with the object of reopening the Burma Road. This plan was approved against Churchill's distaste for all ground operations in that country of jungles and high mountains, and his vigorous preference for landings in the Dutch East Indies or Malaya. Provision was also made for a substantial expansion of the capacity of the air-route over the Hump of the Himalayas into China, and for the establishment of air bases in China for the B-29 super-fortress, then only just going into production. These and various other approved programs were the most substantial allocation yet made for expansion of operations in and for China. They were in response to Chiang Kai-shek's anguished and disturbed warnings that Chinese resistance might end. Most of them, however, were later deferred or reduced because of demands from other combat theaters or in deference to opposed British views.

The main features of this advancing program were summarized for Stalin in a joint message from Roosevelt and Churchill, sent off as soon as the Conference ended. It was untouched by the resentment they both felt at the criticism which—as other pages will tell—they had been receiving from Stalin during the last few days of the Conference about the determination of Italian surrender terms. There is every reason to believe that the sections of the report which interested him most were those that looked toward the Channel crossing. He was told that the great bomber offensive would be continued on a rapidly increasing scale, to prepare the way; that American forces would be assembled during the coming months in the United Kingdom for the operation; and that this would be begun by a joint United States-British force, which would be enlarged steadily, after a bridgehead was obtained, by entry of additional American troops. "This operation will be," the summary stated, "the primary American and British air and ground effort against the Axis." The whole program was set forth as one which the Americans and British had resolved on, of their own will. They did not ask Soviet assent or approval; and they did not promise the Soviet government that it would be carried through regardless of the prospect when the time came around.

The expedition to the toe of Italy which set out one week after the Quebec Conference dispersed, went well. It brought the shaking Italian house down. On the evening of September 8th an armistice was announced. Italian resistance ended as the first landing ships were discharging their men on the beaches around Salerno. This was the day for which Churchill had been waiting. He was back in Washington. For the full formal conference (September 9th) held at the White House with the President and Chiefs of Staff he had his ideas in order. The memo he read was vibrant in every line, and Mediterranean green.[6]

He expounded the need for developing public understanding of the purpose which had been approved by the Combined Chiefs of Staff, to convert Italy into an active agent against Germany. Besides winning over the Italian fleet and air force, he wanted to get Italian divisions in the battle lines against the Germans. They were to be aided to play a part in the fight within their country and then were to be rewarded by better treatment and relaxation of the terms of surrender.

His proposals for immediate action were:

1. That after Naples was captured the Allied troops should keep on northward until they encountered the main German line. This he apparently thought would be well north of Rome, for he added that he was strongly convinced that "we should be very chary of advancing northward beyond the narrow part of the Italian peninsula" unless the Germans retreated to the Alps.

2. To try to work out an agreement between the Italian troops in the Balkans and the local partisans. Then he had in mind the opening of supply ports on the Dalmatian coast, and then, when and as a defensive line in Italy was established, it might be possible, he conjectured, to spare some of the Allied forces in the Mediterranean Theater, "to emphasize a movement north and northeastward from the Dalmatian ports." This was the first time Churchill openly suggested, I believe, that Allied troops be used in that region.

His mind was also astir with hopes of producing far-reaching reactions in Bulgaria, Romania, and Hungary, and that these might even impel Turkey to enter the war. He evoked the same overflowing vision in an appeal to the President a month later in behalf of still another venture in which the British were already engaged: the capture of the islands in the Aegean. "The Germans . . . have to apprehend desertion by Hungary and Rumania and a violent schism in Bulgaria. At any moment Turkey may lean her weight against them. We can all see how adverse to the enemy are the conditions in Greece and Yugoslavia. When we remember what brilliant results have followed from the political reactions in Italy induced by our military efforts, should we not

[6] Churchill prints this memo in *Closing the Ring*, pages 133–37.

be shortsighted to ignore the possibility of a similar and even greater landslide in some or all of the countries I have mentioned?" [7]

But the Americans, Eisenhower included, were not carried away either by the forecasts of momentous gains which might flow from the eastward ventures which Churchill proposed, nor by his estimates of how little extra combat forces and shipping would be needed for them. Churchill then and later thought this the loss of a chance to earn great war prizes at small cost, and the American unwillingness—especially in regard to the Aegean Islands—harsh, and unappreciative of the great value of the Italian operations which he, Churchill, had sponsored. About this Churchill later allowed himself one of his very few bitter remarks, "The American staff had enforced their view; the price had now to be paid by the British." [8]

17. The Arrangements for the Italian Surrender

All the while (from May to September) that the Americans and British had been conceiving these strategic military plans, they also had been considering how to handle the looming Italian surrender. The problem had been talked over with Eden when he was in Washington in March. The President had then stressed his opinion that we should insist on total surrender with no commitments to the enemy as to what we would or would not do subsequently. But the need for a program for the period after the military collapse was recognized. The President had asked Hull to try to work one out; then to discuss it with the British; and, if we got "a substantial meeting of the minds" with them, to talk it over with the Russians.

As this effort proceeded—the various drafting stages of which form too prolonged a story to be retold here—Churchill had been troubled by various trends in American wish and purpose. He was distressed because American propaganda continued to emphasize the demand for "unconditional surrender" rather than the tolerance which might be shown to those who submitted. And he was upset because the Americans seemed bent, not only on suspending the authority of the ruling king, Victor Emmanuel, but also on getting rid of the monarchy in Italy once and for all. For Churchill was firmly against doing that—

[7] *Ibid.*, page 210.
[8] *Ibid.*, page 220.

being convinced that it was essential to keep the monarchy in order to enlist Italian military (especially naval) cooperation, to serve as the only dependable basis for order in Italy, and to prevent a period of chaos and perhaps a surge of Communism.

Despite these different slants of inclination, Roosevelt and Churchill, in the public statements and appeals which they made to the Italian people during May and June, had conveyed substantially the same message: as victors they would not be inhuman. After Italy threw out the Fascist regime and expelled the Germans, it would be given the chance to live in freedom and take its place as a "respected member of the European family of nations." This had been confirmed in a joint declaration to the Italian people broadcast by the President and Prime Minister on July 17th as Allied troops were battering their way over Sicily toward the Straits of Messina. The accent was on the need to get rid of Mussolini and of separation from Hitler and Nazi-controlled Germany. No explicit demand for unconditional surrender was made.

Such had been the broad sketch of Allied intentions before the Italian people when, a week later (July 25th), Mussolini was removed from office by a combination of elements in the Italian Army, near the throne, and in the Fascist Grand Council. The King had appointed General Pietro Badoglio head of the new Italian government. He had once been a close companion in arms with Mussolini, as the head of the Italian armed forces which had so cruelly conquered Ethiopia. But he had become alienated from the regime since he was blamed for the woeful Italian campaign in the Balkans in 1940. Badoglio had wanted to form a government of party politicians. But, at the King's wish, he had made up a ministry of civil servants without party connection.

The people had rejoiced, expecting peace and further political change to follow quickly. But the King had been against any action which might bring on a conflict with the Germans. The new government had proclaimed "The war continues. Italy, cruelly hurt in its invaded provinces, in its destroyed cities, keeps faith in its pledged word. . . ." And the day after taking office, Badoglio had assured Hitler that he wanted to maintain the alliance and continue the war. A mission had been flown to Hitler's headquarters to reassure him of Italy's faithfulness and to propose a meeting with the King and Badoglio. However, the inner intention at this juncture was to try to convince Hitler that the whole war was lost and to persuade him to join in an effort to arrange a compromise peace. Hitler had instead suggested a future talk between Foreign Ministers and Chiefs of Staff. He was sure that Badoglio's heaped-up assurances were false, exclaiming to one bearer of them,

Italy and Surrounding Areas

"This is the biggest impudence in history. Does the man imagine that I will believe him?" He suspected that Badoglio had already tried to make peace with the enemy and had been repulsed. That was not so. Badoglio was at that moment still hoping that he could quit the war with the permission of Germany, that Hitler would either release Italy from the Alliance or join it in seeking peace. He was afraid of forcing the separation by his own act of will. However, on July 31st the decision had been taken to seek an armistice with the Western powers. Thereafter difficulty in finding a secure method of making contacts with the Allies alone delayed initiative.

Hitler was already taking measures to prevent the Allies from getting control of northern Italy whether or not Badoglio made peace with them. During the fortnight after Mussolini's expulsion, he issued orders securing German control of the routes south into Italy, moved eight strong divisions across the frontier into North Italy, assembled forces near Rome to take command of that capital, and, as Italian resistance in Sicily failed, began to pull his troops out of that island into Italy. In sum, step by step, the Germans carried out an integrated plan to take control of much of Italy in case of Italian defection, while pretending to believe the assurances of the Italian government that it would stand fast.

The American and British authorities could only guess at what was going on in Italy during this fortnight, at the scheme upon which the King and Badoglio might be engaged, and at what Hitler would do when the crisis came. But as their forces curved through Sicily toward the Straits of Messina, they tried to get their armistice terms ready for use on demand. All the earlier attempts had left unreconciled various differences of judgment—the Americans finding fault with the latest British drafts submitted to the Combined Chiefs of Staff particularly on the scores that there was no provision for unconditional surrender and that continued recognition of the Royal Italian government was contemplated.

Roosevelt, exultant at the news of Mussolini's downfall, sent a message to Churchill (July 26th) summarizing his thoughts and proposing consultation. He said that he hoped to get an arrangement "as close as possible to unconditional surrender." But once the Italians had submitted themselves to Allied dispensation, he thought they should be treated with lenient justice. He was eager to get all the military help possible, ". . . the use of all Italian territory and transportation against the Germans in the north *and against the whole Balkan peninsula,* as well as use of airfields of all kinds." [9]

[9] *Closing the Ring,* page 55. Churchill's italics.

All these ideas Churchill thought fine and said so in his answer to Roosevelt. Hopefully he enlarged upon the range of military aims to be accomplished in the armistice. The Italian government was to be required to order the end of all resistance to the Allies; to turn over, at least demobilize, its fleet; to try to bring about the surrender of the German troops in Italy, particularly those south of Rome, and to withdraw all Italian forces from the Balkans.

To grasp these chances, Churchill was quite willing to consort with the King and the Badoglio government. His attitude was clearly set forth in the first statement of his thoughts on this subject that he sent to the President as the change in government was taking place. "I don't think myself that we should be too particular in dealing with any non-Fascist government, even if it is not all we should like. Now Mussolini is gone, I would deal with any non-Fascist Italian government which can deliver the goods." [10] And in the House of Commons on the 27th, the day after Badoglio took office, he asserted, "It would be a grave mistake, when Italian affairs are in this flexible, fluid, formative condition, for the rescuing powers, Britain and the United States, so to act as to break down the whole structure and expression of the Italian state."

Badoglio, on this same day, tried to shake off past association with Fascism by declaring the Fascist party dissolved and suspending all political activity until after the war.

Roosevelt went along with Churchill's lenient attitude. He even acted to discourage charges that the King and Badoglio remained of the Fascist stripe, which might arouse American opposition to dealing with them. When the Office of War Information (on July 26th) broadcast to Europe the opinion that, "The essential nature of the Fascist regime in Italy had not changed" and quoted a columnist who spoke of "the moronic little King," the President rebuked that propaganda agency. And at the first chance (on July 27th) he disavowed the broadcast. Despite whatever uneasiness he may have felt, he was again giving rope to elements he detested—for practical reasons—the hope of military gain and need for political order. He was again distressing some of his most ardent supporters. He might again be shaking the belief of the most active anti-Fascist elements in Europe and the Soviet Union in the sincerity of his war aims. All these he tried to reassure in a broadcast made on July 28th. In this he carefully reaffirmed that

1. "Our terms to Italy are still the same as our terms to Germany and Japan—unconditional surrender."

2. "We will have no truck with Fascism in any way, shape or manner. We will not permit any vestige of Fascism to remain."

It is not easy to blend these firm vows with the offhand tone with

[10] *Ibid.*, page 56.

which he commented to Churchill (on July 30th) on what he had been saying in his speeches and press conferences:

"There are some contentious people here who are getting ready to make a row if we seem to recognize the House of Savoy or Badoglio. They are the same element which made such a fuss over North Africa. I told the press today that we have to treat with any person or persons in Italy who can give us, first, disarmament, and, second, assurance against chaos, and I think also that you and I after an armistice comes could say something about self-determination in Italy at the proper time." [11]

But Churchill had no misgivings and was not swayed by the risk of criticism. That conservative warrior answered on July 31st that he was not in the least afraid of recognizing the King and Badoglio, provided they could do what was wanted for Allied war purposes. These, he added, would certainly be hindered by chaos, Bolshevism, or civil war. Thus, he said he would deprecate any statement about self-determination at this time.

At this juncture the correspondence between Washington and London in regard to how Italian political affairs should be handled in and after the surrender had been interrupted by initiatives taken at Eisenhower's headquarters at Algiers.

There preparations were being hurried for operation AVALANCHE, the seizure of the Naples area by amphibious assault. While doing so, Eisenhower and his staff had set hard to work on projects for bringing the war in Italy to an end, perhaps even before Allied troops landed in the country. The soldiers at Algiers were out after a quick military success, with the limited means allowed them.

For that end, Eisenhower's staff wrote out two texts. One was an appeal to be broadcast by him to the Italian people to stop fighting. In this, the nature of the treatment to be accorded them was stated in popular form. The other was a set of armistice terms to be signed by the commanding officers in the field. This was a terse document of twelve short articles stating the measures about military matters which the Italian government would become obligated to take. It did not characterize the surrender as "unconditional." But the program of military submission was thorough; it included acknowledgment of the supreme authority of the Allied Commander-in-Chief to establish military government in Italy. He would remain free, subject to the instructions of the Combined Chiefs of Staff, to decide, as events went along, how to deal with the Italian government and people.

Churchill disliked Eisenhower's initiatives for several reasons. First,

[11] *Ibid.,* page 64.

he did not think it wise to broadcast armistice terms in popular form to the enemy nation. He thought it both more prudent and proper that the Italian government should know our full demands in clear detail. He was alertly on guard lest some rather vague understanding might be brought about between Eisenhower and the Italian authorities. Second, he thought the armistice terms should cover civil as well as military requirements. Third, he believed that it would be much better to have any discussions with the Italians about terms conducted by envoys appointed by himself and the President rather than by the commanding general in the field. He was visualizing the diplomatic solution.

General Marshall did not take to the idea of broadcasting a popular version of armistice terms any more than had Churchill, and the President was persuaded. Eisenhower's broadcast was converted into just another general appeal, repeating the assurance of "honorable conditions." This evoked no immediate response in Italy but later reports told of an impressed audience.

The "short" armistice terms—the military ones—which Eisenhower submitted came through the mill better. They were revised by the Joint Chiefs to make them more precise. They were revised again to satisfy Churchill's misgivings, and to win his assent. This was cheerfully given. But he made it clear that he was agreeing to their use only in case of emergency, since no accord had yet been reached on more comprehensive terms.

Thus Eisenhower had within a week of Mussolini's expulsion an agreed set of armistice terms which he could present if the Italians suddenly sued for peace. But he was compelled to wait for the occasion. During the next few weeks, as the Sicilian campaign was being won, the Badoglio government started to bargain—not for surrender but for a military agreement with the Allies.

While Eisenhower was waiting for the chance to present his "short terms," the Americans and British in Washington had resumed their interrupted study of the "long terms." The points at issue became confused as the fatiguing sessions tried tempers. The student of the cluttered argument that went on will not find it easy to be sure who wanted what or why. And as the stubborn differences between the American and British views about the political aspects of surrender persisted, Roosevelt tried to outwit the problem. He began to doubt whether anything more than was set down in the terms sent to Eisenhower was necessary. "Why," he asked Churchill, "tie his [Eisenhower's] hands by an instrument that may be oversufficient or insufficient? Why not let him act to meet situations as they arise?" [12]

[12] *Ibid.*, page 65.

The matter was still unsettled when, on August 4th, Churchill sailed from England to meet the President at Quebec. While he was at sea it had been agreed that another article should be added to the "short terms," to guard against misunderstanding in the event they were used. This article notified the Italian government that "Other conditions of a political, economic and financial nature with which Italy will be bound to comply will be transmitted at a later date."

By this time the Italians had taken the first steps toward arranging for discussion of armistice terms. On July 31st, while his vows of fidelity to the German Alliance were still warm, Badoglio, with the approval of the King, had decided to send an envoy to Lisbon to put himself in touch with the British Embassy there. Marchese D'Ajeta, Counselor of Legation, was chosen; his rank was modest enough to make his trip pass as a routine transfer. The report spread in Rome that he was taking Ciano's jewels out of the country.

D'Ajeta had talked with Sir Ronald Campbell, the British Ambassador in Lisbon on August 4th. He portrayed the Italian government and people as eager to get out of the war and break with Germany. But since, he went on, the Germans might at any time enter on military occupation of the country—making prisoners of the King, the government, and the military heads—they would need help if they were to take the risk. Thus he suggested that prior military and political accords be reached between the United Nations and Italy. This it will be observed was quite a different line of exit from the war than "unconditional surrender." Campbell listened coolly. In relaying an account of this talk, he commented, "D'Ajeta never from start to finish made any mention of peace terms and his whole story . . . was no more than a plea that we should save Italy from the Germans as well as from herself, and do it as quickly as possible."

Impatient for an answer, the Italian government sent off a second envoy, Berio, also a member of the Italian diplomatic corps, to Tangier to consult the British diplomatic representative there. His instructions were more positive. He was to state that the Italian government wanted to discuss armistice terms. But the plan in mind looked to a concert of action with the Allies and not a simple, or unconditional, surrender. He was sent to urge the Allies to attack in the Balkans—in order to cause the Germans to transfer troops from Italy—and also make a landing in Northern Italy; the Italian armies, the idea was, would then join in the fight to free Italy of the Germans. Events were to show that the Badoglio government offered what it could not deliver—the will of the Italian army really to engage itself in hard battle against the Germans.

On the same day, August 6th, that Berio was making such proposals to the British Consul at Tangier, the Italian Foreign Minister, Guariglia, and Italian Chief of Staff, General Ambrosio, were meeting at Tarviso with Ribbentrop and General Keitel. The Allies had been advised that such a conference was pending and asked not to be misled by the occurrence. At that grisly session of deception ". . . Guariglia declared that the change of government of Italy was purely an internal affair, and that Italy held to Badoglio's declaration that 'the war continues.' Ambrosio then went on to complain that Germany placed little faith in Italy's declared word; in Italian military circles they were astonished at the numerous German divisions which came in part unannounced. It was Southern Italy which was threatened by invasion . . . but the German divisions were concentrated near Rome and in the North, leading to the suspicion that German troops had other intentions than the defense of Italy. Keitel then stated that this questioning of German good faith was quite unacceptable, and he proceeded to express indignation that instead of thanks for the generous German aid in Italy's emergency, the German moves were viewed with suspicion . . . Ambrosio reaffirmed the intention of the Italians to march by the side of the Germans with all their strength." [13]

Eden had sent word to Churchill, who was on shipboard on his way to Quebec, that he thought the second Italian initiative was a genuine attempt to negotiate. Churchill and Roosevelt also treated it as such in the answer which they prepared. But before this reply was transmitted to the Italian envoy at Tangier, still a third Italian emissary, with more authority and more of the steam of purpose behind him, had left for Madrid—General Guiseppe Castellano, Assistant to the Chief of the High Command, who had played a leading part in the dismissal of Mussolini. The wavering of the King and Badoglio about the next step had seemed to him not only timid but tragic for Italy, dooming it to German occupation. By constant effort he had managed to persuade Badoglio, who in turn persuaded the King, to act more boldly, to send someone who would have genuine authority to reach an agreement. He had been given the job. But the King would not give him credentials or written orders. Fear of German vengeance on Italy and the government and himself was too strong. So the mission was arranged under military auspices. He was instructed to negotiate only with Allied military representatives, and to agree with them only on a common plan of action against the Germans.

Castellano had turned up at the British Embassy in Madrid with a letter for the British Ambassador, Sir Samuel Hoare. He told the Am-

[13] McGaw Smyth manuscript.

bassador that he came with the full approval of both the King and Badoglio to arrange an armistice. Like those before him, he asked that the Allies save Italy from the further consequence of its alliance with Hitler's Germany. The Italian government, he said, was willing to undertake to evacuate its forces at once from the Balkans and Croatia, and agree to swing the Italian army, navy, and air force over to the Allied side. Hoare told him that he would report this bid at once. Since any attempt to negotiate in Madrid was extremely dangerous, for there were German agents watching every person in the British Embassy, he advised Castellano to hurry on to Lisbon, where the British government might send someone with authority to carry on the discussion with him. Castellano took this advice.

On August 16th the campaign in Sicily ended—after most of the German forces had gotten away to the Italian mainland. On the next day Roosevelt joined Churchill at Quebec. And on the next day after that (August 18th) he and Churchill, on the basis of a memo of the Combined Chiefs, agreed that the answer to Castellano was to be made through Eisenhower. He was to send two of his staff officers, one American and one British, to Lisbon to meet Castellano. They were to inform him that the unconditional surrender of Italy would be accepted on terms expressed in a document to be given him. The document was the "short" armistice terms which had been entrusted to Eisenhower. The Italian envoy was to be told in addition that the extent to which these terms might be modified in favor of Italy depended on the measure of help which the Italian government and people gave during the rest of the war. It was to be, after all, a military surrender.

The American general, Walter B. Smith, Eisenhower's Chief of Staff, and the British general, Kenneth W. D. Strong, on Eisenhower's staff in charge of military intelligence, were sent to Lisbon at once. There, during the night of August 19th–20th, they found Castellano thinking still of a deal that would avoid formal surrender and treat Italy as an ally. The generals, in the answers they made, sternly stuck by their instructions. Castellano was given a copy of the "short terms," with the statement that the Italian government would have to accept or refuse them as they stood. This was supplemented by a memo stating the actions which the Allies wanted the Italians to take against the Germans, and the political rewards for their military cooperation.

Castellano was delayed in getting back to Rome with this Allied answer. While he was waiting for a safe chance to do so, still another peace envoy, General Zanussi, attached to the General Staff of the Italian army, was sent to Lisbon.

In the meantime, the Americans and British at Quebec had at last managed to agree on the "long terms." These set down the policies and measures in all spheres—political, financial, and administrative—which were to be executed in Italy after the acceptance of unconditional surrender. Now a confusing fuss ensued. On August 26th, just as soon as Roosevelt's concurrence in these "long terms" had been won, the British Foreign Office hastened to instruct its Ambassador at Lisbon to present them to Zanussi. Campbell did so (also acquainting him with the same memorandum that had been given Castellano, promising an easement in return for help against the Germans). And the next day, the 27th, the Combined Chiefs of Staff instructed Eisenhower to use them, instead of the "short terms," in any future negotiation.

This upset Eisenhower and his staff. They were doubtful whether Castellano would be able to persuade Badoglio and the King to go through with the act of surrender even on the basis of the "short terms" he was carrying back to Rome. To supplant these at this late juncture with another and more confronting set of terms would, they feared, imperil the chances of obtaining a quick surrender; and that they were most eager to get before landing in the Naples area. So Eisenhower appealed to the Joint Chiefs for discretion. Macmillan, his English political adviser, matched him in the earnestness of his advice. The order was relaxed. Eisenhower was told to try to get the "long terms" signed; but, if he found that this would mean costly delay, to effect an armistice on the basis of the "short terms," making clear that this was only a partial, in a sense preliminary, statement of the conditions of peace.

General Zanussi, with the "long terms" still in his briefcase, was suspect in the eyes of Allied Headquarters. Both his purposes and authority were in doubt. So he was hustled away from Lisbon to Algiers before he could, or at any rate before he did, radio the text of the "long terms" to Rome. Generals Smith and Strong talked with him at Algiers and were convinced he could be trusted. But he was kept in Algiers, while his interpreter was sent back to Rome with a message urging the Italian government to accept the military (short terms) of the armistice at once, and to send Castellano to Sicily to sign them.

Castellano had managed to get back from Lisbon to Rome. There he did not find much objection to the military terms which had been presented to him, but mounting fear of the Germans. From the King down all wanted the announcement of the armistice to be delayed until after the Allies had landed, and then only when they were in Italy in enormous force (fifteen divisions), particularly near and north of Rome, to protect the government. Instructed to this effect, Castellano was sent down to Sicily. There on August 31st he explained this proposal to Generals Smith and Strong. They told him sternly that it was not acceptable; that the Italian government must either take the terms offered and announce the end of fighting at the time of the Allied main landing, or continue to be regarded by us as an enemy. They made much of the authority given Eisenhower to ease the conditions if Italy gave help in the war. And they implied that if the Italian government lost this chance for a military armistice, it was likely to fare much worse later on. But both Eisenhower and Alexander were much worried over the battle ahead if the Italians did not help, and so in the last hours of negotiation they promised to take special military measures in support of Italian defense of Rome.

The King and the Badoglio government were thus faced with the choice between the risk of becoming captive to the Germans or of being unspared by the Allies. On September 1st Badoglio got the King's assent to acceptance of the offer which Castellano had transmitted. Thereupon word was sent to Eisenhower, "The reply is affirmative."

But even then the Italian government loitered over the measures necessary to give effect to the decision. Early on the morning of September 3rd the Allied landing-craft left Sicily for the toe of Italy. This brought an end to the anxious delay, and Castellano was authorized to sign an acceptance of the short armistice terms. He signed that afternoon at the command post at Cassabile. General Smith signed on behalf of Eisenhower, who came up from Algiers and witnessed the occasion.

The Supreme Commander in the Mediterranean area believed this action sufficient for the immediate purpose. Further, he thought that the more comprehensive set of terms too harsh. But, grimly obedient to orders, he had General Smith that same evening give Castellano a copy of them for presentation to his government with a note explaining their nature. The longer document began with the statement, "The Italian Land, Sea, and Air Forces wherever located, hereby surrender unconditionally." [14] In the "short terms" the nature of the surrender had not been named; here it was stamped out plainly. Castellano protested against both the procedure and the substance, and said he doubted whether his government would ever accept these additional terms. To moderate the Italian reaction to this primer which spelled out the whole set of conditions under which Italy might be required to live, General Smith gave Castellano a note addressed to Badoglio which read, "The additional terms have only a relative value insofar as Italy collaborates in the war against the Germans." The message which Roosevelt and Churchill had sent from Quebec was sanction for this notice that the terms were malleable.

[14] Paragraph 1 after the Preamble.

The fact that an armistice had been signed was kept most secret. The idea was to let it be known just before the Allied troops landed at Salerno. Simultaneously the Italian forces and people would be ordered by the Badoglio government not to oppose but to cooperate.

It had been planned that an airborne force which was to capture the airfields near Rome should be dropped on September 8th, the same night that the Allied expedition was to start for the Salerno beaches. But Badoglio (through General Maxwell Taylor, who had been secretly brought into Rome to make the needed arrangements) urged that the airborne operation be called off since it would be a disaster for all. It was cancelled at the last moment, and wisely so. The Italians could not, even if they had been determined and willing to endure heavy losses, have protected and sustained this airborne force against the capable and well-equipped German divisions which were moving on Rome. Thus the prospect of capturing the capital by one quick daring stroke was closed. The Allied armies were going to have to fight long and exhausting battles before they got to the Holy City.

Badoglio faltered further. The day before the Allied expedition was to start for Salerno, he tried to cancel his acceptance of the armistice accord. He had not expected the landing would be made before the 12th. He sent word to Eisenhower that, "Due to changes in the situation brought about by the disposition and strength of the German forces in the Rome area, it is no longer possible to accept an immediate armistice as this could provoke the occupation of the Capital and the violent assumption of the government by the Germans." The members of his armed forces and of his civil government, it has since become known, were badly divided between those who wanted to act boldly on the Allied side to win better future treatment for Italy and save the House of Savoy, and those who were cautious, afraid of the Germans, and mistrustful of Allied promises. The King himself at this last juncture refused to take or assign the lead.

On getting this news from Eisenhower's headquarters at Algiers, Roosevelt and Churchill at once decided that the armistice announcement would have to be made as planned, no matter what the Italian government did. Eisenhower was angrily of the same opinion. He hurried off a reply to Badoglio, saying that he was going to broadcast the news of an armistice that night (September 8th) and that if the Italian government failed also to do likewise, he would disclose the whole record to the world, cancel the armistice accord, and dissolve Badoglio's government.

That evening Eisenhower went ahead with his broadcast. He stated that, acting for the United Nations, he had signed an armistice accord with Marshal Badoglio, and that, "The Italian government has surrendered its armed forces unconditionally." Badoglio caved in. About three hours later he followed suit. He told of the armistice accord, and then went on to say, "The Italian forces will, therefore, cease all acts of hostility against the Anglo-American forces wherever they may be met."

The Allied convoys were drawing close to the Salerno beaches. That night German troops began to crowd in upon Rome. In accord with the pledge, the main Italian fleet units left the ports of Genoa, Spezia, and Taranto for Malta. The next morning the Royal Family, Badoglio, and chief members of his government fled to an Adriatic port, and thence to Brindisi, which became the seat of their government.

The document that had been signed accorded the United Nations the right to exercise control over Italy in whatever measure they wished, and to issue to the Italian government any orders they saw fit. But it was also a "conditioned" surrender. Roosevelt and Churchill and Eisenhower all had promised the Italian people that they would be treated humanely, given a future chance to choose their own form of government, and be allowed to regain a respected place in the world. They had also promised to reward Italian military help in the war against Germany.

The tortuous way in which armistice terms had been prepared, the delay and confusion as to which set were to be used, caused the Soviet government to think it was being kept in the dark. This happened despite a real effort to keep it informed and give it a chance to comment on what was being done. To appreciate the full impact of these Italian surrender negotiations on relations with the Soviet Union, that side of the story ought also to be known.

18. The Soviet Side Again: Summer of 1943

Communication with Moscow about the arrangements for Italian surrender was intertwined with discussion of many other matters. So I shall tell of it as one phase of the ups and downs in the current of association with Stalin in this July-September period.

It will be recalled that primarily because of Stalin's displeasure over the postponement of the cross-Channel invasion, contact with him had become caustic. During July it had almost lapsed. The idea that Roosevelt might meet with him alone had remained in suspense. But events within Italy and the need to decide plans for carrying forward the war had caused a resumption of correspondence with the sullen head of the Soviet state.

The Soviet press had been paying little attention to the Sicilian campaign. Such reports upon it as had appeared were usually bordered by the reminder (*Tass* report on July 23rd) that no matter how brilliantly successful these operations might be, they were ". . . not a second front which is necessary for the speedy destruction of Hitlerism." Yet the whole Soviet press exulted over the downfall of Mussolini (on July 25th), repaying old taunts. But Stalin was not heard from. Perhaps his silence was not purposeful. He was at the front during most of July, directing Soviet resistance to massive German attacks and he stayed there until the Germans were stopped and the Russians had recaptured Orel and Bielgorod in early August.

On July 26th Ambassador Winant, after talking with Eden about what was happening in Italy, had reported to the President and Hull that Eden made much of the point that Russia ought to be brought into the consultations about how to deal with the Badoglio government and about surrender terms. Winant himself, commenting on this advice, had observed, "When the tide turns and the Russian armies are able to advance we might well want to influence their terms of capitulation and occupancy in Allied and enemy territory." Ambassador Standley in Moscow was similarly alerted by reports of a talk which Ilya Ehrenbourg, the leading political journalist, had with American press correspondents. This Russian public advocate was reproachful about the President's disavowal of the O.W.I. broadcast attack upon Badoglio and the King. Given to sneering, Ehrenbourg had gone so far as to ask whether, if we were going to do business with these Fascists, would we also consort with Goering or his like in Germany?

While the decision probably had been long under consideration, it was at this time (July 28th) that the Soviet Foreign Office let Standley know that Ambassador Maisky would not be sent back to London. He was to be kept in Moscow as one of the Assistant Commissars for Foreign Affairs. The more informed observers took this transfer of a man known to be friendly to the West as a sign that Moscow wanted to show its stiffer expression. The more hopeful construed it to mean that the Soviet government was disturbed by its difficulties with the West and wanted Maisky to guide it in future discussions. Standley was at first inclined to ascribe the shift to the second purpose.

Still, on July 30th he had strongly advised Hull not to lag in telling the Soviet government what was being done about Italy. Hull had at once asked Winant to discuss with Eden whether the time had not come to accede to the Soviet request—made a month before—to have one of its diplomats visit North Africa in order to study the situation there. He had also submitted to the President an informative message about the course of events in Italy which might be sent to Moscow as a joint American and British report. As soon as it was approved (August 1st) Hull had asked Winant to discuss it with the British Foreign Office.

Winant had then learned that the Soviet Embassy in London had already been seeking information about the Italian situation. Days before, the Foreign Office had given it a copy of a statement of the British position in Italy which had been prepared for the use of the British Embassy in Washington. It had also turned over a summary outline of the then latest draft of Instrument of Surrender (the "long terms") which the British had submitted to the Combined Chiefs. In doing so the Foreign Office had made clear that this was provisional, pending agreement with the American government, and was still open for revision. Sobolev, the Soviet Chargé d'Affaires, after consulting Moscow, had told the British Foreign Office that the Soviet government regarded these "long terms" as corresponding to existing conditions and that it saw nothing wrong in them. By that time the "short terms," as revised, had been approved, and Eisenhower had been authorized to present them if necessary for military reasons. The British—Clark-Kerr in Moscow to Molotov—had then proceeded to give the Russians a copy of the "short terms" with an explanation of the circumstances in which they might be used. On this text the Soviet government made no comment. It could hardly have been sure of the status of these two different sets of terms, or which was the more likely to be brought into play when the time came.

Hull had next sent off a message to Molotov, amended to take account of what had passed between the British and Soviet governments. This friendly statement (given to the Soviet Minister for Foreign Affairs on August 5th) was a short memo in the name of the American government only. It informed him that Eisenhower was being authorized to accept unconditional surrender from anyone who could offer it and to take whatever measures seemed to him necessary to preserve order, protect Allied forces in Italy, and prepare further military operations. It recorded the understanding that the British government had already acquainted him with "our joint ideas on the terms of surrender to be exacted from Italy." Then (in paraphrase) it read:

"The government of the United States continues to share the view that it is essential that the U.S., British, and Soviet governments keep each other fully informed about military developments in the various areas in which their respective armed forces are operating and also that they maintain constant touch with each other about such developments of a political nature as may arise from the immediate military developments. Any suggestions which the Soviet government may now or later care to offer would therefore be welcomed by the American government. It would also be glad to answer any questions the Soviet government might want to ask about the Italian situation."

Hull let Eden know at once of this message to Molotov. At the same time he asked Winant to impress on Eden the opinion that he thought the Foreign Office should have consulted their American associates before passing on to the Soviet government matters still under discussion between them; that by neglecting to do so it might give the impression in Moscow that the British government was trying to act as intermediary.

The Soviet government had not asked any questions for several weeks about further developments in Allied attitude and intentions toward an Italian surrender. This may have been just as well. For Hull himself had only a balcony view of what was going on. The American and British groups who were trying to complete the "long terms" were still at odds over several important matters, including what should be done about the Italian Crown and about the scope of military government.

During these weeks Churchill was, as has been told, resolved if possible to have the Italian surrender arranged formally and through diplomatic channels. He was in no mood to take heed of any deranging thoughts the Russians might have. For he had not received any answer to the recent messages which he had sent Stalin on other matters. While on his way to meet Roosevelt at Quebec, he told a shipboard companion that he wanted to send Stalin a cable of congratulations on the capture of Orel, but since he had heard nothing from Stalin about our progress in Sicily, he had decided to say nothing. He wondered aloud in jest whether the President would care to join him in such a message, ending with, "It may not have come to your attention, but considerable military operations are going on in the Mediterranean which have resulted in Mussolini's retirement." Perhaps Churchill was too sensitive; the march across Sicily could have seemed to the Russians like a skirmish compared to the stretched-out life and death struggle in the Kursk-Orel-Kharkov region about which later Churchill was to write, "These three immense battles of Kursk, Orel, and Kharkov, all within a space of two months, marked the ruin of the German army on the Eastern Front." [15]

[15] *Closing the Ring*, page 259.

When the Prime Minister got round to sending Stalin a message of congratulation, it contained no hint of hurt or humor. Stalin, who was back in Moscow, cheered by the works of the Red Army, sent him a prompt (August 10th), friendly answer. He explained his silence by his absence at the battlefront. Churchill, informing the King on the next day of his arrival at Quebec, remarked, "Your Majesty will also have noticed that I have heard from the Great Bear and that we are on speaking, or at least growling, terms again." [16] "Great Bear" was more apt than "Uncle Joe."

On the next evening (August 11th) Standley and Clark-Kerr went together to tell Stalin and Molotov the latest secret news which their government had sent on to them. It was that Italian emissaries had turned up at Lisbon and Tangier to talk about the Italian separation from the Axis. On hearing this, Stalin said that it was necessary to beware of Badoglio; he was tricky, not to be trusted, and would try to deceive Hitler, the King of Italy, and of course the British and Americans. One cannot help but wonder whether Stalin knew of the Guariglia-Ribbentrop meeting a few days before at Tarviso. Clark-Kerr answered that he did not believe the Americans and British would be fooled by him. The Marshal, both Ambassadors felt, was cool on this occasion—and suggestive in his leave-taking remark, "With the Italians out of the way, now, you should be able to open a Second Front."

A few days later (on August 16th) Molotov made known that Litvinov, the Soviet Ambassador in Washington, was being recalled and would not return. The reason given was that Stalin wanted him close at hand for advice. But press speculation connected the change with Russian resentment at his failure to persuade the Allies to start the invasion of France. It was properly surmised that the Soviet government wanted a more disciplined and rigid exponent of its purposes in that post.

The last of the Germans were hurrying to escape from Sicily. Roosevelt and Churchill at Quebec were rejecting Castellano's proposal that the Allies work out with Italy a joint plan of military action; their answer made through Eisenhower will be recalled: unconditional surrender on the basis of the "short terms," and an auxiliary promise that these might be made easier as a reward for Italian help against the Germans.

Immediately they informed Stalin of these latest Italian overtures

[16] *Ibid.,* page 81.

and of the order they were giving Eisenhower.[17] They said that they thought the Italian proposal firm and in good faith, but did not intend to offer the Italians any inducement to switch sides. They explained that by putting Eisenhower in a position to arrange a quick military surrender, they were seeking the full advantage of haste and surprise. In particular they were trying to avert the risk that German troops might take control of Italy before the landings to be made at the tip of Italy and then at Salerno below Naples.

By this time, Churchill and Roosevelt and their Chiefs of Staff were immersed in discussions of that program of world-wide strategy which was to engage the western Allies to the cross-Channel operation. So the next scrape which occurred with Stalin over events in Italy was ironical.

Even though the Americans and British, who were trying to complete the final draft of the "long terms," were still snagged on some main points, Churchill sent the latest available version to the British Ambassador to be passed on to Stalin. It arrived in Moscow on the 20th in slightly imperfect form (there was one garbled sentence and the closing sentence of twelve words was missing). But Clark-Kerr delivered it at once anyhow. For reasons obscure, the small and not meaningful defects in the text incensed Stalin. Or, perhaps not wishing to state plainly his dislike of some of its provisions, he chose to display his feelings this way. In a message for both Churchill and Roosevelt which in the typescript bore the date of August 22nd, delivered through the Soviet Embassy to the White House, he acknowledged the report. But he then went on to say in effect that Eden had not told the truth when he said to Sobolev in London that Moscow was being kept fully advised about the negotiations with Italy. For, he continued, in this latest message long passages were omitted and the concluding paragraph was lacking. And although Clark-Kerr, when giving him this poor text, had assured him, Stalin continued, that he would get the complete and perfect text, three days had passed and still he had not received it; and he could not understand a delay in the transmission of such important information. Actually Clark-Kerr had sent Molotov on the 22nd a full corrected text. But apparently Stalin did not learn that he had done so until after this grumbling communication to Roosevelt and Churchill was sent.

[17] The original text of this message, from which the exact time of its dispatch could be ascertained, has not been available. My only source is Sherwood, *Roosevelt and Hopkins,* page 745; and in a footnote on page 958 he states that it is dated August 16th, But this may be incorrect, for there are reasons for thinking that it was not transmitted to Moscow until the 18th.

That message was not, however, entirely negative. Stalin now urged the immediate adoption of arrangements for regular consultation on all matters concerning the defeated partners of Germany. This had been under consideration for some time. The British government in July had suggested to the American and Soviet governments that the three of them create a European commission (1) to coordinate the execution of surrender or armistice terms to be imposed on the enemy; and (2) to work out long-range plans about security and economic matters. Hull, after consulting the President, had answered that he favored the idea, but thought the commission should have only the first of these two assignments. Perhaps in the interval the British and Soviet governments had discussed the idea further. For now Stalin said to Churchill and Roosevelt (as recorded in awkward English paraphrase):

"I believe the time is ripe to organize the Military-Political Commission of the representatives of the three countries: the United States, Great Britain, and the Union of Soviet Socialist Republics with the purpose of considering the questions concerning the negotiations with the different governments disassociating themselves from Germany. Until now the matter stood as follows: the United States and Great Britain made agreements but the Soviet Union received information about the results of the agreements between the two countries just as a passive third observer. I have to tell you that it is impossible to tolerate the situation any longer. I propose that the Commission be established and that Sicily be assigned at the beginning as its place of residence."

This important message was relayed from Washington to Quebec on the 24th. That night, Roosevelt came into the room before dinner saying, "We are both mad"; and they were. Harriman tried to lighten the mood. He asked the President if he recalled the sentence in another rejoinder that Churchill had made to an earlier recrimination by Stalin (about the second front), "I am entirely unmoved by your statement." Harriman then went on to tell, with Churchill overhearing, that the Prime Minister had shown him this answer before it was sent off to Stalin, and asked for his comment; that he had only asked the Prime Minister if that sentence was entirely accurate. The President roared with laughter. The Prime Minister snorted. Though Eden and Ismay tried to get him to take an easier view of the episode, he would not listen to any excusing talk. After dinner, talking with Harriman, he remarked gloomily that he foresaw "bloody consequences in the future" (using the word "bloody" in its literal sense); and that he thought Stalin an unnatural man—with whom there would be grave trouble.

Further word on these subjects was on its way from Stalin to Roosevelt and Churchill via Sobolev, the Soviet Chargé in London. I do not know whether it was received at Quebec before or after the next series of messages were sent out from there on the 25th—but probably before. Stalin, after commenting on current proposals for meetings of the Heads of State or Foreign Ministers (with which our acquaintance will shortly be brought up-to-date), again stated his ideas about Italy and the Political-Military Commission. He acknowledged without apology receipt of the joint message in which he had been told of the instructions given Eisenhower, and of the full corrected text of the "long terms." These, he calmly went on to say, seemed to him to comply fully with the aims of unconditional surrender and so did not evoke any objections. But anyhow, he added, he considered the information sent him absolutely inadequate to allow him to judge the measures taken in the negotiations with Italy; and he thus repeated his opinion that the time had come to convoke the Political-Military Commission about which he had spoken in his previous reply.

On the 25th, final agreement having just been reached between the Americans and British on the final text of the "long terms," a copy was hurried off at once to Moscow with instructions that Clark-Kerr and Standley should communicate it to Stalin. He was to be told that any comments would be sympathetically examined but that the Soviet government must appreciate that the time factor might not make it possible to give effect to any new proposals. The two gave this final version to Molotov for Stalin on the night of the 26th. Neither before then nor then was the idea stressed that these terms were discretionary with the Allies, and after acceptance could be eased if the Italians gave military help against the Germans.

At the same time the two Ambassadors passed on the Roosevelt-Churchill personal message for Stalin telling him of the great decisions taken at Quebec about military operations in 1943 and 1944, the substance of which has been summarized in earlier pages. It is probable that this report, which pointed definitely toward the desired cross-Channel operation, earned the amiable response that followed about the way in which this secondary Italian surrender transaction was being managed. For, on the next morning, without further ado, Molotov sent a message of approval. Further, the Soviet government authorized Eisenhower to sign on its behalf.

There the matter rested until the Italian government authorized Castellano to accept the Allied offer and to go to Sicily to sign an armistice. Roosevelt and Churchill at once (on September 2nd) hurried a joint message to Stalin, telling him this news. Eisenhower, having been given discretion, they went on to say, it was not certain whether the document to be signed would be the short military terms (which Stalin had seen but not commented on) or the complete terms (which he had definitely approved). In conclusion they told Stalin that they were assuming he was willing to have Eisenhower sign on behalf of the Soviet government, whichever way he decided to handle the situation. Molotov at once answered that the Soviet consent to having Eisenhower sign on its behalf was meant to apply to the short terms also.

The "short terms" were presented by Eisenhower as "Commander-in-Chief of the Allied Forces, acting by authority of the Governments of the United States and Great Britain and in the interest of the United Nations." The agreement was signed by General Walter B. Smith in behalf of Eisenhower. The Soviet government did not have any representative present.

The signed surrender agreement endowed Eisenhower with full authority to enforce the armistice terms, and presumably with the right to form and direct any organization needed for that purpose. It did not indicate which of the United Nations should have part in the work of supervision and control of Italian affairs. Before long the Soviet government was to claim a share in this authority. It also was to press Stalin's proposal for the formation of a tripartite military-political commission to consider all negotiations with governments separating from the Axis. But these emergent problems can best be told in connection with the story of the later phases of Italian surrender, and will be left till then.

All during this improvised converse with the Soviet government over the Italian surrender, correspondence with Stalin about a meeting of Heads of State, or of Foreign Ministers, had been continuing. Despite annoyance at Stalin's gruff suspicion, Roosevelt had remained hopeful of the outcome of a meeting with him. His train of purpose, as sketched out early in September, in the course of his talk with Harriman about going to Moscow as Ambassador, was in consonance with the prevailing thought of the period. He recognized that Russia had the power to grasp whatever parts of Central and Eastern Europe it wanted. But he planned to try to get it to abstain from doing so by making the resultant world reaction clear. He meant to appeal to the (presumed) Soviet wish for collective security and an equal place at the council tables. He was also going to try to satisfy Stalin's wish for more direct security by agreeing to join in the sponsorship of such protective measures as the dismemberment of Germany. He hoped his views could be made more persuasive by offers of American help in repairing war damage in the Soviet Union. In sum, in return for moderation and trust, Russia was to win merit, recognition of its place among the great powers, promises of protection against future enemies, and aid in regaining a normal, peaceful life. All this and more it might have had.

Roosevelt's wish for a first meeting alone with Stalin had given way to the natural flow of his close association with Churchill in the management of the Italian surrender and the formulation of world-wide joint strategy. So their most recent invitations to Stalin proposed a meeting of the three. To these he answered (in that message received in Quebec on August 25th, the other parts of which bearing on the Italian surrender have been noted) that he could not then or in the near future leave the embattled front. This, it may be remarked, was not an excuse; the Germans were still moving fresh divisions to the east, and all the main Soviet Commanders reported directly to Stalin. Churchill made one last attempt by offering to go to Moscow, and then he and Roosevelt gave up. They fell in with the idea of having the Foreign Ministers meet first and soon. The correspondence turned to the nature of that meeting: time, place, and program. Churchill wanted London. Roosevelt was willing to have it in some more remote spot, where the conference would be more protected against reporters—perhaps Casablanca or Tunis. Stalin wanted Moscow. The others gave in. All agreed on October.

And then, on September 8th, the day before the Salerno landing, Stalin said he would afterward go as far as Iran to meet Roosevelt and Churchill. He found Roosevelt's proposal of a time between November 15th and December 15th acceptable. The President answered quickly that he regarded the time of their meeting as fixed, but was hesitant, for reasons of official business, about going as far away from Washington as Iran.

Thus as the hard campaign for Rome set in, the three members of the coalition bent toward each other again. The sun of success blanches out grievances. The Red Army, having secured the safety of Moscow, was fast fighting its way west on an immense front stretching down to the Black Sea. The whole vast line which Hitler had flung forward with all the energy and stamina of German youth in a mad cause, was being battered back. The stream of congratulations flowed again. Responding to a joint message from Roosevelt and Churchill telling him that their troops were on the Naples beaches, Stalin (on September 14th) sent the first words of praise in months: "There is no doubt that the successful landing at Naples and break between Italy and Germany will deal one more blow upon Hitlerite Germany and will considerably facilitate the actions of the Soviet armies at the Soviet-German front." [18] That

[18] *Closing the Ring,* page 144.

was proving to be so. Hitler was still refusing to take away any of his main reserves from the Soviet Front. But he was moving strong divisions, ground and motorized, into Italy and the Balkans, and being compelled to use much of his strength there and consume much of his hoarded oil supply so that soon there would be a lack in the east.

The time was clearly near when the decision-makers would have to meet. The impetus of both military and political events was making this imperative. The possibilities as well as the advantages of more closely concerting the assaults upon the German forces clamored for consideration. If, as was hoped, recent victories in the field were followed swiftly by even greater ones, decisions would soon have to be made about the countries won from the German grasp. Unsettled issues of political principle, purpose, and power hovered between the members of the coalition. This was being evidenced currently in Italy. Since the disposition of the questions that were arising in that country affected the pattern for later events and discussions, this narrative of coalition experience must revert to them.

19. The Italian Evolution into Co-Belligerency

While the tough campaign for the Naples area was being fought out, aspects of association which had been passed over in the hurried military armistice signed September 3rd had to be faced. Badoglio was urging that Italy be granted the status of ally or quasi-ally. "Can we make," he was querying General MacFarlane, the liaison officer with the King and his government at Brindisi, "the transition from victims of an armistice to be beneficiaries of an alliance?"

On September 18th Eisenhower asked for new instructions. He recommended that the Badoglio government be accepted as a co-belligerent provided (1) it absorbed new elements and thus became more representative of the Italian people; (2) it promised to hold free elections and to convoke a constitutional assembly; (3) it left the way open for the possible eventual abdication of the King in favor of his son or grandson.

His object was to inject more fighting will into the Italians. Up to then, the active military aid they had given had been less than looked for. As reviewed by Eisenhower to Marshall just a few days before (September 13th): "Internally the Italians were so weak and supine that we got little of any practicable help out of them. However, almost on pure bluff, we did get the Italian fleet into Malta and because of the Italian surrender were able to rush into Taranto and Brindisi where no Germans were present."

But in this later message of recommendation to the Joint Chiefs he weighed past performance rather in relation to future possibilities: "The benefits we have already obtained from the Armistice are tremendous. We have BUTTRESS [the attack on the toe of Italy], GOBLET [landings on the instep of Italy] and MUSKET [landing on the heel of Italy] almost without fighting and will shortly have BRIMSTONE [Sardinia] and FIREBRAND [the capture of Corsica] not to mention the fleet. Nevertheless we have a hard and risky campaign before us, in which our relationship with the Italians may mean the difference between complete and partial success."

To these observations he added, "I realize that the line of action which I have suggested here will provoke political repercussions and may cause considerable opposition and criticism. Accordingly, I recommend that the burden be placed on us, on the grounds of military necessity, which I am convinced should be the governing factor."

These proposals seemed eminently sound to Churchill. His escalating mind converted them into a program. But even though this was carried out and Italy was thus transformed into a co-belligerent, and therefore some of the long armistice terms could no longer be carried into effect, he thought the Italian government ought to be required to sign them. For this Churchill and the War Cabinet had a practical reason: to establish the full legal authority of the Commander-in-Chief so that he would not have to haggle with the Italian government over his commands and demands as his troops fought their way north. Moreover, they wanted to be surer that Italy would not manage to escape all compulsion to make some amends for the harm it had done either because of military necessity or as the result of political maneuver.

Churchill set out these ideas in separate messages which he hustled off to Roosevelt and Stalin. The one sent to Washington was crossed in transit by one which Roosevelt had written to Churchill. In this the President transmitted the text of a directive to be given Eisenhower when and as Churchill concurred. This differed in its shading from Churchill's proposals. It gave the Supreme Commander more freedom to flex his policy to suit military purposes. And it tried to forefend against the risk that Allied acceptance of the King and the Badoglio government would entrench them in power, contrary to popular will. More concretely, the main features of this Roosevelt directive were:

1. Eisenhower was told to withhold the long terms pending further orders.

2. He was authorized on the basis of military necessity to recommend

a relaxation of the provisions of the armistice, to enable the Italians to fight the Germans.

3. On condition that it declared war on Germany, the Badoglio government was to be permitted to carry on as the government of Italy and to be treated as co-belligerent. But only on the clear understanding that this was in no way to prejudice the untrammeled right of the people of Italy to decide on the form of government they would eventually have.

4. The Allied military government and the appropriate functions contemplated for the armistice control commission were to be merged into an allied commission under the Allied Commander-in-Chief, which was to have the authority to furnish guidance and instruction to the Badoglio government in all realms.

Roosevelt transmitted the substance of this directive to the American Embassy in Moscow to be passed on to Stalin for his information and comment, but did not solicit his concurrence. By the time Stalin got it (on the evening of the 22nd) his answer to Churchill's message was written and on its way. Stalin told the Prime Minister that he agreed with his ideas, including the opinion that the Badoglio government should be required to sign the long armistice terms. His only reservation was that he saw no reason for softening any of them—except insofar as they could not be realized in those sections of Italy held by the Germans.

The need to give Eisenhower guidance in the negotiations with the Badoglio government was deemed so urgent that neither Churchill nor Roosevelt waited for comment from Moscow before acting. Churchill informed Roosevelt that he concurred in the proposed directive. In regard to the time for presentation of the "long terms" he said he would defer to the President. On thus hearing from Churchill, Roosevelt went ahead. On the 23rd he authorized Eisenhower to proceed with the directive. When Stalin's answer to Roosevelt was received two days later, it indicated that the Marshal maintained his doubts as to the need for relaxing the armistice terms. And he was puzzled about the section of the directive centering the authority to guide and instruct the Badoglio government in a commission under the Allied Commander-in-Chief. More will presently be heard on this point of the wedge that divided the Allies on the question of how and by whom policy in Italy was to be made during the armistice period. Here was a scrimmage in the making, or several of them.

During these same days, Eisenhower's political advisers, Macmillan and Murphy, were wrangling with Badoglio over the "long terms." He was much distressed at the idea of signing them. He was trying to get

Italy accepted as an ally and was being told it was not possible. His protests ranged over three points. One was that General Castellano on the 3rd of September had not agreed to an unconditional surrender. The question of whether or not he did is a tempting one for the detective of political criss-crosses and ambiguities. But I shall not devote the short day to it. Badoglio's next ground for protest was that the Allies had basically changed the obligations imposed and accepted on September 3rd. For this assertion, which was in effect a charge of bad faith, he had only the evidence of his own opinion of what the armistice meant. Lastly, he complained that various provisions of the long armistice could not be carried out. This was true for several reasons—the most important of which was that the Germans controlled so much of Italy and the Badoglio government so little.

While this bedraggled debate with Badoglio was going on, Churchill (on September 24th) veered again. Macmillan had advised him that he thought Badoglio could be made to sign the "long terms" within the next few days, and the longer the delay, the more the haggling. The Prime Minister now told the President he thought it was best to hurry to get this done and thus avoid possible later trouble. In view of the fact that Stalin in his message to Churchill had said that he also favored this action, the President now decided to go along with them. Thereupon, revising his directive, he told Eisenhower to try to secure Badoglio's signature on the "long terms" if it could be had quickly.

At this juncture a rift developed between the King and Badoglio. Badoglio was urging the King to agree to declare war on Germany. But the King was refusing, at least until the government had been broadened and was installed in Rome. The Germans, he argued, still occupied more than five-sixths of Italy and would certainly resort to barbarous reprisals. Further, he did not want to give countenance to the pledge that the Italian people would later on decide their own form of government on the ground, as he expressed it MacFarlane, "That he thought it would be most dangerous to leave the choice of post-war government unreservedly in the hands of the Italian people."

Eisenhower's deputy, General Smith, went down to Brindisi to talk with Badoglio and to arrange for him to meet with Eisenhower at Malta. Badoglio managed to get the King's consent to sign the "long terms." But he tried to hedge in regard to the statement to which the King objected—the untrammeled right of the Italian people to choose their own form of government after the war; a monarchy, he argued, was necessary for the stability and unity of the country.

Badoglio left Brindisi for Malta to meet with Eisenhower. There he tried again to get the terms of the long armistice changed—"to be spared," as Churchill has put it, "the clause of unconditional surrender." His main purpose may have been to save Italian pride. But so stubborn was his stand that Eisenhower was compelled to warn him that if he did not sign the terms as they were, the gravest consequences would follow; and that Italy would be treated as a defeated and occupied country. He signed on the 29th.[19]

Eisenhower then gave him a letter which said that it was recognized that some of the articles in the document were already superseded or could not be carried out at once. And, further, that it was to be understood that the terms of both the "short" and "long" armistice agreements might be modified from time to time if military necessity or the extent of cooperation by the Italian government indicated that this was desirable. According to Badoglio's later account, Eisenhower also promised him that this surrender document would remain "absolutely secret." [20] Roosevelt and Churchill had agreed that it might be so.

Eisenhower sought a promise of an immediate declaration of war upon Germany. Badoglio, adapting his position to the King's wishes, demurred. Eisenhower made it clear to Badoglio that his government would have to assume a definite anti-Fascist complexion if it were to be ranged alongside the Allies, and therefore urged him to proceed quickly to place it on a broader liberal basis.

The concluding exchange of comment shows how far national pride can twist the view of history. Eisenhower thanked Badoglio for his effort and expressed the hope that much good would come from this meeting. Badoglio answered, according to the note which Murphy made of the talk, by referring ". . . to the situation in 1918 when the Italians . . . gave the decisive blow to the Germans, that at that time

[19] Shortly afterward Eisenhower recommended several changes in the long terms. Among them were (1) to change the title from stark "Instrument of Surrender" to "Additional Conditions of the Armistice with Italy"; (2) to make the last sentence of Paragraph 6 of the Preamble to the terms read ". . . and have been accepted *unconditionally* by Marshal Pietro Badoglio, Head of the Italian Government *representing the Supreme Command of the Italian land, sea and air forces and duly authorized to that effect by the Italian Government*" [later insertions *italicized*]; and (3) to omit from Paragraph 1 (A) of the text which had read, "The Italian Land, Sea and Air Forces surrender unconditionally."

Roosevelt and Churchill were agreeable. On October 1st Roosevelt advised Stalin of the proposed amendments and asked Stalin whether he concurred in making them. Stalin answered that he had no objection. So in the final outcome, the text provided for unconditional acceptance of terms which were definite—and conditional in the sense of being limiting.

All the changes made were finally incorporated in a protocol signed on November 9th. All relevant texts are to be found in *Documents Relating to the Condition of an Armistice with Italy (September–November 1943)*, H. M. Stationery Office, Cmd. 6693.

[20] Badoglio, Pietro, *Italy in the Second World War*, page 107.

there were with the Italian Army three British divisions and one American regiment all of whom cooperated closely in the German defeat."

The American and British governments were still quite far apart as to the degree of political change that ought to be brought about in Italy and as to whether it ought to be made sooner or later. The President, Hopkins, and Hull, being of the same mind, acquiesced in these war transactions with the Badoglio government and the King as passing expedients, justified only by military benefits and the need for orderly government while Allied forces were still engaged there. They wanted and looked toward a change which could transfer control to other political elements in Italy, those who had had no association with Mussolini and Fascism. Similarly, in regard to the temporary tolerance of King Victor Emmanuel, they believed that as an individual he had shown himself timid and unfit; and that because of his compliance with the Mussolini regime he should resign and turn over the authority to his grandson under a regency. Furthermore, they were on guard against political tricks which would prejudice the future chance of the Italian people to decide whether they wanted any monarch or any form of monarchy.

Churchill was not disturbed in the same way by the associations being formed with the King and the Badoglio government. He did not have such qualms as the Americans about keeping these former associates of Fascism in power. He was more tender in passing judgment on kings, and governments legitimatized by kings. Besides that, he was more worried about the chances of disorder or even a recurrence of Bolshevism in Italy, and less worried about the resentment (and "intrigues," as he called them) of the leftish political groups that opposed Fascism. So he thought it prudent to sustain the authority of Badoglio and the King at least until the situation was well under control; and he wanted to go slow in reviving political parties in Italy and compelling the Badoglio group to share or yield power to them.

This irritable tussle over the nature and timing of the changes to be brought about in the Badoglio government and the treatment of the House of Savoy ended in another temporary compromise. The effort to persuade, or perhaps even to coerce, Badoglio to make a cautious start on transforming his government was to be sustained. But the decision about its ultimate fate and the future of the monarchy was to wait until Rome was taken and many more Italians would be free to record their wishes. So reconciled for the time being, in the fortnight between the signing of the long armistice terms (September 29th) and the Italian declaration of war on Germany (October 13th), Americans and

British both nudged the Badoglio government toward a reformation; the British with finger tips, the Americans with thumbs.

Badoglio remained loath to heed the advice that he make over his government on the grounds that the leaders of the liberal groups were "ghosts of a former era." But he yielded rather than risk dismissal. Eisenhower induced him to adopt the essential points in careful words —and to announce the program on the occasion of declaring war on Germany. He told the people that he was going to "complete" his government by asking representatives of every democratic political party to share in it. He explained that this measure would not impair their chance to determine their own form of government when peace was restored.

In the joint declaration which Roosevelt, Churchill, and Stalin issued (on October 13th) accepting Italy as a co-belligerent, they noted Badoglio's announcement about his political intentions with approval and underscored its meaning. Thus the way was left clear, with Soviet assent, to continue the triple tactic of at one and the same time, (1) working with the King and Badoglio government; (2) seeking to bring other democratic elements into it; and (3) preserving the chance for the Italian people to decide later who they wanted to govern them, and whether they wanted the king they had, or any other king.

Badoglio, to glance forward, tried to get leaders of the political parties to accept posts in his government. But they would not take office under him. And the demand that King Victor Emmanuel give up his throne and depart grew impatient. But this is part of the later story.

※※※※※※※

20. Temporary Concord about Italy: Autumn 1943

※※※※※※※

The Soviet government had followed these further developments in Italy from afar. Although it did not dissent from the policies pursued, it was dissatisfied. Its wishes and efforts focused on transferring authority to make and execute decisions from the Supreme Commander as representative of the United Nations to a special military-political commission (MPC) in which the Soviet government would have an equal place and perhaps a veto power.

The story of the confused controversy that ensued over this proposal retains interest. It will be recalled that Stalin in peremptory messages to Roosevelt and Churchill had (August 24th and 25th) complained that he did not feel adequately informed about what was occurring in

Italy, and that he thought the time had come to establish a joint military-political commission and set it to work at once ". . . with the purpose of considering the questions concerning the negotiations with the different governments disassociating themselves from Germany."

This proposal had been left in suspense—possibly because it had not seemed urgent, since Stalin had approved the text of the long armistice terms which stipulated how Allied authority over Italy was to be exercised. Paragraphs 36 and 37 of this agreement read:

"(36) The Italian Government will take and enforce such legislative and other measures as may be necessary for the execution of the present instrument. The Italian military and civil authorities will comply with any instructions issued by the Allied Commander-in-Chief for the same purpose.

"(37) There will be appointed a Control Commission representative of the United Nations charged with regulating and executing this instrument under the orders and general directions of the Allied Commander-in-Chief."

Roosevelt had chosen to assume that these provisions took care of the problems that Stalin had been raising about Italy. For, in a message which he had sent Stalin on September 5th (concerned mainly with the prospective meeting of Foreign Ministers), while making only passing mention of Stalin's proposal, he had inserted a paragraph into the draft which, as polished and paraphrased, read: "Why not send an officer to General Eisenhower's headquarters in connection with the commission to sit in Sicily on further settlements with the Italians? He would join the British and Americans who are now working on this very subject."

Stalin had the impression that his recommendation was being shunted off. There was a note of annoyance in his answer of September 8th to Roosevelt. He considered, he had said, the most important question, as before, to be the creation of a military-political commission of representatives of the three countries with its meeting place "for the present instance in Sicily or Algiers." And that ". . . the dispatch of a Soviet officer to Eisenhower's staff could in no way take the place of the Military-Political Commission which is necessary for the direction on the spot of negotiations with Italy (and also with the governments of other nations falling out with the Germans)." He had added that much time had already passed and nothing had happened.

Roosevelt and Churchill had sent parallel replies to Stalin on the 10th. The President said that he agreed to the immediate establishment of the military-political commission; and suggested that it have its first meeting in Algiers on the 21st. But he cautiously hedged around the functions to be ascribed to it, remarking that, "Full information will be given of course in regard to the progress of current and future negotiations but they [the Commission] should not have military powers. Such authority would have to be referred to their governments before final action." Churchill also approved the idea of creating such a commission. What he may have said about its prospective activities is not known.[21]

Stalin, in his acknowledgments (of the 12th) to the President and Prime Minister, had answered that he considered the question concerning this commission "basically as solved." He said that he was appointing Vishinsky, Assistant Commissar for Foreign Affairs, as the Soviet plenipotentiary representative; that Bogomolov, Soviet Ambassador near the Allied governments in exile in London, was to be his assistant; and that a group of responsible military and political experts and a small technical staff would be attached to them. He agreed that the commission might start work toward the end of September, and remarked that he did not object to having its first meeting in Algiers on the understanding that the commission itself could determine later whether or not to proceed to Sicily or to some other place in Italy. Finally he said that he found Churchill's statements regarding the functions of the commission to be "correct" but believed that they could be more precisely defined after the commission's initial experience not only with respect to Italy but also to other countries.

It turned out that the American and British governments had quite a different conception from that of the Soviet as to what this MPC was to do, particularly about the part it might play in the direction of Italian affairs.

This prime divergence came to the fore in the notes exchanged apropos of the President's directive of September 23rd to Eisenhower. He was therein instructed to prepare to give effect to paragraph 37 of the "long terms" by organizing a control commission under his command, and to center in it the functions of Allied military government in Italy and the authority to guide and direct the Badoglio government in all realms. In the note which, on September 25th, Molotov presented to the American government commenting on this directive, he questioned the need to set up the Allied control commission under Eisenhower at all, since, to quote, ". . . as is well known, after the ratification of the detailed armistice terms there is established by the decision of the three governments the military-political commission, as a result of which the question of a control commission envisaged in Article 37 of the detailed terms should be considered as falling away."

[21] In *Closing the Ring,* pages 281–82, Churchill quotes portions of his message of September 10th to Stalin, but not what he may have said about the military-political commission.

Moreover Molotov's note said that the Soviet government thought that the MPC ought to have the duty of coordinating and directing the activities not only of the Allied civil but also the military organization on enemy territory in regard to armistice terms and control over their execution. So it believed that the commission should be given the function of issuing orders to the Badoglio government on political, administrative, and military matters in this realm, while the Commander-in-Chief should direct military operations. An announcement which the Soviet government published in the press that same day was based on these ideas. Its tenor, taken together with the selection of Vishinsky, who was senior Assistant Commissar in charge of relations with the United States and Great Britain, as the Soviet member of the commission, shows how seriously its duties were regarded. The Soviet conception was in accord with its usual practice of subjecting military operations to constant political control; the Political-Military Commission was to be a group of political representatives or commissars to guide the military as well as civil organizations in occupied territories. It was historically significant since it would have accorded the Soviet government a main part in shaping the political development of Italy. And possibly the American and British governments would have had an equivalent share in determining policy later for the defeated German satellites in the east, though this is most doubtful in regard to countries bordering the Soviet Union.

However that may be, the American and British governments did not conceive that the MPC should have power to give orders to the Commander-in-Chief or take the place of the Allied Control Commission. In their scheme the MPC was to be a liaison and advisory group, and a center of consultation. As balm for rejecting the Soviet proposal (note of September 25th) to dispense with the Allied Control Commission in favor of the MPC, the British Foreign Office was inclined to give the Soviet Union greater share in the Control Commission. The State Department was not against such an arrangement. But the War Department did not like it. It thought the Soviet government ought to be satisfied with a place on whatever over-looking group was to be constituted.

The first meeting of this newly conceived group (originally named in the diplomatic exchanges as the Military-Political Commission, then as the Mediterranean Council, and finally as the Advisory Council for Italy) was postponed because Vishinsky fell ill. But the time thus gained for discussion did not produce a convergence of ideas of the governments that were to form the commission. It merely gave further opportunity for the repetition of their separate conceptions.

Other countries besides the Soviet Union were pressing for a part in the execution of the Italian surrender terms and the control of Italian affairs—the French Committee of National Liberation, Greece, Yugoslavia, China, and Brazil. Were they also to be invited to become members of the Advisory Council, or associated with it? Or, ought some new system be devised? Proposals were written out and interchanged in the fortnight before the Foreign Ministers met in Moscow in October. But nothing was settled. The whole range of questions was allowed to wait upon this meeting.

There, to look forward and to precede the account of other business done at that meeting, Eden and Hull sponsored a plan which was largely posed on suggestions received from Eisenhower. These rested on the opinion that it was essential that the Commander-in-Chief continue to look to the Combined Chiefs of Staff for both military and political instructions; but consistent with this the suggestions were more evolutionary and flexible than any previously discussed.

At the first talk of the Foreign Ministers about Italy (on October 22nd) Eden advanced two proposals. One he described as very much in the line of the original suggestions put by the Soviet government. It contemplated the forming of a political-military commission to concern itself with all questions *affecting Europe* arising out of the progress of the war except those pertaining directly to military operations. It should have, as he conceived it, the widest possible consultative powers but no executive function. The second was a scheme which dealt with the arrangements for controlling the execution of Italian armistice terms. This offered a program in three phases. During the first, which was to last until an Italian government was installed in Rome, a skeleton Allied Control Commission (presumably U.S.-British) was to operate under the authority of the Commander-in-Chief. During the second phase, to last from then until the campaign in Italy or in designated parts of it, was over, there was to be as well an Inter-Allied Advisory Council of which the Soviet government would be a member. During the third and last phase, the Commander-in-Chief was to give up his presidency of the Control Commission, and that larger Advisory Council would take over from him the executive direction of the work of control.

Molotov began his comment on these proposals by stressing how hard the Soviet government had found it to learn what was going on since it had had no inside representative either in North Africa or Italy. He showed once again suspicion of any intent to change the approved armistice terms; and once again Eden assured him that they remained in force in toto and could be changed only by common consent of all three Allies. Molotov avowed that the Soviet government attached the greatest importance to the course of political events in

Italy; and he stated that in view of the part which Fascism had played in starting the war, the Soviet government was strongly in favor of a quick change to a democratic system. He came forward with a statement of seven principles for the direction of Italian political affairs which his government thought ought to be put into effect at once.

Neither Eden's three-phase program nor Hull's attempt to convince Molotov that our policies would be in strict accord with the principles advanced by the Soviet government corresponded to Molotov's wish to have a Soviet representative on the spot and in the know. But the spontaneous American and British response in favor of the Soviet set of principles may have caused him to fit in with what was by that time an almost operative plan rather than to try to upset it completely. In any case, he did not renew the Soviet suggestion that the Allied Control Commission be discarded, or explicitly ask for equal place in its organization. Instead he urged that the Advisory Council be created at once. Hull and Eden said they were ready to recommend this to their governments, subject to Eisenhower's assent. They did so at once, but the answers were slow in arriving. Discussion between the three officials in the meanwhile showed that there was still not a clear understanding about the membership of the Advisory Council. Britain wanted Greece and Yugoslavia on it. Molotov did not. The difference was bridged by providing that at the start the council should have only four members, but the other two were to be added as soon as possible.

The American and British governments acceded to the Soviet wish that the Advisory Council be brought into being without delay. The accord reached and set down in the protocol of the conference specified that this Advisory Council was to observe Italian affairs and the operation of the control system in Italy, and advise the Commander-in-Chief, as President of the Control Commission, on relevant policy questions. But it was not to concern itself with military matters. And the Commander-in-Chief was to retain ultimate authority subject to orders received from the Combined Chiefs of Staff.

Later on it will be seen the Soviet government was to maintain that the Italian setup was a good and fair model for use in countries liberated by the Red Army, a position which the British and Americans were to contest on various grounds, one being that in Italy they were merely applying a code of principles which the Russians had taken the lead in formulating.

A little more note may be taken of the proposal made by Molotov, and adopted, that the three governments should jointly declare themselves in favor of putting into effect certain "urgent political measures," the seven principles for the direction of Italian political affairs of which mention has just been made. The first among these was "the democratization of the Italian government by means of the inclusion of representatives of Anti-Fascist Parties." Others concerned the restoration of individual and group freedoms, the extinction of all Fascist institutions and organizations, the removal of all Fascist institutions and organizations, the removal of all Fascist and pro-Fascist elements from government and other places of influence, amnesty for political prisoners, and the arrest of the chief war criminals.

British and American aims and preferences were thoroughly consonant with these measures—but with a difference in pace and care for consequences. Hull allowed himself to display his true feeling about Fascism by saying ". . . that if he had his way, he would take Hitler and Mussolini and Tojo and their arch-accomplices and bring them before a drumhead court-martial and at sunrise on the following day there would occur an historic incident." While vigorously agreeing with Molotov that all "democratic" elements must have full political opportunity in Italy, they were cautious about how far and fast the Allies ought to move to determine Italian political evolution. The joint memo which Eden and Hull gave Molotov explained how the Allies were faithfully following the very policies which the Soviet government had in mind while maintaining the care and control necessary during this period of hard and active military operations.

Messages to London and Washington cleared the way for a joint declaration. By skilled selection of formulas, agreement was reached on a text, which was issued at the close of the conference. The first article of this read, "It is essential that the Italian Government should be made more democratic by the introduction of representatives of those sections of the Italian people who have always opposed Fascism." This pledged the controlling Allies to bring about such a change in the Italian government; and it encouraged Italian political leaders to demand it. Thus, while it did not cramp the Allies by rigid obligation, it exposed them to pressure.

The question of what would happen to the King and the monarchy was left untouched for the time being: ". . . nothing in this declaration," another paragraph read, "is to operate against the right of the Italian people ultimately to choose their own form of government."

This "Declaration regarding Italy" was one of the soothing achievements of the Moscow Conference. It augured well for harmony as victory brought joint responsibilities.

PERIOD FIVE

To the Conference of Foreign Ministers in Moscow, October 1943; the First Coherent Consultation about Political Matters

21. Political Troubles: Poland, Czechoslovakia and the Balkans, Autumn 1943

Our account of the coalition engagement with Italy has outstripped the tale of simultaneous difficulties over developments in other areas which the tide of war was reaching.

Of all the troubling issues, those concerning Poland had remained most obdurate. The whole problem of the future of the country, and of its frontiers, lay in ambush for Secretary Hull as he went to meet with Eden and Molotov at Moscow. To grasp the situation as it was when they met, it is necessary to glance back.

On January 6, 1943, the Soviet government had again made it bluntly plain that it meant to claim permanently the areas of Poland which it had occupied soon after the Germans had marched into that country. It had notified the Polish government-in-exile that henceforth those refugees who had come from the former eastern provinces of Poland which were now regarded as part of the Soviet Union would be treated as Soviet citizens. The Polish government had protested this pronouncement as illegal and unacceptable. It had tried to get the American and British governments to back it up. The British government had again been sympathetic but not disposed to do anything positive. Roosevelt (on February 16th, 1943) had similarly given the Polish Ambassador in Washington the sense of being opposed to the Soviet claim, but of not being willing to allow that opinion to rule his action. He had explained that the moment was not good for American intervention in Moscow; that the Soviet armies were winning great battles while, in contrast, the American offensive in North Africa was being held up; and that the Soviet government was complaining that it was being left to carry so much of the burden of the fight against Germany.

The Polish government-in-exile had remained convinced that it ought not and could not compromise in this dispute over its eastern frontiers. Apart from any question of justice, it had felt that it did not have the constitutional right to give up any territory; and that if it should do so, it would lose the support of the Polish army and people. That this fear had genuine basis had been made clear when on March 4th General Anders, Commander-in-Chief of the Polish divisions in the Middle East, in an Order of the Day which he issued to his forces, had once again rejected Soviet claims.

The British government had become oppressed and irked by this conflict—and by the stand of the Polish government-in-exile. The Foreign Office had felt disturbed by this threat both to the wartime coalition and to the prospect of peaceful adjustment of other questions with the Soviet Union later on. Eden had given voice to these anxieties during his visit to Washington in March 1943. He had then told the President and Hopkins that the Poles were being very troublesome about their aspirations. The Prime Minister, Sikorski, he said, seemed to be conspiring with the governments of the small states of the Balkans to gain support for his aims; and that these were "very large," and unreal, and influenced by an anticipation that by the end of the war both the Soviet Union and Germany would be much weakened and the Polish forces and people would have a greater part to play. The President had maintained his cautious reticence. He had said merely that the great powers would have to decide what Poland was to get at the peace conference; and that he did not intend to bargain with Poland but to do what was best for the peace of the world. Even then, however, he had concluded that the Poles would have to compromise with the Soviet Union on frontiers; to yield to it something in the east, and accept compensation in the west, in lands from which the Germans were to be expelled—East Prussia and perhaps other areas.

During this same period the Soviet schemers had begun to foster a rival government for Poland which would do what was wanted. With Soviet help, Polish communists in Russia had started to organize and to set themselves up as a "Union of Polish Patriots."

Then in April the Soviet government had broken relations with the Polish government in London. The rupture was occasioned by a revival of reports about unexplained events which had taken place far earlier. When in the summer of 1941 the Polish government-in-exile had set about forming an army out of Polish prisoners of war and refugees in the Soviet Union, it was puzzled because many fewer Polish officers were located than had been expected. No one admitted knowing where they were or what might have happened to them. They were last known to have been in prisoner-of-war camps in that part of Poland which the Russians had seized, but from which later they had been forced by the Germans to retreat. The Polish government had tried in every way to find out about these missing officers, but had not been able to learn anything. It had brooded over their mysterious disappearance.

On April 13th the Nazi radio had spread reports that the Soviet government had murdered these Polish officers. With a virtuous show of horror it had proposed that there ought to be an international inquiry.

The Polish government had decided that it could not ignore these allegations. On April 16th it had announced, through its Ministry of National Defense, that it was asking the International Red Cross to send an investigating group to the region of Katyn, where the graves were. It had explained that although the Poles were used to German lies, in view of the abundant details which the Germans were diffusing about the finding of the bodies, and their flat statements that these men had been murdered by Soviet forces in the spring of 1940, it felt compelled to seek an impartial investigation of the facts on the spot.[1] After so announcing, the Polish government had gone on to instruct its Ambassador in Moscow to ask the Soviet government to comment on these German allegations.

Churchill had foreseen that the Soviet government might strike back hard, and had tried to avert the blow. Lord Halifax, the British Ambassador in Washington, had told Hull on April 21st that, being worried, Churchill wanted to send a message to calm Stalin, and would like to know whether the President would do the same. But the President was away from Washington and Hull had not responded.

The Soviet answer to this Polish action had been hard and abrupt. On the 24th Stalin notified Churchill and Roosevelt that the Soviet government was again about to break relations with the Polish govern-

---

[1] It is unclear whether the Prime Minister of Poland, Sikorski, was fully advised that the statement was to be issued and, if he was, whether he favored or resisted it. On May 1st he said that he had not been consulted, but the accounts given by various Polish colleagues make this seem doubtful. What is certainly clear is that the military elements in this government, and the leaders of the Polish Army, felt that Polish honor and human justice made it imperative to break silence on this question and to hold the Soviet government up for judgment. Whoever within the Polish group had sponsored the statement, some of them soon began to regret it.

However that may be, on May 1st Sikorski asked Harriman in London to let the President know that he, Sikorski, now recognized that the statement had been a great mistake. He went on to say that no matter what the rights and wrongs, he would try to disregard his feelings in order to get on with the war. He asked Harriman whether the United States would not do its very best to induce Moscow to patch up the quarrel and that to do so he would go as far as he could, consistent with the dignity and the views of his colleagues and people. Sikorski seemed to Harriman tired and worried and anxious to go to the Middle East as soon as possible in order to bolster the morale of the Polish Army there.

A few days later he wrote a letter to the President substantially to the same effect. In the course of this he explained, "Our invitation to the International Red Cross to investigate the circumstances of the death of thousands of Polish Officers recently brought to light by the Germans, may be criticised in some quarters. However, in view of the fact that many Poles, both here and in the Middle East, had near relatives or comrades-in-arms who had been killed in that neighbourhood, it was very difficult for us to ignore the news. I trust that you realize that this action on the part of the Soviet Government was not a sudden or isolated one, but the climax in a sequel of events all directed against the Polish nation and the Polish Government."

ment. He denounced it for acting on the vile German slander before giving the Soviet government a chance to comment; and he said his government viewed this action as proof of its suspicions that the Polish government was hostile and under German influence. Churchill had again tried to dissuade Stalin. He had told him that he thought the Polish government had been foolish to associate itself with these charges, but on the score of "We have got to beat Hitler—and this is no time for quarrels and charges," urged him not to break relations. Roosevelt had made a similar appeal, but too late to have affected Stalin's decision.

The Soviet radio had announced the break on April 26th. Two days later the Union of Polish Patriots in the Soviet Union had issued a declaration also denouncing the Polish government-in-exile. Thereafter, the whole question of who would govern the new Polish state had been cast into open dispute. And this had become entangled with the matter of future Polish frontiers. From that time on the Polish government-in-exile was to be confronted with the demand that if it wanted to get back on good terms with the Soviet government it would first have to accept Soviet ideas about frontiers.

A tense wait followed, during which neither the American nor the British government, while longing to foster a reconciliation, had seen any effective chance for bringing this about. It was one of those spells in which the Soviet government was blowing a gale toward the west for what it called the "second front" while the American and British governments were feeling indignant at Soviet disparagement of their war effort and aid.

And then General Sikorski, Prime Minister of the Polish government and Commander-in-Chief of the Polish Armed Forces, was killed in a plane accident over Gibraltar. Sad in itself, for Sikorski was a man of great quality, the loss had gloomy meaning. For he was the person best able to keep the differing groups within the Polish government-in-exile working together, best qualified to guide them, and least scorned in Moscow. On the 14th of July a new Cabinet had been formed. The leader of the Polish Peasant Party, Mikolajczyk, had been made the Prime Minister. He did not have the persuasive influence that Sikorski had had. But he was an able man, a moderate liberal whose political career had shown honesty and balance. The new Cabinet contained some elements which might be expected to take a compromising course toward the Soviet authorities. Others were convinced that they would be as ruthless as need be to prevent an independent Poland from emerging from the war; to them any concessions to the Bolshevik oppressors was surrender; and surrender that would earn no justice.

In August the American and British governments had tried to interest Stalin in an accord with Poland which bypassed the question of frontiers and responsibility for the mass murders at Katyn. Stalin had taken six weeks to answer the proposal, by which time (September 27th) the meeting of the Foreign Ministers was close in sight. He had rejected it. The rupture in relations, he had answered, had not been caused by the matters which the American and British governments had raised, but by the hostile direction of the Polish government in London as shown by the way in which it sponsored accusations originating in Germany about the dead Polish officers.

The American and British governments hoped that when the Foreign Ministers met in Moscow they would be able to repair this break between the nations linked in the struggle against Germany. But the definitions which the Polish government put forward of what it deemed Poland's just requirements showed how deep the fissure had become.

On October 6th, the day before Hull left for Moscow, the Polish Ambassador gave him a long memo which virtually asked that the United States and Britain not only support its position but become its protectors. Among the requests made were (1) that the Americans and British should give a joint guarantee of Polish independence, integrity, and security. (2) That if, for military reasons, Russian occupation of Polish territory could not be avoided, it was essential that this be regulated by an understanding with the Polish government-in-exile. This, the Ambassador explained, ought to provide that the Polish government would take over the administration of Poland as soon as it was liberated; and warned that unless there was such a provision the Soviet Union would try to rule Poland through their Polish communist followers. (3) And as further defense against such a turn in events, that American and British troops should be stationed in Poland while the Soviet Army was there.

Again the Polish government restated its reasons for rejecting the Soviet boundary proposals. Even though the Soviet government should, in compensation, support Polish claims to some German territories in the west, the memo argued, these new frontiers would make Poland dependent on its eastern neighbor and enable the Soviet Union to use her as a springboard for extending its domination over Central Europe and Germany in particular. These reasons were, it may be remarked, cogent—both in the light of previous history and of the history that followed. But they did not affect the opinion of the American government that there was no chance to bring about a favorable settlement of the boundary question at that time, and that only harm might be done by trying.

Before leaving London for Moscow, Eden had a talk with the new Polish Prime Minister. He was more forthright than Hull. He warned Mikolajczyk that unless the Polish government agreed to give up the eastern areas, there was little chance that Russia would renew relations with it or agree to entrust it with the rule of liberated Polish territories. Mikolajczyk has recorded that he ". . . was flabbergasted to hear Eden echoing those thoughts as if they were routine, not contemptible." [2] After recalling Britain's past vows not to recognize any territorial gains taken by force, Mikolajczyk said, "If we give up this territory which, actually, we are not empowered to yield, it will be only the beginning of Russian demands." [3] Thus, leaving a memo on the position of the Polish government, the same in substance as that given to Hull, he made it clear that he was not authorizing Eden to discuss the frontier question.

Though the subject of Poland was listed close to the top of the original agenda, it was not formally discussed until near the end of the Moscow Conference. Thus it was not allowed to mar the spirit of congeniality which—as will be told—prevailed. For there were clear signals that it might; as when Litvinov, at one of the dinners, poured out a torrent of abuse against the Poles. They had been, he said, responsible for much of the agony of Europe—having played along with the Germans at the League of Nations meetings at Geneva, despoiled Czechoslovakia after Munich, and connived against Russia. They must, he asserted, learn to live as a small national state within their correct boundaries, and give up the idea that they were a great power. And when their interests collided with Russia's interests, they would have to give way.

With the Russians hostile and the Americans wary, it is not to be wondered that the formal discussion was brief and led nowhere. Eden told well of the reasons why the British government was so eager to bring the Soviet-Polish quarrel to an end. Molotov indicated that he thought the question one for the Soviet government to settle; that, while it would listen to what others might say, it would in the end do what it thought necessary to have its way in Poland. He was curt—not to Eden, but about the Polish government-in-exile. He affirmed that the Soviet government wanted to see an "independent" Poland; but its government would have to be "friendly" to the Soviet Union, and the group in London was decidedly not. When Eden said that the Polish

[2] From the book, *The Rape of Poland,* by Stanislaw Mikolajczyk, published by McGraw-Hill Book Co., Inc., 1948, page 45.
[3] *Ibid.*

Prime Minister and Foreign Minister had both told him that they wanted to resume good relations with Moscow, Molotov said it was the first time he had heard of any such desire. Hull, when his turn came round to talk, merely made an innocuous comment—to the effect that if two neighbors fell out, those who lived nearby, without going into the causes or merits of the dispute, were entitled to tell the two that they hoped they would patch up their quarrel.

The entry made in the final Protocol of the Conference said merely about this item on the agenda—"An exchange of views took place." That was all that could be said. The talk did not even touch on the question of where Poland's future frontiers were to be. Because of the attitude of the Polish Prime Minister, Eden felt unable to do so. For Hull this was a relief. He had, as he later told, no intention of lifting the lid on a "Pandora's box of infinite trouble"—Russia's various boundary claims, including Poland.[4] For he could not have accepted the Soviet position without outcry in the United States; and he could not have defended the position of the Polish government-in-exile without imperiling the Four-Nation Declaration on which his purposes in Moscow centered. He had the cheerful impression, for reasons that may remain hard to grasp even after the story of the Declaration is read, that although the talk about Poland in Moscow had settled nothing, the Declaration would mean ". . . everything to Poland in the future."[5] For the time being we must leave the subject to take account of connected developments concerning the adjacent country of Czechoslovakia.

The government of the Republic of Czechoslovakia, with Benes at its head, had also taken refuge in London. The country over which it had once ruled had been entirely broken up. President Benes and his colleagues had not brooded over Munich. But they had not forgotten it, nor what had followed.

The Czechoslovak leaders had little cause to think kindly of Poland. For the Poles, in that tragic year after Munich, had joined in the dissection of their country, invading it when the Germans had, and taking part of it (Teschen). But they were ready for a reconciliation—one that would mean the return of their lost lands after the Germans were driven out. Further than that, President Benes developed a lively interest in a possible federation between Poland and Czechoslovakia after the war.

Relations with the Soviet government were more at ease than those of the Poles. Benes had explained to American and other diplomats dur-

[4] *Memoirs,* page 1273.
[5] *Ibid.,* page 1315.

ing 1942 that he thought that his government had less cause to be fearful of Communism than the Poles because the social and economic structure of Czechoslovakia was in better balance and because the Czechoslovak people knew that Communism was a step backward, not forward. And early in 1943 the Soviet government had given Benes informal assurances that it was willing to have Czechoslovakia restored as an independent country after the war, with its former territories; and that it would not intervene in its domestic affairs. This had seemed to provide satisfactory ground for a treaty that would define the basis of their cooperation in the war against Germany and afterward.

With these promises in hand, Benes had gone to Washington in May. There he had expounded his ideas to the President and Churchill (in Washington for the Trident Conference) and had talked at length with Hull and Welles. They had all listened with attracted mind to his far-reaching comments on many features of postwar Europe, marked by a belief that it would be possible to get along well with the Soviet Union. He had notified them of his wish for an understanding with Stalin about the future of Czechoslovakia and its position in Europe; of his intention of making a treaty with Russia that would regulate their mutual relations. Though nothing conclusive may have been said by the President, Benes had gotten the impression that he and the State Department would be pleased rather than displeased if this were accomplished.

But the British government had been disturbed by the project. Upon his return to London from Washington Benes had made his intentions clearer to Eden, dwelling on the reasons why he thought a treaty with the Russians was not only justified but advisable. Among them were: that the people of Czechoslovakia, still living under cruel German rule, needed this reassurance; that it might well prepare the way for a three-cornered agreement between Czechoslovakia, Poland, and the Soviet Union against future German aggression; and that it would prevent possible Hungarian or Polish designs against Czechoslovakia at the end of the war.

Eden had protested (in three talks on June 22nd, 24th, and 30th). He recalled that when Molotov had been in London in 1942 he had told the Soviet Foreign Minister that he thought it undesirable that either the British or Soviet government should enter into treaties about postwar matters with the smaller Allies, since that might cause disturbing competition among them. Molotov had agreed, Eden said, to this self-denying rule. So the British government had felt obligated to abstain from any similar arrangement. Besides, he had told Benes, he was afraid that the treaty in mind might be regarded as placing Czechoslovakia in the Soviet camp, and so both hurt Allied efforts to restore relationships between the Poles and the Soviet Union and cause strain in the relations between the Poles and the Czechoslovak government. He had suggested that the same purposes might be served, without such harmful effects, by an understanding which might be expressed in the form of a joint Soviet-Czech declaration. Benes, however, had continued to think that only a treaty would be adequate.

The British government had inquired about the Soviet view of the question. Maisky, on July 2nd, had brought Eden a message from Molotov. This said that the Soviet government wanted to develop its earlier mutual assistance pact with Czechoslovakia into a twenty-year treaty similar to that which it had with Great Britain; and it observed that nothing in that treaty precluded this other measure. In the talk that ensued, the Foreign Secretary voiced the same objections which he had explained to Benes. Maisky had denied their validity, and had gone on to say that British opposition would not be understood in Moscow and relations between the two countries would be hurt. He had said also that the Soviet government would be willing to indicate publicly at the time that it signed the treaty with Czechoslovakia that it wished the pact to be turned into a tripartite accord which would include Poland.[6] Eden had remarked that if that were done, British objection would be partly met.

But in talking afterward with Benes, Eden had been firm in his opposition—emphasizing in particular that by making a treaty with the Soviet government at this time, when Moscow would not deal with the Polish government in London, the Czechoslovak government would be isolating it. He had gravely advised Benes to wait at least until the Foreign Ministers had the chance to talk it over.

The Czechoslovak government had been equally active in making its judgments known to the American and Soviet authorities. It did not want its position vis-à-vis Russia to become closely linked with the Polish problem. And on the positive side, it thought that the treaty in mind could be a model for states in the middle European zone and create the conditions for the requisite friendly cooperation of the small nations in this area with both the Soviet Union and the Western great powers. As later described in his Memoirs, Benes thought that a treaty of the sort which the Soviet government was willing to sign would ". . . show the world . . . what the Soviet Union wanted and what policy it intended to follow; that far from driving them apart it should

[6] The treaty as signed had a so-called Polish clause. This in effect recorded the agreement between the parties that if Poland wished to adhere to the treaty, it would be given the chance to do so "after mutual agreement"; and then the treaty would become trilateral.

and could draw the Soviet Union nearer to Great Britain as well as to the United States and that it could finally set the minds of all the other Allies at rest with regard to the aims of the Soviet Union." [7]

The American government had maintained a prudent silence, while the Soviet government had continued to keep its invitation to Czechoslovakia open. Decision waited upon the Moscow Conference.

There, to anticipate the tale of what occurred, Eden tried to get Molotov to defer the completion of the treaty. Failing in that, he urged the Soviet and American governments to join the British in a common vow to abstain from any agreement with smaller allies during the war except by common consent. Molotov did not agree to this; he claimed it was both proper and advisable for each to remain free to conclude accords with bordering Allied states for their mutual security and the protection of frontiers, such as the one which the Soviet and Czech governments wanted to make. In the glow of trust and of satisfaction which followed agreement (apparent or real) on many other matters, opposition to this controversial treaty faded. The way was cleared for Benes to go to Moscow and complete it.

For the sake of continuity the further history of this action may be told here, even though we outrange the narrative of other events. Benes went to Moscow in December, just after the three Heads of State had met at Teheran—where nothing had happened to disillusion him. Following his first talks with Stalin and Molotov he reported to his colleagues in London that, "The political discussions and negotiations have taken place up to this time in the utmost harmony, friendship and cordiality"; and toward the end, after a review of every phase of the Czechoslovak situation, he confirmed that, "There is complete unity of views."

In the text of the treaty that was signed (on December 12, 1943) much that is right is to be found, and nothing wrong without insinuating that fair language might conceal devious purpose. It provided for mutual aid during the war and mutual protection against Germany after the war. It obligated each not to enter into any pact directed against the other. And it pledged each to act after the war ". . . in accordance with the principles of mutual respect for the independence and sovereignty, as well as of non-interference in the internal affairs, of the other state." Furthermore, Stalin agreed with Benes that when the Red Army entered Czechoslovakia, native military units would enter with it, that the local internal order would be respected, and that the liberated areas would be progressively handed over to Czechoslovak civil administration. As regards frontiers, Benes was convinced

[7] *Memoirs of Dr. Eduard Benes,* page 244.

that the Soviet government would support its pre-Munich frontiers—which meant that Poland would have to give up Teschen, which it had grabbed. These terms, and the promise of Soviet favor for the expulsion of the German minority, were the very substantial reasons for Benes' conclusion that the negotiations were "wholly successful."

The Soviet wish for this treaty could still at this time be construed as a measure to assure that there could not be any grouping of unfriendly states along its frontiers—an acceptable political arrangement for security and good neighborly relations. The Czechoslovak wish for it could be construed as sensible recognition of the prospect that Soviet forces would soon be in their country, able to dominate it if Moscow so willed, able to help it if they made friends. Better, the Czech government concluded, to take the risk of joining up with Communism than of relying again solely on the protection of the West.

Benes also reached an understanding with the Czechs in Moscow and Soviet officials there that the Czechoslovakian government should be reorganized. The local Communists were to be given one-fifth of the places. He discussed with them his program, which included nationalization of the arms industries, progressive social legislation, and greater sectional autonomy. The Communists had promised in turn not to try to collectivize farms or other industries. Benes thought this understanding was a reliable basis for domestic order and harmony.

Along with the strain, during this autumn of 1943, over Polish and Czechoslovakian affairs, the Western Allies were trying to soothe the fierce antagonisms which had come to the surface in Yugoslavia and Greece. As of the hour, unity was wanted for military reasons. Beyond the hour, it was essential to avert civil wars after the Germans were expelled, civil wars in which one side would be looking to the West for support and the other to the East.

The young King Peter of Yugoslavia and his government had been in exile ever since the Germans entered their country. After a short stay in Jerusalem they had moved to London. There they tried to maintain their connections with what was going on in their country, but suffered from a growing separation. Local resistance movements had grown up despite every hazard and form of cruel repression. The record of their heroic struggle has been well told by others who were part of it. This is only a passing glance at the way these events entered into the relations between the three great Allies and their strategy.

General Mihailovich was the leader of the first national bands known as Cetniks who had taken up the fight. When, in the fall of 1941, tales of their activities began to come out of Yugoslavia, the government-in-exile had gotten in touch with him; and in January 1942 had designated him as Minister of War. Most of his followers were Serbs, many of them conservatives. They were hard-pressed, poorly armed, and the Germans revenged themselves cruelly on the relatives and friends they had left in Belgrade and other towns. To survive, they had reduced their activity, and here and there had entered into "live-and-let-live" agreements with the local Germans and Italian commanders. Other resistance groups had arisen—men with less to lose, desperate and hardy. These had come to look for leadership to the man who called himself Tito, a bold and able Communist, trained in Moscow. They knew the wild mountains, had gained in numbers, and by tactics of surprise made themselves a terror to the Axis occupation forces. Tragically, these two resistance groups had come to regard each other not only as rivals but as enemies.

The British government had hastened to make liaison with Mihailovich. As early as October 1941 the Middle East High Command had parachuted in staff officers and dropped weapons, medical supplies, and other essentials. Communications were established which enabled Mihailovich, through British channels, to keep the government-in-exile informed of the situation within Yugoslavia, the progress of his actions, the movement of German troops throughout the Balkans, and also to receive instructions. But still, Mihailovich gradually had lost the confidence of the British military authorities.

They were impressed by the far more determined and damaging activity of the partisans under Tito. So, beginning in May 1943, the British had begun to send over by air small parties of British officers and men to work with them also. Within a few months many such liaison parties were scattered among the roving bands and camps. This was done, as Churchill wrote later, ". . . in spite of the fact that cruel strife was proceeding between them and the Cetniks, and that Tito was waging war as a Communist, not only against the German invaders, but against the Serbian Monarchy and Mihailovich." [8] Rea-

[8] *Closing the Ring,* page 463. Brigadier Fitzroy Maclean, who was Commander of the British Military Mission to the Partisans, in the account of his work and adventures in Yugoslavia, tells of a talk that he had with Churchill some months later (at Cairo in November 1943) about the fact that the movement led by Tito which the British were supporting was likely after the war to have its closest ties with the Soviet Union. As told in Maclean's book *Escape to Adventure,* pp. 309–10: "The Prime Minister's reply resolved my doubts. 'Do you intend,' he asked, 'to make Jugoslavia your home after the war?' 'No, sir,' I replied. 'Neither do I,' he said. 'And, that being so, the less you and I worry about the form of government they set up, the better. That is for them to decide. What interests us is, which of them is doing most harm to the Germans?'"

son enough for this was found in the fact that these partisans were keeping large Axis forces frantically busy, forces which otherwise might have been used on the Eastern Front or in Italy.[9]

There hardly seems need to recall how, at every talk with the Americans about strategy during this spring and summer, Churchill and his military colleagues had advocated that more be done to enable these Yugoslav guerrillas to extend their activities: by getting weapons and supplies to them, by liaison and instruction parties, by commando forays to distract the Germans, and the like. Churchill was trying to open the way for the greater strategic projects that were lodged in his mind. These, as later revealed, conceived that when the battle in Italy allowed, Allied forces might cross the Adriatic, land in Yugoslavia, and there combine with the partisans in thrusts toward Vienna and Germany; perhaps also at some point in the region to join up with the Soviet Armies.

For military purposes, both the immediate and the greater possible ones, the British government had tried to get the Yugoslav resistance groups to work together against the Germans. It had striven at the same time to protect the threatened position of the King and the government-in-exile; and to preserve a chance for the Yugoslav people to decide later on in an orderly way who should govern them. For it could be foreseen that if the dissension went on it might turn into a prolonged civil war; or the confederation of Yugoslavia might fall apart; or the Communist elements, after destroying the opposition, might be able to impose permanent control over the country.

The British had sought to persuade the Soviet government to help bring about an accord. That government had veered and tacked in its attitude toward the rival resistance groups. Until the autumn of 1943 and even after the British had begun to support Tito, the Soviet authorities had seemed friendly toward the Cetniks. In September, on British advice, the Yugoslav government moved from London to Cairo to be at hand if and when the Allies made a landing on the Adriatic shores. At a reception which the Soviet Embassy in London gave for the departing King and his Cabinet, Bogomolov, Ambassador near the government-in-exile, eulogized Mihailovich's heroic movement, which was doing such invaluable work in diverting German divisions from the Russian front.[10] That the Soviet government had by then tried out

[9] At Teheran, Churchill told Stalin and Roosevelt that British Intelligence estimated that thirty Axis divisions were being kept engaged in the Yugoslavia-Greece-Albania area by resistance, *Closing the Ring*, page 467. Stalin said he thought this estimate was far too large, and on several later occasions repeated an opinion that British information was not good.

[10] Peter II, King of Yugoslavia. *A King's Heritage*, pp. 177 *et seq.*

Tito, and had found him not as subservient as Stalin wished, can only be surmised.

When Eden was in Moscow in October 1943 for the Conference of Foreign Ministers he suggested to Molotov that the Soviet government use its influence to bring about some practical accord between the followers of Tito and those of Mihailovich. He related that the British government had made it plain to the King that it might have to drop Mihailovich unless he engaged in certain defined operations against the Germans and that the King had promised to order him to do so if an agreement was reached on a common policy for Yugoslavia. He outlined for Molotov working plans for uniting the two factions, allowing them to carry on in separate areas. Hull—keeping the United States out of Balkan troubles—when called on to comment, said he had nothing to add.

In Greece the situation had reached a critical climax. Others, among them Churchill, have given memorable accounts of the cruel struggle waged by the hardy resistance groups in the bare mountains and valleys against the Axis oppressors and each other. So all that will be told here, and that in a fragmentary way, is how the situation became a problem for the coalition.

The King of Greece, a staunch friend of the Allies, and his government-in-exile, largely royalist politicians, had moved between London and Cairo. This regime was treated as the recognized government of Greece. But it had little to do with the emergence and activities of the resistance groups within Greece. One of these (EDES) centered around a Colonel Zervas, who was originally republican in sympathy but anti-Communist. The other (ELAM-ELAS) was Communist in origin, control, and purpose. The British government had felt impelled to give whatever help it could to each and every faction fighting the Italians and the Germans. It had small missions attached to the headquarters and combat camps of both Greek organizations. But in this land where the British had so often found brave adventure in the cause of liberty, they had met disappointment. For the two groups had taken to fighting one another, and to challenging the government-in-exile.

In an effort to satisfy popular feeling within Greece, the government and the King had announced, in July 1943, that they stood for a constitutional monarchy, and promised free elections to determine the form of government after liberation. But neither of the resistance groups had been content with that. In August they had asked the King, who was then in Cairo, not to return to Greece before the Greek people, in a plebiscite, proved that they wanted him back. They had also asked that men of the resistance from inside Greece be given Cabinet posts, including those of the Minister of Interior and Justice. The King had found these demands arbitrary; he had claimed the right to return to Greece as soon as possible, and afterward submit the question of the monarchy to a plebiscite.

But before rejecting the demands, the King had sought advice from Churchill and Roosevelt, who were then at Quebec. Churchill was sternly in favor of the answer which the King wanted to make. He was convinced that the only way to avert civil war and to give the Greek people a genuine opportunity to choose their government was to postpone the settlement of political disputes until after Greece was liberated; and then only after a period of restored peace and quiet—under Allied military watch—to allow a true and free choice. He had not wanted small groups within Greece, particularly the Communist-led group, to have a chance, while the war was on, to gain control by intrigue or violence. Roosevelt had promised Churchill that the American government would maintain the same position.

In early October, when the Communist groups directly attacked the others, the British government suspended its air drops to them. Churchill feared that they might, with the aid of surrendered Italian weapons, take over the government in a rapid coup, after the Germans evacuated. So through the British missions in Greece he had tried ". . . to limit and bring to an end the civil war which had now broken out in the ruined and occupied country." [11] For that, Soviet cooperation was wanted but was not forthcoming. And against the chance that this attempt would fail, he was planning to hurry British forces into Greece in the wake of the retreating Germans, to hold the situation until the Greek people could decide in an orderly way what sort of government they wanted. If this became necessary the British hoped the Soviet government would not object or encourage the Communists to resist.

Eden, at one session of the Conference of Foreign Ministers at Moscow, reviewed what the British were doing. He evoked no response from either Molotov or Hull.

In review, the British alone were showing active concern over what would happen in this area, east and northeast of Italy, after liberation. Churchill and his colleagues felt that it would be a failure in foresight to allow civil war and disorder to run free, and leave local Communist forces an open and broken field—hence their effort to sustain the authority of the governments-in-exile, to moderate the rivalries between resistance groups, and to restrain their political pretensions. They

[11] *Closing the Ring,* page 538.

wanted Western troops present in that part of Europe to protect it from having its traditional way of life quenched out. Thus they were trying—and would keep on trying—to enlist American cooperation in joint military operations across the Adriatic, in Greece, and in the Aegean (of which effort much more will be told). The Soviet government was watching the local conflicts without distress, and being noncommittal when its cooperation was asked.

The American government was uncertain, sharing Churchill's desire that the peoples of these small countries should have freedom and order, but not sharing his inclination to rely on monarchies and discredited conservative groups. Besides, it did not want to be drawn directly into these Balkan troubles, nor into taking sides between the British and Russians. So it kept aloof from the current diplomatic efforts to arrange tranquilizing compromises and combinations.

∰∰∰∰∰∰∰

22. The Pursuit of Political Principle

∰∰∰∰∰∰∰

This course suited Hull. For he was afraid that if he got involved in these disputes, it would spoil his chances of success in the greater purpose he had in mind, which was to change the basis of political conduct of national states. Over each disjointed problem the interested and rival powers were poised—ready to contest, bargain, and threaten. This had been the customary way in the past by which questions of frontiers, political affiliations, and the like got settled. He wanted to bring it about that all such exercises of national power and diplomacy would in the future be subordinated to rules of principle.

Committees of devoted men, both in and outside the American government, had striven to formulate a set of adequate principles which would fulfill this end. The thoughts which guided them may be conveyed by brief extracts about the work of three of the subcommittees grouped under the Advisory Commission on Postwar Foreign Policy.[12]

About the work within the Subcommittee on Political Problems: "International security was regarded as the supreme objective, but at

[12] The story of the work of the parent committee and subcommittees is told in *Postwar Foreign Policy Preparation 1939–1945,* Washington, Department of State, 1949, written by Harley A. Notter, Adviser to the Assistant Secretary for United Nations Affairs. Quotations pages 101, 123, 128–29.

the same time the subcommittee held that the attainment of security must square with principles of justice in order to be actual and enduring."

About the work of the Subcommittee on Territorial Problems: "A fixed conclusion . . . was that the vital interests of the United States lay in following a 'diplomacy of principle'—of moral disinterestedness instead of power politics. . . ."

About the work of the Subcommittee on Security Problems: ". . . emphasis was laid upon the necessity, as the most imperative basis for assurance of peace and security after the war, of a firm pact among the chief victor powers agreed upon prior to the conclusion of the war."

Out of these conceptions there had been shaped a text of a joint declaration setting forth the principles by which the nations were to be called upon to abide. The President had approved it. Hull had submitted it to the British at the Quebec Conference in August. Eden had liked it and said that he thought it offered a good basis for an approach to the Soviet government. Churchill had concurred. Thereupon a copy had been sent to Moscow. The response had been disappointing. The idea had been allowed to rest till Hull got to Moscow. In the interval, Soviet treatment of the Polish government, in particular, had increased misgiving about Soviet political and territorial aims.

But, surprisingly, the business of reaching accord on a general declaration of the variety which the Americans had in mind was done rather quickly and easily at Moscow. Hull, early in the Conference, made a touching exposition of the benefits that all nations would derive by pledging themselves to the rules of conduct contained in the text which the Americans and British had conceived. Eden backed up his presentation. Molotov encouraged them both by saying, "The Soviet government was very favorably disposed toward the principles set forth in this Declaration and therefore welcomed it."

The framework of principles which made up the Declaration of the Four Nations on General Security, issued by the Conference, was vaguely magnificent rather than sturdy. Its main points may be recalled to aid fading memory.

The preamble contained a mutual pledge to continue the war until their enemies ". . . laid down their arms on the basis of unconditional surrender." This was the first time the Soviet government formally endorsed such a policy.

The main substantive sections of the Declaration as signed by Molotov, Eden, Hull, and Foo Ping-sheung were:

207

"2. That those of them at war with a common enemy will act together in all matters relating to the surrender and disarmament of that enemy.

"4. That they recognize the necessity of establishing at the earliest practicable date a general international organization, based on the principle of the sovereign equality of all peace-loving states, and open to membership by all such states, large and small, for the maintenance of international peace and security.

"5. That for the purpose of maintaining international peace and security pending the reestablishment of law and order and the inauguration of a system of general security, they will consult with one another and as occasion requires with other members of the United Nations with a view to joint action on behalf of the community of nations.

"6. That after the termination of hostilities they will not employ their military forces within the territories of other states except for the purposes envisaged in this declaration and after joint consultation."

On three points this Declaration fell away from the original text which Hull had brought to Moscow. To earn assent, several changes were made which loosened the hold of principle upon practice.

The rule contained in paragraph 2 had in the original American proposal, read: "That those of them at war with the common enemy will act together in all matters relating to the surrender and disarmament of that enemy, *and to any occupation of enemy territory and territory of other states held by that enemy"* [my italics].

Molotov had urged that the underscored clauses be omitted. His objections were diverse. One was akin to that which the American and British governments had advanced in regard to Italy: that it might interfere with military operations. Another went to the depths of the question of whether the coalition was joined together in one war over the whole of Europe or two connected ones. For this provision might be construed to mean that, on request, Soviet forces should be allowed to take part in the occupation of areas recaptured by the American and British forces such as Holland, Belgium, and France; and that American and British forces should be granted a similar right to participate in recaptured areas bordering on the Soviet Union. Faced with this grave question, all had agreed to drop the clause in the Declaration.

The rule in paragraph 5 had, in the original American proposal, read: "That for the purpose of maintaining international peace and security pending the reestablishment of law and order and the inauguration of a general system of security, *they will consult and act jointly in behalf of the community of nations"* [my italics].

Eden explained that this could be taken to imply a four-power dictatorship and that the British Dominions, particularly Canada, objected to it. The significant clause had been amended to avoid this possible reaction.

The most revealing change was the one made in the rule expressed in paragraph 6 of the Declaration. This had, in the original American proposal, read: "That they will not employ their military forces within the territories of other states except for the purposes envisaged in this Declaration and after joint consultation *and agreement*" [my italics].

This provision was linked in intent with the discussions between the British and Soviet governments as to whether they should promise each other not to enter into agreements with the smaller countries of Europe except after consultation and agreement, and it was directly connected with the imminent Soviet-Czech treaty. At issue was the question whether the Soviet government should retain the unfettered chance to enter into exclusive agreements with neighboring countries toward which its armies were headed.

Molotov was willing to agree to *consult* before entering into such accords, but he was not *willing to submit to a veto over action*. In support of his position he could and did cite various existing British as well as Soviet treaties, granting the right to send and keep their forces in the territory of other countries. When Eden and Molotov sought Hull's opinion on this issue, he took refuge in rambling. In the end the requirement of common consent was dropped. The obligation assumed was that of exposure to opposition through consultation. Eden tried hard to supplement this clause in the Declaration by a separate proposal which he put forward—that the three great governments at Moscow agree to abstain from concluding any agreements with smaller powers *during the war* except by common consent. This, he argued, would prevent a scramble for special position. But the Soviet government would not assent to this either.

Hull did not try to relate the Declaration explicitly to the question of frontiers. It is not hard to surmise why Molotov was willing to let the question rest. The Soviet government had said over and over that it regarded its western frontiers as settled, and this position had not been challenged. Moreover, the language of the Declaration left the Soviet government free to assert later any protuberant territorial claims it might have. But, though Stalin and Molotov might have thought so, neither Hull nor Eden regarded their discretion as acquiescence in Soviet claims—either those already known, or others that might be made in the future. Hull seems to have been convinced that the Declaration pledged its sponsors mutually to be guided by objective principles in settling issues in this field, though it is hard to find any adequate basis for this deduction in its cumulous provisions.[13] The lectures against independent action and isolation, in contrast to the benefits of cooperation that he gave Stalin and Molotov, were hints that they were expected to take heed of the views of others on such matters as frontiers. This was Hull's way of trying to convey a thought without putting it into plain words.

Indefiniteness in this field made it easier to reach accord in Moscow on other matters—military and political. But it left a void of misunderstanding—as will appear.

Before Molotov agreed to allow China to be one of the originating sponsors of the Declaration, he made quite a lot of trouble—trouble lasting a week, and ending only after dark hints that unless he gave in the American government might not be able to continue to cooperate with the Soviet Union. There is no more ironical episode in our tale than this one.

Molotov contended that China was so weak and dependent, as shown by its failure to expel the Japanese, that it was not entitled to such high place, and could not be counted on to play an equal part with the rest in making the Declaration effective. He also pointed out that since China had no interest in European affairs its appearance as an original sponsor might make the Declaration less acceptable to the European countries.

Hull exerted himself hard to win Soviet assent. He wished to encourage the Chinese government and people to endure and fight on. He hoped that if the Soviet Union and China were brought together in the small band sponsoring common rules for future peace, they would settle their own direct differences in friendly fashion. Thus he mustered every reason he could to justify the award for China. Speaking privately

---

[13] The only ground would seem to be the indirect reference in the preamble of the Declaration to the Atlantic Charter; and the first two articles of that statement, to the principles of which the Soviet Union had subscribed, read: "First, their countries seek no aggrandizement, territorial or other; second, they desire to see no territorial changes that do not accord with the freely expressed wishes of the people concerned." But the Soviet government had allowed itself leeway when on September 24, 1941, it expressed agreement with the principles of the Charter. Its statement had been: "Considering that the practical application of the principles will necessarily adapt itself to the circumstances, needs, and historical peculiarities of particular countries, the Soviet government can state that consistent application of the principle will secure the most energetic support on the part of the government and peoples of the Soviet Union."

Hull probably did not recognize that he failed to have his *intent* effectivated in the text of the declaration.

to Molotov, he went so far as to say he thought it would be impossible from the American point of view to omit China; if that were done it would in all probability have ". . . the most terrific repercussions, both political and military, in the Pacific area. This might call for all sorts of readjustments by my government to keep the political and military situation in the Pacific properly stabilized." And also that if China were excluded, American public opinion would be deeply rent by the news that the American government had joined with the Soviet government in Moscow to throw China out of the war picture.

Eden warmly supported Hull. While still unwilling to have large combat resources devoted to the China Theater, Churchill evidently put aside the misgivings he had recorded in a minute, written a year before in connection with proposals for world government after the war: "It sounds very simple to pick out these four Big Powers. We cannot however tell what sort of a Russia and what kind of Russian demands we shall have to face. . . . As to China, I cannot regard the Chungking Government as representing a great world Power. Certainly there would be a faggot vote on the side of the United States in any attempt to liquidate the British overseas Empire." [14]

Molotov came around, provided the Chinese would sign the Declaration before the Conference ended. This was arranged. Surmises are possible as to the reasons why the Soviet government gave in. Hull's hint that the American government might divert to China some of the war help it was giving the Soviet Union might have had effect. Or it may be that its opposition had derived in part from a wish not to offend Japan, and that the victories being won by the Red Army in Europe and by the American forces in the Pacific caused it to lose fear of doing so. This is what Hull and Harriman were inclined to think. It is probable also that the Soviet turn of mind in this matter was connected with its decision to inform the American and British governments that it would join the war against Japan as soon as Germany was defeated. This was told Hull only after the Conference was over. But Ambassador Harriman got the scent of the coming event some days before and, after informing the President on October 27th of the Soviet acceptance of China as one of the sponsors of the Declaration, he went on to say ". . . a number of indications have been given us that the Soviet government is disposed to cooperate in the Pacific after the collapse of Germany, to some extent at least. They no longer appear to fear Japan and I have a feeling that after the termination of hostilities in Europe they want the Pacific war ended as soon as possible."

This Soviet acceptance of China not only cleared the way for adoption

[14] *The Hinge of Fate,* page 562.

of the Four-Nation Declaration but also eased the final work on other affiliated statements of principles upon which the Foreign Ministers had also been engaged.

One of these related statements was aimed to express more precisely the rules that were to govern the relations between the large powers and the smaller states *of Europe* in particular. The British government was the initiator. Its proposal was entitled, "The Question of Joint Responsibility for Europe as Against Separate Spheres of Influence," a title later changed at American suggestion to read, ". . . as Against Separate Areas of Responsibility." The prime paragraph of the text presented by the British, read: "[The issuing governments declare] that for their part they will not seek to create any separate areas of responsibility in Europe and will not recognize such for others, but rather affirm their common interest in the well being of Europe as a whole."

Although it had opposed the inclusion of any provisions in the Anglo-Soviet treaty about territories, the attitude of the American government toward this proposal was ambiguous. Hull favored the principle but was loath to involve the American government in any definite obligation to see that it was made effective. The President wanted to keep clear of responsibility for the future pattern of relationships within Central and Eastern Europe, since he feared that it might lead to a call to keep American troops in Europe permanently. Accordingly, Hull suggested that this definite political rule proposed by Eden should be embraced in some broader and universally applicable accord such as the Four-Nation Declaration.

Molotov acted the innocent, dismissing as preposterous the idea that the Soviet government would be interested in separate zones or spheres of influence. He said he could guarantee that the Soviet Union had no disposition to divide Europe into separate zones. Then, in effect, he agreed with Hull that it would be better to consider the points in question within the general scope of the Four-Nation Declaration. The encouragement of confederations among the smaller states, he criticized as premature and even harmful. But, he said, the Soviet government would be willing to consider it later on. Actually events were to show that the Soviet government was determined to remain free in its dealings with the neighboring states, and also that it was utterly opposed to any groupings among the smaller powers which it did not sponsor and could not dominate.

In the upshot the British attempt to get a joint and conclusive statement of policy on these two questions—spheres of responsibility and confederations—was melted down into the more fluid vows of the Four-Nation Declaration.

Another foray into principle at Moscow led by the British was aimed toward the formulation of rules to guide policy in the administration of the areas that were being captured from the Germans, or were soon to be.

This survey has told something of the problems already presented to the members of the coalition by French and Italian political developments. They were more manageable than others in sight—Yugoslavia and Greece, or it might be first Romania, Bulgaria, or Poland. The course of war was stimulating deep political and social changes in all these countries. There were rivals for power in each. There were clashes between groups inclined toward Western political ideas and connections, and those inclined toward Soviet Communism. There were unsettled issues of frontiers and reparations. Would the members of the coalition deal with these matters together or separately? Would they treat them as a joint responsibility, or would each try to exploit them for its own greater advantage?

In September the American and British governments had consulted Moscow in regard to a public statement they wanted to issue—defining the course they proposed to follow in enemy territories captured by their forces and in liberated areas on the Allied side in the war. Correspondence—the intricate details of which I shall not review—had revealed variant ideas in Moscow.

In the administration of *former enemy countries*—which would remain under the control of the Allied command—all were in agreement that "democratic" elements must be introduced. But the American and British governments had thought that as long as the war against Germany continued, the decision as to the time and degree of such participation ought to be left to the Allied Military Command in each area. The Soviet government, however, had wanted this question to come within the purview of the Military-Political Commission which Stalin had proposed, and which was then being given form. This, tersely to foretell, emerged from the Moscow Conference as a committee of diplomatic representatives of the three countries, authorized merely to make studies and recommendations, named the European Advisory Commission (EAC).

As regards *liberated* areas, the British and Americans had favored a loose formula which seemed to mean that, subject to military necessity, responsibility for law and order would as soon as possible be turned over to national governments. The Soviet government had wished that also to be decided by the MPC.

In face of these differences, the proposed statement had been allowed to wait until the Foreign Secretaries met in Moscow. In the interval, the British had drawn up a new formulation. The State Department had objections to parts of it, but at Moscow Eden submitted it anyhow.

Hull was wary. He was unready to accept the responsibility that lurked in the suggested accord. He assured his colleagues that he recognized that it was desirable that their three countries should have a common policy. And he avowed that he wanted to see the principles of democracy which inspired the draft prevail everywhere and in all fields. But he thought that since the conditions that had to be taken into account would be different in each country, they would be well advised to deal with each separately. All agreed that the topic was too hard for haste. It also was assigned to the attention of the new committee of three—EAC. There it was allowed to languish while, as later pages will tell, the Allies squabbled unhappily. Then at Yalta, in February 1945, by which time separate spheres of domination in Europe were all but formed, it reemerged as the Declaration on Liberated Europe.

Secretary Hull took along with him to Moscow still another declaration in which he was eager to have the British and Soviet governments join. This dealt with the treatment to be accorded dependent peoples, those living in colonies and in mandates. In a moderate yet definite way it affirmed that policy of the governing countries should be such as to lead them gradually to independence. It looked toward change in the political status of many or all of these countries by intent and consent; and it contemplated the use of various types of trusteeships as intermediate measures.

The President had shown a lively belief in this line of policy and often stressed its justice and political soundness. So he was firmly behind this initiative, although he knew the British thought it would be unwise and threatening. They were unwilling to hobble the government of their Empire by fixed rule, or subject it to outside interference. As far back as November 1942, in a famous speech, the Prime Minister had firmly stated that his government would never share jurisdiction over its Empire with other countries. There was no sign that he had changed his mind in the least since he had declared in that speech, "Let me, however, make this clear, in case there should be any mistake about it in any quarter. We mean to hold our own. I have not become the King's first Minister in order to preside over the liquidation of the

British Empire." De Gaulle had shown the same attitude and spirit about the French Empire; he was bent upon salvaging every acre of it.

Hull put his proposal before the conference. Molotov said his government attached great importance to it and urged that it be studied. Eden said his government was against it, and not ready to discuss the question. Thus it remained a suspended item in the record of the Conference and in the later talk between the Allies. As the Soviet Union showed itself grasping for more power, the aggressiveness of American purpose in this field waned.[15]

Several times, in telling of proposals before the Conference, reference has been made to the lingering wish within the American government to keep clear of the quarrels in Europe, and its fear of becoming obliged to keep troops in Europe indefinitely. But at the same time it was eagerly taking the lead in the formation of a collective world organization to maintain the peace. While still not wanting to be dragged into the incessant wrangles between European states, it had abandoned any conception of isolation.

In the summer of 1943 the Americans and British had agreed to go forward with plans for a permanent collective security system, and to do so while the war was still being fought. Several reasons, all good, converged in favor of moving with the momentum of the war, not waiting until it might be spent. While still engaged in the anguished experience, nations would give more eager attention to plans for preventing war in the future. And, while under the spell of war cooperation, they would find it natural to agree to act in concert for the future. Then, too, if the purpose could be accomplished quickly, it might bring victory nearer. The proof of unity might wipe out the sustained hope of the Germans and Japanese that division might occur among their enemies; and, conversely, the prospect of a new international order after the war might make submission seem less awful. Lastly, there was the pleasing thought that if the United States clearly showed that it would take part in collective effort to prevent future aggression, other countries might feel it less necessary to try to provide for their own security by other measures; and thus it would be easier to work out fair peace settlements. More especially, it was hoped that by forming, while the war was still on, a system for maintaining peace, the Soviet government could be prevailed upon to moderate its requirements. In figurative summary, the end of other great wars had left the nations still within

[15] It reasserted itself at the conference at Dumbarton Oaks and San Francisco. Our efforts resulted in the "Declaration Regarding Non-Self-Governing Territories." Chapter XI of the U.N. Charter.

a coil of serpents; by this measure the coil was to be unwound and the nations freed to breathe as friends.

The intent had been written into the text for a Four-Nation Declaration which Hull had taken to the Quebec Conference; and there it had been officially approved. The weeks before he left for Moscow brought evidence that most of the American people had learned their lesson, and had come to regard the creation of such an agency as one of their postwar aims. This turn of judgment had been strong enough to subdue partisanship. In September the leaders of the Republican Party, meeting at Mackinac Island, Michigan, had endorsed American participation in a postwar security organization.

The great remaining question that appeared in the analyses produced in the State Department was whether the Soviet Union would join in a genuine collective arrangement. It was thought to be in the throes of a major decision of the same sort which the United States had faced at the end of the First World War. Would it decide to live in isolation, relying on its own power and size for its security and welfare, or would it accept the restraints and responsibilities of cooperation in order to secure its benefits?

At Moscow, the Soviet government showed itself ready to support this great future project, and agreement was quickly reached on small changes of language needed to suit all. The final statement, as included in the Four-Nation Declaration (and quoted earlier in this section), marked a further evolution in Roosevelt's thought, a marked conversion of his earlier belief that what would serve best was a continuation of the war coalition to police the peace which it would win and shape. Churchill's ideas had also changed. He had leaned toward the plan for basing any world peace organization on regional ones. Perhaps such a system had appealed to him as better enabling the British Empire and the smaller countries of Europe to hold their own against the massive American and Russian states. But gradually he also had come to adopt the same idea of one all-embracing organization. And so, it seemed, the Soviet government had genuinely also.

In the last session of the Conference (October 30th) Molotov showed more of a hurry than the others to give effect to this element in the Four-Nation Declaration. He proposed that the Conference set up a commission at once to draw up plans for the new organization. It was Hull who demurred, saying he was afraid that if this was done, political groups in the United States might attach wrong meaning to it, and that he thought a less formal method better for the time being, by an exchange of views through usual diplomatic channels.

The text of the Declaration was signed on October 30th under the lenses of the movie cameras. This mutual pledge was one of the most deep and gratifying achievements in Hull's long public career. With its promise in mind, the current troubles and clashes over particular situations which were discussed at Moscow probably seemed to him transient and secondary. He knew that there was no ideal solution for most of them, none pleasing to all. But on one basis or another they would get settled, and then, over the longer run of years, as the world found content in its new peaceful order, the quarrels about the outcome would be forgotten. The ready Soviet will to share in the great design, along with its endorsement of those principles which even in their mutilated form he regarded as the essential basis of good international relations, seemed a bright omen for the future. The Soviet Union, he now thought he had reason to hope, even to expect, would not retreat into isolation, nor on the grounds of security make unjust or threatening demands, nor indulge in measures which its war partners opposed. Principle, not power, was to hold dominion over the actions of all nations.

All these noble hopes found words in Hull's appraisal of the Declaration. But among the students some were skeptical of its value even at the time. To them the fact that the Soviet government had agreed to join in conceiving an international security organization was no warrant of its future conduct. The test would be in practice, not in profession.

23. Moscow Conference of Foreign Ministers; German Questions and Other European Political Matters, October 1943

These talks about principles to guide conduct were animated by the sense that the war was being rapidly won. It was expected that some other members of the Axis would soon follow Italy and seek to break the connection. The purpose of some overtures, it could be foreseen, would be to test out Allied solidarity by offering a tempting separate peace to one or the other. Slight efforts of this sort had, in fact, already been made to draw the Soviet government into talk about a possible separate peace with Germany—notably in September by the Japanese government, which was eager to be the intermediary. Of this and of the Soviet rejection of this bid Molotov had informed Hull, and possibly Eden.[16]

The Allies were mutually pledged not to make such a peace with a common foe. Each had accepted the idea that in loyalty to this pledge it ought not carry on negotiations with an enemy unknown to the others. But a need was perceived to supplement this pledge not to act alone by a positive engagement to act jointly in the handling of any and all solicitations. Moreover, it was recognized that the time had come to have agreed armistice terms ready for the asking. The Foreign Secretaries at Moscow reached an accord on this first question, of peace-feelers, and began discussion of the second question, armistice terms.

Each of the three main Allies had a serious interest in the terms of any armistice or peace made with any of their enemies, large and small. But they did not have equal interest in all respects, or an equal claim to direct each particular negotiation. Several causes made for distinctions in degree of responsibility, if not of ultimate right to decide. There was an accepted assumption that the country that bore the chief weight of battle on any front was entitled to the leading part at least in any preparatory discussions about the possible surrender of the forces on that front; as for example, Britain and the United States in Italy, the Soviet Union in Finland, the United States in the Pacific. This was regarded as all the more natural when, as in Italy, fighting continued in the enemy country even after local surrender.

The case of Romania, discussed during the Conference at Moscow, illustrated the problem. Secret agents, in touch with some leading individuals inside and outside the Romanian government, had appeared in Cairo and were trying to sound out the British government about terms. The Soviet and American governments had been advised of this approach. Eden in Hull's presence (on October 25th) asked Molotov what he thought ought to be done. Molotov answered that the only basis should be "unconditional surrender"; but then he added that he saw no purpose in going ahead with talks with these factions in Romania because they had nothing to offer. Eden assented, saying that his government felt that the Soviet government was entitled to decide any such questions concerning Romania and Hungary and Finland as well—since only its forces were engaged in active warfare against these countries. Hull said he had nothing to add to Eden's remarks. The British government had informed the Romanian agents that no approach could be considered that was not addressed to the American

[16] *Memoirs*, page 1264.

and Soviet governments as well as to itself, and would have to be an offer of unconditional surrender to all three principal Allies.

In sum, the idea was accepted that there would have to be variety and flexibility in the bases on which the three dealt with one another in different situations. But it was agreed that each should keep the others promptly informed and try to act in concert with them. This was expressed in a resolution of the Conference reading: "The governments of the United Kingdom, the United States of America and the Soviet Union agree to inform each other immediately of any peace-feelers which they may receive from the government of, or from any groups or individuals in, a country in which any one of the three countries is at war. The three governments further agree to consult together with a view to concerting their action in regard to such approaches."

This was a healthful accord. It barred out any secret separate negotiations. But for assured and smooth practical effect, the Italian example showed the need to have in hand, when the peace overtures came, an agreement on policies to govern the granting of the armistice and the regime to follow after it. To that end, the Foreign Ministers at Moscow exchanged ideas as to what was to be done about Germany and Austria, and made plans to have their exploratory talks developed into texts.

The prime enemy was Germany. Yet before the meeting at Moscow, the three main Allies had not engaged in any systematic discussion of the many aspects of German surrender and the treatment of Germany thereafter.

The review of these subjects with Eden in March 1943—of which a summary was given when telling of his visit to Washington—had been cursory. Since then, despite much work in committees, the American and British governments had wavered and differed. Both had been perplexed during the quarrelsome mid-term of 1943 about Soviet tactics and intentions toward Germany. Soviet broadcasts had been telling the German people that only the National Socialist elements among them would be treated harshly. Stalin had averred (as in his Order of the Day on May 1st) that it was not his aim to destroy the German Army— as distinguished from the Hitlerite army. The Soviet government had brought together German captives, of all parties and classes, from prisoner-of-war camps in Russia, and taught them to form a Free German movement. This had set about urging the German people by radio to get rid of Hitler and form "a real national German Government with a strong democratic order" (broadcast July 20, 1943). Soon afterward, Soviet authorities had also encouraged the formation of a

Union of German officers in the Soviet Union. Field Marshal Paulus, head of the army that had surrendered at Stalingrad, gave himself to its activities. This group had begun to appeal to the German Army to stop fighting, upset the Hitler regime, and seek friendship with Russia.

Officials in the State Department and Foreign Office had observed these Soviet initiatives with distaste and some anxiety. The note which was being struck was softer than that of unconditional surrender. Even assuming that this line of activity was being carried on either as war propaganda or as warning to the West, it exposed the American and British governments to risks and disadvantages in the development of their decisions about Germany. They had been afraid that if they came out openly for partition, they would leave the way clear for Russia, through its Communist supporters, to set itself up as the champion of political unity of the German people. These suspicions were akin to those which the Soviet government had had about Allied procedure in Italy. Soviet diplomats, in fact, privately excused the line which their government was casting toward Germany by that comparison.

Uneasiness over Soviet tactics had attended the American and British preparatory work upon German matters prior to the Moscow Conference, and had cauterized the impulse to be extremely harsh. The State and War Departments had labored hard with the many-sided problem. The President had approved the result of their work—a comprehensive outline of policy to be put before the Conference by Hull, well described by its title, "Basic Principles Regarding German Surrender." Hull gave a copy to Molotov, saying, "This is not a formal United States proposal but something to show a slant of mind. It is just a personal suggestion you and I can talk about. Then, if you like, we can talk to Eden about it and see what he thinks. I can make the proposal mine, or you can make it yours." [17]

This American paper proposed that in coming to an agreement the three governments should take nine principles as a guide. Among the more familiar were: (1) That Germany, in accordance with the principle of unconditional surrender, should be called upon to sign an admission of total defeat. As phrased, this left a chance to forego insistence on the most literal form of unconditional surrender, without leaving room for bargaining about terms. (2) That Germany was to submit to occupation—to be effected and maintained by contingents of British, Soviet, and American forces. (3) That all Nazis be eliminated from government and every vestige of the Nazi regime be extinguished. (4) That the German government must release all political prisoners, and deliver to the United Nations persons who might be accused of war

[17] *Ibid.*, page 1285.

crimes. (5) That German armed forces were to be demobilized and all weapons given up. Additionally the paper looked toward deep changes to be effected in the German political structure. It was recommended that Germany be turned into a broadly-based democracy, operating under a bill of rights to safeguard individual liberties. In this connection it was properly remarked that if such a form of government were to succeed, the German people would have to be allowed a tolerable standard of living and Allied control measures ought not to exceed those necessary for security. The program visualized that authority should be diffused between federal units. No attempt was made to define these, but it was suggested that the Allies encourage any movements which might emerge within Germany in favor of diminishing Prussian influence in the Reich.

Who has ever seen Molotov's face "radiant"? Yet Hull thought it was, when, on the day after this proposal was made, the Soviet Foreign Minister came to him and said in effect, "I have shown this to Stalin and he is enthusiastic. It expresses Russia's thoughts about Germany exactly as if we had expressed them. . . ." [18] If this could be believed, there was no further need to worry over Stalin's courting of the German people and army in his propaganda.

Eden also told Hull that he thought the proposal in general well drawn and satisfactory. It was agreed that some items in it needed more complete analysis; and for that purpose it should be consigned to the new consultative committee which the Conference was arranging to establish (EAC). Anyone listening in on the friendly conclave of ideas about Germany at Moscow might well have thought that this Committee would have little trouble in completing a joint accord on surrender terms and control arrangements for Germany. But, in fact, the consultations in store were to be so trying and lengthy that the job was not finished until Allied troops were inside Germany, west and east.

What of the opinion that, in addition to all these other measures for reducing and changing Germany, the world would not be able to rest easy unless that country was broken up into several separate states? Since the tentative discussion with Eden in March, differences of opinion about this matter had appeared within both the American and British governments.

The divisional officers in the State Department, worried over the ways in which Russia might extend its influence over a dissected Germany, were against partition. So was Hull, but on another score—as he had told Eden at Quebec that it ". . . might merely create a German national slogan for union." But the President was still inclined to

[18] *Ibid.*, page 1285.

think it must be done, since no measure short of that could prevent the Germans from again trying to make themselves masters of Europe. However, he did not want the United States to become subject to calls on its military forces for the direction of European affairs after the war; that task should, he thought, be borne by the British and Russians, and perhaps the French. This may have been one of the reasons why he did not give Hull, before the Secretary left for Moscow, any conclusive instruction on this vital question of partition.

Churchill and his colleagues were also of two minds. He doubted whether it was advisable, and most, but not all, the War Cabinet felt the same way. Certainly the Prime Minister was not ready to say yes or no. So in the memo he gave Eden to guide him at Moscow, Churchill had sonorously muffled the issues: "We repudiate all territorial expansion achieved by Germany or Italy during the Nazi or Fascist regimes, and further we consider that the future structure of Germany and the position of Prussia as a unit of the German State should be subject to an agreed policy among the three Great Powers of the West." [19]

The discussion at Moscow reflected these hesitations. Both Hull and Eden candidly told of differences of view among their colleagues and advisers. Molotov was a bit surprised to learn that the American government did not seem to be more intent on bringing about dismemberment. After making sure of that, he in turn disavowed any fixed Soviet policy in the matter. He said tactfully that there was a strong sentiment in the Soviet Union in favor of partition, but the Soviet government felt that it had to pay attention as well to public opinion in Great Britain and the United States. In short, he left the Soviet government with as much leeway as the others. But he did not storm at British or American hesitations, or, as he was to do on some later occasions, accuse them of wanting to follow a "soft" policy toward Germany.

In the American proposal, the question of Germany's future frontiers was touched on only in one sentence. "This," it read, "is a matter which should come within the purview of the general settlement."

The discussion of the subject at Moscow was almost equally brief. Molotov asked whether this meant that Germany might be allowed to keep any of its conquests. Eden and Hull both assured him that it did not mean this; and also that on one frontier question their governments were already agreed—that Germany would have to give up East Prussia. All three had well in mind, no doubt, the quarrel between the Soviet and Polish governments as to where the new frontier between them was to lie, with its bearing upon how much of Germany might

[19] *Closing the Ring,* page 283.

be given to Poland. But they forebore from trying to figure out what was to be done about that side of the German question. The postponement gave the American and British governments more time for protests and persuasion. It gave the Soviet government more time for penetration of the areas in dispute.

By so passing by the problems of partition and frontiers, the three Foreign Secretaries were able in cheerful good faith to approve the notation in the official protocol of the Conference after Item 7 (Treatment of Germany and other Enemy States of Europe), "An exchange of views took place which showed an identity of views on the main questions."

About Austria, the Foreign Ministers were pleased to find that the identity of their ideas was complete. So then and there they agreed upon a declaration about the future which they intended to provide for that country. Austria was to be liberated. The union with Germany that had been imposed upon it in 1938 was to be made null and void. Austria was to be free and independent. But the Austrian people were to be called upon to accept some responsibility for their part in the war, which they could begin to discharge by helping to throw the Germans out of their country.

Though none ever disavowed any part of this program for Austria, ten years were to go by after the end of the war before the Allies could agree upon the terms of the treaty with Austria which carried these provisions officially into effect.

24. Moscow Conference; Military Discussions

Concurrently with the disposition of this wide range of political questions, active discussion of military matters went on in Moscow. They had been edged into this conference of Foreign Ministers, but once in they at times almost deposed other claimants for attention.

In all the weeks before October, in every message about the projected conference of three Heads of Government that was to follow the Moscow meeting, Stalin had shown that his main interest in this encounter would be to make sure that the cross-Channel operation was carried out. Churchill had been ready, in person, to tackle the subject. But since he feared the outcome of a conference with Stalin unless the

Americans and British had fixed upon their joint plans beforehand, he had tried to get Roosevelt to agree to prior talks between the two of them and their military staffs. But Roosevelt had not thought any such preliminary meeting necessary. So the Prime Minister had yielded to Stalin's urgent wish by offering to send General Ismay, his personal representative on the Chiefs of Staff, to Moscow along with Eden; and it was arranged that the American government would have a similarly qualified officer present.

Then Stalin, on September 29th, had thrust military matters to the very forefront by proposing that the first item of discussion at Moscow should be "to consider measures for shortening the time of war against Germany and her Allies in Europe." The explanatory portions of his note made clear that he had in mind above all else the invasion of Western Europe across the English Channel. Churchill and Eden had been upset by what they regarded as an attempt to displace the questions most needing the attention of the Foreign Ministers, and as an effort to crowd them into a final decision about the invasion. But Roosevelt had dealt with the suggestion smoothly by telling Stalin that he would welcome a full exchange of views on military plans and strategy at the Moscow meeting, but only as a step toward the decisions that would have to await the prospective conference to follow between himself, Churchill, and Stalin. Hull had feared interference with the business he most wanted to do. But he recognized that Stalin would have to be satisfied about military prospects before he could be induced ". . . to come in with us on the political decisions." So the Secretary of State had assented to having military representatives in the American conference group around him at Moscow; and to have them engage in talks about military matters, subject to orders they were given in Washington. As will be learned, when in Moscow, he did what he suavely could to disassociate himself and his work from theirs. He tried to keep out of their discussions, turning the assignment over, as far as feasible, to Ambassador Harriman and General Deane, senior American Military Officer assigned to the mission. However, because of the close link between military matters and some of the political questions which Hull was presenting, and because Molotov (who was a member of the Defense Committee of the Soviet government) did take part in the talks about military matters, Hull was also drawn into them.

At the very first meeting of the three Secretaries (October 19th) Molotov suggested that before starting on any other matters they have a look at military ones. He had ready an English translation of Soviet proposals—proposals for shortening the war.

There were three: (1) The Anglo-American invasion of Northern France coupled with powerful blows of Soviet forces on the ". . . main German forces on the Soviet German front." In this connection the Soviet memo said it was necessary to ascertain whether the statement made by Roosevelt and Churchill early in June 1943 to the effect that the invasion would start in the spring of 1944 remained valid. (2) Joint suggestion to the Turkish government that it enter the war at once. (3) A demand of the Swedish government that it place air bases at the disposal of the Allies.

Both Hull and Eden said they would have to consult their governments before taking a definite position in regard to these proposals, and they hurried to do so. Since the invasion was to be a combined U.S.-British operation, the Americans and British at Moscow wanted to make a combined answer about it, not separate ones. The return instructions received from the U.S. Joint Chiefs were clear: The Russians might be told squarely that the Quebec statement was still valid. But the incoming advices and comments which Ismay and Eden got from their superiors were less definite, and dissimilar. By radio they received one memo offering guidance, which had probably been prepared and sent before Eden's first report from Moscow had been received. This seemed to confirm the provisional decision made at Quebec that the primary U.S.-British ground and air effort would be the invasion of northern France—with target date May 1, 1944. While restating the three conditions that the British government thought should be satisfied before that operation was launched, it went on, however, to express every confidence that these conditions could be brought about and to indicate how it was hoped to bring them about. But the response which Churchill sent to Eden on the 20th was more diffuse. The reply reflected his lurking doubts about the prospects of the invasion and his longing to try out alternative ways of bringing Germany down—as is more relevantly told in the coming account of the discussion of the second Soviet proposal.

Generals Ismay and Deane made their exposition of American and British military operations and plans on the 20th. This followed the line laid down in the memo of guidance that had been received by Ismay (the message from Churchill to Eden not yet having been received). They first made the point that at every single Anglo-American military conference the thought uppermost ". . . in all our minds has been so to arrange our affairs as to insure the maximum possible diversion of enemy land and air forces from the Russian front." They then explained that it should not be inferred, however, that the Americans and British could concentrate the whole of their combined resources against the Axis in Europe; that it was essential to maintain and extend unremitting pressure against Japan.

Next they summed up the series of operations in Europe decided upon at Quebec, which were in various stages of execution, leading to a cross-Channel invasion in 1944. This last was to be attempted ". . . as soon as practicable after weather conditions in the English Channel became favorable." Subject, also, it was said, to the need of bringing about conditions which would give a reasonable prospect of success. These were, first, a substantial reduction in the strength of German fighter forces in Northwest Europe before the assault began; second, that German reserves in France and the Low Countries must not be on D-Day more than about twelve full-strength, first-quality mobile divisions; and third, that Germany be unable to transfer from other fronts more than fifteen qualified divisions during the first two months of combat. "We are fairly confident," the Deane-Ismay statement went on, "that these conditions would be fulfilled."

When Ismay and Deane finished, Molotov tried to reduce what they had said to a simple acceptance or rejection of the first Soviet proposal. Failing in this, he said that what the Soviet government had been told of the results of the Roosevelt-Churchill conference at Quebec had left it uncertain as to whether the earlier decision to start the invasion in the spring of 1944 was still in force or had been changed. Eden remarked that he thought there was some misunderstanding. "As far as he knew, the May decisions had been confirmed by the Conference at Quebec, and therefore the answer to Mr. Molotov's question is 'Yes,' subject to the conditions quoted by General Ismay in his statement. All the preparations for the operation were going ahead." General Deane then spoke in an even more positive tone to the same effect.

Both Hull and Harriman informed the President that they believed that these affirmations had convinced the Soviet officials of the sincerity of American-British intentions. But Harriman predicted, on the basis of past experience, that they had not heard the last of the subject. He was correct. Later in the Conference (on the 28th) at another restricted meeting the Russians again tested the probabilities. Marshal Voroshilov examined one of the attached conditions—that the enemy should not have in Northwest Europe at the planned day of invasion more than twelve divisions of mobile troops. He asked what would happen if the Germans had a few more. General Ismay explained the reason for this condition: it was expected that the Germans would demolish the ports in Northern France so that they would not be usable for sixty days after capture, and would retard the rate of the buildup of the invasion forces. But he went on to say that the estimate of twelve divisions was an approximation; that it did not look at the present moment as though Germany would have divisions to spare near the front; and that all Allied air strength would be set to smash their ways of movement— roads, railroads, etc.

Over again Molotov put the same dogmatic question, "whether the affirmation made at Quebec regarding the cross-Channel operation in the early spring of 1944 was still valid." Over again Eden answered ". . . that the decision made at Quebec is still valid. This decision, however, is not a binding legal contract; although we will do all in our power to work out the plan which we are following for the common aim." Hull limited himself to remarking that Ismay and Deane had explained American and British preparations in the frankest manner, and that the Soviet officials would be kept well informed as to all future developments.

Molotov then accepted the fact that an unqualified promise was not to be had, and gave thanks ". . . for the expressed views in which he himself joined." But he evidently did not want to expose himself to the same sort of misunderstanding that had followed upon his earlier talks on the same subject when he had visited London and Washington in 1942. He proposed that they make their discussion of written record in the protocol of the Conference. His idea was to have the British and American views on each point written on one side of the page, and the Soviet views on the other side. He explained that what he was after was a mutually accepted record that all could count on.

Eden said that he thought it would be possible to agree on such a summation. Hull was more cautious. He said that any such statement would have to be referred to the President and Joint Chiefs of Staff first, since he did not want them to think that this conference of Foreign Secretaries was trying to take over their functions. In reporting to the President about Molotov's suggestion, as he did at once, the Secretary said that he would see to it that in any statement that went into the record of the Conference it would ". . . be made clear that we have made no commitments. Our position will be that Generals Ismay and Deane were authorized only to impart decisions already made and to describe preparations which are under way in carrying out these decisions."

That evening Eden had a private conversation with Stalin. He gave the Marshal a Russian text of General Alexander's sobering estimate of the situation on the Italian front which Eisenhower sent to Churchill.[20] Eden explained that he wanted Stalin to know that Prime Minister Churchill was anxious about the situation in Italy, and ". . . insistent

[20] The full text is to be found in *Closing the Ring*, pages 243-247.

that the battle in Italy should be nourished and fought out to victory whatever the implications on 'Overlord.' " [21] Stalin asked whether this report meant a postponement of that operation. Eden said that he did not know but the possibility must be faced; and he went on to quote the passage in the latest message he had received from Churchill affirming that the British were determined to do their very best for OVERLORD but that there was "no use planning for defeat in the field in order to give temporary political satisfaction." [22] Stalin then asked whether the postponement would be one or two months. That query also, Eden said he could not answer conclusively; all that he could say was that every effort would be made to launch OVERLORD at the earliest possible moment at which it had a reasonable prospect of success.

Stalin did not recriminate or accuse. He expressed the opinion that the Allies in Italy would be well advised to take up a defensive position north of Rome and use the rest of their forces for OVERLORD rather than try to push through Italy into Germany; and he approved the idea of a synchronized landing in Southern France, the better to force Hitler to disperse his forces.[23]

The Protocol of the Conference gave effect to Molotov's proposal. It first reproduced Molotov's original memo on measures to shorten the duration of the war. Then, in parallel columns, it recorded what the American and British representatives said about these proposals and what the Soviet representatives said. The entry in the Soviet column was temperately trustful—being merely to the effect that Molotov had noted the American and British statements, and expressed the hope that the plan of invasion of northern France in the spring of 1944 would be carried out on time. Its tenor harmonizes with the impression which Stalin was imparting to Eden and Hull.

Of what had preceded the second of the Soviet military proposals— that the three powers join in urging Turkey to enter the war at once— we ought briefly to tell. In an effort to bring this about earlier in the year, Churchill had made a special trip to Adana after the Casablanca Conference. He had been rebuffed, to his great chagrin, since his im-

---

[21] *Ibid.*, page 291.

[22] *Ibid.*

[23] Eden told Hull at once about this talk with Stalin, and Hull immediately, on the basis of what Eden told him, informed the President in paraphrase that "Stalin's attitude was very reasonable and realistic. The British impression of the meeting was entirely favorable. Stalin agreed that the Italian operation must be supported and that the defense should be established north of Rome. He accepted the fact that delay of OVERLORD might be necessitated by an adverse situation in Italy and suggested that Italy might constitute the Second Front. He urged, however, that the OVERLORD concept should be adhered to."

aginative mind conceived that if Turkey joined them the Allied assault might sweep over the whole Mediterranean and Aegean. But the Turkish government had been fearful of the German and Bulgarian armies and air force near its frontiers. They also were wary of the Russians, being afraid that they would take the chance to annex part of Bulgaria (Dobruja), thus forming a common frontier in Europe with Turkey, and then try to force it to yield control of the Dardanelles Straits. Russians rough and Russians smooth were familiar characters to the Turks.

At Churchill's initiative the Soviet and Turkish governments had thereafter engaged in diplomatic talks about their relations and aims in the Balkans and Eastern Mediterranean. These had been amiable but without issue. Then in September the Russian press had begun a campaign against Turkish neutrality. This had worried the Turks since they still did not feel protected enough against the Germans to enter the war, and suspected that the Russians wanted to push them into a disaster so they would not be able to evade the Russian clutch after the war. The Soviet government had also shown mistrust because Britain had continued to send arms to Turkey despite its determined neutrality, thinking the British were trying to create a barrier to Soviet advances in this region.

While Turkey was thus resisting both persuasion and pressure, Churchill and Roosevelt and the Combined Chiefs of Staff had begun to change their minds about wanting Turkey to enter the war at this time. Because of the limited resources allotted for combat in the Mediterranean, they were inclined to think it best that Turkey wait until better armed before becoming involved.

But when the Russians, at the Moscow Conference, proposed joint action to get Turkey into the war, Churchill's attention quickened at the possibility that this might be made part of a large-scale campaign to gain entry into Europe from the southeast. He asked Eden at once to find out whether the Russians would be attracted to the idea of having the British act through the Aegean, involving Turkey in the war, opening the Dardanelles and Bosphorous Sea so that the British naval forces and shipping could aid the Russian advance and ultimately give them "our right hand along the Danube. . . . It may be," his message to the Foreign Minister went on, "that for political reasons the Russians would not want us to develop a large-scale Balkan strategy. On the other hand, their desire that Turkey should enter the war shows their interest in the Southeastern theatre." [24]

Knowing from the way in which Molotov and the Russian generals were pressing Deane and Ismay that they were set on the invasion of

[24] *Closing the Ring,* page 286.

Northern France, Eden was restrained in the way in which he presented Churchill's thought about the matter of getting Turkey into the war, not explicitly pursuing its development into a major campaign from the southeast. In his first exposition he said in summary effect that while the British government thought that under current conditions Turkey as a partner in the offensive would probably be more of a liability than an asset, it would gladly consider doing what the Soviet government wanted. But his attitude took a different deflection after getting another message from Churchill ending in the conclusion that the Russian wish to have Turkey enter the war ought not to be discouraged —if they, the Turks, should come in "of their own volition . . . We should agree in principle and let the difficulties manifest themselves . . ." [25] Eden adjusted his subsequent comments to this advice, broaching the further idea that even if no way was found to induce or coerce it to enter the war, Turkey might be brought to allow the Allies to use its railways, territorial waters, and airfields to go after the Aegean Islands, especially Rhodes. About these proposals, as about Molotov's, Hull would not express an opinion before finding out what the President thought.

Molotov was convinced Turkey would not hold out against joint presentation, backed by a threat to deprive it of any more weapons. But the matter might have been left to rest until the Heads of Government met except for a coincidental event. The British had sent a small expedition to Leros, an Aegean Island on the way to Rhodes. That faced disaster unless Turkey gave active assistance. As well explained in the official British history of the strategy of this period, "Whereas the capture of the Dodecanese had originally been designed to precede action by Turkey, action by Turkey was now required to secure possession of the Dodecanese." [26] Churchill determined to demand of Turkey the

[25] Ibid., page 289.
[26] History of the Second World War, Grand Strategy, Volume v, by John Ehrmann. This gives a full and most interesting account of Churchill's attempt to persuade Roosevelt to agree to allocate necessary means for an assault on Rhodes and the other islands of the Dodecanese—even though that should cause a slight delay in the start of OVERLORD, and of Roosevelt's regretful refusal. This caused the British detachments that after the collapse of Italy had been landed on several of the smaller islands, Cos, Samos, and Leros to become dependent on Turkish facilities and help.
As traced on pages 100–101 of this account, "The Turks had indeed already given valuable help. They did not challenge British warships proceeding through their waters, and through September ferried supplies to Samos. The commanders in the Middle East now wished them as a first step, to extend their service by carrying supplies from Samos to Leros and to agree to receive and pass on British troops who might later be forced to leave the islands.
"By the end of October, however, these demands had grown. Despite continuous operations by air forces from both the Middle East and Italy, the constant patrols and

needed help under penalty of ending British shipment of military equipment. Eden arranged to meet the Turkish Foreign Minister at Cairo, before returning to London, in order to confront the Turkish government with the choice. He was also planning to ask Turkey to allow British submarines and merchant ships to pass through the Straits into the Black Sea, the better to bring aid and supplies to the Soviet Union.

Molotov thought the measures rather palsied. But the British stuck fast to the point that if a formal demand to enter the war was made and rejected, the chance of getting Turkey to help it hold the Aegean Islands would also be lost. After Eden promised that if he failed in his errand the British government would be ready within a month to consider a formal joint demand on Turkey to enter the war at once, Molotov grudgingly gave in. He and Eden signed a memo obligating their governments to try to get Turkey into the war by the end of 1943, and to ask Turkey to provide at once facilities, such as the use of air bases, for British and Soviet forces. A few days later Roosevelt agreed to join in these petitions; the U.S. Joint Chiefs were not opposed on condition that no British or American planes, ships, or fighting men were diverted to the eastern Mediterranean, which in the opinion of the responsible commanders were needed for OVERLORD or operations in Italy.

Of the failure of the effort made to get Turkey to accede, a further account will be given in connection with the resumed discussions of the subject when the three Heads of State met at Teheran.

Another deterrent to the flow of good feeling within the coalition was cleared away during this Moscow Conference when Stalin and Eden settled the rude quarrel which had been going on since early September over arrangements for resuming the northern convoys to the Soviet Union. The tale of this disagreeable accompaniment to the discussion of all other affairs may be very briefly told.

Deliveries of various war supplies to the Soviet Union, despite determined purpose and the great expansion of the southern route via Iran, fell in September again below schedule. This had been due in part to the great demands on shipping and naval vessels for current operations in the Mediterranean, the Pacific, and Burma, in part because ship-

---

supply of the islands were taking a heavy toll of ships. . . . But the necessary air support could never be effective from bases so far removed from the scene of operations; and on 29th October the Chiefs of Staff informed the Prime Minister that either Leros must be reinforced and sustained entirely by submarine, or some six squadrons of fighters must be operated from landing strips in south-west Anatolia within the next three weeks." This and subsequent quotations from *Grand Strategy*, Vols. v and vi, London: Her Britannic Majesty's Stationery Office, 1956, are used by permission of the Comptroller of H. M. S. Office.

ments over the northern route had been suspended during the long summer season. In September Molotov had informed the British government that the Soviet government would have to insist on the urgent resumption of the northern convoys, and expected His Majesty's government to take all the necessary steps during the next few days.[27]

Both the American and British governments, while accepting no blame, had recognized that the Soviet complaints merited attention. On October 1st Churchill had informed Stalin that a series of four large convoys would sail in November, December, January, and February. But he had it of record ". . . that this is no contract or bargain, but rather a declaration of our solemn and earnest resolve"; and that he thought the Soviet government ought—in order both to help these convoy operations and in the name of common decency—to give British Service personnel, stationed in North Russia for war work, better treatment and more freedom of movement, and allow an increase in their numbers.[28]

Stalin's response of October 13th had been contentious. He had said that Churchill's statement lost value because it was not a firm obligation, but only a promise which the British government might renounce at any time, regardless of how the Soviet armies at the front might be affected. "Supplies from the British government to the USSR, armaments and other military goods," he continued, "cannot be considered otherwise than as an obligation, which, by special agreement between our countries, the British government undertook. . . ." [29] The British government had not, it may be recalled, pledged itself to get these supplies to Russia, but only to do its best to do so. Stalin had also repelled Churchill's request for relaxation of the over-severe restraints and regime under which the British personnel in the north were being compelled to live.

Churchill had almost thrown up his hands, and might have done so if there had not been such imperative military reasons for patience. He had mastered his irritation. On October 18th he had asked the new Soviet Ambassador in London, Gusev, to call on him. He had explained that while tempted to retort to Stalin in kind, he was not doing so since it would only make the difference worse; and thus he was leaving the matter up to Eden to settle on the spot in Moscow. So saying, the Prime Minister had handed over Stalin's "offensive" message to the Soviet Ambassador, who vainly tried to give it back to him. Churchill had at once informed Eden of what had been said and done.

[27] *Closing the Ring*, page 261.
[28] *Ibid.*, page 264.
[29] *Ibid.*, page 267.

Eden had thereupon discarded the combative opening statement with which he had been ready to defend the British view and adopted the same tone of companionship in arms which Churchill had used in his talk with Ambassador Gusev. He assured Stalin and Molotov that the British government was eager and resolved to carry these convoys through if it could be done without excessive loss. It was determined to make every effort within reason to deliver the goods. But, he continued, the task imposed a great strain on the British Navy, which still was being forced to cope with German submarine warfare of great range and destruction. So, he concluded, if because of some sudden development, his government found that it could not send all four convoys through, it did not want to be made to bear harsh blame.

Molotov called at the British Embassy in Moscow in person to make it plain to Eden that the Soviet government greatly valued what these convoys would bring. Stalin hinted that his rude refusal to accede to Churchill's requests for better treatment of British personnel was because he thought the British government was taking the attitude that the convoys were a gift to the Soviet Union, an act of favor or charity. That, he said, did not seem to him a true description. Eden denied that the British government had ever regarded the convoy operations in that light. It recognized that they were part of a combined war effort. But it was not willing to be coerced into doing what it thought foolish, and it was not willing to have its men, while engaged in that war effort, oppressed.

In the outcome it was agreed that the convoys would be resumed on the understanding that the British would be free to cancel them if need be. The Soviet government promised to change its treatment of the British personnel a little for the better. So, to foretell, the first convoy in the new series left England in November, before the three heads of government met at Teheran.

Stalin had that coming meeting in mind when he imparted to Hull the news about Soviet military plans which the Americans were most eager to hear.

Harriman, as told, gathered enough from Molotov in the course of the Conference to feel warranted in sending a message to the President forecasting that the Soviet Union would join in the war against Japan after the struggle in Europe was over. At the dinner which Stalin gave on the night of the last day of the Conference (October 30th) he said this in plain words to Hull. They were talking about cooperation and the meeting that Stalin was soon to have with Roosevelt and Churchill, when suddenly Stalin, in Hull's words, "astonished and delighted me by saying clearly and unequivocally that, when the Allies succeeded in defeating Germany, the Soviet Union would then join in defeating Japan," and that he might so inform the President.[30] This was said without any reservations or conditions as to needed military assistance or political rewards.

While Stalin was letting Hull know this, Molotov was telling Harriman and Eden in a flat tone that after dinner a movie would be shown that dealt with Japanese penetration of Siberia in 1921. Eden pretended to be shocked, saying that this did not seem an appropriate picture for a neutral country to be showing. Harriman countered by saying he thought it was fine and appropriate. Then, remarking that he would understand if Molotov did not care to join the toast he was about to propose, Harriman lifted his glass to drink to the day "when we would be fighting together against the Japs." Molotov said, "Why not—gladly—the time will come." Harriman said, "Bottoms up" and they all drank what was left in their glasses.

Hull, Harriman, and Deane did not wait until morning to let Washington know this news. Hull was already glowing over what he thought the Conference had achieved. This brightened the glow. The President and the Joint Chiefs of Staff enthused. They at once began to try to figure out how advance planning with the Russians for this event could be started.

Stalin and his colleagues had, no doubt, reached their decision to enter the Pacific war because they thought it to Soviet advantage. It may also be surmised that by telling the American and British governments of their intention that early, it might gain useful credit with them: perhaps greater certainty that OVERLORD would be carried out in May; perhaps an easier acceptance of its aims in regard to relations with its neighbors in Europe and its frontiers. All this may have been, and probably was, appreciated by the diplomats in Washington and London. But this confidential promise was taken also to be cheerful evidence that while the Soviet government was hard to deal with, it wholly intended to remain within the coalition.

[30] *Memoirs*, page 1309.

PERIOD SIX

The Convocation of the Heads of State at Cairo and Teheran, November 1943; When the Three Wills Came Nearest Concordance

---

25. On to the Cairo and Teheran Conferences, November 1943

THE Conference at Moscow dispersed in a mist of congeniality. The last paragraphs of the American minutes of the final session of the Conference stand as proof of the sense of genuine accord:

"In closing the Conference of the three Foreign Secretaries in Moscow Mr. Molotov expressed warm appreciation of the unfailing cooperation which he had received from the Secretary and Mr. Eden and to which he in large measure attributed the success of the Conference.

"The Secretary said he was sure he was expressing Mr. Eden's sentiments when he said that he had never seen a better example of skill and cooperation than Mr. Molotov had displayed during the Conference. . . .

"Mr. Eden warmly seconded the Secretary's remarks and proposed that at any future meetings of the three Foreign Secretaries Mr. Molotov be selected as permanent Chairman.

"The Conference ended on this note."

So did the dinner in the Kremlin after the close of the Conference. At moments Stalin was jocular—as when he poked fun at Molotov, saying that while he thought his Foreign Secretary was responsible for Chamberlain's actions, he did not think he was entirely responsible. Hull found his host in a most agreeable state of mind no matter what subject was discussed, and noted particularly that he spoke of the need for collaboration in a most favorable way.

The Secretary of State was elated by his belief that the ideal of bringing national states together in collective support of peace and justice—the vision for which Woodrow Wilson had died—was on the way to realization. He regarded Soviet subscription to the Four-Nation Declaration as a fine augury that it would cooperate in making fair and harmonizing peace settlements. Next to these and other signs of Soviet goodwill, the Soviet's stubborn resolve to have final say about relations with its neighbors did not seem to him of great moment. And he was pleased that the Soviet government did not at Moscow bring up the question of postwar frontiers. With undue optimism he thought this postponement to be advantageous; that as relations between the allies deepened into trust, Russia would be less intent on particular frontier lines.

Such impressions shaped Hull's report to the President and to the

American people of the results of the Conference. The address which he made to a joint session of the two Houses of Congress soon after his return remains as memorial to his hopes. An extract will remind how high and far-flung they were: "As the provisions of the Four-Nation Declaration are carried into effect, there will no longer be need for spheres of influence, for alliances, for balance of power, or any other of the special arrangements through which, in the unhappy past, the nations strove to safeguard their security or to promote their interests."

The applause of Congress and comments in the press and radio showed that the American public wanted to believe these affirmations and was prepared to play its part—to accept the burdens and risks of collective action. This was shown by the action of the Senate in approving on November 5th, while Hull was on his way home, the Connally Resolution—overleaping the one which the House of Representatives had passed before Hull left for Moscow. This resolved, "that the United States, acting through its Constitutional processes, join with free and sovereign nations in the establishment and maintenance of international authority with power to prevent aggression and to preserve the peace of the world."

Roosevelt and Churchill, while not being carried away, were much impressed by the outcome of the meeting. The President—without any reference to the item which probably pleased him most, the Soviet promise to enter the Pacific war—described the Conference as "a tremendous success." "When this thing started," he went on, "there were a great many cynics who said 'Oh, they will all agree to disagree,' and 'There will be a lot of suspicion and they won't get anywhere.' But the spirit of the whole Conference has been amazingly good. I think Mr. Hull deserves a great deal of credit for that spirit, and I think the Russians and the British deserve equal credit. It has been—what we called in the old days in the Navy—a 'happy ship.'"

Churchill in a message to Harriman called the results of the Conference "prodigious" and told his audience at the Lord Mayor's Day Luncheon (November 9th) that "We have all been cheered by the results of the Moscow Conference. . . ." and called the Four-Nation Declaration "all-important."

Not everyone in the official circle was as sanguine—for example, Harriman, Bohlen, and other officials in the State Department concerned with Soviet affairs. Harriman, who had had the chance to see and hear all that went on during the days of the Conference, was not sure that anything dependable had been achieved. He felt the Secretary of State, through his sincerity, warmth, and devotion to ideals of international cooperation, had made a genuine mark upon the minds of Stalin and his colleagues, and that as a result their mistrust was lessened and their inclination to try to find joint solutions for problems increased. But he believed that the inclination of the Soviet government to work with us would continue only if it were satisfied with the military actions in the West—since the war was still uppermost in its mind. And he was bothered by possible misunderstanding that might follow the Russian assumption that the 1941 Soviet frontiers had been accepted and it had been granted freedom to settle its relations with its neighbors. Thus in a personal message to Churchill, while bowing before the adjective "prodigious," Harriman went on to add, "We cannot, however, assume too much." He could not help but wonder whether later events might not make Hull's words sound as sad as those which Chamberlain had spoken after his return from Munich.

What Stalin and his associates were saying about the Conference could be taken as confirming both the hopes and the cautions. In his speech on November 6th Stalin referred to the decisions of the Moscow Conference as shining proof that the relations between the Allies, and their fraternity in arms, were growing firmer. The long articles in the Soviet official press were almost radiant. But a talk made by Litvinov to representatives of other United Nations in Moscow, without advance notice to either American or British officials, could be taken to indicate some points which the Soviet government wanted to impress widely: that frontiers had not been discussed; that the Soviet frontiers were untouchable and defended only by the Red Army; that the British and Americans had not objected to the idea of demanding unconditional surrender from the German satellites.[1]

The Moscow Conference having cleared so fine a prospect of co-operation for great ends, Roosevelt looked forward the more eagerly to his meeting with Stalin, and Churchill too. Before starting on the final great move in the war against Germany, consultation for the purpose of concerting military action was becoming essential. Beyond that, the chance beckoned to reach agreement upon questions which the Foreign Ministers had left unsettled, such as Poland, and to carry the alliance in war forward into the peace. Roosevelt had the buoyant notion that he could form a warm personal relation with Stalin of the

[1] This was probably based on the fact that when, on October 25th, Molotov made this assertion, neither Hull nor Eden objected. Harriman, who was present on this occasion, told Litvinov later that his reference to the application of unconditional surrender to Finland might give the impression that Hull had associated the American government with Molotov's statement; and since, as Litvinov knew, this was not so, there might be troublesome repercussions in the United States.

same sort that he had with Churchill, so that he might work with him in the same open and intimate way. He was determined to try—not for power or out of vanity, as has been so often suggested; in some measure out of curiosity and admiration perhaps; but surely and basically because he thought that if peace was to thrive, the Soviet dictator must be brought to know us better and trust us more.

Plans for this meeting of the three Heads of State had been still up in the air when the Foreign Ministers met at Moscow despite the many messages which had passed back and forth about time and place. On October 20th Stalin had sent the President an expanded explanation why he felt he could not go farther than Teheran, to any of the other places proposed by the President and Churchill. All his colleagues agreed that it was imperative that he keep in constant personal contact with Soviet military operations. Besides, he was of the opinion that conditions in Teheran—security, privacy, health, and the like—were better than they would be elsewhere. Roosevelt had been disappointed. As he had explained in his next message to Stalin, a trip to Teheran would expose him and his colleagues to double risk and trouble—the dangers of crossing the mountains twice and the chance of delay in delivery and return of official documents requiring his signature. "Therefore," he had said, "with much regret I must tell you that I cannot go to Teheran and in this my Cabinet members and the legislative leaders are in complete agreement." He had gone on to suggest Basra instead, remarking that if they met there it would mean that he would travel 6,000 miles outside the U.S. while Stalin would only have to travel 600 miles outside Russian territory. But he had added that he would gladly go ten times that distance to meet Stalin if it were consistent with his duties, since he regarded a meeting between the three as of the greatest possible importance not only for the better disposition of immediate matters of common interest but also for a peaceful world for generations to come.

This personal appeal the President had entrusted to Hull as he, in the closing days of the Conference at Moscow, seemed to be attracting Soviet friendliness. The Secretary had taken it himself to Stalin and backed it by a personal plea. Stalin was not to be budged. He had answered that the question was a very hard one and he would have to think about it and consult his colleagues. Molotov had then spoken up to say that every one of the top Soviet officials, civil and military, were of the opinion that Stalin ought not to absent himself while important military operations were on; or, in any event, that he should go only to places where direct and secure daily communications could be maintained.

Stalin had then troubled Hull and Harriman, who was with him, by observing that it might be best to put off the meeting with Roosevelt until the spring of 1944, at which time Fairbanks, Alaska, might be an appropriate place. Hull had not wanted to fail the President. Nor did he want to risk long delay in the advancement of plans for the collective security organization. So he had spoken up against postponement, telling Stalin that both he and the President felt that the meeting was needed in the near future. He said he was afraid that if the three governments waited until the end of the war before formulating the basis for their postwar program, by then unity within and between them would have dissolved. At this time, dominant American opinion was in favor of international cooperation, but a chance remained that—if something went wrong with the war or in relations with other countries—it might reverse itself. Stalin in turn had tried to convince Hull that his refusal to yield to Roosevelt's wish was not due to lack of desire to meet the President or any thought of advantage, but only to proper care for his own responsibilities. Explaining his thought further, he had gone on to say that he thought that the Germans had used up most of their reserves, while the Soviet forces had not, and so there might soon be a chance, which might not come again for fifty years, to inflict a decisive defeat upon them and he did not want to miss it by being out of touch.

Was Stalin finding reasons to make sure that the meeting would take place in circumstances and at a time most favorable to himself? Or, as Harriman thought, and so reported to the President, did he really desire to meet Roosevelt as soon as possible but was deterred only by his intentness on prosecuting the war and the insistent demands of his associates? Who is to know? It was true that because of the way in which the Soviet command system was organized about and under Stalin personally, loss of close contact might have led to difficulties, loss of opportunities or worse in Soviet military operations. As the course of battle on the Eastern Front in November during the conference at Teheran was to show, the situation on the Eastern Front was not wholly secure. But other reasons probably figured in Stalin's willingness to wait; by the next spring he would know whether the Allied armies were going to cross the Channel; by then also, if things went well, the Red Armies would have acquired for the Soviet Union the primary power to influence the future of its neighboring states—one of Stalin's most decided aims.

Meanwhile, Churchill had been growing restless. For, whether or not a meeting with Stalin was arranged, he felt it imperative that he and Roosevelt and their military advisers should meet soon; that before seeing the Russians they should have another thorough talk about the military plans and operations in which their forces were to be mingled—particularly OVERLORD, and the effect of OVERLORD on activities in the Mediterranean. His messages to the President argued that such prior consideration was due and in order since at the start of OVERLORD British forces were to be equal to the American, and twice as strong in Italy and three times as numerous in the rest of the Mediterranean. He was troubled by some features of the joint plans as they stood, and wanted consideration of some corrections. In sum, he had told Roosevelt that he felt very much in the dark and unable to think or act in the forward manner that was needed.

Roosevelt's first response (on the 22nd) to this proposal that plans for OVERLORD be jointly examined again had been equivocal, giving Churchill the impression that there was a strong current of opinion in American circles which seemed to wish to win Russian confidence even at the expense of coordination of the Anglo-American war effort. This interpretation overlooks the complementary reasons why the Americans were not eager to have a preliminary review with the British alone. They could foresee that Churchill would once again urge the extension of operations in Italy, the Adriatic, and the Aegean, even though it meant delay in OVERLORD; and they could be fairly sure that the Russians would stand on their side in this argument.

However, Roosevelt had come about in the message which he sent Churchill a few days later—on the 25th, while Hull in Moscow was trying to persuade Stalin to go to Basra, and failing. He had seemed cheerfully to assent to the idea of a meeting with the British or, at any rate, of going *somewhere* to see *someone* soon. It read, "It is a nuisenza to have the influenza. [Dr.] McIntire says I need a sea voyage. No word from Uncle J. yet. If he is adamant, what would you think of you and me meeting with small staffs in North Africa, or even at the Pyramids, and toward the close of our talks getting the Generalissimo [Chiang Kai-shek] to join us for two or three days? At the same time we could ask Uncle J. to send Molotov to the meeting with you and me. Our people propose November 20." [2]

Two days later on the 27th, having been told in the interval that Stalin would not go beyond Teheran, Roosevelt had tried out still another notion. He had asked Churchill what he thought of suggesting to Stalin that he have someone sit in on the British-American military staff conferences to listen, note, and make proposals. The idea had alarmed Churchill. He had told the President that he thought it would result in intolerable delay in the making of decisions. He had then gone

[2] *Closing the Ring*, page 314.

on to repeat more bluntly than before that he regarded the British and Americans as having the right to meet together and alone to discuss movements of their two forces, a fundamental and a vital right. This was so, but the President and the Joint Chiefs were not sure that they wanted to use that right.

At this juncture the President had definitely decided to fit a conference with Chiang Kai-shek into his program. Thereupon the projects for conferences had gotten twisted up with each other; a conference *a deux* with Churchill, *a trois* with Stalin, *a deux, trois,* or *quatre* with Chiang Kai-shek.

The President was still unreconciled to the choice between seeing Stalin at Teheran or not at all. He had Hull, who was busy sealing up the accords reached at Moscow, try once more to coax Stalin to fly down to Basra and meet with Churchill and himself, if only for a day, and then allow Molotov to remain to continue the discussions. But Stalin, even at the congenial farewell dinner, had also stuck to his answers and his reasons for them.

In his report to the President (sent on the 31st after showing it to Eden before dispatching) Hull had tried to make sure that Stalin's attitude should not be construed to mean that he did not want to co-operate. He urged that the effort to develop a closer military compact should be pursued anyway, and also the work of formulating a postwar program. For, his mind ran, unless the sincerity in both words and actions which Stalin had shown during the Conference was false, which could hardly be believed, he would presently come to the point of meeting with the President and Churchill.

To follow this tangled and touchy tale to the point where assents met: on hearing from Hull, the President decided to go ahead and arrange conferences with Churchill and Chiang Kai-shek anyhow. On October 31st he told Churchill he would meet him in Cairo about November 20th; and he told Chiang Kai-shek to make plans to meet him and Churchill at Cairo about November 25th. Both answered that this schedule was agreeable.

A few days later, Stalin's formal reply to the pleas which Hull had made before leaving Moscow arrived at the White House. This repeated his explanations of why he could not go farther than Teheran and his offer to send Molotov, his Chief Deputy, to meet with the President and Churchill any place they chose.

Whereupon the President gave in. He did so probably because he concluded that he could not achieve his main purposes unless he talked with Stalin himself; possibly also because this message persuaded him that Stalin's reasons were meritorious. He sent back word (on November 8/9) that he would be leaving Washington for Cairo, where he would be joined by Churchill; and he had found that it would be possible for him after all to go on to Teheran. This, he said, greatly pleased him because he thought it vital that he and Churchill should meet with Stalin, if only for two days. Such a meeting of the three would have, he thought, a far-reaching effect on opinion in the three countries and hurt Nazi morale; it would destroy any anticipation Hitler, Goebbels, and the rest had that their enemies would divide. The President's full plan was to have American and British military staffs begin work at Cairo, and thus he told Stalin that he hoped Molotov and —contrary to Churchill's wish—a Soviet military representative might also join them there. Then, he reckoned, the preliminary work having been done, the whole gathering should leave for Teheran on the 26th to meet with Stalin and Soviet military staffs for three days, or as long as Stalin felt he could be away from Moscow. Thereafter he and Churchill and the U.S.-British military staff could return to Cairo and complete their work. Stalin—after a delay due to grippe—agreed to this arrangement and said that Molotov and the Soviet military representative would arrive in Cairo by November 22nd for the talks there.

The Prime Minister had previously said he was willing to go to Teheran, if that was the only place the three could meet. But, as told, through all the turns in arrangements, he had wanted an adequate first chance to get together with the Americans, particularly on military matters. Now he learned that Roosevelt was proposing that the Chinese arrive at Cairo on the 22nd, the very first day that the Combined Chiefs of Staff could get together. Next he learned, indirectly through Harriman and Clark-Kerr (on the evening of November 11th), that Molotov and the Soviet military advisers would also be at hand in Cairo from the start.

Chagrined as he must have been, all that the Prime Minister asked in the message he hastened to send the President was that in order to give the Combined Chiefs an adequate chance to do their work, the appearance at Cairo of Molotov and other Soviet officials be postponed until November 25th at the earliest. The President passed over Churchill's anxieties lightly. He told Churchill (on the 12th) that he had just received a conclusive answer from Stalin, saying he would go to Teheran:

"His latest message has clinched the matter, and I think that now there is no question that you and I can meet him there between the 27th and the 30th. Thus endeth a very difficult situation, and I think we can be happy. In regard to Cairo, I have held all along, as I know you have, that it would be a terrible mistake if Uncle J. thought we had ganged up on him on military action. . . . It will not hurt you or me if Molotov and a Russian military representative are in Cairo too. They will not feel that they are being given the 'run around.' " [3]

Churchill was not satisfied by this jovial response. He told Roosevelt that arranging the meeting with Stalin was a great step forward. But then he gravely repeated that he still regarded it as essential that the British and American staffs should have "many meetings" before being joined by the Russians and the Chinese; and that the British government could not abandon its right to full and frank discussion with the President and American military/officers about the vital business of the intermingled armies. So he concluded by saying that while there was no objection to the President and himself talking with Molotov before seeing Stalin, he was convinced that the presence of Soviet military representatives would cause grave embarrassment and trouble.

On this same day (but after this message to Roosevelt was sent) the Prime Minister heard from Stalin that "for certain reasons of a serious character M. Molotov, to my regret, cannot come to Cairo." Roosevelt was similarly advised. It can be guessed with assurance that the reason why Stalin had decided not to send Molotov to Cairo was that he learned—just how is not of record—that the Chinese were going to be there at the same time. But the Soviet government did not want the avoidance of this association to be regarded as significant. Thus when he and Harriman talked about it (on the 16th) Molotov said that he could not have left Moscow anyway at that time—since Stalin's slight illness was throwing so much work upon him. Vishinsky, Molotov's deputy, on his way to Algiers to serve on the Advisory Council for Italy, stopped over at Cairo briefly as an observer.

By the 22nd, Roosevelt, Churchill, and Chiang Kai-shek and their military staffs were all in Cairo. The British and Chinese might or might not get in each other's way. But, still, the President was intent on keeping the schedule, and soon after his arrival he sent word ahead to Stalin that he thought their talks would be over by the end of the week; that he, Churchill, and their staff officers could then go on to Teheran and meet the Soviet group on the afternoon of the 27th, if that suited Stalin's convenience. "I am," he concluded, "looking forward with keen anticipation to our talks."

He was bent on wiping away any impression Stalin might have that the Americans and British were combining in advance—as though it were ever possible to clear that mind of suspicion!

It may be foretold here that the President continued to act in the same

[3] *Ibid.*, pages 318–19.

way while at Teheran. He avoided Churchill's approaches before the Conference opened, and until after his own talks with Stalin were well underway. A simple personal thought may have made his course seem proper. Churchill had spent much time alone with Stalin the year before; now it was his turn to get to know the man, and his best chance was by seeing him without other company. It came about thus that Churchill, perhaps afraid of being unpleasantly surprised, also sought meetings at Teheran with Stalin alone. But the three of them met together each day at the formal Conferences and each night at dinner. And here it may be noted that Roosevelt did not manage to achieve that same pitch of personal geniality with Stalin as Churchill had during one long night of his visit to Moscow in 1942, and never again. Their dealings at Teheran under the friendly surface and admiring words remained basically official and impersonal. But before telling of them, it is in order to stop off with the President and Churchill at Cairo, where Chiang Kai-shek had come to meet them.

26. The First Cairo and Teheran Conferences: Far Eastern Matters

The President had urgent business with Chiang Kai-shek. The situation in China had been growing poorer in every respect. The country was cut off from the outside world except by air over the High Himalayas. Not enough could be brought in over that route even for the most urgent needs of the Chinese armies and the American combat air force located in China. Chiang Kai-shek and the Chinese government felt much neglected. They complained, and not without reason, that despite their resistance to Japan and the suffering endured, they were promised less aid than any other member of the coalition against the Axis; and that what they actually got was always less than what was promised.

Their military leadership was timid, intriguing, and given over to the thought that without much greater help no offensive operations against the Japanese, either in China or in Burma, should be taken. This attitude, in turn, had caused General Stilwell (who was in command of American forces in the China-Burma-India Theater, and assigned as Chief of Staff to Chiang Kai-shek) and General Marshall to conclude that neither the Chinese government nor Chinese military organization were taking their due share in the war effort.

The economic condition of the people of China was also bad—inflation was running wild—and the supplies of essentials scarce and badly distributed. Corruption was thought to be spreading deeper and farther within the Chinese government. Its measures against opponents and critics—not only Communists but moderate reformist groups—were becoming more harsh. Almost all American officials in China, civilian and military, were reporting that the government was losing popular support.

Out of these strained circumstances there came into existence a fear that the Chungking government might fall out of the war—either because it was not able to carry on any longer, or because it yielded to defeatism, or because of resentment at being left out in the cold. Thus, ever since the summer, the President had felt the need for a personal meeting with Chiang Kai-shek to explain global strategy to which China's needs were being subordinated, to improve Chinese morale, and to plan military operations which could bring relief to China.

When Roosevelt invited Chiang Kai-shek to meet with him and Churchill at Cairo, the Generalissimo had replied that he would gladly do so provided he could see them before they saw Stalin. If that were not possible, he had said, he would prefer to wait until another time. Roosevelt had contrived that the Generalissimo should have the chance to enjoy the first say.

Churchill and the British Chiefs of Staff were unhappy at the President's action in having the Chinese come to Cairo before they had had adequate opportunity for consultation with the Americans. They were afraid that Roosevelt, with what they thought an excessive notion of the part that China would play in the war and peace, might enter into unwarranted engagements with Chiang Kai-shek; that he might give promises that would upset their plans for Europe.

But the President was not deterred. While the American and British military staffs were conferring, Roosevelt immersed himself in talks with the Chinese—to Churchill's annoyance. An echo of his baffled wishes can be heard in what he later wrote about the Conference:

"The talks of the British and American Staffs were sadly distracted by the Chinese story, which was lengthy, complicated and minor. Moreover . . . the President, who took an exaggerated view of the Indian-Chinese sphere, was soon closeted in long conference with the Generalissimo. All hope of persuading Chiang and his wife to go and see the Pyramids and enjoy themselves till we returned from Teheran fell to the ground, with the result that Chinese business occupied first instead of last place at Cairo." [4]

In the course of the talks with Chiang Kai-shek decisions of great moment were reached. These concerned, first, plans for prospective military operations in the China-Burma-India Theater; and, second, the disposition of the Japanese Empire after defeat. Regrettably, as far as is known, no complete or orderly American record of these consequential talks with the Chinese exist, and the historian must rely on secondary sources.

The Americans brought projects for clearing the land route from India through Burma into China, and for driving the Japanese out of Burma. About this program there had been a sharp division in American military circles. The American General in charge of air operations in China, Chennault, was dead against a land campaign in Burma. But Stilwell was fiercely for some such operation. He thought it essential to build up Chinese armed strength and the best way, in fact the only practical way, to employ China's human combat resources. The War Department agreed with him; they had another reason, a wish to use China as an air base for long-range bombing of Japan.

The Chinese also brought several inchoate plans which had been hastily mapped out on the plane while coming from Chungking. In their presentation to the American military staff these got bunched together in a way that displeased skilled and orderly minds, and were judged unusable.

The British, who would have had to provide substantial forces for a ground campaign in Burma, were skeptical as to both the sense and the success of this strategy. Churchill viewed it as an error born of our obsession with China. Victory in Burma, he thought, would be merely the right to fight on longer and harder in swamps and jungles that later would fall to the winner anyhow. Even if the campaign succeeded, he reckoned that the land route to China would become available too late to be of any real importance in the war; and, anyway, he did not attach much value to the possible Chinese contribution in winning the war against Japan. His judgment and inclination led him toward a wholly different course in the Southwest Pacific; toward regaining Singapore, Sumatra, and possibly Hong Kong, thereby—along with what MacArthur's advancing forces and the American Navy were doing in the Central Pacific—destroying the Japanese lines of communication and closing in on Japan from sea and air.

[4] *Ibid.*, page 328.

But, despite the hindrances to a clear and firm accord with the Chinese, and despite British reserve, a plan to drive the Japanese out of Burma and open the Burma Road was adopted. Or at least so it seemed. The President and Chiang Kai-shek agreed that the means ought to be provided for a determined ground offensive in North Burma by Chinese, British, and American troops. This offensive was to be coordinated with amphibious operations south of Burma (Operation BUCCANEER: an attack on the Andaman Islands), safeguarded by the British Navy in the Indian Ocean. Upon this Chiang Kai-shek had insisted with marked emphasis, averring at the First Plenary Meeting that "the success of the operation in Burma depended in his opinion, not only on the strength of the naval forces established in the Indian Ocean, but on the simultaneous co-ordination of naval action with the land operations." [5] The ground campaign was also to be supported by an air operation to prevent Japanese movement of troops and supplies.

But Churchill obstinately refused to promise that British forces would carry out any amphibious operations south of Burma or in South Burma at a fixed date. He disputed Chiang Kai-shek's idea that this was essential to winning the land campaign in North Burma. The President went along with Chiang Kai-shek's contrary opinion—which was that the Japanese were strong in Burma; that they would fight very hard to keep it; and that the land campaign would be too dangerous unless the Japanese were prevented from sending in troops and supplies through South Burma ports or over from Thailand, and were engaged on two fronts. Churchill has recorded his act of dissent: "The President, in spite of my arguments, gave the Chinese the promise of a considerable amphibious operation across the Bay of Bengal within the next few months. . . . On November 29, I wrote to the [British] Chiefs of Staff: 'The Prime Minister wishes to put on record the fact that he specifically refused the Generalissimo's request that we should undertake an amphibious operation simultaneously with the land operations in Burma.' " [6]

The argument over this project was so stubbornly sustained because it bore directly upon the question of what operations could be undertaken in Europe during the next six months; or so it was thought. The amphibious tasks near or in South Burma would have required naval forces, cargo ships, air strength, and possibly even land divisions for which other commanders in other theaters had other uses. But the contest centered on the scarcity of landing and tank-landing craft. Of

[5] *Grand Strategy,* Volume v, page 163.
[6] *Closing the Ring,* page 328.

these—to state the issue tersely at the expense of details—the more for Burma, the fewer for Italy and the Aegean, and that is where Churchill wanted to have them.[7]

When the President and Prime Minister and their military staffs flew off to Teheran, this unadjusted difference hung between them—and the President was involved in a promise to Chiang Kai-shek. The difference still remained unadjusted when, after their talks with Stalin, they returned to Cairo. But by then Churchill had new and telling reasons why the employment of amphibious craft and forces to Burma at this time was not justified. At Teheran it had been decided not only to start the invasion in the coming May but also to make a landing in Southern France at the same time. This increased the prospective need for landing craft and made it necessary at least to hoard all that were in Europe. Furthermore, Stalin had reaffirmed his secret assurances that the Soviet Union would enter the war against Japan. In view of this, the Prime Minister contended it could no longer be deemed essential to hurry to open a land route through Burma into China.

Roosevelt could not deny the bearing of these reasons, but he was much distressed at the idea that the *whole* plan for Burma on which he had agreed with Chiang Kai-shek might be upset; and that possibly the Generalissimo might be so hurt and discouraged that China might virtually stop fighting. But he felt compelled to give in. For, unless the British would assign the naval and landing forces needed for the operation, it was out of the question; and any stronger effort to induce or compel them to do so might have caused a deep division affecting the greater joint program that was worked out in Teheran. That, as the President explained to his disconsolate military advisers, would be ruinous.

[7] The British Chiefs of Staff got the impression, whether justified or not, that the U.S. Joint Chiefs of Staff were willing to agree to postpone the start of OVERLORD to July 1 if necessary to undertake the amphibious operation south of Burma, while leaving desired minimum of assault shipping for Italy and the Aegean. As recounted in *Grand Strategy*, Volume v, page 167, at the meeting of the Combined Chiefs of Staff on November 25th "General Brooke explained that the operation in south-east Asia could be carried out provided that 'Overlord, was postponed; and General Mashall said he quite understood this point. But he reiterated that in his opinion 'Buccaneer' was essential, and when the British raised the possibility that it might be postponed, the Americans revealed the President's personal interest in the operation. As Ismay reported to the Prime Minister, the American Chiefs of Staff seemed to accept the postponement of 'Overlord' with equanimity, but not of 'Buccaneer'; and it was therefore left at this, that if further discussions led the British Chiefs of Staff to view that our proper strategy was to do 'Overlord' as quickly as possible and either to postpone or to abandon 'Buccaneer' they would have to take it up with the Prime Minister and request him to raise it on the highest level. On the eve of the Teheran Conference, the position seemed to be that the Americans (given the appropriate Russian pressure) might accept the British strategy for Europe, if the British would accept the Americans' strategy for south-east Asia."

So at the last he sent word to Churchill, "BUCCANEER [the amphibious operation against the Andaman Islands south of Burma] is off." Churchill in passing on this news to Ismay quoted, "He is a better man that ruleth his spirit than he that taketh a city." [8] He knew how hard it was for the President to reverse himself, and that General Marshall would be sharply disappointed and General Stilwell resentful. About Chiang Kai-shek's reaction he was not much concerned—perhaps not as much as he ought wisely to have been, since the Generalissimo felt China had once again been badly treated—and relieved of obligation to take special risks and burdens to drive the Japanese out of Burma.

However, Chiang Kai-shek's pleas for an expansion of the air route between China and the outside world were in contrast given high consideration. As a result of decisions of the Combined Chiefs of Staff, a very substantial increase was made in the resources devoted to the flights over the Hump—of bombing and transport planes, service, ground, and air forces. These were not easily spared and perhaps not fully appreciated. An entry which Secretary of War Stimson made in a memo a year later (October 3rd, 1944) denotes how much they seemed to him to cost: "The amount of effort which we have put into the 'Over the Hump' airline has been bleeding us white in transport airplanes—it has consumed so many. Today we are hamstrung in Holland and the mouth of the Scheldt River for lack of transport planes. . . . The same lack is crippling us in northern Italy. This effort over the mountains of Burma bids fair to cost us an extra winter in the main theater of the war." [9]

For whatever disappointment Chiang Kai-shek suffered at Cairo over the treatment of his requests for military aid, other decisions made there and confirmed at Teheran offered great consolation and promised China great gain after victory.

While at Cairo, Roosevelt, Chiang Kai-shek, and Churchill agreed upon a declaration of vast scope. Of the history of its sponsorship and authorship much is still to be learned. But what is known shows it to have been an American initiative, scrutinized by the British, welcomed by the Chinese, and tacitly approved by the Russians.

Many of the Far Eastern questions which awaited disposition (Manchuria, Korea, Formosa, Indo-China, and the Japanese islands in the Pacific, including the Kuriles) had been casually reviewed on October 5th at a talk which Hull and his State Department staff had with the President, before the Secretary left for the Moscow Conference. But

[8] *Closing the Ring,* page 412.
[9] *On Active Service in Peace and War,* page 538.

no attempt had been made to coagulate the loose ideas in the flow of talk either on this occasion or in any later discussion in this field which Roosevelt may have had with the State Department. No memo or any other kind of record has yet been found which tells with whom, if anyone, he may have consulted about these matters before leaving for Cairo or Teheran; or which informs whether the idea of issuing a statement about them was an improvisation at Cairo or whether it was conceived in the White House before he departed.

In any case, though still opposed to all attempts to dispose of European territorial issues, at Cairo the Americans had no qualms about settling those which loomed in the Far East. They took the lead at Cairo in proposing some form of statement which would simultaneously (1) forestall any impulse to bring about a peace with Japan which would allow it to retain the means to resume its efforts to dominate Asia (2) gratify Chinese desires and thus invigorate its combat effort. It was decided to state these intentions in a declaration to be embodied in the public communiqué to be given out right after the conference with the Chinese. This was composed in haste and without known further communication between the statesmen at Cairo and their Foreign Offices in Washington and London. The first draft found in the American files was either dictated by Hopkins (probably in bed with maps on the floor beside him) or revised by his hand.[10] The President looked it over, adopting most of Hopkins' suggestions. Churchill also examined it with care, touching up its language. Whether or not it was informally discussed with Chiang Kai-shek also is not of record, but probably so.

One momentous paragraph of the Declaration as issued meant the complete dissolution of the Japanese Empire. This read:

"The Three Great Allies are fighting this war to restrain and punish the aggression of Japan. They covet no gain for themselves and have no thought of territorial expansion. It is their purpose that Japan shall be stripped of all the islands in the Pacific which she has seized or occupied since the beginning of the first World War in 1914, and that all the territories Japan has stolen from the Chinese, such as Manchuria, Formosa, and the Pescadores, shall be restored to the Republic of China. Japan will also be expelled from all other territories which she has taken by violence and greed. The aforesaid three great powers, mindful of the enslavement of the people of Korea, are determined that in due course Korea shall become free and independent." [11]

[10] Dated November 24th, the day after the first formal meeting with Chiang Kai-shek.
[11] Statement on Conference of President Roosevelt, Generalissimo Chiang Kai-shek, and Prime Minister Churchill, Cairo, December 1, 1943. The statement made no reference to the Soviet Union or to the fact that the Soviet government had been, as will be told, consulted before it was issued.

The needs of war and the spirit of retribution were being given their way. No one present at Cairo seems to have urged that these matters had best not be settled until it was possible to know more of what China might look like at the end of the war, and of how the Soviet Union would be behaving. Nor does anyone seem to have asked consideration for the plight in which the people of Japan would be left on their four small and rocky islands.

In October China had been accepted as one of the original signatories of the Four-Nation Declaration. At Cairo and Teheran China was being assigned a place on the Executive Council (then spoken of as the Four Policemen) of the international security organization-to-be. By the Cairo Declaration, reducing Japan to a small insular state and allocating much of its empire to China, it was being granted a much enlarged base of power—for good or bad.

In sum, at Cairo and Teheran, China was deeded vast areas, great potential influence, and top responsibilities. This was done, the record indicates, because it was deemed morally fair, and because it was thought to be helpful in the war. But this attitude and purpose might not have eventuated in these conclusive decisions so easily and so early in the war had it not been for the hold which two general beliefs had on the American official mind. One was that the Chinese people had the latent qualities to become a great nation, and would, in recognition of the chance being conferred upon them, prove to be reliable and friendly partners of the West. The other was that China would have a sufficiently unified and capable government to control and properly administer its greater domains. On these Roosevelt and Churchill and their advisers, civil and military, risked the whole future of the Far East, and the position and security of their countries in the Far East.

Toward the second, American policy then and thereafter yielded to wishful thinking. Not long before the meeting at Cairo, the American government had stepped in to avert an impulse within the Chinese National Government to try once again to eliminate their Chinese Communist opposition by force. Chiang Kai-shek had pledged himself to deal with this quarrel only by peaceful means. Concurrently, the American government made a more and more active effort to try to bring about such a peaceful adjustment. But no solution had come into sight.

Stalin had stayed away from Cairo, and had kept Molotov away, because he did not want the Soviet government to be associated with the Chinese government in a conference. Anyhow, Roosevelt and Churchill agreed that Stalin ought to be told of the Declaration before it was given out to the world. Soon after their arrival at Teheran, Harriman and Clark-Kerr bore a copy to Molotov for comment by Stalin. Within hours (this was November 28th) Molotov sent back word that Stalin was pleased at having been consulted but that he had "no observations at all to make. . . ."

When two days later Roosevelt and Churchill lunched with Stalin, they tried to find out more of his thoughts about future settlements in the Far East. Japan, it had been agreed, would have to give up all its external territories. Some—Manchuria, Formosa, and the Pescadores—were being awarded to China. But the rest—the islands south and north of Japan, including the Kurile Islands (the southernmost one of which is but a few miles away from the northernmost of the Japanese home islands) and Sakhalin—would fall to someone else. Would the Soviet government claim these—and perhaps more besides?

The occasion must have seemed conducive to considerate talk of their national aspirations after victory. For the American and British Staffs had just agreed upon a combined strategic program for Europe and the Pacific (about which more later); they had told Stalin of this program; and Stalin had shown himself to be greatly satisfied with it. He had reaffirmed that the Soviet government would enter the war against Japan as soon as Germany was defeated. Both Roosevelt and Churchill had been glad to hear that again.

Churchill opened the area of discussion by asking Stalin whether he had read the Cairo communiqué. Stalin answered that, although he could make no commitments, he thoroughly approved of it and of all its contents.[12] He then went on to say that he thought it right that Korea should be independent, and that Manchuria and Formosa and the Pescadores Islands should be returned to China. But, he added, the Chinese must be made to fight harder—they had not yet really done so.

Then, after some discussion of China's great size, the talk circled about the question of arranging to provide the Soviet Union with better access to warm-water ports on its various sea frontiers. Churchill said that he thought that such a huge land mass as Russia should have satisfactory access to such ports; and that he thought this could be settled at the peace conference, agreeably as among friends. Stalin answered that the question could be discussed at the proper time. But, he hastened to go on, since Churchill had raised it, he would like to inquire about the regime of the Dardanelles; as England no longer objected, would it not be well to relax that system of regulation? Banter followed about the historic British-Russian rivalry and conflict in this section of the

[12] As recorded in the memo made by Bohlen of this talk. Another American memo of the same talk, however, does not include the phrase "although he could make no commitments."

Levant. The President ended it by turning attention toward the approaches to the Baltic Sea which he had already discussed with Stalin; and he went on to develop a scheme of forming a "free zone" of the old Hanseatic cities, with the Kiel Canal under international control. Stalin said he thought that would be a fine idea.

Then he swung farther around the compass by asking, "What could be done for Russia in the Far East?" Churchill said that he would be interested to know what the Soviet government had in mind. Stalin answered that it might be better to wait until Russia was taking an active part in the Far Eastern war before telling. But, he added, the Soviet government did not have a good all-year-round open port in the Far East; Vladivostok was only partly ice-free, and, besides, it was covered by the Straits of Tsushima, which the Japanese controlled. The President thereupon observed that perhaps the Soviet needs in this area could be met in the same way that he had already suggested in connection with its wish for a better outlet in the Baltic—that is, by establishing a free port. He mentioned Dairen as a possibility. Stalin remarked that he did not think China would like such an arrangement. Roosevelt answered that he thought that they would like it if the free port was under an international guarantee. Stalin said then that would not be bad.

The available records of this luncheon discussion on the 30th may omit parts of what was said. Or, Roosevelt and Stalin may have also talked about these Far Eastern questions in one of the three private chats they had at Teheran (on November 28th, 29th, and December 1st). For soon after his return to Washington, Roosevelt, in telling the Pacific War Council of the points on which he had found understanding at Cairo and Teheran, was more definite. He recounted that (1) Russia, having no ice-free port in the Far East, wanted one; and that Stalin looked with favor on making Dairen a free port for all the world, with the idea that Russian trade could move over the Manchurian railways and through this port in bond. (2) Stalin had agreed that the Manchurian railways should become the property of the Chinese government. (3) Stalin wanted all of the other half of the Island of Sakhalin and all the Kurile Islands for Russia.

This report ought to come to mind recurrently as the narrative proceeds. For it indicates to what an extent matters that are generally thought to have been decided at Yalta in February 1945 were foreshadowed at Teheran more than a year before. Stalin, at any rate, so alleged later in connection with the rewards that he claimed as conditions for entering the Pacific War. As relayed by Harriman to the President (on December 15, 1944), "He [Stalin] said the only consideration he had not mentioned at Teheran was the recognition of the status quo in Outer Mongolia. . . ."

It will be seen presently how Stalin's claims upon the Manchurian ports and railways later took a drastically different turn from any touched on at Teheran. But in the form presented there, none of the Soviet territorial wishes disturbed the President. He told the Pacific War Council, in sum, that he had been gratified to find that both Stalin and Chiang Kai-shek saw eye to eye with him on all the major problems of the Pacific. Therefore he felt it would not be hard to reach agreement about the control of the Pacific after the defeat of Japan. With this view of the prospect, it is natural that the American government should not have thought it necessary to adjust its military plans for the Far East so as to gain first entry into territories about whose future there might be argument.

The projects for which the Joint Chiefs of Staff were eager to get Russian cooperation started were entirely based on military objectives. At their request Roosevelt gave Stalin two memos on the Far East.

One of these concerned prospective air operations against Japan. This memo stated that it would be of the utmost importance when the Soviet Union entered the war to bomb Japan from the Soviet Maritime Provinces. The American aim was to use the greatest bombing force possible from that area—up to 1,000 "heavy" bombers. Bases would be needed for their maintenance and operation. Therefore it was requested that planning be begun at once to accommodate this large American force in the Maritime Provinces.

The other paper suggested similar advance planning for naval cooperation in the Northwest Pacific. It asked whether, since the Soviet Far Eastern ports might be threatened by land or air, the Soviet government wished an expansion of the American base facilities to accommodate the Soviet submarine and destroyer forces. It inquired also what help the Soviet government could give if the Americans attacked the northern Kurile Islands. And it requested the Soviet government to indicate what ports in the Maritime Provinces, if any, the American naval and cargo ships might use.

Stalin shunted off these proposals for air and naval cooperation in the Pacific Northwest. He told Roosevelt that he had not had time to consider them and would discuss them later with Harriman. His answers indicated that he thought it was premature even to discuss such projects with the Americans lest, despite the promise of complete secrecy, the Japanese might learn about it. Then it is probable that even at first glance he did not like certain features of the American plans. It was to become evident that the Soviet government did not want large contingents of American air and naval forces living in and operating from any part of its Far Eastern territory. Beyond that, it may be wondered whether Stalin and Molotov thought that the presence of strong American operational forces in this region might stand in the way of certain Soviet territorial claims in the Northwest Pacific upon which their minds were already set.

On the whole Roosevelt and his advisers left Teheran with a cheerful impression of Soviet attitudes and intentions toward the Chinese National Government. The relations between the two had become distant, almost inimical. But Stalin had subscribed without reserve to the Cairo Declaration which was sure to bring credit to the Kuomintang regime. He had spoken no word of favor for the Chinese Communist opponents of the government. He had had nothing but warm praise for what the Americans told him of their plans to equip the Chinese government armies, to try to effect political unity and reform, and to bring economic help to the Chinese people.

In fact, at this time our current strain over the Far East seemed to be with the British rather than with the Russians. Churchill and his advisers were, as told, against the use of substantial armed forces in Burma. They would not engage in amphibious operations south of Burma. They seemed more eager to clear the Japanese out of the Southwest Pacific than to free China. They seemed to think that even if aided, the Chinese would contribute little to the winning of the war. They were skeptical as to whether the future China would have either the strength or self-restraint to be a good partner in the Pacific. These ideas and attitudes were construed, at least by Hopkins and some members of the Joint Chiefs and State Department, to mean that the British were more interested in preserving their Empire than in bringing the war to the quickest possible end.

27. Teheran and Second Cairo Conferences: Military Matters

As the three heads of government got together for the first time at Teheran in November, the great struggle in Europe was moving toward its climax. They were aware that to finish it, concerted assaults from west and east would be needed, yet victory was clearly glimpsed ahead of the tanks and planes and plodding soldiers. But over the same horizon grim possibilities were discerned of civil wars, social disorder, dissolution of empires, quarrels over frontiers. In this setting of circumstance the discussion at Teheran about European affairs spread over three main areas. They were (1) the plans for concerted strategy against Germany, (2) the growing list of unsettled political situations to be faced, (3) the conception of the future international security organization. Each of these conjoined the others. There was no sharp separation between them either in thought or in the flow of decision. But just as in negotiation they could be taken up only one by one, so in narration. First, in this section, military matters.

At Moscow, a few weeks before, after hearing the U.S.-British statement of intentions about the cross-Channel operation, Stalin and his advisers had seemed to lose suspicion and to have gained appreciation of what the Allies were doing in the meanwhile to engage German strength. However, soon thereafter the Russians had been extremely hard-pressed on one large segment of the front, southwest of Kiev. The Germans were desperately trying to restore the balance, in part by moving divisions from Italy and the Balkans to the Eastern Front. This had revived dissatisfaction among the Soviet leaders, and complaints began to reappear in their notes to the British and American governments during this interval.[13] Yet these had been constrained as compared with the sort of communication which Stalin and Molotov had sent the summer before.

The Americans and British were still arguing among themselves about the best strategic course to be discussed with the Russians. The

---

[13] Especially a note from Molotov to Harriman of November 6th. The answer to this message was delayed probably because the President was at sea on his way to Cairo. When in the interval, on November 16th, Harriman called on Molotov to explain a related matter to him, Molotov referred to the fact that General Antonov, Deputy Chief of Soviet Staff, had, since their talk on November 6th, given General Deane information to the effect that seven German tank divisions and six German infantry divisions had recently been transferred to the Soviet Front—from France, Molotov emphasized, not from Italy. Whether this was meant to be a correction of what he had told Harriman on November 6th, or whether he was referring to additional German troop movements, is unclear. Harriman said he would inform Washington at once.

The War Department had sent Harriman material for answering the Soviet imputation that the Allies were failing to do everything they could to prevent the transfer of German forces to the east. It was of the opinion that British estimates of German strength in the Italian-Balkan war areas were roughly correct, and had gone on to state that, anyhow, Eisenhower was being authorized to keep temporarily in the Mediterranean some landing craft that were to have been sent soon to Great Britain for OVERLORD; and that this should make it possible to step up operations in Italy.

mood in which the two staff groups set off for their rendezvous at Cairo-Teheran has been described by General Frederick E. Morgan, Chief Staff Officer to the Supreme Commander (Designate), and in charge of the preliminary planning for the cross-Channel operation: "Just before I had left Washington I had seen the U.S. Chiefs of Staff take off for Conference Sextant at Cairo and Teheran. They had left muttering imprecations about the adjectival British and their perfidy particularly in relation to their Mediterranean ambitions. I had reached London in time to see the British Chiefs of Staff before they set off equally pugnacious and determined to put the Americans straight once and for all over this strategy business." [14]

Churchill, in harmony with his staff, still longed to grasp the chances they thought were now open. His ideas, as exposed in the preliminary talks at Cairo, meant only one thing to the U.S. Chiefs of Staff—that the Prime Minister was resuming his advocacy of strategic diversion into Southeastern Europe, away from the Channel shores. Their opposition may have caused him to adjust the presentation he made at Teheran, but did not down him.

The three renowned travelers stated their views in their first talks at Teheran. In this briefing of their statements I shall be trying to traverse rather than cling to the sequence of their remarks.

Of the three, Roosevelt alone kept maps of the concurrent Pacific operations on the table while they talked about the war in Europe. He dwelt on the size of the American forces engaged in the Pacific—over a million men and most of the American Navy. He traced the progressive results of our efforts. He explained the plans of campaign for the Far East on which, as he put it, the Americans and British had agreed at Cairo. The unsettled difference between himself and Churchill over the scope of the actions to recapture Burma was not reviewed with Stalin.

Having thus protected the large American operations in the Pacific, the President then went on to affirm that he thought Europe still the first and most important theater of war. He assured Stalin that all the many talks between himself and Churchill had revolved around the question of how best to lessen the pressure on the Soviet armies; and he traced how this wish had eventuated in the plan that had been adopted at Quebec in August for an immense cross-Channel invasion to start the following May. This remained, he affirmed, the supreme objective, and he was definitely opposed to any other ventures which might delay its start, reduce its force, or imperil its outcome.

Churchill avowed and avowed again his devotion to the decision that

[14] General Frederick E. Morgan, *Overture to Overlord*, page 227.

259

had been made at Quebec to invade France. But his vigorous analysis and proposals totaled to the conclusion that various other promising operations open to the Allies ought not, should not, need not be foregone for the sake of starting OVERLORD at the very beginning of summer. He stressed the need to continue to sap and diffuse German strength in the time remaining before OVERLORD; and he argued that this could be done without either impairing or seriously retarding that project.

Of the various ways of doing this, the ones that danced in and out of his presentations were: (1) to carry the campaign in Italy to the capture of Rome and beyond to a line extending roughly through Pisa and Rimini. (2) A concerted attempt to induce or compel Turkey to enter the war. (3) Either in connection with Turkey's entry or otherwise the capture, by blockade or by landing, of islands in the Aegean. This accomplished, he pointed out again, the way would be open to operate transport lines through the Straits of the Dardanelles and the Black Sea into Russia—a quicker, easier, and larger route of supply than any existing; and if later so decided, a possible entry into the Balkans from the southeast. (4) Small forays across the Adriatic to supply and support the Yugoslav partisan fighters. (5) After the line in Italy was stabilized north of Rome, to make a landing in Southern France. (6) Or instead, at that time, to send an expedition to the head of the Adriatic for the purpose of trying to force a way through the Ljubljana Gap and then on toward Austria and Southeastern Hungary.[15]

[15] Actually Churchill was not the first to bring this last project into the realm of talk between the three Heads of State at Teheran. Perhaps this was because, at Malta en route to Cairo, he had talked it over with Eisenhower, and Eisenhower had expressed the opinion that the operation would be uncertain and sure to require large forces and much time; and he had also said that he knew the President would oppose the use of any U.S. forces in this region, since he thought it was a morass.

This makes it harder to understand how and why it was Roosevelt who broached this plan in the first talk on November 28th. But he apparently had a different line of advance in mind—a landing at the head of the Adriatic to join up with Tito's partisans and then advance northeast into Romania in conjunction with the Soviet advance from Odessa. Sherwood, in *Roosevelt and Hopkins*, page 780, writes that this curious improvisation of the President's ". . . surprised and disturbed Hopkins by mentioning the possibility of an operation across the Adriatic for a drive, aided by Tito's Partisans, northeastward into Romania to effect a junction with the Red Army advancing southward from the region of Odessa. Hopkins thereupon scribbled a note to Admiral King: 'Who's promoting that Adriatic business that the President continually returns to?' To which King replied, 'As far as I know it is his own idea.' Certainly nothing could be further from the plans of the U.S. Chiefs of Staff. Churchill was quick to associate himself with Roosevelt's suggestion, but Stalin asked if the continuation of operations in or from Italy would in any way affect the thirty-five divisions which he understood were earmarked for OVERLORD. Churchill replied at some length that they would not."

When in June 1944, after OVERLORD had begun, the argument over whether or

For this supple program of strategic variations the Prime Minister had good arguments to which he clung fast. The campaign in Italy would engage German forces that otherwise would have to be met either on the Soviet Front or in France. The other operations were the best way to use, rather than keep idle in the interval before OVER-LORD, the Allied forces already in the Mediterranean area, especially in the Middle East. They could garner great military gains by small means, maybe even bringing about the surrender of German satellites—Bulgaria, Romania, and Hungary. They could attract on the Allied side Turkish soldiers and, more effectively the Greek and Yugoslav partisans. Surely, he contended, these possibilities, all within reach, were enough to warrant some flexibility about the starting date for OVER-LORD. Supplementary to such positive arguments, he introduced the contention that these intervening operations were needed to prepare the way for OVERLORD; to create the conditions—most recently stated by General Ismay at the Moscow Conference—which his government had attached to British engagement in the cross-Channel invasion.

Here this account of these military discussions may pause for the briefest of comments on two controversies that have ever since commanded interest concerning Churchill's purposes in the strategy he advocated.

Throughout the talks at Teheran, and in his reminiscent record, the Prime Minister has indignantly maintained that his proposals were not influenced by a wish, or any fragment of a wish, to abandon OVER-LORD or to postpone it indefinitely.[16] Military historians, with greater knowledge and more space for details about the plans proposed and for figures and maps, may be able to arrive at more final deductions about this point than I. But some impressions are evident. Churchill's affirmations may be judged to have been basically sincere. He was faithful to the plan that had been adopted for the cross-Channel operation and did nothing with mere obstructive intent. In fact, one new consideration had emerged to sway his judgment in favor of the invasions: foreknowledge that a new danger to Britain—rockets and guided mis-

_____

not to send an expedition into the Istrian Peninsula was resumed, Churchill reminded Roosevelt of what he had said at Teheran. Roosevelt then explained ". . . that at Teheran he had only contemplated a series of raids in force in Istria if the Germans started a general retirement from the Dodecanese and Greece. But this had not happened yet." Winston S. Churchill, *Triumph and Tragedy*, Boston: Houghton Mifflin Co., 1953, page 66.

[16] See Churchill's rebuttal of these "legends" and the idea that he tried to lure the Americans into a mass invasion of the Balkans in *Closing the Ring*, pp. 254 and 344–346.

siles—would be launched by the Germans from nearby sites in Northeast Europe.[17] Still his intimate talk continued to reveal fear of that crossing of the bar, and a most ardent wish to be sure that it could not turn into a long and awful battle in the trenches. So he was most receptive to every other possible venture which might result in making OVERLORD an easier task; bold in his acceptance of more limited risks and losses that might be thereby incurred; and definitely given to underestimating the combat difficulties and costs and expenditure of time that would have been required for what he wanted to do before OVERLORD.

The other imputation regarding Churchill's strategic proposals is to the effect that they were inspired by a political aim rather than by military estimates. The design commonly attributed to him was to assure that the western forces rather than the Russian would be the liberators and occupants of as much as possible of southern and central Europe—particularly Greece, Yugoslavia, Austria, Hungary, and Czechoslovakia. But the record suggests that this purpose became active only later; that during the period of Moscow-Cairo-Teheran Churchill, like Roosevelt, conceived that the three Allies would be companionable parents of freedom and order in these countries, neither divided in affiliation nor rivals for influence. Certainly at Teheran Churchill gave no hint that his strategic proposals were animated by any purpose other than military. True, in the course of talk, he recognized that operations in the Balkan and Eastern Mediterranean areas would bring local political questions to the fore and might influence political developments. This must have been in his mind when, at that meeting on the 29th in which he made his last long plea for his ideas, he affirmed that the British had "no ambitions" in the Balkans, that all they wanted to do was to nail down the thirty or so German divisions in the area. After saying this, he suggested that perhaps Eden, Molotov, and someone speaking for the President might meet and advise the Conference on the political aspects of such measures. Did "our Soviet Friends and Allies," he asked, for example, see any political difficulties in the course advocated? If so, the British wanted to know, for they were determined to work harmoniously with them. Stalin abruptly rejected the suggestion, saying merely that he saw no need for any such political subcommittee. The President said nothing one way or the other.

[17] Before October 1943, the British had reliable knowledge that special structures for this purpose were being built in Northern France. On October 25th Churchill had informed Roosevelt, "There are at least seven such points in the Pas de Calais and the Cherbourg peninsula, and there may be a good many others which we have not detected." *Ibid.*, page 237.

After these scanty conjectures about the inspiration of Churchill's strategic ideas, the narrative must revert to the discussion that went on at Teheran. Neither Roosevelt nor Stalin nor their military advisers tried to dispose of Churchill's arguments point by point. Of the two, Churchill thought the Russians the less resistant. He has recorded that impression in his reminiscences. "I could have gained Stalin, but the President was oppressed by the prejudices of his military advisers and drifted to and fro in the argument. . . ." [18] That is a legitimate description of Roosevelt's treatment of the Prime Minister's proposals.

Stalin saw no need to play upon American-British differences, and he did not do so particularly. He expressed warm appreciation of the American and British war effort in the Pacific, en route to his main object. That was the same as ever—to get the greatest relief in the fight against the Germans on the Soviet Front in Europe. For that, he said that he and his military advisers both thought that the planned operation in Northern France was still the best. To the Allied actions in Italy he granted real but only confined value; the Alps would always bar the way to Germany where decisive victory lay. He did not directly discuss a possible entry by British-American forces into the Balkans from the Adriatic side. He agreed that it would be helpful if Turkey entered the war at once, thus opening the way to the Balkans from the east. This he thought would be a better point of entry than Italy, but also a long way from the heart of Germany. In sum, from the Russian point of view none of these operations, not even the capture of Rome, was really important.

But OVERLORD was major. So he advocated that no other operation should be allowed to reduce the strength of an Anglo-American attack through Northwestern France and a supplementary move through Southern France. As for Churchill's point that the months between the expected capture of Rome and the start of OVERLORD should not be wasted, and English and American troops ought not to remain idle for that period, Stalin proposed then that the invasion of Southern France should be undertaken some two months *before* OVERLORD.

Thus his conclusion was that whatever other operations might or might not be tried, while they were together they should settle the essentials of OVERLORD: fix a definite date, select its commander, and agree to effect a landing in Southern France before or about the same time. The great inducement that Stalin could and did hold out to have these decisions made then and there was that it would enable the Soviet government to plan great simultaneous assaults on the Eastern Front.

[18] *Ibid.,* page 346.

Thus the Americans and British could be sure that the Germans would not be able to enlarge their forces in France while the invasion was underway.

Whether or not the long exchanges of ideas produced a real coincidence of judgment, they did end in a cheerful compromise. On November 30th, the British and American military staffs agreed on a joint strategic program. This Roosevelt and Churchill quickly approved. The two main points first stated were: that OVERLORD was to be launched during May 1944; and that there was to be a supporting operation in Southern France on as large a scale as possible, dependent on the number of landing craft available.

When Stalin was told of this, he said he was content. The Red Army, he continued, would undertake offensive operations at the same time and would demonstrate by its actions the importance it placed on this decision. His flat statement of intention was highly valued by the American military commanders, and hardly less so by their British associates. Both counted upon it in their planning for OVERLORD and in their final decision, as the date neared, to go through with the operation. And—to surge ahead with a notation about the future event—then when this promise was kept and the Soviet armies did start their great offensives roughly on schedule, and did keep all the German forces in the east engaged, the Western military commanders were not only appreciative but impressed. They—and their numbers included the Supreme Commander of OVERLORD, General Eisenhower—were convinced of the reliability of Stalin's word, so firmly convinced that the belief stood much abrasion before it crumbled.

At the same meeting on the 30th the President also expressed his great satisfaction that agreement had been reached on so sound a program. Churchill rose with his usual resiliency. In resonant words he said that now that the decision had been taken he felt that OVERLORD should be delivered with smashing force. He emphasized the need for close and continuous contact with Stalin and the Soviet General Staff so that ". . . all parts of the narrowing circle shall be aflame with battle."

There was consolation for the Prime Minister in the fact that the program adopted did not entirely foreclose any of the other operations on which his heart was set. It was agreed that the campaign in Italy should be carried forward; and that another effort should be made to bring Turkey into the war; and that help should be extended to the Yugoslav partisans. Marked success in any of these ventures might still open better routes toward the defeat of the Germans than through Southern France. Churchill was counting on the expansibility of U.S.-

British production and manpower. For, as he said in his closing remarks, he could not believe that the great resources of the United States and Great Britain could not make available what was needed "for all our needs." Strategic dogma, not basic scarcity, he probably thought the real obstacle to his ideas.

Upon their return to Cairo, the Americans and British completed their combined program of action, taking various executory decisions in behalf of a prompt and great OVERLORD and landing in Southern France. Of the gist of these, Roosevelt and Churchill told Stalin in a joint message on December 8th.

The discussions at Teheran about the relations of Turkey, Iran, and Finland to the war were supplementary to these main decisions, but important enough to be reported separately.

It will be recalled that at the Moscow Conference the British and Russians had agreed to demand military facilities of Turkey at once, and to follow this up by pressure to have it enter the war before the end of 1943; and that subsequently Roosevelt had consented to join in this dual effort. Molotov and Eden had been formally notified to this effect by Harriman on the 10th of November.

But by this time (November 11th–12th) the chances of gaining Turkish cooperation were known to be adverse. Eden's mission to Cairo had failed. The Turkish Foreign Minister had refused to allow British forces to use air bases and other facilities in Turkey—being afraid that these half-measures would cause the Germans to retaliate on Constantinople and Ankara. And he also had turned definitely away from the whole measure to have Turkey enter the war. The Turkish government was still too beset by coinciding fears. One was of German ability to damage the country. The other was that Turkey later on would not be strong enough to resist possible Soviet claims; of which the Foreign Minister had two in particular in mind—the absorption of Dobruja as a Soviet province, thus giving Turkey a common border with Russia in the north, and demands for control over the Dardanelles Straits.

There the matter rested until the three Heads of Government reviewed the situation at their meeting in Teheran. By then Churchill turned out to be the most eager advocate of having Turkey come into the war. His talk spread a golden glow around the enterprise, making it seem not only attractive but thrifty as well. For, he kept drilling on the point, if the Allied forces then in the area were not used in the Eastern Mediterranean and Aegean soon, what Germans could they fight in the interval? Only one division, or at most two or three, he estimated, would be required, and some squadrons of fighter planes and antiaircraft regiments; and all of these were already nearby. As for the landing craft that would be needed, he was ready to take them from anywhere that they could be had.

In contrast, Stalin, by the time of Teheran, seemed to have become almost indifferent to whether or not Turkey came into the war. The reasons remain a matter of conjecture. His explanation was based in part on his conclusion that Turkey could not be led into the war, and in part on his fear that Allied forces might be dispersed if it did. Still, he agreed to embolden Turkey by promising that if Bulgaria turned against it, the Soviet government would at once make war upon that country.

Roosevelt also became chary. His military advisers, especially Marshall, were alarming him over the chance that if any operation in the Eastern Mediterranean developed, it would suck up resources needed for OVERLORD—"burn up our logistics right down the line." Still he, like Stalin, consented to another try at bringing Turkey into the war, provided the help required was not such as might delay or diminish OVERLORD.

It was agreed that President Inonu should be asked in the name of the three governments to come to Cairo. He was to be received by Churchill and Roosevelt, with Vishinsky in attendance as wanted. They would try to convince him that it was to the advantage of Turkey to enter the war; while if she refused to do so, ". . . she would forfeit her chance to sit at the Peace Conference. She would be treated like other neutrals. We would say that Great Britain had no further interest in her affairs and we would stop the supply of arms." [19] Actually, in this preparatory review of what was to be said to Inonu, the Prime Minister went a little further. He said that if Turkey was obdurate he personally would favor a change in the regime of the Straits. Molotov grasped at the remark. But Roosevelt shifted the line of thought by saying that he would like to have the Dardanelles made free to the commerce and fleets of the world, whether or not Turkey entered the war.

Roosevelt and Churchill competed for the first chance to greet Inonu at Cairo. Roosevelt sent his son-in-law in the Presidential plane to Adana to fetch him. Churchill sent his son, Randolph, in his official plane on the same errand. Inonu chose the American insignia. The meaning of the talks that ensued will be clearer if told in connection with later events.

Iran was serving as an essential military base. It was occupied by Soviet troops from the north and British troops from the south. Amer-

[19] *Ibid.*, page 392.

ican service forces were operating the transport system that ran from the Persian Gulf to the Soviet frontier, the great southern route of supply for the Red Army. The Iranian government and people accepted the presence of these foreign elements as incident to the great war that was going on about them.

The British government had taken the initiative in trying to minimize the hardship this caused Iran, and in arranging for assurances that this wartime occupation would not mean any permanent impairment of Iran's independence. It had entered the subject on the Moscow Conference agenda in an item called "Common Policy in Iran." Its idea had been that the three countries whose forces were in Iran should join in a public declaration stating that when the war was over these would be withdrawn. The proposal had briefly presented a problem to Hull and the American delegation because our troops were in Iran in a different capacity than the British and the Russians—they were engineer battalions and would be removed when the railway was turned over to its Persian owners. Therefore, and because of a wish to avoid close association with the political problems of Iran, Hull had suggested that instead of a joint declaration each of the three might make a separate statement of their intentions. Molotov at Moscow had also been cautious. As excuse for postponement he had said that the Iranian Ambassador in Moscow had just called his attention to the fact that in the Soviet-Anglo-Iranian Treaty of 1942 (under which permission was given to station troops in Iran) it was envisaged that an Iranian representative should be present whenever questions relating to that country were discussed. The subject had thereupon been left for further study and consultation at Teheran.

There the three Heads of State dealt with it in private talk outside the regular sessions of the Conference. After some little difficulty in persuading Stalin to join in a clear-cut declaration, agreement was reached. General Patrick Hurley, who had played an animating part in the whole project, then took the signed original copy to the Shah. Though it was not quite as definite as the Shah desired, he signed it. The text was publicly released after Roosevelt and Churchill got back to Cairo.

It was received with delight by the Iranians. It gave them four things they wanted: it nourished their self-respect; it acknowledged their part in the war; it promised consideration for their economic problems at the end of the war; and it affirmed a joint wish to maintain Iran's independence, sovereignty, and territorial integrity. That the American government was a party to this statement increased its value in their minds.

But even while at Teheran the Russians were thus agreeing to keep away from the warm waters of the Persian Gulf, they were making it known that they intended to get more extended outlets in the cold waters of the Gulf of Finland leading into the Baltic Sea.

The time was at hand, the American and British governments thought, to convince Finland that its fight was lost and it would be very well advised to drop out of the war. This was desired on military grounds: the Finnish-German lines were still close to Leningrad, and that city was still being heavily shelled and half-besieged. But there were other reasons as well. The American and British people liked and admired the Finnish nation. They had tried to dissuade it from allying itself with Hitler; and the American government had refrained from breaking relations up to then. They would be very sorry to have Finland disappear as an independent country, as might occur if it fought until overwhelmed by the Red Army.

The President made his try late in the Conference (on December 1st), when he thought that the congenial completion of other business might cause his plea for leniency to be well received. He remarked to Stalin that he would like to help in every way to get Finland out of the war before their big coordinated operation started in May. Stalin then let it be known that the Finns had already asked through the Swedish government about Soviet intentions, saying that they wanted a chance to talk with the Russians but were afraid of losing their independence. Stalin had sent word back to the Finnish government that the Soviet Union had no intention of violating Finnish independence if Finland did not bring it about by its own conduct; and that the Soviet government was willing to receive a Finnish delegation in Moscow, but would like to know in advance what proposals the Finns had in mind. Just that day (December 1st), Stalin added, the answer had come and in his opinion showed that the Finns were not yet in earnest in their wish to get out of the war.

Both Roosevelt and Churchill sought to mediate. Roosevelt asked whether it might be useful if the American government suggested to the Finns that they send a delegation to Moscow. Stalin said that he would not object but nothing useful would come of it if the Finns stuck to their present ideas. When the President observed that it might be easier to reach an agreement with some other Finns rather than with the existing pro-German government, Stalin said that would be better. But then he added that he did not care much who the Finns sent; and that they might send the Devil himself, provided they met the Soviet terms.

These terms he summarized: Finland would have to break all relations with Germany and expel all Germans from Finland; the Finnish Army must be demobilized; the Treaty of 1940—made after Soviet victory over Finland—should be restored. In addition, the Soviet Union, he said, would require certain positions formerly within Finland in order to protect Leningrad against such assault as had been made upon it; it wanted to get and keep Viupuri (on the Karelian Isthmus) and Hangoe (at the end of another small peninsula and about the most southwestern point in Finland), but if the Finns found it too hard to cede Hangoe, it might accept Petsamo instead. Lastly it desired compensation in kind for fifty per cent of the damage done by the Finns to the Soviet Union. Stalin defended these terms as not over-reaching or too harsh. He argued that the territorial acquisitions were necessary for Russian security, and justified the demands for compensation by the fact that the Finns had kept twenty-one divisions on the Soviet Front and, along with the Germans, had kept Leningrad under fire for twenty-seven months.

Without disputing these justifications, both Churchill and Roosevelt tried to get Stalin to soften his terms. They made it clear that they would oppose the absorption of Finland. They tried to see whether the Soviet wish for protective space for Leningrad and for its naval and air power in the Baltic might not be satisfied by less. And they warned against the imposition of excessive reparations. Stalin listened good-naturedly. He did not agree to retract any of the listed terms. But it may be that the opposed pleas and arguments caused Soviet authorities to be somewhat less demanding later on.

∞∞∞∞∞∞∞

28. Teheran: Political Principles and Decisions

∞∞∞∞∞∞∞

At Teheran, the Heads of Government directed most of their discussions toward seeing if they could agree on what to do about the current political situations which were encircling the battlefields. But now and again their talk was liberated to range over the whole map of the political future after the war.

In his second private conversation with Stalin (on November 29th) the President caught Stalin up with the current flow of his ideas about the postwar organization in favor of which the governments had declared themselves at Moscow. It should have three main elements, he proposed: (1) A group of forty or more countries, of all parts of the world. It was to be authorized to discuss all international questions freely and to advise the two smaller bodies in which the power of decision and action were to reside. These were to be (2) an executive committee made up of representatives of four signatories of the Moscow Declaration and six other selected countries around the globe. This was to be qualified to make recommendations for settling disputes—but not to impose its views. (3) A group which the President called The Four Policemen—the USSR, the United States, the United Kingdom, and China. This would have the authority to deal at once with any threat to the peace and with any sudden emergency which required action. To illustrate, the President said that if the Four Policemen had been at work when Italy attacked Ethopia, they could have closed the Suez Canal.

Stalin wondered whether the world would rest easy under the Four Policemen. He thought that European states would resent having China able to apply pressure upon them; and in any event he did not think China would be very powerful at the end of the war. He suggested, as a possible alternative form for this organization, European and Far Eastern Committees—with Great Britain, the United States, and the Soviet Union on both. Roosevelt recalled that Churchill had had somewhat the same idea as Stalin: three regional committees (the third one being for the Americas).[20] But he added that he doubted if the American Congress would agree to American participation in an exclusively European committee, which might be able to force the dispatch of American troops to Europe. Stalin pointed out that the Four Policemen might also require the sending of American troops to Europe, whereat the President said that he had envisaged only the sending of American planes and ships to Europe, and that England and the Soviet Union would have to handle the land armies in the event of any future threat to peace.

Stalin showed that his chief interest was in making sure that the new organization would be able and willing to prevent a revival of German strength. He did not think the measures so far discussed for preventing this were sufficient; and that there was need for "something more serious than the type of organization proposed by the President." He reverted to the arrangement which Roosevelt had mentioned to Eden months ago: that the international organization, besides having the power to make decisions, should control "strong points" not only within Germany and Japan, and near their borders, but even farther

[20] Churchill, *Closing the Ring,* page 363, comments that the President does not seem to have made clear that he, Churchill, also contemplated a Supreme United Nations Council, of which the three regional committees would be the components.

away. Roosevelt again commended the idea. Then at lunch the next day with Eden and Hopkins, Molotov enlarged on Stalin's idea. Since France, he thought, had shown that it did not want to defend itself, it could well be asked to turn over places like Bizerte and Dakar—which might be placed under American or British control. Eden said any such step would have to be very carefully weighed; perhaps France could make a contribution by placing their bases under some United Nations control in a way that would not hurt its pride. Hopkins talked about the American wish for naval and air bases in the Pacific, the Philippines, Formosa, and perhaps some of the Japanese mandated islands. But he said the President was unsure as to how this was to be arranged; the United States did not want sovereignty over any of these areas. The whole scheme, it may be said curtly, was left in a fog; no one knew which places might be selected, how control was to be acquired, who would equip, man, and operate them.

Roosevelt seems to have become hesitant as between the various, vaguely formulated possibilities. For, in a subsequent talk alone with Stalin on December 1st, he remarked that he thought it would be premature to consider with Churchill at Teheran the proposals about world organization which he had outlined to Stalin. The conception of a small policing body, he continued, was just an idea on which future study was required. Somewhere in the course of this talk, Stalin let Roosevelt know that he had changed his mind and come to agree that the organization ought to be world-wide and not regional. The whole subject was in the end relegated to the future, on the understanding that each of the three would continue diligently to examine the complexities which had come into view. These were to turn out to be less tough than some which were not discussed at all at Teheran—for example, what would happen if the Four Policemen should quarrel among themselves.

If they did quarrel it was most likely to be over territorial questions. At Teheran Stalin indicated more fully than before at least some of the claims which the Soviet government would make. Of those directed toward the Far East we have already told. In Europe, the Soviet government sought (1) approval of its determination to retain roughly all the areas which it had acquired during its period of association with Germany, as enumerated in connection with earlier discussions of an Anglo-Soviet treaty; (2) the cession from Germany of that part of East Prussia which lay on the Baltic Sea, including the city of Koenigsberg; and (3) the acquisition from Finland of points close to Leningrad.

In sum, it might be said that the attitude of the Soviet government about territorial questions, as revealed at Teheran, was that if it could get what it wanted, the United States and Great Britain could take what they wanted, provided it was not something that the Soviet Union wanted. This was its rule, not the restraining precepts of the Atlantic Charter to which the Soviet government had professed to adhere.

In contrast, the inclination of the American government was virtuous but ineffectual. It wanted fair principles to govern, and it wished to avoid responsibility for any wartime territorial settlements. For these reasons it tried to get its associates to leave them open until the war was won—when there would no longer be a need to take military considerations into account and when decisions might be farther-sighted.

The approach of the British government was more flexible. It tended to take a pliant view of such Soviet wishes as seemed to it to be reasonably grounded on security, history, or any other acceptable basis. Churchill's view of the matter *at this time* was expansively disclosed at that luncheon on November 30th at which the talk of the three Heads of State, as already told, ranged over the question of access to warm-water ports. He remarked that it seemed to him important that the nations who would govern the world after the war should be satisfied and have no territorial or other ambitions. If that question could be settled in a manner agreeable to the great powers, he felt that the world might indeed remain at peace. So he appeared to regard Soviet proposals about its western frontiers unobjectionable. But as regards other territorial questions where it was thought Soviet presence would be an unjustified intrusion—Western Europe, the Middle East, and the African Coast—the British government showed a front of resolute denial. Further, Churchill and Eden were disturbed at the prospect that Soviet territorial ideas might reduce Europe to an unhappy and divided collection of numerous small dependent states—a "pulverized" Europe. To prevent this, at Teheran they sought ways to bring the smaller European states into groups—councils, federations, alliances.

Even this scant summary indicates how necessity and expediency were tugging at the reins of decision.

As the military plans for the final assaults on Germany were being completed, the three sought a level of agreement on what to do about Germany afterward. It became plain that all the hints and demi-promises which had been coming from Moscow that the German people and army would be spared if they threw over Hitler were only tactical deceptions. Stalin's confidential words at Teheran were hard with anger over what the Soviet people had endured, and firm with conviction that unless the German state was smashed to bits, it would find some way to rise again. Churchill seemed to appreciate both the feeling and the fear, without allowing them wholly to rule his judgment. He was worried, as even a person with more trust in Soviet nature might well have been, by the thought that with Germany down, the will of the Soviet government might be supreme in Europe. Roosevelt was inclined, like Stalin, to give full vent to the reasons for treating Germany and the Germans harshly. He seemed ready to rely on measures of self-control and mutual accords to keep future Soviet activities, like American and British, within just bounds.

All the plans to ensure the complete surrender of Germany, the extinction of Nazism, and the exercise of stern watch which had been discussed by the Foreign Secretaries at Moscow, the Heads of State confirmed. Stalin stated that he judged them to be "all very good but insufficient." On the next day, talking alone with Roosevelt, Stalin said that he thought Churchill was too hopeful about the chance of keeping Germany under control. His belief that his British associate was not really determined to make sure that Germany could not again menace the peace was sharpened by the differences that emerged at the conference session that same day over military plans. Thus at dinner that evening he teased—it might almost be said taunted—Churchill. Several of his remarks could be taken to mean that he thought that the Prime Minister nursed a secret affection for Germany and wished the Germans to have a soft peace. He repeated his belief that unless more adequate ways for keeping Germany down were evolved, it would rise again within fifteen or twenty years to plunge the world into another war. Thus he urged that at least two other measures that went beyond those which they all had in mind ought to be taken.

One of these he and the President had touched on in their talk about future world organization: that the three of them ought to keep possession of important strategic points in the world so that, in his words "if Germany moved a muscle she could be quickly stopped." The other was that 50,000 at least, perhaps 100,000, of "the German commanding staff" ought to be liquidated.[21] Churchill took strong exception to what he termed the cold-blooded murder of soldiers who had fought for their country. It was all right, he said, to make war criminals who had committed barbarous acts stand trial and pay, but he objected vigorously to executing men for political purposes. Roosevelt took a bantering

[21] Churchill's remembrance of this talk as set down in a memo to his Undersecretary for Foreign Affairs, Cadogan, on April 19, 1944 was, "Stalin spoke of very large mass executions of over fifty thousand of the Staffs and military experts. Whether he was joking or not could not be ascertained. The atmosphere was jovial, but also grim. He certainly said that he would require four million German males to work for an indefinite period to rebuild Russia." *Closing the Ring*, page 706.

tone about what must have been to him both a grisly subject and a disagreeable clash—saying that he would put the figure of the German Commanding Staff who should be executed at 49,000 or more.

On the next day, December 1st, the three reverted to the subject about which the month before the three Foreign Secretaries had all hesitated—whether or not Germany ought to be divided into several states. Now Stalin said firmly that he was in favor of bringing this about. Roosevelt, though acquainted with the opposing reasons, agreed. Churchill said he did not object in principle, but he was more interested in separating Prussia, which he thought was the core of German militarism, from the rest of Germany.

Roosevelt then sketched a plan which he said he had thought up sometime ago but which he was still turning over in his mind: that Germany might be divided into seven parts. Five would govern themselves. The other two might be placed under United Nations or another sort of international control: some kind of free zone might be formed which would include a Kiel Canal Zone and the former Hanseatic cities of Bremen, Hamburg, and Lubec; and some sort of international trusteeship might be formed for the Ruhr and the Saar.

Churchill outlined an alternative plan of division: that Prussia be separated from the rest of Germany and kept isolated; and that various southern states (Bavaria, Baden, Wurtenberg, Saxony, and the Palatinate) also be detached, and become part of, or fit in with, a confederation of other states on the Danube. When Churchill asked Stalin what he thought of this idea, Stalin scoffed at it. He said, in substance, that all Germans were alike and all of them fought like devils. He said that he liked the President's plan much better, as more likely to result in having Germany remain weak. And he added with emphasis that he was all against embracing any parts of Germany in a larger confederation, since that would give the Germans a better chance to revive a great state under their control. Roosevelt remarked that he agreed that all Germans were aggressive and stubborn fighters, but that he thought it was possible to direct their loyalties to small units such as he had in mind.

Churchill ably argued back. He predicted that if Germany was divided into small independent parts, and these were not attached to other combinations (where they could establish a viable existence and new loyalties), sooner or later they would reunite and challenge their opponents. To which Stalin in effect answered—not if Soviet Russia could prevent it. Then Churchill tried to bring out the obverse meaning of the course which Stalin and Roosevelt were favoring. He asked Stalin whether he contemplated that the whole of Europe would be composed of little states—separate, disjointed, weak. Stalin answered that he did not; only Germany should be divided up and weak; and he added that "he supposed for example that Poland would be a strong country, and France, and Italy likewise. . . ." The answer could hardly have seemed convincing, since Stalin in other bouts of talks was rebuking France for its weakness, and reviling the Polish government in London for its ambitious notions of the place it could hold in Europe.

This lively preliminary flourish of knives over the body of Europe ended without any definite conclusion as to whether or where the incisions were to be made. It was agreed that the European Advisory Committee should take up the study of the subject where they were leaving off.

A few days after the end of the Conference, one of the American participants summed up in a memo what the full application of the policies favored by Stalin and Molotov at Teheran could mean: "Germany is to be broken up and kept broken up. The states of eastern, southeastern, and central Europe will not be permitted to group themselves into any federations or association. France is to be stripped of her colonies and strategic bases beyond her borders and will not be permitted to maintain any appreciable military establishment. Poland and Italy will remain approximately their present territorial size, but it is doubtful if either will be permitted to maintain any appreciable armed force. The result would be that the Soviet Union would be the only important military and political force on the continent of Europe. The rest of Europe would be reduced to military and political impotence."

But neither Roosevelt nor his chief advisers seem to have been left with such gloomy forebodings at this time. One reason may have been that they were under the impression that Stalin would be content to live within the Soviet borders as then constituted and claimed, and really wanted peace around his country. Another reason may have been because they got the sense that Stalin was working for Russia rather than for the cause of international Communism. They noticed that he almost always talked about "we Russians" or "Russia will do this" or "Russia will not do that." Correspondingly he seemed to treat the cause and prospects of international revolution rather lightly, suggesting that the others need not fear it, as when, while discussing whether Russia wanted to dictate the form of social and political systems in the neighboring states, he said, "We won't worry about that. We have found it not easy to set up a Communist system." Still another reason may have been the idea that these issues of size, frontiers, relative power of the countries of continental Europe may have been deemed of only passing importance. If, it may have been thought, the three main members of the war coalition worked together in the new international political organization, such questions could be adjusted satisfactorily; while if they quarreled and failed to be true to their saving purpose, all of Europe would face a dark future howsoever they were settled at the moment. Such thoughts glimmered in the air as the Conference at Teheran ended.

The association of the three during the days of this first time spent together were marked by Roosevelt's efforts to win over Stalin, Churchill's stubborn attempt to get recognition for strategy which he knew differed from that of the other two, and Stalin's relaxed bluntness.

The relations between the three men swayed with the currents of their conferences. Roosevelt used his whole repertoire in his effort to get on close and trustful terms with Stalin. This included an occasional derisive sally at some of Churchill's ideas, which the Prime Minister no doubt perceived and appreciated. Stalin seemed to take to the President. He treated him as the senior member, with deference. He appeared eager to know what was in the President's mind and pleased by what he learned. Churchill and Stalin were more outspoken with one another. Ever since their flareup during Churchill's first visit to Moscow, they had been in the habit of swapping opinions rather frankly and of disagreeing with zest. Only once at Teheran did their differences verge on angry dispute. That was at dinner on the 29th at which, as has been told, Stalin seemed bent on provoking the Prime Minister. For he went so far as to say to him ". . . that just because the Russians were simple people, it was a mistake to think they were blind and could not see what was before their eyes." No man of greatness ever placed his temper at the service of a good cause more admirably than Churchill. He rebutted the accusation firmly without becoming personal. The President was jocular, helpfully so.

As the three decided what they could agree on and postponed what they could not, opposition and mistrust gave way to a hopeful sense of achievement and of friendly unity between themselves and their countries. Fragments of the toasts exchanged at dinner the following night (the 30th), just after accord had been reached on strategic plans, on being disinterred, still convey the feeling. Churchill in his toast described Roosevelt as a man who devoted his entire life to the cause and defense of the weak and the helpless and to the promotion of the great principles that underlie democratic civilization. As for Stalin, he was worthy to stand as one of the great figures of Russian history and merited the title of "Stalin the Great." Stalin answered that the honors were due not to him but to the Russian people since it was easy to be a great leader of such a people. Roosevelt at the end of his main toast spoke of the hopes for a better world which the Conference had justifiably raised. He said that the rainbow, the enduring symbol of hope, could now, for the first time as a result of this Conference, be discerned in the sky.

On parting, each of the three had a sense of harmony of purpose. They felt satisfaction at what they had done together. The joint public statement issued on December 6th, while they were on the way home, is still a stirring record of their beliefs and sentiments. Its first sentence they had rewritten themselves because the draft submitted had not sounded positive enough: "We express our determination that our nations shall work together in war and in the peace that will follow."

Other sections read:

"The common understanding which we have here reached guarantees that victory will be ours.

"And as to peace—we are sure that our concord will make an enduring peace. We recognize fully the supreme responsibility resting upon us and all the United Nations, to make a peace which will command the good will of the overwhelming mass of the peoples of the world, and banish the scourge and terror of war for many generations. . . .

"We came here with hope and determination. We leave here, friends in fact, in spirit and in purpose."

The individual statements made or authorized by each after the Conference were in harmony with the spirit of this joint declaration. Who can doubt that Roosevelt meant what he said to the American troops who were stationed at Camp Amirabad near that city in Iran:

"I got here four days ago to meet with the head of Soviet Russia and the Prime Minister of England to try to do two things: The first was to lay the military plans for cooperation between the three nations looking toward the winning of the war just as fast as we possibly can. And I think we have made progress toward that end. The other purpose was to talk over world conditions after the war—to try to plan for a world for us and for our children when war would cease to be a necessity. We have made great progress on that also."

Never again perhaps was his assurance so unmarred. Looking back at what had been decided at the series of coalition conferences at Moscow, Cairo, Teheran, and again Cairo, he could count many accords that he valued. In the military field, there were the strategic plans for Europe (OVERLORD and ANVIL—code name for the projected landing in Southern France), the allowance of freedom of operations in the Pacific, the reaffirmation of the Soviet promise to enter the Pacific War; in the area of general political principle, the Four-

Nation Declaration of Moscow and the code of policy for Italy; in the approach to peace settlements, the Cairo Declaration about Japan and China, the Declaration protecting Iran, the promises to preserve the independence of Austria and Finland, the reprieve for Poland (of which I will shortly tell). And looking farther forward, there were the expressions of determined intention to form and work together in a permanent organization to preserve the peace.

Churchill's view was closer to the ground, but still pleasantly tinted. Recalling later his state of mind after Teheran, he wrote: "Surveying the whole military scene, as we separated in an atmosphere of friendship and unity of immediate purpose, I personally was well content." [22] While recognizing that some of the political questions that had arisen for discussion might turn out to be very troubling, that possibility seemed remote and speculative. His judgment was that, "It would not have been right at Teheran for the Western democracies to found their plans upon suspicions of the Russian attitude in the hour of triumph and when all her dangers were removed." [23]

Stalin seemed just as pleased as Roosevelt. He, too, could count many causes for satisfaction. The Soviet government had been given a firm pledge that the invasion of the West would start within a few months. Soviet territorial aims in Europe had been advanced, and he had managed to get all proposals that might have resulted in opposed strength discarded or deferred. The promise to enter the Pacific War left time and opportunity to decide what advantage might be secured in that connection. Substantial as these benefits were, it is quite possible that Roosevelt's responsiveness may have caused Stalin to think that they would be even greater than they turned out to be, and more easily had.

In any case, the Soviet press and radio went all out in enthusiastic comment about the results of the meeting. The press was unreserved in its praise. Special meetings were held in factories and elsewhere throughout the land at which political spokesmen explained the significance of the joint statement. Listeners at these gatherings reported an interesting answer to a comment that was frequently made, in effect, "But we have often heard much the same before—that the second front was soon to start." The answer given was, "But this time Stalin left Russia to attend the Conference and that means that this time it is the real thing."

Responding to a farewell message from Roosevelt, then back in Cairo, the day the joint statement was issued (December 6th), Stalin said, "Now it is assured that our peoples will act together jointly and in

[22] *Ibid.*, page 405.
[23] *Ibid.*

friendship both at the present time and after the end of the war." He ended with the remark that he also hoped that "our meeting at Teheran cannot be considered as the last and that we will again see each other." [24]

But events and the daily rub of give-and-take were soon to test the durability of these avowals. By the turn of the year, signs that Soviet wishes were expanding could be detected. The Soviet press again began to rail against any opposition to them. Soviet officials seemed to become as rigid as before in dealing with such matters as arrangements for cooperation in military operations and Lend-Lease schedules. They presented their claims for what they wanted as a matter of right, and were silently stubborn about American requests which they did not want to grant. By January Harriman was again lamenting how much energy and patience were needed to carry out any piece of official business with them; and he was recommending that we regulate our responses so as to awaken the Soviet government to the fact that it was expected to give as well as get. The flux of his feeling is recorded in the message which, on January 22nd, he sent to Churchill, congratulating the Prime Minister on his safe return to Britain after a bad illness in Carthage. In paraphrase, "The Russian Bear is demanding much and yet biting the hands that are feeding it." The surmise of the American Embassy in Moscow was, as given in its periodic report on trends in the Soviet press, that "influential elements in the Party and the Government which are inherently suspicious of foreign influence, including the NKVD and certain isolationist circles, are alarmed by the popular enthusiasm for international collaboration resulting from the Moscow and Teheran Conferences and are urging caution."

Of all the issues that tried the harmony within the coalition which resounded at the end of the Teheran Conference, none did so as deeply as those concerning Poland—which affected in their spread the future situation of all the peoples and states of Central Europe.

[24] Roosevelt's first message to Stalin after leaving Teheran was dated December 3, presumably sent from Cairo. Then on the 6th he and Churchill sent a joint message informing Stalin of the results of their further conference. Stalin answered the same day. Then Roosevelt asked Harriman to deliver to Stalin a sealed letter about the contents of which Harriman was not told, and which he delivered to Stalin on December 18th. On the 21st Stalin acknowledged this letter and one sentence of the acknowledgement reads, "I am glad that Fate gave me the opportunity to render you a service at Teheran. I also attach great importance to our meeting and to the talks there. . . ." Roosevelt's letter may have been nothing but a letter of thanks to Stalin for giving him quarters within the Soviet Legation grounds. Or it may have referred to a private talk he had with Stalin over the embarrassment which the Polish question gave him. Or it may have dealt with a wholly different matter about which I know nothing.

PERIOD SEVEN

Teheran to the Cross-Channel Invasion, June–July 1944: Despite Grave Contention over Poland Military Cooperation Proceeds

---

29. Poland Again and the Region Thereabout

AMERICAN officials had been disconcerted to find out during the Moscow Conference how condemnatory an attitude the Soviet government took toward the Polish government-in-exile. That regime had felt let down by Hull's apparent unwillingness to fight for its fate and its conceptions of what was due to Poland.

In anticipation of the meeting of the Heads of State at Teheran, this Polish government submitted (on November 19th) fresh statements of its views. The memo for the President which the Polish Ambassador in Washington gave Hull contained an appeal to persuade Stalin to resume relations and to allow the government-in-exile to return to Poland when Soviet troops crossed the former frontiers. If the Soviet government refused, it forewarned, the Polish government would regard the Soviet entry into Polish territory as an invasion and be compelled to take resistant political action, and its adherents in Poland would remain underground. With reference to frontiers, this memo stated that the Polish government-in-exile could not consider giving up "its eastern territories to the Soviet Union even if it got as compensation East Prussia, Danzig, Oppeln and Silesia." A memo presented to the British government for Churchill was to the same effect. But it explained the operations of the underground forces in Poland more fully and summarized the instructions which the government in London had sent these forces.[1]

To sustain these written presentations of his views, Mikolajczyk asked Roosevelt and Churchill several times for the chance to talk with them personally (somewhere in North Africa or Cairo) before they met with Stalin. Roosevelt had replied that this would not be possible but that he hoped to see Mikolajczyk in Washington a little later on. Churchill, answering through Eden, explained his refusal in part by a fear that if he met Mikolajczyk first, Stalin might cancel the whole conference.

[1] The instructions are summarized in Mikolajczyk's note to Churchill dated November 16, 1943, printed in *The Rape of Poland*, pages 267–8. One paragraph stated: "The entry of Soviet troops on Polish territory without the previous resumption of Polish-Soviet relations would force the Polish government to undertake political action against the violation of Polish sovereignty while the Polish local administration and army in Poland would have to continue to work underground. In that case the Polish government foresee the use of measures of self-defense wherever such measures are rendered indispensable by Soviet methods of terror and extermination of Polish citizens."

At Teheran, Roosevelt had left it to Churchill to take the lead. The Prime Minister did so after dinner on November 28th, the first day of the Conference. He seems to have appealed to Stalin rather than to have argued with him. His manner of address implied that he appreciated that Soviet decisions would have to be accepted. He recognized, he assuringly remarked, that there was nothing more important than the security of Russia's western frontiers. Poland might, he continued, move westward like soldiers taking two steps "left close." If that meant that the Poles trod on some German toes, it could not be helped, for there must be a strong Poland.

Having thus intimated that the British attitude was not going to be too rigid, he asked Stalin whether they should try to draw frontier lines. Stalin said yes. Churchill had then added that he did not have any power (from Parliament) to do this, nor had the President (from Congress), but he thought that the three of them might, while they were in Teheran, try to agree informally on a policy which they could recommend to the Poles with the advice that they accept it. Stalin inquired whether this should be attempted without Polish participation. Churchill answered that he thought so and that the subject could be discussed with the Polish leaders after the three of them had agreed among themselves. Eden, who had joined them while this talk was going on, had remarked that he was encouraged by a statement which Stalin had made earlier that evening at dinner—that the Poles could go as far west as the Oder River. Stalin turned toward him and asked him whether he thought that the Soviet government was going to swallow up Poland. Eden answered that he did not know how much the Russians were going to eat, and how much they would leave undigested. Stalin said they did not want anything belonging to other people, though they might take a bite out of Germany. Eden said that what Poland lost in the east she might gain in the west. Stalin answered "possibly," he did not know. Churchill ends his account of this talk by telling, "I then demonstrated with the help of three matches my idea of Poland moving westward. This pleased Stalin, and on this note our group parted for the moment." [2]

Roosevelt was not an auditor of this conversation. And Hopkins said little when, at luncheon two days later, Eden and Molotov reverted to the subject. But the President did not want Stalin to think that this aloofness meant either indifference or dissent. So, on December 1st, after a luncheon of the three, Roosevelt told Stalin that he would like to continue the conversation alone. When Stalin called on him early that afternoon, shortly before the three were to meet again, the President

[2] *Closing the Ring*, page 362.

began by saying that he wanted to talk frankly about a matter which related directly to internal American politics—Poland. According to the American (Bohlen) memo made of this conversation, the President went on to explain that a national election in the United States was due in 1944; that while he would rather not run again he might have to if the war was still in progress. There were between six and seven million Americans of Polish extraction in the United States and he did not want to lose their votes. Then, in the probably misleading language in which this talk is recorded, he added that

". . . personally he agreed with the views of Marshal Stalin as to the necessity of the restoration of a Polish state but would like to see the Eastern border moved farther to the west and the Western border moved even to the River Oder. He hoped, however, that the Marshal would understand that for political reasons outlined above, he could not participate in any decision here in Teheran or even next winter on this subject and that he could not publicly take part in any such arrangement at the present time."

In telling Stalin that he found no fault with the general ideas of shifting Polish frontiers to the west, Roosevelt, according to his own later interpretation, did not mean to bestow his approval on any particular frontier line—specifically the Curzon Line. But Stalin and Molotov both understood him to be doing so. Or, so they were to assert the following October when Churchill visited Moscow, even though, in the interval, Harriman had told Stalin (most plainly in June 1944 on getting back from Washington) that the President was still puzzled and troubled over what ought to be done about Lwow and the oil region.[3] When this misunderstanding was revealed, the Ambassador wondered whether the meaning of what the President had said in their informal private talk at Teheran might have been accidentally twisted in translation. However that may be, by sidestepping the question at Teheran as he did, Roosevelt left Churchill and Stalin unhindered to continue their attempt to draw frontiers for the new Poland.

Roosevelt did not inform Churchill of what he had said to Stalin in this confidential talk between the two. And when, minutes afterward, the three gathered together, it was he, despite his professed wish not to be involved, who made the first reference to Poland by saying that he hoped talks could be started soon to bring about the resumption of relations between the Polish and Soviet governments. Stalin asked gruffly with what Polish government these talks were to be conducted —since the one in London was in contact with the Germans, joining with the Nazis in slandering the Soviet government, and killing parti-

[3] See pages 455 and 459.

sans who were fighting the Germans. He would, he asserted, want a guarantee that all these activities would end, and he was not sure that the Polish government-in-exile would ever cease them and become the kind of government it ought to be. Then, having made his critical attitude clear, he said, however, that if the Polish government in London acted satisfactorily, and began to fight the Germans, that the Russians would be ready to treat with it. For, he concluded, the Soviet government was in favor of the reconstitution and the expansion of Poland at the expense of Germany.

Stalin's harsh words did not destroy the cheerful effect left by his closing affirmation. Churchill—perceiving that he was to get a chance to mediate—proceeded to seek further guidance as to how he might handle the disputed boundary question. He invited Stalin to define his ideas about Poland's future frontiers more precisely. Stalin did so. The Poles, he declared, could not be allowed to try to seize what he called Ukraine and White Russian territory—territory which had been restored to the Soviet Union in 1939; and he said that the Soviet government intended to cling to those 1939 frontiers, for he thought them just and ethnographically correct. Eden asked whether this meant the Ribbentrop-Molotov line.[4] Stalin said: call it what you will, he still considered it fair and right. Molotov had another rejoinder. He said it was generally called the Curzon Line. Eden contradicted him, saying that there were important differences. Molotov denied that fact.[5] Maps were procured and the conferees separated into two loose groups, poring over the lines they bore. I shall not try to pursue here the confusingly recorded intricacies of this fluid discussion.[6] It is sufficient to record that when Eden suggested that the Curzon Line was intended to pass to the east of Lwow, Stalin said that was not so, that Lwow should remain on the Russian side and the line should go west toward Przemysl.[7] It seems probable that this point was still not cleared up when the group turned its attention to the western frontiers of Poland and began to study the Oder River line on the map. Roosevelt's only part in this

[4] *Closing the Ring,* page 395.

[5] In the central part of the line, the Curzon boundary and that agreed on between Molotov and Ribbentrop on September 28, 1939 are the same—following the Bug River to the Galician frontier. But in the north the Curzon Line awarded the large district of Bialystok to Poland, while the 1939 accord, by following the Bug River farther before striking north, allotted it to the Soviet Union. In the south also (in Galicia) the 1939 deal yielded a little more territory.

[6] The account given by Churchill in *Closing the Ring,* pp. 394–397, besides being of very lively interest, is probably as complete and accurate as any could be.

[7] *Ibid.,* page 396. Stalin was correct. Eden probably had in mind an alternate boundary line (between Poland and mandate for Galicia) which was discussed at the Paris Peace Conference in 1919. For a description of the line contained in Lord Curzon's note of July 1920, see the Appendix.

stretch of the conversation had been to inquire about the size of the territories involved in the suggested border changes. Having been told this, he asked Stalin whether he thought a transfer of population on a voluntary basis was possible, and Stalin answered that he thought it entirely so.

Churchill, intent on getting a definite arrangement that he might put up to the Poles in London, summed up for Stalin what he took to be the result of their talks. In effect, the new Polish state was to lie between the Curzon Line (subject to interpretation in detail) and the Oder River in the west, including East Prussia and Oppeln. Whether the boundary in the west was to follow the eastern or western Neisse rivers which flow together to form the Oder was not defined. Stalin said that he would accept the Curzon Line as the Soviet-Polish frontier, provided the Russians also got the northern part of East Prussia running along the left (the southern) bank of the Niemen River, including Tilsit and the City of Konigsberg. The acquisition, he explained, would give the Soviet Union an ice-free port on the Baltic and also a small piece of German territory which he felt it deserved. Churchill, in his later account, seems to report Stalin as saying, as well, that it ". . . would put Russia on the neck of Germany." [8] Churchill made no objection to this additional demand. But he did ask again: what about Lwow. Stalin merely repeated that he would accept the Curzon Line.

Despite this, Churchill said he would espouse this formula as the basis of a proposal to be put by him before the Poles in London with strong advice that it be accepted. The British initiative was imprinted by anxiety, by a fear that unless the Polish government-in-exile was quickly reinstated as negotiator, the Soviet government might create a puppet rival, and even abandon the idea of restoring an independent Poland. The President, in conformity with what he had said to Stalin, temporarily relinquished the problem to the Russians and British. This left him free to fight another day—but, alas, by that day the battle was all but over.

The Soviet armies were fast nearing the Polish frontier. Rumors about Soviet intentions to foster a rival Communist-dominated government were growing more definite. So Churchill, taken ill on his way back from Teheran, did not wait until he was well enough himself to attempt to get the Polish government in London to deal with the Soviet government on the terms discussed at Teheran. He asked Eden to try.

On the 20th of December Churchill told Eden to open up the frontier question with the Poles on the basis of the formula agreed on with

[8] *Closing the Ring*, page 403.

Stalin, and advise them to accept. This the Prime Minister estimated would give the Poles a country between 300 and 400 miles each way and 150 miles of seaboard. One sentence in the memo sent by Churchill to Eden for guidance went to the very center of the great issues involved: "You should put it to them that by taking over and holding firmly the present German territories up to the Oder, they will be rendering a service to Europe as a whole by making the basis of a friendly policy towards Russia and close association with Czechoslovakia." [9]

This may be interpreted with the aid of passing time. The Polish government in London was to be converted into one whose necessity and rule would be to get along with the Soviet Union. It would live within frontiers that embraced some territory that had long been part of Germany, from which it would be compelled to expel millions of Germans. The Soviet Union would acquire not only those eastern areas which Poland held before 1939 (which the Soviet government claimed were really Russian), but also some German territory in the north. Thus the two countries (the Soviet Union and Poland) would be bound together by the need to be on guard against any German attempt to recover these lost areas and to reemerge as a strong power.

Looked at in one way, Poland was being invited to be a protector of the peace and staunch cooperator in preventing any future assertion of German will. This is the way Churchill suggested that Stalin's proposition be put before the Poles. Looked at in the reverse way, the Poles were to be bound to remain in association with the Soviet Union whether they liked it or not, because Germany, if and as it ever recovered, would feel injured by both. Poland would never again be able, as it had between the two wars, to try to stand as a neutral between Germany and the Soviet Union, disliking and fearing them both, and ready to conspire against either of them.

The Soviet government deemed that the war experience which its country was undergoing proved the need for the proposed arrangement. But if this were effected, the Soviet Union might be in a position to dominate Europe. This would mean that the task of resisting abuses of its power would fall upon the British Commonwealth and the United States.

But how was the Soviet Union to be prevented from making these frontiers its own without smashing war strategy into bits? And after Teheran, did it not seem sensible to put aside the fear that the Soviet Union would misuse its power in favor of the hope that it would act in the spirit of friendly and just cooperation?

[9] *Ibid.*, pp. 450–51.

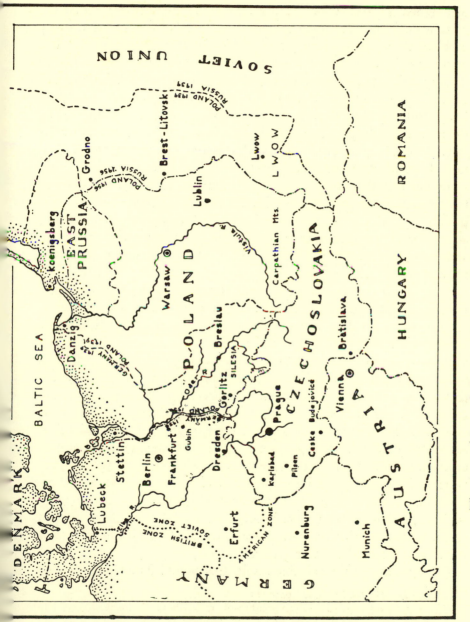

The Area of Struggle Between Germany, Poland, and the Soviet Union

Czechoslovakia was to be a partner in this new association in East-Central Europe, and its President, Benes, was telling the American and British governments that Soviet intentions could be trusted. He had gone to Moscow in December right after the Teheran Conference, and had signed a Czech-Soviet Treaty of Alliance (December 12th). He was, he had told Harriman, wholly satisfied. He thought that every problem between his country and the Soviet Union had been settled. Stalin and Molotov had over and over reassured him that no matter what question might arise they would not interfere in Czechoslovakian internal affairs. They had offered to aid in enlarging and equipping Czech military units then in Russia. They had agreed—as reported by Benes to his colleagues in London—that ". . . our own military units should always enter our territory with the Red Army; that the occupation of our territory should always be left to us provided our numbers were sufficient, that our internal order should be respected and that our territory should be progressively handed over to our own civil administration." [10] Stalin and Molotov had promised to support Czechoslovak claims for the frontiers that existed before the country was broken up and despoiled; the Russian territory would be on the other side of the Carpathians. [11]

It happened that on the same day (December 20th) that Churchill was telling Eden to try to persuade the Poles to go along with the arrangement outlined at Teheran, Benes had another talk with Stalin. Thereafter he told Harriman (and probably Clark-Kerr) that he was even more hopeful than before that the Soviet government would be willing to reach an accord with the Polish government in London if that group adapted itself to Soviet requirements; that is, if it eliminated, in Benes' words, its "irreconcilable reactionaries," took in some new democratic leaders, and accepted the frontier line wanted by Russia. If it would make these adjustments, Benes thought the Soviet government would be willing to make the same kind of treaty with Poland which it had signed with him. The two treaties, he forecast, would become the basis of a three-cornered system which would secure them all against Germany's *Drang nach Osten*. It would also insure Poland against Soviet interference with Polish internal affairs, because Moscow would find no need or cause for such action.

This appraisal of the valuable results that would flow from a Soviet-

[10] *Memoirs of Dr. Eduard Benes,* page 263.
[11] These promises in regard to reestablishment of Czechoslovak forces, reentry into their country, cooperation with the Red Army, turnover of civil administration, and frontiers were officially embodied in a supplementary "Soviet-Czechoslovak Agreement regarding the possible entry of Soviet troops into Czechoslovak Territory," signed May 8, 1944.

Polish treaty was in harmony with the general impressions of Soviet policy which Benes derived from his talks with Stalin and Molotov and which he was freely expressing. As conveyed by him to Harriman just before he left Moscow: he thought the Soviet leaders now felt secure and calm; that they were reposing in the belief that the revolution was achieved and that the Soviet Union was strong and consolidated. With this change their wish and purpose to Bolshevize other countries was waning and in its place had come the determination to participate in world affairs.

Benes, on his way back to London, went down to Marrakech, where Churchill was recuperating, to tell him about his experience in Moscow. Benes in his later account of this talk wrote, "His [Churchill's] reaction was very strong and decided. He felt that the Poles should accept what I was bringing Mikolajczyk from Moscow; that when I reached London I should first tell Eden and then Mikolajczyk, and that then in conjunction with Eden I should urge the Poles as their friend to decide at once to negotiate with Moscow and to accept Stalin's offer." [12] Such was the route which was followed in the next stage of pursuit of a solution for the Polish problem.

30. The Trouble over Poland Continued

As his vigor returned, Churchill took over the lead. On January 6th, 1944, in a message to Roosevelt, he confirmed his intention of going along the line marked at Teheran. As soon as he got back to London, he said, he was going to do his utmost to get the Polish government ". . . to close with this [the Soviet territorial proposal worked out at Teheran] or something like it, and, having closed, they must proclaim themselves as ready to accept the duty of guarding the bulwark of the Oder against further German aggression upon Russia, and also they must back the settlement to the limit. This will be their duty to the Powers of Europe, who will twice have rescued them." [13]

But tension became so vibrant during the next few weeks as to daunt anyone less resolute than Churchill. The Polish government in London was concerned not with its duty to Europe but with its survival and

[12] *Memoirs of Dr. Eduard Benes*, pages 265–66.
[13] *Closing the Ring*, page 452.

place in Europe. It was still intent on regaining most if not all of the area which it had occupied between the wars, and something more from Germany in the west. It felt entitled to emerge from the war as a larger as well as a free power. And it was determined that it would neither change its political color nor become bound to the Soviet Union.

Without consulting either the British or Americans, the Polish government in London on January 5th made a broadcast to Poles reminding them of their rights and fighting duties, and at the same time issued a public declaration to the United Nations covering most of the points raised in the broadcast. The declaration stated that it considered an agreement with the Soviet Union highly desirable but made no mention of a purchase price. It announced that the sovereignty of Poland over its liberated territory would be established as soon as possible. It stated that it expected the Soviet Union would not fail to respect the rights and interests of the Polish Republic and its citizens. It told of the order already issued to the underground in Poland (October 27, 1943) to intensify its fight against the Germans and to avoid all conflicts with the Soviet armies that were entering Poland; and to cooperate with the Soviet Commanders ". . . in the event of the resumption of Polish-Soviet relations."

Benes, having checked his opinions against those of Eden, tried on January 10th to convince Mikolajczyk that in issuing this statement his group had taken a wrong turn; and that they would be better advised to accept the chance which Stalin was offering. Mikolajczyk's response showed that he did not share the opinion of some of his group that Russia would be exhausted at the end of the war, and that he recognized the need of concluding some agreement with the Soviet Union as soon as possible. But he said that even if he, as an individual political leader, could subdue his unhappiness at the proposed frontier adjustments, he did not believe he could overcome the objections of his colleagues.

The Soviet authorities let a week go by before taking note of the defiant public affirmation that the Polish government in London had made. In that week the Red Armies surged across the former Polish frontier. At midnight of the 11th, Molotov asked Harriman and Balfour (who was in charge of the British Embassy in Moscow while Clark-Kerr was away) to call. He gave them copies of a paper, remarking that "As everyone else is talking about Poland it would be wrong for us to remain silent." The Soviet statement was an angry contradiction of the Polish one. It accused the Polish government of giving a false account of the frontier question. The correct view, it averred, recognized that the frontiers of 1941 were in accord with the wishes of the peoples living in the Western Ukraine and Western White Russia. The earlier line had, it was asserted, been imposed by force and was unjust to these peoples and to the Soviet Union. The Soviet government, it continued, wanted to see a strong and independent Poland with which it could be friendly; and if the Polish people wished to enter into an alliance for mutual aid against the Germans this might be done if Poland became a party to the Soviet-Czech Treaty. But this new Poland should be reborn, not by seizing Ukraine and White Russian land, but by seeking the return of Polish lands taken away by Germany.[14]

Other sections of the statement adjudged the "emigrant" Polish government incapable of forming friendly relations with the Soviet Union and of leading an active fight against the Germans in Poland. In fact, the Soviet government declared that it thought it was playing into the hands of the German occupants; while in contrast the "Union of Polish Patriots in the USSR" and the Polish Army Corps under its auspices were operating hand in hand with the Red Army in the battle for liberation.

At once the black question arose whether this exchange of declarations showed so great a separation between the Soviet government and the Polish government in London as to make useless any further attempt to get them to resume relations on the basis of the Teheran formula. And if so, what else were the British and American governments to do? Were they to begin to deny the Soviet territorial claims at the risk of smashing the whole war alliance? Were they to coerce the Polish government in London if they could, even though its soldiers and airmen were fighting side by side with the Americans and British? Faced with such perplexities they had to conserve their optimism, their belief that a compromise could be reached.

Harriman in Moscow retained the impression that the Soviet government, despite its severe public rebuke, was still willing to enter into

---

[14] To record the exact language of this Soviet bid:

"The eastern frontiers of Poland can be established by agreement with the Soviet Union. The Soviet government does not regard the frontiers of 1939 as unalterable. These frontiers can be modified in Poland's favor so that the areas in which the Polish population forms the majority be turned over to Poland. In this case the Soviet-Polish frontier could pass approximately along the so-called Curzon Line, which was adopted in 1919 by the Supreme Council of the Allied Powers, and which provides for inclusion of the Western Ukraine and Western Byelorussia into the Soviet Union.

"The western frontiers of Poland must be extended through incorporation with Poland of ancient Polish lands previously wrested by Germany, without which it is impossible to unite the whole Polish people in its state, which thereby will receive a needed outlet to the Baltic Sea."

an accord with the Polish government in London similar to that which it had made with Benes, provided two main desires were met. One was that the impenitent anti-Soviet members of that government be dropped. The second desire was that the Polish government tacitly recognize the Soviet position about boundaries. Harriman predicted that as the Soviet troops advanced inside Poland the chances of getting an acceptable settlement would wane, that it was probable that the Poles could get a better deal if they acted at once rather than wait, hoping that the British and Americans would pull their chestnuts out of the fire.

Churchill and Eden were trying hard to persuade the Polish government that this was so. Their efforts at mediation brought forth on January 14th a second Polish statement, softer than the first one. This said that though the Polish government could not recognize imposed decisions or accomplished facts, it sincerely wished for an agreement with the Soviet government on terms just and acceptable to them both, and it announced that the British and American governments were being asked to act as intermediaries to get such an agreement.

The President still did not want to share that role. But, following on a talk with Hull, he agreed that Harriman should be told to let the Soviet government know that, without regard to the merits of the issues, we greatly hoped it would respond in a friendly way to this latest Polish offer to renew discussions; more than that, to say that despite a wish not to become actively involved in this dispute, the American government would be glad to use its good offices. By accident, the receipt of this instruction was delayed some days. Before Harriman could act upon it, the dispute became more aroused than ever.

The Soviet government failed to appreciate, or did not care, how hard the more conciliatory elements in the Polish government were trying to mend the break. To abbreviate, it flung out (on the 17th) another answer, treating the latest Polish response as a rejection of its proposals and again accusing the Polish government of hostility.

Churchill decided that the Poles must be brought to realize that they could only lose by continuing to be stubborn. So he put the alternatives to Mikolojczyk on January 20th in curt and ominous fashion. The distressed head of the Polish government has told how the Prime Minister bore down on him in an effort to get him to accept the Teheran formula. The Prime Minister said first, "The British government takes the view that Poland must be strong, independent and free." But then he added, "from the Curzon Line to the Oder." He warned Mikolajczyk that Great Britain and the United States would not go to war with the Soviet Union over Polish frontiers. He explained that the British and Soviet governments would guarantee these frontiers if Poland accepted them, but explained that Roosevelt could not do so.[15] He then told Mikolajczyk of the changes in the composition of the London government which Moscow was demanding, observing, however, that in this regard he could not entertain Stalin's authority to interfere in Polish "internal" questions.

Mikolajczyk said he would have to consult both with his colleagues in London and the political leaders who were living underground in Poland. While waiting to hear from this second group, he continued to seek more positive British and American aid in the efforts to resist Soviet demands. On the score of what the Red Army would do on Polish territory, Mikolajczyk asked them to find a way to send their troops into Poland to help support Polish administration of liberated areas and furnish protection against Soviet forces.[16] To Roosevelt, Mikolajczyk put three questions. One, did he think it advisable now to enter into settlement of European territorial questions? The American answer was that in general we were against doing so, but this attitude did not preclude direct settlements by mutual accord. Two, would the American government participate in bringing about and guaranteeing a settlement? The American answer was that we were ready to use our good offices to help in arranging a settlement, but were not in a position to guarantee it. Three, did the President support Churchill's particular suggestions? This was evaded by the reply that the American government was ready to support Churchill's "endeavors." [17] These were thin answers.

And yet, to leap ahead of other portions of the narrative of coalition business, for a government which was so loathe to become involved in this painful issue, the American government during the following weeks showed a great interest in what might happen next. In conjunction with the British government it tried harder than ever to heal the breach. Guided by instructions from home, both Harriman and Clark-Kerr pursued Molotov and Stalin so diligently into this field of trouble that Stalin became tired of it.

[15] As told by Mikolajczyk in his book *The Rape of Poland*, page 51. However, Hull in his *Memoirs*, page 1438, gives the substance of a note from Mikolajczyk (of January 26th) in which the Polish Prime Minister informed him of Churchill's suggestions, one point of which was, in Hull's summary, "Britain, Russia, and the United States to guarantee this settlement."

[16] The note to the British government making this request was probably written earlier, right after their public appeal for mediation on January 14th. It is dated, as printed in Mikolajczyk's book, pages 273–75, January 16th, but he recounts that he delivered it subsequent to his talk with Churchill on January 20th, *ibid.*, page 52.

[17] As summarized by Hull in his *Memoirs*, pages 1438–39.

In the first of Harriman's talks with Stalin on February 2nd, the Marshal put on the table a copy of a magazine that he said was printed by the Polish underground in Vilno. The headline he wished the Ambassador to note was "Hitler and Stalin—Two Aspects of the Same Evil." The fact that this article had been printed in the previous July did not seem to matter to him, nor that it was an almost unknown sheet. The statement on which he stood was that it was hard to deal with such people; that they might be able to fool Eden, but that this story showed their real character. He thought that the government was under the control of General Sosnkowski and others like him, who really wanted to work with Germany against the Soviet Union. The Poles liked to think, Stalin said toward the end of the talk, that the Russians were good fighters but fools, and that they could let the Russians carry the burden of the war and then step in at the end and share the spoils. They would, he said with all the weight of weight, find out who were fools.

The talk which the British Ambassador had with Stalin on the same day took much the same course. But Stalin did seem to come nearer saying that if the Polish government in London rid itself of those men whom he particularly mistrusted, and brought in men who were "democratic, anti-Fascist, and pro-Ally" he would deal with it. Among the direct answers that he gave to the direct questions asked by Clark-Kerr was that the Soviet government would allow democratic elections in Poland after liberation.

The advice Harriman got from Washington during the next few weeks was sincere but hardly likely to move the stubborn antagonists. Hull asked the Ambassador to impress both the Soviet and Polish governments with the wisdom of not doing anything that might affect full military cooperation, spoil the possibilities of international cooperation after the war, or affect adversely the President's prospects for election. But judgment as well as expediency influenced the American treatment of the situation. Roosevelt thought, and Harriman's and Winant's reports gave ground for the belief, that the Soviet government was not without cause in its refusal to deal with the Polish government until it ejected certain of its members. Some of its inner group were, in truth, making no secret of their hatred and complete mistrust of the Soviet Union. They were saying that the only real hope for Poland lay in a war between the West and the Soviet Union. So at the same time that Roosevelt, through Gromyko, the new Soviet Ambassador in Washington, and through Harriman, was trying to get Stalin not to ask too much or to act abruptly, he was also appealing to Churchill not to be too unbending about the demanded changes in the Polish government.

The prospects were not improved by the responses which Miko-lajczyk got from the group of underground political party leaders inside Poland (The Council of National Unity set up by the government-in-exile) and his Cabinet in London. These, in brief summary, were willing to accept the territory offered in the west. But they refused to cede what was asked in the east, proposing instead a temporary line of demarcation passing east of the cities of Lwow and Vilno, and rejecting the Soviet claim for part of East Prussia. They also proudly affirmed that changes in the Polish government and High Command could not be made in obedience to the demands of a foreign power. Equally firm was the opposition among the Polish fighting contingents who had carried on the fight against Germany with unwavering courage and endurance. For example, General Anders, who was in command of the Second Polish Corps and was in the center of the hardest fighting in Italy, on February 25, 1944 sent a message to his Commander-in-Chief, Sosnkowski, saying that, "all soldiers of the Polish Army in the east will refuse to consider the possibility of abandoning any scrap of Polish territory to the Bolsheviks. . . ."

The tone of the note in which the Polish government informed Churchill of the substance of these resolutions depressed him. At the end of a talk that followed with Mikolajczyk, he turned away with the gloomy remark that, "I'll have a public statement on this matter in the near future." This he made on the 22nd of February in the House of Commons. After referring to Stalin's assurances that he wanted a strong, integral, and independent Poland, the Prime Minister went on to say, "I cannot feel that the Russian demand for a reassurance about her Western frontiers goes beyond the limits of what is reasonable or just. Marshal Stalin and I also spoke and agreed upon the need for Poland to obtain compensation at the expense of Germany both in the North and in the West."

On the last day of February, Clark-Kerr, with a new analysis of Churchill's in hand, again tried to see whether Stalin might grant relief and reprieve to the Polish government, if only because of the deep association between the three Allies. His report began (in paraphrase), "I saw Stalin tonight. It was not a pleasant talk. He attempted to dismiss with a snigger the position of the Polish government as described in the Prime Minister's message." It ended with the comment that, "This dreary and exasperating conversation lasted for well over an hour. No argument was of any avail."

Harriman's following talk with Stalin (on March 3rd) uncovered the same hostile contempt for the Polish government in London. When the Ambassador told Stalin why he had sought the interview, Stalin's first response was one of annoyance. "Again the Poles," he said, "is that the most important question?" He had been kept so busy with the Poles, he went on, that he had not had time for military matters. And then he restated the Soviet position with an even more marked accent of dislike for the Polish government in London than in his talk with Clark-Kerr. He dismissed the idea that if a solution was not found there might be a civil war in Poland, asking, war with whom? between whom? where? How could it happen—since the Polish government had no armed forces of any size inside Poland and its underground was small, just a few agents of the London government? While the Red Army was liberating Poland, he predicted, Mikolajczyk would just go on repeating his platitudes; by the time Poland was freed another government would have emerged inside the country.

As for Churchill's efforts to bring about a reconstruction of the Polish government in London, Stalin thought that he was being deceived and would accomplish nothing. When Harriman remarked that the President feared that on the basis of the Soviet proposals Poland would "get a hand-picked government with no popular movement behind it," Stalin said there were no grounds for this assumption. Poland did not need the elements represented in London—it needed democrats who would look out for the interests of the people and avert chaos and anarchy.

Harriman loaned Clark-Kerr a copy of his report to the President on this talk. The note which Clark-Kerr wrote on the margin after reading it expressed the anguish of many diplomats who for a century and longer had tried to smooth out a concordance about Poland— "My God! Who would be an Ambassador!"

Stalin in a message to Churchill on March 23rd reproached him for not being stern enough with the Poles: "I do not doubt," he said, "that if you had continued to stand firmly on your Teheran position the conflict with the Polish emigrant government would have already been solved."

And, taking heed of word that Churchill was planning to state in the House of Commons that all territorial changes ought to be postponed until the peace conference, and that until then he could not recognize any transference of territory affected by force, Stalin roughly said: "You are free to make any speech in the House of Commons. That is your affair. But if you make such a speech, I shall consider that you have committed an act of injustice and unfriendliness toward the Soviet Union."

Mikolajczyk at this time was again seeking an interview with the

President. The President was still putting him off. The Poles and the Russians seemed so decisively apart on the territorial question that, until one or the other changed its position, he saw no chance for an accord. He was afraid that the publicity that would result from a personal meeting with Mikolajczyk might give the impression that the American government was taking Poland's side. We were—so far has this telling of the trouble over Poland been allowed to outrun the rest of our story—on the brink of OVERLORD, and the invaders counted upon coordinated Russian military assaults in the east to prevent the transfer of German forces to the west. Thus, to quote Hull, "We could not afford to become partisan in the Polish question to the extent of alienating Russia at the crucial moment." [18] The requirements of coalition warfare came first.

As for Churchill—on the verge of those great combined assaults which were to expose the whole future of Europe—he could see nothing but more ulceration about Poland. He was provoked by the stub-

---

[18] *Memoirs.* page 1442.

In accord with the idea that Stalin and Molotov had expressed to the American and British governments that the Polish government in London might begin to make itself over by giving place to democratic Poles then living in the United States, Britain, and elsewhere, they had asked the American government to make it possible for two American citizens of Polish extraction to come to Moscow. These were Professor Oskar Lange of the University of Chicago and Father Orlemanski, a Catholic parish priest from Springfield, Mass. Both of these men were known to be Soviet admirers and sympathizers. Despite the way which Stalin was refusing to give any ground for the sake of arriving at an accord, the President decided that these men should be allowed to go to Moscow.

They went, and were warmly welcomed, made much of in the press, and taken hither and yon. Stalin and Molotov found hours of time to talk with them. They both, it need hardly be said, became more and more enthusiastic in their view that the Soviet position in regard to Poland was fair, and that Stalin sincerely wished to see a strong, free, and independent Poland. These two enlisted advocates for Soviet position told American representatives in Europe in the fullest detail of what they had seen and heard and said. Orlemanski's reports of his talks with Stalin and Molotov were garrulous, almost verbatim, made interesting by their naïvete and the singular way in which he thought he saw a fusion of purpose betwen the Soviet government and the church to which he belonged. The student of this episode will find entertainment in the lively and nonsensical detail in the accounts he gave of his talks, especially a long report written by DeWitt C. Poole.

The Soviet government probably had two purposes in mind in inviting these two men to the Soviet Union. It hoped to educate advocates who would go back to the United States and present the Soviet position sympathetically to Polish communities in the United States. It also, although this may have been an afterthought, regarded this as a step for recruiting Polish individuals with connections in the United States who might take part in another government for Poland that was developing under the auspices of the Soviet government. Lange ultimately did join the Polish government so formed, and served as its first Ambassador in Washington. He is still in Poland, an important member of the Polish Diet.

bornness and pretensions of the Polish group in London. He was hurt and angry at Stalin's treatment of his efforts, at his harsh rejection of British and American pleas that he yield something to Polish sentiment and allow the Poles to prove their friendship without being abject. Soviet behavior revived in him and Eden suppressed memories of how badly the British had been treated by the Soviet government in the past; of the Molotov-Ribbentrop Treaty, which left the West alone; of the insults hurled at them by Stalin. They resolved anew that the Soviet should not destroy freedom in Poland, the country in whose defense Britain had gone to war. As they saw it, enormous British effort had been rewarded only with ingratitude; they had managed to get the Polish government to agree to accept a compromise demarcation line (running east of Vilno and Lwow) for civilian administrative purposes during the war, leaving the final settlement of the boundary until later. Such an arrangement would, they thought, spare the Polish government-in-exile the dire need of agreeing to permanent territorial amputation before being authorized by their countrymen, and still it would have obtained world acceptance of the adjustments which the Soviet government was demanding. And what had they gotten for all this? Insults from Stalin. Soviet policy was to have the Red Army establish boundaries, using force as a substitute for the goodwill of mankind. Teheran had not changed that.

These thoughts and feelings Churchill and Eden made known to the American government through Winant and Harriman. But Roosevelt did not regard this Polish question as vital or clear enough to risk the impact of dramatic action upon the military operations in prospect, and upon his campaign for reelection. Harriman was in Washington in the middle of May. The messages which the President wanted carried back to Stalin were still that he could not take an active interest in the Polish question until after the election; that the Curzon Line, with some adjustments, seemed to him a sound basis for settlement though he remained puzzled about Lwow; that he had put off Mikolajczyk's visit as long as he could, and before agreeing to receive him had secured a promise that the Polish Prime Minister would not make any public speeches while in the United States; and that he intended to tell him that he must get rid of those elements around him which would not cooperate with the Soviet Union if he wished a settlement. Roosevelt also wanted Stalin to know that he hoped that Soviet statements about the Poles would avoid further controversy and would stress the affirmative side of Soviet intentions—friendship and independence for the Poles and freedom of religion—so that arguments over the question should not be aroused during the election campaign.

Before Harriman had the chance to convey these messages, the strain between London and Moscow relaxed and hopes for a possible Soviet-Polish accord revived.

The brightest turn came about by the completion of an understanding between the British and Soviet governments about other troubled situations in Europe—which forms an important story soon to be told.[19] Cheered by that, and because Stalin's messages on other subjects had again become "civil," Churchill once more took heart. Thus he told Harriman, who stopped off at London on his way back to Moscow, when they talked on May 25th that, without seeing clearly how it would be worked out, he was hopeful that a tolerable settlement could be found eventually about Poland. In sum, Harriman was able to report to the President after this talk that ". . . the sun is shining again on the Soviet horizon."

A wish not to neglect any chance of breaking the Russian-Polish impasse marked the first talk which Harriman had with Molotov about Poland (June 3rd) after his return from Washington. The Ambassador explained the President's views in a friendly fashion—while making clear that the American government was still obligated to sustain the Polish government in London and that it would not have anything to do with other Polish groups who were soliciting its attention. What might well have impressed Molotov most in this talk was the restatement which Harriman made of Roosevelt's and Hull's resolve that the understandings for solidarity in Soviet-American relations reached at Moscow and Teheran should be made effective; and in this spirit that the search for agreement on all questions ought not to be checked by minor obstacles. A few days later Harriman was able to report to the President that, on seeing him again, Molotov had told him that Stalin was greatly pleased at the President's attitude.

Thus on the eve of the invasion of France, and of the long postponed entry into Rome, the most disturbing question of Poland seemed to have been brought back into the area of friendship. So also, for the time being, was the management of other emergent and troubling situations in the Balkans. This stretch of dangerous strain was thus passed. The tension had been real enough to have led even to separation, if at that time the armed forces of the three countries had not been just about to become engaged in their greatest assault on Germany. For that purpose, in contrast, the three main Allies had been during this troubled

[19] Sections 34–35–36 will tell of political developments in the whole range of countries south and southeast of Germany, of the consultations within the coalition about them, and of the Anglo-Soviet accord about spheres of influence.

spring managing to cooperate excellently. It is next in order to notice that—before we revert to the tale of their difficulties over emergent political problems.

31. Teheran to OVERLORD, June 1944; Excellent Military Cooperation in Europe

In the weeks after Teheran, the contest between strategic ideas that had been smoothed over at that Conference had broken out again. The battle in Italy was still halted on the line from Cassino to the sea. All the senior commanders in the Mediterranean area had begun to favor an amphibious venture in back of the Germans, a landing just south of the Tiber to join up with a new surge forward of the main armies. The issue presented was whether the means for this operation could be found without postponing or injuring other scheduled actions, particularly OVERLORD. The plan first in mind after Teheran was for a small expedition—one division. However, an amphibious assault on so limited a scale could not, it was judged, be wisely attempted until the main armies were near enough to come at once to the aid of the landing force. But for a larger expedition it could be foreseen that it would be necessary to retain landing craft consigned to OVERLORD and ANVIL, and cease the effort to take Rhodes and other Aegean islands.

Churchill, nevertheless, had directed his powers of advocacy to bring about the larger Italian landing. On December 25th he proposed this directly to the President, asking that the transfer of some of the landing craft then in use in Italy be delayed so that there might be a two-division landing at Anzio on the 20th of January next. "If this opportunity is not grasped," he wrote, "we must expect the ruin of the Mediterranean campaign of 1944." [20] The British Chiefs of Staff shared his desire, having in mind a two-division operation, plus paratroops, with the aim of capturing Rome and advancing to the Pisa-Rimini Line.

The Prime Minister, then still recuperating in the African warmth, had brought together on Christmas Day at Tunis all the senior commanders in the area, among them General Eisenhower, who was soon to leave to take command of OVERLORD; General Wilson, who was to succeed him as Supreme Allied Commander in the Mediterranean

[20] *Closing the Ring,* page 437.

theater; General Alexander, who was in command of operations in Italy; and the naval commanders. Accounts do not convey clearly whether General Eisenhower's acceptance of the proposal was ready or reluctant. He did warn that coastal landing was not likely to cause the Germans to withdraw from Central and Southern Italy, as Churchill was contending; that it was more probable that they would bring more combat troops into the battle south of Rome; and that therefore more than two divisions would be required for this venture.

On December 28th the President had agreed that landing craft might be retained so that the two-division approach over the Anzio beach could be tried about the time Churchill had suggested. But he said that his assent was on the understanding that OVERLORD remain the paramount operation, and that it would be carried out on the date agreed at Cairo and Teheran. Churchill was relieved, being not too much troubled by the President's condition. His confidence that this new Italian venture would not be abandoned for lack of means, is recorded in the message which on January 8th he sent to General Mark Clark, who was to command the Anzio operation, and who did not wholly share his confidence. "I hope they [the staff officers who had gone to Marrakech to talk with Churchill and had just returned] will reassure you completely about the aquatic support our great operation [SHINGLE] will receive. It may even be possible to throw in the equivalent of a third division, which ought to clinch matters. I am deeply conscious of the importance of this battle, without which the campaign in Italy will be regarded as having petered out ingloriously." [21]

As the main armies in Italy began a vigorous offensive against the German lines, the Anzio landing had been launched on January 21st. It ran into great trouble and was almost thrown back into the sea. The troops that were landed on the beaches were saved only by bringing up large sustaining forces. The original plans contemplated the use of about 50,000 men in the Anzio operation; by the end of February about 170,000—more than six divisions—were engaged.

The assault against the German lines at Cassino, which was to have resulted in quick junction with the forces landed at Anzio, had also been checked. The campaign leading to Rome which the hopeful had thought would be won quickly went on into the spring, using up greater and greater Allied forces drawn from many nations. The Germans, too, suffered heavily and were compelled to keep sending in divisions from France, Germany, and Yugoslavia to maintain the fight.

[21] General Mark W. Clark, *Calculated Risk*, page 260.

This could be regarded as justification and consolation, and was so regarded by Churchill and his military advisers. The Americans were rueful.

The Allies had been rebuffed in Turkey also. President Inonu had accepted the invitation which Churchill and Roosevelt had sent from Teheran to meet them at Cairo. Vishinsky had been there as Soviet consultant. For three days (December 4th–6th) Churchill applied all the prongs of persuasion in an effort to move him. The military men tried to convince him that by following a secret strategy of gradual engagement Turkey would safeguard itself against the risk of suffering great damage. But Inonu had not been swayed. His government, he had averred, was disposed to enter the war but was still unprepared to do so. If and when what he thought to be its essential requirements for protection were met, he had continued, "we will come with you." But he had refused to assume any obligation, and promised only to consult his colleagues in Ankara. After some weeks his answer had been received. It had been merely a repetition of an agreement in principle to enter the war—on condition that the Allies first make good Turkish deficiencies in all kinds of combat equipment and provide air support and transport. Their needs in all these respects the Turks reckoned to be very large. The continuation of the talk into February had not overcome Turkish fears and hesitations, nor had British and American reprimands. All ideas and plans for an Allied military campaign based on Turkey lapsed.

Churchill and his colleagues had grieved over what they regarded as a brilliant lost chance to rout the Germans from the southeast. The American government had been sorry, but the Joint Chiefs were also partly relieved at the passing of a possible extra diversionary demand upon combat resources. The Soviet government had turned sulky and assumed the attitude that it was freed from the obligation taken at Moscow to act toward Turkey only in concert with the Allies.

In the greater realms of strategy during these same first months of 1944, Eisenhower and his commanders had reexamined the plans for OVERLORD. They had come to the conclusion that the first attempted landings in France had to be in greater force than had been earlier assigned, and over a wider area.[22] To do that, and to be sure of the

[22] See Forrest C. Pogue, *The Supreme Command,* Chapter VI, "SHAEF Revises Plans for the Attack." Eisenhower on January 23, 1944 formally proposed that the number of divisions in the initial assault should be increased from three to five; and besides an airborne landing in the Caen area, he wanted an airborne division to seize the exit from the Cotentin beaches, with a second airborne division to follow in this same locality within

needed additional landing craft, naval fire support, and aircraft, it had been concluded that it would be advisable to postpone the starting date for OVERLORD. First it had been agreed to put it off from early May (the date originally preferred by the Americans) to late May, and then it was advanced again to the early June moon. The postponement gained one more month's production of landing craft; it afforded that much more time to assemble the means of landing and combat; and it gave the Allied bombing units more chance and better conditions to impede the movement of German reserves and demolish German coast defenses. Besides, it shortened the interval between the landings in Normandy and the new great offensive which the Russians were going to start on the Eastern Front.

The same competition for combat means had caused a revival of debate as to whether the landing in Southern France, ANVIL, should be attempted—either at the same time as OVERLORD, later, or not at all. The British Chiefs of Staff, with Churchill before and after them, had found new ground for doubt in the way that the battle in Italy was going. Churchill (as early as February 4th) had resumed his criticisms of the plan, leaning hard on the opinion that because of the distances between the OVERLORD and ANVIL areas, the rugged terrain which the forces landed in the south would have to traverse, and the defensive strength opposing them, ANVIL was not interwoven with OVERLORD. The British Chiefs of Staff had proposed that the Southern France project be cancelled, and that the allocated forces should be devoted to other operations in the Mediterranean area. The U.S. Joint Chiefs of Staff were willing to postpone, or even cancel ANVIL if Eisenhower thought that essential to strengthen OVERLORD. But they were more strongly opposed than ever to large new ventures either in Italy or farther east on the Mediterranean.

On March 21st General Wilson had asked for a new directive. The orders given him would be most crucial for the next offensive in Italy, which was soon to be resumed—the drive to overcome the Cassino Line on the way to Rome and beyond.

Despite what had happened, Churchill had continued to contend as forcefully as before that it would be a shame as well as a mistake not to leave enough campaign resources in the Mediterranean to do what he thought could be done. During these same weeks of March he was aggravated at the vigorous efforts of the Americans in trying to bring

---

twenty-four hours. The increases were made in the final plan. Both the U.S. 82nd and 101st Airborne Divisions landed on Cotentin Peninsula on D-Day. *Cross-Channel Attack,* page 279, *et seq.*

about a basic reconstruction in the Badoglio government. He was troubled also by American resistance to his wish to recognize the French Committee of National Liberation. Then, too, there was his nasty quarrel with Stalin about the Polish boundaries on which Roosevelt at this time was giving little help. For some or all of these reasons Churchill sought another meeting with Roosevelt, bringing together the Combined Chiefs of Staff as well, for early April at Bermuda. But the President was fatigued, and he did not want to be subjected to Churchill's strong contentions, especially about strategic matters, at this time. On April 8th he went to South Carolina for a rest. Admiral Leahy, who went along with him, remembers himself saying in jest, as they passed markers on a road telling of visits to the area by Lafayette, Washington, and Monroe, that another historical marker should be placed on the highway to tell future visitors that in 1944 Roosevelt also traveled this route to escape the British.[23]

Denied the chance for immediate face-to-face discussion with the President, Churchill had done the best he could at long range, scolding his American friends for their continued belief in the value of ANVIL and their insistence that divisions should be taken away from Italy for that operation. As put by him to Marshall on April 16th:

"What I cannot bear is to agree beforehand to starve a battle [still to reach Rome] or have to break it off just at the moment when success, after long efforts and heavy losses, may be in view. . . . Please do me the justice to remember that the situation is vastly changed [since Teheran]. In November, we hoped to take Rome in January, and there were many signs that the enemy was ready to [retire] northward up the Italian peninsula. Instead of this, in spite of our great amphibious expedition, we are stuck where we are, and the enemy has brought down to the battle south of Rome the eight mobile divisions we should have hoped a full-scale 'Anvil' would have contained. Thus there has been cause for rejoicing as well as bitter disappointment."[24]

The Joint Chiefs of Staff were swayed by this gale of argument. All means required to start the cross-Channel invasion on the new D-Day (two or three days before or after June 1st) and in fullest strength were assured. So they gave in to British insistence that the combat force in Italy should not be reduced or deprived of landing craft and other means of continuing the offensive there. And they agreed to postpone ANVIL without any guarantee that it would be carried out later.

The compromise and interim directive to General Wilson left the future indefinite. On April 19th the Combined Chiefs directed him to:

[23] *I Was There,* page 236.
[24] *Closing the Ring,* pages 513–14.

(a) launch as early as possible an all-out offensive in Italy; (b) develop the most effective threat possible to contain German forces in Southern France; and (c) make plans for the "best possible use of the amphibious lift remaining to you, either in support of operations in Italy, or in order to take advantage of opportunities arising in the south of France or elsewhere for the furtherance of your objects and to press forward vigorously and wholeheartedly with all preparations which do not prejudice the achievement of the fullest success in (a) above." [25]

Under this directive Alexander was enabled to begin his large offensive on May 11th in adequate strength. About twenty-eight Allied divisions in all took part in the campaign (from Great Britain, New Zealand, Canada, South Africa, India, the United States, France, and Poland) besides large naval and air forces. As victory came close at the end of May, Churchill's congratulatory comment to Alexander was in order: "How lucky it was that we stood up to our United States Chiefs of Staff friends and refused to deny you the full exploitation of this battle!" [26] At long last on June 4th Rome was entered.

For the Germans who tramped under the swastika, this was an ominous week and month. Two days before the capture of Rome a large force of American bombing planes had flown from Italy east on shuttle flight to new bases in Soviet territory, at Poltava; no place in the German combat area was thereafter out of range of destruction from the air. Two days after, the great Allied invasion expedition appeared in the morning light off the beaches of Normandy. In the east the huge Red Armies were completing their preparations to pound the whole length of the defending line. The coalition was allowing the Germans no immune or easily protected areas, no rest or reprieve from blast and battle. Military cooperation between its members during this season of the war reached its most enthusiastic and unblighted pitch.

The main narrative may be interrupted briefly to tell of the arrangement for shuttle bombing bases at Poltava, to which passing reference has been made. This had been arranged only after much nagging by us. Roosevelt at Teheran had presented this project to Stalin, leaving with him a memo of the Joint Chiefs of Staff. After keeping the eager American Mission in Moscow waiting for weeks, Molotov had finally told Harriman that the Soviet government had no objection in principle to granting the bases which were desired, and that the Soviet

[25] Forrest C. Pogue, *The Supreme Command,* Washington, D.C.: Office of the Chief of Military History, Department of the Army, 1954, page 117.
[26] *Closing the Ring,* page 609.

Air Command was being instructed to begin talks about their organization and use. But this promise had turned out to be just a preface for another long wait. The Ambassador had concluded that the spirit of Teheran had not yet penetrated the lower ranks of Soviet officials. After further patient effort—and eight talks with Molotov about the matter since Teheran—had brought little results, he had sought an interview with Stalin. That (on February 2nd) had brought a comforting reply. The Marshal had agreed to provide facilities on Soviet airfields for 150–200 American heavy bombers as the initial force to be used in shuttle operations, and also for photo-reconnaissance flights from Italy and England. Having had the command, others obeyed.

Thereafter, arrangements for the shuttle bombing operation had moved forward. The Soviet military organizations had worked in harmony with the Americans to get the bases at Poltava ready. The Russians had been consulted about targets for the first expedition. Russian fighter squadrons had given the bombing force protection and other Russian planes had attacked German airdromes to weaken the German defense. The Commander of the American squadron flew in first in what the Russian press described as a "silver aircraft" with the name "Yankee Doodle" on the fuselage. The commanding Soviet air officer stepped forward as soon as the American was on the ground, to give him a bouquet of flowers. Harriman barely avoided a "victory embrace." A few days later General Eaker (Allied Air Commander-in-Chief in the Mediterranean) pinned the medal of the Legion of Merit with a citation signed by Roosevelt upon the Russian General in Command of the base who was, if anything, more excited than the Americans.[27] But when, in his next talk with Stalin, Harriman thanked him for the bases which had been made available, Stalin calmly remarked, "This is the least we can do to assist." Harriman reported that the Soviet officials were emphasizing to him not only the tactical value of the operation but its great effect on morale, both in the Soviet Union and among the enemy by destroying the Hitler-Goebbels propaganda that the Allies could be divided.

[27] How high the enthusiasm ran among the officers of the American Air Force is shown when General Eaker met Molotov on June 5th. The American General said that he wanted to offer to the Red Army all the Intelligence information we had on the German Air Force and its tactics, and about the battle experience of the U.S. Air Force in Italy and England. Further, he offered to take a Soviet Air Force representative back with him so that he might see the technical equipment of the U.S. Air Force and how it operated. Molotov answered that he was sure that the Soviet air authorities would make use of this generous offer.

These scenes of comradeship-in-arms after the first successful landing at Poltava expressed also the rejoicing in the Soviet Union over the news of the capture of Rome (on June 4th) and the landings in Normandy (on the morning of June 6th). The Americans, British, and Canadians were coming up from the beaches over the rising dunes, where their swing and sweep was seen from Moscow. The "second front"—that particular battlefront in France for which the Soviet authorities had waited since the Germans turned against them in 1941—was in existence.

That vast operation had been set and scheduled definitely at Teheran. Stalin had then thought that General Marshall would command it. But when told that the job was to be given to Eisenhower, he had spoken as though just as well pleased with the selection. To Harriman he had said, "I am satisfied. He is an officer of great experience in amphibious warfare and a man of determination."

The directive given by the Combined Chiefs of Staff to Eisenhower had described his task clearly and succinctly: "You will enter the continent of Europe, and, in conjunction with the other United Nations, undertake operations aimed at the heart of Germany and the destruction of her armed forces. The date for entering the Continent is the month of May 1944. After adequate channel ports have been secured, exploitation will be directed to securing an area that will facilitate both ground and air operations against the enemy."

At frequent intervals Roosevelt and Churchill had kept the Soviet authorities informed in ample detail of the progress of plans and preparations for Operations OVERLORD and ANVIL, as well as the course of the battle in Italy. Stalin had responded with thanks and with brief reports on what was happening on the Soviet front. He had not told in advance about the plans for the Soviet offensive that was to coincide with OVERLORD. He was not asked to do so since Eisenhower did not think it necessary to know them. Churchill and the President had agreed with him. The reason for reserve hinted by the Soviet officials was that secret knowledge the American government got from others would not be absolutely safe in its keeping.

On the 18th of April Stalin had acknowledged with satisfaction a Roosevelt-Churchill report that the cross-Channel operation would take place as then scheduled (early in June) and would be of fullest strength. He had confirmed that the Red Army would at the same time launch a new offensive in order to give maximum support to the Anglo-American operations. As D-Day drew near, Churchill had thrown away his anxieties and had blessed the invasion prospect with his enthusiasm.

It had required the august command of the Crown as well as the grave protests of the War Cabinet and his senior military commanders to keep him out of the first assault wave. And then, as soon as the invading forces had secured a small area and he could no longer be held back, he had paid them a visit.

Stalin had acknowledged the first quick bulletins of progress of the landing in France with his usual formal awkwardness. "We all greet you and the valiant British and American armies and warmly wish you further successes." But when he saw Harriman on June 10th, a few days after the Ambassador's return from the United States, his pleasure found freer flow. On being shown a map marking where the Allied troops had landed and where they were that evening as they talked, Stalin is remembered to have said, in effect, "The history of war has never witnessed so grandiose an operation. Napoleon himself never attempted it. Hitler had envisaged it and was a fool for never having tried it." [28] Stalin in this same talk went on to explain that the concurrent Soviet offensive was being slightly delayed because it was taking longer to clear the Crimea and to transfer troops than had been foreseen. On that very day, however, he said the Soviet forces had begun an offensive against the Finns north of Leningrad, that they would move forward on another part of the front within fifteen days, and that by July the Soviet offensive along the whole line would be at its full force.

The Soviet military actions were carried out on this revised schedule. Stalin did not allow the chance to pass to call attention to this fact. His sense of being regarded with suspicion showed in a remark he made in his next long talk with Harriman (on the 26th) while reviewing the record of the arrangements for the dual offensives, beginning with the agreement at Teheran. Despite this, he said, ". . . some people had some doubt about what he would do." Harriman said he had heard of none. All the top Americans—whom he named—were, he remarked, so sure that the Soviet offensive would be started as promised they had

[28] This is a condensed version of his remarks as they appear in the American memo of the talk. In a message which he sent to Churchill on the next day, June 11th, he said much the same thing. This message, as printed in *Triumph and Tragedy*, page 9, was: "As is evident, the landing, conceived on a grandiose scale, has succeeded completely. My colleagues and I cannot but admit that the history of warfare knows no other like undertaking from the point of view of its scale, its vast conception, and its masterly execution. As is well known, Napoleon in his time failed ignominiously in his plan to force the Channel. The hysterical Hitler, who boasted for two years that he would effect a forcing of the Channel, was unable to make up his mind even to hint at attempting to carry out his threat. Only our Allies have succeeded in realizing with honour the grandiose plan of the forcing of the Channel. History will record this deed as an achievement of the highest order."

not even asked about its size or location. But the Marshal was not to be so easily convinced; he repeated that he thought there had been doubts "in certain quarters."

Stalin's impression that either the Americans or British doubted the reliability of his promise was without ground. But the President and Marshall, and probably others, had had some fear that if the Americans and British did not carry through the plans approved at Teheran, in full as approved there—in particular if they did not make the landing in Southern France when they could—the Soviets might also retreat from the agreement and change their plans. This was a factor, recognized by Churchill, in their opposition to British diversionary proposals elsewhere.

There were, however, some diplomatic officials in lesser posts who suspected that the later selection of points of assault and the timing and pace of Soviet offensives were influenced in behalf of Soviet political aims. Various members of the governments-in-exile of Central and Eastern European states were convinced that this was done. The subject is a complex one and must be left to specialists, with more detailed and expert knowledge, to determine. Thorough study is warranted, for example, of the reasons for the interruption in the advance of the Red Army into Romania during the early summer; of the long pause before Warsaw while the Polish underground army in that city was being destroyed, a most tragic tale which will be found in later pages; and of the direction of forces toward Hungary.

But this is a digression. To repeat, the responsible Americans and British had no real doubt that the Soviet government would do its stint in the east while they were doing theirs in France. Soviet advances cheered and encouraged them, as bringing the ardently sought end near. Their enthusiasm is well illustrated by the compliment which Eisenhower on July 7th, in a note to Harriman, paid to the first successes of the great new Soviet offensive. "I have been tracing Red Army progress on my map. Naturally I got a tremendous thrill out of the rate at which they are demolishing the enemy's fighting power. I wish I knew how to express properly to Marshal Stalin and his Commanders my deep admiration and respect."

Summing up, in this period of the conjoined great assaults, frictions among the Allies over other matters—frontiers, the control of governments, and the fate of kings—did not lessen the momentum or change the course of military cooperation. But it did not prove easy to carry this forward by continuous consultation.

Harriman, guided by talks which he had had with the President, the

Joint Chiefs of Staff, and Eisenhower, consulted Stalin on June 26th about a possible bold step toward fuller coordination of military plans and activities. Now that the American and British armies were on the Continent, and the Russian armies were coming nearer to them, did it not seem necessary, he asked, to set up some close liaison? Would it not be useful to both sides to know the plans and future strategy of the other? Stalin agreed that it would, saying that a consultative group for such liaison should be formed. His assent seemed to be restrained only by the fear that the secrets from Soviet sources would leak out. The danger that this might happen was closely connected in his mind with the fact that American and British newspapermen wrote articles for personal profit. As an example to show that his anxiety on this point was justified, he referred to the seepage into the press of messages that he had sent to Churchill about Soviet proposals to the EAC concerning the treatment of the German army. The Ambassador pointed out that such leaks as there might have been were concerned with political questions. In regard to military matters, he maintained that the record showed that the American and British staffs had kept the greatest secrecy and security. His proofs were hard to dispute: the way in which the Germans were surprised when we turned up in North Africa; their ignorance of where we were going to land in France; and the many times our moves in the Pacific caught the Japanese off guard.

Stalin's response warranted Harriman's report to the President— that he thought Stalin was ready to establish liaison between the Red Army staff and General Eisenhower. But, he added, because Stalin doubted whether secrets would be safe with us, the liaison arrangement would have to be carefully worked out. He recommended that General Deane, the Head of the American Military Mission in Moscow, be used as the channel.

Meanwhile, the Soviet authorities remained on the alert for any signs of default or deception by their Western Allies. And when puzzled, they still seemed to think, as before, that the best route to the truth was through the tunnel of suspicion. During July when the soldiers of OVERLORD were making their position in Normandy firm while the Red Army was forcing its way swiftly through White Russia, the Soviet press tended to carp at the slow rate of advance in France, discounting the idea that German resistance in the west might be harder to break. Then, during August, after the Western forces broke out of their positions in Normandy, and landed in Southern France, and began to surge rapidly east and north, while the Red Army was halted before Warsaw, the Soviet comment shifted. Western successes were ascribed mainly to the fact that the Germans had been compelled to use such great forces in the east that they had no reserves left to meet the assaults in the west. The Soviet leaders were not going to allow their people to admire the military performance in the west too gratefully.

And actually, as will be further traced, consultation with the Soviet authorities about plans for future operations remained fragmentary. The Combined Chiefs of Staff continued on the whole to decide their movements in Europe before discussing them with the Russians; and the Russians did the same. It was not yet essential to act in close concert, or to define in common the precise lines the converging armies would follow.

The only vigorous discussion of strategy that went on during this summer of progress was between the two Allies in the west. No sooner had Rome been taken, than Churchill put the old question in a fresh jacket of circumstance. "Should we go through with ANVIL or should we make a new plan?" He and his advisers had advocated a new-old plan: to continue forward in Italy on a large scale, and go across the Adriatic and strive to reach Vienna. The Americans were no more willing to adopt this plan than ever. But the further tale of military discussions and actions will have more meaning after a review of the many political situations—besides Poland—over which, during this period, the members of the coalition were having trouble. First, those concerning France.

32. Compelling Questions concerning France

The preparation and execution of operation OVERLORD had compelled the Allies to confront many connected questions of relationship with the French armed forces, French political groups, and the French nation. What part were the French forces to play in the reentry operations, and who would command them? Should de Gaulle, as President of the French National Committee and Consultative Assembly, in Algiers, be consulted about the military plans or even be informed of them? How were the invading armies, after landing in France, to manage their relations with the people living there?

The tale of what was done about these matters will be clearer after a summary itemization of some of the main occurrences in the affairs of the French National Committee and France since last we took notice of them—as of the end of June, 1943.

The governments of the three main Allies had been unable to agree upon a common basis of treatment of the French Committee. Roosevelt had continued to refuse to consider any form of public statement that would accord or imply *recognition* of the Committee's claim to speak and act for the whole of the French people. He had been afraid that de Gaulle's growing control—which other historians have traced— might interfere with our military and political plans. He was determined, in the expression he had taken to using, not to give de Gaulle a "white horse" on which he could ride into France and make himself the master of a government there. For these attitudes and opinions his Secretary of State Hull had stood advance guard.

Churchill and Eden, though more often at odds with de Gaulle than not, would have been willing to bear the disadvantages and risks of recognition for the sake of encouraging French national and fighting spirit. But the Prime Minister had been constrained by the thought he had expressed in a Minute to his colleagues on July 13th: "Even if Soviet Russia recognises de Gaulle on account of his recent flirtations with Communist elements, we should still be wise to measure our course by that of the United States. Indeed, in this case it would be still more important not to leave them isolated and give the appearance of working with Russia against them. . . ." [29] So he had continued to try to bring about a reconciliation between the Committee and the American government. But to no immediate avail.

At the Quebec Conference, on August 20th, Hull and Eden had found themselves falling into the sharpest talk experienced in their association over the issue of whether or not specifically to include the term "recognition" in the formula defining their relations with the French Committee. Eden had then said that because of the harm that might be caused by further delay, it might be necessary for each of the two to make its own announcement. Hull had answered, according to his later account, that he very much regretted the divergence but ". . . that if the British could stand it, we could too." [30] Each had written its separate statement, showed it to the other, and given it out (on August 26th) with a friendly nod right and left. As events moved along, it may be interjected, the careful differentiations between the two statements turned out to be of little actual consequence.

[29] *Closing the Ring*, page 179.
[30] *Memoirs*, page 1233.

314

The Soviet statement, postponed, it will be recalled, by request so that it could be issued at the same time, had been more definite than the other two. It had stated a decision: ". . . to recognize the French Committee of National Liberation as representative of the state interests of the French Republic and leader of all French patriots struggling against Hitlerite tyranny and to exchange plenipotentiary representatives with it."

De Gaulle and Stalin were using each other at this time (August 1943) the better to get more of a voice in the management of French and Italian affairs. Moscow could also hope by this gesture that French Communists might gain influence, both within the French Committee and in occupied France. De Gaulle wanted the cooperation of the French Communists in fighting the war and in maintaining order in France after the war. Although he had fished hard for this Soviet recognition, he had told Murphy and Macmillan on August 26th when they called on him with copies of the statements which their governments were about to issue, that while the French Communists were cooperating fully in efforts to liberate France, he reserved his opinion about their postwar aims, and would not allow them to dominate France.

Connected with this issue of recognition had been the question of whether the Committee, as representing France, should be included in the United Nations. Hull had been eager to have it adhere to the principles of the Declaration. The British and Soviet governments had also favored this. But de Gaulle had not been satisfied by this measure of acceptance; he had wanted to be received as a full and regular member. To this the American government had not been willing to assent. The action was to remain in suspense until the end of the war was in sight, by which time the Committee had been recognized as the Provisional Government of France.

Despite this uncertified status, the Committee had been awarded membership on the Advisory Council for Italy. De Gaulle had not been consulted about the armistice terms for Italy nor about the decision to accept Italian military cooperation. This he had taken not only as an affront, but as unfair disregard of the direct French interest in Italian affairs. The President had not wanted to give de Gaulle the chance to interfere in the conduct of the military occupation of Italy; and he had been afraid that the Italians would resent the presence of the French. But during the Moscow Conference in October, when it had been made clear that this new Council was to be advisory in character, the French Committee had been invited to join as an original member. The larger issue of opportunity—whether the Committee was also to be given membership in the European Advisory Commission—had remained unsettled.

During this autumn French political life in North Africa had been, in Churchill's words, "crystallizing into an embryo government for the future"; and de Gaulle's influence became paramount. In September, Giraud, in concert with the Americans, and without letting de Gaulle know what was afoot, had carried out an expedition which expelled the Germans from Corsica. This had angered de Gaulle and his colleagues. They had brought about early in October a reorganization of the Committee. Thereafter there was to be only one chairman, in all probability de Gaulle; and he was to have a veto power over all actions. Giraud, though retained as Commander-in-Chief of French armed forces, was to be subject to the direction of the Committee. He, on November 8th, had resigned from the Committee, though continuing for a little longer as Commander-in-Chief. By then, it may be remarked, the President had lost faith in his effectiveness as a check on de Gaulle, and Eisenhower had lost respect for his ability to organize the French armed forces.

At this juncture Churchill and Roosevelt had been further put off by the action taken by the French Committee about Lebanon. There the national movement for independence which had been promised was being repressed by force by de Gaulle's orders. Of the two, Churchill had been the more aroused. He had been ready to withdraw all favor from the Committee and, in conjunction with the United States, to suspend the arming of French troops in North Africa, unless de Gaulle agreed to allow the local government to operate again. Bending before this threat, the Committee began to negotiate with Lebanese and Syrian leaders for ultimate independence.

A private talk between Roosevelt and Stalin at Teheran on November 28th, by which time the Lebanon crisis was past, had illuminated the whole area of their thought about French affairs. Stalin, who up to then had upheld the Committee, had fallen in with Roosevelt's attitude toward de Gaulle but in doing so had given it a more ruthless significance. He had said he was of the impression that de Gaulle's political activities were unreal, since he acted as though he were really the head of a great state while France was, in fact, a comparatively small power. Furthermore, de Gaulle did not really represent the French people, the real France, which in Stalin's opinion, was still controlled by its corrupt upper and ruling classes; and under Pétain it was still helping Germany and wanting Germany to win. Therefore France, the real France, ought to be punished for its harmful acts and was not entitled to share in the benefits of peace.

It is still to be wondered whether Stalin's revealed animosity was connected with what was going on just then between de Gaulle and the French Communists. Twenty-seven former Communist deputies, released from prison, had been engaging in fervid political activity in North Africa; they had been agitating among the laborers and peasants and urging the Moslems to claim equal rights with the French. De Gaulle had offered them two Cabinet portfolios on condition that he could pass upon their selection, and that they would desist from their separate political efforts in favor of a common and unified policy of the Committee. This offer had been refused. And at this time all Communist elements in North Africa were carrying on a campaign against de Gaulle, accusing him of playing personal politics and neglecting the war effort.

Roosevelt in a passing way had tried to alleviate Stalin's condemnation. He had called Stalin's attention to the growing French military program in North Africa and to the real part being assigned to the French troops in the invasion. But he also said that he did not agree with Churchill's view that France could be quickly restored as a great nation; he, Roosevelt, thought that many years of honest labor by all the French would be necessary before France could ever again become great.

Doubts about French right and qualifications to regain control of various parts of its former Empire—particularly Indochina—also streaked through the talk of the Heads of State at Teheran: whether French rule ought not to be allowed to lapse or be replaced by trusteeships. Stalin insisted that France did not deserve to get Indochina back, and Roosevelt talked as though he thought the same. Stalin emphasized his view that France could not be trusted with any strategic possession outside its borders. Roosevelt showed favor toward the possibility of placing New Caledonia and Dakar under the trusteeship of the United Nations. But nothing final had been decided or arranged.

In reality, the military measures which the Heads of State had approved at Teheran had made their reserve toward the French Committee of National Liberation ineffectual in most respects, and their ideas about the future treatment of France and the French Empire unlikely. They had determined upon operations OVERLORD and ANVIL, the requirements of which would almost inevitably give the Committee the chance it wanted to emerge as the provisional government of France, and enable the French nation to resume its place in Europe and regain control over its broken Empire. But this does not seem to have been appreciated.

In any case, Roosevelt had stayed set against the drive of the Committee to be accepted as the Provisional Government of France. He had wanted to be sure that the French people would be in a position to choose their own government when the country was freed. Hence he had been determined that all French regular forces serving in the invasion should be subject to Eisenhower's orders. While he was willing to entrust the administration of civil affairs in their own country to Frenchmen, he was bent on having this brought about through the Supreme Commander and the French military authorities—thus averting initial domination by the Committee.

These ideas had shaped the first attempts to compose a statement of policy and a directive for Eisenhower in regard to civil administration—a task which, after brief discussion in Moscow, had been turned over to the European Advisory Commission. But the British had soon fallen away from the idea of leaving the Committee on the side. And so had Eisenhower. In Washington, in January 1944, he had tried hard to persuade the President and the Joint Chiefs of Staff that a close working arrangement with the Committee would be helpful, if not essential, to the management of some of the situations he would confront while the invasion went on. But Roosevelt had been adamant. He was still under the impression that many of the French people would not submit to the authority of the Committee, and any attempt to impose it might well lead to civil war. His belief in the danger of such a development was clearly displayed in his prolonged unwillingness, as told elsewhere, to accept the southern zone of occupation in Germany, because in that location our forces would be dependent on the use of French ports and communications running through France.

In March Eisenhower had stressed the need for instructions. So Roosevelt, with Churchill's approval, issued a directive, to enable him to propose a working agreement to the French. This accorded the Supreme Commander conclusive authority in France and the "ultimate determination of where, when and how the civil administration . . . shall be exercised by French citizens." He was allowed to consult the French Committee of National Liberation and might accept its nominations for this work. But he was to be careful not to recognize the Committee or any other French organization as the Provisional Government of France.[31]

On April 9th Hull had unexpectedly swung at least part way round in a speech approved by the President: "The President and I are clear, therefore, as to the need, from the outset, of French civil administration

[31] For a fuller account see *Grand Strategy*, Volume v, pages 327 *et seq.*

—and democratic French administration—in France. We are disposed to see the French Committee of National Liberation exercise leadership to establish law and order under the supervision of the Allied Commander-in-Chief."

Churchill had cheered. The British, who were averse to granting Eisenhower discretion to settle what they considered important political questions, tried to get Eisenhower's directive amended. They feared that for reasons of military convenience—as Stettinius, who was in London at this time, reported—he might fall into another Darlan deal. But Roosevelt had remained unwilling to curb Eisenhower's chance to deal with any and every French democratic group he thought qualified and helpful. And Molotov, after long delay, told him that the Soviet government thought his policy met military requirements. The American and British governments simply could not break their deadlock.

And thus in late April Eisenhower, in despair, had permitted Generals Grassett and Morgan of his staff to start informal talks, based on his directive, with General Koenig, representing the French Committee, on a military level to work out arrangements urgently needed for operational purposes. But that also failed because of the surging pride and resentment at what the Committee regarded as exclusion from association with the invasion. Thus it refused to consider provisions and measures which Eisenhower felt essential; it was unwilling to pay any dues to the circumstances which the Allies expected to confront as they fought their way from the beaches across France. So it came about that at the time of landing there was no formal agreement with the Committee nor any settled program for dealing with civil affairs in France. Eisenhower's military staff had to do what seemed best each place, each day. This, to foretell, worked well; and in the course of it the Americans learned that almost all the French were with de Gaulle in spirit, for a short time living above their differences and prejudices.

The Allies were working in close military cooperation with the French forces in North Africa and Italy under General Le Clerc, who were to take part in the projected landing in Southern France. But they had not confided in de Gaulle the character and details of the OVERLORD plan or its date. Their chief reason had been the imperative need for secrecy. Experience had shown that no knowledge, political or military, was wholly safe within the de Gaulle entourage.

It had been arranged between Roosevelt and Churchill, and by the Combined Chiefs, to have de Gaulle come to London a day before the invasion was to start.[32] He was then to be told of the prospective assault and induced to appeal to the French people to welcome these Allied forces as their liberators. Up to the last moment it was uncertain whether he would come. As reported by Churchill to Roosevelt just before de Gaulle's plane came into sight over the shores of Britain:

"De Gaulle's Committee by a large majority decided that he should accept my invitation to come here. He hemmed and hawed, but Massigli and several others threatened to resign if he did not do so. We expect him on D minus 1. If he arrives, Eisenhower will see him for half an hour and explain to him the position exclusively in its military aspect. I shall return to London during the night of D-Day [then set for the morning of June 5th]. I do not expect that very much can be done with de Gaulle, but I still hope that the word 'leadership' which I am told you approved in Hull's speech [the one of April 9th] may prove serviceable." [33]

Churchill has since told so well of the troublesome time he had with de Gaulle that it is easily visualized.[34] Churchill had explained to him that he had been asked to come because of a sense that the history of the two countries required that the liberation of France should not be undertaken by the British and Americans without telling the French of what was about to be done. De Gaulle had bristled. He would not consent to associate himself with the invasion unless given the right to send messages to Algiers in his own code; to this Churchill had agreed on condition that de Gaulle would not transmit any military information about Operation OVERLORD. Until the afternoon of the 6th de Gaulle had refused to broadcast to France because of the omission of mention of the Provisional Government, and he had also forbidden the French liaison officers with the OVERLORD command to accompany the troops to France. But after Churchill had told him the plans, on grasping their immensity, he had been moved. He had agreed to broadcast a brief separate statement to the French people as soon as the expedition was started on its way—omitting any mention of the Americans; and also to allow some of the liaison officers to proceed.

After their talk Churchill had taken de Gaulle to see Eisenhower, who told him more fully about the plans for OVERLORD. As the

[32] It had been intended to invite him earlier. But the action of the Assembly in Algiers which on May 15th voted that the Committee of National Liberation should thereafter be called the Provisional Government of the French Republic, the refusal of General Koenig to accept Eisenhower's proposals for civil administration, and the demands of the head Committee representatives in London that they be exempted from emergency security measures which forbade foreign missions in London from sending messages in code, caused the change of plan.

[33] *Closing the Ring,* page 627.

[34] *Ibid.,* pages 628–30.

vast expedition began its crossing of the Channel, de Gaulle had broad-cast to France in words which conveyed enthusiasm for the great rescue that was about to occur, and called upon his countrymen to do all in their power to assure its quick triumph: "France, overwhelmed for four years, but never conquered, is on her feet to take part in the fight. For her sons, whoever and wherever they may be, the simple, sacred duty is to fight with all the means at their disposal."

From this point on, the narrative of the gradual lessening of distance between American authorities and de Gaulle and his group may be hurried to its end to make space for other more lasting acts in the life of the coalition. Within a week of the landing, Marshall and Arnold and King, all of whom were watching the course of OVERLORD, urged the President to simplify Eisenhower's task of dealing with the French. Stimson, despite the fact that he shared distrust of de Gaulle, also tried to persuade the President to grant the Committee provisional recognition. He tersely recorded in his Diary (June 14th) that he failed, that the President ". . . believes that de Gaulle will crumple and that the British supporters of de Gaulle will be confounded by the progress of events." [35] Who was misinforming the President? Not the military men in France. They were reporting that the average Frenchman looked to de Gaulle "as the natural and inevitable leader of Free France."

In the address he gave to the Consultative Assembly at Algiers (on June 26th) de Gaulle supplemented his statement of assurance to his colleagues that General Koenig, as Commander of the French forces under Eisenhower, had the same status and rights of recourse to French national authority as any other national commander under an inter-allied system, with praise of Eisenhower ". . . in whom the French government and people had complete confidence for the victorious con-duct of the common military operations." This tribute was a helpful prelude to the visit to Washington which he was soon to make. So was the cooperative way in which the civil and military members of the Committee in France worked with the Americans and British.

De Gaulle's visit to Washington, starting July 6th, marked a decisive stage in the return admission of France to the company of the West. Both Hull and Roosevelt found him more agreeable and reasonable than they expected. He impressed the President with the sincerity of his assurances that he did not intend to force himself or his Committee on France as its future government. On the 11th Roosevelt told the press that the American government had decided to consider the Committee

[35] *On Active Service in Peace and War,* page 551.

of National Liberation as the "dominant" political authority in France until elections could be held to determine the choice of the French people. De Gaulle, who was in Ottawa on his way back to Algiers, was gratified. But he made it plain that he and the Committee were going to claim for France every right of a great nation, just as though they were an established government.

The new bond of friendship was sealed on August 25th, when de Gaulle was enabled to hurry forward and make a triumphant entry into Paris, and when on the next day—more than two months after the Allies landed in France—Eisenhower exchanged letters with General Koenig comprising an agreement on civil affairs made between the Committee and the American government. The first sentence of Eisenhower's statement clearly marked the acceptance of the Committee: "I have been authorized to deal with the French Committee of National Liberation as the *de facto* authority in France, which will assume the leadership of and responsibility for the administration of the liberated areas of France." The British and French Foreign Offices signed an identical accord.

But France was a while longer kept short of the means of self-assertion. Requests for arms for extra divisions—besides the eight being outfitted—were denied by the Joint Chiefs of Staff, as was an attempt to get the means of equipping and transporting a French task force for use in the Far East, to recapture Indochina. In weakness, de Gaulle had not been easy to deal with; in strength, what might he not claim in the name of France? France was still going to have to find its way back into the realm of great powers.

PERIOD EIGHT

Summer and Autumn of 1944; the Channel Crossing Achieved, while Political Issues along the Circumference of Combat Engage the Coalition

33. Political Troubles along the Rim of War: Summer 1944

EACH country on the rim of the main combat area in Europe presented a problem that tested the coalition. All were caught in the wave of war and being tossed about in it, but each was at a different point from the others in the curling crest. In Italy the situation was moving on three uncoordinated planes: in some respects, it was still a former member of the Axis, bound by armistice terms and subject to control; in others it was an associate in the war against Germany; and simultaneously it was the scene of a contest among Italians for control and form of their government.

It had been thought after the Moscow agreement (of October 1943) on control arrangements for Italy, along with the adoption of a joint declaration of the policies to be pursued there, that the question of what part the Soviet Union was to play in the direction of the affairs of that country was straightened out. But it was not.

On November 10th, Eisenhower had formally announced the establishment of the Control Commission. As specified in a directive from the Combined Chiefs to him, this Commission was to (1) enforce and execute the terms of surrender; (2) ensure that the conduct of the Italian government conformed to Allied military needs. In the public announcement it had been explained that this was to be the organ ". . . through which relations between the United Nations and the Italian government are conducted." All communications with the Control Commission on matters of policy were to be channeled to and from the Commander-in-Chief through the Combined Chiefs of Staff. Posts on the staff were to be equally divided between the Americans and British. Sir Henry Maitland Wilson, the new Commander-in-Chief in the Mediterranean Theater, was subsequently named its President.

Steps had been concurrently taken to form the Advisory Council. On November 24th Vishinsky, having recovered from his illness, had arrived in Algiers and entered on his duties as Soviet representative with a large staff and energetic curiosity. The terms of reference under which this Council was to act were still being discussed by the British and American governments. But they were agreed that its assignment should be to observe the operation of the organization which would be enforcing the terms of surrender, and to advise the Allied Commander-in-Chief, as President of this Control Commission, on general policy. They contemplated it should act as a unit and that its members should not approach the Italian government separately.

It had become evident at once that Vishinsky had different ideas on all these and related points. Despite the discussion at the Moscow Conference, he clung to the conception that this Council had deliberative powers—authority to decide the policies and functions of the Control Commission. This was clarified in further wearisome discussions, the telling of which must be left to specialist students of this alienating episode. The Soviet government had seen fit in the end to accept the fact that it could not get the intrusive entry into this western combat area which it wanted.

There had been confusion also over the place of Soviet officials within the organization of the Control Commission. Vishinsky, having an erroneous idea of its structure, had assumed that important posts were waiting for the two high-ranking Soviet military officers whom he had brought with him. The details of this misunderstanding remain obscure. After protracted delay it was agreed to appoint Soviet and French representatives as Deputy Chiefs of Staff to the Deputy President of the Commission, its active head. But no one knew definitely what their standing was. Before long Molotov was raising the question whether the Soviet members of the staff ought not to be given a larger part in the work of the Commission.

And then suddenly the Soviet government had sought by a surprise move to make itself independent of the Control Commission. Hardly had Vishinsky taken his place on the Advisory Council than he told Badoglio that his government wanted to see Italy liberated as soon as possible and that it was anxious to establish relations with the Italian government. According to Badoglio, he had at once repeated the substance of this conversation to General Joyce, the Deputy President and operating Head of the Commission.[1] Whether or not this was so, the Americans and British had been taken aback when it occurred.

Vishinsky had soon thereafter been recalled to Moscow for more important work. Early in March his deputy on the Advisory Council, Bogomolov, had sought an interview with Badoglio; and, after reminding him of the earlier talk with Vishinsky, had asked the Prime Minister whether he was ready to request the Soviet government in writing to accredit a Soviet representative to the Italian government and to receive a representative of the Italian government in Moscow. Badoglio

[1] Badoglio, *Italy in the Second World War*, page 121. General Joyce had invited Badoglio to go with him to the first meeting of the Advisory Council after it had moved from North Africa to Naples.

had said that he would do so. The Soviet government had speedily acceded to Badoglio's request.

The American and British Ambassadors in Moscow, under rushed instructions, had entered protests. In answer to their complaints that this action had been taken without prior consultation, Molotov and Vishinsky had said that they thought the Soviet representative on the Advisory Council had made the Soviet intention known; that at any rate he had been told to do so. The Soviet government had gone right ahead and on March 14th had announced that the arrangement for the exchange of diplomatic representatives with Italy had been completed.

A bleak correspondence lasting over weeks had ensued. Allied forces were still deeply engaged in hard battles in Italy. And the country, as an ex-enemy, was still obligated, under armistice terms in which the Soviet Union had concurred, to carry out all orders issued by the Supreme Commander. In the light of these facts, the Soviet action had been deemed willful and harmful. Thus the State Department had agreed with the opinion which Harriman had sent on March 16th: that if the Soviet government was allowed to get away with this sharp practice, which struck at the spirit of collaboration, it would be an invitation for them to repeat it. The decline since Teheran in the Ambassador's belief that the Soviet government had really adopted the ways of cooperation is indicated by his comment in this message: "When the Soviets do not like our proposals they certainly do not hesitate to be abrupt with us. We may look forward to a Soviet policy of playing the part of a world bully if we don't follow this procedure of firmness now in connection with each incident." Hull had authorized Harriman to make it clear that we thought the act regrettable, threatening to the unity of the coalition and to faith in the trustworthiness of the Moscow agreements.

In the answers which Molotov had made on March 19th, he had vigorously defended what the Soviet government had done, on the grounds that it was necessary to take care of Soviet interests in Italy, and to rectify the unequal position of the Soviet government in dealing with the Italian authorities, as compared with the American and British governments. He had denied that the Moscow or Teheran agreements forbade direct individual relations with the Italian government.

The American and British governments had also rebuked Badoglio with severity. They had accused him of acting behind their backs, which he denied.[2] They had reminded him that he did not have the right to

[2] *Italy in the Second World War*, pages 128–29, states that immediately after that talk with Bogomolov in which he had acceded to the Soviet suggestion, he, Badoglio, had instructed Prunas, the Secretary General of the Italian Foreign Office, to give General

enter into any agreement with a foreign government except by consent of the Control Commission. Badoglio had evaded this reference to the restraint imposed upon Italy by the armistice accord, and had argued that he could not have refused to take a step which seemed to him so clearly in the interests of Italy. The Supreme Allied Commander subsequently had sent him a letter asserting bluntly that the Italian government could not enter into direct relations with any power, Allied or neutral; and that all communications must be through the Control Commission for reasons of military security. Badoglio again had denied that the conditions of the armistice so restrained the Italian government.[3]

The American and British governments had not thought the reasons given by either the Italians or Russians justified their action, but in the end had not prevented the exchange of diplomats. On April 4th the appointments had been announced.[4] Almost at once the American and British governments had also attached diplomatic representatives (Alexander Kirk and Sir Noel Charles) to the Italian government, but they had not accepted Italian representatives in Washington or London.

The reasons why the American and British governments had given in were various. They had not wanted at this time, just when the trouble over Poland was growing acute, to have a spectacular public showdown with the Soviet government. Perhaps they had concluded that, after all, this step could not have any great importance as long as the Allied Commander-in-Chief was in control. Perhaps, also, they had been influenced by the fact that, simultaneously, the Soviet representative on the Advisory Council was working harmoniously with his American and British colleagues. It may be added that ironically Badoglio had soon found the presence of the Soviet "Direct Representative" to his government, Kostilev, troublesome, and had begun complaining about him to the British and Americans.

Despite this tussle over the opportunity to influence events in Italy, the Soviet government had, during the period we have been reviewing, concurred in the political developments in that country. Of the con-

---

MacFarlane, the new Deputy President of the Control Commission, all particulars of the conversation. If this was done, it is hard to understand why the American and British governments did not intervene earlier.

[3] The text of Badoglio's letter is given in *ibid.,* pages 130–31. In this he complains bitterly about the measure of control which the Control Commission was exercising over Italy, and argues that the armistice terms be revised, as obsolete and out of accord with the status of co-belligerency.

[4] The official title given to each was "Direct Representative."

sultations within the coalition about these, more ought to be told.

Talks between Badoglio and political party leaders had broken down at the end of October 1943 over the issue of the abdication of the King. He had carried on with a cabinet that was supposed to have no political character. But as it had become clear that the Germans were going to put up a prolonged and hard defense south of Rome, the unresting demand for a change in government had grown louder. Churchill and the War Cabinet had been all for resisting the furor. This was due partly to appreciation of the help given by Badoglio and the King (the Fleet); partly to the attitude stated by the Prime Minister to the President on November 6th, "Surely we should stick to what we have got till we are sure we can get something better, and this can only be ascertained when we have Rome in our possession." [5] Though troubled, Roosevelt had gone along with Churchill. He had agreed that the Badoglio-King combination might continue to carry on a while longer —more or less in disregard of the principles approved at Moscow. The Soviet authorities had been similarly patient.

At the end of January 1944, after the Anzio landing, Hull had tried to hasten the changes—the reorganization of the government and the abdication of the King. But Churchill and his colleagues had maintained their objections. Circumstances had been on their side; the slowness of the Allied advance made the decision less urgent and caution more natural. So the President once again, despite Hull's grumbling, had given in.

However, the Executive Committee which the remnants of the six Italian anti-Fascist political parties had organized, had gone ahead on its own. This Junta had formulated a program and sought American-British support for putting it into effect. As submitted in the middle of February, the program had called for the abdication of the King and the end of the House of Savoy. But it had become known that, for the time being at least, it would be satisfied if the King stepped down in favor of the Crown Prince—whose powers were to be controlled. A coalition party government was to take over from Badoglio, to keep office until general elections could be held throughout Italy. Strikes and demonstrations led by the leftist parties had been conducted to gain attention for these proposals. The new Supreme Allied Commander in the Mediterranean, General Wilson, and both the American and British political advisers had urged that the program be accepted. The Americans had wanted to have it put into effect. But Churchill had remained in the way and once again Roosevelt had deferred to him.

[5] *Closing the Ring*, page 202.

The Soviet initiative in establishing direct diplomatic relations with the Badoglio government had not seemed to Churchill a reason for change.[6] The Communist movement had been allowed to emerge, along with other Italian political groups. Its leaders in the forum and factories had appeared from hiding, prison, and exile. Its former head, Togliatti, a member of the Comintern, had come direct from Moscow at the end of March and had at once revitalized Communist lines of influence and altered its tactics. The Communists had previously combined with other political parties in the demand for political change and the abdication of the King. But Togliatti, soon after his return, had exhorted the members of his and other parties to collaborate with the Badoglio government pending the realization of one that would derive its authority from the great mass political parties, to allow the question of the King's abdication to wait, and to concentrate on the war against the Germans.

The American government had finally forced the changeover. It had lost patience with reasons for further delay in carrying out one of the main purposes for which it was fighting the war—the extinction of Fascism and suppression of all those who had contributed to it. Through the Advisory Council it sought to bring about a basic transformation of the Badoglio government and the abdication of the King. The British government had at long last given way. It had agreed that the King might be told that the time had come for him to leave the throne. The British member had joined in a resolution of the Advisory Council which stated that it would welcome speedy formation by Badoglio of a government on a broad basis representing all parties.

On April 11th Murphy (who was still acting as the American representative on the Advisory Council as well as political adviser to Eisenhower) had seen the King and made the demand that he retire at once. The King had definitely not wanted to do so. The utmost to which he could be brought to agree was to announce that when Allied troops entered Rome, he would withdraw from public affairs by appointing his son, the Prince of Piedmont, Lieutenant-General of the Realm. Since the British government could not be counted on to force the issue, the American government had accepted the compromise. It had been understood that the ultimate fate of the monarchy was to be decided by plebiscite after the war was won. On the next day, April 12th, the King had signed a Royal Decree and made his announcement.

Soon after, the committee of the Italian parties had agreed, in order to give effect to the resolution passed by the Advisory Council, to enter

[6] See his series of messages to Roosevelt—March 8-15, 1944, printed in *ibid.,* pages 502–05.

a new government in which Badoglio would still remain head, but which was to be made up mainly of their representatives. This was on April 16th. On the 17th, Vishinsky, at a press conference in Moscow, had called attention to the recent decision of the Advisory Council, expressing approval of it as the common viewpoint of the Allies and a step forward in the solution of Italy's political problems.

On April 24th the new government had taken office. Among the chief figures in this new administration were Benedetto Croce, Count Sforza (whom Churchill had tried hard to keep out), and Togliatti, the Communist leader, as ministers without portfolio.

In one respect Churchill's anticipation was soon shown to be correct. Badoglio, in the name of the new government, had become more assertive in his effort to get Italy accepted as an ally. Consent to this would almost certainly have given Italy a right to claim that the armistice terms were no longer applicable, and that Italian territory must be kept intact. It was foreseen also that the Yugoslav, Greek, and French governments would be displeased. Thus the British government had opposed any further change in the nature of the relationship and the American government grudgingly had agreed that it was premature to consider one.

While the new government was taking over the care of a still very miserable Italy, the Allied forces had been finally breaking through toward Rome and thus bringing more of Italy under Italian rule. On June 5th, the day after Rome was entered, the King carried out his promise and transferred the powers of the throne to Crown Prince Humbert, as Lieutenant-General of the Realm. At once the leaders of the Italian political parties in Rome acted to get Badoglio out of office. While the American and British governments were going on with the old familiar argument as to whether this should or should not be allowed, the Italian politicians decided the question. They refused to serve any longer under Badoglio. Without consulting the Allies in advance, they formed a new government under Bonomi, in which Count Sforza was to be Foreign Minister. Churchill was distressed at this, at the discarding of Badoglio in favor of "this group of aged and hungry politicians," but could not prevent it. The new Cabinet pledged itself to assume the obligations taken by the Badoglio government, including both the terms of surrender and the postponement of decision as to what was to be done about the monarchy until the fighting in Italy was over. For a time Italian issues became quiescent among the Allies.

34. Political Troubles along the Rim of War: Summer 1944 (Continued)

During this same period, when Rome was being captured and OVER-LORD launched, hopes also revived for achieving peaceful and mutually satisfactory arrangements for the governing of Yugoslavia.

It will be remembered that during the Conference of Foreign Ministers at Moscow, an essay to enlist Soviet cooperation in a joint effort to unify Yugoslav political groups had led to nothing. A month later, while the Conference at Teheran was assembling, Tito had summoned a political congress. This had instituted a provisional government in which the Communists, though in the minority, were the directing elite. It had claimed the right to represent Yugoslavia and denied all authority of the King and his government-in-exile. It forbade the King to return until after the country was freed. These measures, and rumors of Soviet intrigue, had impelled Churchill to try again to secure Stalin's interest and aid. Stalin had seemed as detached as Molotov had been.[7]

The British government had gone on with its effort to remove obstacles to agreements between the resistance groups and between them and the royal government-in-exile. It had increased its help to Tito's partisans. And since Mihailovich's Cetniks had not shown any renewed will to go after the Germans, it had withdrawn its support from them and had recalled the British missions operating in their territory. For some time past, Churchill had come to regard Mihailovich as "a millstone tied around the neck of the little king. . . ."[8] He had urged the King to remove him from his position as Minister of War in the royal government. Concurrently, the British liaison officers near Tito had been urging compromise and combination with the royal government, to attract into his ranks those Yugoslav elements, especially the Serbs, whose allegiance was to the King.

During the first months of 1944, while the British government had been trying out these tactics, Tito's forces were growing into a strong

[7] This effort may have been encouraged by statements conveyed by Benes (while he was in Moscow in December) that Stalin told him that he favored a continuation of the Yugoslav federation; that he did not like the present government or the King; although he was not averse to the King personally; that he was sympathetic to Tito, but that he was open-minded and would keep hands off the country's internal politics.

[8] On December 30th Churchill had written a note to Eden: "There is no possibility now of getting Tito to accept King Peter as a *quid pro quo* for repudiating Mihailovic. Once Mihailovic is gone, the King's chances will be greatly improved and we can plead his case at Tito's Headquarters." *Closing the Ring,* page 469.

army and winning over more and more of the people. In contrast, the royal government-in-exile—"bedraggled," Churchill had called it in one of his messages—had begun to dissolve. The King and Prime Minister returned to London in March, leaving the rest of the Cabinet stranded in Cairo. By April 1st Churchill was beginning to fear that if the government did not act soon, the last chance would pass. In a Minute of that date which he had sent to Eden, expressing the opinion that decision was imperative, he had noted that, "Since we discussed these matters in Cairo, we have seen the entry of a grandiose Russian Mission to Tito's Headquarters, and there is little doubt that the Russians will drive straight ahead for a Communist Tito-governed Yugoslavia, and will denounce everything done to the contrary as 'undemocratic.'" [9] However the Soviet government still had continued to refrain from any open show of favoritism for Tito in the political talks that were going on and had allowed the British to take the lead.

The young King had at last sadly realized that he had better yield to British advice. He had consented to the formation of a new government, from which Mihailovich was to be dropped. Subasic, a former governor of Croatia, a member of the Peasant Party, and a man of moderate political opinions was chosen to be the new Prime Minister. To Tito, Churchill had sent word that he ". . . should greatly regret it if you [Tito] were at all in a hurry to denounce them in public. . . . The battle in Italy goes in our favour. General Wilson assures me of his resolve to aid you to the very utmost. I feel therefore that I have a right to ask you to forbear from any utterances averse to this new event, at least for a few weeks till we can have exchanged telegrams upon it." [10]

In another message a week later (on May 24th) he had explained to Tito that "My idea is that this Government should lie quiet for a bit and let events flow on their course." The short paragraph with which he had ended this message showed how jovial a tone he was taking with this Yugoslav partisan leader: "Give my love to Randolph [Churchill's son] should he come into your sphere. Maclean [the Head of the British missions to Tito] will be coming back soon. I wish I could come myself, but I am too old and heavy to jump out on a parachute." [11]

The Prime Minister was a-wooing in a spirit of adventure. But he was compelled to go on with his less strenuous but more wearing duties, from which, however, a fortnight later, it will be recalled, he managed to find time for an excursion—sans parachute—to Normandy to have a look at OVERLORD.

[9] *Ibid.*, page 477.
[10] *Ibid.*, page 478.
[11] *Ibid.*

Tito, at the end of May, was being rescued. A strong German attack had been driving his bands back from the coast into the hills. He had appealed for aid to the Allied Commander in the Mediterranean and was given it in good measure. British and American air forces had bombed German troop concentrations and transport, and had given Tito's men protection against German air attacks. Concentric German thrusts, some airborne, had overrun and chased him out of his headquarters in the Bosnian hills. With his staff and the British and Soviet liaison officers he had managed to get through the German lines to a partisan airfield, where Allied planes were waiting. Choosing the one Soviet plane in the group, he had been flown to Bari, and thence taken by British destroyer to the island of Vis in the Adriatic, where he made his new headquarters.

He does not seem to have regarded this act of salvage reason for changing his political aims. But it is quite possible that it did make him better disposed toward an agreement with the government-in-exile of which the British government was still acting as protector. An accord was reached between Tito and Subasic in June, under which Tito's supporters were given top places in the new royal government in return for his promise of cooperation. But the story of this event will follow as part of the pattern of later developments.

In Greece also, largely due to the supple and bold British initiative, a chance for orderly settlement of the internal struggle had come briefly into sight.

When the Italians in Greece surrendered, the Communist resistance groups had acquired much of their equipment. This had upset the balance between the two chief factions and given the Communist one military superiority and a chance to gain dominant political position. Churchill and his colleagues had concluded that a swerve in policy was needed if the situation was to be saved. They had decided that the best way left to secure internal stability would be to have the King yield to a regency of some respected figure, who would be on the spot to take over authority at the time of liberation. So they had urged the King to give way in favor of a temporary regency under Damaskinos, the Archbishop of Athens. But he had refused.

An uneasy truce made in February between the resistance groups had soon dissolved. As in early March the prospect of German evacuation of Greece had drawn near, the Communist-led elements set up a Committee of National Liberation, which was a direct threat to the royal government and its adherents. They had won sympathizers in Greek army and navy units who were in Egypt. At the end of the month these had tried to force the resignation of the Prime Minister by a violent mutiny. Churchill strode forward to suppress it. A message of instruction which he sent on April 9th to Leeper, the British Ambassador to the Greek government in Cairo, describes the ground which he was determined to defend until sponsors of what he regarded as reasonable political principles could be found to carry on the governing of Greece: "Our relations are definitely established with the lawfully constituted Greek government headed by the King, who is the ally of Britain and cannot be discarded to suit a momentary surge of appetite among ambitious émigré nonentities."

But he went on to observe that: "The King is the servant of his people. He makes no claim to rule them. He submits himself freely to the judgment of the people as soon as normal conditions are restored. . . . Once the German invader has been driven out, Greece can be a republic or a monarchy, entirely as the people wish. Why then cannot the Greeks keep their hatreds for the common enemy . . . ?" [12]

While this rebellion was being suppressed, the King of Greece, pushed by the British government, had proclaimed that his government would be made over. Papandreou, leader of the Greek Social Democratic party, had been brought out of Greece to be Prime Minister of the new government, which was to be representative. After sessions as exhausting as only Greek political contests can be, the various main resistance and political groups had agreed to enter his administration, and combine in their fight against the Germans. But, to anticipate, an all party government was not finally formed until early in September when six members of leftist parties entered the Cabinet. It was not destined to last.

During all these twists, Roosevelt had given Churchill a free hand in dealing with the Greek quarrels. When it seemed that they had been soothed, he expressed his pleasure at the way in which the difficulties had been overcome. Churchill had also taken great care to keep the Soviet government informed at all times of what he was about to do and Stalin also had kept hands off. As Churchill later related: "The Soviet Government confined itself to criticism of our actions, and when on May 5 a formal request to Russia for co-operation in Greek affairs was made in Moscow, the reply was that it would be improper to join in any public pronouncements on political matters in Greece." [13] Soviet passivity allowed Churchillian determination to impress the Communists into temporary conformity.

One danger less that disorder or Communism would prevail, Church-

[12] *Ibid.*, pp. 544–45.
[13] *Ibid.*, page 551.

ill could think with relief, and in a country both dear to British hearts and vital to its influence in the Mediterranean. It is not hard to appreciate why his success in controlling the trouble in Greece bred the belief that an agreement which divided responsibility among the Allies was worth more than some inconclusive pledge that such situations could be dealt with only on the basis of joint accord.

In this same period before OVERLORD, the members of the coalition had been engaged in secret discussions about the surrender of two German satellites, Romania and Bulgaria. They were within the long arc of operations of the Red Armies, and the Soviet government felt entitled to the ultimate right of determining what was done.

During March 1944, as the Red Army had neared the Romanian frontier, emissaries had resumed their devious attempt to arrange a surrender. Prince Stirbey, formerly a high court figure well known in Britain, had been sent to Cairo by the main opposition parties, but probably with the knowledge of the government. But hardly had the secret talks gotten under way when Hitler had invited the Prime Minister, Marshal Ion Antonescu, to come and see him. Word of this summons had been sped through neutral channels to the British government, along with the message that in view of the decisions he would have to make, Antonescu felt it essential to know what the Western Allies would do to protect Romania against the Soviet advance. The answer (March 22nd), was a sharp warning against going to see the Nazis; advice to surrender to the three Great Powers and not oppose the Russian troops; and a statement that the terms to be imposed on Romania would largely be determined by the extent to which it contributed to the defeat of Germany. But before this blunt injunction reached him, the Prime Minister was on his way to see Hitler. He did not accept any new obligations toward Germany, but the Romanian divisions in the field continued to fight on against the Russians.

The Red Army was about to cross the Prut River frontier and enter Romania at several points, and for the first time since Hitler's invasion go into territory beyond the claimed borders of the Soviet Union. Thereupon the Soviet government had taken over the initiative. On April 1st it had let the British and American governments know that it was about to issue a statement informing the Romanians of its intentions. This affirmed that the Soviet government planned to take back the provinces of Bessarabia and Bucovina, but wanted no other Romanian territory. It had declared that no compulsion would be used to change the existing social system. Both the American and British governments had praised these avowals as valuable and timely, and had publicly said so.

The Soviet government had then gone on to formulate the armistice terms which it proposed should be applied to Romania. These were lenient. The Romanian forces were either to surrender to the Red Army or change sides and join the Red Army against the Germans. As compensation for the provinces to be ceded to the Soviet Union, Romania was to have the larger part of Transylvania returned from Hungary. There was to be a war indemnity. The Soviet government would not insist on maintaining a regular military occupation of Romania, but would require only that Soviet and Allied troops be allowed to move freely through the country as needed for military operations. The British and American governments had thought these terms suitable. But Churchill had proposed that they too should be admitted into the discussion of political matters. The idea had been well received. Before the middle of April, therefore, the three main Allies had agreed on the terms on which a Romanian surrender might be arranged. These armistice proposals had been passed on to Stirbey in Cairo on April 12th. But they had drawn an ambiguous response. The Romanian troops went on fighting against the Soviet forces, the better trained and equipped divisions in the Crimea fighting hard and ably. The Soviet government had dismissed the idea that a revolt followed by surrender might soon occur in Romania as (in words used by Molotov in talking with Harriman on April 25th) "a pipe dream."

The battlefront in Romania had, thereafter, become stationary for some months as great Soviet offensives farther north, to fit in with OVERLORD, were being prepared. The Romanian government could detect no chance of separating the Allies, and thereby getting better terms; nor of inducing the British and American governments to give protection against the two dangers which it had called down upon itself—German reprisals and Soviet dictation. The King and the opposition during the summer tried to prepare the way for an overturn in Romania, and acceptance of the April terms. But the Allies waited for events to make the submission sure. Nothing decisive happened until August.

So, too, Bulgaria had hung back from the act of surrender. Though fighting at Germany's side against other enemies, it had not gone to war against the Soviet Union. But Bulgarian troops had helped the Germans keep control of the Balkans and had deterred Turkey from joining the Allies. At the end of 1943 Sofia and other Bulgarian cities had been subjected to heavy American and British bombing attacks as a stimulant to surrender. When asked to stop, the Allies had told the Bulgarian government that if it wanted to be spared, it had better send a secret mission to Cairo or Cyprus to discuss terms.

In the following months, consideration had been given as to whether or not Bulgaria might be moved to seek a surrender if told in advance how it would fare. But the impulse to formulate armistice terms had been discouraged by the Soviet government in March, on the score that the question was not urgent and that circumstances were as yet not good. The Red Armies were still quite distant from Bulgaria and it is probable that the Soviet government had thought that when they got closer it would have a greater say in Allied counsels as to what was done about this country.

Those elements in the Bulgarian government who wanted to part from Germany were checked. The Bulgarian Armies continued to stand by the Germans. In answer to Soviet protests that this conduct was not compatible with normal relations and could not be tolerated, it had made no apologies to Moscow and had given no ground. The ending of the answer it made on April 24, 1944 to the Soviet government read: "In conclusion, the Bulgarian government considers it necessary to state once more that it has not changed in any way its relations with the Soviet Union in comparison with its relations at the time of the adherence of Bulgaria to the tripartite pact [March 1, 1941] at which time the Soviet Union and Germany were also allied by another pact."

The situation remained in suspense until the autumn when the Red Army was very close and threatened to invade.

⦿⦿⦿⦿⦿⦿⦿

35. The Idea of Dividing Responsibility for Control of Smaller Countries of Central Europe

⦿⦿⦿⦿⦿⦿⦿

Experience was showing how hard it was to apply the rule of common consent in each of these unstable situations. And decision could not always wait. In brief, the diplomatic methods in use began to seem defective or unsuitable—awkward for war, ineffective for peace. Hence both diplomats and soldiers began to wonder whether an arrangement which made one or other of the Allies the dominant authority in each of these situations was not the sensible way to end the dissension.

338

Fear that as the Red Army spread through Eastern and Central Europe, the Soviet government might seek to impose its will on the whole of the region, was spur to the idea. This worry found words in a Minute which Churchill had sent on May 4th to Eden. It advised the Foreign Secretary,

"A paper should be drafted for the Cabinet, and possibly for the Imperial Conference, setting forth shortly—for that is essential—the brute issues between us and the Soviet Government which are developing in Italy, in Rumania, in Bulgaria, in Yugoslavia, and above all in Greece. . . . Broadly speaking, the issue is, Are we going to acquiesce in the Communisation of the Balkans and perhaps of Italy? . . . I am of opinion on the whole that we ought to come to a definite conclusion about it, and that if our conclusion is that we resist the Communist infusion and invasion, we should put it to them pretty plainly at the best moment that military events permit. We should of course have to consult the United States first." [14]

Possibly as a result of talk with other leaders of the Commonwealth, however, the blunt showdown was postponed while a new bid was entered for an accord. The following day, May 5th, the British government had made a formal request to the Soviet government through its Embassy in Moscow for cooperation in Greek affairs. On that same day, while Eden was talking with Gusev at the Foreign Office in London, he had mentioned the possibility that the Soviet government might well leave Britain to manage the situation in Greece while fighting was still going on there, and that Great Britain might well leave the management of the situation in Romania to the Soviet government during the fighting there. The Foreign Office later said that the suggestion was an off-hand one. Whether or not this is so, the Soviet government had been attentive to it. On May 18th Gusev had told the Foreign Office that the Soviet government favored the idea but, before going ahead with it, would like to know if the American government had been consulted and did not mind.

On the 30th the British Ambassador in Washington, Lord Halifax, had asked Hull how the American government would feel about such an accord. The memo which he gave the Secretary stressed the fact that it was to hold only for the war period and would not affect the rights and duties of each of the three great powers at the peace settlement. The proposal had offended Hull's convictions. He foresaw that—despite assurances to the contrary—even such a temporary working accord might develop into a sphere-of-influence arrangement of the type he thought had always in the past brought conflict. Thus, the Secretary

[14] *Ibid.,* page 708.

of State had objected strongly. And he had continued to object despite the plea that there was no practical alternative, that current troubles were proving that joint consultation would not work well. Nor did the fact that the President still wished to avoid involvement in the Polish or Balkan troubles, at least until the elections were past, seem to him a reason for restraining the statement of his views. In the words in which Hull later recounted his answer to Halifax, he said that he thought ". . . it would be a doubtful course to abandon our broad basic declarations of policy, principles, and practice. If these are departed from in one or two important instances, such as you propose, then neither of the two countries parties to such an act will have any precedent to stand on, or any stable rules by which to be governed and to insist that other Governments be governed." [15]

Churchill had next addressed himself directly to Roosevelt. In a message of May 31st he reviewed the disquieting signs of divergence of policy between the British and Russians in regard to the Balkan countries, Greece in particular. He had said he hoped that the President would approve the proposal as a "practical matter" and added: "We do not of course wish to carve up the Balkans into spheres of influence, and in agreeing to the arrangement we should make it clear that it applied only to war conditions and did not affect the rights and responsibilities which each of the Great Powers will have to exercise at the peace settlement and afterwards in regard to the whole of Europe. The arrangement would of course involve no change in the present collaboration between you and us in the formulation and execution of Allied policy towards these countries." [16]

The way might have seemed to the Prime Minister the more natural since, in the course of talks then going on between himself and the President over zones of occupation in Germany, Roosevelt was again saying that the American government did not want, and would not accept, any role in the region during or after the war. As stated by the President in a memo to Stettinius as early as February 21, 1944, and as told to the British over and over, "I do not want the United States to have the postwar burden of reconstituting France, Italy and the Balkans. This is not our natural task at a distance of 3,500 miles or more. It is definitely a British task in which the British are far more vitally interested than we are." [17]

The President had turned to the State Department to draft an answer to the Prime Minister's appeal. While it was doing so, further word

[15] *Memoirs*, page 1452.
[16] *Triumph and Tragedy*, pages 73–74.
[17] *Memoirs*, page 1612.

came from Churchill on June 8th. In the language in which he expressed his thoughts to Halifax, to be put in appropriate form for presentation to the American government, he again denied that there was any question of spheres of influence. "We all have to act together, but someone must be playing the hand." He went on to aver that it seemed reasonable that the Russians should deal with the Romanians and Bulgarians since their armies were "impinging" on those countries, and that Britain should deal with Greece and Yugoslavia, and remarked that he thought "no fate could be worse for any country than to be subjected in these times to decisions reached by triangular or quadrangular telegraphing." His last paragraph ought to have been winning: "On the other hand, we follow the lead of the United States in South America as far as possible, as long as it is not a question of our beef and mutton. On this we naturally develop strong views on account of the little we get." [18]

Due note was taken of the hint contained in Churchill's message that the agreement in mind might also include Bulgaria and Yugoslavia. This made it seem to Hull more urgent than ever to oppose. The President in his next reply to the Prime Minister (June 10th) followed straight down Hull's route of argument. The Prime Minister's laments over the difficulties of reaching joint decisions were vaguely answered by the opinion that it would be better to try to set up consultative machinery to clear up "misunderstandings" and restrain any impulse to form spheres of influence.

The heart of Churchill's comeback was: "Action is paralyzed if everybody is to consult everybody else about everything before it is taken. Events will always outstrip the changing situation in these Balkan regions. Somebody must have the power to plan and act." Citing what had been done in Greece, he said that if in that crisis it had been necessary to have complicated consultation, the outcome would have been chaos or impotence; instead, working together flexibly, Roosevelt and he had done a good job. And he asked, "Why is all this effective direction to be broken up into a committee of mediocre officials such as we are littering about the world?" As for Romania, he said that he thought it not only natural that the Soviets, who would be in that country in great force, should have the lead, and they would probably do what they wanted anyhow. At the end he asked that the proposal be given a trial of three months, after which it would be reviewed by the three powers.

Hull was away from Washington for a few days. Roosevelt took advantage of his absence and risked his gloom. On June 12th he informed

[18] *Triumph and Tragedy,* pages 74–75.

Churchill that he agreed to this short period of trial, adding, "We must be careful to make it clear that we are not establishing any postwar spheres of influence." He sent this message off without consulting the State Department or telling Hull when the Secretary of State returned to Washington. This caused confusion and agitation.

For, on the same day, the State Department gave the British Ambassador in Washington a memo which it thought the President had previously approved, in which all our objections were again firmly stated.[19] And then on the 17th, still ignorant of the message which Roosevelt had sent to Churchill, Hull wrote the President that it seemed to him more important than before to contest the arrangement since it appeared that Bulgaria and Yugoslavia were also to be included. Along with this letter he submitted the text of another message for Roosevelt to send to Churchill. What happened next defies explanation. The President, perhaps sorry, perhaps to appease Hull, thereupon sent off to Churchill the contradictory message. This not only repeated the charge that an important mistake in policy was being made but also complained because the British had broached the idea to the Russians without first finding out what we thought about it, and might not even have sought our opinion if the Russians had not asked them to get our approval.

The British government, in fact, had, as soon as it received the President's earlier answer, told the Russians that it accepted the general division of responsibility. Churchill took this second "unhappy message" to mean that Roosevelt was really upset about having given in; and so in his next message, which he sent on the 23rd, he put himself out to reanalyze the situation as he saw it. Having again summed up the justifying reasons for his move, he gently ended by observing that in all these situations he was just struggling to bring order out of chaos and that he was keeping the President constantly informed. The President made a simple friendly answer (June 27th), and it seemed as though their correspondence on this subject was temporarily complete.

But at this juncture the Soviet government was heard from. It queried the American government directly about the proposed accord, and meanwhile would not seal it. Churchill argued with Stalin as he had with Roosevelt, telling him on July 11th, "I would ask whether you should not tell us that the plan may be allowed to have its chance for three months. No one can say it affects the future of Europe or divides it into spheres. But we can get a clear-headed policy in each theatre, and we will all report to the others what we are doing. However, if you tell me it is hopeless, I shall not take it amiss." [20]

[19] *Memoirs,* page 1455.
[20] *Triumph and Tragedy,* page 79.

342

On July 15th the State Department informed the Soviet government that it had already agreed to the arrangement for a trial period of three months as useful to the war strategy, but that it was worried lest this lead to the division of the Balkan region into spheres of influence. It expressed the hope that no measures would be taken that would prejudice collaboration or work against a broader system of general security. This tepid answer may have influenced Stalin to let the proposal drag. Then, because the Russians began to encourage the Communist resistance group in Greece, Churchill also desisted for the moment.

In regard, then, to the emergent situations in Central and Eastern Europe, what the American government was saying at this time to the British and Soviet governments was, in substance, (1) that it did not want to become involved at that time in decisions about frontiers or the internal affairs of these countries; (2) that it was against any agreement that might assign separate spheres of influence in this region; (3) that it wished these problems to be settled by consultation and joint agreement, and in consonance with certain general principles which it thought had been endorsed at Moscow; (4) that all countries concerned should give up claims based only or mainly on their need for security, and rather look to the future system of collective security for their protection. In contrast, Churchill was saying that in some of these situations the power to act boldly and without the delay of consultation was essential to prevent civil war, chaos, and disorders spread by Communism; and that in any event it was likely that the ally whose troops were fighting in a country would dominate developments while there. Stalin expounded no theories; he seemed willing either to make a deal or to rely on Soviet ability to see that Soviet interests did not fare badly.

The American government turned aside not only from any agreements dividing the world or any part of it into separate spheres of influence, but also from military plans designed to affect the future balance of influence or power. It did not want to suffer losses or prolong the war. Besides, it was most doubtful whether any military operations within American-British capabilities could check the Soviet Union if it was really determined to dominate East and Central Europe. Rather the other way about: it was thought that military measures of political import would, by arousing its mistrust, cause the Soviet Union to extend its control and revert to isolation. So the American authorities would not use their army, navy, or air force as levers for diplomacy. The question of whether they should or not presented itself in the course of discussion of how to direct strategy in Europe after the entry on the Continent was secure.

36. Southern France or Italy and the Southeast?

As soon as Rome was captured and the beachhead won in Northern France, Churchill revived the question of whether to go ahead with the projected landing on the southern shores of France (Code name DRA-GOON, changed from ANVIL. He thought the new name apt since he had been "dragooned" into it). That operation, it will be remembered, had been postponed in order that the initial landing in Normandy might be larger, and the forces left in Italy stronger. The time was now near, however, when, unless countermanded, landing craft were to be diverted from OVERLORD and divisions taken from the armies in Italy for the venture. Could not these combat resources, the Prime Minister queried, now be better used against Germany elsewhere and otherwise than in DRAGOON?

Churchill and the British Chiefs of Staff hurled this question at their American colleagues early in June and did not quit the resultant argument until four days before the landings were made in Southern France. They were convinced that DRAGOON would be an ineffectual operation. Basing themselves on General Alexander's estimates, they contended that, with the same means, the assault in Italy could be pushed forward in such strength that the Germans would be compelled to send divisions there which otherwise would fight in France, and a landing could be made across the Adriatic en route to Vienna and Hungary. Their thought was that once an entry was gained through the Istrian Peninsula, a large force could be organized in combination with the Partisan resistance fighters in the region, and that the German divisions there in hostile country would be at a great disadvantage. This advance from a third direction, gaining momentum and moving toward a juncture with the Soviet armies, would shake the German satellites and throw the whole defense of Germany into despairing disorder.

The Combined Chiefs of Staff on June 14th decided that the campaign in Italy should continue to have priority as might be required to destroy all German forces south of the Pisa-Rimini Line. But at the same time they determined to proceed to prepare for some assault landing, of about three divisions, to be launched from the Mediterranean around July 25th. Its destination was to be selected later; it might be Southern France, Southwestern France, or the head of the Adriatic.

General Marshall was in England, watching the progress of the battles in Normandy. On June 16th he flew down to General Wilson's headquarters to talk with the Mediterranean commanders. He found Wilson unhappy over the prospect of disbanding joint armies and joint tactical air forces in Italy in order to land in Southern France. DRA-GOON, he contended, could not be launched until August 15th at the earliest without so weakening the armies in Italy that they might not be able to reach even the Pisa-Rimini Line; and if they failed to accomplish that, the Germans would have a very good chance to rest and regroup and maintain resistance in Italy indefinitely. He proposed that the Allies try to get through the Pisa-Rimini Line, go across the Po, and then advance toward Southern Hungary through the Ljubljana Gap, the latter advance to be taken in conjunction with amphibious landings on the Istrian peninsula. General Alexander agreed with him. He reckoned he could accomplish this great advance if not deprived of those five or seven divisions assigned for transfer to ANVIL (DRA-GOON) which would be needed for reserves and rotation of combat units.[21] General Mark Clark, who was in charge of the American forces fighting in Italy, also favored this undertaking. He thought, however, that the French contingents in Italy might be spared for an attack on Southern France, and that they, along with other French divisions in Corsica and North Africa, would be enough to carry out that operation also.[22]

But Marshall disagreed with both the facts and the conclusions. As a reason for not being willing to consider the Adriatic operation, he pointed out that the Germans in Italy might withdraw to the Alps and avoid fighting in the Po Valley; and by doing so they might well be able, without diverting divisions from other fronts, to prevent a break-through toward Austria or Hungary and thus make the extra effort in Italy wasteful. As a reason for regarding a landing in Southern France as essential, he stressed the need at once for another major port where the Americans could debark the many divisions waiting in the United States to be moved across the Atlantic. Eisenhower was of the same decided opinion.

The U.S. Joint Chiefs of Staff resolved again in favor of the landing in

[21] *Grand Strategy,* Volume v, page 347.

[22] He later wrote, "I am firmly convinced that the French forces alone, with seven divisions available, could have captured Marseilles, protected General Eisenhower's southern flank, and advanced up the Rhone Valley to join hands with the main OVERLORD forces. The VI American corps, with its three divisions, could then have remained in Italy. The impetus of the Allied advance in Italy would thus not have been lost and we could have advanced into the Balkans." General Clark tells that he discussed this idea with Marshall during his visit in June 1944. Marshall would not change the plan. In order to get the men, matériel, and air forces for the Southern France landing, the entire VI Corps as well as the French Expeditionary Forces which were fighting in Italy were moved out by the end of July. *Calculated Risk,* page 369.

Southern France and against the acceptance of proposals to commit resources then in the Mediterranean to any large future operation either in Northern Italy or the region called the Balkans. Churchill, and with reason, found the tone of this judgment "arbitrary." So he asked the President to act as an appeal judge. In a series of messages starting on June 25th, he again tried to win Roosevelt over to his belief that it would be needless as well as foolish to ". . . ruin all hopes of a major victory in Italy and all its fronts . . . for the sake of ANVIL with all its limitations. . . ." Thus he pleaded that the forces in Italy should not be deprived of much of their power to destroy the enemy armies there. That is all he asked at that time. But he may well have reckoned that if this request were acceded to, it would soon become evident that it was not essential to make a second landing in France; and then the way to take divisions across the Adriatic would be cleared by consent.

Roosevelt's answer (of June 28th) was, as Churchill has called it, "prompt and adverse." He said he still thought that the plans, including the early assault on Southern France that had been envisaged at Teheran, were best suited to realize the objective—the unconditional surrender of Germany. He went on to recall that at Teheran Stalin had also favored ANVIL as against other operations in the Mediterranean, and so it could not be abandoned without consulting him. Turning to the proposals of the British Commanders which Churchill had passed on to him, he remarked that he thought they disregarded the probable long duration of the campaign to debouch from the Ljubljana Gap into Slovenia and Hungary, and its difficulties of supply. For these reasons, the President flatly said, "I cannot agree to the employment of United States troops against Istria and into the Balkans nor can I see the French agreeing to such use of French troops." And then he added at the end of his message, "For purely political reasons over here, I should never survive even a slight setback in 'Overlord' if it were known that fairly large forces had been diverted to the Balkans." [23]

[23] *Triumph and Tragedy*, page 65. Churchill's later review of this exchange of messages, in the same volume, pages 61–66, is marked by indignation due to the sense that the President either misconstrued or misjudged the proposals made to him. "No one," he wrote (repeating what he had said in the reply he sent on July 1 to Roosevelt's message), "involved in these discussions had ever thought of moving armies *into the Balkans* [Churchill's later italics]; but Istria and Trieste were strategic political positions, which, as he [the President] saw very clearly, might exercise profound and widespread reactions, especially after the Russian advances."

The Prime Minister's judgment (both contemporaneously and when writing *Triumph and Tragedy*) may have been in part due to the belief that the message received from the President of June 29th was an answer not only to his (Churchill's) first message of June 25th but also to the long and temperate exposition of his aims that he sent to the President on June 28th. But it is probable that the President had not read this later presentation of views before approving the reply to Churchill which had been written

At this point it may be observed that if any operation from the Istrian Peninsula toward Austria and Hungary had been undertaken it might well have encountered serious local difficulties—not only operational but also political. The British Commanders seem to have had the blithe assumption that Tito would have been willing to have his forces cooperate with and under the Allied Command. This would have been hard and perhaps impossible to arrange.

If not bothered by such possible complications during June and July when he was arguing with the Americans, Churchill became so soon afterward. This is indicated by the fact that when he saw Tito in Naples (August 12th–13th), he tried to clear them out of the way. In a memo given to Tito by British military headquarters it was proposed that in the event that Allied forces entered Northern Italy, Austria, or Hungary, the Allied Commander would govern all territory that had been under Italian rule at the outbreak of the war; and that Allied forces would have control of the port of Trieste and the lines of communication toward Vienna and the Hungarian plains—Ljubljana and Maribor (in Yugoslavia, Slovenia) and Graz (in Austria). Tito protested, pointing out that since his guerrillas already controlled some of these areas, they should at least be associated in their administration. Subasic, the new Prime Minister of the royal Yugoslav government, was of the same opinion. This issue as between the Western Allies and Tito became acute later on, as will be told.

But for the time being it did not have to be faced. For, to go back, after one last attempt to get a reprieve, Churchill and the British Chiefs

in the War Department. Forrest Pogue in *The Supreme Command,* page 222, gives detailed dates of this correspondence which supports this supposition.

Nevertheless, the statement of Churchill's just quoted is puzzling. There can be no doubt that the British Commanders and the British Chiefs of Staff did urge that, after the entry into the Po Valley, a substantial force should thereafter be sent east toward the Istrian Peninsula, and then northward through the Ljubljana Gap toward Hungary or Vienna. For operations recommended, see Wilson's book, *Eight Years Overseas,* pages 216–219, and *Grand Strategy,* Volume v, pages 345–358.

In the messages asking the President to review the subject for himself, the Prime Minister did not directly or specifically support these proposals. As said, he asked only that there be ". . . justice to the great opportunities of the Mediterranean commanders." But can the President be blamed for assuming that Churchill had deeply in mind not only the seizure of the Istrian Peninsula but a further venture through the northeast corner of Yugoslavia and Austria and/or the plains of Hungary?

Perhaps the Americans, including the President in this message, misused the phrase "into the Balkans." It is possible to argue that no military plan existed for going *into* the Balkans; that an advance into Austria and/or Hungary by way of the Ljubljana Gap was *away* from the Balkans. In short, it may be that Churchill was not denying his strategic intentions but was indignantly rejecting the phrase "into the Balkans" which the Americans seemed determined to pin upon all the British proposals for action toward the East.

of Staff suspended their opposition to DRAGOON and reconciled themselves to the transfer of divisions from Italy. On July 1st Churchill told Eisenhower that he would approve the plan for Southern France. On the next day the Combined Chiefs of Staff instructed General Wilson to make every possible effort to launch a three-division assault —to be built up to at least ten divisions—near the Port of Marseilles by the middle of August. All available Mediterranean resources not required for that forced venture were to be used, he was told, to carry out his existing directive with regard to operations in Italy.

After the invasion forces broke through the German lines in Normandy in July, thereby opening a prospect of getting quick control not only of Normandy but of the whole of Brittany, the British once more urged a change in plan. Churchill urged that the destination of the landing operation be switched from the south of France to some point on the Brittany Peninsula nearer the main battle—Brest, Lorient, or St. Nazaire. But neither Eisenhower nor the Joint Chiefs would agree. Actually all these ports were being most stubbornly held by special German garrisons, and almost certainly would have been destroyed before capture. Roosevelt being off in the Pacific, Churchill addressed a final message of argument to Hopkins in an effort to influence Marshall. In his judgment there was no correlation possible between the armies in the Brest and Cherbourg peninsulas and troops operating against Toulon and Marseilles; and gloomily and mistakenly he predicted that DRAGOON could not influence the course of Eisenhower's battle for ninety days. Hopkins answered that it would be well nigh impossible to divert the operation to Brittany ports for various practical reasons and he was certain that DRAGOON would result in a tremendous victory.

After Roosevelt confirmed this judgment, the Prime Minister gave in, saying, "I pray God you may be right. We shall of course do everything in our power to help you achieve success." But the Prime Minister was hurt by the series of rebuffs, and regretful over what he thought was a great mistake. When Eisenhower (on August 9th) spent an evening with him alone at Downing Street, he complained that the American government was not trying to understand the British position and was indifferent toward the Italian campaign. Eisenhower found him "stirred, upset and even despondent," seeming to think that the success of his war leadership would be affected by the failure to push the Italian drive forward with the utmost strength. "I may," he gravely said, "lay down the mantle of my high office." The Supreme Commander tried to divert the reproaches from himself by remarking that if the Prime Minister had political reasons for backing a campaign in the Balkans they ought to be put before the President; that he, as military commander, was willing to change his plan of campaign if political purposes were to be paramount; but on military grounds he could not. Nor did he.[24]

Apropos of Eisenhower's intimations that he thought that Churchill's strategic proposals might be inspired by political purposes, it ought to be noted that during this stage of discussion neither Churchill nor his colleagues ever openly avowed or admitted that this was so. However, there are ample revelations of Churchill's anxiety that where the Red Armies went, Communism would follow, and it is safe to presume that in addition to the military gains he thought could be won by bringing Western forces into Yugoslavia, Austria, and Hungary, their presence in those countries seemed to him a valuable prudential measure.

It may be asked that if this purpose was in his mind, why did he and his colleagues not say so candidly—albeit confidentially—to the Americans? On this point conjecture can spray in any of several directions. The top American military men—Marshall, King, Eisenhower—paid strict homage to the idea that, in making military plans, their assignment, their only assignment, was to win the war as soon and with as little loss of life as possible. They wanted to do whatever would serve this end, and they did not want to do anything that might interfere with it. Cognizant of this attitude, Churchill may have felt that to argue for an adjustment of military plans on any grounds except that of military advantage would be sure to arouse opposition and spoil the chance of getting a fair verdict. Further, he must have been aware that Harry Hopkins and the President were also inclined to construe his interest in the fate of South and Southeastern Europe as being a special British one rather than a general one. But, to repeat, all this is only conjecture. The argument was carried on solely in terms of what would best make ". . . for the better conduct of the war."

Churchill was not a man to bear a long grudge over differences of this kind. And Eisenhower was an appreciative victor. Thus the summer strain over strategy after OVERLORD did not affect the friendship and mutual esteem between the Prime Minister, Eisenhower, Marshall, and the President. But Churchill's regret and a sense that a mistake had been made did not vanish even after DRAGOON proved easier and more rewarding than the British staff had thought it would

[24] See Pogue, *The Supreme Command,* pages 225–26, Eisenhower, *Crusade in Europe,* pages 281–84, and Butcher, *My Three Years with Eisenhower,* pages 634 and 644, for accounts of this interview.

be. Nor was it assuaged when it also turned out that the forces left under Alexander's command in Italy were, as the President had contended, strong enough to keep driving the Germans north and ultimately across the Po. Thus when the Soviet authorities, with their native Communist associates, set about bringing Central and Southeastern Europe under Communist control, Churchill's determined wish to move east from Italy flared again. More will be heard of the subject.

37. Whether to Apply the Principle of Unconditional Surrender

The events, military and political, which we have reviewed had brought the Allies face to face with the question of whether to stand on the strict "unconditional surrender" formula, or to be adaptable in pursuit of the policy it represented.

At Teheran—where it will be remembered that Stalin outdid the others in the severity of his attitude toward Germany and the Germans —he nonetheless had questioned whether it was advisable, as a wartime measure, to leave the principle of unconditional surrender undefined. He thought that the lack of explanation of what was in store for them served to unite the German people; whereas, if they were told what would be done to them, no matter how harsh, he felt that the day of surrender would be hastened. The condensed record leaves room for wondering whether he really meant to have the Germans *truthfully* told of the measures which, in that same talk, he had said must be taken to assure that Germany could not rise and fight again. The available memos of conversation do not record what Churchill and Roosevelt thought of Stalin's views on this point or what they may have said about them.[25]

[25] The main discussions of the treatment of Germany took place (1) at and after the dinner on November 28th given by President Roosevelt. On this occasion the President retired before the other two, who continued their conversation on this subject after he had left. (2) During a private talk between the President and Stalin on November 29th. (3) At the dinner given by Stalin on November 29th. Such American records of these conversations as I have seen do not contain mention of any talk about the interpretation of the formula of unconditional surrender. Roosevelt, as will be told in the text, had no memory of hearing the subject discussed in his presence. But both Churchill and Eden remembered it as having been mentioned by Stalin to Roosevelt at the dinner on the

In any case, the question had been left hanging. It had to be. For all three governments were uncertain at this time and by no means of one opinion as to what ought to be done about Germany and the German people. But the British officials had thought the matter well worth pursuing. Therefore after Teheran they had urged that an effort be made to draw up a statement of terms which could be communicated to the German people—either in definition of or in place of the outstanding demand for unconditional surrender. On December 22nd the State Department had received a memo from the Foreign Office which, after referring to some talk at Teheran, proposed that the European Advisory Commission be instructed to deal with the subject as soon as possible. Hull had asked Roosevelt for guidance in his answer. The President had replied in a chit which read "This I think should be taken up by Winant with Prime Minister Churchill as soon as the latter gets back. It was not brought up in any way at Teheran in my presence."

Hull had instructed Winant accordingly on December 24th. On that same Christmas Eve, in his radio speech to the nation, the President had tried to construe the principle in a way that might influence the enemy. He said, "The United Nations have no intention to enslave the German people. We wish them to have a normal chance to develop, in peace, as useful and respectable members of the European family."

In psychological warfare, truth and untruth get embraced in the same haze. Whom was he speaking for? Would the terms that Stalin had in mind have afforded the Germans a "normal chance to develop in peace"? Could they be trusted with such a chance?

Churchill apparently also decided that little more could be advisedly said at this time. In an explanatory note to his colleagues on January 14th, after summing up the penalties and restraints which were in store for Germany (though still not finally determined) he concluded: "Enough at any rate is set down above to show that a frank statement of what is going to happen to Germany would not necessarily have a reassuring effect upon the German people and that they might prefer the vaguer terrors of 'unconditional surrender,' mitigated as they are by such statements as the President has made." [26]

When called upon to state his policy in the House of Commons on February 22nd, the Prime Minister's remarks had been as general in

---

29th—after that stretch in the talk in which Stalin advocated the liquidation of at least 50,000 and perhaps 100,000 of the German commanding staff.

Since the question of whether or not it was briefly discussed between the three at Teheran has no particular significance, I abstain from giving further detail or citations.

[26] *The Hinge of Fate*, page 690.

their import as those made by Roosevelt in his Christmas Eve broadcast: "The term 'unconditional surrender' does not mean that the German people will be enslaved or destroyed. It means however that the Allies will not be bound to them at the moment of surrender by any pact or obligation. . . . Unconditional surrender means that the victors have a free hand. It does not mean that they are entitled to behave in a barbarous manner, nor that they wish to blot out Germany from among the nations of Europe."

It may be observed that the way in which the Germans, as they fell back before the Russian armies, were treating subject peoples, prisoners, and refugees did not improve their title to kindness or survival as a unified nation. The concept of stern justice was to clash with the instinct of mercy, and the passion of hatred was to war with the teaching to forgive.

Thus the idea of attempting to announce definite terms for Germany had been dropped for some time. But the thought of doing so in regard to the satellites had arisen again. The Finns had begun to discuss a possible armistice with the Russians. The Soviet government was ready to tell them on what conditions it would make peace. Noting this, Eden had consulted the American and Soviet authorities as to whether something similar ought not to be done in reference to the other satellite states. On March 20th he had suggested, in a memo given by Halifax to Hull, that the fight still being put up by these countries might weaken if the principle of unconditional surrender was dropped, either silently or openly; and their defection might be hastened if they were told—as the Italians had been—that they would be rewarded by contributing to the defeat of Germany. Moreover, he had observed that in order to facilitate surrender, leeway was needed in the discussion of such matters as military cooperation and frontiers. The Soviet government, it was learned a few days later, had agreed with Eden's recommendations.

The State and War Departments had been strongly inclined to concur. In consultation they had prepared the text of a joint statement which might be directed toward Romania, Bulgaria, and Hungary. This did not mention unconditional surrender. In substance it bid these satellites to quit the war at once; assured them that the quicker they did so the less they would suffer; and warned them that the longer they fought on, the more rigorous the terms that would be imposed on them. This was all pretty vague, but it suggested that there was an area for negotiation—as compared to the Moscow Four-Nation Declaration, which decreed unconditional surrender for the satellites as well as Germany.

But after studying this provisional draft and listening again to an exposition of the propaganda and military purposes it might serve, the President had decided it would be better to abstain from even such spongy promises. Thus, when Hull on the 25th passed on to him Eden's suggestion, with a recommendation that it be followed, the President promptly commented, "It would be a mistake, in my judgment, to abandon or make an exception in the case of the words 'unconditional surrender.' " Italy, the President maintained, had surrendered unconditionally but was at the same time, as an act of grace, given many privileges—and the same thing could be done in the event of the surrender of Bulgaria or Romania or Hungary or Finland. He had once again referred to Lee's acceptance of unconditional surrender followed by Grant's generous response. His comments ended, "That is the spirit I want to see abroad—but it does not apply to Germany. Germany understands only one kind of language." With this answer, he also sent back to Hull the copy of the message from Eden, having scribbled on it "No—the British Foreign Office has always been part of this and it is N.G.—F.D.R." [27]

Hull, exceptionally for him, had challenged the President's ruling. On April 4th he had sent him a letter saying he was afraid that the Soviets would not understand our refusal, nor why we should object to doing in the case of Romania what we did not object to in the case of Finland. They might thus, he thought, accuse us of making the Soviet military task harder. The President was sick, but by return messenger he had sent back word to Hull that at all costs he wanted to prevent it from being said that the principle of unconditional surrender had been abandoned, and that there was real danger that it would be abandoned if we made exceptions. "I understand perfectly well," he then continued, "that from time to time there will have to be exceptions not to the surrender principle but to the application of it in specific cases. That is a very different thing from changing the principle. If the Soviet and British governments will advise us of any case of this kind, I am quite sure that we will agree with them. This should be made clear to both of these governments." [28]

Hull, in notes to the British and Soviet Embassies in Washington (on April 11th) had transmitted the President's views without trying to clarify them.

The British and Soviet governments had been apparently satisfied that in practice in dealing with the satellites they would not be hindered by the retention *of the principle, in principle*. Still the British had appealed to the American government to consent to the omission of the

[27] *Memoirs,* page 1576.
[28] *Ibid.,* page 1577.

term *in propaganda* addressed at least to Hungary and Bulgaria. Hull had favored this and had asked the President (on May 10th) whether he would approve our taking parallel action with the British and Russians in authorizing a degree of latitude for propaganda purposes, ". . . having it clearly understood that the exception is authorized to enable the propaganda services to omit reference to the term, though of course there would be no public recantation of the principle as applicable to these countries." [29]

To this the President had made no objection. The way had thus been cleared for the joint statement to the satellites which the State Department had prepared. It had been issued on May 12th. The peoples and governments of Hungary, Romania, Bulgaria and Finland could read that they ". . . still have it within their power, by withdrawing from the war and ceasing their collaboration with Germany and by resisting the forces of Nazism by every possible means, to shorten the European struggle, diminish their own ultimate sacrifices, and contribute to the Allied victory." This, along with the fact that nowhere was it said that they must surrender unconditionally, could be read as meaning that the victors would negotiate with them about terms.

While this play with concessions for the satellites had been going on, the European Advisory Commission had been trying to draw up a detailed instrument of surrender for Germany. There were still differences of opinion on various main issues. But the call for some advance definition of what the doctrine of unconditional surrender would mean in application to Germany had become more insistent.

In the middle of April, preparations for the invasion of France had been in full and tense flow, with hearts beating fast over the coming full encounter with the Germans. When Stettinius, the Undersecretary of State, was in London Generals Eisenhower and Smith had impressed on him reasons for making our intentions clearer. They had thought that by doing so, the German people, as they felt the weight of our assault, might become disposed to give up; while, if we merely repeated the ritual formula, German propagandists would be able to get their people to fight on out of desperate fright of what would happen to them after surrender. They had also thought there was a chance of inducing a movement inside the German Army and the German General Staff to overthrow Hitler and arrange for a surrender. What they had proposed was that the three Allied governments should hurry to agree upon their intentions, and guarantee law and order in the Reich; and then, as soon as Allied forces had won a beachhead in Northwest

[29] *Ibid.*, page 1580.

Europe, Eisenhower, as Supreme Commander, should issue a statement summarizing the terms of surrender and calling on the Germans to lay down their arms. William Phillips, former Undersecretary of State and old friend of the President, who was briefly serving as political adviser to Eisenhower, had agreed with this tactical line.

Stettinius' report on these recommendations had been placed before the President, who was still resting in South Carolina. This message may have seemed to him to be an effort by diplomatic and military officials to bend if not break his position; to turn his policy into one of bidding with promises for German surrender—which could quite possibly end in a conditional negotiated peace. In any case, he had asked Hull to instruct Phillips to let everyone concerned know that he did not want the subject to be further considered without his approval.

This had caused a suspension of discussion within the EAC in regard to any definition of terms for Germany. But the men who were to lead the invasion and their staffs had turned to trying to develop some statement that might be addressed to the Germans. Eisenhower had reviewed the problems involved in the working out of an effective declaration in a memo for the Chiefs of Staff of SHAEF on May 20th. He had encountered two problems for which there was no good solution: (1) the fact that the three main Allies had not yet agreed definitely on the treatment to be accorded Germany after surrender; (2) that an honest exposition of Allied intentions was likely to appear so grim as to offset any reassuring elements in the statement. So he had concluded that, unless these difficulties could be overcome in some way, it would be best to drop the attempt to state Allied demands.

Similarly a last-minute attempt by the President to word a statement which would best these difficulties failed to win Churchill's assent. He was bothered by the same quandary which had balked Eisenhower: any announcement which was not candid about such matters as punishment for war crimes would expose the Allies later to charges of deception, but any that *was* candid would terrify the Germans and cause them to fight all the more fiercely. Roosevelt had hurried to tell Stalin that because of Churchill's objection he was giving up the idea. This had crossed Stalin's answer in transit; he had not liked the proposed pronouncement any better than Churchill. Thus it had come about that the only statements made before or at the time of the landing in France were flashes on military action.

Since this subject is of such active controversial interest, it may be pursued a little further in what must be a summary fashion.

During the time that followed, work was resumed in the EAC on the terms of the instrument of surrender and the directive to be issued for the control of Germany. Various further attempts were made in the State Department, Eisenhower's Headquarters, and among the Combined Chiefs of Staff to compose an acceptable statement of Allied intentions which might affect German resistance.[30] But none came to fruition.

Then in September, American and British ideas of what was to be done about Germany flamed into confusion. As is described in the account to come of the Conference at Quebec: Roosevelt and Churchill initialed proposals that would have kept the German people living at poverty level and forbidden them from again developing a great industrial system of life. The idea was quickly dropped, but frightening versions of it leaked out. The German agencies whose task it was to inject the hormones of fear and hate into German resistance used it with effect. This, they told the German people, revealed the real meaning of "unconditional surrender." The deduction which they flaunted before the German people was that it was equivalent to annihilation; or, as the *Voelkischer Beobachter* typically said, "The German people must realize that we are engaged in a life and death struggle which imposes on every German the duty to do his utmost for the victorious conclusion of the war and the frustration of the plans of destruction planned by these cannibals." [31]

[30] Another line of possible action would have been primarily to give impetus to secret movements to overthrow Hitler by a promise that if that occurred the Allies would review their policies toward terms of surrender and the future treatment of Germany. In this connection, what Allen Dulles, the OSS representative in Switzerland who was in secret touch with members of the group that tried to kill Hitler in July 1944, has written in his book *Germany's Underground*, pages 140–41, is of interest:

"In reviewing my notes of those days (July 1944) I find that the 'Breakers' group was encouraged to proceed by a most innocuous statement in the House of Commons by Mr. Atlee to the general effect that before there could be any fresh consideration of the German situation the Germans themselves should take the first step to get rid of their criminal government. They were also heartened by a statement made about the same time by Prime Minister Churchill recommending that the German people should overthrow the Nazi government. I urged that some similar statement be made from America as I was convinced that whatever the result of 'Breakers' might be, the fact that an attempt was made to overthrow Hitler, whether or not successfully, would help to shorten the war. Nothing of this nature was done."

Whether the issuance of such a statement might have helped the secret plotting that was going on against the Nazi leaders or even caused it to take a different form cannot be known.

[31] Goebbels used it also against German advocates of continuing to hold in the east, while letting in the west—as for example in his article in *Das Reich*, October 21, 1944: "It hardly matters whether the Bolshevists want to destroy the Reich in one fashion and the Anglo-Saxons in another. They both agree on their aim: they wish to get rid of thirty or forty million Germans." See *The Supreme Command*, page 342, and *The Struggle for Europe*, page 549.

It was deemed advisable to try to offset this intense Nazi effort to arouse false fears of Allied vengeance by general statements of the Allied program. Eisenhower on September 28th, as Allied troops and tanks crossed the frontiers of Germany, declared, "We come as conquerers but not as oppressors." The President in a speech on October 21st, after warning that there could be no bargain with Nazi conspirators, again assured the German people that they would not be enslaved. In Eisenhower's Headquarters and among the Combined Chiefs of Staff there was a natural eagerness to go further to convince the Germans that they need not fight on to save their country from devastation or destruction. But when Churchill was consulted in November, he and the War Cabinet thought the time wrong—that since the Western Front was just then stalemated, the Germans might regard it as a sign of weakness. Then, too, unless the Russians gave the same assurances, it would have little effect, the Prime Minister thought, since it was Russian conquest that the Germans feared. So he told Eisenhower (on November 26th) that he thought it best that they just keep going as they were till winter, adding that "In the meantime I shall remain set on unconditional surrender which is where you put me." [32]

At Yalta (to leap far ahead to February 1945) the three Heads of government finally managed to come near enough to agreement to approve sections on Allied aims for Germany as part of the joint statement they issued at the end of the Conference. This said nothing that had not been announced before by Churchill and Roosevelt, but it also bore Stalin's name. It declared: "It is our inflexible purpose to destroy German militarism and Nazism and to ensure that Germany will never again be able to disturb the peace of the world. . . . It is not our purpose to destroy the people of Germany, but only when Nazism and Militarism have been extirpated will there be hope for a decent life for Germans, and a place for them in the comity of nations."

What the Germans as a people had to fear most, I think, after this series of interpretations, was not the black terrors of the "unconditional surrender" formula. It was their own knowledge of the agony they had brought upon the world, and the punishment that might justly be inflicted on them. For the Nazi leaders it was death or prison; for the lesser ones and their associates it was ruin and humiliation. For senior military commanders and staff it was the end of their career and enjoyed power. For other Germans it was foresight of a meager existence in a damaged and occupied country. For almost all there was the frightening possibility of domination by the Russians.

The maintenance of the unconditional surrender formula, it is my

[32] *The Supreme Command*, page 343.

impression, was a minor influence in the fight which the Germans sustained, except perhaps in the very last spell of the war. For what they longed and hoped for was not merely assurance that they would not be oppressed, but a deal with the West which would divide their enemies and allow them to escape penalty and survive as a strong country.

The real question for the Allies—as distinguished from the tactical one—was what was to be done about Germany and the Germans *after* they submitted. That, in my reading of the record, would not have been decided much differently even though some German group—such as that which made its brave attempt in July 1944—had managed to overthrow Hitler and his crowd and had asked for an earlier peace. The Germans had too much to account for; they were too greatly feared; they had lost the usual rights to justice in a humane society. All that protected them—unconditional surrender or not—was the restraint and tolerance of their enemies, and the mutual uneasiness between the West and the Soviet Communist realm.

38. The Treatment of Germany

Progress toward deciding what was to be done about Germany after surrender had lagged behind the talk of what might be said to the Germans.

The European Advisory Commission (on which Sir William Strang of the British Foreign Office met with Winant and Gusev, the American and Soviet Ambassadors to Great Britain) had been asked, it will be remembered, to make recommendations about the terms of surrender and the organization that would be needed to make sure they were carried into effect. But from the start that Commission had been tethered and tripped. Winant was often without instructions; sometimes because one branch of the War Department was still contending that surrender terms and occupation questions were military matters to be decided by the Combined Chiefs of Staff and nobody else; sometimes because various branches of the American government were quarreling over what should be done about the German economic structure. Then there were the trans-Atlantic arguments—the most stubborn of which was over occupation zones.

The Commission had worked to develop three documents. One,

stipulating unconditional surrender, was to be accepted by the Germans. The other two were to be signed by the three allied governments; one of these was concerned with the machinery for the control of Germany after surrender; the other set forth the system of occupation and allotted the zones to be held by the national forces of each of the Allies. It was foreseen that still a fourth agreement would be essential—one that stated the *common* policies to be pursued throughout all of Germany during the period of occupation and control. Without that, the whole system was likely to fail. That was never really completed.

I shall tell the story about each of the three accords separately.

The task of writing out the instrument of surrender to be signed by the Germans was much simpler than it had been in the case of Italy. The only trouble had come in March—because of Soviet anger at accurate stories appearing in the British press about the Soviet wish to use German troops for work inside the Soviet Union after the war. But this had been soon mended. So nearly complete was the work on this document at the time of OVERLORD that when, three days later (June 10th), Harriman told Stalin that the President wanted to talk with him again before Germany collapsed, to settle all questions about that country, Stalin answered that it did not seem as though it would be necessary for three months anyhow and ". . . there seemed to be general agreement as regards the principles of German surrender."

This turned out to be so in the sense that the three governments had recorded their agreement on what they could agree on, and agreed to leave those matters on which they could not agree, undetermined. These reserved questions were vital and had defeated the authority of the EAC. Among them were: whether or not the way was to be left open to use German troops for forced labor; reparations; frontiers; dismemberment. These still remained unsettled among the victors at the time of German surrender. This text, developed in the EAC, was in the final event not used.

On the second document, the one which contained the arrangements for the execution of the surrender terms and the control of Germany after the war, a large degree of accord had also been quickly reached. The plan envisaged a Control Council formed of representatives of the three Allies who would be sharing in the occupation. It was understood that the commanding general of each of the occupying forces would serve both as commander in his national zone and member of the

Control Council. This Council was to have responsibility for all matters which concerned Germany as a whole, while each zone commander would exercise the residue of authority in his own zone.

The system was adopted. It worked until the three governments could not agree on common policies to be applied by the Council in all the zones.

The attempt to settle zones of occupation went differently—being marked by a prolonged clash of desire between the British and Americans.

A British Cabinet Committee had in the summer of 1943 recommended that the occupation forces in Germany should be disposed in three main zones, with the British in the northwest, the Americans in the south and southwest, and the Russians in the east, Berlin to be a separate joint zone. Neither Roosevelt nor the Joint Chiefs had liked the designated allocation. The President had wished the Americans to be in the northwestern area of Germany which could be supplied through the northern ports—Hamburg, Bremen, Rotterdam—and not in the southwestern area for which the lines of supply would run through France. He had not wished to become dependent on French cooperation. This was in part due to the trouble he was having with de Gaulle; in part to his idea that there might well be civil war in France; and perhaps also to the possibilities in mind about the detachment of certain areas or points of the French colonial empire. Additionally, the Joint Chiefs had reckoned that it would be easier to transfer American troops from Europe for the war in the Pacific if the United States controlled the North German ports.

On the plane en route to Cairo and Teheran, Roosevelt had marked out sketchily on the back of an old envelope an alternative plan of division. This differed from the British scheme in two main features: one, it reversed the American and British locations, placing the Americans in the northwest; and, two, it drew the boundary line between the Western and the Soviet zone much farther to the east. But it had some curious zigzags and left unfinished that part of the line which would have divided the British zone in the southwest from the Soviet zone.

It is possible that either at Cairo or Teheran Roosevelt had briefly discussed this subject with Churchill, though the accessible records do not tell of it.

When the EAC met formally for the first time on January 14, 1944 the British member had submitted proposals for zonal division which had been approved by the War Cabinet.[33] These (set down in a proposal circulated on the 15th) had followed the earlier British scheme of allocation, but had defined the zones more exactly. The Eastern zone, assigned to the Soviet Union in this text, ran southward from Lubeck on the Baltic some 200 miles west of Berlin, contained about 40 per cent of former German territory, 36 per cent of the population, and 33 per cent of the productive resources—all exclusive of Berlin. Then in February the Soviet member had submitted another plan in which the dividing line between the Western zones and the Soviet one was substantially the same as in the British proposal, and which differed from it otherwise only in secondary features. He had indicated that the Soviet government was not greatly concerned as to how the British and Americans divided the western part of Germany, but hoped they would settle the matter between themselves soon. Talks between the British and Soviet members had soon thereafter adjusted the differences in detail between their two proposals regarding the limits of the Soviet zone. It should be borne in mind that this was still months before OVERLORD and the capture of Rome. The coordinated Soviet offensives promised at Teheran were regarded with unqualified approval, everyone being eager to have the Russians press on as hard, far, and fast as they could. Whatever the shaping currents of thought or calculation during this first half of 1944, neither the British nor Americans had seemed troubled at having the Soviet armies stationed so far west in Germany as was contemplated in this zoning plan.

Meanwhile Churchill had done his utmost to get the President to accept the original allocation as between the northwestern and southwestern zones. This request he thought justified, as he had explained to the President in February, because (1) when the war ended British troops would be in the northern areas of Germany, with bases at Cherbourg and Le Havre; (2) they already had close liaison with the Dutch

[33] In referring both to the earlier recommendation of the War Cabinet Committee and to the British part in the discussions in the EAC, Churchill is unusually vague. He has written that "At this time the subject seemed to be purely theoretical. No one could foresee when and how the end of the war would come. The German armies held immense areas of European Russia. A year was yet to pass before British or American troops set foot in Western Europe, and nearly two years before they entered Germany. The proposals of the European Advisory Council were not thought sufficiently pressing or practical to be brought before the War Cabinet. . . . The question of the Russian zone of occupation in Germany therefore did not bulk in our thoughts or in Anglo-American discussions, nor was it raised by any of the leaders at Teheran." *Triumph and Tragedy*, page 508.

It is to be noted that the European Advisory Council did not meet until January 1944, which was only five months before the cross-Channel invasion.

and Norwegian forces; (3) they would be better able to ensure the naval disarmament of Germany. Correspondingly, he stressed that the Americans would be in the southern segment of Germany with bases in Brittany; and they would be equipping the French forces and working more closely with them. Both State and War Departments at this time seem to have had the impression that the British were thinking also that it would be easier to support the German population in the northern area; and that they wanted to be in a position to control Britain's great competitor, the Ruhr.

Churchill's explanations had not impressed Roosevelt. He thought it would not be hard to switch about the American and British troops from north to south at the end of the war. Besides, his other reasons for not wanting the southern zone, he had explained to Acting Secretary of State Stettinius on February 21st, were that after the first occupation period anyway, the Americans ". . . will be only too glad to retire all their military forces from Europe." At the end of this memo he added, "If anything further is needed to justify this disagreement with the British about lines of demarcation, I can only add that political considerations in the United States make my decision conclusive."

Sometime thereafter Winant had received from Washington a variant American proposal regarding zonal boundaries. This alternative plan (which it was learned later was based on the off-hand sketch of the President which has been described) besides placing the Americans in the northwestern zone, had circumscribed a much smaller Soviet zone, one starting well east of Lubeck, running southeast to Stettin, and then touching the edge of Berlin. Since this had been forwarded to him without definite instruction, and since its sponsorship was not clearly stated, the Ambassador deferred its presentation to the EAC. He had explained to the State Department various difficulties it would cause, among them that because of the reduction of its zone the Soviet Union would be deprived of the important junction of Gottbus, and that the lines did not correspond with Germany's administrative boundaries.

Then on April 3rd George Kennan, who was in Washington, at Winant's behest and with Hull's approval, had consulted the President. He had pointed out that the plan for zonal division which had been sent to Winant took no account of the earlier proposals on which the British and Russians had virtually settled, and would place the border of the Soviet zone very much farther east than the Russians wished to have it. The President had said he did not object to acceptance of the western border of the Russian zones on which the others had agreed. The Joint Chiefs of Staff had approved doing so (on April 28th), as had Hull. Winant had been instructed accordingly (on May 1st), and so advised his colleagues (on June 1st).[34]

But Roosevelt had continued to want the northwestern zone. Winant, therefore, in the current meetings of the EAC had persisted in this requirement against equally stubborn British refusal to accede to it. In early August, Stettinius, who was Acting Secretary of State, proposed to the President that we accept the southern zone if the British relieved our worries: first, by promising to take over the occupation of France, Italy, and the Balkans, if that should become necessary; second, by allowing our forces to use the ports in the north of Germany and the Low Countries. The President, who was in the Pacific, sent back word to tell Winant that he was waiting for Churchill to give in. Once again he said, "It is essential that American troops of occupation will have no responsibility in southern Europe and will be withdrawn from there at the earliest practicable date."[35] He also remarked that he did not know why it was necessary to discuss this subject with the Russians since it had been agreed that they might police that part of Germany in which they had said they wanted to exercise control.

The pressure on the President to compromise had, however, intensified. Eisenhower and Stimson advised him that an agreement, and a speedy one, was essential because our troops were already in Germany. He had continued, however, to hold out until after a further tussle with the American military advisers and the British at Quebec in the middle of September. Then he yielded. He agreed that the Americans should have the southwestern zone, the British the northwestern one. The dividing line between the two was changed, leaving in the British zone the region of the Saar and the Palatinate, west of the Rhine. The ports of Bremen and Bremerhaven within the British zone were to be under American control, and the Americans were to have a free right of passage to and from the American zone and these ports.

There may not be real point in trying to guess what caused the Presi-

---

[34] Churchill seems to have been forgetful or negligent of this earlier history when, in a comment he made to Truman on April 18th, 1945 in the course of advocating delay in withdrawing American and British forces back from their battlelines into their assigned zones, he remarked, "The occupational zones were decided rather hastily at Quebec in September 1944, when it was not foreseen that General Eisenhower's armies would make such a mighty inroad into Germany." *Triumph and Tragedy*, page 514. As a matter of fact, this earlier American concurrence in what the British and Russians had already arranged settled the question, and this was merely confirmed formally at the conference at Quebec.

Subsequently, agreement was reached to make some adjustment in this dividing line between the eastern and western zones—transferring Mecklenburg into the eastern zone and Schleswig-Holstein into the northwestern zone.

[35] *Memoirs*, pages 1613 *et seq.*

dent to give in. Probably it was the mere weight of advice. Or perhaps it was because the conduct of the French people and their reception of de Gaulle caused his fear of civil war in France to fade. Or perhaps, and this is the notion which the Secretary of the Treasury brought back from the Quebec Conference, because "The President had wanted the British to be in charge of the Ruhr and the Saar so that they would have to implement the [industrial destruction] policy which was outlined in the memorandum initialed by Churchill and himself." [36]

Berlin was located within the Soviet zone. But from the beginning it had been conceived that it should be a separate area of jurisdiction, to be occupied by the forces of all three countries and under their joint administration.

Both the British and Soviet proposals to the EAC had so provided. But discussion of the arrangement—and in particular of the ways of assuring the Americans and British access to Berlin from their zones through the Soviet zone—had been left up in the air because Winant had not known how to proceed. Under the novel scheme of zonal division which had been transmitted to him from Washington, all three wedge-like zones would have met at Berlin, and so each would have access to the city through its own zone. But after he was authorized to discard this, and concur in the British-Soviet line of division between the western and eastern zones, the question of access to Berlin had been left in abeyance.[36a]

However when the Ambassador had been in Washington in May, he had told the Civil Affairs Division of the War Department that he would be willing ". . . to propose [in the EAC] detailed provisions safeguarding American access [to Berlin] by highway, railroad and air." He was confident that concrete provisions could be negotiated in the EAC without great difficulty, since the Soviet representative had repeatedly insisted that there would be no trouble in arranging for transit through the Soviet zone to Berlin, and that the presence of American and British forces in Berlin "of course" carried with it all

[36] Memorandum by the Assistant to the Secretary of the Treasury (White) September 20, 1944, Yalta Documents, page 137.

[36a] Consideration of the whole subject of access to Berlin was delayed because of difference between ourselves and the Russians as to whether separate zones of occupation in Berlin ought to be assigned before actual entry into the city. The Joint Chiefs of Staff had wanted to wait till then, and to leave the matter to the national commanders on the spot who would know what facilities there were for communication, billeting, and the maintenance of order. But the Russians refused to accept the basis of combined administration unless there was prior agreement on zones of responsibility. Many months went by before the Americans gave in, and this delayed consideration until 1945 by the military of the question of a transit accord.

necessary facilities of access.[37] But the Civil Affairs Division had not wanted such an article written in the agreement on zones of occupation. It had thought that it was not possible to foresee what railways and roads would be needed, and which might, when the war ended, be serviceable and which destroyed. So it had insisted that the task be left to the military commanders to arrange when the time came. Thus having received what he regarded as an authoritative military view, Winant had not pressed the question further.

When Roosevelt and Churchill and the Combined Chiefs of Staff reviewed the draft of the proposed accord on zones at Quebec in September, none apparently judged it essential to define the right of access at that time. It seems to have been thought of only in connection with the movement and requirements of the armed forces which would be stationed in Berlin. The need to take care of the wants of the people of Berlin by sending in great quantities of supplies from the Western zones was not anticipated.

In the attempt to complete the system of accords the Allies found their greatest difficulty in deciding (1) what to do about the German economic structure; (2) what attitude to take toward the economic condition and problems of the German people after the war. These questions were connected with that of reparations, but went far beyond.

The German armies and air forces which had overrun Europe rested on great and specialized industries. What part of these should Germany be allowed to retain and reconstruct? In deciding policy about this question and that of reparations, should the victors concern themselves with how the Germans lived after defeat? Should they abstain from actions or demands that would make it very hard for the Germans to feed and shelter themselves, or even if necessary help them? Should they force the Germans to share anything they might have over minimum essentials with the victims of their fury?

No matter how adequate and well-conceived the machinery for the

[37] As told by Philip Mosely in his article "The Occupation of Germany," in *Foreign Affairs,* July 1950. Mosely served as chief adviser and deputy to Winant on the EAC from June 1944, and had full knowledge of the record. Thus General Lucius Clay (who served later as Commander-in-Chief of the American zone in Germany and American member of the Control Council) would seem to have been mistaken in blaming Winant for the flaw, as he did in his book *Decision in Germany,* page 15. There he wrote, "This omission was not accidental and had been discussed with our representative on the European Advisory Commission by Mr. Murphy [Political Adviser to General Eisenhower]. Ambassador Winant believed that the right to be in Berlin carried with it the right of access and that it would only confuse the issue to raise it in connection with the agreement. He felt strongly that it would arouse Soviet suspicion and make mutual understanding more difficult to attain."

control of Germany might be, it was sure to break down ultimately unless the directing coalition agreed on these matters. Winant pointed this out in a long and cogent message which he sent to the President and Secretary of State in the middle of August. But when this seven-thousand-word analytical statement was received, the President was off in the Pacific, absorbed in the conduct of that war; it is to be wondered whether it was read by him with any care.

The State Department had been trying hard to level its ideas on these subjects with those of the War Department and the British Foreign Office. Except for points which it thought ought to be left to the military commanders to settle, the War Department was in general accord with the emergent sketch of policy. But the Treasury deemed it much too mild, and felt that the State and War Departments really wanted to treat the Germans much too charitably.

How severe the President at this time thought he wanted to be with Germany is indicated by a memo which he sent to Secretaries Stimson and Hull on August 26th, after noting certain points of a handbook that was being prepared for the guidance of future military government officials in Germany. In ordering it to be withdrawn, he said,

"It gives the impression that Germany is to be restored just as much as The Netherlands or Belgium, and the people of Germany brought back as quickly as possible to their prewar estate. It is of the utmost importance that every person in Germany should realize that this time Germany is a defeated nation. I do not want them to starve to death, but, as an example, if they need food to keep body and soul together beyond what they have, they should be fed three times a day with soup from Army soup kitchens. . . . The fact that they are a defeated nation, collectively and individually, must be so impressed upon them that they will hesitate to start any new war." [38]

Stimson became worried at this same time because our troops were going into Germany without instruction on vital points of policy. He urged the President to appoint a committee of the Cabinet to assimilate the work already done and prepare a report. The President did so at once, naming Hull, Stimson, and Morgenthau as the Committee, and asked Hopkins to coordinate its efforts.

At a preliminary meeting (held in Hopkins' office on September 2nd) of the departmental assistants, they found themselves in accord on many features of policy. But in two vital fields Harry D. White, speaking for Morgenthau, presented startling proposals.[39] They were

[38] *Memoirs,* pages 1602–03.

[39] A lengthy and detailed comparative study of texts would be necessary to identify precisely the succession of proposals which were under discussion inside the American gov-

much more drastic than the measures which the State and War Departments had in mind. Yet it could be argued, I think, that they were just a runaway ride along the course which Roosevelt and Stalin had marked out at Teheran.

The Treasury plan visualized large transfers of German territory to other countries—Silesia, East Prussia to Poland and the Soviet Union; Saar and adjacent territories to France; the area north of the Kiel Canal to Denmark. The Ruhr and the Kiel Canal were to be made into an international zone which was not to be allowed to trade with the Reich. What was left of Germany was to be divided into two independent states, north and south. One other point was an obvious attempt to fall in with the President's ideas: the task of civil administration and policing of all these units was to be left mainly to Germany's neighbors —which would have allowed withdrawal of American troops in a relatively short time.

What the Treasury proposed in the economic sphere started a fire of controversy which charred all later thinking on the subject. In briefest summary it urged (1) that nothing be done to sustain the German economy or relieve the condition in which the German people might find themselves; (2) that German heavy industries should be either dismantled and given over as reparations, or destroyed, especially those grouped in the Ruhr and Saar.[40]

---

ernment during the next two weeks, for there were a series of uncompleted and completed drafts.

The first set of Treasury proposals were those presented by White at this meeting of Departmental Assistants in Hopkins' office on September 2nd—the Saturday before Labor Day. The President and Morgenthau were at Hyde Park over that weekend. There the President read over slowly and carefully the then available draft and told Morgenthau of certain changes he wanted in it (in particular no planes, no uniforms, and no parades for the Germans). Morgenthau on the basis of his talk with the President and his own further study of the first Treasury draft concluded that its economic features were not sufficiently drastic. In his later words, "My own critical analysis of our first draft was that it left the Ruhr intact, with international control as the only safeguard." This was not so; even this first Treasury draft called for a great reduction in the Ruhr industrial structure to meet two acknowledged purposes: (a) the destruction of war-making potential; and (b) the making of reparations payments by capital transfers. Morgenthau wished to be sure that no residue of major industries in the Ruhr zone could survive. The changes he urged were presented, probably in the form of oral annotations, at the first meeting of the Cabinet Committee on September 5th. They then, perhaps after further amendment, were embodied in the written version considered at the meeting of the Cabinet Committee with the President on September 6th. It is probable that still further changes were made in this draft in the course of turning it into the final version which was taken to Quebec by Morgenthau entitled, "Program to Prevent Germany from Starting a World War III."

[40] As written into the version discussed with the President on September 6th, it read, "This area [the Ruhr] should not only be stripped of all presently existing industries but so weakened and controlled that it cannot in the foreseeable future become an industrial

The Cabinet Committee met in Hull's office on September 5th, on which occasion Morgenthau orally presented his severe proposals. Hull urged that no decision should be made about partition (as distinguished from territorial transfers) until the internal situation in Germany was clearer and we knew more of British and Soviet views. Otherwise the treatment that the Secretary of State had in mind for Germany was neither lenient nor forgiving.[41] Stimson objected to the Treasury proposals on the ground that they would cause "enormous general evils"; that the Germans would be permanent paupers and that a large part of Europe would suffer; and that the hatreds and tensions that would develop would obscure the guilt of the Nazis and poison the springs of future peace. They would, he vehemently argued, breed war rather than prevent it. But Morgenthau remained convinced that nothing less than what he proposed could stop the Germans at some time or other from again trying to extend their domination by force. He stood up also for the opinion that the German people could live even though their heavy industries were banned, and that the rest of Europe could also get along without them.

In two meetings of the Cabinet Committee with the President on September 6th and 9th these opposed views were presented and argued again. But the whole question was left in a greater muddle than before. Roosevelt did not seem—at any rate to Stimson—to take up with the Treasury plan for destroying the industries of the Ruhr. But at moments he showed animated approval of some of the points made in the Treasury briefs; according to Morgenthau's reminiscent account saying at one juncture, "As far as I am concerned, I'd put Germany back as an agricultural country." [42] He seemed untouched by the dark picture painted of how the German people might suffer by losing the means

---

area. The following steps will accomplish this: (a) Within a short period, if possible not longer than 6 months after the cessation of hostilities, all industrial plants and equipment not destroyed by military action shall be completely dismantled or removed from the area or completely destroyed. All equipment should be removed from the mines and the mines thoroughly wrecked. (b) The area should be made into an international zone . . ."

The final version as printed in Morgenthau's book, *Germany Is Our Problem,* differs somewhat in phraseology.

[41] In the memo prepared by the State Department for the President dated September 4th, the pertinent paragraph read: "The primary objectives of our economic policy [for Germany] are (1) the standard of living of the German population shall be held down to subsistence levels; (2) Germany's economic position of power in Europe must be eliminated; (3) German economic capacity must be converted in such a manner that it will be so dependent upon imports and exports that Germany cannot by its own devices reconvert to war production." *On Active Service in Peace and War,* page 571.

[42] Morgenthau's article "Our Policy toward Germany," *The New York Post,* November 28, 1947.

of economic and military recovery. In this mood he thought that if the Germans should have to live off soup kitchens for awhile that was good enough for them. The peoples of the countries who had been twice forced to give up life and endure the cruelest of suffering because of Germany's misuse of power agreed with him. The opinion may be ventured that if at this time the question had been put to a vote of these people—not of economists, or historians, or clergymen—there would have been a vast majority for allowing or making the Germans endure shabby misery for a long time, even though they themselves would also be worse off because of it.

In these White House talks, Hull—judging from the accounts later written by Stimson and Morgenthau—seems to have given each of them the sense that he had come around to his side. Probably the Secretary of State's tactic at the time was just to avoid harsh face-to-face argument with the President, his aggressive colleagues in the Treasury, and his vehement colleagues in the War Department. He allowed the memos which the State Department sent over to the White House to speak for him, and these clearly moved away from Morgenthau's more extreme conceptions. Stimson, in contrast, was outspoken. The Americans who would have to reckon with the consequences first and on the spot would be the army commanders and soldiers for whom he felt responsible. The thought that they, in the line of duty, would have to carry out these policies left him most unhappy, and his depression colored the entry which he made in his Diary about the meeting on the 9th (entry for September 11th): "I have been much troubled by the President's physical condition. He was distinctly not himself. . . . He had a cold and seemed tired out. I rather fear for the effects of this hard conference [Quebec] upon him. I am particularly troubled . . . that he is going up there without any real preparation for the solution of the underlying and fundamental problem of how to treat Germany." [43]

At Quebec, as has often been told, Churchill was persuaded to assent to a course close to that marked out by the Treasury.[44] He and the President on September 15th initialed an agreement which read:

"At a conference between the President and the Prime Minister upon

[43] *On Active Service in Peace and War,* page 575.

[44] This account of what happened at Quebec is put together from (1) Hull's *Memoirs;* (2) the Stimson-Bundy book; (3) memo dated September 20, 1944 by Matthews, Deputy Director of the Office of European Affairs in the State Department, *Yalta Documents;* (4) memo by Assistant Secretary of the Treasury, White, September 20, 1944, *Yalta Documents;* (5) Morgenthau article "Our Policy toward Germany" in the *New York Post,* November 26, 1947; and (6) Record of Conversation between Roosevelt and Churchill at Quebec, September 14, 1944.

the best measures to prevent renewed rearmament by Germany, it was felt that an essential feature was the future disposition of the Ruhr and the Saar.

"The ease with which the metallurgical, chemical, and electrical industries in Germany can be converted from peace to war has already been impressed upon us by bitter experience. It must also be remembered that the Germans have devastated a large portion of the industries of Russia and of other neighboring Allies, and it is only in accordance with justice that these injured countries should be entitled to remove the machinery they require in order to repair the losses they have suffered. The industries referred to in the Ruhr and in the Saar would therefore be necessarily put out of action and closed down. It was felt that the two districts should be put under some body under the world organization which would supervise the dismantling of these industries and make sure that they were not started up again by some subterfuge.

"This programme for eliminating the war-making industries in the Ruhr and in the Saar is looking forward to converting Germany into a country primarily agricultural and pastoral [45] in its character.

"The Prime Minister and the President were in agreement upon this programme."

On his return to Washington, Morgenthau (on September 20th) told a surprised Hull and Stimson something of the history which preceded the initialing of this drastic statement of intention. He recounted that when he first talked to Churchill about it the Prime Minister was angrily opposed and he quoted Churchill as asking with annoyance whether he had been brought to Quebec to discuss a scheme which would chain England to a dead body. Writing later of the scene, he remembered that Churchill ". . . was slumped in his chair, his language biting, his flow incessant, his manner merciless. I have never had such a verbal lashing in my life." But the Secretary of the Treasury rebounded quickly from this castigation. The next day he convinced Lord Cherwell that the policy was practicable and that it would enable Great Britain to recover more quickly after the war. Cherwell had persuaded Churchill to accept the program. But the Prime Minister had not liked the statement in which Morgenthau and Cherwell had expressed this policy. So he had called in his own secretary and dictated his version of what had been agreed. That was the document which the President and Prime Minister had initialed. Morgenthau went on to tell further

[45] The adjective "pastoral," which did so much to condemn and ridicule the plan, was a Churchill addition. The Morgenthau-Cherwell draft which Churchill found unsatisfactory had read: "This programme for eliminating the war-making industries in the Ruhr and in the Saar is part of a programme looking forward to diverting Germany into largely an agricultural country."

that Eden had been much upset and had argued hotly with Churchill over this action. The Prime Minister had held his Foreign Secretary off, and told him not to discuss this subject with the War Cabinet until he, Churchill, got back to London because he was bent on pushing it through.

There is ground for wondering why Churchill put his initials on this accord. One attracting thought was that by eliminating Germany as a competitor, Britain would be able to recover more quickly. Another reason may have been to be surer of American government aid for the restoration of Britain. Morgenthau denied, in answer to a question by Stimson, that Churchill may have been swayed by this consideration. But a sentence in Churchill's succinct later account indicates that it was very much in his mind, the sentence that tells, "At first I violently opposed this idea. But the President, with Mr. Morgenthau—from whom we had much to ask—were so insistent that in the end we agreed to consider it." [46] How could it not have been in his mind since the day before (the 14th) the President had given favorable assent—which fell little short of a definite promise—to a continuation of lend-lease assistance during the period of war against Japan alone, after Germany had been defeated? Munitions were to be provided in the approximate amount of three and one-half billion dollars; this would enable the United Kingdom to transfer labor from munitions industries to the export trades. The other requirements—food, raw materials, machinery and shipping—to be met had been put at about three billion dollars. This prospective help, especially since it was to have been given without conditions that would hinder British export trade, was a real lure. Beyond that, Churchill may have thought that by subscribing to this policy, he would convince Stalin and Roosevelt that he did not care about the Germans and had no concealed wish to use them to maintain a balance of power against the Soviet Union after the war. Or—a final conjecture—did Churchill go along with Roosevelt in this field so that Roosevelt would accept, as he did, the southwestern zone of occupation in Germany instead of the northern zone he had craved? How many possible ways there are of explaining an action that was unwise in a way that Churchill was so seldom unwise!

Both the President and Prime Minister soon found out how stubborn was the sentiment of some of their closest advisers that the measures on which they had agreed were both impractical and unhealthy. Stimson and Hull rebelled against them. Hull found two new grounds for second thought. One was that the Soviet government, which had not

[46] *Triumph and Tragedy*, page 156.

been consulted, might be offended. The other was that if a large credit was promised Britain without conditions, it would upset his plans for inducing that country, as part of the bargain, to conform to the trade policies we advocated.

For whatever reasons, the President began to waver about the policy endorsed in the memo he and Churchill had initialed at Quebec. Both Stimson and Hull got the impression that he had not grasped its full import. On October 2nd Hull got a note from the President (dated September 29th) which marked a compromise. In part this read:

"I just cannot go along with the idea of seeing the British empire collapse financially, and Germany at the same time building up a potential rearmament machine to make another war possible in twenty years. Mere inspection of plants will not prevent that.

"But no one wants 'complete eradication of German industrial productive capacity in the Ruhr and Saar.'

"It is possible, however, in those two particular areas to enforce rather complete controls. Also, it must not be forgotten that outside of the Ruhr and Saar, Germany has many *other* areas and facilities for turning out large exports."

On October 3rd Stimson, at lunch with the President, returned to the subject. The notation that he made in his Diary is amusing: "He [the President] grinned and looked naughty and said 'Henry Morgenthau pulled a boner' or an equivalent expression, and said that we really were not apart on that; that he had no intention of turning Germany into an agrarian state and that all he wanted was to save a portion of the proceeds of the Ruhr for use by Great Britain. . . ."

Stimson tried to bring home to him the meaning of what he had signed by reading the pertinent sentences of the Quebec agreement. His further entry in his Diary read: "He [the President] was frankly staggered by this and said he had no idea how he could have initialed this; that he had evidently done it without much thought." This last observation can be understood only in the sense that under the influence of the ideas described in the note to Hull which has been quoted, he rather hastily approved at Quebec a program that went beyond his intention toward insupportable destruction. The excess aroused a reaction against a line of policy which, if kept within moderate bounds, might well have been carried into effect with coalition accord.

Howsoever that may be, the President drew away from the understanding made at Quebec. He felt badgered and unsure. He let Churchill and Stalin, who were about to meet in Moscow, know that he would rather that they did not make any decisions about Germany until he could discuss the subject with them. On October 20th—to run a little ahead—in commenting on a memo which Hull had sent to inform him on the state of planning for Germany, he wrote, ". . . I think it is all very well for us to make all kinds of preparations for the treatment of Germany, but there are some matters in regard to such treatment that lead me to believe that speed on these matters is not an essential at the present moment. It may be in a week, or it may be in a month, or it may be several months hence. I dislike making detailed plans for a country which we do not yet occupy." [47] In the same answer, however, he indicated approval, subject to further examination of the facts, of most of the more restrained State Department proposals and standards to guide the disposition of German economic, political, and social life.

Churchill too had been retreating with equal speed from the Quebec flash accord. The end was as terse as his comment upon it in *Triumph and Tragedy*. ". . . and in the event, with my full accord, the idea of 'pastoralizing' Germany did not survive." [48] A proposed policy directive which the British government sent on to Washington at the end of October for study contained a far more moderate program for dealing with German economic life and affairs than that which had briefly won favor at Quebec.

39. Attempts to Foster Polish-Soviet Accord

There still seemed enough time to work out a common policy about Germany. But little or none was left by the end of the summer to do so for Poland, through which the Soviet forces were pounding their way.

Roosevelt had, after again telling Stalin that he still did not wish to intervene, at last agreed to receive Mikolajczyk in Washington. They had four talks between June 7th and 14th, 1944, while the invasion of France was getting underway. The President had showed himself re-assuring but nimble in his avoidance of obligation. Poland must be free and independent, he had reaffirmed. He would, he averred, see to it that Poland did not come out of the war injured, and he seemed to suggest this would not be too hard to bring about because while Stalin was a "realist" he was not an imperialist. As regards the frontiers within which the new Polish nation was to thrive, he had said that he still

---

[47] *Memoirs*, page 1621.
[48] Page 157.

did not like the idea of bounding Poland on the east by the Curzon Line; but all he had promised was that, if circumstances allowed, he might eventually try to act as "moderator" to effect an agreement on this rending issue. In a free and easy way he had sketched his idea of a settlement in which Poland, while yielding territory to the Soviet Union in the east, might still retain Lwow, the region of Tarnopol, and the oil and potash area of Drohobycz.[49] In return, in the west, Poland might get Silesia, East Prussia, possibly even including Konigsberg. Mikolajczyk had spoken up firmly against such a transposition of former Polish frontiers—answering, according his own later account, that in his opinion, ". . . Russia had no more right to half of our country than it had to that portion of the United States from the Atlantic to the Mississippi. . . ."[50]

The President had advised the Polish Prime Minister to go and see Stalin and try again to find terms of an accord. In dealing with the Marshal, he had remarked, one had to keep fingers crossed. But still ". . . you Poles must find an understanding with Russia. On your own, you'd have no chance to beat Russia, and . . . the British and Americans have no intention of fighting Russia."[51] Hull had proffered the same advice in sentences that went into coils not easy to trace.[52]

Mikolajczyk had agreed to go and see Stalin and the President had said he would send a message asking the Marshal to receive him.

While these talks were taking place in Washington, Harriman, as asked by the President, had tried anew to find out what chance there was for bringing about a reconciliation. On June 10, after reviewing what he thought would be said to Mikolajczyk in Washington, he had remarked to Stalin that Roosevelt's attitude had not changed since the meeting at Teheran but that he was puzzled in regard to the status of Lwow; that he believed that this was a point to be settled between the Russians and the Poles, and that he was sure that if Stalin would give sympathetic study to it, an understanding could be reached. Stalin's answer had been evasive. ". . . if anything arose in Polish-Soviet relations he would keep the President informed."

Stalin had also said that he thought it would be helpful if Harriman

[49] As recounted in Mikolajczyk, *The Rape of Poland*, page 60. There is a discrepancy between this and the account given by Ciechanowski, Polish Ambassador to the United States, in his book *Defeat in Victory*, page 305. He states that the President mentioned "the city of Lwow, the city and oil fields of Drohobycz, and the region of Stanislawow."

Both Stanislawow and Tarnopol are rather far to the southeast and east respectively in Eastern Galicia. Tarnopol is not far from the Russian border. Stanislawow is quite a distance to the southeast of Lwow, but perhaps more possible than Tarnopol. To have included either in Poland would have meant most of Eastern Galicia.

[50] *The Rape of Poland*, page 60.
[51] *Ibid.*
[52] *Memoirs*, page 1445.

had a talk with members of the Polish National Council—Kremlin-favored—who had recently arrived in Moscow. Because, he explained, they were "living people," not emigrés, and they would have a lot to tell him. Harriman had said he could see them unofficially. On the next day they had called upon him. They had described the Council as being representative of all Polish groups of the Center and Left and as wanting to develop into a Polish Parliament in which all democratic elements would have a place. They had avowed that their first purpose, however, was to get the Germans out of Poland. They had accused the underground movement directed by General Sosnkowski of doing little against the Germans, of killing partisans of the Polish popular movement, and of collaborating with the German Gestapo. But they had said that they would like to get in touch with the former democratic members of the London government, including Mikolajczyk, and believed these men could be persuaded to cooperate with the Council. As for frontiers, they informed the Ambassador that they thought Poland would fare better by cooperating with the Soviets rather than by adopting an adamant position; that they hoped to retain the Galician oil fields and Lwow and expand Polish territory in the west. They suggested that an American military observer be sent to Poland to learn for himself the situation there and to see whether the groups from which they came or the Polish government in London enjoyed the support of the Polish people.

Harriman had recommended to Washington that consideration be given to the dispatch of an observer. Later that day he had tried to find out from Molotov how the Soviet government would regard such a step, but Molotov had evaded. The Ambassador's reports to the President and Hull on his talks with Stalin and with this Polish group had arrived while Mikolajczyk was still in Washington.

If we look at Mikolajczyk's response to American advice together with Stalin's response to Harriman, it is hard to understand the optimism tincturing the message which Roosevelt sent to Stalin (on the 17th) after Mikolajczyk had gone. In this, after again stating that he was not trying to inject himself into the merits of the quarrel and had no definite plan to settle it, he said he wanted the Marshal to know that he thought Mikolajczyk a sincere and reasonable man, disposed to try very hard to have Poland be on good terms with the Soviet Union. He thought his recent visitor would not allow small matters to deter him from trying to find a solution and would be willing to go to Moscow if Stalin would indicate he was welcome. Churchill (on the 20th) had sent a message to Stalin in the same key of deference to Stalin's power to have his arbitrary way, if he would.

And he would. Stalin's answer to the President—like so many other of his messages about Poland—was written with a mind made up. In sum he said that since there was no evidence that Mikolajczyk was ready to advance toward the acceptance of Soviet conditions for a reconciliation, it was hard for him to express any opinion about the usefulness of having the Pole come to Moscow. On this same day, June 24th, Stalin had assured Churchill that he did not want to set up a Soviet administration in Polish territory; that the Poles would have to do it; that the assignment was being turned over to the Polish National Council or its outgrowth since the underground elements directed by the Polish government in London were short-lived and without influence. As for Mikolajczyk, Stalin had said that he would not refuse to see him, but it would be better if he were to address himself to the Polish National Council, whose attitude toward him personally was friendly.

Stalin's answer had taken the President aback. But Mikolajczyk seems to have expected it since, in the interval between Roosevelt's message to Stalin and the answer, the Polish Prime Minister, back in London, had had two talks with the Russian Ambassador to the exiled governments there, Lebiediev. In the second of these, the Ambassador had proposed that the London government dismiss various of its members, including the President, Raczkiewcz, and General Sosnkowski, Chief of Staff. He had also urged that after the government in London was reorganized, it should denounce the step which had led to the break with the Soviet Union—bringing the Katyn murders to the attention of the International Red Cross. Mikolajczyk had laughed at the Soviet Ambassador at this point, and had remarked, "You're asking me, who served as a minister in General Sikorski's government, to denounce that government?" The Russian Ambassador nodded and Mikolajczyk had remarked, "Then we have no other business at this time." [53]

While these messages were being exchanged, the Polish groups who were working hand in hand with the Soviet government had started to take over the administration of Poland. The Soviet officials were becoming more sure that the Red Armies could deal with Polish dissenters as well as with the Germans; and more confident that though the British and American governments might reproach and complain, they would not retaliate or risk a break for the sake of salvaging the Polish government in London.

The Polish National Council on July 21, at Chelm behind the Soviet lines, had formed a Committee of National Liberation. This was domi-

[53] *The Rape of Poland*, page 65.

nated by Polish Communists and reliable Communist sympathizers. Among its members were Bierut, who was soon to be designated as the President of the rival Polish government, and General Berling, the officer in command of the Polish forces that were fighting as part of the Red Army.

After his rebuff, the President had desisted from any immediate further attempt to influence Stalin. But Churchill had tried to avert further acts which might displace the Polish government in London once and for all. Warning Mikolajczyk of this impending danger, the British government had urged him to act at once on Stalin's lukewarm offer to receive him. Despite the conditions looming before him, Mikolajczyk had agreed to go. Churchill, on the 25th, had hastened to advise Stalin. On this same day the Committee of National Liberation had issued a manifesto to the Polish people and declared Lublin the capital of Poland. The day after (the 26th), the Soviet government had signed an agreement with it defining relations between the civil administration in Poland and the Soviet High Command in Poland. This had entrusted the Committee with the administration of Polish liberated territory. Eden had stated in the House of Commons that His Majesty's government continued to recognize the Mikolajczyk government.

Mikolajczyk, learning of the agreement between the Soviet government and the Committee of National Liberation while en route to Moscow, had had the impulse to turn back. But both Churchill and Roosevelt had urged him not to, and he had resumed his journey. On the 28th the President, having heard from the Prime Minister that Mikolajczyk was on his way, sent a message to Stalin expressing the hope that Stalin could work out the whole situation with him to the best advantage of "our common effort." In reality, the chance that either the Soviet government or the new Polish Committee would yield in any degree was small, smaller even than Mikolajczyk and his colleagues realized, since they still thought the Soviet forces would need their cooperation to deal with the Polish people. But in fact, the Soviet rulers did not feel that need and had no intention of giving up anything they wanted just to please the Polish government in London or its supporters. This was clearly forecast in the answer which Vishinsky had given to Harriman's query on the 29th about what the Soviet government was going to tell Mikolajczyk. Vishinsky had answered that Mikolajczyk was coming with full knowledge of the Soviet position, that it was up to him to do the talking.

Mikolajczyk had arrived in Moscow on the afternoon of July 30th. This was the eve of the start of a tragic attempt by Polish underground fighters in Warsaw to expel the Germans from their city.

40. Poland Continued; and the Warsaw Uprising

This was a desperate and most courageous action. It was ignited by sparks blown in from Moscow and the battlelines that stretched east of Warsaw. In late June the Soviet armies had started a great offensive at Vitebsk on the main Polish front. By the end of July they had smashed the central German defensive line, crossed White Russia, and advanced three hundred or more miles.

In the light of what happened later, a forecast which Molotov had made to Harriman on July 5th ought to be reported. In summarizing for the Ambassador the strategy of the current Soviet offensive, he had said that the Red Armies in White Russia were headed for Konigsberg, and then intended to move southwest through East Prussia and North Poland, going around Warsaw. It was contemplated, he had said also, that the liberation of Warsaw would be left to the Polish partisans and army after German communications to the west had been severed. There might also be, he had added, an advance in Southern Poland. Harriman probably had had this talk in mind when, on July 19th, in response to a request by the State Department for an estimate of Soviet intentions, he sent on surmises, first, that General Berling's Polish Army (part of the Soviet Army) might be held in reserve for use in liberating Poland; and, second, that Warsaw might possibly be bypassed by the Red Army so that Berling's Army, with the cooperation of the partisans, might in appearance, if not in fact, take Warsaw after its communications from the West had been cut, if the job did not turn out to be too hard.

If such had been the original strategic Soviet plan, I do not know if it was unswervingly followed, or whether, as the advance rolled on, it was decided that the Red Army might, after all, try a frontal thrust for Warsaw. The course of the Russian armies during the next month through Central and Southern Poland toward the Vistula and Warsaw gives ground for believing that a change of plan providing for such an attempt was considered, favored for a time, then dropped. If this was so, the final decision to halt before Warsaw may have been either (1) because, as the Poles in London and Churchill came to believe, Stalin wanted to wait until the Poles in Warsaw were wiped out; or (2) because the Soviet advance in the northern part of the line was stopped early in August, thus not completing the swing through East Prussia north of Warsaw to cut communications to the west; or (3) because,

as Stalin said, the Red Armies had to stop at the Vistula in front of Warsaw to bring up weapons, and German defense strength in Warsaw was far too strong.

On July 22nd the Poles in Warsaw intercepted a radio call from the Commander of the Fourth German Panzer Army to his units ordering them to retreat west of the Vistula.[54] On the 24th, the Red Armies, having crossed the Bug River in Central Poland, entered territories west of the Curzon Line and captured Lublin. On the night of the 26th —the day that the Soviet government announced that it was signing an accord entrusting the civil administration of Poland to the National Committee of Liberation—Soviet troops reached the Vistula, about 57 miles southeast of Warsaw. Within the next two days they captured Bialystok and Brest-Litovsk, which covered the two main approaches to Warsaw from the east. The official Soviet war communiqué for the 28th announced that the Soviet Army ". . . advancing on Warsaw from the south and east on a front almost 50 miles wide . . . were at points within 40 miles of Warsaw." That night the Warsaw railway yards were bombed for the third time. Praga, the industrial suburb on the eastern bank of the Vistula, came under Russian artillery fire.

The Commander-in-Chief of the organized underground army in Warsaw, General Bor, was impatiently waiting his chance, on edge, to take over the city ahead of the Red troops. Before Mikolajczyk left London for Moscow, he had sent a message for General Bor saying, "At a sitting of the Cabinet of the Republic a common resolution was taken authorizing you to proclaim the rising at a moment to be chosen by you. If possible let us know of it beforehand."

This was known as Operation TEMPEST. It was an elastic order leaving the local leader in each Polish town to decide whether or when to utter the word.[55]

[54] General Bor's account of these developments reads: "Far more important than the flight of the Germans [out of Warsaw] or the reaction of the people was the news which reached us from the front. About July 22, our monitoring service intercepted a call from the commander of the 4th German Panzer Army issuing uncoded wireless orders to his units. The army was completely routed in the Zamosc sector. The dispersed and beaten units were ordered to withdraw to the west on the other side of the Vistula. . . ." Bor-Komorowski, *The Secret Army*, page 207.

[55] The Cabinet resolution was taken on July 25th. Mikolajczyk's message was sent off to the government delegate in Poland sometime between then and the 27th. I do not know whether it was received and passed on to General Bor before or after he radioed to London, "We are ready to fight for Warsaw at any moment. I will report the day and hour of the beginning of the fight."

General Anders, the Commander of the Polish Corps in Italy, was opposed to the idea of any general uprising. General Sosnkowski, the Minister of War, who was at the time in Italy with Anders, agreed, and sent on July 28th and 29th two messages to General Bor

On the evening of the 29th a radio station in Moscow known as the Kosciuszko Station broadcast an appeal from the Union of Polish Patriots to the people of Warsaw which began: "No doubt Warsaw already hears the guns of the battle that is soon to bring her liberation. . . ." It then proclaimed, "The Polish Army now entering Polish territory, trained in the USSR, is now joined to the People's Army to form the corps of the Polish armed forces, the armed arm of our nation in its struggle for independence."

It called upon the people of Warsaw to join the battle:

"For Warsaw, which did not yield, but fought on, the hour of action has already arrived. The Germans will no doubt try to defend themselves in Warsaw. . . . They will expose the city to ruin and its inhabitants to death. . . . It is, therefore, a hundred times more necessary than ever to remember that . . . by direct active struggle in the streets of Warsaw, in its houses, factories and stores we not only hasten the moment of final liberation but also save the nation's property and the lives of our brethren.

"Poles, the time of liberation is at hand! Poles, to arms! There is not a moment to lose!" [56]

Mikolajczyk on the next evening (the 30th) had his first talk with Molotov. The Commissar for Foreign Affairs was distant, asking, "Why did you come here? What have you got to say? And, according to the account which Mikolajczyk later published, "We'll take Warsaw soon; we are already about six miles from Warsaw." [57]

Mikolajczyk does not tell of passing on this statement either to Warsaw or London. Nor was there any contact between the Red Army units by then so close to Warsaw and the Polish underground groups

---

stating ". . . in the present political conditions, I am absolutely against a general rising, the political outcome of which would inevitably result in changing one occupation for another. Your appreciation of the German situation should be sober and objective. Any error on this point would cost us dear. It is necessary at the same time to concentrate all political, moral and physical forces against the annexationist plans of Moscow." Anders, *An Army in Exile,* page 201.

These messages may not have gotten to Bor until after he had taken action. In any case, this prudent advice was directly countered by a later message sent by President Raczkiewicz from London, and on August 2nd Minister Kwapinski (Mikolajczyk's deputy during his absence) confirmed to Bor that "In connection with the suggestions of the Commander-in-Chief as to avoiding open sortie and full action in accordance with the plans you have set out, the Polish Government does not see it possible to change its previous instruction and your decision. The question of armed action and going out into the open is entirely in your own competence. This includes insurrection." Bor-Komorowski, *The Secret Army,* page 208. By this time the insurrection had begun.

[56] *The Rape of Poland,* page 69.
[57] *Ibid.,* page 71.

in the city who were waiting for their arrival. The Soviet commanders did not try to get in touch with them. Perhaps they did not know who they were or where to find them. No code system of communication had been arranged. The group in Warsaw did make some sort of effort to connect, but failed for reasons not known. The harsh way in which the Red Army had up to then treated the resistance groups attached to London who had made themselves known did not encourage others to place themselves in its service.

By the 31st, the Red Army was spread along the Vistula on a wide front, and had entered towns less than 10 miles northeast and 12 miles southwest of Warsaw. The German forces inside the city seemed exposed to a massive attack from both these directions, and heavy shelling and perhaps direct assault from the east. That night General Bor gave the order to start Operation TEMPEST the next day (August 1st) at five in the afternoon.[58] His decision may have been hastened by the fact that by this time the Germans were treating the people of Warsaw most cruelly; there were more and more arrests, deportations, executions, forced labor. The order sent into the streets against the Germans over 35,000 men with their civilian auxiliaries, who between them had only small supplies of weapons, munitions, food, drugs. Among these there were only a few Communists. Five German divisions within or near the city, and other units, were hurried to the scene of revolt.

General Bor hastened to send out urgent reports and appeals to London for aid. But who could have given substantial relief quickly except the Red Army across the Vistula? It did not move the next day, nor the next, nor send planes over Warsaw. The Moscow radio made no mention of what was going on in the city. No Soviet liaison officers came through or around the German lines. When, on the 2nd, Mikolajczyk told Molotov of the reports about the revolt that he had received via London, Molotov made no comment. The Soviet press for that day an-

[58] Fervent national pride and an excited wish to justify Polish claims dominated the decision. The flow of feeling which entered into it has been described by Stefan Korbanski, an active member of the Polish underground army in Warsaw. The impulse to act was made the more intense by the thought of what ". . . the western world would say if the Russians were to conquer Warsaw unaided. In that event Stalin would have no difficulty convincing the Allies that the Home Army, the Underground Government and the Polish Underground as such were a fiction . . . no one could have foreseen that the Russians would deliberately halt the offensive. . . . The date of the Warsaw rising, however, was decided subsequently, during a secret session of the Home Army which had taken into consideration an additional factor, namely that the Germans had placarded the city with posters summoning all males, except young boys and old men, to report for building fortifications." *Fighting Warsaw*, pages 347-48.

nounced that General Bulganin would be its liaison with the Polish Committee of National Liberation.[59]

On the next day, the 3rd, Mikolajczyk, along with his Foreign Minister, Romer, had his first talk with Stalin. But this concerned itself with the broader issues of Soviet-Polish relations, and took no special cognizance of the fight going on in Warsaw. At first Stalin belittled the underground movement directed from London. He said he could not trust it to cooperate with the Red Army; and that it was making a lot of trouble for him. By abstaining from argument and instead telling of its operations, Mikolajczyk got Stalin to listen. But then Stalin said that he was not interested in mobilizing a large part of the Polish population into the army. The Poles could do more, he thought, by restoring a stable life behind the lines. Turning to frontiers, Stalin asserted that he would deal only with a Polish government that recognized the Curzon Line. In return, the Soviet government was willing to accord it the Oder Line in the west, including Breslau, Stettin, and East Prussia. But—and there went one of the consoling points Roosevelt had made— Konigsberg and the area around it would have to remain in the Soviet Union. As the talk went on, Stalin added that perhaps if Mikolajczyk's group reached an accord with the Committee of National Liberation, some small changes to the benefit of the Poles might be made in the Curzon Line. He said he hoped this would come about, for if it did not he would have to deal with the Committee, anyhow. Mikolajczyk said he was ready to try. Whereupon Stalin said he would ask the Committee to send representatives to Moscow to begin talks as soon as possible.

The Polish government in London had informed Washington of the revolt in Warsaw and of General Bor's appeals for help. Romer had told Harriman at once of Mikolajczyk's talk with Stalin, and the Ambassador hurried off a report upon it. But nothing positive was heard on either subject from either the President or the State Department.

The British government, taking heed of the Polish appeals, decided to try to air-drop equipment and supplies on Warsaw by long night flights from Italy. Churchill told Stalin of his decision to do so, remarking that it might help Soviet operations; and no doubt hoping to set an example for the Soviet army and air force. But the first British try failed badly—only a very few of the planes reaching the beleagured city. And Stalin's answer to Churchill on the 5th, sent off after Stalin had talked

[59] Soviet press, August 2, 1944. Full name, Nikolai Aleksandrovich Bulganin. In the year 1957 Marshal Bulganin, Premier of the Soviet Union.

with Mikolajczyk, was, as the recipient has described it, "prompt and grim." It mocked at the action within Warsaw. Stalin said that the Polish statements about what they were doing were untrue; that the Polish underground army in Warsaw was small, and it did not have artillery, planes, or tanks; and so he could not imagine how it thought it could take Warsaw away from the Germans, who had four tank divisions there.

At Stalin's signal, the Polish Committee of National Liberation had sent its spokesmen to Moscow. In his first real talk with them (on the 6th) Mikolajczyk had appealed to them as Poles to get help for Warsaw, if only ammunition, which was almost gone. General Rola Zymierski, Commander in Chief of the Polish formation in Russia, said that he had asked the Soviet military people to drop ammunition and arms, and had been told that this could be done only at a spot some 30 kilometers away from the center of the city. He also said that he had been informed the Red Army advance had been slowed down by the appearance of four new Panzer divisions, but that an effort was being made to surround the town by a large enveloping movement north and south; and that the Polish divisions of the Red Army under General Berling were being moved into the line east of Warsaw. Whether or not this was a truthful account of the Red Army's situation and intentions as of that moment; or whether the Soviet government was misleading the Lublin Poles also; or whether this explanation was a secret understanding worked out between the Soviet government and the Lublin Poles for transmission to Mikolajczyk, is part of the story left open to conjecture.[60]

Mikolajczyk's following talks with the representatives of the Committee (on the 7th and 8th) revealed the full impact of what was asked in return for help. The discussion was dominated by Bierut, who was chairman and whose impressive manner and statements caused Mikolajczyk to become distressed and anxious. It was proposed to Mikolajczyk that he should not return to London but go to Warsaw as soon as he could. Then when the new government was formed, four out of its eighteen Cabinet posts would be assigned by the Lublin group to independent parties. Of these the chief one would be for Mikolajczyk, who would be named Prime Minister. Mikolajczyk rejected the proposition vigorously, telling Bierut that he was being asked to sell out the Polish people. The impasse was not eased when later, on the 8th, Mikolajczyk and the Committee group talked out their differences again in the

[60] This information regarding the interview between the two groups of Poles on the 6th about the Warsaw situation is derived from the reports which the American and British Ambassadors in Moscow sent their governments after talking with Mikolajczyk.

presence of Molotov, who assumed the role of big brother. Mikolajczyk stubbornly repeated that he thought that what was proposed to him was unfair to the Polish people and in a way disgraceful. Nor did he change this view when General Rola privately urged him at least not to return to London but instead go to Warsaw. General Rola warned him that if he did not do that it was more likely than not that the Committee of National Liberation would set up a government without him which the Communists would dominate. Mikolajczyk, in telling the American and British Ambassadors of this, remarked that he would be a swine if he took the advice.

Thus, with the separation more ominous than ever, Mikolajczyk on the 9th went to have a final talk with Stalin. When Mikolajczyk referred to the situation in Warsaw, Stalin said that he had expected to capture the city three days before (on the 6th) but had been prevented by the arrival of four Panzer and other German divisions to defend the crossing of the Vistula. He still seemed doubtful as to whether a real struggle was going on inside the city—saying, according to Mikolajczyk, that the Lublin Poles told him there was not any fighting going on. In answer to Mikolajczyk's pleas that aid be dropped from planes, Stalin said that the Soviet Army had already tried to send two officers into Warsaw and both had been caught trying to land and were killed by the Germans. Mikolajczyk later wrote that he found out this was untrue.[61] But, anyhow, before the talk was over, Stalin avowed that he wanted to help the Warsaw fighters and would do his best to do so. Mikolajczyk rushed a message to London reporting that Stalin had given a promise to supply help to Warsaw, particularly to drop arms at once from aircraft. Whether Stalin's proffer warranted so definite a report, there is no way of being sure.

Mikolajczyk also gave both Harriman and Clark-Kerr the sense that this parting talk with Stalin was a step toward reconciliation. This impression was confirmed, though only briefly, by a message which Stalin sent to Roosevelt on August 9th about his interchanges with Mikolajczyk. After stating that he was sure that the Polish Prime Minister was not well informed about conditions in Poland, he said that he thought that the talks might be a beginning toward agreement since both Polish groups said that they wanted to work together to unify all the democratic forces in Poland. The President (on the 12th) thanked Stalin for this roseate message. He earnestly hoped that the talks would produce a solution ". . . which will permit an interim legal and truly representative Polish government to be formed." That was all.

[61] *The Rape of Poland*, page 78.

But the Soviet armies so near Warsaw still did not attempt to reach the city and rescue the Poles. Molotov spread word through the Embassies that the enveloping movement on which the Soviet armies were engaged would take time; that at the moment, in fact, the Germans were counterattacking.

Churchill again (on the 12th) asked Stalin whether he would not and could not find a way to get help to the valiant fighters in Warsaw. They were securing almost none of those supplies which, at great risk, were being flown for them through the nights from Italy. Roosevelt, having taken a week to think over appeals from the Polish government in London, now approved a plan whereby the American Army Air Force should fly from France at high altitudes by day, using heavy bombers both to carry the supplies and to bomb nearby German airfields, with fighters to protect the bombers. For such an undertaking, Russian concurrence was needed, as the bombers would have to cross the Soviet battlelines and land behind these lines at the Poltava air fields which the Americans used for shuttle bombing. This plan was put up to the Soviet government through military channels. But Harriman also on the 14th presented it to Molotov ". . . as political considerations are involved."

The first answer was given in a letter which the Ambassador received almost at once from Vishinsky. This said that he had been instructed by Molotov to say that the Soviet government ". . . could not go along . . ." with the project, as it regarded the Warsaw uprising as a ". . . purely adventuristic affair in which the Soviet government could not lend a hand." [62]

Upon receiving this letter from Vishinsky, Harriman and Clark-Kerr asked for an interview with Molotov. On the score that he was not in Moscow, Vishinsky received them. They told him that they thought that the Soviet decision was a great mistake which would have grave repercussions in Washington and London. Vishinsky's answers gave ground for the belief that the Soviet government had decided to grasp the chance afforded by the Warsaw tragedy to so cover the London government with blame as to destroy it in the eyes of the Poles within

[62] In a message which Stalin sent to Mikolajczyk later on, the same view was more flatly stated. "After a closer study of the matter I have become convinced that the Warsaw action, which was undertaken without the knowledge of the Soviet command, is a thoughtless adventure causing unnecessary losses among the inhabitants. In addition, it should be mentioned that a calumnious campaign has been started by the Polish London government which seeks to present the illusion that the Soviet Command deceived the Warsaw population.

"In view of this state of affairs, the Soviet Command cuts itself away from the Warsaw adventure and cannot take any responsibility for it." *The Rape of Poland*, page 82.

the country. They led Harriman to include in his report (of August 15th) a grim reflection: "If the position of the Soviet government is correctly reflected by Vishinsky, its refusal is based on ruthless political considerations—not on denial that the resistance exists nor on operational difficulties."

The next evening Vishinsky, having asked Harriman and Clark-Kerr to call, gave them an answer in writing so that, as he explained, it might be perfectly clear. This was: "The Soviet Government cannot of course object to English or American aircraft dropping arms in the region of Warsaw, since this is an American and British affair. But they decidedly object to American or British aircraft, after dropping arms in the region of Warsaw, landing on Soviet territory, since the Soviet government does not wish to associate themselves either directly or indirectly with the adventure in Warsaw."

As soon as Harriman and Clark-Kerr could get to Molotov they tried to impress him how greatly their governments were distressed and disturbed by the cold Soviet disregard of the state of the rebels in Warsaw —who were fighting Germans. At first Molotov was vague as to why the Soviet attitude had hardened so during the week since Stalin had told Mikolajczyk he would try to deliver aid. But presently he admitted that there had been a change and hinted that it was due to radio and newspaper criticism of the operations of the Red Army inferring that the Soviet government was abandoning the Poles in Warsaw on purpose. Molotov thought that the Polish government in London was responsible for these stories. He saw nothing that could be done to save it or the rebels in Warsaw from their folly.

When Harriman got back to the Embassy after this talk he found a further instruction from Washington awaiting him. This authorized him to say to Stalin or Molotov that the President himself hoped that the Soviet government would cooperate in aiding the Polish underground forces in German-occupied Poland; but whether it did or not, the U.S. military forces intended to do so—insofar as they could feasibly. This was the first bold statement of the American will as regards Warsaw that had been sent to Moscow.[63]

[63] Either the State Department or the Defense Department, or both, soon became worried lest it was *too* bold. In a message to Harriman on the 19th it raised the question as to whether it was desirable to continue to press the Soviet government further in regard to the use of bases in its territory for these Warsaw rescue operations. It left it to Harriman's discretion as to whether or not to do so. But it told him to bear in mind the importance of being able to continue with the shuttle bombing of Germany, remarking that, "Our military authorities attach first importance to this consideration." It went on to point out that the British might not have this equally in mind and were showing a tendency to go considerably further than the President was ready to go. It concluded with the obscure comment that since the Soviet government was not trying to prevent our

Harriman sent off a letter to Molotov at once, telling him of our intentions to give such help to the Poles in Warsaw as we could. This was followed up on the 20th by a message in which the unhappy but unwearied Churchill persuaded the President to join him, despite his reluctance to become personally engaged in Polish affairs: "We hope," they said to Stalin, "that you will drop immediate supplies and munitions to the patriot Poles in Warsaw, or will you agree to help our planes in doing it very quickly?" [64]

On that same day two items showed how differently the Soviet government had come to view the situation in Warsaw. The press reported that on the night before Soviet planes had dropped leaflets on Warsaw describing the uprising as the work of an irresponsible clique in London and encouraging the population to cease resistance and save their lives. And the Soviet military office delayed answer to the usual advance notice of another planned shuttle bombing flight over Germany to end at Poltava in order to be sure that none of the planes might drop supplies for Warsaw.

Stalin answered the joint Roosevelt-Churchill message on the 22nd. He now heaped all the blame for what was happening in that city on others. The authors of that rebellion, he said, he regarded as criminals who were causing the death of good people by throwing many almost unarmed citizens against German guns, tanks, and aircraft. Further than that, he said their action had had bad military consequences, since it had caused the Germans to concentrate their forces in the Warsaw region.[65] Direct assault upon the city, he continued, was unprofitable for the Red Army; but it was doing everything it could to smash the German attack around Warsaw which was underway and to go on the offensive to free the city for the Poles. He did not refer to the request that relief planes be allowed to land behind the Soviet lines.

Churchill was eager to send an answer right back, saying that the planes were going to be sent anyhow, leaving it up to the Soviet authorities to give or bar refuge to any that might have to come down behind the Soviet lines. But Roosevelt would not join him, since he did

independent operations it was felt that Harriman had already achieved his chief purpose by what he had done. This puzzled Harriman, who so informed Washington.

The reference to the President's views is also puzzling in the light of the joint message which he and Churchill sent to Stalin on the 20th, the next day.

[64] *Triumph and Tragedy,* pages 135–36.

[65] It may be contended that this worked to the advantage of the Russians by absorbing German reserve forces which would otherwise have been available to defend Romania and Bulgaria south of the Carpathians. By the middle of August only two of the eighteen German panzer divisions in the east were south of the Carpathians. The Soviet forces started on the 20th a masterly campaign along a 300-mile line between the Carpathians and the Black Sea.

not think that such action would help the general war prospect.[66]

During the next fortnight the Poles in Warsaw fought on, separated into isolated units, besieged and dying. That center of misery was not to be forgotten despite great actions on the main fronts. Churchill continued his fervent appeals to Moscow and Washington for some measures to prove at least that this reckless band was not deserted. And in early September, in Churchill's phrase, the Kremlin "changed its tactics." On the 9th the Soviet government agreed to cooperate in attempts to drop supplies from the air. Even as it did so, it repeated its disavowals of any responsibility for what had happened in Warsaw; going further, in fact, it reproached the British government for not warning it in advance that the uprising would take place and asked whether this was not a repetition of what had happened in April 1943 when the Polish "emigré" government, without British objection, came out with their slanderous statements about the Katyn massacres.

During the nights beginning September 13th, small groups of Soviet planes tried to drop food to the people within Warsaw. The Germans got most of it. On the 18th, after several days' delay caused by the weather, the American Air Force sent over a large group of bombers which dropped supplies from high altitudes and then landed behind the Soviet lines. The Soviet Air Force aided by bombing the German airfields and keeping the German planes out of the air. But these dropped supplies also scattered, and the besieged got almost none. The large Soviet army on the bank of the Vistula opposite Warsaw was stationary while other units carried the battle forward south and north of the city. When General Berling insisted, four infantry battalions of Polish troops were ferried across the river and tried to join up with those fighting within the city. But they suffered great losses and the survivors had to be brought back.

During these tardy attempts to sustain or rescue the survivors in Warsaw, Churchill, Roosevelt, and their military staffs were in conference at Quebec. There they seem to have found nothing new to say or do either about the Polish situation in general or the fight in Warsaw. When, on September 23rd, Harriman called on Stalin to give him the joint Roosevelt-Churchill message informing him of the decisions made at Quebec, he asked Stalin whether the battle for Warsaw was going to his satisfaction. Stalin said it was not. The Vistula had proved to be a tremendous obstacle; the Germans kept the crossing under such steady, heavy shelling that tanks could not be moved across; without tanks, frontal attack could not be made because of the overlooking position

[66] Roosevelt's messages to Churchill, August 26th and September 5th. *Triumph and Tragedy,* pages 143–44.

of the Germans on higher ground. Harriman did not remind Stalin of the way in which he had belittled similar explanations of the difficulties of crossing the Channel and landing on the beaches of France.

The end was near. On October 2nd the remainder of the fighting Poles in Warsaw surrendered after sixty-three days of most awful struggle. The lost force was the strongest element in the Polish Home Army. As Churchill wrote of this final outcome: "When the Russians entered the city three months later they found little but shattered streets and the unburied dead. Such was their liberation of Poland, where they now rule."[67]

The Lublin administration had been, during this period, extending its reach and working on close terms with the Red Army. It was trying to assure foreign diplomats and newspapermen that it was independent and representative of the mass of the Polish people. It presented itself as a coalition group, not a Communist one. The policies which it professed to favor were moderate and tolerant.

Concurrently, the Polish government in London had begun moving from its transfixed posture of opposition to Soviet desires. On getting back from Moscow to London, Mikolajczyk had started intense consultations with his group and the chief figures in their underground in Poland. By the end of August they had agreed, after harsh disputes, upon a plan which marked a new effort to satisfy the Soviet demands. This had been submitted to the Soviet, American, and British governments on September 1st with an explanation that its terms were not to be regarded as final but as the basis for discussion after the liberation of Warsaw.

A willingness to shake off the control of those elements which had governed Poland before the war and to become truly democratic was evidenced in some of the main features of this new plan. It visualized the conversion of the government into a coalition of the four main prewar political parties and the Polish Socialist Party (Communist) on equal terms. This new government was to be entrusted with the administration of liberated Polish lands. Elections were to be held as soon as practicable; and after these elections a new constitution was to be enacted. An agreement was to be negotiated at once with the Soviet government for the conduct of the war against Germany, the prevention

[67] *Triumph and Tragedy*, page 145. It might be noted here that later in October—after the struggle in Warsaw was over—when Churchill visited Moscow, in one of the variant explanations which Stalin gave him for not trying to take Warsaw by frontal attack, he said that the Soviet Army would have been compelled to destroy the city and the people in it, and they had not wanted to do that, and for the same reason had restrained their air attacks.

of renewed German aggression, and a durable Soviet-Polish alliance, respecting the independence of both states. Alliances and close friendships were also to be maintained with Great Britain, France, and the United States. Boundary questions were to be settled on these broad principles: (1) the new Poland was to have no less territory than Poland before the war; (2) the main centers of Polish cultural life and sources of indispensable raw materials were to be left within Poland; (3) the final boundaries were not to be settled until the elected government was in existence. In the meanwhile, Polish armed forces would operate under the Supreme Soviet Command in the Eastern Zone. And during the Soviet occupation of Germany, the Russians were to be allowed to keep troops in Polish territory to protect their bases and lines of communication.

The British government had thought highly of this program. The American government had passed up the chance to express an opinion about it. The Soviet government had ignored it, on the ground that any such proposals had to be worked out with the Lublin Committee.

Mikolajczyk, still in London, was hanging back from any renewal of the discussions with that rival group. Because of his zeal in trying to find bases for an accord with the Soviet government, his position within the London group was threatened. And he did not want to go on a mission in which he would find himself compelled to consider any arrangement resembling that which had been proposed to him at Moscow in August.

Thus the Polish rift still stayed open after the surrender at Warsaw. The Soviet government and press continued to treat the Polish Committee of National Liberation as a ward and began to provide some food for the hungry Poles in the liberated areas. That Committee continued to berate the London government, accusing Mikolajczyk of having become more obdurate after his return to London. It tried to get and prove its popular support by organizing meetings within Poland of members of the former political parties—those very parties which Bierut, in talk with Harriman, had said were dead. It sought to convince the Polish people that the government in London had deserted them and were all Fascists. At the same time, it appealed to the American and British governments for food, machinery, and technical help for the restoration of living and working conditions within Poland.

But this study of what happened must wait. For our long saunter over this most trampled area of coalition relations—Poland—has taken us out in advance of other parts of the field of events, decisions, and conferences during the summer and early fall of 1944.

PERIOD NINE

From the Second Quebec Conference in September
1944 to the Conference at Dumbarton Oaks;
Plans to Conclude the War and Efforts to
Conceive for Peace after the War

THE concurrent events of the late summer of 1944 may be scanned as they appear in review at the meeting between Roosevelt, Churchill, and their staffs at Quebec in September—an important interim session in which the Western Allies agreed on the whole range of their future strategy.

Churchill, smarting over the disregard of his ideas of strategy after OVERLORD, and bothered by the American inclination to defer decisions about European questions, had sought another chance to review the whole outlook with Roosevelt face to face. But the President had not been eager to hear the Prime Minister's vehement arguments all over again. So he had put off another meeting with him while trying to see whether Stalin could not be prevailed upon to join them. On July 17th, three days before he was nominated for a fourth term, Roosevelt had sent another message to Stalin, saying that since things were now moving so well and fast perhaps Stalin could meet with the two of them in the reasonably near future. Churchill, he said, had the same thought. The President had suggested some time in the middle of September and had remarked that the north of Scotland would be a good central place for the conference.

Stalin had answered (on the 22nd) that while the Soviet armies were involved in battles on so wide a front, he could not leave Russia and interrupt his direction of "front matters." He had added that all his colleagues also considered it "absolutely impossible" for him to do so. Roosevelt had accepted the fact that he would have to wait before seeing Stalin, remarking, however, in his acknowledgment of the 28th, "We are approaching the time for further strategic decisions and such a meeting would help me domestically."

But Churchill, with the smashing advances of the Red Army, especially in Southeastern Europe, weighing heavily in his thoughts, kept on expressing in worried messages to Hopkins (Roosevelt being off on his Pacific trip) his sense that another British-American review of strategy was urgently needed. Thus after Roosevelt returned to Washington in the middle of August, a meeting with Churchill and the British Chiefs of Staff had been arranged for September. Quebec was chosen as a pleasant and convenient place, and being in this hemisphere less likely to create an impression of a conference about political matters which left Russia out in the cold than would a meeting in Europe or England.

Never before had the two war leaders and their staffs had such a vast panorama of military action before them as at Quebec. The two groups, during congenial but hard-working days and nights, set a strategic program which determined the main lines of effort for the rest of the war in Europe. And notably, and for the first time, primary attention was given to the war in the Pacific and the mainland of Asia. Campaign plans for that vast area were brought back into the field of joint consultation, out of which they had largely slipped.

The round-the-world vista which they regarded as they talked ought to be brought back to mind.

Eisenhower had by then taken personal command of the great Allied armies in France, over a half-million combat troops, for whom a way was being blasted by a dominant air force. These armies were engaged in three main efforts at the same time. They were trying to clear the northern Channel regions of France, Belgium, and Holland with their great ports. Brussels had been won on September 3rd, Antwerp on September 4th (but the approaches to the port were still barred), and Le Havre on September 12th. In the center they were driving forward toward the Saar region. Liège and Luxembourg had been captured, and the American and British divisions were headed for the German frontier on a long front, the first break having been made in the Siegfried Line. To the south the troops had reached the Moselle River and gone on to Nancy. Junction had been made between the Americans and the French forces which had hurried up from Southern France (the ANVIL divisions) forming a line south to the Swiss frontier. The German armies were in disorderly retreat. The summer campaign had turned into an exhilarating pursuit, which however was coming to a pause about this time.

Eisenhower's report to the Conference at Quebec visualized the development of the assault by encirclement of the Ruhr and Saar, and advances on a broad front aimed in the general direction of Berlin from both north and south.[1] He was asking freedom to take any or all routes toward and into Germany, as permitted by the supply situation. But some of his commanders were convinced that if the assault was con-

[1] In his strategic conception, as summed up in a note of September 15th to army group commanders, Berlin was named as the ultimate goal after the Ruhr, Saar, and Frankfurt areas had been seized ". . . by the most direct and expeditious route, with combined U.S.-British forces supported by other available forces moving through key centers and occupying strategic areas on the flanks, all in one coordinated, concerted operation." *The Supreme Command,* page 290.

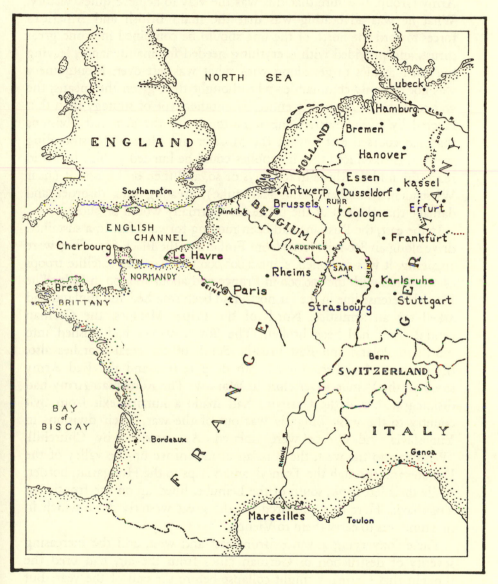

Northwest Europe

centrated along one route, the break into Germany and on to Berlin could be carried through that autumn. General Montgomery, in command of the great British and Canadian forces organized into the 21st Army Group, was sure that this was the way to achieve quick victory. What he was advocating was that the main British and American forces toward the north of the line should be combined into one great thrust, and provided with everything needed for maintenance, leaving the other armies to get along with what was left over. Montgomery was not the only commander who thought that, given the means, the war could be more quickly ended by another type of strategy than that favored by Eisenhower. General Patton, with the armored divisions that had coursed east toward the Moselle and Metz with astounding speed, was convinced that if supplies could be hurried to him he could reach the middle Rhine in ten days or so, and then on beyond it (near Wiesbaden, Mannheim, and Karlsruhe), creating such disorder and damage that the rest of the battle for Germany would be short.

In the east, the Russians had been moving forward fast in a sustained drive along an 800-mile front from Finland to the Black Sea. They were engaging, it was reckoned, some 2,000,000 German and satellite troops as compared with the 700,000 in France and about 300,000 in Italy. The Finnish defense line in the far north had been smashed and Finland had asked for an armistice. North of the Pripet Marshes, the German central front had been broken. The Soviet armies had pushed into Northern Poland and East Prussia. South of the great marshes also, the Germans had been forced into deep retreat and the Red Army stood on the Vistula River close to Warsaw. The Romanian Army had disintegrated, and the Germans had made a hurried exit from that country to the west. Bulgaria was out of the war. Their divisions in Yugoslavia and Greece were isolated. As described by Churchill, "Wheeling to the west, the Russian armies drove up the valley of the Danube and through the Transylvanian Alps to the Hungarian border, while their left flank, south of the Danube, lined up on the frontier of Yugoslavia. Here they prepared for the great westerly drive which in due time was to carry them to Vienna." [2]

These converging advances from east and west, and the increasing severity of destruction of German cities from the air, had bred the thought that Germany might collapse before the end of the year. But neither Roosevelt nor Churchill were convinced by predictions to that effect which appeared more and more assuredly in the British and in some American military intelligence reports. [3]

[2] *Triumph and Tragedy,* page 83.
[3] For example, the British Joint Intelligence Committee had concluded as early as mid-

In the Pacific also, bright chances were beckoning to eager spirits. American naval task forces were breaking into the Japanese chain of outer island defenses in the Central Pacific. Vital supply lines between Japan and the south were being cut, ending the inflow of oil and preventing support for the Japanese forces scattered among the island bases. The Japanese fleet was being so weakened that all chance that it might regain control of these Pacific areas was past. By early August, Saipan and Guam and Tinian had been captured. The American Air Force thus secured fields from which its long-range heavy bombing planes could strike in great strength at the home islands of Japan. The northward movement of the forces under General MacArthur, by large skips, had gone faster than even blithe hopes. While the Quebec Conference was on, Morotai Island, well on the way to the Philippines, was taken and the route to the Philippines lay open.

These two lines of assault were converging toward the Philippines, Formosa, and the China Coast. The President, after talking with MacArthur and Nimitz at Honolulu (July 27th–28th), had decided in favor of MacArthur's program: that the next main move to be made should be to retake the Philippines. Then while the Conference was going on at Quebec, the American Joint Chiefs of Staff approved a daring action, to bypass the southern Philippine Islands and strike directly at the central portion of the Philippines—the Island of Leyte.

Within China, in contrast, the military situation was blacker than ever since the start of the war. Japanese armies had struck south and toward the coast. They were severing all connection between the provinces controlled by the Chungking government and the seaboard. They had captured some of the bases which the American Combat Air Force in China was using, and the fall of our large base at Kweilin was imminent. There was a chance that the Japanese might be able to take Kunming, the chief American air center in the south and the China terminus of the air supply route over the Hump, or move west and reach Chungking itself, and drive the Chinese government into even more remote refuge.

These events were causing a grave crisis in Chinese-American military relations. Roosevelt and the Joint Chiefs were urging Chiang Kaishek to confer full powers of command over the Chinese forces upon his American Chief of Staff, General Stilwell. The Generalissimo was

---

July that although it was impossible to predict when the German collapse would come ". . . it is . . . equally difficult to see how Germany can, if Allied attacks on the three major fronts are ceaselessly pressed home, prolong the struggle beyond December." And on September 5th the Committee was "prepared to hazard that the end would come quite soon, although no precise date could be given." *Grand Strategy*, Volume v, page 398.

holding back until he could be sure about the limits of the authority which Stilwell was to exercise, and as to how he would use it. In the midst of the conference at Quebec, a positive message was received from Stilwell, which forecast the imminent loss of the Kweilin air base and warned that the Japanese might win in Burma unless Chiang Kai-shek retained and enlarged the dwindling Chinese force that was engaged in combat in that country, which he was refusing to do. Coming at the time when the Combined Chiefs of Staff had just agreed on a grand plan of operations against Japan, for which the greatest possible Chinese military contribution was wanted, this report was most upsetting. Mingled with dissatisfaction over the Chinese military performance was an unhappy difference over the policy to be pursued toward the Chinese Communists. Stilwell, supported by the War Department, was urging the Generalissimo to throw some of the divisions being used to maintain a blockade of the Communist area in China into the fight against the Japanese. The State Department and General Hurley (the President's special representative in China who had just arrived there at the time of Quebec) were also urging Chiang Kai-shek to enter into some plan of military cooperation or unification with the Chinese Communists—as one element in a program for the formation of a unified constitutional government.

The President, on the advice of the Joint Chiefs, sent off from Quebec (September 16th) a stern summons to Chiang Kai-shek to recognize that the whole situation in China was threatened with disaster unless he placed Stilwell in effective command. In sum, the whole prospect of what could be expected and planned for the Chinese theater of war was not only uncertain but tinged with criticism and a sense of failure.

It may be interjected here that Chiang Kai-shek, shocked at this message, made up his mind that no matter what the consequences he would not place Stilwell in charge of China's armed forces. The effort which Hurley was making to work out the terms of the assignment broke down. The Generalissimo proceeded (on September 25th) bluntly to ask that Stilwell be replaced. By this decision he lost his best chance of becoming a ward of the American government. Had he done what was asked of him, the United States would have become responsible for the fate of the Chinese government. Chiang Kai-shek's claim upon our help would have been stronger, and probably our backing of his regime against the Communists would have been quicker and sturdier.

In Burma the battle was still a grim one. During the early part of the year a Japanese attempt to force a way into India had been stopped. The Allied effort to secure the land route across Burma into China had also failed. British, Indian, Chinese, and American forces were con-

tinuing their operations despite the summer deluges and the awful heat and dampness.

It now seems surprising that, despite the faltering course of the campaigns in China and Burma, the decision makers at Quebec did not anticipate that Japan could be quickly beaten down to final defeat. It is now hard to understand why they did not appreciate that the compounded forces (including the Soviet)—air, sea, and land—which would be directed against Japan could not long be resisted by even the most resolute people. But the planners at Quebec were far from sure of that and dared not count upon it; neither were Stalin and his military advisers, as the record tells.

In any case, the Combined Chiefs of Staff at Quebec took as the planning date for the end of the war against Japan an 18-month period after the defeat of Germany. This extended estimate had many consequences. One of them was to create the belief that there would be ample time to build up the Chinese armies, the armies of the Kuomintang government; and ample time to send Allied forces into China either over the Burma Road or by sea.

Such was the military situation and outlook over the main combat areas which were before the President, Churchill, and their military staffs when they met at Quebec.

Differences of judgment and desire turned out to be quickly adjustable. Victory is a soothing unguent.

The decision was made to press on with all priority on the Western Front, to destroy the German armed forces, and to occupy the heart of Germany. The plan approved provided that this was to be done by striking both north and south of the Ruhr. But it leaned toward the view that the main effort should be along the northern line of approach rather than toward the south.[4] No definite ruling was made about Montgomery's desire for a single, more powerful thrust across the Rhine. Eisenhower was left with much discretion as to how to distribute his forces along the whole line, and any and all sections of it.[4a]

[4] The report adopted read:

"We have approved General Eisenhower's proposals and draw his attention

(a) to the advantages of the northern line of approach into Germany, as opposed to the southern, and

(b) to the necessity for the opening up of the northwest ports, particularly Antwerp and Rotterdam, before bad weather sets in." *Triumph and Tragedy,* page 157.

[4a] The subsequent directive issued by Eisenhower (on October 28 after a meeting at Brussels with Tedder, Montgomery and Bradley) certainly seems to have visualized that the primary line of attack would be in the North. The pertinent sections read

". . . 6. The general plan subject always to prior capture of the approaches to Antwerp is as follows:

(a) Making the main effort in the north, decisively to defeat the enemy west of the

No major units were to be withdrawn from Italy until results of the offensive underway then, including the invasion of the Po Valley, were determined. General Wilson was also authorized to retain the landing craft then in that area for possible use in the Istrian Peninsula. This gave marked satisfaction to Churchill.

For wanting to have this operation—leading to Vienna or Hungary or both—undertaken, the Prime Minister had more and more telling reasons than before. As well summed up in the official British account of his thought: "The march on Vienna, as the Prime Minister saw it . . . met every demand at this stage of the war. It would provide the Western Allies with a coherent strategy for the winter; it might lessen, or counter, the danger of excessive Russian ambitions; and it would form an appropriate contribution, within the limits of the British effort to the common victory." [5]

Churchill and his military advisers thought the venture might still prove possible before the end of 1944 if the Germans in Italy were routed. So he was able cheerfully to inform the War Cabinet (on September 13th), "The idea of our going to Vienna, if the war lasts long enough and if other people do not get there first, is fully accepted here." [6] Wilson was instructed to submit by October 10 a plan for capturing the Istrian Peninsula with the assault shipping already in the Mediterranean, about which a decision was to be made by the 15th. In the meanwhile, only minor units were available for possible landings in Greece and for commando activities in the Adriatic.

A far-flung program for the defeat of Japan was adopted. The prolonged delay in the realization of Stalin's promises to start preparatory Soviet-American staff talks had left its mark. The plans were not contingent on the active participation of the Soviet Union in the Pacific war, but were adjustable to that event.

The Joint Chiefs of Staff had in July already accepted as a basis for planning the concept of an invasion of the industrial heart of Japan. As had been propounded by the Joint Chiefs to the Combined Chiefs on July 11th:

"Our successes to date, our present superiority in air and sea forces, and the prospective availability of forces following the defeat of Ger-

---

Rhine and secure bridgeheads over the River; then to seize the Ruhr and subsequently advance deep into Germany.

(b) To conduct operations so as to destroy the enemy in the Saar, to secure crossings over the Rhine, and to be prepared to advance from the Saar in accordance with the situation then prevailing. All of these operations to be timed so as best to support the main effort to which they are subsidiary." *Grand Strategy*, Vol. vi, page 32.

[5] *Grand Strategy*, Volume v, page 394.
[6] *Triumph and Tragedy*, page 155.

many, lead us to believe that our concept of operations . . . should envisage an invasion into the industrial heart of Japan. While it may be possible to defeat Japan by sustained aerial bombardment and the destruction of her sea and air forces, this would probably involve an unacceptable delay." [7]

At Quebec this view was endorsed by the Combined Chiefs and approved by the President and Prime Minister.

As immediate steps in the execution of this program, the Philippines were to be captured; landings were to be made on Formosa, and possibly along the coast of China. The British fleet, and maybe part of the Royal Air Force, were to take part, under United States Supreme Command, in the final great assaults upon Japan.

The battle in Burma was to be carried on until the whole country was won and the Burma Road opened. The British Commonwealth forces, ground and air, that were already engaged in or designated for that theater would carry on their fight. The United States, which was already providing large numbers of service troops in India and Burma and along the supply lines, and devoting large air resources for the air transport route from India, was to increase that contribution, but it was not to supply any ground combat forces except some special brigades of airborne troops. The Chinese government was to be warned not to call back any of the soldiers it had in Burma, as Chiang Kai-shek was bent on doing.

But except for these strenuous measures to reopen and expand ways in and out of China, that theater of war was left for a while longer toward the end of the list of priorities. Greater help was to wait upon the success of these measures and the end of the war in Europe.

Lastly—and this was a staple item in all the major decisions of the Combined Chiefs of Staff—it was resolved to carry through the schedule of supply operations for the Soviet Union and its armed forces. In prospect, it was reckoned that the Soviet needs for the war in Europe would soon wane. But it was expected that deliveries for reconstruction would expand, and that the flow of supplies for Soviet forces in the Far East would have to be greatly augmented.

Neither the President nor the Prime Minister nor the Combined Chiefs consulted the Soviet authorities while reaching these decisions. But as soon as they were made, a joint message was hurried off to Stalin telling him about them. This was a continuation of the effort to arrange more thorough coordination of military action with the Soviet Union in both Europe and the Far East. The American government was

[7] Ray S. Cline, *Washington Command Post: The Operations Division*, pages 338–39.

moved, in addition, by a wish to get Soviet cooperation for the effective conduct of the war in China and for the achievement of a stable, unified government in China. Of the important discussions on these several matters that were connected with the Quebec decisions, more is worth telling.

∞∞∞∞∞∞∞

42. Questions around the Quebec Conference

∞∞∞∞∞∞∞

Despite the agreement reached at Teheran for the coordination of the offensives against Germany, cooperation between the American, British, and Soviet staffs had not developed significantly. The location and movement of German military forces had become regular. The Americans and British were giving the Russians their own operational reports and the Russians were responding at intervals—on request and along more general lines. But little actual consultation had taken place about advance plans, and liaison for that purpose continued to be as tiresome as before. Stalin had rejected suggestions that the Commander-in-Chief in the west might maintain direct touch with Soviet field commanders. All communications still had to be passed through the American and British Embassies or Military Missions in Moscow and be formally presented by them to the Foreign Office. If important, they were submitted to Molotov or Stalin. When they smiled and gave plain orders, a special course of consultation for a particular purpose sometimes, but not always, got underway. When, as more usual, they asked for more time to consider, nothing happened.

All proposals regarding cooperative planning and preparation for action in the Pacific had suffered delay. Few of the Americans or British concerned seriously doubted that the Soviet Union would at some time or other, and in some way or other, enter the war against Japan. But fear of prematurely arousing Japanese retaliation at this stage did not seem a wholly adequate reason for the continued delay by the Soviet government. That was taken to mask the wish to keep full freedom to decide when it would enter the war, what part it would play, and possibly what reward it might get for doing so.

It will be recalled that Roosevelt had tried at Teheran, the past December, to get joint work in motion. He had given Stalin memos on several proposals for joint planning for naval and air operations in the Northwest Pacific. Time and again Ambassador Harriman had tried to

402

extract answers from Molotov. Each time he had promised to arrange the necessary talks with the Soviet military authorities, but only minor results had followed. Then on the 2nd of February Stalin had explained to Harriman that the Soviet Union could not at that time take part in operations against Japan because its forces in the Far East were still too small. Before doing so, the Soviet Air Force would have to be re-equipped, and four infantry corps would have to be transferred to the Far East. That could not be done, he had said, until German resistance in the west had weakened. So he had ruled out until the summer, at least, any consideration of immediate activities. But he had said that planning talks about basing American air forces in the Far East might be carried on. Six fields could be made available for three hundred American planes, and there would also be a Soviet bombing force. But, he had added, the question of whether these fields should be located on Kamchatka or near Vladivostok would have to be further examined. He would, he had promised, ask the Chief of the Red Air Force in the Far East to come to Moscow. Then the fields for the American planes could be selected, and if the number was not enough, new ones could be built. At the end Stalin again made the point that if Japan was provoked into action prematurely, the territory available for these air bases might be lost.

More time had elapsed without any more word about the matter. On March 3rd Harriman had asked Stalin when the head of the Soviet Air Force in the Far East was expected in Moscow, and had been told "soon." He also asked Molotov the same question almost every time he saw him, but Molotov had said he did not know. That was the status of consultation regarding joint planning for joint action against Japan when on March 30th the Soviet government concluded two new agreements with Japan—one about fishing rights covering a five-year period, and one by which Japan promised to liquidate its concessions in Northern Sakhalin Island. This act could have been thought to mean that the Soviet Union would make a deal with Japan rather than go to war against her. The President and his advisers had recognized that this Soviet-Japanese agreement was a signal that the chance existed. But they had not become anxious. They had accepted with a resigned sigh the continued delay in the start of joint planning.

The messages and memos of this period leave the impression that neither the President nor the Joint Chiefs appreciated how strong was the Soviet reluctance to have large American air establishments within that part of the Soviet Union. They also suggest that the Soviet government was not in as much of a hurry as was the American government to end the war against Japan. The ultimate schedule on which it timed the program of cooperation suggests that it was allowing decisions to wait until, having procured supplies from us, it could conduct the whole campaign from the north against Japan—ground, sea, and air—with its own forces. Continued postponement was allowing the situation to evolve in a way that would lead to the conclusion that American activities in this region were not needed.

The Americans had thought that once the invasion of France was underway, Soviet caution might give way. Harriman had again reviewed American proposals for cooperation in the Far East in his talk with Stalin on June 10th. He had explained that the President and Joint Chiefs of Staff were now compelled to think about what was to be done with our air force after the defeat of Hitler. So they would greatly like to know how soon Stalin would be ready to start secret talks on the use of bases in the Soviet Far East, and also about the coordination of naval plans. Stalin's answer had given a clue that the Soviet Union, when it entered the Pacific war, was not going to play a secondary role. Before discussing plans for American air and naval action, he had wanted to know more about the field of operation for the Soviet armies. The question was, he remarked, one of joint cooperation in waging war on land and sea as well as in the air.

Stalin had then spoken more affirmatively than before. He had said the American heavy bombing forces could get the use of six or seven air bases in the Vladivostok region. To stock supplies, especially fuel, he had advised full use of the sea route across the Pacific since the Japanese were not interfering with it. He had also brought up the proposal that the United States might provide several hundred four-engine bombing planes for the Red Air Force in the Far East—since the Russians had only two-engine bombers. Harriman had told him that General Arnold was ready to begin to deliver them in the autumn after agreement had been reached in regard to American operations from bases in the Soviet Far East.

Despite its greater immediacy, this talk had failed, like previous ones, to hurry Stalin into action. Harriman had not been able to pin Stalin down to a date for the initiation of detailed staff planning. All he could be brought to say was that, "No time should be lost and the sooner the discussions started the better it would be." And the procedure had continued to be rigid; and the start made had been small.

By the end of summer Ambassador Harriman and General Deane were irked by the way the Soviet authorities seemed to be ignoring our requests and proposals. They were convinced that we could check this trend only by changing our way of doing business with the Soviet government and by taking direct issue with it whenever our interests were involved. Conformably, Harriman had joined with General Deane in a recommendation that we suspend shipment to the Soviet Union of all industrial equipment not needed for current war effort and various related measures of the same sort. The better to explain the reasons for this advice, Harriman had asked to be allowed to return to Washington at once. Hopkins answered (on September 12th while the Conference at Quebec was starting and the talks at Dumbarton Oaks were reaching their final critical stage) that he wanted to hear what Harriman had to tell him, but he thought it would be a mistake for the Ambassador to leave Moscow just at that moment. So he asked Harriman to delay his departure until given a green light. Whether these messages from Harriman and Deane affected the strategy for the defeat of Japan which the Combined Chiefs of Staff and the President and Churchill approved at Quebec is hardly to be known.

But at any rate, Harriman reviewed with Stalin the many past proposals we had made for closer military cooperation when, on September 23rd, he gave Stalin the joint report from Roosevelt and Churchill about the results of their Conference at Quebec. Once again Harriman told Stalin that the President was most eager to begin talks about Pacific operations. The first questions Stalin put showed that he was still on guard against being thrust into the war before the time was safe and the chance suited him. He asked how discussions could best be held and what was to be discussed—was it a question merely of making plans or of fixing dates? Harriman answered that the purpose was to plan; the date for putting the plans into effect was dependent upon the ending of the war with Germany.

Stalin then asked if the President and Prime Minister still thought Russia's entry into the Pacific war essential. Was there, he asked, any change in thinking on this point? Harriman and Clark-Kerr assured him that there was no change. Stalin then said in effect that if this was so, he found it peculiar that the joint message did not refer to Russian participation, and that it was not taken into account in the planning. Harriman explained that the Combined Chiefs could not do so since they did not know what part the Soviet Union would play; that they could not plan for the use of Soviet resources until Stalin was ready to start talks; and that the plans could be changed to coordinate them with the Soviet program. Stalin rejoined that the Russians for their part must know what plans its Allies had in mind, particularly what tasks were to be assigned to Soviet forces. Harriman said he might be sure that these matters would be clarified as soon as the Soviet officials were ready to talk about them. Stalin said he was ready now; that the discussions could start in a few days; that he would give the orders and fix the time.

Stalin prolonged his questioning. He asked whether he was correct in understanding that we wanted not only the use of air bases in the Far East but also the active participation of Soviet troops in the Pacific war. Turning his thoughts backward, he said that the President "had suggested" such participation; that the Russians had agreed to do so after Germany was defeated; that they were still ready to do so.[8] "However," he concluded, "if the United States and Great Britain desired to bring the Japanese to their knees without Russian participation, the Russians were ready to agree to this."

Harriman, in his report to the President after this talk of September 23rd, said he thought that Stalin was now ready and willing to cooperate, but did not want to do so without a fresh invitation. He believed it was clear that if we took the initiative and suggested what we would like the Russians to do rather than wait for the Russians to advance proposals, we would get greater cooperation. General Deane was asking the Joint Chiefs of Staff for full instructions. Harriman recommended that he be authorized to discuss our Pacific strategy with the Red Army staff and to propose the full measure of what was wanted of the Soviet forces.

The President (on September 28th) asked Harriman to tell Stalin that he had never doubted what had been settled at Teheran, and that he was glad that talks in this realm were about to start. On the same day the Joint Chiefs of Staff sent Deane a statement of the objectives to which they thought the Russians might best direct their effort. Harriman, referring to what Stalin had told him on the 23rd, at once let Molotov know that Deane now had the necessary authority to start talks, and instructions in regard to the questions which Stalin had raised. But days continued to pass without an answer.

Harriman was asked by the President to try again. On October 4th, on the occasion of presenting a replica of a bust of Roosevelt to Stalin, the Ambassador passed on the President's message, and reminded Stalin that General Deane was ready to get on with the talks at once. The Marshal said that he had ordered his commanding generals in the Far East to come to Moscow to bring him up to date on the situation in that region; and then conferences could be arranged between these officers and General Deane. They were begun a week later, when Churchill and his military advisers were also in Moscow. But before we tell of these conversations, it is necessary to bring other matters

[8] The first draft of the American memo stating in English this comment of Stalin's uses the word "demanded" but this was later changed to "suggested."

within the scope of the narrative. First of all, the concurrent talks about Chinese affairs that had been going on with Stalin and Molotov before and right after the Quebec Conference.

The American government had been trying to enlist Soviet cooperation in straightening out the situation in China. When Harriman was in Washington in June, the President had asked him to talk over with Stalin the current Soviet troubles with China and to outline the sort of pattern we wanted to see develop there. The President at that time had believed that Chiang Kai-shek was the only one who could hold China together, and therefore his government should not be undermined. He thought it would be disastrous if China broke up into parts and there was civil war, ending its effective resistance to Japan. He had been hopeful that the Soviet government would show patience in bringing about an adjustment of the quarrel between Chiang Kai-shek and the Chinese Communists in the north. The American government was then seeking consent from Chiang Kai-shek to send a group of military observers to Chinese Communist headquarters in Yenan, and the President was willing to promise that if they went we would share what we learned with the Soviet government.

In that same first long talk after his return, on June 10th, Harriman had explained these views to Stalin. He had reminded the Marshal that the President had said at Teheran that Chiang Kai-shek was the only man who could hold China together. Stalin had confirmed that he agreed with that. Harriman had then said that the American government felt that Chiang Kai-shek ought to be induced both to reach a settlement with the Communists in the north so that all could unite in the war against Japan, and to liberalize his internal policies. At this point Stalin had commented that "this is easier said than done." And, responding to Harriman's remark that he knew the President would be glad to have the Marshal's views, Stalin had gone on to say that he also thought Chiang Kai-shek was the best man under the circumstances—unfortunately no one better had arisen and so he must be supported. But, he had continued, Chiang Kai-shek's faults must be borne in mind; the Chinese had fought better five years ago than at present; many of the men around Chiang Kai-shek were crooks or traitors; and everything that went on was known to the Japanese at once. Chiang Kai-shek's refusal to use the Communists in the fight against the Japanese he thought stupid, for he had explained, "The Chinese Communists are not real Communists; they are 'margarine' communists." Still he had added ". . . they are real patriots and they want to fight the Japanese."

In the course of this talk Stalin had also said that he thought the United States should and could take leadership in China since neither the Soviet Union nor Great Britain could do so. But he had suggested that this leadership must be flexible; new men outside the Chiang Kai-shek entourage might come up, and if they did they ought to be supported and given authority. Stalin had then gone on to charge that Chiang Kai-shek and his group were spreading unfriendly and false propaganda about the Soviet Union. But despite that, he had concluded, the Soviet government would continue to base its policy toward China on its treaty of friendship and nonaggression of 1924. To current incidents on the frontier between Outer Mongolia and Sinkiang, Stalin did not seem to attach much importance. He admitted that the Soviet government had helped its Mongolian ally, but thought the situation was quieting down. To what he intended China to yield in Manchuria, he had made no allusion.

On the whole Harriman had gotten the impression, which he had reported to the President, that he thought Stalin wanted the situation in China so to develop that when the Soviet Union joined the war against Japan its forces could cooperate with the Chinese forces.

Later in June the Soviet government had been advised of the substance of the long talks between Vice President Wallace and Chiang Kai-shek and of the efforts being made by our diplomatic and military representatives in China to bring about some sort of accord between the Kuomintang government and the Chinese Communists. Such little comment as could be gathered seemed to confirm Soviet willingness to let us keep the lead in China and conform to it.

This impression had been refreshed when, at the end of August (the 31st), Hurley and Nelson stopped off at Moscow en route to Chungking and reviewed again with Molotov all aspects of Sino-Soviet relations. The Soviet Foreign Minister had rehearsed relations so as to give the sense that the Chinese government was not appreciative of the way in which the Soviet Union had refrained from taking a part in the Chinese internal fight; and that Chiang Kai-shek lacked gratitude for what the Soviet government had done to get him released after his capture by rebellious rivals in 1936. Then Molotov had made some statements which were to leave a lasting imprint on Hurley's mind, and which perhaps swayed thinking within the State Department. "The Soviet government," he had said, "could bear no responsibility for internal affairs or developments in China for which at times it had been unjustifiably held responsible." It ought not, he had continued, be blamed for or associated with conditions in China. In parts of that country the people were half starved and miserable; and thus they called themselves "Communists"; but they had no relation to Communism; they used the name as a way of expressing their discontent over their condition; but if these were improved they would forget that they were "Communists"; and so, if the United States helped these unfortunate people there would be fewer "Communists" in China. Further, if the Chinese government itself did a better job in that respect, did what needed doing, their people would be better off and there would be fewer dissatisfied elements in China. This statement of his view of the Chinese situation Molotov had completed by saying that the Soviet people would be very glad if the United States helped China and the Chinese people to improve their economic and political position, to seek unity, and to choose their best people to run their affairs.

These remarks on matters known to engage the sentiment of the American people as well as their idea of national interest were, no doubt, designed to please and allay mistrust of proposals the Soviet government was soon to make about its assignments in the Pacific War. But it is probable that these statements of policy toward China were at this time sincerely meant. Little or nothing is known to indicate that the Soviet government had up to then given aid to the Chinese Communists. Whether or not the Russian Communist Party may have been doing so through its own secret channels is harder to judge; but it also was probably being watchful rather than active.

Presently the story will pick up again the trail of these arrangements about Soviet entry into the Pacific War and Chinese affairs. But first, so that the whole area of coalition activity may be in mind, we must glance again at what was happening in Europe, and of the talks going on at Dumbarton Oaks in Washington, during this same autumn period after the Quebec Conference and before Churchill's visit to Moscow. As, in reality, each segment of these doings rubbed against the rest, so they must in the telling of them.

43. Southern and Eastern Europe Falling from the Nazi Grasp: Finland, Romania, Bulgaria

To visualize the whole scene during this late summer and autumn of 1944, our gaze must swing back to Europe—to events in the countries of Southern and Eastern Europe which were beginning to fall from the Nazi grasp. Each of these became a separate case and cause of discussion among the members of the coalition. But before telling of them one by one, we may make a brief sweep of comment about the forward flow of Soviet forces and influence throughout the whole area.

The ultimate intentions of the Soviet government remained obscure. It saw to it that the governments which came into power in the countries along its borders were well disposed to the Soviet Union and feared it. But it did not seem to be trying to impose on them in haste Communist economic or social systems. The Soviet rulers avowed that they did not wish or plan to interfere in the internal affairs of these countries, and at times ostentatiously refrained from doing so. They accepted "popular front" governments in which local Communists were associated, in minority part, with Socialist, peasant, and other political groups. But at the same time they encouraged Communist and other parties of the Left to take control and pursue energetic programs —demanding speedy arrest and trial of all persons associated with pro-Nazi regimes or known anti-Communist tendencies, and calling for extensive changes, notably land reform.

In the formulation of armistice terms for the Axis satellites the Soviet government demanded quick and heavy deliveries in kind to the Soviet Union as reparations. Because of the size and variety of these claims Soviet control over their national economy was almost certain to ensue, if only temporarily. Under the armistice terms control commissions were created of which the chairmanships were, on Soviet insistence, assigned to the Soviet members, who were usually military commanders; this put the Soviet government in a position to influence or dominate economic, social, and political affairs in these countries, even against British or American wishes. But it was still not clear whether the Soviet government would use these powers to impose its will. It might be content with securing support and supplies for its armies, and with contributions that these countries could bear to the repair of war damage; and, as long as these countries were acquiescent, allow them to exercise political freedom. Or, it might insist that they become subordinate to its rule and system.

The comment which the American Embassy in Moscow made in the interim report which it sent on October 20, 1944, based on the Soviet press for the preceding period was prophetic:

"Political ferment and economic upheaval in these countries appear unavoidable in these circumstances. In orthodox Marxist ideology they are recognized as the ideal conditions for a revolutionary movement; and the effective local Communist parties, which appear to be the only groups with a well-defined program and strong backing, may be expected when the moment is propitious to take advantage of the situation in an attempt to gain the controlling voice in government for themselves."

The American government did not believe, however, that this was inevitable. Then and therefore it did what it could to prevent this from happening by appeal to principle and diplomatic exertions. But it did not want to get too involved in any of these fractious situations, nor jeopardize Soviet cooperation in what were deemed greater and more enduring causes—winning the wars and creating a system to maintain peace after the wars. The British government was more anxious and contesting; but, as will be told, it tried to avert a protracted struggle against the Soviet Union by an agreement about spheres of responsibility.

The Finns finally gave up in September. The rutted road that led to a surrender may be hurriedly retraced. The Finnish government had been repulsed by the armistice terms laid down by the Soviet government in February. On March 3rd it told the State Department it would not yield to them, or be able to carry out some of the main terms even if it did. It could not, as asked, undertake to intern the German troops that were in Finland, for it would not be able to do this without Soviet help, and it did not want to admit the Russians into Finland. It was not willing to demobilize the Finnish Army, as asked, for that would be needed to maintain neutrality. And it would not accede to the frontiers Moscow was proposing.

In March the Soviet government had stated its terms more precisely. It would allow the Finns, after retreating behind the proposed new frontiers, to maintain an army on a peacetime basis. As reparations it wanted six hundred million dollars, to be paid in kind over five years. It would agree not to demand the return of Hangoe and the Hangoe region (which it had had under lease from Finland) if instead it got Petsamo and the Petsamo region. These terms also the Finns had refused. In sum, the Finnish government had argued that if Finland tried to meet these requirements it would not be able to stand as an independent nation. So all negotiations for the time being had come to an end.

The American government had then reluctantly concluded that the Finns would act only when forced to do so, and then fare worse. The President had thought that perhaps their fears of what would follow their surrender might be quieted if the three main Allies joined in a declaration of the same sort they had made about Iran—confirming that the Finnish people would be masters in their house. Harriman had asked Molotov what he thought of the idea. On June 7th Molotov had answered that the Soviet government did not think that this would be worthwhile since the question of resuming talks with Finland had ceased to be an actual one. Three days later, however, Stalin had again assured Harriman that he wanted an independent Finland. But he said the Finnish lines were still a mere twelve miles from Leningrad and must be pushed back to give security to that city. Only hard blows, he had added, would cause the Finns to change their government and their policy. "They are," Stalin said, "a serious, blunt people and sense must be hammered into them." On this same day the Soviet forces had started a heavy attack on the Karelian Peninsula.

Whether or not as a result of this new blow, about June 20th the Finns had sought to resume talks on conditions of surrender. Stalin had refused, unless the Finnish government formally stated that it was willing to give up. It would be no use, he had explained, because the government in power in Finland was under German domination. The next turn in Finnish diplomacy had seemed to confirm this judgment. Ribbentrop had visited Finland; the Finnish government had reaffirmed its solidarity with Germany; and more German troops had been sent into Finland. Thus fighting on that stiff front had continued while our forces moved over France and the Soviet forces moved into Poland. The United States had rather sadly on June 30th broken relations with Finland, the country that, for its upright qualities, had once been its favorite among the small European states.

But soon afterward it had become apparent that the Finnish position was beyond salvage. The Russian armies had advanced rapidly toward the Baltic Coast, cleaning the Germans out of the way. The German troops had begun to leave Finland to escape defeat or capture. On August 1st Foreign Minister Ryti, who had signed the pact with Ribbentrop, had resigned; and soon after, the pact was denounced. On the 25th the Finnish Minister in Stockholm had asked the Soviet government to receive a Finnish delegation in Moscow to arrange an armistice. Hostilities had been suspended on September 5th. An armistice was signed on September 19th by Soviet General Zhdanov.

The terms imposed upon the Finns were eased somewhat in the course of the final talks. As signed, they provided: (1) That the Finnish forces were to be withdrawn behind the Soviet-Finnish frontier line of March 12, 1940. (2) This was to be the boundary except that in the far north Finland ceded Petsamo to the Russians and granted them a naval base at Porkkala-Udd; the Russians in return, however, gave up the right they previously had to a lease on the Peninsula of Hangoe. (3)

Finland was to pay three hundred million dollars in six years, a reduction by half of what the Soviet government had originally asked, and Finland was allowed one year longer to make the payment. (4) The Soviet forces were not to occupy Finland. The administration of the country was to remain Finnish.

The Finnish peace envoys returned home from Moscow, relieved on the whole that the independence of their country had been preserved.

Romania had already submitted and signed an armistice.

The lines in the south between the Carpathian Mountains and the Black Sea, where Romanians had been fighting alongside the Germans, were weakly supported because some of the best German reserve divisions had been moved to the central front in Poland. The Russians had smashed through, captured Jassy, and at the same time landed on the Black Sea coast. On August 23rd, as it was becoming clear that nothing could stop the Red Army from reaching Bucharest soon, King Michael in combination with some army officers and political leaders had taken courage and dismissed the Antonescu government. A new one had been appointed—a coalition of moderately conservative, Socialist and Communist elements. The King had announced that hostilities would end at once, and the acceptance of ". . . an armistice offered by the Soviet Union, Great Britain, and the United States."

The conditions that had been offered and rejected in April were only some rudimentary principles. So on the very next day (the 24th) Harriman and Clark-Kerr had suggested to Vishinsky that an effort be made to complete the understanding between their three countries. The Americans and British had two points in particular in mind. One was the determination of the amount of reparations to be demanded from Romania. The other was the arrangement for watching over the fulfillment of the armistice terms. Among the wishes stated in the British invitation to discussion were (1) that an Allied Control Commission should be appointed; (2) that the British government should have separate political representation in Romania—to which it was recalled Molotov had agreed on April 11th past, in a letter to Clark-Kerr. Vishinsky had answered both that because of changed conditions the subject needed further study.

At this point the Soviet authorities had taken the lead away from the Americans and British in bringing about the Romanian surrender, and deciding and imposing the armistice terms. At 2:00 a.m. on the morning of August 25th, Molotov had asked Harriman and Clark-Kerr to call. He read them a statement which the Soviet government was planning to release that same morning. To both Harriman and Clark-

Kerr this seemed, as it was, in accord with past understandings. The statement, issued as the Ambassadors were returning to their Embassies, said:

"The Soviet High Command believes that if the Rumanian armies cease military action against the Red Army and if they join arm in arm with the Red Army in carrying the war of liberation against the Germans for the liberation of Rumania or against the Hungarians for the liberation of Transylvania, the Red Army will not disarm them, and will let them keep all their arms, and will fully aid them in fulfilling this honorable task."

Molotov that same day had publicly repeated the assurances which he had broadcast the previous April that, "The Soviet government decrees that it does not pursue the aim of acquiring any part of Rumanian territory other than Bessarabia or of altering the social structure of Rumania as it exists at present."

The next day Molotov had informed Harriman and Clark-Kerr of the terms which the Soviet government had in mind for the preliminary armistice. These were the same as the ones that had been jointly approved in April with some small moderating changes. He had said that the Soviet government wanted to have the armistice signed in Moscow, and therefore wished the Romanian representatives to come there. He cheerfully agreed that the American and British governments, through their Ambassadors, should take part in the talks with the Romanians. To all this the American and British governments had assented.

The short preliminary armistice had been accepted on August 27th.[9] The Soviet government had announced the suspension of hostilities. But the Red troops had kept advancing west and south in pursuit of the German forces. As they did so they disarmed the Romanian troops and took away their equipment and supplies; and the Romanian Army began to disintegrate. Within a few days Bucharest was evacuated by the Germans, and the Russians entered. By September 1st the Red Army had reached the Danube and was spreading along the frontier of Bulgaria.

The new Romanian government had been eager to have the formal armistice concluded quickly so that orders would be sent to the Soviet troops to cease their harassment of the Romanian forces and to carry out the promise made in Molotov's broadcast of August 25th. But it was

[9] *Tass* on August 27th, 1944, published the April 12th conditions with this statement: "These conditions were rejected by the former Rumanian government of Marshal Antonescu.

"The Rumanian King Michael and the new Rumanian government of General Sanatescu have expressed their agreement to acceptance of the conditions."

kept waiting for about two weeks while Molotov, Harriman, and Clark-Kerr argued.

The Soviet government had been determined to have the deciding voice about terms and pretty much of a free hand in the subsequent treatment of Romania. It justified this claim on various grounds; that Romania was a neighbor; that the Soviet Union had suffered most from Romanian alliance with Germany; that Romanian troops had caused destruction in Russia as far as Petrograd; and that the Red Army had brought the country down to defeat.

The American government had been displeased and alarmed over the way in which the Soviet forces were imposing themselves on Romania, and at the Soviet refusal to assign it and the British effective parts in the arrangements for control. But it was not willing to contest the situation so stubbornly as to cause major damage to our general relations with the Soviet government. Besides, the Joint Chiefs of Staff were urging that our first aim should be to bring about the formal armistice quickly, so that some of the Romanian army might be preserved as an effective fighting force against the Germans. Thus, while Harriman had been instructed to do what he could to modify those features of the Soviet proposals which we did not like, he was told to use discretion as regards to how long and hard he opposed.

The British government was more stubborn in its effort to curb Soviet domination. It stood out against Soviet demands for reparations so heavy as to cause the Romanian economy to collapse and Romania to become subservient to the Soviet Union. It tried to make sure that it would have a real part in the control of Romania during the armistice period, and a chance to maintain direct relations with the Romanian authorities.

While these matters were being argued, the Soviet forces had continued to move fast and far over the country—though by then Romania had declared war on Germany. Finally, on September 12th, the armistice was signed. The Romanians tried to get solid assurance that all Soviet troops would leave Romania when the war against Germany ended. But they were told this was unnecessary since, as Molotov expressed it, "What the Romanians wanted was implicit in the whole Convention." But they did manage to get recorded in the minutes of the negotiation that "it would be unnecessary to add to the proposed articles, because it was a matter of course that the Soviet armies would leave Romanian soil at the end of hostilities."

Harriman, in his report of September 14th two days after the formal armistice was signed, predicted that it would mean that the Soviet

High Command would get unlimited control over the economic life of the country and police power throughout the land—at least during the armistice period. And he forecast that the Russians would deal with the various political groups in Romania according to the degree each bent to Soviet wishes, as was being done in Poland and Bulgaria. The State Department authorized new protests and arguments, which washed against the Kremlin walls like the autumn rains.

Nor did the American and British governments obtain satisfaction of their wish for adequate participation in control arrangements. To condense summarily, the provision to which at the end Clark-Kerr and Harriman, under instructions, gave reluctant assent read, "An Allied Control Commission will be established which will undertake until the conclusion of peace the regulation of and control over the execution of the present terms under the general direction and orders of the Allied (Soviet) High Command acting on behalf of the Allied powers."

Molotov made it plain that: first, the Soviet High Command alone would have authority to issue orders to the Romanian government; second, that the Soviet member on the Control Commission would exercise executive power for the Commission; and third, that the function of the British and American members was to be what the Soviet government regarded as analogous to that of the Soviet representatives attached to the Control Commission in Italy.

On September 20th Vishinsky sent Harriman and Clark-Kerr a statement of Soviet plans for the organization of the Allied Control Commission. This provided that the British and American part in the work of the Commission was to be indeed subordinate. Each was to be allowed only five officials on the staff; they were to be permitted to deal with Romanian officials only through the top officers of the Commission, all of whom were to be Russian; and they were to have to ask permission of the chairman of the Commission before making trips into the country. Vishinsky also claimed that this corresponded with the position of the Soviet members of the staff of the Allied Control Commission in Italy.

Clark-Kerr protested. On September 23rd he informed Vishinsky that the British government proposed to appoint a separate British diplomatic representative in Romania with a suitable staff—quite apart from the British section of the Control Commission and quite independent of the Soviet authorities. In answer, the Soviet government remarked, "In this case also the Soviet government considers the analogy with Italy to be correct, where the Soviet government have their own political representative. . . ." It answered American protests which were to the same effect as the British in the same way, and it similarly acceded to the American wish to have a political representative in Romania—a foreign service officer with the rank of Minister.

As later pages will tell, the Soviet government wielded decisive power and authority in all Romanian matters. Neither the American and British members of the Control Commission nor their diplomatic representatives could influence it.

One brief postscript on one point in these armistice terms for Romania. The Soviet government had long before made it clear that it was going to require the return of the Province of Bessarabia and Northern Bucovina to the Soviet Union. This was carried out in the armistice agreement.

The Soviet government had also promised the Romanians that if they joined the war against Germany and Hungary, Romania should get back from Hungary all or part of Transylvania. This promise was carried out in the article of the accord which read: "The Allied governments . . . are agreed that Transylvania (or the greater part thereof) should be returned [from Hungary] to Rumania, subject to confirmation at the peace settlement. . . ."

These were irreversible steps, made while the war was on, toward the settlement of European frontiers.

Bulgaria, too, was quitting the war during this early autumn and being taken into the Soviet orbit. Despite the fact that as an ally of Germany it had served the Axis cause, the Soviet Union had not gone to war with it. Thus, although Soviet armies ringed Bulgarian northern frontiers, the task of preparing armistice terms had at first fallen to the British and American governments. They were virtually agreed by the end of August. The Soviet government had been asked for its views upon the terms formulated. On August 22nd Molotov had said he thought they were satisfactory. If and when, he had said also, they were discussed with the Bulgarians, a Soviet official might take part as an "observer."

Then the Bulgarian Cabinet had fallen. The succeeding one, headed by Muraviev (a right-wing leader of the Agrarian Party), on the night of September 4th–5th, issued a statement of policy which pledged the country to a strict unconditional neutrality. It denounced the pact with Germany and said that the German troops in Bulgaria be disarmed and that if they resisted, Bulgaria would break relations with Germany. Further, it announced that it would carry on negotiations with the United States and Great Britain for an armistice and that it would pursue a policy of ". . . the most sincere relations founded on trust with fraternal Russia." *Tass* at once published the opinion that this action did not go far enough, and that Bulgaria must join the Allies or suffer the consequences. It should, this official statement said, follow Finland and Romania and separate itself completely from Germany.

Then suddenly, late in the next afternoon, Molotov asked Harriman and Clark-Kerr to call. He gave them copies of a statement which the Soviet government was about to issue. This was a declaration of war against Bulgaria. Molotov evaded questions as to whether Soviet troops would enter Bulgaria. Asked also whether he expected to start armistice negotiations with Bulgaria, and how and when, he said that depended on what the Bulgarians did. The assumption arose that the Soviet government wanted to influence the shaky course of political events within Bulgaria; by the threat of invasion to bring about another change of government, placing in power groups that the Soviet government preferred to the ones on whom it was declaring war.

Almost at once the Bulgarian government asked the Soviet government for an armistice. It was worried about breaking relations with Germany. But on the 8th it did so. The Soviet troops had begun to pour into Bulgaria. During the day and night of September 8th–9th, the Muraviev government was overthrown. The power was taken over by an association of political parties and groups, calling themselves the Fatherland Front, in which the Bulgarian Communists were prominent though not dominant.

After these events the Soviet government asked that the armistice negotiations be held, not at Cairo, as had been planned before the Soviet Union had declared war on Bulgaria, but at Moscow or Ankara. To this the American and British governments agreed. The original idea had been that the armistice should be signed by General Wilson, Commander-in-Chief in the Mediterranean, on behalf of all the United Nations—in the same way as General Eisenhower had signed the Italian armistice and General Malinowski had signed the Romanian armistice.[10] But the Soviet government now asked that instead this important formality be assigned to a Soviet general. The British resisted the suggestion.

They also stood out against the Russians on several leading issues. They insisted that the Bulgarian government be obligated to take all its troops out of Greece and Yugoslavia before the armistice was signed, or very soon thereafter. The Soviet government wanted them to be allowed to stay in certain parts of these countries, an attitude which seemed to indicate assurance that Soviet orders would from then on

---

[10] See Wilson, *Eight Years Overseas,* pages 234–35. He blames the American and British Ministers at Cairo for dragging out the discussions, thus giving the Russians chance and reason to enter the negotiations.

control Bulgarian forces. The Soviet government wanted to grant Bulgaria the status of a co-belligerent. The British government was not willing to do so. The Soviet government wanted the Allied Control Commission in Bulgaria—the agency that was to supervise the execution of the armistice—to be under the direct authority of the Soviet High Command, as was the similar body in Romania. Neither the Americans nor the British were satisfied with that.

To anticipate, just before Churchill began his talks with Stalin in October, it was agreed that the Bulgarian government must undertake, as a condition for an armistice, to withdraw all its troops from Greece and Yugoslavia within fifteen days. It did so. Then, as one feature in the division of spheres of responsibility made by Churchill and Stalin, the Soviet Union was accorded dominant influence in Bulgarian affairs. Armistice negotiations were soon thereafter completed in Moscow. The terms were much the same as those for Romania. No reparation payments were required, however—the leniency being justified by the fact that the Bulgarians had inflicted no damage in Russian territory. And in the agreement with Bulgaria somewhat more explicit reference was made to the participation of British and American representatives in the work of the Control Commission, and it was provided that the primacy of the Soviet High Command over the Commission should last only until the end of the war against Germany.

44. Southern and Eastern Europe Falling from the Nazi Grasp: Hungary, Yugoslavia, Greece, Italy

The resistance of the other German satellite, Hungary, was also crumbling. The country had been under German occupation since March 1944, the real ruler being a member of the German SS, Veesenmayer, the German Minister in Budapest. The Hungarian troops had been brought back from the Eastern Front as far as the Germans would allow, in order to defend the Carpathian line. By the middle of August the Red Armies had neared Hungarian frontiers. The surrender of Romania, and the announcement of Russian support of Romanian claims against Hungary, had brought about a Cabinet crisis and on August 30th a new government had assumed office. It was Regent Horthy's final attempt to restore Hungarian autonomy.

At the end of August the head of the Hungarian diplomatic mission in Lisbon had tried to get in touch with the British Ambassador there. The purpose was, he said, to find out what conditions would be exacted by the "Anglo-Saxon powers" if Hungary broke with Germany. He claimed that he was authorized to pass the information on to Budapest. The British government had instructed its Ambassador in Lisbon to have an answer conveyed indirectly to the effect that the Hungarian government must surrender to all three of the major Allies and "must work their passage home." There was still no accord between the Allies about the terms that might be presented. The British and American members of the EAC had for some time past tried to get their Soviet colleague to join in preparation of terms but he had not responded. Nor did he after the Soviet government had been informed of this preliminary sounding.

By the middle of September, the Hungarian attempts to find a way out of the war became more definite. On the 16th Harriman, as instructed, sent a letter to Molotov saying that the American government had received what purported to be a message from the Hungarian government that it had decided to ask for an armistice on certain conditions—which, since they were never considered, need not be detailed here. Harriman informed Molotov that the State Department had not yet answered, but he recalled that American foreign representatives were under orders to deal with any such approaches by saying that if Hungary wanted an armistice it should address its request for terms to all three of the principal Allies and appoint an authorized representative to receive and sign their terms. Four days later Vishinsky answered that the Soviet government agreed with this way of replying to any and all Hungarian offers.

On the night of September 22nd–23rd, before the American government had sent its answer to Regent Horthy, there arrived at Caserta in Italy a Hungarian airplane carrying General Nadoy, a former officer of the Hungarian First Army, who was reputed to be a close associate of Horthy. On that night the Soviet troops had crossed the Hungarian frontier, the first step on their way from the foothills of Transylvania toward the broad plains. Nadoy told General Wilson that he was authorized by Regent Horthy and the Hungarian government to ask for an armistice. He said that they were ready to do what they could to shorten the war, but he pointed out that it was going to be difficult for Hungary to get out of the war without disaster because the Germans were in occupation. He also said that the Hungarian authorities were expecting a Soviet attack and realized that it could not be stopped; that Soviet occupation of Hungary was inevitable; and that their objective was to seek to moderate its hardships. General Nadoy asked whether the Allies could give the Hungarian government and armies help in their effort to take action against the Germans.

The British government thought that General Nadoy would be a suitable channel for transmission of armistice terms. Thus it proposed to the American and Soviet governments that as soon as the accord on these terms could be completed, they be given to him. Would not the Soviet government please tell its representative on the EAC to get together with the British and American members at once? As for giving the Hungarians help to get rid of the Germans, that was a matter for the Soviet government to determine. The Soviet government took no notice of this plea to cooperate. It was biding its time and waiting for the Hungarians to address themselves to it.

On October 6th the Red Army, aided by some Romanian units, began a heavy attack, seeking to reach Budapest from the southeast, while at the same time also striking down from the Carpathian region in the North. Horthy had already sent special envoys to Moscow, who had carried a personal message to Stalin. In telling Harriman and Clark-Kerr of this, Molotov also informed them that these envoys had suggested certain conditions for their surrender which the Soviet government had refused; and that it, in turn, had presented to the Hungarians certain preliminary conditions. These Molotov now asked the American and British governments to consider urgently with Soviet officials in Moscow. The terms turned out to be very nearly the same as those which the British government had proposed in the EAC. Among them were: that Hungarian troops should be evacuated from Yugoslavia, Czechoslovakia, and Romania in short order; that this withdrawal should be controlled by a joint Allied Military Mission under the chairmanship of the Soviet representative; that Hungary was to declare war on Germany; that the Soviet Army would help Hungary in this action.

On October 8th both the American and British governments approved these terms. Molotov at once presented them to the Hungarian envoys in the name of the three main allies, just before Churchill arrived in Moscow. But, as will be told later, the time for their use had not yet come.

In Yugoslavia the prospect after liberation was still riven by internal divisions. Churchill had brought about on June 1st a remodeling of the Yugoslav government-in-exile. The new Prime Minister, Ivan Subasic, shoved by the British, had concluded an agreement with Tito a fortnight later. Thereunder Subasic recognized Tito's (the National Committee's) "temporary" administration of the country, and had promised to reshape the Yugoslav government-in-exile further so that it would be composed only of progressive democratic elements. In return Tito had agreed not to force decision as regards the future of the monarchy during the war.

Churchill's mind was thrashing about restlessly—upset by the course of the campaign in Italy, the way in which control over Yugoslavia was passing away from elements whose friendship to the West was dependable, and especially by the civil war in Greece. He had determined to try to correct these situations by going to Italy to talk with the men who could influence the turn of events.

In August Tito had come down to American headquarters at Caserta. Churchill was nearby to observe the landing in Southern France. In a talk on the 12th, the Prime Minister had reviewed the combat situation on both the Eastern and Western Fronts. He remarked that the Allies must reckon with the chance that the German divisions in the Balkans would have to be driven out by force. He asked Tito where, if the Western Allies could send forces across the Adriatic to reach the Istrian Peninsula, the Yugoslav guerrillas might cooperate; and he explained how much it would help if Tito's partisans could open a small port on the Yugoslav Adriatic Coast to receive supplies by sea. Tito said that although the German opposition within Yugoslavia had recently become stronger and Yugoslav losses were very heavy, he could raise substantial forces in Croatia and Slovenia and ". . . he would certainly favour an operation against the Istrian peninsula, in which Yugoslav forces would join." [11] In September, as the narrative will tell, Tito abruptly reversed himself, going so far as to tell Stalin that if the British forced a landing in Yugoslavia he would offer "determined resistance." [12]

Tito had described the situation within Yugoslavia, saying that the groups under Mihailovich were being helped by the Germans and Bulgarians and that his partisans were still fighting them, and so he saw little chance of reconciliation. Churchill had emphasized that the British government wanted a strong, united, and independent Yugoslavia. He dwelt on the obligation of the British government to King Peter. Tito had said that he was not able to do anything about the King until after the war, when the people would decide for themselves. He had assured Churchill that, as he had stated publicly, he had no wish to introduce the Communist system in Yugoslavia and went on to tell

[11] Churchill, *Triumph and Tragedy*, page 89. And Clissold, *Whirlwind, an Account of Marshal Tito's Rise to Power*, page 195.
[12] *Tito*, by Vladimir Dedijer, page 234.

Churchill that the Russian mission at his headquarters had spoken against such action.

Subasic, at Churchill's invitation, had joined them at Naples. He and Tito had conferred. They agreed on a number of "practical questions" such as uniting all Yugoslav naval forces under a common flag. They also arranged to issue simultaneous statements soon. Then Tito and Subasic both had left Naples to return to Vis to continue their discussions.

But despite these efforts and the fact that the British were more and more actively trying to sustain Tito's forces against stronger German measures to destroy them, relations with the British took a turn for the worse. General Wilson, who was most earnestly trying to convince Tito of Allied goodwill by deeds, met with increasing hindrance and suspicion. The demands upon the British grew and Tito's accusations of breaches of faith became more frequent and trivial. As Wilson has recounted,

"With the approach of Russian forces to eastern Jugoslavia and the early possibility of the liberation of Belgrade, it appeared that Tito might want to move his Headquarters from Vis to nearer the capital; I therefore asked him to keep me informed of his immediate plans and suggested that should he be considering moving I would appreciate his having the MacLean Mission accompany him so as to ensure that the coordination of operations was not interrupted. Tito assured me of his cooperation and agreed to keep me informed of his intended movements. However, on the night of 21st September he boarded an aircraft and flew away from Vis to an unknown destination, leaving his Chief of Staff as his representative." [13]

Tito had gone to Moscow without telling his British rescuers and supporters. The chief reason he gave later for this visit was the need to coordinate the operations of his forces with those of the Red Army who were beginning to come into Yugoslavia south of the Danube. The first junction between small units had been made as early as September 6th, and to mark it Tito had issued an "Order of the Day." He had determined that it should be his soldiers, not the Russians, who would liberate Belgrade. But for this he needed Russian help, and Stalin promised him a full tank corps. He wanted to be sure of how far the Russians were coming into his country and when they would leave. On these points also Stalin gave him full satisfaction, as recorded in the joint communiqué that was published on September 28th, 1944. Otherwise, this meeting between Tito and Stalin was argumentative. Stalin

[13] *Eight Years Overseas,* pages 233-34.

found Tito too independent in the statement of his opinions, too much his own man acting as an unafraid equal. Tito, in turn, was displeased by the advice which Stalin pressed upon him: cautiously to work with middle-class Serbian politicians, and to allow King Peter to return—that is, to return temporarily until a knife could be slipped in his back.[14]

During the rest of the autumn, the fight to drive the Germans out of Yugoslavia began to go excitingly well. Bulgarian troops, after the capitulation of that country, joined in the fighting. Tito's guerrilla units and the British commando groups accelerated and extended their activities. All the larger islands of the Adriatic were captured. Dalmatian ports were cleared of mines. In short, all the enemies of the Axis were fighting well together to rid Yugoslavia of the Germans. But they were uneasily at odds about its future.

The internal conflict in Greece was even more acute. The agreement that had been signed the past May for an "all party" government (the so-called Lebanon Agreement) had begun to go to pieces in July. EAM—the political group spurred on by the Communists—had repudiated it. The imminence of civil war, while the day was approaching when the Germans might evacuate Greece, had kept Churchill and his colleagues greatly disturbed. He had advised his Chiefs of Staff that it might be necessary to deal with a political crisis which he thought of major interest to British policy.

After his arrival in Italy, Churchill had pressed forward with his protective arrangements for Greece. Papandreou, the Greek Prime Minister, had come to see him on August 21st, and was advised to continue in office and defy the opponents who were assailing him from several sides. Churchill had also determined to prevent a possible attempt by Greek guerrilla bands clustered around the Communists to grab power as the Germans yielded it. General Wilson had begun to plan a landing of British forces when and as it might be found necessary; this operation was regarded by Churchill as a measure to give greater force to diplomacy and policy rather than as an actual military campaign, and was to be confined to Athens and its approaches, with possibly a detachment at Salonika. His idea was that units should be parachuted in and that as soon as they had secured the ground the Greek government was to fly in and begin to function.

On August 17th Churchill had explained his ideas and plan to Roosevelt and had asked him if he would agree to having this expedition

[14] For what purports to be, and probably is, Tito's own account, partly in form of spoken dialogue between himself and Stalin, see Dedijer's *Tito*, pages 231–34.

prepared. On the 26th Roosevelt had answered that he did not object to having preparation made so that a sufficient British force would be ready to go into action if needed to preserve order in Greece when the Germans evacuated the country. He had said that he was agreeable to having General Wilson use for this purpose such American transport planes as he could spare. Then at Quebec Roosevelt and Churchill and the Combined Chiefs of Staff had completed and approved the plan.

When Harriman and Clark-Kerr went to see Stalin (on September 23rd) in order to deliver to him Roosevelt and Churchill's joint message about the military decisions reached at the Quebec Conference, they informed him of the contemplated landing operation in Greece, saying that it might be made in the near future. Stalin remarked that he thought the plan all right and it was high time that this be done.

While this venture was being made ready for use if necessary, the British continued to try to unify the resistance movements in Greece and to get a consolidated government. At a conference arranged by General Wilson at Caserta, the heads of the opposed guerrilla armies (Communist and Nationalist) agreed to place their forces under the orders of a British commander from Supreme Headquarters, and to restrain their followers and end their rivalries. Zones of operations were agreed on. But the account of what happened as the Germans began to withdraw from the country will fit better into the next and later account of the sweep of events in this region.

Over Italian affairs the strain had grown less. The American and British governments had continued to have different views about the pace at which their relations with Italy ought to be adjusted, and to be at odds over changes within the government. But these differences were not allowed to get out of hand. The Soviet government did not seriously attempt to interfere in the evolution that was taking place. Perhaps it had decided that if it left the Americans and British alone in Italy, the better the chance they would leave the Soviet government alone in areas falling under its military control—Romania, Bulgaria, Hungary.

The Italian government under the new Prime Minister, Bonomi, by midsummer had settled down well to its job. When Churchill visited Roosevelt at Hyde Park after the Quebec Conference they had found themselves nearer together than before. On September 26th they jointly announced that they would continue to transfer control over Italian affairs in a gradually increasing measure to Italian administration. To mark the purpose, the Allied Control Commission was renamed the Allied Commission.

The American government wished to go further and resume full diplomatic relations with Italy. The Soviet government wanted to also. But the British government hesitated. It pointed out (in a telegram of October 20th) the strangeness of doing so while still technically at war with Italy.[15] And if this proposed step were taken, could Romania and Bulgaria—who had also changed sides in the war—be refused similar consideration? But despite these misgivings of the British, the American government and those of the other American Republics announced on October 26th that diplomatic relations with Italy would be inaugurated. The State Department explained that it was seeking to reach, as soon as possible, a state of peace with Italy. It was worried over the continued political crisis in that country and thought it essential to encourage in this way the groups that were fighting with us against the Germans and standing for democratic government. The administration cannot be too severely condemned if it thought this measure might also improve the prospects of the Democratic Party in the American national elections, just a few days off.

Other crises of change in the Italian government were soon to occur, and other upsurges of trouble between the Americans and British. But events bore out the later reflections of Secretary of State Hull on the Italian situation at the time he left office in November 1944: ". . . the President and I felt that Italy, after more than two decades of Fascist domination, had made gratifying progress toward embracing the concepts and forms of democracy. We had no illusions that the task would be easy in a country economically prostrate, but we did have hopes that the basic good sense of the Italians, plus the lesson of the terrible catastrophe into which Fascism had plunged them, would keep them headed in the right direction." [16]

Here, for the sake of wholeness, this tale of strategic decisions, diplomatic activities, and the struggles of nations in the breaking waves of the war must briefly pause. For while the three great members of the war coalition were engaged with these measures, eager officials were trying to look beyond them. If, the premise was, countries could be brought together in a common vow for peace and for concerted will to have it, then differences between them would be transient and soluble.

[15] It also stressed the paradox of doing so while the American government was still refusing to exchange Ambassadors with the French authorities in Paris. This was done within the next few days. On October 20th the French Zone of the Interior was set up; the French Committee of National Liberation was on the 23rd recognized as the Provisional Government of the French Republic, and an American Ambassador was named.
[16] *Memoirs*, page 1569.

Thus while trouble brewed over the whole of Europe east of the Rhine and over Asia from Manchuria to the Indies and the Indian Ocean, devoted delegations were trying to beget a charter for the United Nations. They were gathered in the house and grounds of Dumbarton Oaks, where every room and vista is touched with grace—grace from the past for which the future would be in want.

45. The Conference at Dumbarton Oaks— September 1944

The American government was determined to bring the nations together in a collective system to maintain the peace before the war ended. There was some opinion adverse to doing this on the score that only when the state of the world after the war was known, and peace treaties were concluded, would it be possible to judge whether the United States ought to enter any such league of nations. For, it was argued, the proposed organization would find itself obliged to sustain and defend the resultant situation. The White House and State Department did not deny that in going ahead before peace terms were agreed on trouble might be met later. But they tended to dismiss the risk as small, for they thought it had to be taken for the sake of their imperative reason. The drawn-out agony of war had led to an almost universal longing for a new basis of relations between nations which might prevent future conflicts. But this wish might wane in the relief of victory. And then, as in 1919, the great purpose might be killed by false fears, relapse to older ways of thinking, minority objections or partisanship.

When had there ever been, when would there ever be, a peace treaty that some countries did not think wrong and unjust? The pains of peace-making, the officials directing foreign policy thought, must not be allowed to deter the treatment which alone could make and keep the nations well. Not only that; they hoped that if before final peace terms were set there was an operative system to which all nations could look for mutual protection, they would find it easier to agree on terms, and on fair—not fear—terms.

Hull's answers to members of the Foreign Relations Committee of the Senate who (on May 2nd, 1944) had questioned whether a security organization might not find itself committed to enforcing a "bad" peace, convey the blend of thought and aspiration which guided American policy:

"I commented," he recalled in his Memoirs, "that the Senate would of course pass on the peace treaties and therefore would itself have much to do with the adoption of a good or a bad peace. I then asked what we should do if the peace agreement were not quite to our notion. Would we abandon all idea of an organization to keep the peace, or would we proceed with determination . . . to perfect the peace and, if necessary, to develop further and perfect further the proposed organization to keep the peace?" [17]

This reasoning might have been battered on close examination by those who knew and appreciated how far, even in the autumn of 1944, many of the features of the postwar world had been *already* settled, either by accords such as those reached at Cairo and Teheran or by the movement of armies. But I do not think that, even so, the American (or British) government would have faltered in its purpose or program. For as McNeill has written, the Americans ". . . tended to think of the establishment of an international organization as a sort of talisman which would possess a powerful virtue to heal disputes among the nations." [18] In brief, it was both an ideal and a balm.

The concept of an association of free nations for common protection and welfare had come to appear the most comfortable as well as the most effective way to ward off future wars. We had tried isolation. We had tried neutrality. We had tried exhortation. All had been found wanting. We had no faith in balance-of-power arrangements, and did not want to maintain large armies after the war. Having come to know the pits and ambushes along these paths, we sought to clear a new path for the nations—first at Dumbarton Oaks, then at San Francisco.

Since the project had been confirmed at Teheran memo-writers and drafting committees had gone hard to work upon it. The American and British official constitution-makers had begun to exchange ideas, and to try to draw the Soviet government into the circle of authorship.

[17] *Ibid.*, page 1660. And on another occasion (May 12th), "A good peace will be much facilitated by keeping alive the beneficial and softening doctrines and policies contained in the Atlantic Charter, the Moscow Four-Nation Declaration, and the Connally Resolution. Otherwise, when the fighting is over, there will be no program halfway perfected even tentatively; our leadership will be gone; and each country will already be preparing to hoe its own row in the future. This government, however, acting through the Senate, can probably prevent a bad peace, and, failing that, will have nothing to do with it. We will not fail for the reason that we shall be supported by the small nations and probably by most of the large nations." *Ibid.*, 1661.

[18] William Hard McNeill, *America, Britain and Russia, 1941–1946*, page 501.

But all this member of the coalition had said in effect—taking many weeks to say it—was that it had no objections to the topics in mind but did not want to be obligated to discuss them in the order proposed.

By the end of April the State Department had thought its provisional proposals definite enough to submit to the examination of members of Congress and outside authorities. Hull was not to be deterred by what he regarded as lesser matters—such as the unresolved future of Poland. "I stressed," he later informed the readers of his *Memoirs,* "the necessity for unity especially among the United States, Russia, and Great Britain, if this postwar international undertaking were to succeed. Malcontents in this country, I pointed out, were doing their best to drive Russia out of the international movement by constant attacks and criticisms largely about minor incidents or acts." [19]

The talks had brought so much encouragement and assurance of support that at the end of May Hull had announced that the American government was able to begin discussion of plans for the new organization with foreign governments.

The British government had been favorable. But the Soviet government had been slow to respond. It had to be prodded. Harriman, under instruction, had kept reminding Molotov that we were eager to start the talks, "the sooner the better." Both he and Clark-Kerr had emphasized that these would be informal and everything done would be subject to final acceptance by the governments. At last on July 9th the Soviet government had said that it was ready to begin.

The evolution of the President's ideas away from his early predilection for an arrangement akin to an armed alliance could be traced from the public statement which he had issued on June 15th. In this, the accent was upon (1) the fact that the organization was to be a fully representative body; and (2) that "We are not thinking of a superstate with its own police forces and other paraphernalia of coercive power." The members were merely to agree to have forces available for joint action when necessary to prevent war. The change had been also reflected in the memos which the American government had submitted in July to the Soviet and British governments outlining its ideas and suggesting a program of discussion. These had stated that it was expected that after the four main Allies had provisionally agreed upon a plan, it would be discussed with the other United Nations, and that this might lead to further talks between the main Allies and to changes in the proposals which they would ultimately adopt. The Soviet government had observed that this was a new element in the American proposals. But it had nevertheless agreed to enter into preliminary talks.

[19] Page 1659.

These had been scheduled for early in August. But the British had first asked for a little more time for study, and then the Soviet government had asked for still a little more time. So the discussions had not actually started until August 21st, when three serious and well-trained delegations had sat down to their task at Dumbarton Oaks.

The work went well. A concordance of purpose prevailed—perhaps because it was not tested by the strain of dealing with any of the particular problems of the war or of peace-making. In a sense this voyage was a trip on a high-altitude plane; it flew over the storms in between that present and the future.

There was some difference of opinion about the range of activity of the Assembly—the body on which every member was to have a place. The Americans persuaded the others to agree that this all-embracing part of the structure might have greater scope and freedom than they at first were inclined to grant.

The matter of what countries were to belong to the new organization at the start presented a series of questions—so many and so involved in detail that those who want to know about them will have to turn to other sources. One was startling. Gromyko, the head of the Soviet delegation, asked that all sixteen units of the Union of Soviet Socialist Republics should have initial and separate membership. The surmise of some observers at the time that this proposal was mainly due to a wish to win support among the constituent nationalities of the Soviet Union is probably correct, particularly among the peoples of White Russia and the Ukraine who were being brought back into the Soviet federation. In putting the request forward the Soviet government may have thought it was not disguising reality much more than the presumption that the other American Republics were truly independent of the United States, or that the other members of the British Commonwealth followed the senior leadership of Britain of their own free will. The international Communist leaders have never been willing to believe that powerful countries like the United States or the United Kingdom would honestly allow their friendly affiliates to have effective free political will. Whatever the impelling reasons, the notion upset the American and British governments. President Roosevelt was afraid it might cause so great an uproar that the American people would turn against the whole project. He had Stettinius tell Gromyko so at once, and hastened to let Stalin know that he was against it. The Conference left the request in suspense.

The conferees had some trouble in agreeing on the composition of the Security Council—in which it was supposed that the ultimate powers of decision and action would be centered. No one questioned the right of Great Britain, the United States, and the Soviet Union to permanent places in this body; and it was agreed that a similar place should be kept open for France. But there was argument as to whether China should have a permanent seat, as the American government advocated. The day was to come when it wished the wish had not been granted! Of the eleven members, it was agreed that the other six should be elected by the Assembly for short terms.

All these and many more differences were, either at Dumbarton Oaks or later, adjusted without serious trouble. But one other turned out to be lastingly hard—that which was called the question of "voting procedure" in the Security Council. In reality the problem embraced several connected basic issues. The first of these was of ultimate import: to what extent would the great powers share with others the right to shape and decide policy and action?

The five main Allies who were to have permanent seats on the Council were to be a minority in that body of eleven, the other six of whom were to be elected by the Assembly. What votes were to be required for a decision? The Soviet government thought a simple majority rule sufficient; the British government thought it would be more advisable to require a two-thirds majority; the American government was willing to agree to either practice. But all of the five permanent members were to be protected by a provision requiring the assent of each and every one for any decision of substance.[20] In other words, each was to be able to prevent any action by the Council to which it objected: a right to veto.

However, it had not been decided before the Conference whether a

[20] I do not think a clear understanding was reached either during the exchange of proposals before the Dumbarton Oaks Conference or at that Conference in regard to the realm within which unanimous consent of the permanent members would be essential, even in regard to disputes in which they were not directly involved. Hull and the American delegation seem to have believed that the use of the veto power was to be limited to situations involving the employment of force or sanctions. As stated in his *Memoirs,* page 1663:

"In all the discussions with my associates in postwar planning, two important conditions had been understood and repeatedly stated in connection with the veto. The first was that none of the permanent members of the Council would exercise its right of veto capriciously or arbitrarily. It would call this power forth only on a matter of the gravest concern to itself, never on secondary matters and never in a way to prevent thorough discussion of any issue. . . . The second condition was that we were thinking largely of the application of the veto power to military or other means of compulsion."

But I do not think the Soviet government, and perhaps others, thought that they would be obligated to show such restraint. I leave this quesion—which in the postwar period has caused flaming contention—to the specialists who will have gone over both the texts and the record of discussions more thoroughly than I have.

permanent member should be entitled to exercise this right *even as regards disputes in which it was directly involved*. The area of decision was a terraced one, rising from stage to stage: was concurrence to be required (1) before the Security Council was allowed even to discuss such a dispute? (2) before it could make any recommendations for settlement? (3) before it could take any action to induce or compel an objecting member to heed its recommendations? And, beyond that, were each to be obligated to submit to a decision of the Council against which it might have objected?

If the need for concurrence was required in *all* these stages, then in effect each permanent member would have the power to prevent the Council from doing anything at all about a dispute in which it was involved. It would have to be persuaded to consent, for in no degree could it be coerced. This might put a premium on bargains between the great powers at the expense of the small ones. If, to take the other extreme, directly affected permanent members gave up all right to check the activities of the Council, then each would be subject to the verdict of a majority of the members and conceivably mistreated by an unfriendly coalition. The resultant bad feeling might be ruinous and destroy the organization.

The complexities of the subject became more and more evident as study and consultation at Dumbarton Oaks continued. The Soviet delegation insisted on the full stretch of the veto power. The American delegation tried to get the others to agree that each of the permanent members should renounce this right at least in the earlier stages of consideration of a dispute in which it was involved. Roosevelt addressed himself directly to Stalin about this issue on September 9th (in paraphrase): "We and the British both feel strongly that in the decisions of the Council, parties to a dispute should not vote even if one of the members is a permanent member of the Council; I know public opinion in the United States would never understand or support a plan of international organization which violated this principle." He added that he thought the small countries would also reject such a plan. Just what did the President have in mind in this loosely phrased appeal? Would the American government have been willing, if the Soviet government had been, to forego the right to prevent the Council from imposing a decision upon us, even perhaps by threat of sanctions or force? The question did not have to be faced since the message was without effect.[21]

[21] Hull recounts that two days after the Conference opened the President approved ". . . our new position that the votes of the nations involved in cases before the Council, including the great powers, should not be counted in the Council's decisions on such

Stalin started his answer by remarking that he had been under the impression that at Teheran Roosevelt and Churchill had agreed with him on the unanimity rule without any such great limitation as was now being suggested.[22] Then he explained why he could not consider any departure from this rule. The Soviet government, he said, had to take account of the fact that certain influential foreign circles had "ridiculous prejudices" which hampered an objective view of the Soviet Union; these were opposed to the unanimity rule because it would stand in the way of their wish to constrain the Soviet Union. Moreover, the Soviet government was, he said, afraid of being isolated and out-maneuvered in a dispute in which it was a party. But the Soviet government would like to be believed when it avowed that it did not want to do anything with which the others disagreed. And he suggested that other countries should consider further what the consequences would be if the great powers did not preserve their unanimity. Correlative to these reasons, he explained in talk with Harriman, he thought the smaller powers ought not to be allowed, by raising a dispute with one of the larger ones, to cause trouble between them—as they had done in the past. This point, it may be remarked, did not often figure in the American comment upon the rights of the smaller powers and their title to equality.

In all this comment by the Soviet government there was a sad lack of realization that the prospect of unanimity was most blurred by its own acts. Its policy at this time was, as Harriman and Kennan were pointing out in their analysis, a dual or ambivalent one: always to keep itself in a position to impose its own will in matters deemed vital to the Soviet security or prestige, even while wanting and seeking continued co-operation. Balance in this duality was easily lost. Unless the Soviet government was willing to trust the intentions of its Allies more, and

---

cases." He adds, "There was still some difference of opinion among us, however, as to whether this abstention from voting should apply only to the pacific settlement of disputes in which one or more of the major nations were involved, or should apply also to enforcement action." *Memoirs,* pages 1677–78.

Adequately to trace the evolution of the American official position on this subject of voting procedure would tax the patience of all except the most interested student, since it went through various phases and involved various ambiguities.

[22] Such records of the talk at the Teheran Conference as are available to me do not indicate that the question was definitely or explicitly discussed. It will be recalled, however, that the plan then outlined by the President visualized not only an Executive Council—which was to be authorized to recommend settlements but not to have power to impose decisions—but also a body talked of as "The Four Policemen" which would have the power to do so. It seems to have been presumed that in this the four main Allies would always be in agreement and act together. Thus, Stalin had a valid basis for his impression that the President too thought that the executive power of the organization would be exercised only when and if all the main Allies were in agreement.

refrained from measures that seemed to them to signify a wish to dominate Europe, quarrels might at any time occur. The Soviet Union, like the United States and Great Britain, could have genuine and positive unanimity as among equals only by contributing to it in due measure. No rule of voting procedure could assure it. Stalin and his colleagues were caught in a crotch of their own making. The unqualified rule of unanimity which they sought could guard the Soviet Union against lesser perils, but not against the greater ones that would follow alienation from its Allies.

The delegations at Dumbarton Oaks finally produced a compromise in this field which they submitted to their governments. Under this formula the Security Council would have been enabled to engage in efforts at peaceful settlement of a dispute without having to take into account the vote of parties to the dispute, even though they were permanent members. But the permanent members would have retained their veto, even when they were involved in the dispute, over any decision of the Council that contemplated or required the use of force of any kind. Neither Roosevelt nor Churchill, who were then together at Quebec, liked this proposal. Even if they had, it is most doubtful whether it would have been acceptable to the Soviet government. Thus it came about, after four weeks of conference, that an impasse was reached on this issue.

Hull seems to have been surprised at this, shocked in the belief he had nursed since the Moscow Conference that the Soviet government would, if dealt with fairly and patiently, settle all questions in consultation. He was at the same time becoming disturbed over Soviet claims of right to dictate what was done about Hungary, Romania, and Bulgaria. He sent Harriman, on September 18th, a perplexed query, which said he was beginning to wonder whether the Soviets had decided to reverse the policies "apparently" decided on at Moscow and Teheran of cooperation with the Western Allies and to pursue a contrary course. He invited the Embassy to comment on this question, particularly as regards the causes of the change in Soviet policy. The inquiry bewildered the Embassy. Had the scores of messages it had sent on the many signs of Soviet disregard of American and British wishes not been understood?

Harriman, it will be recalled, had been so irked that he had asked just a few days before to be authorized to return to Washington to report to the President, and had been asked to postpone the visit because it was thought that he might be able in Moscow to help bring about an agreement on this veto question. He had tried—to no avail—as has been told.

434

Provoked by that, he and George Kennan, the Counsellor of the Embassy, had prepared a careful interpretive report on Soviet policy. They had dispatched it on September 19th, before receiving Hull's query, with the thought that it might aid the President in answering Stalin's most recent message on the veto question. After Hull's inquiry came, they followed it up with a still longer analysis (sent on the 20th).

The main purport of these two reports was that they thought the Soviet government was determined not to allow the Security Council to deal with any dispute to which it was a party, most especially when it concerned its neighbors. The Ambassador recalled that at the Moscow Conference Molotov had said that the Soviet government was ready to consult with the American and British governments on most matters, but that in those between itself and its Western neighbors he would agree only to keep them informed. He observed also that neither Hull nor Eden had objected at the time, and thought that Stalin and his colleagues might well have concluded, therefore, that we were satisfied with that. Thus the Ambassador said he was not sure that any basic change was taking place in Soviet policy; recent events were simply revealing what it had always been; that as soon as the Soviet government was sure that it would win the war and could do without us if necessary, they began to put this policy into effect. While it was not possible, these reports concluded, to predict how far the Soviet government would insist that neighboring countries obey its orders, it clearly intended to have a positive sphere of influence over them; and thus would not be willing to forego the right to prevent the Council from mingling in any disputes it might have with them. In paraphrased summary:

"Stalin and his chief advisers do think it important to associate in a major way with the other great powers in world affairs. But they have thought they could settle the conditions by themselves, by their political and military strength. Stalin could not forego that association without causing grave concern among the Russian people. But there are powerful groups within Stalin's circle who are unwilling, where Soviet interests are affected, to give up the right to act independently and to allow Russia to become dependent on an untried world organization in which it would be associated with countries which it does not fully trust. Stalin does not think it inconsistent to pursue these two methods simultaneously in order to serve what he believes is the security and interest of the Soviet Union."

After these interpretive judgments, the Ambassador cautiously hinted that it might be in part our fault that the Soviet Union believed it could get the best of both methods. He remarked that it would be possible to arrive at an agreement with the Soviet Union only if the U.S. Government took a definite interest in the solutions of the problems of each country as they arose. The same critical thought had been more outrightly expressed in an earlier memo of Kennan's: "An international organization for the preservation of peace and security cannot take the place of a well-conceived and realistic foreign policy . . . and we are being . . . negligent of the interests of our people if we allow plans for an international organization to be an excuse for failing to occupy ourselves seriously and minutely with the sheer power relationships of the European peoples."

The import of these messages—which contained definite suggestions to the same effect—was that we ought to be taking a more observant and firmer interest in the current affairs in Central Europe than we had been; and if necessary should match Soviet disregard for our ideas with disregard for theirs. If that were done, the Ambassador thought, some unpleasant situations might follow, but presently the Soviet government would accede to our views.

It is not of record whether these messages influenced the decision reached by the President and Secretary of State not to appeal Stalin's message of September 15th about the veto question. The President resisted advice to accept the Soviet view. For the Joint Chiefs of Staff—speaking through General Stanley Embick, who was one of the military members of the American delegation at Dumbarton Oaks—did not want anything to occur which might cause the Soviet Union to stay out of the Pacific War. As Hull later made known: "During the Dumbarton Oaks Conference our military advisers . . . were willing to go farther than many of the political advisers in agreeing to Russia's position that the veto should be applied without exception." [23]

The President decided that since so many matters had been settled at Dumbarton Oaks, while no solution to the veto question was in sight, it was advisable to suspend the talks. Those who had hoped to have the large gathering for the adoption of a charter of the United Nations before the year 1944 had run out, were disappointed. The first and main stage of the Conference, the one in which the Soviet government took part but not the Chinese, was adjourned on September 28th. The second, with the Russians absent but the Chinese present, was begun at once and was over by October 7th.

Each of the four governments issued (on October 9th) a short identical statement as introduction to the record of the work done at Dumbarton Oaks. This said that, "The governments which were represented

[23] *Memoirs,* page 1470.

in the discussions in Washington have agreed that after further study of these proposals they will as soon as possible take the necessary steps with a view to the preparation of complete proposals which could then serve as a basis of discussion at a full United Nations conference."

The anticipatory note of this public statement seemed warranted. The governments of the great winning powers had agreed on the nature and structure of a flexible collective system for peace and security, and on the way it should operate. The range, depth, and rigidity of the differences which lay beneath the one big space in the accord was not appreciated.

The world in general hailed the outcome with uncritical, glad satisfaction. Despite the signs of difficulty that crept into each day's news, the American and British people were still counting on a continuation of cooperation with the Soviet Union after the war. Only a few critics averred that this could not be, and that the war alliance would be followed by a struggle for mastery between a world-wide revolutionary Communist movement and the West.

The President on October 9th expressed his satisfaction ". . . that so much could have been accomplished on so difficult a subject in so short a time." Churchill let the identical statement about the results of Dumbarton Oaks speak for itself.[24] He was not, and could not be, carried past troubling actualities. He was not wholly pleased with accepted strategic plans; he was disturbed over the efforts of insurgent elements in the liberated countries of Europe to gain control; and he was becoming fearful that the Communist Soviet Union might make itself the master of the Continent. So he had decided to go to Moscow to find out whether and how the situations which were worrying him might be settled in accord with the theme of harmony sounded at Dumbarton Oaks. He arrived in Moscow on October 9th, the day the statements were given out.

Roosevelt had asked him to postpone discussion of the veto question until the three of them should meet. He obliged, with Stalin's assent.

[24] See his cool summary of the work done at Dumbarton Oaks, *Triumph and Tragedy,* pages 209–10.

PERIOD TEN

From the Churchill Visit to Moscow in October 1944 to the Yalta Conference; Wartime Political Accords and Coordination of Strategic Programs

46. Churchill in Moscow, October 1944: European Affairs, Military and Civil

━━━━━━━━━━━━━━━━

CHURCHILL had concluded that it was imperative that he talk with Stalin rather than continue the unrewarding exchange of communications that had been going on. Stalin was saying that he could not leave Russia for another personal meeting. On September 23rd, when Harriman had called on Stalin to report about the Quebec decisions, he thought him to be, after a long bout of grippe, "more worn out than I have ever seen him and as yet not fully recovered." The Ambassador had passed on a message from the President that he would have to wait until the American elections were over, but had in mind a meeting in the latter part of November and thought that the Mediterranean would be a pleasant and mutually convenient place. Stalin had agreed that such a meeting was very desirable. But he had gone on to say that he was afraid that his doctors would not allow him to travel— even to the warm Mediterranean—since they thought that any change of climate would have a bad effect. Harriman had tried to get him to take a lighter view of the medical advice, saying that by the time November came around he might have some new doctors. Stalin seemed to enjoy the thought, but did not encourage the possibility.

So, as there was no other way, Churchill had decided to make the hard trip to Moscow again to see the immovable head of the Soviet state "with whom I always considered one could talk as one human being to another."[1] On September 27th he had indicated his grave sense of the errand by saying in his message to Stalin that after his return from long talks with the President (at Quebec and Hyde Park) he could assure Stalin of their intense conviction that the hopes of the world rested on agreement between Britain, the U.S., and the Soviet Union. And then he had said, "I will gladly come to Moscow in October if I can get away from here." Two days later, after telling Roosevelt of Stalin's complaints about the bad effect of travel, Churchill informed him:

"In these circumstances Anthony and I are seriously thinking of flying there [Moscow] very soon. . . . The two great objects we have in mind would be, firstly, to clinch his coming in against Japan, and secondly, to try to effect an amicable settlement with Poland. There are other points too concerning Yugoslavia and Greece which we would

[1] *Triumph and Tragedy,* page 214.

also discuss. We should keep you informed of every point. Averell's [Harriman] assistance would of course be welcomed by us, or perhaps you could send Stettinius or Marshall. I feel certain that personal contact is essential." [2]

Roosevelt had made no direct comment either about Churchill's initiative in going to Moscow or on the area of discussion which Churchill proposed to traverse. In his first answer (of the 30th) he had merely said that he would direct Harriman to give him any desired help, but it did not seem either practicable or advantageous to be represented by Stettinius or Marshall. On this same day, Stalin had informed Churchill that he would gladly welcome him in Moscow in October— or Eden if Churchill could not come—and he had sent his best wishes. Churchill had found this response "most friendly" and made up his mind to go.

Hopkins had been nervous about the outcome of a meeting of the two without Roosevelt. On learning that the President was about to send a message to Churchill which he thought implied that the President was content to have the Prime Minister speak for the American as well as for the British government, Hopkins had persuaded him that he ought to be more on guard. Hopkins had cancelled this message and written another, which Roosevelt had sent off to Stalin on the 4th of October. This began by saying that the President was sure that Stalin understood: ". . . that in this global war there is literally no question, political or military, in which the United States is not interested. I am firmly convinced that the three of us, and only the three of us, can find the solution to the still unresolved questions. In this sense, while appreciating the Prime Minister's desire for the meeting, I prefer to regard your forthcoming talks with Churchill as preliminary to a meeting of the three of us which, so far as I am concerned, can take place any time after the elections here."

Then he went on to say that if it was agreeable to Stalin and Churchill, he would like Harriman to be present at their talks, but only as an observer: "Naturally, Mr. Harriman would not be in a position to commit this government relative to the important matters which you and the Prime Minister will, very naturally, discuss." [3]

But the precaution had puzzled Stalin, as well it might have. He had sent back word to Roosevelt that he was somewhat embarrassed, as he had supposed that Churchill was coming to Moscow in accordance

[2] *Ibid.*, page 216.

[3] The Department of State: The Conferences at Malta and Yalta, referred to hereafter as the *Yalta Documents,* page 6.

with an agreement reached at Quebec, but this did not seem to be so. He did not know, he had gone on to say, what questions Churchill and Eden would talk about; that they had not told him; that they had merely said they wanted to come if he did not mind; and that of course he was telling them that he would be glad to see them.

The President had sent much the same notice to Churchill as he had to Stalin. In regard to Harriman's presence he said, "While naturally Averell will not be in a position to commit the United States—I could not permit anyone to commit me in advance—he will be able to keep me fully informed and I have told him to return and report to me as soon as the conference is over." [4] The President had also reviewed his ideas of the assignment with Harriman. He had explained that he hoped the Stalin-Churchill talks would be no more than exploration leading up to a full-dress meeting between the three. He had counselled the Ambassador to bear in mind that he and Hull were greatly concerned in any and all the subjects that Stalin and Churchill would discuss, and so it was important that they be left with complete freedom of action after the Churchill-Stalin talks were over.

Churchill had answered on October 5th that he would be glad to have Harriman sit in on all principal conferences. But, he had added, he was sure that Roosevelt would not wish to preclude private tête-à-tête talks between himself and Stalin or between Molotov and Eden. On his arrival at Moscow on October 9th, Churchill advised Harriman accordingly. He also sketched out for Harriman the realm of probable talk, and what he intended to say, including his idea of trying to work out some sort of arrangement for spheres of influence in the Balkans. In passing this information on to the President, Harriman asked whether, since such matters were going to be discussed, the President wanted him to try to be included even in the private talks between Stalin and Churchill. The President answered no, that he was to be present only when invited and then only as a listener and reporter.

As the narrative will tell, Harriman was kept at the side of Churchill and Stalin in all their talks except a few intimate ones in off hours. Churchill and Eden kept him fully and quickly informed; they solicited his opinions, and turned over to him and General Deane—as the American government definitely desired—the lead in the discussion of plans for Soviet participation in the Pacific War. But Roosevelt's personal absence was the insulation which he wanted until the elections were over, between himself and those twisted European questions for which he thought no altogether happy solution was likely to be found.

[4] *Ibid.*, page 7.

443

The exchange of military facts during this Moscow visit was candid and extensive. The Russians drew assurance from what they were told of U.S.-British plans; the British and Americans were happily impressed by those of the Soviet government. Each accepted the other's program without criticism or fear or rivalry.

The British, Soviet, and American military men (General Brooke for Britain, General Antonov for the USSR, and General Deane for the United States) reviewed the European military scene on the 14th of October, with Churchill and Stalin now and again taking the lead away from them. Together their expositions were a comprehensive chart of the situation at the time and of the prospects. The main features of the situation and strategy on the western fighting fronts were described by the British and American participants:

1. They had all the soldiers needed to win on the Western front. But the speed of their advance was dependent on the flow of supplies and maintenance facilities.

The plan was first to reach the Rhine, then force crossings north and south of the Ruhr to encircle it; then the main axis of the movement forward would be directed on Berlin. At the same time there would be (a) a thrust on the southern front toward Frankfurt, turning then northeast toward Leipzig; (b) the American and French armies which had come up from Marseilles would go through Belfort Gap, across the Rhine, and move east. All this, Churchill said, depended on Russian armies preventing the Germans from shifting troops west. Stalin stated that they would.

2. Alexander's push in Italy had passed the Gothic line on the Adriatic side in the late summer. Clark's Fifth Army was striving to get over the crest of the Apennines in the center. While Churchill was in Moscow, this struggle was at its most intense pitch and the Allied commanders in Italy were hopeful of being able to drive the Germans across the Po, and force them at last to pull out of Northwest Italy. But it may be noted that the climax of the battle in the center of Italy was reached a few days later (between October 20th–24th) and then, in Alexander's words, "assisted by torrential rains and winds of gale force, and the Fifth Army's exhaustion, the German line held firm." [5]

3. A possible plan was outlined for a British landing on the Istrian Peninsula and thence across Northwest Yugoslavia and through the Alps; and on to Vienna, there to join up with Soviet forces coming from the east.

Churchill and Stalin talked this over in the course of a long and congenial dinner on the 11th. At Teheran Stalin had almost derided such

[5] *Triumph and Tragedy,* page 222.

operations as of little use—a long way from the heart of Germany. Now, unexpectedly on this occasion, he encouraged them. The Marshal fell to talking about the tactics of envelopment which had served the Red Army so well at Stalingrad and which he was using in Hungary and around Warsaw. He enlarged on the idea that direct assaults against the German defense lines along the Rhine and in Italy would be more costly than need be. He wondered whether instead it would not be better to try to encircle these strong positions. The existing line in Italy might be, he remarked, held by fifteen of the twenty-five divisions of Allied troops in that country, and the other ten might be sent through Istria to flank the Germans and assist in the advance of the Red Army through Hungary into Austria.

Then during the formal military discussion on the 14th, Stalin and General Antonov repeated the suggestion. In accordance with the agreement which Stalin had reached with Tito Russian troops in Yugoslavia were not going to advance farther west than Belgrade; they were going to leave it to Tito's forces to clear the Germans out of the rest of the country. Stalin said he would be glad to see the British move north from Istria, go through the mountains, and join the Soviet columns which would be, he hoped, coming west from Hungary in the neighborhood of Vienna.

It is impossible to resist conjecture why, at this time, and for the first time, Stalin favored such a strategy. Was it only because he wanted this threat at the flank or rear of the German lines in the south, to be sure that they would not be able to shift forces to his central front or Hungary, where it was becoming apparent that the Germans were going to contest every mile? Or was he also displaying his sincere intention to conform to the chart of "spheres of responsibility" which he and Churchill had marked out a few nights before—as will soon be told? Or was he trying to embroil the British in a clash with Tito, whom he knew had grown opposed to having them land in Yugoslavia?

Although this novel bid of Stalin's for coordinated operations in the south strongly appealed to Churchill and his military advisers, they felt compelled to forego any immediate step toward its fulfillment. Brooke said an amphibious operation against the Istrian Peninsula was being prepared. But it could not be attempted until more ground had been won in Italy and landing craft brought around from the south of France. Actually, the circumstances bearing on the chances of going forward with this plan were as adverse as ever. The President and Joint Chiefs of Staff were at this time rejecting Churchill's appeals to deflect two or three divisions of troops from France to Italy, on the ground that it would be unwise to deprive the forces in France of this infusion of strength in order to subject them to the attrition of a winter campaign in Italy. Then Allied attempts to clear the Scheldt and open the port of Antwerp were dragging. And then, even while Churchill and Stalin and their military advisers were enthusiastically discussing the Istrian possibility, Tito was being critical of British activities, and of their entry into any of the Adriatic ports—even those small ventures made in order to bring help to his partisan fighters. He was sending word to General Wilson that the Yugoslav people were disturbed by the presence of the British forces and suspicious of their intentions. This change in Tito's attitude may possibly be explained by his dissatisfaction with the subordinate role assigned to the Yugoslav forces in the Allied project for Istria, Austria, and Hungary, expounded in a memo which General Wilson's Chief of Staff gave him.[6]

To foretell, the successive plans which General Wilson submitted to the Combined Chiefs of Staff all tended towards the conclusion that it would not be feasible to attempt a landing either on the Dalmatian coast or Istrian Peninsula before February 1945. Even Churchill, deeply disappointed, judged that any advantage that might be won by an action started so late would not be enough to justify the immediate relaxation of the campaign in Italy that would have been required. In December the project was definitely renounced.[6a]

4. The British were proceeding with their plans for sending forces into Greece: at first paratroopers and air commando groups, then larger units. They had two missions: to hurry the Germans out of Athens, occupy the city and its approaches; and thereafter, to harry the German retreat north. The Germans withdrew from Athens on the 12th and on the next day Wilson began sending paratroopers to take over the nearby airfield. A few days later the recognized Greek government, headed by Papandreou, moved into the capital. But it was doubtful whether this regime would be able to extend its authority over the country, to disperse the several guerrilla bands and build up its own army and police. Despite Stalin's aloofness, the Greek Communists were going to make the title which Churchill gained in Moscow—a free hand in the direction of Greek affairs—a shaky one.

Correlative to this review of situations in the west, General Antonov then described operations and plans of the Red Armies on the eastern fronts. In very general summary they were:

1. In the north—the Baltic States and Northern Finland—operations

[6] *Ibid.*, pages 90–91.

[6a] A comprehensive account of the proposals and plans considered between October and December 1944, and the circumstances affecting the decision, is in *Grand Strategy*, Vol. VI, pages 47–56.

would be carried out until all German forces there were defeated or compelled to retreat; the thirty German divisions in that area were cut off from any escape except by sea.

2. Towards the south of their line, the Soviet forces would concentrate on the occupation of Hungary and encircle as many as possible of the twenty-three German divisions in that country. The attack in this area was to be the main immediate Soviet offensive. From Hungary, he explained, the Red armies would be directed through Austria to take Vienna. This would open up a route into Germany to the west of Czechoslovakia, then to the northwest in the direction of the Oder at Breslau.

3. On the central front (from Lithuania to the Carpathians), where the Germans had two-thirds of the divisions they were using in the east, the Soviet armies would at the same time maintain continuous pressure. The timing of the attack against East Prussia and the encircling of Warsaw would depend on the progress of the operations in the north and south.

4. After the Baltic situation was cleared up and Hungary forced out of the war, the Soviet armies would address themselves to their ultimate job—the invasion of Germany. It was hard to tell yet from which direction this would take place, maybe from the east, maybe from the south, maybe from both.

Harriman sent the President a summary of this exposition of plans and intention, and General Deane sent a more detailed account to the Joint Chiefs of Staff. Thus the American military organization had a clear advance knowledge of the course that the Soviet armies would travel, and the relation to the Allied advances from the west and Italy. The Soviet armies during the campaigns followed the strategy outlined.

It is notable that in all this talk of military actions and plans there was no spoken word or even hint by anyone that they were or would be influenced for political ends, to get control of any particular area in the east or west. Nor did any participant seem to have the sense after the talks were over that this was being done; or if they had, they did not make it of record then. Perhaps this was because, early in their talks, Churchill and Stalin reached a working accord assigning the lead in some parts of the region of trouble to Britain, leaving the lead in other parts to the Soviet Union.

Churchill had been sorry to desist from his earlier attempt to arrange with the Russians for a "divisions of responsibility" in the Balkans. The American government, it will be recalled, had opposed it.

447

The Soviet government had slid out of it, ostensibly because of regard for American opinion. Early in August it had in a tricky way sent a mission from Italy to the Communists (EAM) in Northern Greece (which had been assigned to Britain in the uncompleted understanding). Churchill had looked upon this as an act of bad faith. He had thus stopped trying to revive this diplomatic arrangement until he met with Stalin. But it had continued to seem to him the only way to get a clearheaded policy toward each of the Balkan countries in face of military and political upheavals, to avert local turmoil or civil war, and to avoid conflict with Soviet and local Communist forces. He had been open in explaining his ideas and intentions to Roosevelt and Stalin.

At his first talk with Stalin on the night of October 9th, with Molotov and Eden present, Churchill, after arranging to have the London Poles invited to come to Moscow, put his proposal on the table. What happened then—and it happened fast—cannot be better told than it has been by Churchill himself.[7]

"The moment was apt for business, so I said, 'Let us settle about our affairs in the Balkans. Your armies are in Rumania and Bulgaria. We have interests, missions, and agents there. Don't let us get at cross-purposes in small ways. So far as Britain and Russia are concerned, how would it do for you to have ninety per cent predominance in Rumania, for us to have ninety per cent of the say in Greece, and go fifty-fifty about Yugoslavia?' While this was being translated I wrote out on a half-sheet of paper:

Rumania	
Russia	90%
The others	10%
Greece	
Great Britain	90%
(In accord with U.S.A.)	
Russia	10%
Yugoslavia	50–50%
Hungary	50–50%
Bulgaria	
Russia	75%
The others	25%

"I pushed this across to Stalin, who had by then heard the translation. There was a slight pause. Then he took his blue pencil and made a large

[7] *Triumph and Tragedy,* pages 227–28. Churchill in this later account incorrectly includes Harriman as being present during this talk. He was not.

tick upon it, and passed it back to us. It was all settled in no more time than it takes to set down.

"Of course we had long and anxiously considered our point, and were only dealing with immediate wartime arrangements. All larger questions were reserved on both sides for what we then hoped would be a peace table when the war was won.

"After this there was a long silence. The pencilled paper lay in the centre of the table. At length I said, 'Might it not be thought rather cynical if it seemed we had disposed of these issues, so fateful to millions of people, in such an offhand manner? Let us burn the paper.' 'No, you keep it,' said Stalin."

The story of what had taken place, and its meaning, was told to Harriman only little by little, and he passed it along to the President as learned. In the first joint message which Churchill and Stalin sent to Roosevelt on the 10th of October they said merely, "We have to consider the best way of reaching an agreed policy about the Balkan countries, including Hungary and Turkey." At lunch on that day Harriman was told that in the first draft of this message to the President, Churchill had included the phrase (to the best of Harriman's memory) ". . . having regard to our own varying duties toward them." Stalin had suggested that this phrase, which clearly implied spheres of influence, be omitted. On hearing this, Harriman said to Stalin, with Churchill listening, that he was sure that the President would be glad that the phrase had been eliminated since he thought that subject should be dealt with by the three of them. Stalin said he was pleased to hear Harriman say that and, reaching behind Churchill's back, he shook Harriman's hand.

In his next message to the President (October 11th) Churchill made a careful bid for approval. "It is absolutely necessary," he said, "we should try to get a common mind about the Balkans, so that we may prevent civil war from breaking out in several countries, when probably you and I would be in sympathy with one side and U.J. with the other. I shall keep you informed of all this, and nothing will be settled except preliminary agreements between Britain and Russia, subject to further discussion and melting down with you. On this basis I am sure you will not mind our trying to have a full meeting of minds with the Russians." [8]

On this same day, the President got from Harriman a more definite explanation of what the British were trying to do and why—based mainly on what Eden told him. The Ambassador said that Churchill

[8] *Ibid.*, page 229.

449

had been using the term "spheres of influence," but that Eden was stating that his aim was merely to work out a practical arrangement as to how the problems of each country were to be dealt with and what the relative responsibility of the Soviet Union and Britain was to be in each case.[9] The Prime Minister and Foreign Secretary, Harriman continued, thought that in Romania, on the basis of the armistice terms, Russia would have a pretty free hand anyhow; and they were seeking to persuade Molotov to accord the British and American elements on the Control Commissions in Bulgaria and Hungary more authority than was being allowed in Romania, and equal place with the Soviet elements after fighting ended in these countries. In Yugoslavia they were trying to get the Soviet government to work with the British and American governments to bring all the Yugoslav factions together. As for Greece they sought a Soviet promise to keep hands off and to induce the Greek Communists to play a constructive part in the national government. The Polish situation was deemed different from these, needing a specific solution involving all three countries, which they were trying to bring about.

It might well be borne in mind that the American government at this time was making a similar effort to get Soviet cooperation to bring about an accord between the Chinese National government and the Chinese Communists. Stalin and Churchill seemed willing to have the American government take the lead in directing the political evolution of that country; and the American government was assuming it. Similarly, it was understood that Britain could be to the fore in dealing with Southeast Asia.

The President's response to these several accounts from Moscow about the assignment of spheres of responsibility in the Balkans was meager and noncommittal. His only comment (on October 11th) to Harriman on getting the Ambassador's first report was, "At the present time my active interest in the Balkan area is that there be taken such steps as are practicable to insure against the Balkans getting into an international war in the future." On the next day, the 12th, in acknowledgment of the joint message which Stalin and Churchill had sent him two days before, he told them, "I am most pleased that you are reaching a meeting of your two minds as to the international policies in which, because of our present and future common efforts to prevent international wars, we are all interested." Although this response might have been written out before he had gotten Harriman's fuller report

[9] Churchill, in a letter to Stalin which he decided not to send but which he has printed in *ibid.*, page 231, described the percentages that had been agreed on as "A good guide for the conduct of our affairs."

on what was in mind (the one sent from Moscow the day before), in all probability the President had seen that before it was sent off to the conferring Heads of State.

In short, the evidence is that Roosevelt had come to agree with Churchill that some such arrangement as the one reported was advisable, if not essential. But he continued to restrain official interest in Eastern and Central European matters except as they might affect sentiment in the United States. He was determined to have a lot to say, once the elections were over, about the settlements in the Pacific. But, since he thought is was nearly impossible to find happy solutions for many European problems, he wanted to remain as clear of them as he could, except for those involving Germany.

The staff of the State Department was more aware of the need for vigilance in regard to the political situations developing in Central and Eastern European countries. But it tended to regard the disputed issues as lying between Russia and Britain rather than of more universal significance, and so was inclined to view the activities of both as an attempt by each to benefit at the expense of others, and therefore unfavorable to future peace. This led the Department to adopt an attitude of critical reserve, and to pursue a strategy of postponement. It tried to arrest the march of armies, the clash of civil wars, the forays of diplomacy by repeated affirmations of the view that principle should govern European postwar settlements, not proximity or political affiliation or power.

Churchill and Stalin went forward with their adjustment of responsibility, assuming that it would not again be upset by Washington. For Greece, their accord meant that the British were enabled to carry on without Soviet interference. For Yugoslavia, they agreed upon a joint message to Tito and Subasic, urging them to meet again and work out their problems together. They announced that they were going to try to bring about a union between the Royal Yugoslav government and the National Liberation movement; and that they recognized the inalienable right of the Yugoslav people to settle their future constitution for themselves. For Bulgaria, they completed the armistice terms. Molotov would not grant Eden's request that the American and British members be given more voice in the Control Commission for that country, but he did concede that it should be bettered when the war against Germany was over.

Over what was to be done about Hungary, the tussle was harder. That country was thought by the Americans and British to be of the West, and outside the historic fling of Russian or Slavic power. Still, it had joined in the assault on the Soviet people when they were suffering all but mortal hurt, and helped the Germans much. As told, the preliminary armistice terms which the three Allies had formulated together had been sent on to the Hungarian government under the Regent, Horthy, just before Churchill arrived in Moscow. The Red Army had crossed the frontier, reaching Debrecen on the 10th. The Horthy regime quickly accepted the proffered preliminary terms, and Molotov (on the 13th) hastened to put before the British and Americans the Soviet proposals for the longer period. Stalin had agreed on paper that the British should have a part equal to that of the Russians in the direction of Hungarian affairs. But what the Soviet government now asked made it clear that this balance would be hard to maintain. It sought control arrangements that were almost the same as the ones adopted for Romania—in which country Russia had been accorded the most say—and would have allowed the Soviet Commander-in-Chief to impose his unrestrained will on Hungary. Also, it asked for reparations which, while not an unjust fee for the suffering and damage endured, were very heavy for so small a country in so drained a condition. The Soviet authorities wanted to reduce Hungary's military and industrial potential, and were not bothered by the chance that this might cause suffering and disorder. Perhaps they were swayed by the thought that economic distress would weaken the conservative elements who had governed Hungary, and hasten the emergence of groups who would seek support in Moscow. The American government came out of its shell to protest. Molotov was stubborn, but he agreed to reduce the sum to be demanded by almost half.

This argument over armistice terms for Hungary turned out to be premature. Events again upset the negotiations. The Hungarian government lagged in carrying out the preliminary terms. The Soviet government called upon it to do so within twenty-four hours and, even more, to break relations at once with the Germans, start fighting them, and withdraw all Hungarian troops from Romania, Yugoslavia, and Czechoslovakia. These Russian demands were overborne by a German ultimatum. On the 15th the Budapest radio announced that the Regent had asked an armistice. The German SS had tried to capture the radio station to prevent this, but had been resisted until the news was broadcast. Early the next morning German squads, led by Skorzeny, the rescuer of Mussolini, attacked the Burg, and the Regent gave up to them, and abdicated. A puppet government took over. The massed Red Army began to advance from the south. German divisions grasped control of the western section of the country. Part of the Hungarian Army continued to fight on the side of the Germans, while another part began to join the Russians in fighting the Germans. Discussions and decisions among the main Allies as to how to organize the armistice for Hungary waited upon the course of the great campaign still to be fought in that country.

47. Churchill in Moscow: The Attempt to Reach Accord on Poland

·∞·∞·∞·∞·∞·∞·∞·

Poland was not on the list of countries toward which Churchill and Stalin bounded the respective responsibilities of their countries. But of all the issues which took Churchill to Moscow, this was probably the most compelling one. The Prime Minister had the sense—and it came out harshly in his talks with Mikolajczyk in London—that Poland's cause was being lost as time went on, and that chances of a settlement which would allow a truly independent Polish state to emerge were getting poorer. Eden was even surer this was happening. He thought it essential that there be no further delay in making over the Polish government in London, and reaching an accord with the Lublin group.

One of the first things Churchill and Stalin agreed on was to invite Mikolajczyk and two of his acceptable associates to Moscow at once. Churchill hurried off a message to Mikolajczyk, saying that he and his friends were expected to come—to talk with the Soviet government, himself, and the Lublin Polish Committee. He said that a refusal would be regarded as a definite rejection of his advice, and relieve the British government of further responsibility toward the Polish government in London. He also advised Roosevelt of what he was doing.

Mikolajczyk, who up to then had said he would not go to Moscow a second time to submit his case to Stalin again unless he had some advance reassurances, gave in. He hastened and got to Moscow on the 12th. His freedom to negotiate with the Lublin Poles was, however, restricted, for his colleagues in London had pledged him to stand fast on the terms of a memo which had been given to the Allied governments on August 30th past. This, it will be recalled, had provided that each of the former five political parties, including the Communist, should have equal place in the new government. About frontiers it had stipulated that the new Poland should be at least as spacious as before the war, and include "in the East the main centers of Polish cultural life and the sources of raw materials. . . ."

In his first talk of consequence with Churchill and Stalin on the 13th (Harriman and Clark-Kerr also being present) Mikolajczyk based his statements on this memo. He was friendly but defiant. "Our aim," he asserted, "is to bring about an agreement between Poland and Russia, not between Russia and a handful of Poles—arbitrarily and unilaterally chosen by a foreign power." [10] Churchill tried to lead him along the path of compromise. But his stubborn answer was that he had come to realize it was not possible merely to merge the Polish government in London with the Lublin Committee; that it was essential to go deeper and construct a wholly new government in which all Polish democratic elements should have a part—each of the five political parties to have an equal part at the start until there could be elections. Stalin's comment was blunt. Mikolajczyk's proposals, he said, had two great faults. First, they ignored the Committee of National Liberation, which he said was doing important work in the liberated areas of Poland, and had a large army and much popular support. Second, they were not responsive to Soviet suggestions about frontiers; if the Poles wanted good relations with the Soviet Union they must recognize the Curzon Line. "You," Mikolajczyk rejoined, "are ignoring the Polish government that created strong armies, a navy, and an air force and that now fights on all fronts."

The ensuing discussion brought forth only more positive statements of the differences. Churchill asserted that the British government supported the Soviet proposal—not because Russia was strong but because it was right: ". . . it would be understood of course . . . that the Allies would pursue the war against Germany so that Poland would receive other territories including Silesia and East Prussia which would offset her territorial losses in the East. On this basis there would be a great Poland; not the same one as was established at Versailles, but still a real home where the Polish people could live in security and prosperity." [11]

Mikolajczyk flung the offer aside. He said flatly that he could not agree with either Stalin or Churchill and could not accept the Curzon Line. Stalin would have a low opinion of him, he continued, if he agreed then and there to abandon forty per cent or more of Polish territory and five million Poles. He could not do so, and the boundary

[10] Mikolajczyk in *The Rape of Poland*, pages 93–98, gives a vivid account of this important talk. This comports in a general way with Churchill's and American records but varies in significant detail and effect not only from these but also from the official minutes of the Polish Delegation. These are on pages 115–124 of *Polish Documents, Report of the Select Committee on Communist Aggression*, House of Representatives Report 2684, Part 4, 83rd Congress, 2nd Session.

[11] Memo by Francis B. Stevens, Secretary of the American Embassy in Moscow.

question would have to be settled not by him and his group but by the Polish people. Stalin interrupted to deny that there were five million Poles in the disputed territory and to say that the people who lived there were mainly Ukrainians and White Russians. Mikolajczyk went on to say that even if he gave this territory, there would still be no guarantee that the Polish people would be independent. Stalin asked whether the Soviet Union threatened Poland. Mikolajczyk's answer was in effect, though not in words, that it did—as attested by the fact that it was not allowing Poles abroad to return to their country. He had not realized, he said, that he had come to Moscow to partition Poland. Stalin retorted that he had evidently come to partition the Ukraine and White Russia.

At this juncture, Molotov said he wished to advert to what had been said on the Polish question at Teheran; that he would like to repeat what Roosevelt had said, and asked the others who had been present there to correct him if his statement was inaccurate. His memory was that "Roosevelt had said that he considered the Curzon Line right but did not feel it advisable to publish a statement to that effect." Thus, he continued, it must be concluded that the opinion of the British, American, and Soviet governments on the question of the Soviet-Polish frontier was unanimous.[12] Mikolajczyk was surprised and shocked by this statement, which for the moment no one contradicted or amended. He asked whether he might learn what western frontier had been contemplated for Poland at Teheran, and Molotov told him that the Oder had been proposed without objection by anyone. Churchill said the British had supported it (the Oder), and Eden remarked that the idea had been that the frontier could be moved as far west toward the Oder as the Poles wished to go. Molotov confirmed that this had been the understanding. Churchill added that all of East Prussia west and south of Konigsberg was to go to Poland, and Stalin concurred in this statement.

Churchill then asked whether Mikolajczyk would consider a formula by which the new united Polish government would accept the Curzon Line *as a working arrangement* subject to the right to discuss details at the peace conference. Mikolajczyk said flatly that he was not authorized to accept such a declaration. Then, when Churchill remarked that this seemed to him by far the best chance to get agreement on the creation of a united Polish government, Mikolajczyk said that he could not agree, that he had heard that the Committee of National Liberation was claiming Lwow. Churchill answered that the great port of Danzig was more valuable then Lwow. Stalin interjected that the Soviet govern-

12 *Ibid.*

455

ment did not trade in Ukrainian soil. He denied that the Committee was claiming Lwow, saying that anyhow it would not get it. But he went on to tempt by stating that the Russians were willing to give Poland in the west not only Danzig but Stettin as well. For this Churchill offered British support also. But Mikolajczyk was not moved either by the plea or the new inducement. Whereupon Stalin remarked that he wanted to make it clear that the Soviet government did not assent to Churchill's formula regarding the Curzon Line merely as a working arrangement; that the Soviet Union could not have one frontier one day and another the next. At this point, according to Mikolajczyk's later account, "Churchill held up his hands, looked up to the ceiling in despair and wheezed. We filed out silently." [13]

Later that same evening, October 13th, Churchill and Stalin met with leaders of the Polish Committee of National Liberation, headed by Bierut, the chairman of the Polish National Council. Harriman listened. The conduct of this group left no doubt in Churchill's mind that although it was claiming a predominant place in any new Polish government, it was not truly independent. He got the definite impression ". . . that the Lublin Poles were mere pawns of Russia. They had learned and rehearsed their part so carefully that even their masters evidently felt they were overdoing it." [14]

Bierut and his group went into long, hostile criticisms of the Polish government-in-exile as reactionary, as fighting the Committee of Liberation, and as promoting civil war in Poland. They argued that it was they, not the London government, that stood for the Polish people and democracy. Before compromise between the Polish factions was possible, they insisted, the democratic Constitution would have to be recognized; and the basic principles for which the National Committee stood would have to be accepted. Of these, land reform, which had been awaited for two hundred years, they said, was in the forefront; the government had promised it but had never carried it out.

As regards frontiers, Bierut said that there should be friendly relations with the Soviet Union, and since the Committee wanted freedom and independence for the Poles they were ready to accord it to the Ukraine and White Russia; and so they wished to settle the question of Polish boundaries by recognizing the Curzon Line as the basis for the eastern frontier and to request Allied support for the rectification of Polish western frontiers by the return of historic Polish lands stolen by Germany. On this point Churchill said that as far as he and Marshal Stalin were concerned, Bierut was beating on an open door.

[13] *The Rape of Poland*, page 97.
[14] *Triumph and Tragedy*, page 235.

But after listening long to Bierut's other strictures, Churchill snorted and said that in a nutshell the Committee wanted him to believe that all right was on its side and all wrong on the side of Mikolajczyk; that he had also heard hard words from the London group. But, he continued—still trying to serve the purpose he had at heart—they had come together to reach an agreement. His eloquence went unheeded. The group continued with its list of accusations, caustically blaming the London Poles for the futile sacrifices made in the revolt at Warsaw.

Churchill and Eden tried once more (on the 14th) to get Mikolajczyk to agree to some formula on boundaries that Stalin would accept. Failing in that, Churchill again tried to get Stalin to give a little, and failed again. More flatly than ever, Stalin asserted it would have to be the Curzon Line—with possible small adjustments up to seven or eight kilometers. Churchill then said that although he was not sure of Roosevelt's position he thought the President might want to appeal strongly to Stalin to be generous to the Poles and allow them to keep Lwow. To this Stalin made no comment.

Up to the very end of his stay in Moscow, Churchill kept up his efforts to soften the opposed positions. But their repetitive course always struck the same difficulties. Churchill, in his search for unity, had to listen to Molotov's imputation that an attempt was being made to circumvent the agreement reached at Teheran; had to hear Mikolajczyk dismissed by Stalin as a "blackmailer"; and to bear with Mikolajczyk's even more stormy reproaches.[15] Once while doing so his patience broke and he accused the Polish government in London of wanting to wreck the peace of Europe, and he warned Mikolajczyk that unless the government accepted the Curzon Line it would be finished and the British government would drop it. Mikolajczyk has recorded his reaction in remembered dialogue which may have been steepened by his emotion:

"Mr. Churchill, I once asked you for permission to parachute into Poland and rejoin the underground. . . . You refused to grant me that permission. Now I ask it again."

"Why?" he asked, surprised.

"Because I prefer to die, fighting for the independence of my country, than to be hanged later by the Russians in full view of your British ambassador!"

The outburst was forgiven. Churchill appreciated that Mikolajczyk and Romer, the Foreign Minister who had come with him to Moscow, really desired a compromise and were sincere in their wish for friendship with the Soviet Union, but that of their circle they were almost alone in these ideas and sentiments.

[15] As later told by Mikolajczyk himself, *The Rape of Poland*, pages 98–99.

Between the two contending Polish groups the differences gaped large. The Committee, while willing to accept Mikolajczyk as Prime Minister of the proposed new government, would allow his associates at most only one-quarter of the Cabinet portfolios. The utmost that Mikolajczyk's group was willing to concede was that it should retain one-third of the places, yield another third to the elements in the Committee, and fill the rest with men from within Poland.

Churchill verged on depression over what looked like blank failure. He was disturbed because of the harm to the future state of Europe. He was worried also because of possible reaction in America and upon the President; he was afraid of the effect there if nothing came of these talks in Moscow; and no less afraid if Mikolajczyk was forced to settle on Stalin's terms. Then, just before the gathering at Moscow dispersed, reasons for believing a tolerable solution might still be found reappeared. Mikolajczyk came round. He told Churchill that upon his return "he was going to urge upon his London colleagues the Curzon Line, including Lwow, for the Russians." [16]

On Churchill's last day in Moscow (the 18th) Stalin saw Mikolajczyk again. It was, according to Churchill, a ". . . very friendly talk. Stalin promised to help him and Mikolajczyk promised to form and conduct a Government thoroughly friendly to the Russians. He explained his plan, but Stalin made it clear that the Lublin Poles must have a majority." [17] Then that night, after dinner, the drift of Stalin's comment to Churchill encouraged hope that he would cause the Lublin Committee to be reasonable; the issue seemed to reduce itself to the question of whether the London government should have only one-third of the places in the reformed government, since Mikolajczyk was to be its Prime Minister, or more. Churchill argued that unless it was given at least half, the Western world would not believe that an independent Polish government had been set up. The conversation was unfinished and inconclusive.

Still a curious streak of optimism trailed on, as displayed in Churchill's summing up of the prospect for Roosevelt on the 22nd, "I am hopeful that even in the next fortnight we may get a settlement. If

[16] Churchill so informed the President of his report on October 22, *Triumph and Tragedy*, page 241. This is confirmed in a memo by Harriman, recording that on the 18th Mikolajczyk told him that if Stalin continued to insist that the Curzon Line be accepted, he and Romer would return to London and try to get their colleagues to agree to it. Then, provided Stalin gave him reasonable assurance of an equitable and workable accord about the formation of a united Polish government, he would return to Moscow.

[17] *Triumph and Tragedy*, page 240. This is confirmed by Harriman's memo of his talk with Mikolajczyk on the 18th. But the impression given by Mikolajczyk in his own later account is different. *The Rape of Poland*, pages 99–100. The official Polish memo bears out Churchill's and Harriman's version.

so I will cable you the exact form so that you can say whether you want it published or delayed." [18]

A resumption of the discussions was expected after Mikolajczyk consulted his Cabinet in London and his commanders. The President and the State Department waited upon their course and the advent of the American elections. They would say nothing before then, but thought that if in the interval no solution was found, they might be able to salvage one later. But they were not going to allow the current chapter in the sad struggle over Poland that had gone on for two centuries to destroy plans for permanent peace, or for cooperation in bringing the Pacific war to a quick end. Poland was the bread of the martyrs.

Let us revert briefly, as of historical interest, to the flurry caused by Molotov's statement during the meeting with Mikolajczyk on October 13th that Roosevelt had, at Teheran, approved the Curzon Line, but had not thought it advisable to say so publicly. No one in his audience either confirmed or denied—at the moment and in Mikolajczyk's presence—this version of what Roosevelt had said at Teheran. Harriman later explained to the President why he had not done so: because Molotov did not refer to him for corroboration and he was present only as an observer, he had thought it would only make matters worse if he tried to correct Molotov's statement.

He had asked Churchill at dinner that night about the episode, and the Prime Minister had told him that to the best of his memory of what had occurred at Teheran, although the President showed interest in hearing his views and those of Stalin, he had not expressed any opinion one way or the other. But Molotov may have been alluding to what had or had not been said at a talk between Roosevelt and Stalin at Teheran on December 1st—at which Churchill had not been present. Stalin clearly had that particular conversation in mind when Churchill, a few days later (October 16th), said that his memory of the talks at Teheran did not conform to Molotov's statement that the President had accepted the Curzon Line. Stalin answered gruffly that "he was his own witness" and that the President had done so in a "separate talk." [19] Churchill did not pursue the question of what Roosevelt may have said in the past; he remarked merely that not knowing the President's views he could not speak for him, but he believed that the President felt that the Poles were entitled to Lwow.

[18] *Triumph and Tragedy,* page 241.
[19] See preceding pages 284–85 for the American record of this talk between Roosevelt and Stalin on December 1st, 1943 at Teheran and page 459 for Roosevelt's reference at the Yalta Conference to the attitude on the subject which he had expressed at Teheran.

In the interval Mikolajczyk had sent a letter to Harriman on the 16th saying how much he and his colleagues had been surprised and upset by Molotov's disclosure. Well they might have been if the recalled version which Mikolajczyk set forth in this letter of what Roosevelt had said to him in Washington in June 1944 was accurate, rather than an emotional misconstruction.[20]

Harriman answered Mikolajczyk that his understanding was that the President had not, at Teheran, agreed to the Curzon Line; that he had made it plain that he did not intend to take any position on this boundary question either privately or publicly.

48. Churchill in Moscow: Soviet Entry into the Pacific War

In all matters European—military and political—Churchill and his advisers took the initiative with the Russians, bore the rub of argument and decision. Harriman was the observer, the confidante, the liaison with the President who wanted to know everything that was said and done without entering into the record. But on questions connected with the war against Japan and the future of the Pacific, Churchill stepped aside, passing the lead to the Americans—Harriman and General Deane.

Agreement among the three Allies on strategic plans and schedules was urgently needed if they were to have the advantages of coordinated assault upon the common enemy. Events were beckoning them to hurry. It was only in China that the Japanese were still advancing, and there against unequipped, underfed, badly led, straggling troops. In Burma, though fighting with utmost stamina, they were just managing to hold on to their last positions. More of the Japanese merchant shipping fleet was at the bottom of the Pacific than still afloat. Its navy and air force were badly smashed; the next great engagements might finish them off. The lines of communication to the bases and sources of supply in the Southern Pacific were under constant destroying attack.

The talks at Moscow could go forward with the knowledge of great

---

[20] According to Mikolajczyk, he had been told by the President that the American government opposed the settlement of territorial questions before the war ended; that only Stalin and Churchill had agreed to the Curzon Line; that the President had made it clear he did not regard this as satisfactory, and that at the appropriate time he would help Poland retain Lwow, Drohobycz, and Tarnopol and get East Prussia, including Konigsberg, as well as Silesia. *The Rape of Poland,* pages 59–61.

impending ventures. Air assaults on the air fields between the Philippines and Japan in preparation for the landing on Leyte had been started; MacArthur's great expedition was on its way there; and once that was won the plans called for a quick progression of attack upon Luzon and other island positions. There were also to be operations on the Chinese coast, of use for blockade and air bombardment, and a possible fling at Formosa. If all these actions succeeded, by the end of 1944 the Japanese detachments scattered over the South Pacific—in Burma, Thailand, the Malay Peninsula, and the Dutch East Indies— would be isolated and vulnerable. The Americans would have air bases so close to the Japanese home islands that these would be at the mercy of our great, and growing greater, heavy bombing force. Then, after Germany was defeated, there would be the great American and British forces that were fighting in Europe—ground, air, and naval—that could be devoted to the final stages of the struggle against Japan, wherever needed to complete their expulsion and destruction.

All this was—must have been—visible to the American and British strategists at the time of these discussions in Moscow. But they were seen not in the calm afterwards of the study, but in the suffering and danger of each day of war that was being lived through: the agony of landing on beaches and struggling up hills through fire and flame, the Kamikaze suicide torpedo bombers who flung themselves against the bridges of blockading ships, the planes that hit peaks in the Himalayas or were found by the Japanese antiaircraft guns. The outcome might be certain, but the Japanese were deemed to have it in their power to determine how much and how long an ordeal would yet have to be endured.

There would be very large Japanese armies in the home islands, China, and Manchuria still to be overcome, both the American and British Chiefs of Staff envisioned. For the expected fearsome last land battles, the huge Red armies were wanted to take part of the crush off the Americans and Chinese. Thus the American government had continued to wish for a second or third front on the mainland of Asia, much as the Russians had wanted one in Europe. The British were as eager to have the Russians come into the Pacific War as the Americans, and on the same simple grounds.[21] On October 4th, in a review of his intentions for the President, Churchill had said, ". . . We want to elicit the time it will take after the German downfall for a superior Russian Army to be gathered opposite the Japanese on the frontiers of Manchukuo, and to hear from them the problems of this campaign. . . ."[22]

[21] *Triumph and Tragedy,* page 215.
[22] *Ibid.,* page 219.

The Americans were then waiting Stalin's signal to start talks with Soviet Chiefs of Staff about Russia's part in the Pacific War. It had been contemplated that these would be, at the beginning anyhow, between the Americans and Russians only. But here was Churchill, coming along with a complement of senior military advisers. The American Military Mission in Moscow and Harriman, on first learning of this, were uneasy. They were concerned lest the Prime Minister's initiative might either retard or confuse the detailed discussions of plans that were needed. But there was no cause for worry. Churchill readily consented that Harriman and Deane should participate, if the President approved, in all his talks about the Far East; and that the primary purpose should be to get Stalin's responses to the questions and proposals presented by the U.S. Joint Chiefs of Staff.

Harriman hurried word to the President that he was satisfied that a meeting of this kind would develop information of great importance that could not be obtained quickly in any other way, and would aid rather than hurt Deane's subsequent talks. Moreover, he said he was sure that Churchill would make it plain to Stalin that, though the British would bear their full share in the Pacific, planning was an American responsibility, and that the consultations to follow would be Soviet-American and not three-cornered, the British being kept informed. The President answered that Harriman was correct in assuming that he would want it made clear that the Pacific campaign would remain an American command. But he left the way open for Churchill, as a preface to eliciting information about Soviet plans, to outline to Stalin the contemplated strategy in the Pacific, centering perhaps on what part the British were going to play. It was for Harriman and Deane to work out how to link up their staff talks with Churchill's presentation. That proved easy to do.

The chance came on October 14th in the course of the review of military situations and projects, the European segment of which has already been surveyed. General Brooke, in duet with Churchill, told what was being done and planned for Burma, China, and Southeast Asia, and what the British military effort in the Far East was to be. Then General Deane summed up the course of the war in the Pacific thus far, and the further objectives in mind, ending in the invasion of Japan. This section of his exposition ended with the statement: "The most important factor in the development of the overall strategic situation will be in the part which the Soviet Union is to play. Plans have been developed for all possible lines of approach against Japan from the east, south and west. However . . . these plans can be most effectively selected and applied if they are thoroughly concerted with plans to be developed for operations against Japan from the north."

Stalin asked how the American military authorities thought the Soviet armed forces could best be used. Deane explained the plans which had been transmitted to him by the Joint Chiefs. In summary, he said they would most like the Russians to enter the Pacific War as soon as possible and in all available strength; and that they felt it urgent to start to prepare for combined operations at once. He enumerated the tasks which it was hoped the Soviet forces would first of all carry out:

1. To make the Vladivostok Peninsula and Trans-Siberian Railway secure;

2. To conduct along with American air forces a joint attack on Japan from the Maritime Provinces and Kamchatka;

3. To cut off movement by sea and air between Japan and the Asiatic mainland;

4. In conjunction with American naval forces to secure the supply route across the Pacific to the Maritime Provinces—which would involve Soviet military occupation of Southern Sakhalin;

5. To destroy Japanese ground and air forces in Manchuria. This last was to be the principal and ultimate object of the Soviet forces.

On the next day (the 15th) the Soviet authorities gave their answer. It was full and opened up a prospect of immense intervention. After reviewing five possible operational routes south for the Red land armies, General Antonov presented an estimate of the Japanese forces that would be met. Anticipating large transfers from Japan and China, he forecast that the Japanese could (or would) assemble in Manchuria some forty, perhaps up to fifty, well-equipped divisions.[23] To deal with such a force, Antonov went on, the existing Soviet army in the Far East would have to be doubled in size—from the thirty divisions to sixty.[24] This was to be done by transfers from the west. The Soviet tactical and bombing air forces in the Far East were also to be greatly increased. It was understood that a large American bombing force would be operating along with the Russians from Soviet bases.

These and connected tasks would take, Antonov estimated, about three months after Germany was defeated. At this point Stalin spoke

[23] This was a much higher fix, it may be noted, than any the Americans and British were making, and excessive. It turned out to be at least double the number of Japanese that were met in Manchuria when the Russians finally marched in.

Actually in October the Kwantung Army was being depleted to defend the Philippines and Formosa, and for the advance in China. Later it was enlarged, but it never became half as strong as Antonov's forecast.

[24] Antonov, however, was calculating that Russian divisions had 10,000 men, while he estimated that the Japanese divisions in Manchuria counted 18,000 men.

up, ". . . he believed that sufficient supplies could be accumulated in three months to maintain the Soviet forces for a period of one and a half to two months. This would be sufficient to deal a mortal blow against Japan." Then, after Harriman had affirmed that the American government was ready to start to furnish the extra supplies for the enlarged Soviet forces in the Far East as fast as it could without interfering with shipments for the war in Europe, Stalin had repeated that the Soviet Union would be ready to take action against Japan in about three months after the collapse of Germany. "In three months—yes. After the building up of supplies, in several months."

Harriman, as instructed, renewed the earlier American offer to send the Soviet Air Force four-engine bombers and to train their crews. Stalin said he had heard that the deliveries of these planes presented many problems, so he would not press for them; but if the difficulties could be met, he would like to have them at once, and to have the training of the crews in Russia start soon. He once again confirmed that bases for the American bombing forces in Kamchatka and the Maritime Provinces would be provided.

It was arranged that the Americans and Russians should carry these discussions into further detail. For this they met on the 17th again, and then the sphere of Soviet operations was drawn more definitely. Stalin was ready with the requested list of the supplies which the Soviet government sought from the United States in connection with its entry into the war. These were to form the reserve stock which would assure that the campaign could be carried on even though the Port of Vladivostok was closed. The total was over a million tons in addition to those supplies already scheduled to be sent to the Soviet Union under the current Fourth Protocol.

Stalin outlined the plans for vast ground campaigns which he had in mind. He asked Harriman whether the Joint Chiefs were considering joint land operations. Harriman answered that they were not, that it was contemplated that only Soviet forces would be used in Manchuria. Stalin then said:

"If we are thinking seriously about defeating the Japanese, we cannot be limited to the Manchurian region. We shall strike direct blows from different directions in Manchuria. But to have real results we must develop outflanking movements—blows at Kalgan and Peking. Otherwise the assaults in Manchuria alone will produce no important results. I do not believe that the major battles will be so much in Manchuria as in the south where Japanese troops are to be expected to be found when they withdraw from China. The problem that faces us is to prevent the Japanese from withdrawing from China into Manchuria.

464

Our objective is to see to it that the Japanese forces in China cannot be used by the Japanese in Manchuria. That is my observation. Regarding the other objectives set forth by General Deane—I have no objection."

Later on he expressed agreement with the American decision to abstain from operations in China except for some landing on the coast to take airfields. "The Americans," he said, "would cut off the Japanese garrisons on the southern islands and the Russians would cut off the Japanese land forces in China. He agreed that this was the proper plan—however, it would be difficult to effect it." Conjunctively he remarked that the American design to invade Japan was a "grand undertaking."

As for naval and landing operations in places near the Maritime Provinces, he fell in with the proposals of the Joint Chiefs, and identified in detail what he would be pleased to have the Americans do. "All the sea positions," he volunteered, "should be strengthened and then the northern Korean ports should be occupied by Soviet land and sea forces." In answer to a question, he also said that he wanted American naval forces in the Japan Sea.

General Deane remarked that, "As Marshal Stalin has outlined his operations the two plans were in coordination."

To foretell, the President and the Joint Chiefs were enthusiastic about the Soviet program. The great visualized spread southward of the Red Army caused no alarm. They did not want to have to use large American ground forces in China and Manchuria, and placed little reliance on the Chinese armies. American plans, especially air and naval, were readjusted to conform to the combined intentions. Orders were given to see that the Soviet Union got what it needed for its part in the Pacific War. Save for a few special items, such as hospital ships, seagoing tugs, and certain types of aircraft, what had been asked for was scheduled and gradually sent. Extra shipping wanted in all combat theaters was assigned to the route to Siberia. The Soviet government, in order that shipping might be saved, agreed to do without many of the supplies it was to have received under the Fourth Lend-Lease Protocol.

The satisfaction of the American government at all this progress and preparation for Soviet entry into the Pacific War was not spoiled by the fact that Stalin had made it clear that the Soviet government expected a reward for doing so.

When, on October 15th, Stalin had extended his assurance that the Soviet Union would enter the war three months after the collapse of

Germany, he had gone on to say that, however, ". . . there were also certain political aspects which would have to be taken into consideration. The Russians would have to know what they were fighting for. They had certain claims against Japan."

This was the first time that Stalin had made clear that, *before* entering the war, he would want to have a precise understanding in regard to what the Soviet Union was to get out of the defeat of Japan. Most of his desires, it will be recalled, had been sketched out to Roosevelt at Teheran. But up to then Stalin had allowed it to be supposed that the Soviet Union would come into the war against Japan in the same way that the United States had come into the war against Germany, leaving national claims to be settled in due course after victory. Neither Eden, substituting for Churchill, who was ill on that day, nor Harriman, who was without instruction in the matter, made any immediate comment on this revelation of how Stalin intended to proceed.

Eden told Churchill of it. But the Prime Minister let it pass, perhaps because he thought the subject was in the realm of greater American interest. Harriman included this news in his reports to the President, and Deane presumably in his to the Joint Chiefs of Staff. Neither reacted; there was no objection such as was being maintained against similar Soviet attempts to secure advance recognition of its claims in Europe. The available records do not tell why. But it is possible that the knowledge gained of the vast scope of prospective Soviet land operations stimulated the opinion that it might be well to have an understanding about Soviet claims before the Soviet armies began to march. They would be sweeping around and through all parts of Manchuria. They would be continuing their advance to Kalgan and Peking within Northern China and perhaps beyond, if that was where Japanese armies were to be met. They might also be coming by land and sea to take the ports and towns of North Korea. These movements would place them not far from the regions dominated by the Chinese Communists. Our plans did not include any steps to forestall or restrict the spread of the Soviet forces in the north. How, then, could it be assured that they would withdraw, that they would not use the presence of their soldiers to impose their desires upon China?

Foreknowledge, then, of what the location of military forces was likely to be at the end of the war against Japan might well have influenced the President to act as he did—that is, to prepare to settle with Stalin what the Soviet Union might be promised. This could be regarded either as a tribute to be paid because the Soviet government could and would exact it anyhow; or as a fair penalty for Japan (for its aggression) and China (for its weakness) to suffer, and a fair reward for the Soviet Union to receive.

Churchill had a better chance to talk continuously and freely with Stalin than at any time before, and he used it well. They reviewed subjects of joint interest in set meetings, with staffs and colleagues present. But they took many meals together, as well; met alone or in small company at any time in the afternoon, evening, or late night; and once, on the 17th, stayed together, glass and bottle near, till almost four in the morning.

The social occasions were lightened by good humor—open display of warm feelings by Churchill, touches of admiring or teasing regard by Stalin. As when at supper, served between acts of a special ballet at the Opera House, someone, on raising his glass in a toast to the Big Three, alluded to them as the Holy Trinity, Stalin japed, "Churchill must be the Holy Ghost, for he flies about so much." Mingled with their talk about public business, there were turns of comment or reminiscence which seemed to flow between men who meant something to each other as individuals, not merely officials in conference—as when, in their revel of talk into the early hours of the morning, Stalin spoke long of his days of exile in Siberia.

Of this experience Churchill was later to write, "There is no doubt that in our narrow circle we talked with an ease, freedom, and cordiality never before attained between our two countries. Stalin made several expressions of personal regard which I feel sure were sincere. But I became even more convinced that he was by no means alone. As I said to my colleagues at home, 'Behind the horseman sits black care.'" [25] Perhaps so, but quite far behind right then. For Stalin at that time had reason to be jovial, even jubilant. Soviet forces had attained assured superiority along the whole of the Eastern Front in Europe in whatever direction they might choose to take.

All three Allies thought much good had come out of the Churchill visit to Moscow. It was judged that the stress over many political situations in Europe—actual and prospective—had been eased, and dangers of dissension lessened.

But more than these half-sewn compromises, the concert of strategy for going on with the war in both Europe and the Pacific was esteemed of great value. The British and the Americans could feel sure that the Germans would not be able to strengthen their resistance in the west by moving in forces from the east. The Russians could have a corresponding sense of protection for their armies on the Eastern Front. The Americans and British could count on the robust Russian troops to subdue the Japanese in Asia, and if need be help in the invasion of Japan. The Russians could be fairly sure that before they were called

[25] *Triumph and Tragedy,* page 238.

upon to do so, the Japanese power to sustain a long fight would have been broken. They had just made clear their vast plan for operations in Manchuria and no objection had been met; and they had summed up their huge requests for weapons and supplies for use in the Far East and had every reason to think most would be granted.

Both Churchill and Stalin in their public statements as well as in their private reports expressed their sense of accomplishment in words marked by unusual warmth.

Thus Churchill wrote to Stalin on leaving Moscow on October 20th: "Eden and I have come away from the Soviet Union refreshed and fortified by the discussions which we had with you, Marshal Stalin, and with your colleagues. This memorable meeting in Moscow has shown that there are no matters that cannot be adjusted between us when we meet together in frank and intimate discussion." [26]

A week later in the House of Commons he said, "I am very glad to inform the House that our relations with Soviet Russia were never more close, intimate and cordial than they are at the present time. Never before have we been able to reach so high a degree of frank and friendly discussions of the most delicate and often potentially vexatious topics. . . ."

How different a mood of judgment from that of the spring before the second front, and from that which was again soon to descend upon him! The studious recorder can hardly evade the curious conclusion that Churchill's view of what might be hoped and expected of the Russian rulers were more volatile than Roosevelt's, that his spirit kept closer rhythm with passing experience.

Stalin spoke to the same effect as Churchill—telling the President: "On my part I can say that our conversations were extremely useful for the mutual ascertaining of views. . . . During the conversations it has been clarified that we can, without great difficulties, adjust our policy on all questions standing before us, and if we are not in a position so far to provide an immediate necessary decision of this or that task, as for example, on the Polish question, but nevertheless, more favourable perspectives are opened. . . ." [27]

To his own people on November 6th he said substantially the same thing: "The recent talks in Moscow with Mr. Churchill, the head of the British government, and Mr. Eden, the British Foreign Secretary, are to be viewed as an even more striking indication of the consolidation of the United Nations front, held as these talks were in an atmosphere of friendship and a spirit of perfect unanimity."

[26] *Ibid.*, pages 242–43.
[27] *Yalta Documents*, page 9. Message dated October 19th, received by Roosevelt on the 22nd.

Roosevelt took a complaisant view of the course and outcome of the talks, even if he was not quite as openly pleased. His anxiety that Churchill and Stalin might, together and without him, make decisions which he would not like had turned out to be needless. His wish not to be drawn into the settlement of questions that might hurt his prospects at the election, now only a few weeks away, had been respected with care. And, most important in his eyes, was the progress made in joining together the assaults from East and West against Germany, and the knowledge that the Soviet Union would throw its huge forces into the fight against Japan within three months after Germany was defeated.

Whatever their inmost thoughts and fears were, seemingly none of the three foresaw how brief a time this circlet of satisfaction would last. Some of the loose political accords conceived at Moscow began to prove so disappointing that by the beginning of January (the 8th) Churchill, in the course of correspondence with Roosevelt about their joint plans for meeting with Stalin—which was at long last about to come off—wrote: "What are your ideas of the length of our stay at Yalta? This may well be a fateful Conference, coming at a moment when the Great Allies are so divided and the shadow of the war lengthens out before us. At the present time I think the end of this war may well prove to be more disappointing than was the last." [28]

But before telling of the events that inspired this foreboding, we ought to take note of the reemergence of France as another country to be reckoned with in these attempts to demarcate the world after the war.

<hr/>

49. The Further Recognition of France

<hr/>

On his return to London from Moscow, Churchill got news that the American government had abruptly decided to accept the French Committee of National Liberation as the provisional government of France. He had been trying to persuade the President to take this step. He had cited the many ways in which he thought the Committee had shown itself qualified and acceptable. It had cooperated well with Supreme Allied Military Headquarters. Under its guidance a free and orderly civilian life had been restored throughout the provinces and cities of the liberated sections of France. De Gaulle had absorbed in his

[28] *Triumph and Tragedy,* page 341.

executive organization new members from the resistance groups and political parties inside France, including the Communists. Firm plans had been announced similarly to enlarge the Consultative Assembly, to which the Committee reported, by including members from inside France; to call it together in Paris in November; to increase its authority over the executive; and to prepare the way for free national elections at the earliest suitable time. Along this whole course of action the French people had warmly approved the leadership of the National Committee.

Alluding to these solid reasons, on October 14th from Moscow Churchill had suggested to Roosevelt, ". . . that we can now safely recognize General de Gaulle's administration as the Provisional Government of France." [29] Roosevelt had still held back, telling Churchill that he preferred to wait until the French had set up a real Zone of the Interior, and the Consultative Assembly had actually been made more representative. "I should," he said, "be inclined to hang recognition on the effective completion of both these acts." [30]

Within hours after Churchill had been so advised by Roosevelt, the Joint- Chiefs of Staff received word from Eisenhower that he had reached an agreement with the French Committee regarding the formation of a Zone of the Interior under French control, to be announced on the 23rd. Roosevelt had at once sent off a secret and personal message to Stalin, in which he said that it was expected that the French, by agreement, would in the very near future set up a real Zone of the Interior; and that he thought that when this was done it would be an appropriate time to grant this recognition. "I am informing you," the message concluded, "of our intentions in this regard in advance in the event that you may wish, when the Zone of Interior is set up under French administration, to take some similar action." [31]

Then without waiting for Stalin's answer, the State Department— the President being out of Washington—bounded into action. It hustled off urgent messages to Molotov and the British Foreign Office, informing them that the President had decided to recognize the Provisional Government in France concurrently with the announcement by the French of the creation of the Zone of the Interior, which was expected on October 23rd. The British Foreign Office at once let de Gaulle know it would take the same action. By special efforts of diplomatic staffs,

[29] *Ibid.*, page 247.

[30] This, as printed, is dated October 20th, but it may have been written a day or two before.

[31] This message was transmitted by George Kennan, who was in charge of the Embassy since Harriman had left for Washington, in a letter to Molotov dated October 21st. Churchill, at this time, was en route home by air from Moscow to London via Cairo.

the announcements of the three governments were timed to be simultaneous. The reasons for the American procedure had been circumstantial rather than purposive, but it is not to be wondered that Churchill was startled, and perhaps briefly under the impression that the Americans had been either careless or sharp toward him and the Russians.[32]

Ambassadors were at once accredited by all three Allies to their posts in Paris. The formal readmission of France as a main member of the war coalition was a healthy step forward that gave satisfaction. But it was soon to become evident that the French had ideas of their own on some of the most difficult of European problems, especially Germany, which were going to make it harder to arrive at a common policy. France was saved for the West. But its impassioned claims and opinions were sometimes going to distract the efforts of the United States and Great Britain to hold their own in times of difficulty with the Soviet Union.

De Gaulle lost no time in claiming a part and chance second to none in all decisions having to do with war settlements and postwar arrangements. The new Provisional Government had been assured by agreement reached at Dumbarton Oaks of a place on the Security Council of the United Nations Organization. But it did not seem to be in haste to secure its title to that role. In contrast, it urgently pressed its previous petition for membership as an equal on the European Advisory Commission, which was working on terms for Germany. The Soviet government was first to propose that this be accorded. The others assented, though not without misgiving, for the new member was almost certain to want to review the past work of the Commission. It was agreed that each should extend the invitation on Armistice Day, November 11th. This was done and the French member began to take part in the discussions of the Commission soon afterward.

By then, as will be told, the French Provisional Government was seeking a separate zone of occupation in Germany and a separate command. In order first to take over more of the battle line on the Western Front, and then to be able to share adequately in the occupation of Germany, de Gaulle renewed the request for equipment for eight more

[32] In *Triumph and Tragedy,* page 249, he prints the text of the message which he dispatched to Roosevelt after learning of the American decision. Its opening sentence was, "I was naturally surprised at the very sharp tone taken by the State Department, and on arrival here [London] find the announcement is to be made tomorrow [meaning the 23rd]. We shall of course take similar and simultaneous action. I think it likely that the Russians will be offended. . . ."

Obviously he did not know of the preparatory notification which the President had sent to Stalin.

divisions of troop recruits from metropolitan France. Churchill told him (during a joyous visit he paid to Paris for Armistice Day ceremonies) that the British government would favor the French taking over the occupation of as much of Germany as their capacity allowed. In informing Roosevelt of this in a message on November 15th, he explained, "One must always realize that before five years are out a French Army must be made to take on the main task of holding down Germany." [33] The Joint Chiefs were in favor of providing the means for this French rearmament, and more, as soon as they were available. But the President doubted whether he had the authority. His comment, when so advising Churchill (on November 18th), shows that he still did not foresee any need to keep American forces in Europe to support his diplomacy: "I, of course, sympathize with the French point of view and hope that we may all be able to help her meet postwar responsibilities. You know, of course, that after Germany's collapse I must bring American troops home as rapidly as transportation problems will permit . . ."

This alarmed Churchill. If, he said in his return message, after Germany's collapse American troops were brought home that fast, and: ". . . if the French are to have no equipped postwar army or time to make one, or to give it battle experience, how will it be possible to hold down Western Germany beyond the present Russian occupied line? We certainly could not undertake the task without your aid and that of the French. All would therefore rapidly disintegrate as it did last time." [34]

The President's answer (on the 26th) to this was not too reassuring: that it should be possible to get enough equipment for the French occupation force from the defeated German Army; and, in any event, he did not have as yet authority to equip "any postwar foreign army" and the prospect of getting it from Congress was not good.

De Gaulle seemed to have achieved a real basis of easy friendship with Churchill and the British government. In the daily conduct of both civil and military activities in France his administration was getting on well with General Eisenhower and the Allied High Command. His first contacts with the new American Ambassador, Caffery, were going pleasantly. The American government was relaxing its guard against French participation in high councils of the Allies.

But de Gaulle was not satisfied to remain dependent on British and American good will for the gradual acquisition of favor, influence, and

[33] *Ibid.*, page 253.
[34] *Yalta Documents*, pages 286–87.

strength. He exerted himself to make his relationship with the Soviet government secure. It is possible to identify at least two ways in which he hoped the closer association with Moscow would justify itself. It might steady the position of his government and the situation in France, for the French Communists were a numerous political party and he was trying hard to get along with them, especially with Thorez, whom he thought "the best of the lot." It might increase his weight in dealing with the British and American governments.

So, soon after his warm reunion in Paris with Churchill, consulting neither the American nor the British government, de Gaulle let Stalin know that he would like to go to Moscow to contact the leaders of the Soviet government. The trip was arranged for the end of November. Stalin informed Churchill of the prospective visit, remarking that he did not know its objectives. Churchill hastened to assure him (on November 25th) that he was glad that de Gaulle was going to see him and hoped that the two of them would talk over the whole field of European affairs together. He developed his thoughts about the widening of the circle of association; the British government, he said, had not given consideration to a Western European bloc; that he trusted first of all to the British Treaty of Alliance with the Soviet Union and close collaboration with the United States as mainstays of a world organization to insure peace; and he thought that any European arrangements ought to be subsequent to and subordinate to such a world structure.

De Gaulle, on arrival in Moscow on December 2nd, was accorded the full honors due a Chief of State. On December 2nd, probably just before his first talk with de Gaulle, Stalin sent roughly identical messages to Roosevelt and Churchill to let them know that he expected that de Gaulle would want to discuss two questions in particular: (1) The conclusion of a Franco-Soviet pact of mutual assistance similar to the Anglo-Soviet Pact. About that, Stalin commented, "We can hardly object but I should like to know your view on this subject. Please give your advice." (2) The possible extension of the eastern frontier of France to the left bank of the Rhine. Stalin pointed out that such an action might compete with the scheme for forming a Rhenish-Westphalian province under international control now being studied. About this also he asked the views of his American and British associates.

Quickly, after his first talk with de Gaulle, Stalin let Churchill and Roosevelt know that de Gaulle had raised these questions, and told them of his answers. He had said that there would be a need for close study of the proposal of a Franco-Soviet pact and particularly the question of who would ratify this pact in France under present circumstances. In regard to extending the frontiers of France to the Rhine, he had stressed the complexity of the question and expressed the idea that it could not be solved without the knowledge and consent of all the main Allies. The account which Bidault, the French Foreign Minister who accompanied de Gaulle, gave Harriman and the British Chargé d'Affaires in Moscow of this same talk, can be regarded either as varying from or adding to Stalin's report. The French Foreign Minister said that at this first meeting Stalin had proposed a *military* alliance with France, explaining that he had in mind mutual protection against possible German aggression in the future; that de Gaulle had indicated this was acceptable; and that subsequently the French delegation had submitted a preliminary draft along the lines of the Anglo-Soviet Treaty but not identical. Bidault explained that it was contemplated that this treaty would be within the framework of the international security organization.

Whether Stalin's or Bidault's version of this talk is the more nearly correct, memory will note the striking difference in Stalin's tone and policy in regard to both de Gaulle and France from those he had displayed at Teheran a year before. Instead of ridicule of de Gaulle's leadership, as not representing the real France, there was now sympathetic regard. The attitude that France ought to be made to pay hard and long for yielding to the Germans was subdued. The idea that many of the French colonies ought to be detached was allowed to languish in silence.

Churchill responded first to Stalin's request for advice, on December 5th. He informed the Marshal that the British government would not object to a Franco-Soviet pact of mutual assistance similar to the Anglo-Soviet Pact; on the contrary, he thought it desirable as an additional bond. He went on to remark that it might be best of all if a tripartite treaty were concluded, embodying the existing Anglo-Soviet Treaty, in this way making the obligations of the three identical and linked together from the start. About the several proposals—to change the eastern frontier of France to the left bank of the Rhine, or to form a Rhenish-Westphalian Province under international control, or other alternatives—the Prime Minister said he was not ready to state a definite opinion. He thought that the decision might be postponed until the peace settlement, thus allowing more chance for discussion between himself, Roosevelt, and Stalin and also in the EAC, of which France was now a member.

Roosevelt had asked Churchill for his views before answering Stalin's inquiries, and his reply (sent on the 6th) blended with Churchill's. In telling Churchill of the answer he was making to Stalin, the President remarked that although he appreciated the advantages Churchill saw in a tripartite pact, he was somewhat afraid of the effect which this might have on the formation of the international security organization. But he added that he realized it was a subject of primary concern to the three countries involved.

Harriman had a long and candid talk with de Gaulle on this same day, December 6th. This threw more light on the area of negotiation. Neither Stalin in his reports to Roosevelt and Churchill, nor Bidault in his talk with Harriman, had specified what the Soviet government wanted. Latent in the idea of an effective military pact was an arrangement assuring both members of quick access to Germany—France by control of the Rhineland, the Soviet Union by control of Poland. De Gaulle admitted that he hoped, by assenting to the Soviet wish to transfer to Poland all the territory east of the Oder River, to get Stalin's approval of the Rhine as Germany's western frontier, and the plan for placing the Ruhr under international control. He confirmed that Stalin had reserved decision on these French aspirations.

Then he told Harriman that Stalin had asked him to send a representative to the Polish government in Lublin—which was a new element in the possible bargain. De Gaulle was vague as to the import of the response he had made to this suggestion. Harriman impressed upon him how greatly disturbed the American and British governments would be if he granted recognition to the Lublin group.

Then when Harriman saw him again later that same evening at a reception, de Gaulle told him that he had in the interval talked with Stalin again, and that he had made it clear to Stalin that he wanted to wait in the hope that the different Polish factions could be harmonized, and that in any event he could not take this step without first consulting the American and British governments.

De Gaulle said he was afraid that the Soviet government intended not only to try to expand its influence in Eastern Europe but to incorporate some of the neighboring states within the Soviet Union. He predicted that this would meet with resistance, and that although the Soviet government would succeed in imposing its will on some or all of these countries, there would be prolonged political uncertainty and instability in them. Then, turning his thoughts back to France, he said that the Communist Party in his country took its orders from Moscow; that he thought it would abandon its revolutionary aims but that under the guise of urging radical social programs would continue to create trouble. He was satisfied that the Soviet government would use the French party as a means of furthering its own policy rather than in an effort to bring about a Communist France.

Despite this grasp of the portent of Soviet aims, de Gaulle continued to want a treaty of alliance with the Soviet Union. Stalin—probably influenced by the reply which Churchill had made to him—suggested the alternative of a three-country pact, including Great Britain. That, de Gaulle argued, would be premature, since in his opinion there were still too many matters to be worked out between the British and French governments. Stalin did not insist. But he and Molotov tried very hard to get de Gaulle to give in about Poland, to desert the Polish government-in-exile in London, and to agree in connection with the signing of the Franco-Soviet Pact to assign an official representative to the Lublin government.

At the dinner which Stalin on the 9th gave at the Kremlin for the French, Harriman noted that Stalin was in high humor but de Gaulle was stiff and cold. Stalin thought wine might thaw him, or broad humor, as when he called Bulganin over and said, "Bring out the machine guns. Let's liquidate the diplomats." Molotov was again urging recognition of the Lublin government. De Gaulle and Bidault were again refusing. De Gaulle left the Kremlin soon after the dinner was over, believing that he would have to leave Moscow the next morning empty-handed—without the treaty which he desired. Bidault stayed on to talk with Molotov, while Stalin regaled his other guests. Late in the night he sent a message asking de Gaulle to return to the Kremlin. When he did, Stalin appealed to him once again to support the Lublin Committee, emphasizing the need for a friendly Poland to avert a possible future German threat. But de Gaulle stood firm. Equivalently Stalin continued to reserve his position in regard to the eastern frontier of France. Both proposals were, in the upshot, dropped. At six-thirty in the morning of the 10th the Franco-Soviet accord was signed.

It was a rather simple mutual assistance pact. The chief value to each party was protection against the chance that the other might, either before or after the war ended, make a bargain with or about Germany of the wrong sort. The accord was welcomed by the people of both countries and so won popularity for its authors. But the experience did not bring Stalin and de Gaulle or their associates close together, or produce real trust. Neither had been able to win over the other as much as he had hoped. De Gaulle was displeased because he had not secured Soviet support for his claims upon Germany, and displeased by his impressions of Soviet policy. Stalin found de Gaulle awkward and stubborn; and, if the scornful view of French conduct which Stalin had exposed in the past is recalled, probably thought French claims presumptuous. But the official announcement of the pact and the press treatment in both countries were marked only by friendly satisfaction.

It may be that de Gaulle thought that this new bond with the Soviet Union would gain for him admission into the next prospective meeting of the Heads of State. Churchill favored the idea; Stalin was lackluster; and Roosevelt opposed it.

De Gaulle in identical notes to the American, British, and Soviet governments served notice that if the great allied powers should decide in advance, without French participation, questions which interested France directly or indirectly ". . . the Provisional Government of the French Republic evidently could not consider itself bound by any of the decisions taken without it and, consequently, such decisions lose some of their value." [35] The warning did not affect the President, and Churchill and Stalin did not press him. The three were finding it hard enough to agree upon a time, place, and program for their talks; unless imperative, why make it even harder?

To soften the effect of his firm refusal to have de Gaulle at Yalta, Roosevelt asked Hopkins to stop off in Paris to call upon him. The American government was in increasing measure striving to satisfy French wishes. Policy was being transformed gradually in accord with the recommendations which the State Department and Joint Chiefs of Staff made to the President shortly before he left for that Conference, ". . . to treat France in all respects on the basis of her potential power and influence rather than on the basis of her present strength" [36] In sum: (1) The President approved in principle French requests made in the EAC for equal French participation in the surrender, occupation, and control of Germany, and informed the Soviet and British governments accordingly. (2) But the President and the State Department maintained their reserve about French aspirations to assimilate the Rhineland, if not at once, eventually. (3) The Combined Chiefs of Staff approved a recommendation by Eisenhower to equip eight additional French combat divisions as soon as possible. (4) However, the President continued to defer decision on de Gaulle's request, supported by the British, that we also provide weapons for a postwar army, which presumably would have been employed not only for the occupation of Germany but for the general defense of France.[37]

While these events, attendant upon the reemergence of France as an important element in the life of the coalition, were going on, the situation on the Western Front was being dangerously threatened by a

---

[35] *Yalta Documents,* page 296.

[36] Briefing Book Paper on France. *Yalta Documents,* pages 300–304.

[37] See telegram from Acting Secretary of State Grew to Ambassador Caffery, January 27th, *Yalta Documents,* page 299.

German offensive in the Ardennes. Of this and developments in the other main combat areas, it is well to take account before traveling on to the conference at Yalta.

⊷⊶⊷⊶⊷⊶⊷⊶

50. Before Yalta: Coordination of Strategy on Eastern and Western Fronts

⊷⊶⊷⊶⊷⊶⊷⊶

The Germans had prevented the Allied armies from achieving their strategic objective—from reaching the Rhine in the northern and most important sector of the front. In Italy also they were frustrating Allied efforts in the water-soaked valley of the Po. In both areas they had been aided by harsh weather, floods, and cold which grew worse each passing day. The Germans had sent to the west the large reserve forces which they had managed to organize within Germany, and also had transferred divisions from the east.[38] Thus Eisenhower had lost his hope of decisive success before winter set in. The Allied air commanders were

---

[38] Wilmot, *The Struggle for Europe,* pages 621–22, after studying both Allied and German military records, figured that at the end of 1944 the Western Allies were engaging 100 German divisions—76 on the Western Front and 24 divisions in Italy. This corresponds roughly with the estimates presented by General Marshall at the first plenary session at Yalta (February 4, 1945); 79 German divisions in the west against 78 Allied, as of ten days before, and 27 German and Italian Fascist divisions in Italy facing about an equal number of Allied divisions. *Yalta Documents,* pages 577–78.

Wilmot also estimated that Hitler had at the end of 1944 on the whole length of the Eastern Front only 133 divisions, compared with 157 divisions when the Normandy invasion began. Of these, 58 were cut off or tied down in the north and in Hungary. So he computed that the Germans had only 75 divisions to hold the main Central front running 600 miles from the Carpathian Mountains to the Baltic Sea. Figures given by General Antonov, the Deputy Chief of Staff, and Stalin at this same session at Yalta are in close accord. Antonov said that on the route to Crakow, the area of the great current Soviet attack, the Germans had "up to 80 divisions," including only four armored. "We set up a grouping calculated on having a superiority over the enemy: in infantry, more than double; in artillery, tanks, and aviation, a decided superiority." Stalin said the Soviet Army had 180 divisions on this central front, of which 100 were used in the attack. The German divisions were ordinarily much larger than the Russian ones but many of those in the east were not up to full strength. *Yalta Documents,* pages 578, 582, 587. On December 14th Stalin remarked to Harriman that "the Russian big superiority was not in men but rather in the artillery and in the air but to utilize them there must be good visibility."

478

similarly frustrated; they were troubled by signs that the German fighter air force in the west was becoming stronger, and were afraid the Germans might get their jet planes into the battle first.[39]

In contrast, the Soviet advances on the Eastern Front had surpassed expectations. Great German armies were cut off in the north with their backs against the Baltic. In the south, after occupying Belgrade, the Red armies had pushed up the Valley of the Danube and were threatening with defeat other large German forces in Hungary. But they were massing their greatest strength along the central front in Poland and completing their preparations for a delayed offensive that was to carry them into Silesia and on to Berlin. This is what the Allies on the Western Front were counting on, this great push from the east which would make the Germans unable to meet their scheduled thrusts to and across the Rhine.

In the earlier phases of the war the Soviet Union had constantly solicited greater cooperation in action from the Western Allies. Now it was the turn of the American and British military authorities, eager to guarantee success for the offensives in the west which were planned for the coming spring, to grasp for assurances that their Soviet ally would press on with its attacks and sustain them. Thus the way in which Hitler directed resistance on the two fronts caused at least a temporary reversal of the flow of the sense of military dependence between the Western Allies and the Soviet Union.

The commanders on the Western Front, from Eisenhower down, were eager to know when the next Soviet offensive would begin, and on what scale. General Deane had made several attempts to find out. These having failed, Harriman tried. On his return trip from Washington he had stopped off to see Eisenhower, the better to inform himself of the Supreme Commander's views about Soviet cooperation. Then on December 14th, he had explained to Stalin that Eisenhower wanted to act in concert with the Russians and to give the Russian armies whatever support they needed, and so desired to know about the situation on the Eastern Front. Stalin had remarked dryly that Eisenhower must know what had already happened, and that what he probably wanted to know was what the Russians were going to do. Before informing him about that, he would rather wait until after he had conferred with his staff. Then he had gone on briefly to tell of recent vagaries in

[39] Wilmot, *ibid.,* estimates that at the end of December more than two-thirds of the Luftwaffe's aircraft were deployed for action against the U.S.-British air forces, and that the concentration of fighter forces against the West was even greater.

the weather, and to say that the Russians were waiting for a good spell before starting their big actions so that they could use their superiority in artillery and in the air. He promised he would give Harriman a more comprehensive picture in about a week. The Ambassador stressed the utility of such information; that Eisenhower could use his assault strength gradually or quickly, and knowledge of Russians plans would be of great value in deciding what was best. Stalin answered merely, "His wish will be met." But the days passed. Harriman was not called to the Kremlin to hear any fuller exposition of Soviet plans, and the one meeting which Deane had with Antonov yielded little.

In that same December week the Germans struck in the Ardennes, in the wintry snow and ice, where a front some seventy-five miles long was weakly held. For this assault Hitler had collected all the forces that he dared take away from anywhere else, including some good and strong armored divisions. He had the excited hope of being able to break through the Allied lines to the Meuse River and then, by turning to the north and northwest, reach the Port of Antwerp, destroying the supply lines on which the northern Allied armies were so dependent, and also of dividing them. This rash and threatening action during the first few days worried the Allied Commanders, deranged their plans, and obliged them to divert from other projected operations.

This turn in the situation further stimulated the wish to know how soon and in what strength the Russians were going to engage the Germans. So, on the 21st of December, Eisenhower asked the Combined Chiefs of Staff to make another effort to get this information. He advised them that a few German divisions from the east were appearing on the Western Front, and if more were to come that must affect his decisions about future strategy. But, he continued, "If . . . it is the Russian intention to launch a major offensive in the course of this or next month, knowledge of the fact would be of the utmost importance to me and I would condition my plans accordingly. Can anything be done to effect this coordination?" [40] He added that he was disposed to send a senior member of his staff to Moscow to give and procure information that was still lacking.

Two days later, December 23rd, Roosevelt had sent a message to Stalin in which he made it appear that the initiative came from himself, not from Eisenhower. He said that he wanted to order Eisenhower to send a fully qualified staff officer to Moscow to talk over with Stalin the relation of the situation on the Western Front to that on the Eastern. He asked Stalin to answer him quickly ". . . in view of the emer-

[40] *The Supreme Command,* pages 405–06.

gency." Churchill sent a similar message. Stalin answered that he would be glad to receive and talk with the special visitors from Allied headquarters in the west.

Eisenhower decided to send his deputy, Air Chief Marshal Tedder. The group set out for Moscow early in January. Bad weather all along the flight route held them back. Eisenhower fretted. Churchill volunteered personally to try to find out what Eisenhower wanted so keenly to know. "Shall I try?" he asked. Eisenhower answered that he would be pleased to have him do so.

Churchill lost no time. On the 6th of January he sent a message to Stalin which ended by stating that since the Supreme Commander might have to make great decisions all would be grateful if Stalin could tell him whether to count on a major offensive on the Vistula front or elsewhere during January. Stalin answered at once. He repeated to Churchill what he had said to Harriman—that they had been waiting for clear weather to take advantage of their superiority in artillery and in the air. This was, he commented, still unfavorable. "Nevertheless, taking into account the position of our Allies on the Western Front, G.H.Q. of the Supreme Command has decided to accelerate the completion of our preparation, and, regardless of the weather, to commence large-scale offensive operations against the Germans along the whole Central Front not later than the second half of January." [41] Churchill hurried to tell him, "I am most grateful to you for your thrilling message."

No doubt this news of Soviet intentions lightened Eisenhower's worries. But that it did not wholly dissipate them is indicated by the image of possibilities which lingered in his mind a week after its receipt, as outlined in a message to Marshall on January 15th. If, his analysis ran, the Germans withdrew part of their forces from Italy and Norway, and if the Soviet offensive on the Central Front should be weak and ineffectual, the Germans might then manage to keep as many as one hundred divisions on the Western Front and prevent a spring offensive. He expected to have under his command by that time some eighty-five divisions, including larger French components.

Tedder and his staff group had at last arrived in Moscow. On the same day (the 15th) that Eisenhower was exposing his anxieties to Marshall, Stalin was telling the visitors from Supreme Headquarters more about what the Soviet Army proposed to do. Stalin said that the great Russian offensive in the center of the front, using 150–160 divisions, actually had been started while the group was on its way to

[41] *Triumph and Tragedy*, page 279.

Moscow; that it would go on from two to two and one-half months. Its ultimate objective was to reach the line of the Oder, but of course he did not know whether or not it would. He was thoroughly confident that his armies would wear out and destroy the Germans as they were doing in the fight around Budapest. But he anticipated that the struggle would be stubborn and would not end before the summer.

When Tedder expressed satisfaction, Stalin said that, in order to help out the West, preparations for this offensive had been speeded up and it had been started without waiting for desired weather conditions. As for thanks: "We have no treaty but we are comrades. It is proper and also sound selfish policy that we should help each other in times of difficulty. It would be foolish of me to stand aside and let the Germans annihilate you; they would only turn back on me when you were disposed of. Similarly, it is to your interest to do everything possible to keep the Germans from annihilating me."

Tedder made an attempt to find out whether the Western Allies could count upon a continuation of this Russian offensive long enough to protect their armies in the spring operations being planned in the west. He asked whether the Russians would keep the Germans fully engaged from the middle of March to the middle of May. Stalin said that while he could not promise to sustain a full-scale offensive throughout that period, the Soviet Army would continue enough activity to deter the Germans from transferring any forces to the Western Front. That is as far as he would go and as definite as he could be induced to be, at least by Tedder.

Eisenhower and the Joint Chiefs of Staff were much relieved and pleased by this prospectus of the Soviet program. So was the President, who, having received a direct report from Stalin about his talk with Tedder and the current Soviet offensive, answered with appreciation.

So were Ambassador Harriman and General Deane. But neither of these permanent representatives took it for granted that this marked any lasting change either in Soviet policies or ways of doing business with their Allies. A memo which Deane submitted to the Joint Chiefs on January 22nd after Tedder left indicates the weary doubts imprinted by their day-by-day experience. Deane observed that it was quite possible, indeed quite common, for visitors who came to Moscow for a short time, to be misled by the general warmth of the reception they received and the avowals they heard. But it all too often turned out that unless the agreements they thought they had reached were in writing, precise and detailed, the Soviet government did not feel itself deeply obligated. Many of the characteristic ways and fixed attitudes of the Soviet authorities were likely to continue to hinder military collaboration. Those were by then familiar to all Americans who dealt with Soviet officials: mistrust of foreigners; a ban against personal association, no matter how important the common working interest; the deep and comprehensive security measures and lack of confidence in those of the United States and Great Britain; fear of hampering their operational freedom or infringing on their political interests or aims abroad; an unwillingness to allow foreign observation of what they were doing, in the liberated or occupied countries; their wish to keep the Russian peoples ignorant of foreign ways and conditions. These, Deane thought, would continue to check collaboration, especially since the Soviet government did not think it essential except in basic, great moves. But he qualified this conclusion by remarking that he discerned a growing realization of the advisability of closer coordination as the armed forces in Europe drew nearer together from east and west.

Events were to confirm in the main these reservations about Soviet treatment of secondary Allied military requests and proposals for the concert of military operations. But I think it quite possible that after thorough examination of the many projects pressed by the American military organization, the qualified historian would conclude that Soviet resistance was not always unjustified. To generalize and run fast, leaving the field to others, some of our schemes may well have called on the Soviet government for excessive effort and resources compared to the anticipated military result; and some others carelessly brushed Soviet pride. The one proposal which was put up to the Russians with the greatest tenacity—bases for the American strategic bombing forces in the Maritime Provinces—turned out to be unnecessary.

But such grievances and doubts as existed were submerged, in the early months of 1945, in satisfaction over the way in which the Russian offensive on the Eastern Front was improving the prospects of the U.S.-British assault upon Germany from the west. This, to borrow from the future tale, found expression in the first talk between the three Heads of State at Yalta (on February 4th) when they reverted briefly to the Soviet act of mutual aid of which we have just told. Stalin stressed the fact that the Soviet government had not been obligated by any agreement made at Teheran to conduct a winter offensive; that neither the President nor Prime Minister had asked or demanded that it should do so; but when it became clear to him that they wished it to do so, he had given the orders. This, he observed, was in the spirit of Soviet leadership which carried out not only their formal obligations but went farther and acted on what they conceived to be their moral duty to their Allies. Interjectorily, the contrast will be noted between this self-praising view of the Soviet decision and the one of simple common interest which Stalin had made to Tedder.

The President had agreed with Stalin that at Teheran it had been understood merely that each partner would move as quickly and as far as possible against the mutual enemy. Churchill remarked that the reason no request had been made of Stalin was because he and the President had felt complete confidence in the Marshal, the Russian people, and the efficiency of the Russian military; and so no attempt had been made to strike a bargain; and he had always been sure that when an offensive was possible the Red Army would attack. Discreetly abandoned, evidently, was the suspicion that the Red Army may have deliberately suspended its early offensive on the Central Front before Warsaw until the rebellious Poles in the city were doomed.

This mood of satisfaction was appropriate. By the beginning of February, the Red armies had advanced 200 miles through Central Poland, past the German frontier, far into Upper Silesia, and were less than 100 miles from Berlin. They had crossed the Vistula both north and south of Warsaw, and on January 17th had captured that city, and were then moving on toward the lower Oder River, Stettin, and Danzig. Still farther north the Red divisions had overrun East Prussia and controlled all of it except Konigsberg. These impressive results, before the start of the spring offensive from the west, began to make it seem possible that German resistance might collapse first along these eastern lines of combat.

Yet, perhaps because of the experience in the Ardennes, Eisenhower and the U.S. Chiefs of Staff had been cautious. They remained sure that the careful strategy which they favored was sounder than any other. This provided in its first phase for attempts to reach the Rhine all along the line before trying to force a crossing. Then, in the next phase, simultaneous thrusts across the river were to be made in order to establish bridgeheads north and south of the Ruhr. And in the next, and it was hoped decisive, phase, there was to be a main advance from the lower Rhine on to the plains of Northern Germany, and farther south a secondary operation from the Mainz-Karlsruhe area to Frankfurt and thence toward Kassel. The British military leaders, the Chiefs of Staff, and Field Marshal Montgomery, supported by Churchill, were pleading, inside and outside the meetings of the Combined Chiefs, for a greater concentration upon one main thrust in the north. In this way alone, they thought, could a quick, conclusive victory be achieved. But the Americans believed the wider-spread attack to be more and more flexible. This difference of judgment, as later pages will tell, arose again before the march across the Rhine got underway.

One other point of interest in the discussions about strategy ought briefly to be noted. In his December 14th conversation with Harriman about the position on all fighting fronts, Stalin had renewed the suggestion he had made to Churchill in October that the Allies detach certain of their forces in Italy for an advance across the Adriatic. He had said that he knew that neither Eisenhower nor his staff needed his advice, but that if he should offer any it would be that it was desirable that they transfer five or six divisions from the Italian front to Dalmatia for an advance on Zagreb so that they might join hands with the Russians in Southeastern Austria; and he had traced the action which he had in mind on a map. The German forces in Italy, he thought, would then either be forced to withdraw or be captured. The Russians, he explained, would be able to advance as far as Vienna and he thought it would be very satisfactory if eight or ten Anglo-American divisions met them there. Harriman had explained that Churchill had been eager to do this, that study had shown difficulties in connection with amphibious operations and bad winter weather in the upper Adriatic, and that decision had been postponed until spring.

Churchill had had the idea of sending General Alexander to join in Moscow the SHAEF group headed by Tedder to discuss such a Balkan operation. Roosevelt, on January 2nd, told Churchill that he had no objection to having "a representative from the Mediterranean theater" go on this errand, but suggested that the assignment might better be given to the American deputy to Alexander. But the idea seems to have been dropped following upon a report from Field Marshal Wilson to the Combined Chiefs on January 8th—that his forces would soon have to go on the defensive in Italy. Shortly afterward, in fact, the Combined Chiefs, with Churchill's concurrence, decided that three of the Canadian and British divisions then in Italy should be sent to enlarge Montgomery's forces in France.

Stalin had also casually suggested to Harriman that the army under General Devers which was at the southern end of the line in France might possibly break through to link up with the Russians near Vienna. The Combined Chiefs passed that by as conflicting with other thrusts into Germany which were being projected.

All these and many other strategic plans and proposals were soon to be more thoroughly discussed among the American and British Chiefs of Staff at Malta; and then further talked through with the Soviet Chiefs of Staff at Yalta—the Conference for which the Americans and British were on their way at the end of January.

PERIOD ELEVEN

The Conferences at Malta and Yalta; February 1945; Constant Military Understandings and Inconstant Diplomatic Compromises

51. On to Malta and Yalta; February 1945

THE assembly of the three Heads of State and their military advisers
had been, as we have seen, long deferred. Roosevelt had looked forward to the reunion. However, he had put it off until after his inauguration on January 20th. This enabled him to take care of the closing
business of the current session of Congress and prepare his presentation
to the new one. It is probable that because of the drag in the war in
France and Italy he foresaw that there would be more time than he had
thought to reach settlements about the peace. Stalin had not been disturbed by the further wait. But Churchill had been, fearing that there
would be a serious hiatus in the concert of Allied policy during which
important matters would moulder. But he had gracefully acquiesced.

The President had also veered about in regard to traveling as far as
the Soviet Black Sea coast to meet with Stalin. In October he had told
the Marshal that he was willing to go there. But then he had become
very loath to do so. Reports that the area was unhealthy and unsanitary
bothered him—perhaps not so much on his account as because of fear
that the men who were to go with him and the crew of the ship that
was to carry him might fall ill. He wished to travel by sea to the
rendezvous and to live on the ship; and it was uncertain whether it
would be possible to arrange to enter the Black Sea. Then, also, he had
become worried lest at that distance rapid mail communications with
Washington, necessary for the conduct of public business, might fail.
For all these reasons he had tried to induce Stalin to come to Italy, or
to Sicily, or to Malta, or to Cyprus or any other pleasant spot in the
Mediterranean. But Stalin had continued to avow that on the advice of
his doctors he would not be able to attend a meeting elsewhere than at
some point in the Soviet Union. —

Bored or irritated at this cautious obstinacy, Churchill at one point
seemed quite reconciled to accepting Molotov as a substitute for Stalin.
He had the cheerful notion that in that case the conference might be
held in London, and that Roosevelt might pay Britain his long-
promised visit and go on for review of the armies in France. But
Roosevelt had not thought that he could do the business in mind with
anyone but Stalin. So in December he had reconciled himself to traveling to the Crimea. Churchill had repeated that he would go wherever
the President was willing to go. Thus they had all finally settled on
Yalta.

The President had at once begun to plan to leave by warship for the Mediterranean as soon as possible after the inauguration. Since his doctors thought that he ought not to fly at high altitudes over the mountains between Italy and Yalta, it was suggested that the cruiser *U.S.S. Quincy,* which was to carry him across the ocean, might instead go to Malta. Churchill was almost boyishly pleased that the President would, after all, put in at some spot under the British flag, and at this island in the Mediterranean which had stood up so valiantly. His enthusiasm expressed itself in the short rhymed sentences which have amused the world:

> "No more let us falter!
> From Malta to Yalta!
> Let nobody alter."

In similar happy vein he had suggested to the President that the code name for their conference might be ARGONAUT.[1] That *did* catch the President's fancy. In welcoming the suggestion that their voyage might be remembered by that name, he had added, "You and I are direct descendants."

Churchill was still anxious over the course of operations in Northwest Europe; and, before meeting with the Russians, he wanted to have another thorough joint review of strategic plans for the Western and Italian fronts. Perhaps also, he was on the alert against the possibility, suggested by not too well-founded dispatches from the British Ambassador in Washington, Lord Halifax, that U.S. Joint Chiefs might again try to alter the whole strategic program in favor of the Pacific War.[2]

Thus the Prime Minister had asked the President whether it would not be possible for him to spend two or three nights at Malta and let the staffs confer unostentatiously. After the President said he was sorry that he would not be able to do so, it was arranged that the U.S. Joint Chiefs should arrive at Malta in advance of himself and Churchill, so that they might have preliminary talks with their British colleagues.

Roosevelt had said that he did not think that he and Churchill ought to stay at Yalta for more than five or six days. With this in mind, and appealing to the President's great wish to complete the work started at Dumbarton Oaks, the Prime Minister suggested that Stettinius also be

---

[1] According to Greek legend a member of the band which sailed with Jason on the ship Argo in search of the Golden Fleece. It is supposed to have landed at Colchis on the Black Sea coast south of the Caucasian Mountains.

[2] *Triumph and Tragedy,* page 339.

sent ahead to Malta for preliminary talks with Eden. He had adverted to the benefits resulting from the talks between the Foreign Ministers at Moscow before the Teheran Conference and had jestingly added "I do not see any other way of realizing our hopes about World Organization in five or six days. Even the Almighty took seven." Roosevelt answered that Stettinius would not be able to leave Washington in time for any extended preliminary talk with Eden, but that he was going to send Hopkins to London soon. After a season of coolness, Hopkins was again being used for the more top and tousled tasks of diplomacy. The President evidently thought him more fit for the jousts against the knights (and nights) of Malta than the novitiate he had elevated to be Secretary of State.

The British and American military staffs began their conferences at Malta on January 30th. They found quick agreement on most of the questions that had still been undecided between them. So their provisional report was almost ready to present to Churchill and Roosevelt when they arrived.

The British (and possibly Russian) fears that the Americans might be over-eager to pursue the war against Japan were allayed. The rule that the first objective was the unconditional surrender of Germany at the earliest possible date was retained. But the combat resources in sight were great enough to permit a concurrent resolution to press on also against Japan—this being safeguarded by a provision which, as written into the final report of the Combined Chiefs, read, "The effect of any such extension on the over-all objective is to be given consideration by the Combined Chiefs of Staff before action is taken." With a cheerful look ahead, this indent of purpose specified that upon the defeat of Germany, the United States and Great Britain, in cooperation with the other Pacific powers and with Russia, should direct their full resources to bring about the unconditional surrender of Japan at the earliest possible date.

It was agreed that the first phase of the new offensive on the Western Front should be hurried. Eisenhower sent word to the first meeting of the Combined Chiefs at Malta on January 30th that he thought ". . . the factor of time . . . had now become of great importance in view of the Russian advance. It was felt that on the Western Front freedom of movement could be counted on until the 15th of March. . . . In view of the present diminution of German offensive capabilities in the West, it was essential to get to the Rhine in the North as soon as possible. . . ." [3]

[3] *Yalta Documents,* page 471.

This was the tag end of a difference which had existed since October between Eisenhower and Montgomery and their respective service chiefs over the conduct and direction of the Allied assault on the Western Front.

The British had vehemently and insistently protested against the strategy of a "broad front." They had argued that concentration on one main line of attack was the best way to gain a decisive result. After two meetings with Eisenhower, Montgomery had written a letter (on November 30th) which put his views in unsparing language. After judging adversely the results of recent attacks in different sections, he urged a reversion to Eisenhower's early directive (of October 28th) which contemplated a concentration of strength in the north, as well as a change in the pattern of command.

On this point the author of *Grand Strategy* comments, "This last factor [the suggested extension of Montgomery's command], indeed, was of some importance in the argument. For the stress laid by the British on the relation between strategy and command influenced the Americans, already suspicious of the argument on command, in their attitude to the strategy. They had never sympathized with Montgomery's case of a single subordinate [i.e. to Eisenhower] land commander. They were less disposed to accept it now from the British Chiefs of Staff in view of reports received of his recent behaviour. For Montgomery, already unpopular with American officers, had notably increased his unpopularity since the Ardennes offensive, by the attitude of superiority which they conceived him to have adopted." [3a]

Both the main substance of what Montgomery wrote in this letter and its tone had irritated Eisenhower and Bradley. The unadjusted differences had survived a notable effort to reach an agreement at a special meeting in London on the 12th of December which Eisenhower and Tedder attended with the Prime Minister and Chiefs of Staff, and had claimed the unremitting attention of the Combined Chiefs of Staff.[4]

The argument was resumed strenuously at Malta and Yalta. The two staff groups were agreed that the main drive should be in the north—in the Ruhr area of the Rhine. But the British were worried about several features of the campaign plans which they thought the Americans had in mind.

They were afraid that Eisenhower might not try to cross the Rhine even in the north, until there were no Germans left anywhere west of its curving length. Eisenhower dealt with this apprehension by a mes-

[3a] *Grand Strategy,* Vol. VI, page 72.
[4] A lucid account of this sharp and sustained argument, in all its detailed and documented continuity, is given in *ibid.,* pages 34–37, 69–76, 87–89.

sage to General Walter Bedell Smith, who represented him at these Malta conferences: "You may assure the Combined Chiefs of Staff in my name that I will seize the Rhine crossings in the north just as soon as this is a feasible operation and without waiting to close the Rhine throughout its length. Further, I will advance across the Rhine in the north with maximum strength and complete determination immediately the situation in the south allows me to collect necessary forces without incurring unreasonable risks." [4a]

The British were also concerned lest Eisenhower would not provide enough force for the northern drive to enable it to effect a decisive smash through the German lines. Therefore they proposed that the plan should be based on the whole effort being made in the north, with every other operation subsidiary. To this the Americans were unwilling to commit themselves. They contended that no matter how much force was devoted to that section of the front, the actual northern crossing of the Rhine could be made only in limited strength. They wanted to be sure that the Germans would not be able to assemble enough force in the Ruhr area to defeat the Allied thrust there. General Smith brought Eisenhower's assurance on this matter also: that he intended to put into the northern effort every single division that could be maintained logistically (i.e. kept fully equipped and supplied). The southern advance, he confirmed, was not intended to compete with the northern, but ought to be strong enough to draw off German forces to protect the Frankfurt area, and provide an alternative line of attack if the main effort failed. The British conceded either to this reasoning or to the superior numbers of the Americans on the Western Front.

It is more than possible that into this separation of opinion there entered not only differences of military judgment but competition for command.[4b] Able controversial books have been written by the admirers or defenders of Eisenhower and Montgomery, exploring these matters on many levels descending from high strategy to personal aspersion. I will prudently abstain from entering further into an argument which still engages many veterans of these great campaigns.

To conform to the assurances which Eisenhower extended, changes were made in the plans of operations for the winter and spring of 1945. Reworded paragraphs were approved by the Supreme Commander and noted by the Combined Chiefs. On February 2nd Churchill and Roosevelt were informed that complete agreement had been reached. They were satisfied with the result.

[4a] *The Supreme Command*, page 414.
[4b] Reconciliation of judgment was also hindered by British mistrust of the way Eisenhower construed assurances, and American resentment at the lack of faith in Eisenhower's leadership.

As explained by General Marshall and Field Marshal Brooke to Stalin and his military staff at Yalta, the American and British forces would put their main effort into two converging thrusts toward the line of the Rhine from Dusseldorf north. All the divisions that could be maintained would be put into these attacks. It was hoped that they would drive the Germans east of the Rhine, making possible a crossing of the river north of the Ruhr. In addition, large numbers of airborne troops were to be landed east of the Rhine. It was considered possible to cross the Rhine in the north after March 1st, but ice would make any attempt before then hazardous. There were plans also to deploy, on the axis Frankfurt-Kassel, such forces as would be available after providing thirty-six divisions, with ten in reserve, for the northern thrusts and essential security elsewhere along the front.

Neither Stalin nor the Soviet staff found any fault with this scenario of operations on the Western Front. It was written out, act by act, in the Final Report which Roosevelt and Churchill approved at Yalta.

The Combined Chiefs of Staff made changes in the plans for the Mediterranean theater. As recorded in the final report approved at Yalta:

"We have reviewed our strategy in the Mediterranean in the light of the development of the situation in Europe and of the fact that the enemy is at liberty at any time to make a voluntary withdrawal in Italy. We have agreed that our primary object in the war against Germany should be to build up the maximum possible strength on the Western Front and to seek a decision in that theater.

"In accordance with this concept we have agreed to withdraw certain forces from the Mediterranean Theater and to place them at the disposal of the Supreme Commander, Allied Expeditionary Force, and to redefine the tasks of the Allied Supreme Commander, Mediterranean." [5]

Accordingly, it was decided that three British and Canadian divisions should, before March 15th, be transferred to Northwest Europe, and two more as soon as their equivalent could be spared from operations in Greece, and also part of the tactical air strength then in Italy. In consenting to these switches of fighting forces, Churchill may have been influenced in part by the eagerness of the Canadians to have all their divisions brought together on the Western Front. His assent was consonant with the wish of the British Chiefs of Staff that Montgomery should have irresistible might at the north of the line. Thus expired the Prime Minister's long-sustained attempt to find the means of effecting

[5] *Yalta Documents,* page 829.

an entry into Southeastern Europe and to make a junction with the Russians near Vienna or in Hungary. But he still clung to the crux of his purpose, remarking, as he gave approval to the decision, "that he attached great importance to a rapid followup of any withdrawal or of any surrender of the German forces in Italy. He felt it was essential that we should occupy as much of Austria as possible as it was undesirable that more of Western Europe than necessary should be occupied by the Russians." [6]

There also emerged from the staff conferences at Malta plans for the Far Eastern theaters of war of joint interest—China, India-Burma, and Southeast Asia.

The prospect in China was brightening. The Japanese had failed to reach the main base of American air operations at Kunming, and their chance to wipe out the resistant Chinese armies and government at Chungking had vanished. Despondent doubts that it might ever be worthwhile to pay a fee in lives and equipment to invigorate the Chinese military effort were beginning to yield to hope.[7] However, the need for mass Chinese armies to finish off the Japanese was declining in view of the prospective Soviet entry into the war. Similarly, the value of air bases in China was depreciating as the Americans captured island positions nearer and nearer Japan and the Russians promised bases in the Maritime Provinces.

The statement contained in the Final Report was indefinite: "The primary military object of the United States in the China and India-Burma Theaters is the continuance of aid to China on a scale that will permit the fullest utilization of the area and resources of China for operations against the Japanese." [8]

This did not envisage mere passive attendance upon events in Europe and China. Proposals were being revived in the Joint Chiefs for eventual land operations in China to which the United States would contribute equipment, technical service, training personnel, and some small combat units. They included a plan (Code name RASHNESS) to have Chinese divisions march overland from the interior to the coast and gain

[6] *Ibid.*, page 543.

[7] General Marshall, who had been one of those discouraged by the poor Chinese performance in the past, at the meeting of the Combined Chiefs on February 2nd described the changes that were occurring: "In the first place certain well-trained Chinese troops were now in China, having been transferred there from Burma. Secondly, the opening of the Burma Road had meant that the first artillery for the Chinese Army had been able to go through. Thirdly, if operations in Burma continued to go well, additional trained Chinese troops could move back to China, and it was hoped that an effective reinforced Chinese corps would soon be in existence." *Ibid.*, page 544.

[8] *Ibid.*, page 830.

control of the Canton/Hong Kong area; and open a port there through which the United States could send supplies and weapons and possibly troops; and thereafter, the combined force would concert action with other Chinese columns to drive the Japanese north, where the Russians would be waiting for them.

Current plans for clearing the Japanese completely out of Burma were confirmed and extended. By then the battle for North Burma was all but won. Chinese, Indian, and British troops had converged on the battered Japanese forces. On January 26th the Chinese troops who had marched west across the high mountains from Yunnan met with those other Chinese divisions that had fought their way east from India. The road into China was open. The first convoy of trucks crossed the frontier the next day. Some hard fighting was still ahead before the Japanese in Central and Southern Burma were killed or forced by hunger and sick exhaustion to surrender.

Looking ahead, the Combined Chiefs in their Final Report instructed the Southeast Asia Command (under Lord Mountbatten) after Burma was won to proceed to the liberation of Malaya and the opening of the Straits of Malacca. But it was laid down that the U.S. combat forces then deployed in the India-Burma Theater were to be regarded as a reserve for China, and not to be available for operations in Malaya or elsewhere in the region unless there was a fresh agreement. Churchill, as he looked through the planning telescope toward this area, commented on the split of interest which the Malta Conference was revealing: "It now appeared that the American and British operations in this part of the world were diverging. The American effort was going on in China and the British effort was turning to the south." [9]

This meant that the American government retained a free hand in the making of operational plans for China and the Northern Pacific; and these, as adjusted to form a coordinated strategy with the Russians, had an effect upon what occurred later in North China, Manchuria, and Korea. Similarly, the British were unhindered in determining the later movement of their naval and landing forces in Southeast Asia. This bore upon the way and time in which subsequent British recovery of Singapore and the Federated Malay States, Dutch recapture of the East Indies, and the French return to Indo-China, transpired.

Having thus conjoined their views, and given them agreed and definite form, the American and British military men flew off for Yalta. There they expected to complete the concert of action with Soviet forces in Europe and the Far East. The President and Churchill in their separate planes flew after them through the cold night.

[9] *Ibid.*, page 544.

The President had seemed to various friends and visitors to be looking poorly before he left Washington, though he assured one and all that he felt fine. The sea voyage had allowed some rest and left a touch of tan. He had enjoyed the brief stay in Malta. But still, when the Presidential plane landed at the airfield at Saki in the Crimea, and as Churchill watched him come down the lift from the "Sacred Cow," he thought he looked "frail and ill."

As for Britain's Prime Minister, the world had come to take it for granted that he could stand any amount of travel and survive; even as Stalin, in a talk with Harriman, by way of excusing his refusal to leave the Soviet Union, had spoken of the Prime Minister as ". . . the healthiest old man . . . a desperate fellow." But Churchill's family and his doctors had not forgotten the dangerous spell of pneumonia after the conferences at Teheran and Cairo; his daughter Sarah, and his doctor Lord Moran, were with him. That he did indeed need watching over was shown when, on the journey from England, he developed a high temperature and was forced briefly to take to bed at Malta.

Together, the President sitting in an open car and Churchill walking beside him, they inspected the Guard of Honor at the airfield at Saki before going to the refreshment room, where Molotov was waiting to meet them. Stalin was, to all appearances, hale and hearty again.

It was understood before the meetings that each of the three Heads of State would be free to raise any subject he wished for discussion. No formal order of business was prepared in advance—in the spirit expressed by the President in one of his earlier messages to Stalin (November 18th)—"We understand each other's problems and as you know, I like to keep these discussions informal, and I have no reason for formal agenda." In my telling of their work, rather than mark the calendar of their sessions, I shall follow the topography of the historical landscape they traversed.

52. Yalta: Military Discussions, Europe and the Far East

The first decision which the Heads of State made at Yalta was to open their conference with a discussion of military matters.

The staffs deployed their views among themselves, went away to formulate their decisions, and then submitted them to the Heads of State for review and approval. The American and British staffs continued to meet from time to time as they had at Malta to touch up their

Combined Report. Concurrently, they got together with the Soviet military staff. On the side the Americans and Russians developed their coordinated plans for the Northwest Pacific. Over all this work the Heads of State maintained close watch. Their yes or no were the final words.

The record of the talk about coordinating efforts against Germany gives no signal of competition between the Western Allies and the Soviet Union for renown or political advantage to be won by advancing the farthest possible. Each showed a wish to have the other push its attack with all possible speed and vigor so that the Germans would not be able to transfer troops between east and west and their reserves would the sooner be used up. Thus no attempt was made to reach agreement as to the places or lines along which the armies coming from the east and from the west should stop. Their destination was to be decided by the course of battle; the question of where and how long the armies of each would *remain* was left to the makers of political arrangements.

What each had to tell the other of its recent victories and prospective plans was impressive. Stalin and his military advisers reported on the progress up to then of the main offensive on the central part of the Eastern Front which they had begun in the middle of January, and of the accompanying assaults in the north and the south. During the first three weeks they had broken the enemy defense all along the line and advanced over three hundred miles in the direction of their main drive. Soviet troops were at the Oder River north of Frankfurt (*not* Frankfurt-on-Main) and farther south on the Central Front they had captured much of the Silesian industrial area. They were only about forty miles from Berlin. In the flanking attack in the north, they had cut the main roads and isolated some twenty-six German divisions in the Courland area; and they had broken through the German defense positions in East Prussia, and were at the edge of Konigsberg. In Hungary they were gradually exhausting the German forces and moving towards Budapest. In all, they had destroyed some forty-five German divisions, and had almost completely dispersed the tank divisions that had originally faced them on the Central Front.

Stalin's expectations, as revealed in his first talks with Roosevelt and Churchill, were high. In sum, he thought the German front had been smashed and the Germans were finding it very hard even to repair the breaks. But the exposition made by Antoñov at the first plenary Staff meeting (on February 4th) contained some ominous forecasts. It bespoke a grave respect for the resistance that even a battered Germany might still be able to make against the larger Red attacking force. He said that much fierce fighting was still anticipated before the Russians could get farther west: "The Germans will defend Berlin for which they will try to hold up the movement of the Soviet troops in the area of the Oder River, setting up the defense here at the expense of withdrawn troops and of reserves being moved over from Germany, Western Europe, and Italy."

This brought out what the Soviet authorities wanted of the Americans and British. A few German divisions, known to have been on the Western or Italian fronts not long before, had appeared on the Eastern Front. The Russians were afraid that in their last desperate defense the Germans might transfer many more divisions (up to 30 or 35) from France and Italy and Norway in the near critical future unless prevented by the violence of the attack from the west, and that whatever reserves were still inside Germany might be concentrated on the Eastern Front. What the Soviet staff thus asked was: that the offensives on the Western Front and Italy be hastened and maintained so sturdily that all enemy forces there would be fully engaged; and that air assaults should be conducted against communications to prevent the removal of troops to the east from these fronts or Norway.

General Marshall for the Americans and Field Marshal Brooke for the British exposed the whole Allied scheme of current and prospective operations on the ground and in the air. They told of their plans to start the main offensive north of the Ruhr and the secondary one to the south within a very few days; then they would force a way across the Rhine in March as soon as the condition of the river and the country permitted. They thought that the actual crossing of the Rhine, when they expected to come up against the most stubborn and dense German defense, was likely to be their time of greatest trouble and danger. It was while being engaged in that operation that they thought they would most need protection against an accession of German forces from the east and from within Germany. They were the more concerned because it was anticipated that during the second half of March and April Soviet action in the east might be hindered by thaw and mud, giving the Germans the chance to release forces for the west. Thus what the British and Americans wanted was assurance that the Russians would do everything they could at that time to maintain such continuous pressure on the German lines in the east that this could not happen.

This analysis of the dangers that might arise on the two fronts gave convincing precision to the advantages of coordination toward which the Heads of State were in favor. At their first meeting, with the military staffs of the three countries present, they made this plainly known. Churchill affirmed with his usual directness, "It was imperative that the two offensives should be integrated so as to get the best results." Roosevelt agreed. Stalin said that he recognized that the recent offensives from east and west had not been well synchronized and that steps ought to be taken to do better in the future.

The subsequent talks ensured that they would do better. The program of assault in the west which the Americans and British had adopted assured the Soviet armies in the east much, if not complete, immediate protection against enlargements of the German forces on that front. The Russians were told, however, that while every effort would be made, it might not be possible to prevent the Germans from moving some troops from Italy to the east. The terrain, the rivers, the marshy valleys, and the mountains would aid the Germans in scheduling and hiding their troop movements during the bad winter months. For the first time the Soviet authorities seemed greatly impressed by the smashing results of the ever-extending Allied bombing activities. Just a few days before, 1,000 bombers had joined in a single attack on Berlin; they were striking at more and more places in Eastern Germany; and they had already destroyed all but a small fraction of the German oil production.

The Soviet military staff responded with a similar pledge to do everything in their power to prevent the shunting of German forces away from the east during March and April. General Antonov, the spokesman, quoted Stalin as saying that the Russians would continue operations on all fronts as long as weather permitted. There might be interruptions, he continued, because of the need to reestablish communications; but the Soviet Army would do all possible to make these short and to continue the offensive to the limit of its capacity. Stalin confirmed these promises.

The three military staff groups concluded their discussions of strategy in Europe with professions of belief in the intentions and good faith of the other. The course of operations in the west and east confirmed the reliability of the accord reached for mutual protection.

Once again at Yalta Stalin agreed that there should be more consultation between the military staffs of the three countries in behalf of closer coordination in both strategy and operations. The President and the U.S. Joint Chiefs favored direct liaison between Eisenhower, Alexander, and the Soviet General Staff by having them deal with one another through the American and the British Military Missions in Moscow. As General Marshall tersely asserted at a meeting with the President and his advisers on February 4th ". . . with the Russians within 40 miles of Berlin there was not time to go through the Combined Chiefs of Staff." Churchill was reluctant to authorize this straight route of consultation, fearing that Eisenhower would get involved in the settlement of matters that were more properly the business of the superior authorities. The President put it up to Stalin, who agreed, and the Prime Minister, it may be inferred, consented to allow it.[10] Actually the President went on to urge direct liaison between Eisenhower, Alexander, and field commanders of the Russian armies in the east on such matters as the employment of air forces and the coordination of day-to-day action. But this direct intercourse between theater commanders, Stalin debarred as not necessary for the time being.[11]

When, it will be told later, rapid communication on over-all strategic questions became imperative, Eisenhower addressed himself directly to Stalin as Commander-in-Chief of the Soviet forces, and Churchill thought that by so doing he was exceeding his authorization and his authority.

The discussions about the Pacific War were taken up where they had been left at the end of the Churchill visit to Moscow the past October. The Russians were informed that we proposed to continue the liberation of the Philippines; and then after seizing the Bonin Islands, about the first of April to try to capture Okinawa (in the Ryukyus), which would give us air bases and an advance naval base menacingly close to Japan. The Japanese defending air force was no longer a serious hindrance to our bombing squadrons. A recent attack in which we had used 120 planes had left Kobe in ruins; and plans to expand the assailant force to about 1,800 operational planes were already underway. What was left of the Japanese Navy would not be able to sustain a major engagement. Japanese merchant shipping had been reduced from about 7,000,000 to 2,000,000 tons.

The President and Marshall were also aware of another development, not included in the portrayal of the situation given to the Russians, which, if realized, would make that superiority even more crushing. They had been told before leaving for Yalta that they could quite possibly expect to have a new projectile of far greater destructive power than any in use. General Groves, head of the Manhattan Project, had informed Marshall in a letter on December 30th that the first specimen should be ready in August, the next before the end of the year, others at shorter intervals thereafter. It was forecast that the explosive force of this first projectile would be equivalent to 500 tons of TNT; and that the next one in the series would have twice that force.[12] Presum-

---

[10] But Churchill was surprised when Eisenhower construed the agreement to authorize him to correspond with Stalin, as Commander-in-Chief of the Red Army. See pages 606–07.

[11] *Yalta Documents,* page 645.

[12] *Ibid.,* pages 383–84.

ably, Churchill also knew of the state of progress on this new weapon, though the open record does not tell.

But the decisive effect that this weapon could have upon bringing about the end of the war was not realized on the basis of this first report and any others that may have been received before the Yalta Conference.[13] This is puzzling in the light of our later knowledge of the development of nuclear weapons. Neither the President nor Joint Chiefs have explained their thoughts on the subject. The historian is therefore compelled to seek (or invent) the reasons. Several together seem to provide a plausible if not evidenced explanation. First of all, the customary prudence in which military men are schooled must be borne in mind. They are taught that it is best not to count on any weapon until it exists and has proved itself. Then after all, even if this forecast was borne out, only a few of the new missiles were to have become available for use in the twelve months ahead. Then the predicted explosive force—500 to 1,000 tons of TNT—while many times more than any single bomb then in use, was no greater than the load being taken to Germany by a single flight of bombers. Each of the bombs that was made and dropped on Hiroshima and Nagasaki had 10,000 to 20,000 tons of high explosive strength!

In any case, neither the establishment of our command of the air and seas near Japan nor this forecast of a new weapon that would make that command indisputable caused the Joint Chiefs of Staff to make any substantial changes in their plans or schedules for the further conduct of the war against Japan or waver in their opinion that Russian entry would be of great value.

The operational plans had been confirmed by the Joint Chiefs shortly before their departure from Washington. These, as reviewed on January 22nd, were to culminate in "Invading and seizing objectives in the industrial heart of Japan." In a memo sent to the President on the next day the Joint Chiefs had restated their conclusions about the part which the Soviet Union ought to play in the Pacific war. Their definition of

---

[13] The purpose of this report was to define the time-table of Pacific operations for the Argonaut Conference. It repeated, and thus reaffirmed, the following paragraph from a memo of the Joint Chiefs of December:

"1. The United States Chiefs of Staff have adopted the following as a basis for planning in the war against Japan:

"The concept of operations for the main effort in the Pacific is:

"A. Following the Okinawa operations to seize additional positions to intensify the blockade and air bombardment of Japan in order to create a situation favorable to:

"B. An assault on Kyushu for the purpose of further reducing Japanese capabilities by containing and destroying major enemy forces and further intensifying the blockade and air bombardment in order to establish a tactical condition favorable to:

"C. The decisive invasion of the industrial heart of Japan through the Tokyo Plain."

"... basic principles in working toward USSR entry into the war against Japan" began as follows: "Russia's entry at as early a date as possible consistent with her ability to engage in offensive operations is necessary to provide maximum assistance to our Pacific operations. The U.S. will provide maximum support possible without interfering with our main effort against Japan." [13a]

The Final Report submitted by the Combined Chiefs at Yalta on February 9th to the President and Churchill conformed to the strategic policy approved in Washington. The sobriety with which the military advisers measured the ability of the Japanese to keep on fighting is attested by that sentence in their report which reads: "We recommend that the planning date for the end of the war against Japan should be set at 18 months after the defeat of Germany." To repeat, this was the most prudent military line. It did not debar effort to bring about surrender by naval and air action alone, or rule out the hope that the surrender might come quickly, maybe even before or without Soviet participation. The President was aware of such possibilities. In his private talk with Stalin (February 8th) in connection with the discussion of air bases in the Far East he again said that he hoped it would not be necessary to invade the Japanese islands; and that he hoped by intensive bombing to be able to destroy Japan and its army and thus save American lives.

Dubious as the Americans and British were as to whether the Japanese would surrender before their land armies were wiped out and their home islands invaded, Stalin and the Russians were even more so. Their whole plan of operations in the Pacific, and their way of explaining these plans, indicate that they anticipated that the Japanese might be able to invade the Maritime Provinces of Siberia as well as put up a very hard battle in Manchuria and in the home islands. Despite all their chance to observe the damage that had been done by the Allied bombing forces in Europe, they apparently still did not appreciate the havoc that could be brought down from above if command of the air was complete.

The discussions between American and Soviet military staffs, under the gaze of Roosevelt and Stalin, to fit together their operations against Japan, went smoothly. Again, as in Europe, there is no admission in the record that the resultant design was influenced by political purposes. These were dealt with in a separate secret accord between the Heads of State.

The Soviet officials confirmed the date in mind for Soviet entry into

[13a] *Ibid.*, page 396.

the Pacific War—about three months after the defeat of Germany. The Americans confirmed that this would suit their provisional schedule of operations; they should at that time be getting set for their first landing in Japan. There was a similar concordance between the plans that each had developed: the Americans admired the Soviet program; the Russians had nothing but praise for the vast range of American enterprise.

The discussion at Yalta of two of the particular projects that had often before been considered with Stalin was revealing, for it showed how hard all thought the struggle against Japan was still going to be.

Were the Americans to secure air-bases in the Maritime Provinces? Once again at Yalta the Joint Chiefs presented the request, and at their behest the President again put the question to Stalin. It was made plain that we were willing to supply the Soviet Air Force with whatever equipment it might need to make operations conducted from these bases joint or combined. The answer finally given was that bases would be made available, but not near Vladivostok—farther north in the Komsomolsk-Nikolaevsk area. The Americans accepted this as the best they could get.

Were the Americans to try to keep open a sea route to the north of Japan into the ports of the Maritime Provinces? That was one of the reasons they had thought of trying to make an amphibious landing in the Kurile Islands. Closer study had convinced them that it would be hard to find the means in 1945. But since the Soviet authorities still seemed to think that despite the advance accumulation of supplies, an open sea route would be needed, the decision was deferred.

There were other unmarked edges and blank spaces in the approved chart of coordinated operations. No attempt was made to determine how far south into China Soviet ground forces might go in pursuit of the Japanese. No definite provision was made for American landings in the Kwantung Peninsula or Korea but they were not banned. Whether it was thought impractical or unwise to decide these operational questions so far ahead of the actual course of battle, or whether they were avoided as being too delicate, the record does not indicate. But at Yalta neither the Americans nor the Russians seemed bothered by these imperfections in the broad accord they reached.

The Soviet government had managed to develop a position which enabled it to secure in advance a promise of reward for entering the Pacific War. By maintaining the posture of neutrality it had allowed the Japanese government to believe that a continuation of this policy was purchasable, and that government was bidding. By maintaining a

menacing aloofness toward China it had allowed the Chinese government to fear how it might be treated, once the Soviet Union was free
to use its force and influence against it. By maintaining that it was
willing to stay out of the war against Japan unless its help was wanted,
it had allowed the American government to worry over the risks and
costs of having it stay neutral. But during the same days that the plans
for military cooperation were being completed, Roosevelt and Stalin
were reducing to writing an agreement as to what the Soviet Union
was to get after victory.

53. Yalta: The Secret Accords about the Far East

In the talks in October with Churchill and Harriman, Stalin had
said that he would go through with the program of participation in the
Pacific War only if certain desires of the Soviet government were
satisfied. This connection made by Stalin has, ever since, I think, cross-
circuited judgment about the Far Eastern accord that was signed at
Yalta. It has given that the cast of a bargain in which the American
government bartered away some strategic territories and impaired Chinese sovereignty for the sake of securing help in defeating Japan; and,
to make the matter worse, for help that in the end was unneeded. But
that was not the sole nor perhaps even the main reason for making the
accord.

Even though the Soviet government had not asked such payment in
advance, some disposition of most of the subjects treated would have
been in order, if not right then, soon after. There were at least three
convergent sets of unsettled problems which the heads of government
would have had to consider anyhow:

1. The Cairo Declaration had stated that Japan was to be deprived
of its whole Empire. China, it was stipulated, was to regain control
over Manchuria, Formosa, and the Pescadores Islands. But what was to
happen to the other parts of the Japanese Empire? Were the Kurile
Islands and the southern half of Sakhalin, its first defense barriers to
the north and east, to be taken away from Japan; and, if so, to whom
were they to be awarded? What was to be done about the Japanese
Mandated Islands to the south?

2. What course was the Soviet government going to pursue toward

China? Quarrelsome situations in the border regions were a threat both to peace in this North Asian region and to the hope of harmony among the great powers in the Council of the United Nations.

3. What attitude was the Soviet government going to take toward the internal quarrel going on in China? Would it cooperate with the United States in its exertions to bring about a unifying accord between the Chinese government and the Chinese Communists? Or would it, as soon as it could spare the means and risk the trouble, aid the Chinese Communists? Or would it, perhaps, pursue a more sinuous diplomacy, directed toward causing China to fall apart, with the hope that if this happened the Soviet Union would extend its influence or control over the northern border regions?

The accord made at Yalta was an attempt to extrude from Russian terms for entering the Pacific War solutions for this whole range of questions.

Before tracing the actual negotiation of the accord, it is well to refresh our memory about the state of China at this stage of the war. There was no longer any danger that the Japanese would be able to gain control of the whole of China and destroy its organized government. But otherwise conditions were woeful. The interior regions were cut off from the food-producing provinces of the east, and from the coast. There was no trade with the outside world. Inflation ruled. Poor workers in the cities, students, officials, and soldiers were finding it very hard to live. The rural economy was suffering from eight years of neglect and destruction; in many places there was a lack of farm labor, livestock, fertilizer, and tools which reduced production and supply of the main crops. Ninety per cent of the railways were out of operation; roads were very poor and trucks few and worn out. In brief, the people in free China—and in those sections occupied by the Japanese—were managing to keep alive and going, but miserably so.

The conflicts among the Chinese people and the political parties were unreconciled. The Kuomintang government was at odds with smaller democratic groups. The loyalty of many officials—governors of provinces, mayors of cities, commanders of armies—was venial and uncertain. Most importantly, the Chinese Communists in the north were openly defying the authority of the government, and rejecting its terms of cooperation. Life in the areas they controlled was reported to be scant and hard also. But production was being kept up better, and rice and other essentials were being more fairly and honestly shared. Experienced visitors to Communist headquarters at Yenan were impressed by the confidence of their leaders and the popular support of their army and civil administration. These were outspoken about their plans for expanding their realm. The National Government was convinced that their aim was to capture the whole country by taking advantage of the misery and confusion of war. It was maintaining an armed blockade of Communist areas.

General Hurley, to whom the President had assigned the task of bringing about political and military unity in China, was trying hard. His active, almost fervid, efforts kept in check the impulse of both sides to resort to arms. Not allowing himself to be depressed by failure of his first attempts, he was, during this Yalta period, keeping the two sides talking to each other. On the third of February (the day before the Yalta Conference opened) the National Government had submitted a proposal for the convocation of a consultative conference of all parties which was to prepare the way for a unified, constitutional government. Chou En-lai, the leading Communist official who was in Chungking for talks with Chiang Kai-shek, had said he believed his party would take part in this conference. In short, during the Yalta meetings, there seemed some basis for hoping that what Hurley called in one of his reports "this dreary controversial chapter" would end in a political arrangement if not in a reconciliation.

American policy in and toward China was based on the supposition that it must and would end, and that political and military unification within that country would follow. In fact, our whole Pacific policy was becoming dependent on the realization of that aim. The President and the State Department hoped that Stalin's favor and help could be won for a peaceful settlement of the Chinese internal quarrel, or at least that they might get assurances that the Soviet government would not make it harder to bring about unification by encouraging the Chinese Communists to be unyielding, as were the Polish Communists.

But if the scanty American records contain the whole story, the President devoted only passing attention to this aspect of the accord on the Far East. They tell of only one brief exchange of comment on February 8th after Roosevelt and Stalin had agreed to enter into a written understanding about the political conditions under which the Soviet Union would enter the war against Japan. The President is recorded as saying merely ". . . that for some time we had been trying to keep China alive" and Stalin commenting dryly ". . . that China would remain alive." Then Stalin went on to say that some new leaders were needed around Chiang Kai-shek. The President remarked that he thought progress was being made in bringing the Communists together with the Chungking government; and that ". . . the fault lay more with the Kuomintang and the Chungking government than with the so-called communists." [14] The memo of this talk ends with Stalin's limp observation that ". . . he did not understand why they did not get together since they should have a united front against the Japanese. He thought that for this purpose Chiang Kai-shek should assume leadership. He recalled in this connection that some years ago there had been a united front and he did not understand why it had not been maintained." [15]

But could this have been all that the two men said to one another about this vital feature of the Chinese situation? That is hard to believe. Perhaps Roosevelt thought Stalin's statement, his show of aloofness and willingness to allow the Americans to handle the problem, enough for the purpose. Or perhaps he sensed that Stalin could not be induced to give a positive promise. Or perhaps he believed no more could reasonably be asked, since he regarded the conservative elements in the Kuomintang to be the real obstructors of fair unity rather than the Communists. Most of the American military men in China so thought at the time; and most of the group in the State Department concerned with Chinese affairs felt that it was Chiang Kai-shek who ought to be forced to give in the more, or be dropped by us.

Whatever the reason, Roosevelt did not get explicit assurances from the Soviet government that it would use its influence to cause the Chinese Communists to be conciliatory, in return for his assent to Soviet terms for entering the war. He seems to have left it up to the Chinese government to win this cooperation for itself—as one phase of the improvement in Sino-Soviet relations which he was bent on bringing about.

At every chance the American government had been preaching the sense and benefits of mutual friendship to the Soviet and Chinese governments. Chiang Kai-shek, despite his fear and mistrust, had shown an eager wish to arrive at an arrangement with his menacing neighbor to the north. He had sought various chances to discuss terms with it. He had assured Vice-President Wallace during his visit to Chungking the previous June that he would continue to do so. At that time he had proposed that the President might act as "middleman" or arbiter. Wallace had told him that he did not think that the President could do so, or that the American government could become a party to or guarantor of a Sino-Soviet agreement. But he had said he thought it would be willing to use its good offices to get them together. Chiang Kai-shek had said he would welcome that; and if the American govern-

[14] As printed in *Yalta Documents*, page 771.
[15] *Ibid.*

508

ment would "sponsor" such a meeting, he would go more than half-way to reach an understanding. From time to time Stalin and Molotov had been approached with this suggestion. They had always averred that they wanted to be friendly with China. They had held the Chinese responsible for the friction, and had spoken indignantly over the constant attempt of the Kuomintang to blame them for the internal troubles of China, thereby excusing its own faults and failures.

Then in November the Russian Chargé d'Affaires in Peking had spoken to Chiang Kai-shek's oldest son about a possible meeting between his father and Stalin. Chiang Kai-shek had thought of sending this son to Moscow to learn what was in store. While this was still under consideration, the President—with his knowledge of Soviet war plans in the Far East fresh in mind—had (on November 18th) sent Chiang Kai-shek an enigmatic message. He had asked Hurley to tell the Generalissimo that not only from his point of view but also from that of the Russians, a military agreement between all Chinese forces was much to be desired. He could not, the President had added, explain his thoughts more fully at that time; Chiang Kai-shek would simply have to take his word for it. When giving Chiang Kai-shek this message, Hurley was told he might emphasize the word "Russians." There can be little doubt that Chiang Kai-shek understood this as a signal that the Russians were going to enter the Pacific War and would presently be marching southward. He had hurried his efforts to get in touch with the Soviet government. In view of the weight of the errand, he had decided that Soong rather than his son had better be sent to Moscow. He had asked Stalin to receive his Foreign Minister. Stalin had answered that he would be glad to do so. But he had suggested that the visit be put off until the latter part of February or the early part of March. This meant that Stalin had chosen to test American and British response to the claims he was going to make before discussing them with Soong. On February 4th, the day of the first formal session at Yalta, Hurley informed Washington that Stalin had just confirmed the arrangements for the Soong visit; but a few days later—probably after his talk with the President on February 8th about Soviet desires in the Far East—Stalin had asked Soong to postpone his visit until later in March or early April.

It will be recalled that at that momentous meeting on October 15th while Churchill was in Moscow, Stalin, after confirming Soviet intention to enter the war three months after Germany was defeated, had served notice of Soviet desires in the Far East; and that Harriman and Deane had made no comment, expecting him to enlarge on the subject, but he had not done so. Stalin had evidently thought it best to reserve discussion in this field until he met with Roosevelt. And the President had shown no hurry to find out more exactly what Stalin had in mind —perhaps because he did not want to risk friction which might upset joint planning for Soviet entry into the Pacific War; perhaps because he was waiting to see the outcome of the negotiations between Chiang Kai-shek and the Chinese Communists. Whatever the reason, he had waited.

When Harriman returned to Washington, the President had shown curiosity as to what Stalin's claims were going to be. In the course of sketching out (on November 17th) his surmises, the Ambassador had stressed the importance of bringing about a settlement between Chiang Kai-shek and the Chinese Communists before the Soviet Union was in the war. For he feared that if there were none, the Red armies in Manchuria would back the Chinese Communists, as they were backing Tito in Yugoslavia, and then Stalin would demand much more of Chiang Kai-shek. It was on the next day, it may be recalled, that the President had told Hurley to whisper the word "Russians" to Chiang Kai-shek. The President had instructed Harriman on his return to Moscow to ask Stalin to clarify what he wanted.

Harriman had, on December 14th, done so and Stalin had responded freely.

He had talked first of Dairen. At Teheran, he had remarked, the President had said that Dairen should be returned to Russia under a lease. Pointing out the area he had in mind on a map he had fetched from the next room, he encircled the southern part of the peninsula with a blue pencil—including Port Arthur as well as Dairen. Harriman had asked whether the President had not at Teheran suggested that Dairen be internationalized as a free port. The Ambassador said he thought the President preferred that sort of arrangement to a lease, as being more in accord with current ideas. Stalin had said that he did not remember exactly, that the record could be easily checked.[16] In any case, he had gone on, the possibility of internationalization of the port "could be discussed." How well this phrase served him!

Then Stalin had proceeded to state two other desires which he said had also been mentioned in talk between himself and the President at Teheran. One was the Soviet wish for a lease on the Manchurian Railways. Harriman had asked whether, if this were granted, China would remain sovereign in Manchuria, and Stalin had answered that he did not intend to interfere with that sovereignty. In reporting this answer to the President, the Ambassador had observed that there could be no doubt, however, that with control of the railway operations and

[16] See page 255.

with the probability of Russian troops to protect the railroad, Soviet influence in Manchuria would be great. The other requirement was the transfer of South Sakhalin and the Kurile Islands to the Soviet Union. Russia, Stalin had explained, had no free outlet to the Pacific; all were either held or blocked by "the enemy."

Finally, he listed a desire which had not been touched on at Teheran —to have an agreement recognizing that Outer Mongolia would, as Stalin put it, ". . . maintain its status quo as an independent entity."

Harriman had informed the President that he would not pursue the discussion of these terms unless instructed to do so. Roosevelt had judged it best to allow them to rest unremarked until he should meet with Stalin.

At Yalta he continued to wait until Stalin brought up the subject. There it was considered outside the regular business of the conference, in a few brief patches of private talk between Roosevelt and Stalin, with Harriman and Molotov acting as aides.

Just before the fifth regular session, Stalin and Roosevelt had a detailed talk about military plans and prospects for the final assaults on Japan. After each had expressed satisfaction over the cooperative attitude of the other, Stalin remarked that he would like to discuss the political conditions under which the Soviet Union would enter the war against Japan. He referred to the talk he had had with Harriman in December. The President answered that Harriman had reported to him in full. Then he went on to state what he considered the Soviet Union could ask with just title. Perhaps by the show of free and ready assent he was trying to make it a little harder for the Russians to press for more. He saw no difficulty, he began, about turning over to Russia at the end of the war the southern half of the island of Sakhalin and the Kurile Islands.[17] As for the wish for a warm water port in the Far East, the President said that Stalin would recall that at Teheran he had suggested that the Soviet Union be given the use of such a port

[17] Divisional committees in the State Department had prepared memos on these subjects which are included in the *Yalta Documents*, pages 379 ff. and 385 ff. Neither memo was included in the Briefing Book taken along to Yalta.

The one on southern Sakhalin recommended that an effort be made to get the Soviet Union to agree to designate this as a trust area; but then said that if the Soviet Union was not satisfied with that, the American position should depend on the circumstances existing at the time. The one on the Kurile Islands recommended that the Northern and Central Kuriles should be placed under international trusteeship, with the Soviet Union as administering authority; but that the Southern Kuriles should be retained by Japan, subject to the principles of disarmament to be applied to the whole of Japan.

There are indications in both of these memos that the officials who wrote them discussed the subjects with colleagues in the War and Navy Departments. I do not know whether the Joint Chiefs of Staff were asked for any formal report on these matters.

at the end of the southern Manchurian railroad, possibly Dairen on the Kwantung Peninsula. There were two ways, he continued, in which this might be done; it might be leased by China to the Soviet Union or it might be made into a "free port" under some form of international control. Of the two, the President continued, he preferred the second, since he hoped that the British would agree to give Hong Kong back to China and that then China would make it into an internationalized free port also. After an interval in the talk, Stalin remarked, ". . . the Russians would not be difficult and he would not object to an internationalized free port." [18] Then he went on to say that there was another question: the Soviet Union wanted the use of the railways of Manchuria, and he specified what lines he had in mind. The President did not contend that the Soviet Union could get reliable "use" of these lines by some customary sort of trade and traffic agreement with China. He accepted the idea that a special arrangement was necessary and justified. He answered that there were two possible ways of dealing with this matter: the lines might be leased by the Soviet authorities and operated directly by them, or they might be placed under a joint Chinese-Russian commission.

Leaving this and other points unsettled, the talk had then passed on to the question of when Chiang Kai-shek might be advised of Soviet intentions and requirements. But before it ended Stalin observed that he thought it would be well if, before leaving Yalta, the three powers should set down in writing their agreement regarding the conditions on which the Soviet Union was entering the Pacific War. Roosevelt said that he thought this could be done.

Stalin grasped the initiative. On the 10th, as the work of the Conference was coming to a compressed end, Molotov asked Harriman to call, and gave him an English translation of a paper entitled "Draft of Marshal Stalin's Political Conditions for Russia's Entry in the War against Japan." In the two-day interval, evidently, Stalin concluded that the Soviet Union must have and could get an exclusive lease on both Port Arthur and Dairen; and also that it should again secure all the rights which the Czarist regime had once had over the Manchurian railroads without control by a joint commission.

On the spot Harriman explained to Molotov that he thought there were three amendments the President would want. Two of them were: acceptance of his proposal that Dairen and Port Arthur should be free ports and not under lease to the Soviet Union; and that the railroad should be operated by a Chinese-Soviet commission. The third was concerned with obtaining Chiang Kai-shek's concurrence and I shall discuss it separately.

[18] *Yalta Documents*, page 770.

After consulting the President, Harriman wrote out the desired changes and transmitted them to Molotov. Later that same crowded afternoon—on the last long day before adjournment—the Conference met in formal session. After this was over, Stalin told Harriman that he was willing to have Dairen made into a free port under international control, but that he would want a lease of Port Arthur since it was to be a naval base. Harriman said that Stalin would have to talk this over with the President. The Marshal walked across to the President and repeated his proposal about the two ports. The President consented. Stalin then accepted the idea that the railroads should be placed under a Chinese-Soviet commission. The talk of the two map-makers was shortly afterward interrupted. But before leaving the conference room Harriman asked Stalin whether he would prepare a revised draft and Stalin said that he would.

The text which was produced overnight, in addition to incorporating the amendments agreed upon, contained some entirely new language. This is italicized in the text of the two pertinent paragraphs as they came back from Stalin.

"2 (b) the commercial port of Dairen shall be internationalized, *the preeminent interests of the Soviet Union in this port being safeguarded* and the lease of Port Arthur as a naval base of the USSR restored,

"2 (c) the Chinese-Eastern Railroad and the South-Manchurian Railroad which provides an outlet to Dairen shall be jointly operated by the establishment of a joint Soviet-Chinese Company, it being understood that *the preeminent interests of the Soviet Union shall be safeguarded* and that China shall retain full sovereignty in Manchuria."

The practical application of these new vaulting phrases was not talked out. Despite advice from Harriman that they ought to be eliminated or that their import ought to be clarified, the President let them pass. His view was that their meaning was well understood between himself and Stalin; and that the "preeminent" Soviet interests recognized were only toward (1) having access to Dairen as an international free port, and (2) having unimpeded use of the specified railways for Soviet transit traffic. This was a lax and hazy treatment of demands on which for almost half a century grave quarrels had centered.[19]

[19] During that half century the American government had fluctuated in its stand towards similar claims, adapting itself to circumstances and the disposition of the American people to risk war. Sometimes it had unyieldingly refused to countenance or recognize Russian or Japanese acquisitions in the region, sometimes it had acceded to them. This feature of the Yalta accord appears far less sensational when compared with: (1) the notes exchanged by Secretary of State Root and the Japanese Ambassador in Washington, Takahira, on November 30th, 1908, wherein it was stated that "the policy of

The President had the choice of opposing these and the other Soviet demands, or of leaving them for the Chinese to grant or deny, or of agreeing to support them. He chose the third course. By doing so he probably did not agree to anything with which Chiang Kai-shek would not have been forced to grant anyhow, perhaps less. But he made the United States responsible for what the Soviet government exacted. And when later it turned out that Soviet participation in the Pacific War was not needed at all, his compliance came to seem foolish. To echo Churchill, those who have never tried to serve several good causes at the same time, each beset by risks, will be most harsh in condemning the error.

The third Soviet suggestion was handled by bandaging the text. In their first short talk (February 8th) about the ports and the railways, Roosevelt had let Stalin know that he had not yet talked these arrangements over with Chiang Kai-shek and so could not speak for the Chinese government. But the draft which Molotov had given to Harriman on the 10th paid no attention to that. It read flatly that, "The Heads of the three Great Powers have agreed that these claims of the Soviet Union should be unquestionably satisfied after Japan has been defeated." This would have obligated the President and Prime Minister to support the Soviet terms unconditionally—no matter whether the Chinese government found them acceptable, no matter how the Soviet government behaved. Harriman had told Molotov that he was sure that the President would not want to dispose finally of these matters without the concurrence of the Generalissimo.

On returning to Livadia Palace, Harriman urged him to get Stalin to omit this clincher of obligation. But the President did not think it essential to go so far, and was afraid that by trying to do so he might seem to be bringing the whole value of the agreement into doubt. His dilemma was real: to make a promise to cause China to pay a toll it might resent was to risk reproach, or worse; to refuse bluntly was to leave China exposed to whatever bargain Moscow might later impose.

---

both Governments was to be directed to the maintenance of the existence of the status quo . . ." The status at this time embraced Japan's special position in Manchuria with all rights and privileges pertaining thereto. See A. W. Griswold, *The Far Eastern Policy of the United States,* pages 129-131, and P. C. Jessup, *Elihu Root,* Vol. II, page 684, and (2) the provision in the Lansing-Ishii accord of November 2, 1917, which stated that the Governments of the United States and Japan recognize that "territorial propinquity creates special relations between countries, and consequently, the Government of the United States recognizes that Japan has special interests in China, particularly in the part in which her possessions are contiguous." This was supplemented by a declaration by Japan of respect for the open door and the independence and integrity of China of a sort which the Soviet government later on agreed to issue and might have issued if the American and Chinese governments had pursued the matter more diligently than they did.

In any case, and with what history indicates was faulty judgment, he decided that the delicate problem could be met by adding a new qualifying provision in the text reading, "It is understood that the agreement concerning the ports and railways referred to above requires concurrence of Generalissimo Chiang Kai-shek." [20] He told Harriman that he regarded this provision as ruling over the other. Besides, he thought that Stalin was aware that under the American Constitution any agreement that he entered into with foreign governments must be provisional and subject to the approval of Congress. This, it may be remarked, was pertinent to the legal validity of the agreement and perhaps even to his ability to carry it out. But it was not conclusive in regard to the moral or personal obligation which the President assumed.

Stalin agreed to include this new sentence—suggesting however that Chiang Kai-shek be asked also to concur in the provision regarding the maintenance of the status quo in Outer Mongolia. Thus both provisions remained, one following the other, in the text that was signed. [21] The President and Stalin do not seem to have discussed what would have happened if Chiang Kai-shek did not concur. But the whole record suggests that neither Roosevelt nor Stalin thought it likely that Chiang Kai-shek would refuse his consent.

The two found it hard to decide when and how Chiang Kai-shek should be told of their understanding and asked to abide by it. Neither of them trusted that this accord, connected as it was with the Soviet promise to go to war, could be kept secret if told to Chiang Kai-shek. Stalin suggested that he thought it would be safe and time enough to let the Generalissimo know about it when Soong came to Moscow at the end of April; for by then, he thought, Soviet forces on the Manchurian front would be strong enough to take the risk that Japan might learn of its intention and move first. The President agreed to leave it up to Stalin to choose the time when Chiang Kai-shek should be told. And when Stalin said that he would rather that the American government first consult Chiang Kai-shek, since he was an interested party, the President undertook to do so through Ambassador Hurley.

In so going forward with matters of such evident concern to China, the President may have been moved by the thought that the Chinese government would be getting in return what it most wanted—protec-

[20] *Yalta Documents*, page 897.

[21] *Ibid.*, page 984. The provision in the signed text thus read, "It is understood that the agreement concerning Outer Mongolia and the ports and railroads referred to above will require concurrence of Generalissimo Chiang Kai-shek. The President will take measures in order to obtain this concurrence on advice from Marshal Stalin."

tion against Soviet hostility and possible Soviet cooperation with the Chinese Communists. For in the agreement there was a final paragraph which read, "For its part the Soviet Union expresses its readiness to conclude with the National Government of China a pact of friendship and alliance between the USSR and China in order to render assistance to China with its armed forces for the purpose of liberating China from the Japanese yoke." [22]

Nothing in the original records so far seen throws direct light on what the President thought of the value and implications of this item in the accord.[23] A good surmise is that he anticipated that the mere concourse laid out in this agreement would lead to an improvement in Sino-Soviet relations; and that the pact of friendship and alliance that was to be made would secure the position of the National government of China. The way in which Stalin, even in the course of their talk at Yalta, had developed his demands does not appear to have caused Roosevelt to worry because this mere statement of attitude left the Soviet government free to bargain with China later on for a still greater payment for its friendship. But, to repeat, of all elements in the accord the least is known about what Roosevelt and Stalin thought would emerge from this one.

Churchill and his Foreign Office aides had known that the American and Soviet governments were drawing up an accord about Russian territorial desires in the Far East. Just before the plenary session on the 10th, Stalin had told the Prime Minister what he was proposing to Roosevelt. Perhaps he was sounding out Churchill in regard to the American wish to have the ports placed under international control in view of a reference the President had made that a similar regime might be formed for Hong Kong. All that Churchill has told us about his answer is, "I replied that we would welcome the appearance of Russian ships in the Pacific, and were in favour of Russia's losses in the Russo-Japanese War being made good." [24] It is unlikely that, because of the lack of time, either he or Eden discussed the subject again with Roosevelt.

When in the closing hours of the Conference the completed accord

[22] *Ibid.*

[23] Churchill, in *Triumph and Tragedy*, page 389, wrote that Stalin categorically agreed to support the Nationalist Chinese government. But he does not make clear whether this is merely his interpretation of the meaning of the final paragraph in the accord, which is given above, or whether Stalin in his private conversation with him on the afternoon of the 10th or on some other occasion gave this assurance orally. Harriman, in a statement presented to the *Joint Committee on Military Situation in the Far East*, page 3334, stated that the President ". . . had also obtained Stalin's pledge of support for Chiang Kai-shek."

[24] *Triumph and Tragedy*, page 389.

on the Far East was brought to the table for signature along with the others, Churchill signed without demur. He has recorded in *Triumph and Tragedy* the reasons why he was so obliging: "I must make it clear that though on behalf of Great Britain I joined in the agreement, neither I nor Eden took any part in making it. It was regarded as an American affair and was certainly of prime interest to their military operations. It was not for us to claim to shape it. Anyhow we were not consulted but asked to approve. This we did. . . . To us the problem was remote and secondary." [25]

Perhaps the Prime Minister was swayed by the thought that it was essential to concur in order to maintain the position of the British Empire in the Far East.[26] It may be wondered also whether he did not regard his compliance as a fair return for the initiative that was being ceded to Great Britain in Southeast Asia.

As agreed, the existence of the accord was guarded by silence. It was not mentioned in the joint communiqué issued at the end of the Conference. None of the three sponsors referred to it in their public reports on the Conference. This secrecy served several purposes. It preserved Soviet military security. It postponed any possible reaction to the agreement by either the Chinese government or the Chinese Communists. It averted active debate within the United States which might have impaired the unity of the Allies. But ever since, the secrecy has caused the agreement to be regarded in a sinister light. Undoubtedly this is one of the reasons why so much dramatic interest has been attached to it, and why its importance has been so exaggerated in public controversy.

In the long run, its main consequence may well prove to be its effective confirmation of the decision reached at Cairo—that Japan was to forfeit its whole Empire and position on the continent of Asia—rather than in what the Soviet Union got.

But the doubts and disputes came later. The sponsors separated at Yalta with the sense that by their agreement about what was to be done in the Northern Pacific area they had added another segment to their coalition and smoothed the way for China to enter more fully into it.

[25] *Ibid.*, page 390.
[26] Stettinius in his later account records that he was told by one of his friends in the British government that Eden had tried to persuade the Prime Minister not to sign the agreement; that Churchill said he was going to sign "in order that Great Britain might stay in the Far East," and also because ". . . he had great faith in President Roosevelt and felt that he could rely completely on the President's judgment in the matter." *Roosevelt and the Russians*, pages 94–95. Churchill in *Triumph and Tragedy* makes no allusion to any such talk with Eden.

A provisional understanding was also reached about Korea. In the Cairo Declaration the American, British, and Chinese governments had made of public record their resolve ". . . that in due course Korea shall become free and independent." In that same talk on February 8th, Roosevelt raised the question of how this was to be given effect. He asked Stalin what he thought about a trusteeship for Korea composed of Soviet, American, and Chinese representatives; and suggested it might be maintained for twenty to thirty years if necessary to prepare the people for self-government. Stalin said the shorter the period the better. He asked if any foreign troops would be stationed in Korea. The President said no. Stalin expressed approval. The President then said he did not think it essential to invite the British to participate in the trusteeship for Korea, but felt that they might be offended if left out. Stalin said they most certainly would be offended. In fact, he added, the Prime Minister might "kill us."

This coincidence of ideas about Korea was not stated in the secret accord, or otherwise. No thought was given then to finding out whether the Korean people would agree to a trusteeship rather than claiming immediate independence.

54. Yalta: Polish Issues

In contrast to his bold willingness to face the remaining territorial questions in the Far East, the President at Yalta was careful to avoid responsibility for what might be done about Poland. The problem distressed Churchill, worried Roosevelt, and provoked Stalin.

The hope which the Prime Minister had carried away from Moscow in October had been entirely vain. The differences between the two groups had gaped wide open again. The Lublin group had treated the government-in-exile (still recognized by the United States and Great Britain) with hostility and scorn. The Soviet government was accusing the leaders of the Polish underground directed from London of sabotage and murder, and was imprisoning its members. The Red Army commanders in Poland and their local Polish friends were refusing to allow the British or Americans to send observers or liaison officers into the country. The Poles in exile throughout the world who longed to return to their homeland were afraid to go back or were refused entry.

Mikolajczyk, as soon as he got back from Moscow, had consulted his colleagues in London as to whether or not to accept the terms Stalin had proposed. Before reaching a decision he had tried to define again how far the British and American governments would support him. He had addressed a series of questions to Churchill. He had asked whether the British government (1) would support the proposed extension of the Polish frontiers in the west even if the American government did not agree with them; (2) would favor the extension of this frontier to the Oder River, including Stettin; and (3) would guarantee the frontiers and independence of the new Poland. The British government had answered (on November 2nd) that it would support the proposed advancement of the Polish frontiers in the west and that it thought the Polish government should have the right to extend its territory to the Oder. It would be willing to give the suggested guarantee, but only jointly with the Soviet government.

Mikolajczyk, by personal letter and through his Ambassador in Washington, sought Roosevelt's response to these questions, while appealing to him to intercede with Stalin about Lwow and the oil fields. The State Department had urged the President to give some indication of American views on the disputed issues. It had been arranged that Harriman, who was to start back from Washington for Moscow via London, should give Mikolajczyk a letter outlining the position of the American government and at the same time should say that if desired, he (Harriman) would, on arrival in Moscow, explain to Stalin why the President thought Lwow should be left to Poland. Roosevelt's policy was, in Hull's apt phrase, ". . . to refrain from stretching the United States upon a bed of nettles." [27]

The letter, signed by Roosevelt, was sympathetic in tone but careful in promise. Once more it affirmed that the United States government stood hard and fast for a strong, free, and independent Poland. And it went so far as to say that the American government would not object to any agreement which the Polish, Soviet, and British governments might reach about the future frontiers of Poland, including the proposed compensation from Germany. But it would not promise to guarantee the frontiers that might be set in such forced circumstances. It excused itself in the letter on the ground that the security organization planned at Dumbarton Oaks would have the responsibility for seeing that boundaries were not violated.

Harriman had shown Churchill and Eden this letter before giving it to Mikolajczyk. They had thought it might clarify the situation. He had then (on November 22nd) passed it on to Mikolajczyk. That tried man was pessimistic over what was happening both in Poland, where

[27] *Memoirs,* page 1448.

Communist influence over the Lublin committee was getting more marked, and in his circle in London. He had told Harriman that he was convinced he could not get enough support for his program of reconciliation with the Soviet government and Lublin Poles. His associates, he had explained, were certain that the Soviet government was bent on communizing Poland; and intended to wait until Poland was liberated, to retain within Poland a resistance to Russian domination; and to hope that at some future time American and British influence might be brought to bear on Russia to induce it to allow the Polish people to choose their own government. So he did not now think it fair to ask the President to try to get Stalin to compromise about Lwow and the potash and oil fields.

Mikolajczyk had, in fact, decided to resign. As he wrote later, he felt that: "We were becoming increasingly isolated. The Big Three regarded us either openly or privately as *saboteurs* of their unity. . . . My own cabinet felt that what I had agreed to represented too much of a compromise, though I explained to them that they were on the verge of being cut off from the Polish people by the threatened recognition of the Lublin group by all major Powers." [28]

Churchill and Eden had felt that under the circumstances they could not try to dissuade Mikolajczyk from resigning. The American government had sighed. The new Cabinet that had been formed in London after Mikolajczyk gave up office was anti-Soviet—except for its Prime Minister, Arciszewski, an old Socialist leader who had been brought out by plane from Warsaw. Yet the American and British governments were still committed to treat it as the legitimate government of Poland. Thus if the Soviet government should decide to disregard it entirely and accord the Lublin Committee full recognition, the break in the coalition would be marked and open. At that time more than most, with trouble on the Western Front, such an alienating quarrel had been feared.

The danger broke down Roosevelt's disinclination to get deeper into the Polish problem. During the next fortnight he urged Stalin several times to abstain from any main decisions about the Polish question until the three of them could meet. In particular he asked the Marshal to desist from recognizing the Lublin group as the Provisional Government of Poland. He stressed that only a small part of Poland had as yet been liberated and the Polish people had thus not had a chance to express their political wishes. But the Soviet government had, on the last day of 1944, gone ahead and announced that it would regard the National Committee as the Provisional Government.

[28] *The Rape of Poland*, pages 104–05.

Both the President and the Prime Minister had suppressed their indignation. They were paying the full price for coalition and Soviet military cooperation. Perhaps also for future peace they were accepting a situation which in its full later consequences would haunt the peace. But they had remained resolved not to deal with the Polish Provisional Government as then composed. They had clung to the hope of persuading Stalin when they met with him to join them in making that government more representative of all elements in Poland, and in arranging that the Polish people should have a quick and genuine chance to choose their own government and decide their own constitutional structure. On these terms Churchill was ready to confirm his acceptance of those boundaries which Stalin had laid down in October; and the President, though still bent on trying to keep Lwow for Poland, was resigned to giving in, if need be.[29]

But the auguries had grown darker in the weeks before the Yalta Conference. Up to then the Soviet government had proposed that the western boundary of Poland should be on the Oder River, possibly including the cities of Stettin and Breslau. Suddenly there were signs of an aim to push that frontier even farther west. For example, there was a long article in *Pravda* by the Propaganda Minister of the Polish National Committee, advocating that the new frontier on the Oder should run to the confluence of the lower (the Western) Niesse, and then south *along the Niesse* to the Czech border near the city of Gorlitz. Several million Germans lived in the areas which now for the first time it was proposed should also be ceded to Poland. These presumably, with the other six millions or so living east of the Oder, were to be sent back to Germany. If Poland was controlled by the Communists, they would be pressing close upon all Germany and Western Europe. Moreover, it was a boundary which sooner or later would have to be defended by force. So when they had set off for Yalta, the President and Prime Minister could not tell what new claims might confront them.

The Polish question was a disheveled presence in every conference hour. It was discussed in the private talks which Churchill, Stalin, and Roosevelt had with one another; in the group meetings of the Foreign Ministers; and at all but one of the plenary sessions. It became the testing ground between the West and Communist Russia—between two conceptions of security.

[29] In regard to former inhabitants of the disputed areas who were released from former German control in Italy and France, the Soviet government was already claiming that all coming from places roughly east of the September 1939 boundaries were Russian. American Army Group Headquarters were on the whole abiding by the rule that such "displaced persons" were of the nationality they claimed to be.

The repetitious argument always came back to the same two issues: (1) What were the frontiers of Poland to be? The answer to that was more than a determination of how much room the Polish and German peoples would have to live in. It would have a great bearing upon (2) Who was to govern Poland? The answer to that was very likely to settle whether or not Poland was to be a revolutionary state and permanently a dependent part of the Soviet zone of control.

In their very first talk on the subject, Roosevelt made his try at getting Stalin to relent a little about the eastern frontiers. He pleaded rather than argued. He recalled that at Teheran he had said that he thought the American people were in general favorably inclined to the Curzon Line as the eastern frontier of Poland but that if the Soviet government would allow Lwow and the oil deposits in that province to remain in Poland, it would have a very salutary effect.[30] Churchill then said that he would stand by his statements that the British government would support the Curzon Line despite criticism, for he felt that after the agonies which Russia had suffered in defending itself and in liberating Poland her claim was founded not on force but on right. However, should Russia make the magnanimous concession suggested by Roosevelt, it would be most prized.

Stalin's answer was to the effect that the Soviet government was as determined as the British or American that Poland should have a sufficient basis to be a strong and independent state. Poland was the border country, the corridor, through which Germany had struck at Russia twice in thirty years. This could happen because Poland was weak. He wanted it in the future to be strong and powerful enough to protect this route with its own forces. But, he continued, he could not accept the President's suggestion. The Soviet Union was entitled to have Lwow and Lwow Province, which were to the east of the Curzon Line. The Russians, he declaimed, had had no part in determining that this ought to be the frontier line between the Soviet Union and Poland back in 1919. Lord Curzon and Clemenceau had fixed that. The Russians had not been invited and the line was established against their

[30] This is based on the Bohlen notes of this meeting as given in *Yalta Documents*, page 667. The Matthews notes of the same meeting give a somewhat different impression of Roosevelt's remarks. "There are six or seven million Poles in the United States. As I said at Tehran, in general I am in favor of the Curzon line. . . . The Poles would like East Prussia and part of Germany. It would make it easier for me at home if the Soviet government could give something to Poland. I raised the question of giving them Lvov at Tehran. It has now been suggested that the oil lands in the southwest of Lvov might be given them. I am not making a definite statement but I hope that Marshal Stalin can make a gesture in this direction." *Ibid.*, page 677.

will. Lenin had opposed giving Bialystok Province in the north to the Poles, but the Curzon Line gave it to them, and he had already retreated from Lenin's position. He could not return to Moscow and face the people, who would say Stalin and Molotov had been less sure defenders of Russian interests than Curzon and Clemenceau. It was therefore impossible for him to agree to the proposed modification of the line. In order to compensate Poland, he would rather have the war go on, though it would cost Russian blood. For now he proposed that Poland's western frontier be carried to the more westerly of the two Neisse Rivers. The American Embassy had been correct in its forecast.[31]

Molotov followed up this statement at the next session of the Conference (on February 7th) in a written note. Churchill stood up against the further distention of the western frontier. Poland should not be given more land in the west than it could properly handle; "it would be a pity," he said, "to stuff the Polish goose so full of German food that it got indigestion." [32] Many British people were going to be shocked by the plan to move large numbers of Germans out of the transferred territories by force. Even though Poland's western boundaries were extended to include only East Prussia and Silesia as far as the Oder, there would be about six million Germans to be moved. That number Churchill thought could be handled—leaving aside moral grounds.[33] But if the line were carried still farther west, the problem would be much harder and the opposition much stronger.

Roosevelt did not intervene in this clash of assertions. But after the session he circulated a proposal in answer to that made by Molotov. This said that the American government would not object if the Polish eastern frontier were set at the Curzon Line with small changes in Poland's favor, as suggested by Molotov. But "while agreeing that compensation should be given to Poland at the expense of Germany, including that portion of East Prussia south of the Koenigsburg line, Upper Silesia, and up to the line of the Oder, there would appear to be

[31] Mikolajczyk's latest proposals about the western frontier of Poland, as set down in a memo to the State Department and as summarized by it in a message to Yalta transmitted on February 6th, read: ". . . that in the west the new frontier should include East Prussia, Danzig, the region of Oppeln, the region of Gruenberg on the left bank of the Oder and, northward, the whole right bank of the Oder including Stettin." *Yalta Documents,* page 953.

[32] *Ibid.,* page 717.

[33] As summarily stated in Churchill's later account "If Poland took East Prussia and Silesia as far as the Oder, that alone would mean moving six million Germans back to Germany. It might be managed, subject to the moral question, which I would have to settle with my own people." *Triumph and Tragedy,* page 374.

little justification to the extension of the western boundary of Poland up to the Western Neisse River." [34]

The issue was left in suspense while the three Heads of State and their Foreign Ministers devoted themselves to arduous argument over the creation of a new government which they could all recognize. It was still unresolved when the negotiators had to decide what, if anything, must be said about frontiers—in the Declaration on Poland which was to be part of the published report on the Conference.

Churchill thought something must be said; otherwise the whole world would wonder what had been secretly decided. He observed that the three of them seemed to be agreed upon what the eastern frontier of Poland was to be. And he had approved the idea that Poland should receive compensation in the west up to the line of the Oder River if the Poles so wished. But, he continued, he had received a message from the War Cabinet strongly deprecating any reference to a frontier as far west as that which Stalin had suggested.

What Roosevelt said at first was apparently hard for his associates to understand, and remains hard for the student of the available records to interpret now.[35] His hesitation is evidenced by his statement that, "I do not believe we should say anything in the communiqué. I have no right to make an agreement on boundaries at this time. That must be done by the Senate later." [36] But Stalin and Churchill persisted. Stalin argued that they ought at least make known that they were agreed on the eastern frontiers, and Churchill suggested that it might be possible to state as well that the three powers recognize that Poland should receive substantial accession of territory both to the north and to the west, but that final decision must be kept open pending discussion with the Poles.[37] The President said he did not object to that in principle, but would like to see it stated in writing, and asked Churchill to draft it.

A text was produced by the Foreign Ministers and brought in for examination. It was in the form of a statement of agreement between

[34] *Yalta Documents,* page 792.

[35] Three sets of unofficial notes are printed in the *Yalta Documents.* One of these, the most systematic and least cryptic, was made by Bohlen, who was interpreter for the Americans, the other two by Matthews and Hiss, members of the American delegation; Bohlen, pp. 898–99, 905–06; Matthews, pp. 907, 911; Hiss, pp. 912–13, 917–19. They are condensed and divergent; and all that is reasonably certain is that Roosevelt was dubious as to whether anything at all ought to be said about the subject in the published report of the Conference.

[36] As recorded in the set of notes which, on this point, appear to me to be the fullest and most reliable (the Matthews notes). *Yalta Documents,* page 907. Compare Hiss notes: "I cannot agree on Pol boundaries at this time. It must be done by the Sen later." *Ibid.,* page 912.

[37] Bohlen notes, pp. 898–99; Matthews notes, p. 907; Hiss notes, pp. 912–13.

the three powers. The President again explained that he did not have the authority to accept any such formal obligation in the name of the American government. To ease past the difficulty, he proposed three changes of language which turned it into merely an expression of the views of "the three Heads of Government." As thus amended, the paragraph in the Declaration on Poland which was made part of the communiqué, read:

"The three Heads of Government consider that the Eastern frontier of Poland should follow the Curzon Line with digressions from it in some regions of five to eight kilometers in favour of Poland. They recognize that Poland must receive substantial accessions of territory in the North and West. They feel that the opinion of the new Polish Provisional Government of National Unity should be sought in due course on the extent of these accessions and that the final delimitation of the Western frontier of Poland should thereafter await the Peace Conference."[38]

The Russians had not given up without a last try. Molotov had urged that the second sentence read: "It is recognized that Poland must receive substantial accessions of territory in the North and West, *with the return to Poland of her ancient frontiers in East Prussia and on the Oder.*"[39] Roosevelt asked how long since these lands had been Polish. Molotov said very long ago, but they *had* once been Polish.

"President (laughing to Prime Minister): Perhaps you would want us back?

"Prime Minister: Well you might be as indigestible for us as it might be for the Poles if they took too much German territory."[40]

Stalin withdrew the proposal.

Thus it was decided that Poland was to be large. But who was to govern the country? And were the Polish people to have a free and fair chance to determine that? By this last day, after exhausting talks, the Conference had agreed upon verbal formulas in regard to these issues.

The American and British governments recognized that the time had gone for a "fusion" of London and Lublin. The only type of solution left was deemed to be the creation of a *new* and more representative interim government in Poland pledged to hold free elections as soon as conditions permitted. Roosevelt brought along a proposal designed to give effect to this plan, and placed it before the Conference early (Feb-

[38] *Yalta Documents*, page 980 (final text).
[39] *Ibid.*, page 905. [My italics]
[40] *Ibid.*, Matthews notes, page 911.

ruary 6th). This—in brief—looked toward the formation, through the agency of a small group of Polish leaders, of a government made up from the five Polish political parties. Churchill used all his powers of persuasion in the service of some program of this sort. He tried to salvage at least a segment of the Polish government group in London—the group which had stood with Britain in the darkest time of the war—by suggesting that there ought to be places in the interim government for men of good will like Mikolajczyk, Grabski, and Romer.

Stalin was bland and accusatory. He remarked that he thought Churchill's tongue had slipped, since he said that the three of them at Yalta ought to create a government for Poland. For, he continued, that could not be done without consulting the Poles and getting their consent. But it would be hard to bring them together; the principal personalities in the Provisional Government would not want to talk of fusion with the London group. Still, Stalin continued, he was ready to go along with any attempt to create unity that might succeed. Should the three of them ask the Lublin Poles to come here (to Yalta), or would it be better to see them in Moscow?

After his first exposition the President refrained from taking part in the long review of the situation in which Stalin and Churchill engaged, of which I have marked merely the main channel. But as soon as the meeting was over, after consultation with Churchill, he sent a letter to Stalin. This reaffirmed the determination that the Polish question should not cause a breach between them. It suggested that as a next step they might invite to Yalta the heads of the Lublin government and two or three other individuals, representing different Polish elements selected from a list he submitted. Then he, Stalin, and Churchill could consult with this small composite Polish group as to how to develop a new temporary government, and perhaps jointly agree with them on a provisional government ". . . which should no doubt include some Polish leaders from abroad such as Mr. Mikolajczyk, Mr. Grabski and Mr. Romer." Then the American government, and he felt sure that the British government also, would be ready to examine with Stalin the conditions under which they would disassociate themselves from the London government and transfer their recognition to the new Provisional Government. Finally, the President thought it would be understood that any interim government so formed would be pledged to the holding of free elections in Poland at the earliest possible date.

Stalin tried to get in touch with the leaders of the Lublin group before the next meeting of the Conference on the 7th, but he could not reach them by telephone. On reporting this he said that he doubted whether the other Poles could be located in time for them to come to

Yalta. So it was agreed that it would not be possible to carry on the necessary consultations with the Poles at Yalta; that would have to be done later on. The Conference then, and to its end, devoted itself to considering the basis on which this later consultation with the Poles should be conducted.

Should the new Provisional Government merely be an enlargement of the one that had emerged from the Lublin Committee, by giving places to a few eminent Poles from inside and outside Poland? That is what Stalin and Molotov wanted. Or, should it give way to a wholly new one, made up of some of the members of the existing Provisional Government, representatives of other democratic elements that were still in Poland, and Polish democratic leaders at the moment abroad? That is what Churchill and Roosevelt and their advisers wanted. The issue was, at bottom, the vital one of who was going to be in control.

Rights and wrongs, facts and sentiments—all were tossed about in the ensuing breakers of discussion. Churchill emphasized that if the Polish government in London were wholly brushed aside, the British people would cry out in anger and the many Poles who had fought in the skies over Britain and on the Western and Italian Front would feel betrayed. The British government, he concluded, could consider transfer of recognition only if a genuinely new start were made by all on more or less equal terms, and if fair elections would follow later. Stalin spoke in the name of the Poles who had stayed in their country and shared in the suffering and "the great festival of liberation." He made much of the Soviet need for a stable and friendly government behind the lines of the Red Army as it fought its way to Berlin.

But the most persuasive point which Stalin and Molotov made was that the differences concerned only the question of the composition of the government *during the short period before the whole of Poland was liberated and general elections could be held*. How long, the President asked Stalin (on February 8th), did he think that interval would be? Stalin's answer was: "In about one month unless there is a catastrophe on the front and the Germans defeat us." And then with a grin, "I do not think this will happen." [41]

Molotov and Stalin reverted to this point at every remaining twist of the argument. After all, if the new Provisional Government was to give way so soon to an elected one, was it essential to maintain the dispute? To trace the trailing discussion over formulas, of the exact selection of conditions and phrases, we would have to dissect tediously the cadavers of the various discarded drafts. It is enough, I think, to mark the fact that a revised proposal which the Americans had submitted (on

[41] *Ibid.*, Matthews notes, page 790.

the 9th) read as follows: "That the present Polish Provisional Government be reorganized into a fully representative government based on all democratic forces in Poland and including democratic leaders from Poland abroad, to be termed 'The Provisional Government of National Unity.' " [42]

And that the formula to which, at the end, Churchill and Roosevelt gave their resigned consent read: "The Provisional Government which is now functioning in Poland should therefore be reorganized on a broader democratic basis with the inclusion of democratic leaders from Poland itself and from Poles abroad. This new government should then be called the Polish Provisional Government of National Unity." [43]

The President and Prime Minister yielded the central structure of their defense against the domination of Poland by the elements that were supported by Moscow. For this formula left the existing Provisional Polish Government, though called upon to absorb other elements, in the seat of authority. How clearly one and the other perceived this cannot be deduced with certainty. They could hardly have failed to be aware that the Soviet government could maintain—as Stalin later did—that "There [at Yalta] all three of us, including President Roosevelt, proceeded on the assumption that the Provisional Polish Government, functioning now, as it does, in Poland and enjoying the confidence and support of the majority of the Polish people, should be the nucleus—that is to say, the principal part—of a new reorganized Government of National Unity." [44]

If we assume that they foresaw that the Soviet government might so interpret this ambiguous formula, their choice was of the hardest. If they left Yalta without any accord, what would prevent the Lublin group, with Soviet help, from grasping undiluted control? And what would happen to the prospect of free and unhampered elections as soon as the war was over? About these, Churchill and Roosevelt got as firm and clear promise as could be had. The text upon which they were agreeing specified that, before recognition, the reorganized Provisional Government "shall be pledged to the holding of free and unfettered elections as soon as possible on the basis of universal suffrage and secret ballot. In these elections all democratic and anti-Nazi parties shall have the right to take part and to put forward candidates." [45] Whatever chance remained that the Polish people might be free to choose their government and determine their national policies was deemed to depend on this pledge.

[42] *Ibid.*, page 804.
[43] *Ibid.*, page 973.
[44] Stalin to Churchill, April 24th, 1945. *Triumph and Tragedy,* page 492.
[45] *Yalta Documents,* page 973.

But what was this worth? What likelihood was there that an interim government, Communist ruled, would allow itself to be challenged, and quite possibly ejected from office, by an election held in the Western style? The only effective guarantee would have been a provision for international supervision of the elections from start to finish. But it was taken to be obvious that Stalin would reject any such plan as unnecessary and offensive. The idea the President and Churchill advanced was more deferential—only that it should be stipulated that "the Ambassadors of the three powers in Warsaw following such recognition would be charged with the responsibility of observing and reporting to their respective governments on the carrying out of the pledge in regard to free and unfettered elections." [46] Even that Stalin and Molotov did not like. They objected to it on the score that the Poles—they did not clearly say which Poles—would be offended by it.

Roosevelt apparently decided that it was useless or almost so to protract the argument over possible supervision of the elections, meaning as it might have, a prolongation of his stay at Yalta. His responses during the last formal discussion of the subject (on February 9th) were tinged, I think, by a longing for an end to the labor of debate. [47]

Churchill threw himself earnestly into pleas for retaining the original American proposal. In a private last-minute talk with Stalin before the final plenary session (on the 10th) he tried to wrest from him at least assurances that the three Ambassadors in Warsaw would be allowed to move freely through Poland so that they could find out what was going on. Stalin said that the Soviet government would not interfere with them, and that he would give the necessary instructions to the Red Army. But, he added with a shrug, the matter would have to be arranged with the Polish government.

The brief clause substituted for the American proposal on this point was ineffectual. It stipulated merely that when the new Provisional Government was recognized, Ambassadors would be exchanged, ". . . by whose reports the respective Governments will be kept informed about the situation in Poland." [48] Churchill, telling later of his talk with Stalin on this point, curtly wrote, "This was the best I could get." [49] But all it was was a poor chance to argue again another day.

The duty of continuing the argument and of securing what had not been secured at Yalta was imposed upon the American and British Ambassadors at Moscow. In this assignment they were to meet with Molotov as a special committee.

[46] *Ibid.*, page 804.
[47] *Ibid.*, page 848.
[48] *Ibid.*, page 980.
[49] *Triumph and Tragedy*, page 385.

55. Yalta: German Questions

The Germans, clinging to their malignant leadership, were fighting on and would continue, it seemed, until the very earth fell away from them or they were buried in it. They had survived great defeats in the past and would survive this one. What measures, acceptable to the conscience of our times, could eliminate the chance that they might rise from the rubble and strike out again?

All three Heads of State at Yalta professed that this aim, and not cruel revenge, should govern their decisions about Germany. They were unanimously determined that Hitler and his supporters and his system of life and government must be abolished. They all felt justified in demanding as retribution the punishment of the war criminals and the payment of reparations. But they tended to separate on how drastically they must act to make and keep Germany weak, and the Germans peaceable. Yet substantial progress was made toward the completion of agreements between the three for dealing with this main and feared and hated enemy.

Agreement on the instrument of surrender was quickly reached. Its basic elements are so familiar that there is hardly need to do more than name them. Germany was to accept unconditional surrender. In so doing, it was to obligate itself to submit to the orders in all spheres of the United Nations. The whole German military establishment was to be disbanded with utmost speed and thoroughness, and German arms of all sorts were to be delivered to the Allies or destroyed. National Socialism as a regime or party or political ideal was to be extinguished. The German people were required to accept whatever measures for the redirection of their life might be imposed upon them.

With almost equal speed agreement was completed on the arrangements for exercising control over Germany after surrender. The essential features have previously been described. Supreme authority in Germany was to be exercised by the American, British, and Soviet Commanders-in-Chief, each in his own zone of occupation, and also jointly in matters affecting Germany as a whole. They were to act together as members of a top organ called the Control Council. This Council, among its other functions, was to (1) insure uniformity of action in the respective zones; (2) make plans and decisions affecting Germany as a

530

whole, on the basis of instructions received by each Commander from his government; (3) control the German Central Administration; and (4) direct the administration of Greater Berlin. Unanimous consent was required for decision within the Council. Thus if the governments of the members could not agree on any main matter of policy, the Council would not be able to act, and decision would rest with the separate zone Commanders.

The zones of occupation for the United States, Great Britain, and the Soviet Union had been settled, though not yet recorded in a formally signed document. The questions left were whether or not to allocate a zone to France and make it a fourth member of the Control Council. It was understood that the Soviet zone was not to be cut down, and any zone for the French would be formed out of part of the American and British areas as already delineated. The President, as told, was disposed to assign a zone to France. But when first talking about this with Stalin and Molotov before the opening session of the Conference, he adopted an indulgent air. He referred to the fact that he would rather have had the United States occupy the northwest zone of Germany, so that it would not have to rely on communications through France. But he had given in to the British, even though what they seemed to want was that the United States should first restore order in France and then turn over control of it to Britain. Stalin by then had probably learned not to take Roosevelt's sallies about Churchill's wiles to be other than what they were. His answer was in the form of a question: did the President really think that France ought to have a zone of occupation? The President answered that it would not be a bad idea, but would be done only out of kindness. Stalin shook his head, as a way of saying he thought so, too.

In the session of the next day (the 5th), both Churchill and Roosevelt spoke in favor of assigning a zone to France. The Prime Minister declared this to be of much importance to Britain. France was not only the nearest neighbor of Germany in the West but the only ally of any strength on which Britain could count. It was needed to stand guard on the left hand of Germany so that Britain might not again be confronted by the specter of Germany at the Channel ports. Roosevelt, he continued, had made it clear that Britain ought not to count on American forces remaining in Europe indefinitely. At this point the President repeated that, "he did not believe that American troops would stay in Europe much more than two years . . . he felt that he could obtain support in Congress and throughout the country for any reasonable measures designed to safeguard the future peace, but he did not believe that this would extend to the maintenance of an appreciable American force in Europe." [50]

At a later session of the Conference in another connection it ought to be noted that the President amended this statement. He explained that he had made it with current American attitudes in mind, that if an international organization along the lines of Dumbarton Oaks was created, the American people were much more likely to take part in world activity.[51]

Stalin remained resistant to the allocation of a zone to France until the Conference was nearly over. If France were granted a zone, he thought it would be hard to refuse one to other countries who had contributed more to the war and suffered more because of the German assault. But, he explained, what really bothered him was not the assignment of a zone to France but the connected proposal that France be given a place on the Control Council. For that, he foresaw, would make it much harder for the Council to conduct its business; France would have ideas of its own and would want to make bargains for its own benefit. So he suggested that they might agree to assign a zone to France on the understanding that it would not be allowed to participate in the Control Council.

Roosevelt was willing to go along with that proposal. But Churchill and Eden maintained that it would not work, and that France could cause more trouble off the Council than on it. At the end, Roosevelt changed his mind. In the last Plenary Session he said so. He explained that he was in part influenced by the thought that if France was awarded both a zone and participation in the Council, it would be easier to get de Gaulle to go along with other agreements that had been reached at Yalta, for example, to join in the Declaration on Liberated Europe. Stalin, having just gotten very much of what he wanted in regard to Poland, gave in.

Joint messages were prepared to inform de Gaulle of the admission of France to an equal place in the occupation and control of Germany. He was pleased and perhaps somewhat appeased. For he had been aggrieved that he had not been asked to take part in the Conference at Yalta, on the score that the Allies were offending the dignity of France and neglecting its interests. To mark his resentment he had refused an invitation from the President to meet him at Algiers after the Yalta Conference was over.

The district of Greater Berlin was deep inside the Soviet zone of occupation. The text of the Agreement on Control Machinery provided

[50] *Yalta Documents*, page 617.
[51] *Ibid.*, pages 660–61.

that it was to be governed jointly by a Komendatura consisting of commandants appointed by the respective zone Commanders-in-Chief. In order to exercise their assignment of authority, the Americans, British, and French needed adequate and unhampered access from their zones through the Soviet zone to the city. But, as told in an earlier reference to the question, the War Department (or at least one branch of it) had thought it unnecessary to define the ways of access in the Protocol on Zones of Occupation. That could be done better, it had reckoned, by the zone commanders when more was known of the state of roads, railways, and the like. The subject had remained in abeyance.

While at Yalta, the Joint Staff Planners recommended that a memo be sent to the British and Soviet General Staffs as follows:

"The U.S. forces in Berlin and certain other areas will be isolated from the main areas of U.S. occupation by territory occupied by other than U.S. forces. There will be need for regular transit by road, air and rail across this intervening territory. The U.S. Chiefs of Staff propose that the general principle be accepted of freedom of transit by each nation concerned between the main occupied area and the forces occupying Berlin and similar isolated areas. They further propose that details be worked out between the local commanders."

The Joint Chiefs consulted their British and Soviet colleagues about entering into some such accord as an interim military measure pending general agreement as to transit to be made in the EAC. To anticipate, the British concurred in this suggestion, but the Soviet staff hung back. The matter was deferred.[52]

After the stir made by the Morgenthau Plan, both Roosevelt and Churchill had been willing to let time do its calming work—before trying again to decide what should be done about German economic activity and existence. Stalin had not hurried them. At Yalta the three tried to develop a common policy to be followed in the whole of Germany.

They were in accord that the Germans were to be left to take care of themselves. They were not to be treated as wards; the occupying powers were not to feel called on to do anything to assure a standard of living better than that needed—in the military phrase—to prevent disease and disorder. It would be only just, all agreed, if they were reduced to about the same standard of living as the other European peoples on whom

[52] This is an incomplete account of what occurred in this matter at Yalta and the months between Yalta and the capture of Berlin. But it is all that I have been able to find out from accessible records without intensive search and consultation. I anticipate that the full story will appear presently in one of the volumes of official history of the U.S. Army in the war published by the War Department.

they had brought such great suffering. But the British were more interested than the other two in preserving enough of the existing economic organization and structure to enable the Germans to take care of themselves on this, or a somewhat better, level. The Russians were ready to subordinate all questions of general welfare to a determination to erase the German economic capacity to make war and to a wish for reparations.

Although having discarded the drastic Morgenthau Plan, the American government still thought controls ought to be used to reduce the capacity of many German industries and to eliminate some entirely, such as synthetic oil and rubber. The British government, which, because of the location of its zone of occupation, would have had to bear the chief onus for the execution of such a policy, was of a divided mind. It was swayed by the same thoughts as the American government, but it was restrained by fear that if the policy were carried far and wide it might have to support the Germans living in its zone, and to reckon with great unemployment. Further, it was afraid of the effect in other European countries which would need German products. The Soviet government felt no compunction about destroying any or all parts of the German heavy industries. It was, of course, not deterred by the possibility that if the Germans were forced to get along without this industrial foundation, the country might be the more easily associated with the Communist regime in the east. But in those branches which would be called upon to provide goods for Russian reconstruction, it recognized that enough capacity would have to be retained for that purpose.

In the end, no attempt was made to define with precision just what the allowable level of German industry was to be, and just what industries or sections of industry were to be suppressed. All that was said in the Final Report of the Conference was that, "We are determined to . . . eliminate or control all German industry that could be used for military production."

The differences of attitude and interest became focused on the issue of what reparations Germany should be required to make. The American government asked no reparations payment except the retention of German assets in the United States, and perhaps raw materials. The British government wanted and hoped to receive some German equipment and German products which would enable Britain the more quickly to repair the war damage. But it was ready to adjust its demands to other considerations of policy. The Soviet government sought very great reparations. It not only wanted them but was determined to have them, and willing to use whatever measure of compulsion was needed in order to get them. Even so—and it repeatedly made the point —what could be had from Germany would fall immensely short of the damage that Germany had done to the Soviet Union and her people.

All agreed that this question needed more specialized and thorough study than could be given during the brief meeting at Yalta. It was arranged that this should be conducted by a Reparations Commission that would start work in Moscow as soon as possible. So the argument that ensued at Yalta dealt with the definition of the principles by which this Commission was to be guided in its work and conclusions.

The Soviet government took the initiative. It proposed that Germany should be required to make reparations not in money but in kind, and in addition to labor services to be rendered by the Germans. In part the payment was to be made by the removal from Germany and shipment to the recipient countries of factories, machinery, ships, railway equipment, power plants, and the like. These were to be selected with two purposes in mind: (1) to eliminate industries primarily useful for military purposes; and (2) to reduce other German heavy industries to about one-fifth of their previous capacity. These removals were to be accomplished within two years after the end of the war. The rest of the reparations payment was to be made by the delivery of goods to be currently produced in Germany, to be provided during a period of ten years. The better to assure that these would be produced and turned over, the Soviet plan contemplated Anglo-Soviet-American control over the German economy, and more directly over those enterprises that were producing for reparations.

The Soviet government proposed that the total amount to be demanded in these two forms should be set at twenty billions of dollars, and of this the Soviet Union should get half. In addition, it stated that it would require German labor and truck services in the Soviet Union to reconstruct the devastated regions. Churchill and Eden protested that this sum was excessive and could not be collected. They maintained that if German industry were so greatly reduced, misery, perhaps starvation, would follow. They forecast that if the attempt was made to enforce the Soviet plan, the United States and Great Britain would again, as after the last war, have to provide the means for the Germans to live; it would mean, in substance, that other countries would be paying German reparations to the Soviet Union. They urged, in consequence, that no decision should be made at Yalta as to the total reparations to be demanded, and also that the period of payment should be shortened.

In the concluding discussion of this issue (at the seventh and last

Plenary Session on February 10th), after Maisky and Molotov failed to overcome these British contentions, Stalin flung himself into the argument with vigor. He asserted that the Germans would be able to pay what the Soviet Union was asking and still live as well as the countries east of them. Supporting this conclusion were the impressive statistical comparisons which Maisky had presented previously. In contrast to the method of collecting reparations attempted at the end of the last war, the Soviet plan, he emphasized, should involve no monetary transfer difficulty; the Soviet government, no matter what the others did, would acquire its due directly. His suspicion that Britain really wanted Germany to be left strong after the war—perhaps revived by its cool stand toward dismemberment, of which we will tell shortly—found sarcastic expression in the remark to the effect that if the British felt that the Russians should receive no reparations at all it would be better for them to say so frankly. He went on to insist that the Conference decide that the Moscow Commission should fix the amount and should take into consideration what he called the American-Soviet proposal that there should be twenty billion dollars of reparations, with fifty per cent to the Soviet Union.[53] Or, as variantly expressed by him a little later in the discussion: ". . . all they were preparing was a figure to be used as a basis for discussions—it could be reduced or increased by the Commission in Moscow." [54]

It is hard to tell whether he was justified or not in calling this an American-Soviet proposal, because the American comment on the issue had slipped so much from side to side. When first it was discussed by the Foreign Ministers, Stettinius' ambiguous remarks had seemed to imply assent to the Soviet ideas. But in the face of the opposed arguments, Roosevelt at this last session suggested that the whole matter be left open for the Commission in Moscow. Then, when challenged by Stalin as to whether that meant that the American government had changed its mind and no longer agreed with the Soviet proposal, the President had answered that he was completely in agreement; the American government was entirely prepared to discuss the sum and principles.[55] Roosevelt may be pardoned for being of several opinions at once. For the guiding line which Stalin was proposing—that the named sum be taken by the Moscow Commission "as a basis for dis-

[53] *Yalta Documents,* Bohlen Minutes, page 901.
[54] *Ibid.,* page 902. As summarized in the Matthews notes, his statement contained an even stronger suggestion that the matter of amount was really left open. "Three, the Moscow reparations commission is given the task to consider the amount to be paid. We bring our figures before the commission and you bring yours (to Churchill)." *Ibid.,* page 909.
[55] *Ibid.,* Hiss notes, page 915.

cussion"—could have several meanings, and Stalin maneuvered confusingly between them in the course of the discussion.

At the end Roosevelt assented to this broad formula: possibly because he believed that it left the question sufficiently open to further examination; perhaps because of the view recorded in a note which, at some time while the matter was being argued, Hopkins passed to him: "Mr. President the Russians have given in so much at this Conference that I don't think we should let them down. Let the British disagree if they want to—and continue their disagreement at Moscow. Simply say it is all referred to the Reparations Commission with the minutes to show the British disagree about any mention of the 10 billion. Harry." [56]

The question was disposed of in this fashion. The pertinent provisions in the Protocol approved by all three read:

"4. With regard to the fixing of the total sum of the reparation as well as the distribution of it among the countries which suffered from the German aggression the Soviet and American delegations agreed as follows:

"The Moscow Reparation Commission should take in its initial studies as a basis for discussion the suggestion of the Soviet Government that the total sum of the reparation . . . should be 20 billion dollars and that 50% of it should go to the Union of Soviet Socialist Republics.

"The British delegation was of the opinion that pending consideration of the reparation question by the Moscow Reparation Commission no figure of reparation should be mentioned.

"The above Soviet-American proposal has been passed to the Moscow Reparation Commission as one of the proposals to be considered by the Commission."

One other item of the agreement on reparations should be noted even in this simplified and condensed account. It provided that the reparations to be exacted from Germany should include the "use of German labor." Stalin and Molotov explained that what they had in mind was using some two or three million Germans for reconstruction work within the Soviet Union during a period of ten years. These workers would be selected from the lesser war criminals first of all, then from the active Nazis, and then from the unemployed.

To the last round of toasts Stalin tried to better the chances of getting all that he asked. In the course of the congenial talks at the table the last time the three dined together (on February 10th), Stalin complained about the outcome of their discussion. He said he feared having to go back to the Soviet Union and to tell the Soviet people that they

[56] Ibid., page 920.

537

were not going to get any reparations because the British opposed. Churchill did not mar the occasion. He answered softly that, to the contrary, he hoped very much the Soviet people would get large reparations. Stalin suggested that it would help him if the public statement that was to be issued conveyed some assurance to that effect. Molotov drew up the sentence in which that was to be made clear: "We have considered the question of the damage caused by Germany to the Allied Nations in this war and recognize it as just that Germany be obliged to make compensation for this damage in kind to the greatest extent possible." This was approved without qualification. But what might be "possible" would depend on whether or not the United States, as before, provided support for the German people while they were paying reparations, and also upon how the victorious powers decided that other primary question—whether or not to partition Germany into several separate states.

All the accords made at Yalta rested on the premise that there would be only one German state, reduced in area by adjustment of its frontiers. But the idea of dividing Germany into several states was still very much alive.

Since their concurrent recoil from the program initialed at Quebec, Churchill and Roosevelt had searched their thoughts for certainty but had not found it. In October, Churchill had briefly discussed with Stalin various possibilities of division—involving also the formation of a Danubian Basin Confederation. But since this talk was only an intermediate flight of ideas, which left all conclusions open for the triple meeting, this account may pass it by.

This is in effect what Stalin did when introducing the subject at Yalta. Thus far there had been only conversation: what now did the three of them propose to do? Churchill said that the British government was still inclined in principle to favor partition. He, personally, thought that the isolation of Prussia and the elimination of her power would remove the arch evil; and that a South German state with perhaps a government in Vienna might indicate the line of great division. But he was puzzled and appalled over the many and profound matters that ought to be considered before any final decision and plan were made. Certainly these could not be thoroughly enough weighed in the few days they were going to spend together at Yalta; they would be dealing with the fate of eighty million people, and that required more than eighty minutes of discussion. Besides, he said, there did not seem to be any need to determine the question right then and there, and it might be better to wait until they were in occupation of Germany before making up their minds.

Roosevelt at first spoke vaguely, by intent or otherwise. He seemed disposed to fall in with Churchill's idea that decision might be allowed to wait upon knowledge of the actual condition of Europe at the end of the war. There are flickers in his remarks which indicate that he thought that if they did wait, the answers as to whether or not to partition Germany, and how to do it, would largely emerge of themselves; that the German people might separate into several states before or during the regime of occupation. But he affirmed that he, personally, still thought it would be a good idea to have Germany divided into five or seven parts, to prevent the possibility that it would again break the peace of Europe.

Stalin sought a decision then and there. Coupling up with this last remark of Roosevelt's, he professed that the three of them all seemed to be basically of the same mind. So he suggested they might record their agreement in principle that Germany should be dismembered, and instruct the Foreign Ministers to work out the details. He proposed further that in order that the Germans could raise no question when the plan was put into effect, a clause be added to the terms of surrender stating this intention. By so doing he seemed to think the German people would be obliged to submit. Although Churchill contended that it was unnecessary since the surrender terms would confer unrestricted authority and power upon the Allies, it was done.

The Heads of State found that they could agree quickly on amending Article 12 of the surrender instrument to read as follows: "The United Kingdom, the United States of America, and the Union of Soviet Socialist Republics shall possess supreme authority with respect to Germany. In the exercise of such authority they will take such steps including the complete disarmament, demilitarization *and the dismemberment* of Germany as they deem requisite for future peace and security." [my italics for the added phrase]

But attempts to determine how to study the procedure for dismemberment were lost in the convolutions of the subject. So that was consigned to a committee consisting of Eden as Chairman and Ambassadors Winant and Gusev. This group was to consider the desirability of associating with it a French representative.

If Stalin in his zeal for dismemberment, or Churchill in his hesitations, had in mind the way in which the decision would affect the power situation or the spheres in which Communism or Western democracy might prevail, they did not say so. Nor did Roosevelt haul such large considerations to the surface.

On separating at Yalta the three Heads of State could feel that they had done what was imminently necessary for dealing with Germany during the period of surrender and control. Stalin would have been more pleased if they had set their mark more deeply and permanently upon that country. But this was against Churchill's instinct. For him not the cold and rigid determination to enforce a program upon the hidden future. Before the Conference started, he had, in a memo to Eden, explained why:

"It is a mistake to try to write out on little pieces of paper what the vast emotions of an outraged and quivering world will be either immediately after the struggle is over or when the inevitable cold fit follows the hot. These awe-inspiring tides of feeling dominate most people's minds, and independent figures tend to become not only lonely but futile. Guidance in these mundane matters is granted to us only step by step, or at the utmost a step or two ahead. There is therefore wisdom in reserving one's decisions as long as possible and until all the facts and forces that will be potent at the moment are revealed." [57]

Roosevelt swayed in between these two attitudes. He spoke as though willing to be unsparing in the treatment of Germany as long as necessary to keep it sober, if not meek. But his responses give the impression that he was fatigued by the weight of the problem, and unsure as to whether the American people would be willing to accept continued responsibility and bear the continued cost of keeping the Germans under prolonged control.

The accord reached at Yalta served their most immediate purposes well—to sustain the concert of military action against Germany until that war was won and to manage German surrender smoothly. Whether thereafter the three great victorious powers would find and really observe common policy that would fulfill the aims of each remained dubious.

56. Yalta: The Smaller States of Europe

In intervals of attention snatched from the greater problems of strategy and peace-making, the three Heads of State glanced at the unsettled situations in the smaller countries about which they were still not at ease or in accord.

Of all of these, Italy had become the most nearly quiescent. It was gradually emerging from the misery of the war. The Germans were still in the northern provinces and held some of the large northern

[57] *Triumph and Tragedy,* page 351.

industrial cities. The government, a coalition of six main political parties, maintained itself shakily from week to week. Rivalry and conflict between them was making further reorganization inevitable; and proposals for change had caused a sharp brush between Churchill and the State Department which had been smoothed over by the time of Yalta.

The Control Commission was easing its restraint and its demands. But it was not doing so fast enough in the opinion of the American government, which was evolving plans to change the status of Italy to that of cooperating ally. The British government, still mindful of the way in which that country had turned against it at the time of greatest peril, was not as ready to forget and forgive. At Yalta members of the State Department and the Foreign Office discussed the differences of viewpoint and found that they were only a matter of degree and timing. The President, just before leaving Yalta, wrote a letter to Churchill saying he was glad to find that this was so. At the same time he urged the need for quickly ending what he called "Italy's present condition of semi-servitude." He was afraid, he explained, that too long a delay would give troublemakers their chance to play upon despair. He was sure, he concluded, that they were in agreement that Italy must be given both material and spiritual food, and he wanted Churchill to know that he was determined to work together with him in Italy as in other areas. Churchill made his usual generous response.

During this period the Soviet Union had not challenged the British-American exercise of authority over the country—which was still a main combat area. The Italian Communists, although assertive in their demands on various matters, such as the punishment of the Fascist elements, did not seem to be exploiting the misery of the Italian people for any revolutionary purpose.

In Greece "a precarious tranquility," in Churchill's phrase, had been achieved. The coalition government which had been patched together had broken up early in December as it tried to disband the guerrilla forces. The groups led by the Communists had tried by tactics and strikes, disorder and terror, to take control. British forces had been engaged in severe street fighting in Athens. They had prevented an immediate upset. But General Alexander had put Churchill on notice (on December 21st) that "the Greek problem cannot be solved by military measures. The answer must be found in the political field." [58]

[58] *Ibid.*, page 310. The campaign was using up far greater fighting forces and resources than had been foreseen. "The occupation of Greece, which in September, 1944 had seemed likely to demand the provision of 10,000 British troops for a short time, absorbed over 60,000 by the end of December, with another 18,000-odd designed to reinforce. . . ." *Grand Strategy,* Vol. VI, page 57.

Churchill and Eden had, on Christmas Eve, turned away from the cheerful light of the occasion and had flown down to Athens. At the time only the small center of the city, the section of the legations and government buildings, was out of the range of fire and tumult; and in his goings and comings the Prime Minister could have been hurt or captured. This exciting errand animated the once young subaltern who had been with the Spaniards during the Cuban rebellion, the British press correspondent in South Africa during the Boer War. In Athens he had been compelled to recognize that the feeling against the King and the existing government was so strong that it would be necessary to displace them or face a prolonged civil war. He had managed to guide the leaders of the various political parties to agree to accept the authority of a regency to be exercised by the Archbishop of Athens, Damaskinos. It was understood that the new government to be formed under him would be composed of a small group of the "best men" led by a vigorous republican, General Plastiras. Churchill had then taken upon himself the uncongenial task of persuading the King to renounce his powers and appoint the Archbishop as Regent. Impressed at the need for haste, he had told the King that unless he consented at once, the Regency would be established anyhow and the British government would recognize it. Roosevelt, in response to Churchill's appeal, had added his plea to that of the Prime Minister's. The King had given in. On December 30th he had announced the Regency and his resolve not to return to Greece unless summoned by fair expression of the national will.

The Archbishop had been installed on the 1st of January with the assent of all parties, including the Communist. Two days later a new government under General Plastiras had taken office. He and his associates were known as vigorous republicans and thus had attracted support even among opponents of the former authorities. But the Communist-led combatant groups could not be prevailed on to lay down their arms. A stiff campaign, mainly by British troops, had been required to drive them from Athens and Attica. Only after this had been done had an armistice been effected (January 15th), preliminary to the arrangement of a peace agreement between the resistant party (EAM) and the government. For the time being the revolutionary forces were scattered. The government in turn had promised fair elections, respect for civil rights, and amnesty.

At Yalta, Stalin showed himself curious about what had taken place. But he assured Churchill that he meant no criticism and had no intention of meddling in the situation. Churchill expressed appreciation of this attitude. The poorly recorded dialogue between the two men conveys an intimation on the part of Stalin that he was observing his part of the bargain which he had made with Churchill in October—that Britain was to have a determining voice in Greece. With knowledge that trouble might at any time start up again among that quick-spirited and contentious people, Churchill valued the assurance. Though having looked forward eagerly to the return sea voyage from the Crimea to Malta, he gave it up and flew straightaway to Athens, to see how the work he had done seven weeks before had stood the political weather. In Athens he found order and enthusiasm—and words for a moving expression of his affection for the country, its past, and its future in a "harangue" (his own word) which ended, "Greece forever. Greece for all!"

Churchill and Stalin had agreed to share equal responsibility for guiding developments in Yugoslavia, and in the months before Yalta had made a genuine effort to work together.

Tito, as President of the National Committee of Liberation, and Subasic as Prime Minister of the Royal Yugoslav government, had announced on December 7th two agreements looking toward the formation of a single new government for Yugoslavia. These provided that King Peter was not to return to Yugoslavia unless and until the people decided to have him back. In the interval the royal power was to be exercised by a Regency Council to be appointed by the King in agreement with Tito and Subasic. In the allocation of executive offices, members of Tito's Committee were to have a dominating portion, but some Cabinet positions were assigned to the Subasic group. The anti-Fascist Council of National Liberation was to have full legislative powers for the time being. But it was stipulated that within three months after the liberation of the whole country free elections should be held for a constitutional assembly which would decide on the future permanent government of the country.

The British government had not been pleased with the terms of these agreements. But it had decided to sustain them as a means of averting continuous agitation and giving diverse democratic elements in that turbulent Balkan country a better chance to survive. The views of the American government had been invited. The State Department was adverse; it correctly concluded that one group would have controlling power in the government and that "The gesture toward the government-in-exile, in the person of Dr. Subasic, seems hardly more than a concession considered sufficient to acquire recognition by other governments, on grounds of an apparent continuity."[59] However, beyond such observations the American government did nothing.

Subasic had followed Tito's example and gone to Moscow to find out

[59] *Yalta Documents*, page 256.

543

what assurances he might get from Stalin. On his return to London he
had advised King Peter to conform to the agreements between himself
and Tito, not to return to Yugoslavia, and to turn over the royal powers
to a regency. But the young King had refused and had issued a public
statement on January 11th explaining that he would not do so because
these actions seemed to him equivalent to abdication and certain to
result in the transfer of all power in Yugoslavia to a single political
group. Persuasion had failed to move him; on the 18th Churchill in the
House of Commons had set a deadline. In defiance of it the King had
summarily dismissed the Subasic government, whereupon the British
government had told the King it would not recognize any new Yugoslav government the King might form. It had told Subasic that the
King's action did not affect the intention of the British government to
see that his accords with Tito were carried out, and for this purpose
the British government was ready to transport him and his government
to Belgrade, together with all the Yugoslav leaders who wanted to go
there, and that it was informing Tito to the same effect. Another attempt had been made to persuade the American government to associate itself with this course of action, but had again come to nothing.

Unable to find any replacement acceptable to the British War Cabinet, the King had reappointed Subasic with a mandate to carry out the
agreement with Tito. But the King and Tito had not been able to agree
on nominations for the Regency Council. Until that was settled, the
Subasic government had remained in London and the accords could
not be put into effect.

At Yalta Churchill proposed to Stalin that they try to get two amendments made in the Tito-Subasic accords. These were: (1) an agreement
that members of the former Yugoslav Parliament who had not collabo-
rated with the enemy should be included in the anti-Fascist Council,
which was to exercise legislative authority; and (2) that the acts of this
anti-Fascist Council should be subject to confirmation by the Constituent Assembly that was to be summoned after the whole of Yugoslavia
was liberated. Stalin, using reasons supplied by Molotov, resisted the
proposal. He argued that this would mean an indefinite delay in bringing the accords into effect. It would be better, he maintained, to wait
until the new system of government was in operation and then to
consult it about the British amendments. Churchill and Eden denied
the fact that discussion of their proposals need cause delay in the execution of the accords. They advocated that they should be put up to Tito
and Subasic at once, since they were reasonable, since they would make
the new Yugoslav government more democratic, and since they would
insure the new government a better reception.

In the closing rush of the Conference, while the formula for Poland was being devised, agreement was also reached on this subject. In form it was a compromise; in result it meant that the Soviet strategy prevailed. Churchill gave up the idea that the Tito-Subasic agreement should be amended before being carried out. Instead, it was settled that he and Stalin should join in messages to Tito and Subasic, urging them to hurry and put the agreement as it stood into effect, by the formation of a new government based on it; and then this new government was to declare that it intended to act in line with the two amendments proposed by Churchill. Roosevelt, after some deliberation, concluded that he could associate himself with the message. It was sent on its way.

Not long after the Conference at Yalta adjourned, Subasic and his group left London for Belgrade. Early in March the three Regents took their oaths; Subasic read the proclamations from the King. A few days later Tito formed a new government, effectively subject to his will.

Looming conflicts over the frontiers between Yugoslavia and Austria and between Yugoslavia and Italy were worrying the British. Eden submitted memos on both situations to the Conference at Yalta.

One pointed out that under the prospective allocation of zones of occupation in Austria, the British would be responsible for the whole length of the Austro-Yugoslav frontier. Trouble might come because the Yugoslav government had advanced claims to border regions of Austria, and their partisan forces might try to take possession of these areas. The British government did not want to stand alone in preventing them. So it suggested that the three powers while at Yalta join in telling the Yugoslav government that pending the final peace settlement the old Austro-Yugoslav frontier should be restored, and ask it to promise to abide by this ruling; and that they would further affirm that the Soviet Union would support any action which the British government might have to take to preserve the integrity of this frontier.

The second memo gave warning of a grave danger of clashes in the Italian province of Venezia Giulia, in the northeast adjoining Yugoslavia. It stated that the British had planned to extend their Allied military government in Italy over the whole of this province up to the 1939 frontier. Tito, however, was refusing to consent. He was saying that he intended to exercise administrative authority over large sections in this province which he claimed for Yugoslavia, in some of which his partisans were already in control. The British government foresaw that, unless precautions were taken, fighting was likely to occur between the Allied military government and these partisans, or between the Yugoslav and Italian partisans. It suggested that they establish at Yalta a provisional line of demarcation in the province between the area to be controlled by Tito and the area to be placed under Allied military government.

The British memos on these subjects were introduced on the eve of adjournment. The Heads of State took note of them and agreed that they should be considered through usual diplomatic channels after the Conference adjourned. There, to foretell, they were caught in the silt.

In Romania the coalition government, which had lacked vigor and stamina, had given way under pressure from all sides. The local Communists and associated elements had intrigued against and plagued it with disorder. The Soviet government, not without some reason, had badgered it about reparations due, and for sheltering Nazi sympathizers and war criminals. The leaders of the more conservative parties had pulled away from it because they did not think it was doing enough to suppress the threat of Communism. The King had found the Prime Minister, Sanatescu, unworthy of his confidence, and ready to act as a tool of the Communists. Thus he had decided that the best chance of maintaining order and some measure of freedom would be to replace his government of politicians by one made up largely of "technicians," men not closely associated with any political party. This had been done early in December, despite fears that the Communists would try to take control by force, and would succeed in doing so if supported by the Soviet officials in Romania.

No immediate attempt of the sort had been made. But in the weeks before Yalta, American observers in the country had reported to Washington abundant signs that the Communists were bent on getting control of the country and the government, and were prophesying that with the encouragement, and sometimes the active aid, of the Red Army and Secret Police they were likely to succeed. Anna Pauker and another Romanian Communist leader had been called to Moscow in mid-January for instruction to launch a campaign for monopoly of power by the National Democratic Front (Communist). This group enlarged its appeals by claims that a real leftist government would be more able to secure for Romania recognition as a co-belligerent; the return of Romanian prisoners of war held in the Soviet Union; the award of northern Transylvania; and economic help, presumably relief from reparations demands.

The Soviet government was making no secret of its dislike and contempt for both the existing Romanian government and the people. The Soviet High Command was ruling with an iron hand. As chairman of the Control Commission, the Soviet member (General Vinogradov) had issued instructions in the name of the Commission without first consulting the British and American members. When reproached, he had tried to excuse his procedure on the score of emergency or military necessity. But in more open talk he had expounded the view that just as the Americans and British members of the Control Commission in Italy made executive decisions about that country, so in Romania he felt entitled to do the same. Molotov stood behind him in his excuses and rejections.

Toward Bulgaria the Soviet government and army were showing a more kindly but also more possessive attitude. The British and American members of the Control Commission were being shunted out of any real part in its operation. The Soviet member was maintaining, with support from Moscow, that under the armistice agreement he was entrusted with conclusive authority. The American and British members were rarely consulted, inadequately informed, and not allowed to travel so that they might see for themselves what was going on; virtually "interned," as Churchill was to say.

The British and American governments took to Yalta their complaints about the way the Soviet chairmen were running the control commissions in these two countries, Romania and Bulgaria. They did not ask for equality. After all, Churchill had agreed that the Soviet Union was to have the lead in both while the war was on. But they did ask to be consulted in advance about political orders, and they would have liked to have gotten Stalin to assent to the idea that after the war was over, and military necessity was at an end, their members would attain authority equal to that of the Soviet chairman. But no time was found to deal with these requests. They were left for more ordinary diplomatic treatment.

In Hungary heavy fighting was still going on, with Hungarian troops engaged on both sides. While the representatives of the new Provisional Government which had been formed at Debrecen waited, discussion of armistice arrangements had been resumed in Moscow between Molotov and the American and British Ambassadors.

Two basic differences with the Soviet government had not been adjustable. One concerned the question of whether the Control Commission should be just an appendage to the Soviet High Command or be a genuine joint authority.[60] Harriman and Clark-Kerr had sternly sought

---

[60] Because of its indicativeness of the Soviet attempt to get predominant influence over Hungary, the text of the original Soviet proposal on the question of control made on December 27th, 1944, is of some interest:

"For the whole period of the Armistice there will be established an Allied Control

to get a full and exact understanding about the rights and privileges that the American and British representatives and staff members would have. As instructed, they were prepared to agree that while the fighting continued, the Soviet chairman should have final say. They had centered their effort on getting a promise that the American and British representatives would be informed about policy directives long enough in advance of issuance to give their governments the chance to protest if they did not agree. Though Molotov at first asserted that this was not feasible, and though he also renewed the comparison with Italy where he averred that there had been no consultation with Soviet representatives for over a year, in the end the Soviet government had acceded to the British-American desire.

But, as regards the American and British claim of fully equal right and authority on the Control Commission after the war against Germany ended, the Soviet government had been unyielding. It was willing to grant the American and British elements on the Commission more privileges and freedom of movement than those accorded their counterparts in Romania and Bulgaria. But it refused to accept the basic rule that the Commission should function as a group of three equals and issue instructions only with the concurrence of all. The American and British governments had given in. This may have been because they had realized that what Molotov had said bluntly at one point in their arguments (on January 8th) was so: "It was not necessary for the Soviet Union to conclude an armistice with Hungary since the Red Army was practically the master of that country. It could do what it wished." However, each of the Ambassadors had put into the records a letter to Molotov serving notice that his government reserved the right at a later time after the defeat of Germany to again present its claim for equality.

The armistice terms had been presented to the officials of the Debrecen government on January 18th, accepted on the next day, and signed by Marshal Voroshilov for the United Nations on the day after that. With the Red Army spreading over the country, groups and elements sympathetic to the Soviet Union had increased their activity and grew in boldness as they grew in strength.

At Yalta the situation got only passing notice.

Commission in Hungary which will regulate and supervise the execution of the Armistice terms under the Chairmanship of the representatives of the Allied (Soviet) High Command and with the participation of the representatives of the United Kingdom and the United States.

"During the period between the coming into force of the Armistice and the conclusion of military operations against Germany, the Allied Control Commission will be under the general direction of the Allied (Soviet) High Command."

Thus in country after country, hitched to the train of victory, trouble trailed. It will be remembered that at the Moscow Conference in October 1943 the idea of placing all situations arising in liberated areas under a canopy of principle had been briefly discussed by the three Foreign Secretaries, and that the task had been found too complex and difficult. Now at Yalta, almost too late for the purpose, the American government vigorously tried again to bring this about.

Memos prepared for the Secretary of State and the President, found in the Briefing Book taken to Yalta, summed up the main objections to the way in which the situation was developing. They were: (1) that the prospect that really representative democratic governments would emerge in many smaller countries of Europe was being curtailed; and (2) that despite the Anglo-Soviet accord about spheres of responsibility, tension and suspicion were growing. The British officials were becoming more and more of the opinion that the Russians were striving to bring governments that were submissive to Communist control into power as far West in Europe as possible; while the Soviet officials were attributing to the British a wish to sustain along Soviet frontiers repudiated governments that would be hostile to the Soviet Union.

Devotees in the State Department of the United Nations project were also worried lest these tendencies stimulate opposition to the Dumbarton Oaks plan on the score that the future organization ". . . would merely underwrite a system of unilateral grabbing." So they prescribed what they hoped would be an antidote—in the form of a joint statement of policies.

This the American government presented at Yalta. The text was named "The Declaration on Liberated Europe." In itself it was little more than another avowal of devotion to ideals which all three Allies had approved many times before. In this proposed creed the Heads of State affirmed ". . . their mutual agreement to concert during the temporary period of instability in liberated Europe the policies of their three governments in assisting the peoples liberated from the domination of Nazi Germany and the peoples of the former Axis satellite states of Europe to solve by democratic means their pressing political and economic problems."

To this end, the declaration obligated them jointly to assist the peoples in any of these states to regain conditions of internal peace and to form interim representative and democratic governments, pledged to the earliest possible establishment through free elections of governments responsive to the will of the people. It stated that "when, in the opinion of the three governments, conditions . . . make such action necessary," they would consult at once on the measures needed to discharge these joint responsibilities.

With some minor changes of language, the Heads of State adopted and issued this declaration. It is hard to judge whether either Soviet or British governments shared the sense of the American formulators that its principles might govern events. Its loose net of phrases allowed easy passage to any determined purpose. The struggle within these countries was not just another chapter in Anglo-Soviet rivalry for influence in Europe. It was part of a world contest between those who looked to Moscow for leadership and those attached to other social ideas and systems. As long as that contest went on, coalition arrangements composed of such mutually hostile elements could be only temporary; and unless it was suspended, the resort to free elections, as the solvent of internal political differences, was certain to be impeded. What would happen if the people of one of the countries on Soviet frontiers elected a government actively opposed to the Soviet Union? What if one of the countries in the West elected a Communist government? Looked at another way, the question was whether the Anglo-Soviet attempt to limit the struggle by a division of spheres of influence should be discarded for excellent political principles which might, however, in the circumstances, have wayward results.

But the effort to enthrone principle, at Yalta and subsequently, ought not to be dismissed as futile. The Declaration on Liberated Europe may have served to sustain the resistance of democratic elements in Central Europe. The principles which it avowed may have affected action for a while and still survive as an inspiring guide for the future.

57. Yalta: The United Nations Organization

The Conference at Dumbarton Oaks had dispersed with the hope that the call to all the United Nations to meet to create the new world peace organization might be sent out soon. But a pause had followed. To the individuals who were attached to this cause above all else, each week that passed was a week of anxiety. Delay was a peril. So they tried hard to secure agreement on those matters which had not been settled at Dumbarton Oaks.

Among these, three were important:

1. What voting procedure was to be followed in the Security Council?

2. Who were to be the initial members of the organization?

3. Should the proposed Charter provide for any kind of territorial trusteeships?

As recounted, the three main Allied governments were agreed that the unanimous consent of all permanent members of the Council should be required for: (a) any verdict determining that a threat to the peace existed or that a breach of the peace had occurred; (b) before the Council could apply enforcement measures. The significant area of difference was whether the consent of all permanent members should also be required before the Council could even take cognizance of a dispute, investigate, and try to settle it by peaceful means. Was each of the permanent members to be able to stop the Council from engaging in efforts of this sort; and was it to retain that right even when it was a party to the dispute?

On November 15th Roosevelt had approved complete recommendations of the State Department about the position to be taken in this field. In sum, these provided: (1) that the Security Council ought to be able to determine "procedural matters" by a vote of any seven members of the Security Council (out of a total of eleven); (2) that for decision on all other matters, the concurrence of *all* permanent members should be required; but (3) that while the Security Council was trying to bring about a voluntary peaceful settlement of a dispute by advice, conciliation or adjudication, then any member of the Council, including the permanent members, *who was a party to the dispute should abstain from voting* [my italics].[61]

This proposal was submitted by the President to Churchill and Stalin with a grave call to cooperate in making evident ". . . that the leadership of the great powers is to be based not alone upon size, strength, and resources, but upon those enduring qualifications of moral leadership which can raise the whole level of international relations the world over." In presenting it on December 14th, Harriman had explained that the President was eager for a quick answer and for a quick accord since he hoped that invitations might be issued in February convoking all the United and other nations to meet to create the security organization.

[61] The text of this proposal as presented to Stalin is contained in the message from Roosevelt to Stalin, sent to Harriman on December 5, is in the *Yalta Documents,* pages 58–60. Neither in this, nor in later drafts or expositions of our proposals, nor in the discussions of Yalta, was there a *positive* definition made of what types of question might be considered "procedural." The fullest enumeration of the principal substantive decisions for which votes of all permanent members was to be required is in the U.S. Delegation memo distributed to the British and Soviet Delegations on February 6th at Yalta, printed in the *Yalta Documents,* pages 684–86. Stettinius and the President followed this closely in their oral statements at this meeting. *Ibid.,* pages 660–67.

Stalin had said that he would let the President have his views as soon as he could, but the subject required careful study and Molotov was ill.

When the answer had come—on the 27th—it said that to his regret Stalin could see no possibility of agreeing to the President's proposal that parties to a dispute should refrain from voting upon efforts of the Council to bring about peaceful settlement. He thought it unwise to authorize the Council to take any measure in the face of objection by any permanent member. He feared that this might bring some of the great powers in opposition to the others, and so undermine the cause of universal security. Molotov this same day had tried to convince Harriman of the soundness and fairness of the Soviet position. He had made a skilled explanation of why the Soviet government thought it essential to maintain unity among the great powers; why it thought no loopholes, no escape which might allow a break between them, should be permitted. He had argued that if there was unity among them when the question of peaceful settlement arose there would be a much better chance of settling any dispute then without the use of force; while, if they should differ during this stage in the consideration of a dispute, any further action to enforce a decision would probably not be possible. That, Molotov had concluded, is what Stalin feared. To quote from the memo made of his statement, "The principle of unity of action must be preserved from the inception of any dispute, it must never be diminished, and there must be no exceptions to it; otherwise, the entire organization would be emasculated."

Harriman had followed his report of this talk with Molotov with an interpretation of the reasons why the Russians were being so uncompromising. Its residue was that they mistrusted the impartiality of the members of the Council; that they took a differing view than we of what it was fair to expect of neighboring countries; that in final effect they did not want to qualify their right to settle disputes in this area by direct negotiation or action, and without any interference.

Word having been received that the British government would accept his proposal, Roosevelt had determined to try again to win over the Russians also. But he was not disposed to treat the issue as a crucial one—as some of the more convinced advocates in the State Department would have had him do. Just before leaving for Yalta, he had let it be known to members of the Foreign Relations Committee of the Senate that he thought he might have to yield to the Russians on this point.

At the third session of the Conference (February 6th) Roosevelt prefaced the presentation of the American proposal by a statement of his belief that it would be feasible and possible for the world to have peace for fifty years even if not for eternity. Churchill spoke up next and said that after careful thought he had come to the conclusion that the proposals made by the President were entirely satisfactory.[62]

Stalin spoke as though still puzzled about the effective meaning of the proposed basis of voting rights in the Council, but the same theme as always dominated his remarks: ". . . the main thing was to prevent quarrels in the future between the three Great Powers and that the task, therefore, was to secure their unity for the future. The covenant of the new World Organization should have this as its primary task. . . ."[63] The fear Stalin had in mind was made clear by his illustration. He and his colleagues, he said, could not forget the events of December 1939, when war broke out between the Soviet Union and Finland. Then, instigated by Great Britain and France, the League of Nations had expelled the Soviet Union and world opinion had been mobilized against it, the Western world going so far as to speak of a crusade against the Soviet Union. Churchill did not apologize for the past. He observed merely that at that time British opinion had been very angry. And his commentary went on to the heart of the problem: ". . . that he saw the force of that [Stalin's] argument, but he did not believe that the world organization would eliminate disputes between powers and that would remain the function of diplomacy."[64]

Roosevelt, in further pursuit of his idea, argued that in any case the nations of the world gathered together in the Assembly of the new organization could not be prevented from discussing differences between the three great powers or those in which they were involved. Therefore he thought that free, full, and friendly discussions in the Council would not stimulate trouble among the great powers but rather would serve to show the confidence they had in each other and in the justice of their policies.

Of a sudden on the day after this discussion, the Soviet government made a surprising change of front. In the middle of the afternoon meeting of the Heads of State on the 7th, Molotov said in a matter-of-fact way that the Soviet government, after listening to Stettinius' explanatory report and Churchill's remarks, felt that the American proposals fully guaranteed the unity of the great powers in the matter of pre-

[62] The condensation of the American proposal later made in *Triumph and Tragedy,* page 354, was curiously inverted. "Mr. Roosevelt's proposals had contained one other refinement. The dispute might be settled by peaceful methods. If so, this also would need seven votes, and the permanent members—that is to say, the 'Big Four'—would all have to agree. But if any member of the Council (including the 'Big Four') were involved in the dispute it could discuss the decision but could not vote on it."
[63] *Yalta Documents,* page 666.
[64] *Ibid.*

serving peace. Therefore, he said, since that had been the main Soviet purpose at Dumbarton Oaks, the Soviet government would accept them.

This statement caused rejoicing. The President said that he felt a great step forward had been taken which would be welcomed by all peoples of the world. The Prime Minister spoke thanks for an action which he felt would bring joy and relief to all nations.

After his acceptance of this proposal on voting in the Council, Molotov hurried on to ask consideration for the request made at Dumbarton Oaks—that all or some of the constituent states of the Union of Soviet Socialist Republics be admitted as original members of the new organization and be given places in the Assembly. What he had to ask now, he continued, was not that all sixteen of these, but only three or at least two, be admitted. The three he had in mind were the Ukraine, Byelorussia, and Lithuania. This request he justified by comparison with the number of votes in the Assembly that the members of the British Commonwealth would have; by the size of these Soviet Republics and the part they played in the war; and by the fact that under the recently amended Soviet Constitution they could maintain independent relations with foreign governments.

The President merely said in effect that he regarded this question as only one of many before them concerning the admission of countries not already members of the United Nations, and that it ought to be studied further by the Foreign Ministers. Churchill said that, bearing in mind the part which the British Dominions had of their own free will played in the war, he had sympathy with the Soviet request. But he asked a chance to consult London before expressing a more definite opinion.

Discussion by the Foreign Ministers led to the production on the 10th of a report on which they had agreed. The pertinent clause read: "It will be for the conference [that is, the organizing conference] to determine the list of original members of the organization. At that stage the delegates of the United Kingdom and the U.S.A. will support the proposal to admit to original membership two Soviet Socialist Republics."

The President had been persuaded that this would do no harm, and that it might elicit firmer Soviet cooperation in the work of the United Nations. But in agreeing to it, Roosevelt, without dispute by Stalin, made clear that he knew that this language cloaked a departure from past standards. It was not, he said, a question of admitting new countries to the United Nations, but of giving one of the great powers three votes instead of one in the Assembly. Later that evening (the 10th) he found some of his American colleagues much upset over the possible dissatisfaction at home about this compromise. Byrnes, a former member of the Senate, was worried by his memory of the way in which Roosevelt, when talking with members of the Foreign Relations Committee of the Senate before leaving for Yalta, had made fun of the Soviet request. He and Edward Flynn, leader of the Democratic organization in New York, were close to dismay at what the Irish in the big Eastern cities might think about an arrangement under which members of the British Commonwealth had six votes in the Assembly, the USSR had three votes, and the United States only one. So, in order to put himself in a position to quiet such criticism if need be, the President wrote a letter to Stalin. He explained that the promise he had given might cause political trouble at home. In order to get the American people and Congress to back up the promise, he might have to ask that the United States be given additional votes. He put the same query to Churchill. Both answered at once that they would not object and would help as needed to bring this about.

The question of whether to include in the Charter provisions looking toward the exercise of trusteeships by the United Nations was settled in the same spirit of amiable compromise.

Roosevelt had been devoted to the principle right along and he had approved an effort at Yalta at least to secure political living room for the idea. Stettinius, on the 9th, proposed to the Foreign Ministers that the invitations to be sent out for the organizing meeting should state in one paragraph that, "The above-named governments have agreed that it would, in their opinion, be desirable that consideration be given at the forthcoming Conference to the inclusion in the projected Charter of provisions relating to territorial trusteeships and dependent areas." But Eden would not accept this and Molotov seemed indifferent.

When the matter was brought before the three Heads of State, Churchill was provoked into lively comment on what he regarded as a disguised crowbar under the British Empire. It is safe to surmise that in what he said he was speaking his mind not only about this particular project, but upon the whole current of encouragement to break loose which had been given to peoples living under British imperial control. He did not agree, he asserted, with one word of this report (of the Foreign Ministers) on trusteeship. Under no circumstances would he ever consent to have forty or fifty nations thrusting interfering fingers into the vital existence of the British Empire. In view of what that Empire had done in the war, he would not agree, as long as he was

Minister, to have one scrap of British territory flung into this area, nor would he consent to having a representative of Great Britain go to any conference where he would be placed in the dock and asked to justify its right to live in the world which the British had tried to save.

Whatever the President had in the past thought should be done about Hong Kong and other British and French imperial outposts, he did not now risk the whole United Nations project by challenging the Prime Minister. He listened and allowed Stettinius to make the soothing explanations. The Secretary of State did so. He said that he and his colleagues did not have the British Empire in mind. They were thinking of the dependent areas that would be taken out of enemy control—for example, the islands in the Pacific.

Churchill relaxed. He said he accepted Stettinius' explanations but would feel better if it were plainly stated that this proposal did not refer to the British Empire. The British government, he added, did not want to extend its rule over any new lands but would not object to consideration of possible trusteeships for territories to be taken from the enemy. How, he asked Stalin, would he feel if it was suggested that the Crimea be internationalized as a summer resort? The Marshal answered suavely that he would be glad to give the Crimea as a place to be used for meetings of the three powers.

In the last final rush of drafting, it was agreed merely that the five governments having permanent seats should consult with one another before the United Nations Conference on the question of providing machinery in the Charter for trusteeships. However, this was on the understanding that any such trusteeships should apply only to (1) the existing mandates of the League of Nations, (2) territories to be detached from the enemy as a result of the war then going on, and (3) any other territory that might voluntarily be subjected to such supervision.

Thus the questions which had stood in the way of calling together a conference to complete the Charter for the security organization and to establish it were deemed to have been settled. The American government was eager that it should be held in the United States, not later than April. The others cheerfully assented. The text of the invitations to be sent out was approved. April 25th was fixed as the date; San Francisco was named as the place.

The end of the Conference was too hurried. Stalin, on learning when the President was planning to get away, told him that he doubted whether they could finish their work properly by that time. Roosevelt said that, although he had three Kings waiting for him, he would, if necessary, stay another day. But by adopting abrupt or ambigious solutions of some of the unsettled issues, by turning over others to the Foreign Ministers, by having drafting groups and staffs work through the night, by starting early in the morning and working through lunch, the Conference adjourned on schedule.

If the President had been more stubbornly patient and more patiently stubborn it may be that certain agreements would have been more clear and more favorable to the Western aims. But would this really have affected later events—unless we had landed troops in China and Manchuria and left them there?

To various members of the American group who saw him frequently, the President did not appear ill or exhausted. It was noted that he tired when discussions were prolonged, and that he seemed to want to avoid sustained argument. But decisions did not seem to burden him as they would a sick or extremely worried man. His hurry to be off, he explained to them as to Stalin, was due to a wish not to be absent any longer than he was going to be anyhow because of his trip to the Middle East and the sea voyage ahead. He did not want to be separated too long from Congress, the people, and the men who were running the war. But when Churchill saw him for the last time, in the harbor at Alexandria, just before the *Quincy* sailed for home, he thought him ". . . placid and frail." So frail, apparently, that as he has since written, "I felt that he had a slender contact with life." [65]

But clearly he shared with Churchill and Stalin, at the close, not only satisfaction over work done but also a kindled sense of common purpose and personal attachment. They all seemed to have concluded from their convocation that good will and unity within the coalition had been tested again and proved reliable. The toasts spoken at the banquet which Stalin gave on the night of February 8th, as their work was progressing, echo mockingly in the record.

Roosevelt, in answer to a toast proposed to him by Stalin, said he felt that the atmosphere at this dinner was that of a family, and that he liked to characterize the relations between the three countries in those words. Stalin, answering a toast addressed to the alliance, was more restrained. He remarked that it was not so hard to keep unity in time of war since there was a common aim clear to everyone. The difficult time would come, he said, after the war, when diverse interests would tend to divide the Allies. But, he concluded, he was confident that the existing alliance, to whose future he drank, would meet this test also, and it was the duty of all of those around the table to see that it

[65] *Triumph and Tragedy,* page 397.

did, and that the relations between them in peacetime should be as strong as they were in war.

Churchill addressed himself to the years ahead. He felt, he said, that all were standing on the crest of a hill with the glories of great future possibilities stretching before them; that in the modern world the function of leadership was to lead the people out from the forests into the broad sunlit plains of peace and happiness. He felt that this prize was nearer their grasp than at any time in history, and that it would be a great tragedy if they, through inertia or carelessness, let it slip from their grasp. History would never forgive them if they did.

PERIOD TWELVE

After Yalta; Corrosion within the Coalition as the Soviet Union Extends Its Realm of Control

58. After Yalta: The Loosening of the Coalition as the War Was Being Won

THE coordinated assaults against Germany which had been fixed upon at Yalta went forward with crushing might. By the second half of March, all German forces west of the Rhine were broken except in the region south of the Moselle. First with unexpected good luck at Remagen, and then elsewhere, American divisions were across the river in number. Several hundred thousand German soldiers had given up and were in prison camps. The German armored divisions had lost much of their equipment and there was no reserve left. The German Air Force no longer had the power to attack, and little strength for defense. The oil supplies were so low that even critical operations were hindered. Transport inside the battered country was in ruins.

On March 23rd, the advance units of an army of one million men under General Montgomery started its main thrust to the north of the Ruhr and across the Rhine—an advance that was to carry it clear through northern Germany to Lubeck. As this army pushed forward, American divisions (Bradley's First Army) moved with great momentum up from the south toward the Ruhr and by the end of March that area, and 300,000 German troops within it, was encircled. Although some hard local battles were still to be fought, in effect Germany's Western Front was gone.

On the Eastern Front the Soviet forces along the Oder River some thirty-five miles from Berlin were waiting upon weather and supplies to begin their final great attack. Elsewhere the Red Army had forced the Germans into ever-smaller areas of last defense, in reality burial plots. The Germans had concentrated ten armored divisions northeast of Lake Balaton in Hungary, and these had been defeated. They were centering resistance in the Bratislava area but that could not last long. They still had sixteen divisions in Latvia but these could not be moved out with their artillery. The Baltic Coast to the east was clear, and Danzig had been captured by the end of March. When Harriman, on the 31st, asked Stalin whether he still thought, as he had earlier, that the Red Armies might be slowed down at about this time, Stalin said that the prospect was better than he had anticipated since the floods had come early that year and the roads were drying. The Marshal added that he believed the Germans would probably make their last stand in the mountains of Western Czechoslovakia and Bavaria.

American observers noticed that during this period of triumph the Soviet press gave little space or attention to advances on the Western Front—except for the usual back-page Tass stories summing up the daily communiqués issued by Supreme Headquarters. The ordinary Soviet citizen was not being kept aware of the way in which operations in the West were going forward and would have been surprised to learn that the damage done by the Western forces to the German Army was comparable to the performance of the Red Army.

Although at Yalta Stalin had approved the idea of consultation between the Soviet and Allied military staffs, to be carried out through the American and British Military Missions in Moscow, this had not led to easy contact. The Soviet military authorities continued to be slow in responding to requests or suggestions of cooperation, and when they did it was usually to evade or refuse. Stalin and his service chiefs seemed content with the general knowledge of campaign plans given and gotten at Yalta; to have the battle roll on in the East and West without more talk or ado. They showed no interest in having an advance agreement as to the routes along which the Soviet and the Western armies should direct their further courses, or how far they would go, or where they might meet. As usual, when they had no complaints, they left it to the West to make the first approaches.

Although victory thus was growing near, accord on many important elements and aspects of the future of Europe after victory between the Western Allies and the Soviet Union was not: the treatment of Germany; occupation zones in Austria; the nature of the government for Poland and its future frontiers; the share to be accorded the United States and Great Britain in the control of Hungary, Romania, and Bulgaria.

Negotiations over some of these questions were becoming set and shrill. The tide of trust that had flowed at Yalta was ebbing fast. Stalin was giving way to suspicion of the American-British conduct of the war and to resentment at their attempts to maintain influence in any region near Soviet frontiers. To the Western Allies it seemed that under the spell of victory the Russians were becoming indifferent to their hard-time vows.

The American and British governments admitted that the Soviet determination to prevent hostile elements in the countries near its frontiers from gaining control was not without fair reason. Such precaution, within balanced measure, could be justified by the need to protect Soviet occupation forces. The American and British authorities were, similarly, keeping an alert watch over political turns in the liberated areas of the West—Italy, Greece, France, and Belgium. The undefined qualification to this principle of freedom of choice went even farther. The Americans and British granted that the Soviet government was within its historical right in hindering the emergence in any of the neighboring countries of a government that had deeper attachment to the West than to it; and the Soviet government did not seem to take it amiss that the British and American governments should be hindering the efforts of Communist elements to gain control in those liberated countries near the Atlantic.

But within the large area of remaining political choice, the American and British governments hoped that the Soviet government would be as willing as they were to respect the right of other peoples to choose the government under which they would live—as proclaimed in the Atlantic Charter and reaffirmed in the Declaration on Liberated Europe. This was an offshoot of the conception that the three great Allies were to remain closely joined, and without fear of one another.

But Soviet actions evidenced an unwillingness to trust the outcome of the democratic political contest, and a ruthless will to make sure that all of Central and Eastern Europe was governed by its dependent supporters. This set purpose was not affected by association in combat or appeals to principle. Nor could it be diverted by the vision pursued at San Francisco of a world in which all countries would join together to protect each and to maintain peace. The Soviet Union wanted space, satellite peoples and armies, additional economic resources, and a favorable chance for Communism to spread its influence.

The American government was disturbed by the signs of these intentions and by the spirit of mistrust behind them. For the thoughts and feelings of the American people were happily centered on the approaching victory, a quick movement of our troops to the Pacific and then back home. The British government with its longer memory of the struggles in Europe was less surprised but even more disturbed. Churchill, who had spoken as though he thought the Yalta accords ended the need for anxiety, began to experience now "deep despond," all the more so since he was failing to get the American government to realize, in his own words, that "Soviet Russia had become a mortal danger to the free world," and thus the need for creating at once a new military front against its onward sweep. Of his mood during those days of March and April when Nazi Germany was going down, he has since told. "Thus this climax of apparently measureless success was to me a most unhappy time. I moved amid cheering crowds, or sat at a table adorned with congratulations and blessings from every part of the Grand Alliance, with an aching heart and a mind oppressed by forebodings." [1]

Such was the blight that fell upon the coalition just as, at long last, the evil that Hitler had summoned up was being destroyed. It was a general process, not merely a series of local and separated situations and difficulties. This ought not to be forgotten as the tales of what occurred here, there, and everywhere are told one by one.

59. The Soviet Spread in Eastern Europe

In Romania a grave crisis occurred within two weeks after Yalta. The infirm Radescu coalition Cabinet was a fair target for opposition and agitation. It was divided, slovenly, slow to begin needed agrarian reform; its local branches still harbored former German sympathizers. In February the American member of the Control Commission, General Cortlandt Schuyler, warned Washington that the Soviet government was not going to allow this coalition to survive. The Soviet officials in Romania were garnering reparations without care for consequences. They were forcing a reduction in the Romanian Home Guard. The attacks of the local Communist and Communist-associated groups were ungoverned and determined. The Soviet chairman of the Control Commission was issuing orders to the Romanian government in the name of the Commission without the prior knowledge or consent of either the American or British representatives.

On February 24th the agitation in Bucharest broke out in mass turn-outs interrupted by gunfire. That evening the Prime Minister spoke on the radio, saying that a handful of Communists were trying to subdue the nation by terror. He was severely reprimanded by the Soviet member of the Control Commission for this speech. The next day, the 25th, the Communist press talked about bloody massacres and called for demonstrations and punishment. Some of the Communist members of the coalition government sent a message to the King, demanding the immediate dismissal of the government led by the "executioner" Radescu. Burton Y. Berry, the American political representative in Bucharest, reported that ". . . the violent elements of the Communist

[1] *Triumph and Tragedy,* page 456.

party increases its demands, distorts facts, and levels charges as the Government's position with the people improves."

The British and American members of the Control Commission requested that it meet. The Soviet chairman refused to call it together. Under instructions, the British Ambassador in Moscow on the 24th, followed by the American Ambassador two days later, sent written protests to Molotov about the way in which the Control Commission was being run, and the pressure being brought against the Radescu government. But in this and later attempts to get the Soviet government to hold an even balance in Romania until elections were held, Churchill, as he has told, felt constrained.

"We were hampered in our protests because Eden and I during our October visit to Moscow had recognised that Russia should have a largely predominant voice in Rumania and Bulgaria while we took the lead in Greece. Stalin had kept very strictly to this understanding. . . . Peace had now been restored, [in Greece] and, though many difficulties lay before us, I hoped that in a few months we should be able to hold free, unfettered elections . . . and that thereafter a constitution and Government would be erected on the indisputable will of the Greek people.

"Stalin was now pursuing the opposite course. . . . But if I pressed him too much he might say, 'I did not interfere with your action in Greece; why do you not give me the same latitude in Rumania?' This would lead to comparisons between his aims and ours. Neither side would convince the other. Having regard to my personal relations with Stalin, I was sure it would be a mistake to embark on such an argument." [2]

Harriman's letter to Molotov, sent on the 26th, said that the American government wanted political developments in Romania to take an orderly course in accord with the Declaration on Liberated Europe; and if they did not, it thought that the resultant situation would be one that called for full consultation between the three governments as envisaged in that Declaration. When on this same day Harriman told Vishinsky of the American dislike of what was going on, the Vice Commissar heaped blame on the Radescu government, led by the Fascist elements, for what was taking place. He said that regime was showing it could not maintain order, which was important since the country was at the rear of the Red Army, and that it was incapable of carrying out the terms of the armistice agreement.

Actually, Vishinsky was on his way to "correct" the situation. He

[2] *Triumph and Tragedy*, page 420.

arrived in Bucharest on the 27th. He rushed to the Palace and recited from a paper the Soviet charges against the Radescu government and asked for its immediate dismissal. He suggested that it be replaced by one based on "the truly democratic forces of the country." The King asked leave to consider. On the next day, the 28th, he told Vishinsky that he was consulting party leaders for the purpose of choosing another Prime Minister. Vishinsky gave him two hours and five minutes to find one and announce the appointment. When the Foreign Minister, Visoianu, who was present, remarked that the King had to follow constitutional practice, Vishinsky told him to "shut up." Then he left the room abruptly, slamming the door as he went.

The King asked Prince Stirbey to form a government. Stirbey reported at three o'clock the next day that he could not do so, that the Communists could not be induced to join it. Vishinsky thereupon sent word to the King that Petro Groza, a tough politician who had tied up with the Communists, was the Soviet choice. The King again consulted his party leaders. Some were ready to accept Groza; others were not. At ten o'clock that same night, Vishinsky went to see the King again to tell him that he wanted Groza appointed.

The King continued during the next several days to try to arrange for a government in which Groza would have a limited mandate, and in which the political parties other than the Communist-dominated ones would have a substantial share. In the meanwhile, in Moscow, both Ambassadors were hammering away at the undentable Molotov. Their written presentations were formal and vigorous. But Molotov cast aside the requests for consultation in the Control Commission on the score that Vishinsky, in Bucharest, was talking with the American and British members.

On the 5th and 6th of March events in Bucharest reached their crisis. The King summoned his Ministers and asked them to make every effort to find a way of participating in a coalition government with Groza as Prime Minister. The Queen Mother, who took part in the discussion, reminded the group that a King of France had put on a red hat, but that had not saved him from the scaffold. The leaders of the two main older parties (Peasant and Liberal) agreed to enter such a government if their groups were given half the Cabinet offices. Groza said his supporters would not consent to that, but still he pressed the King for permission to announce that a government had been formed. The King refused, but consented to an announcement that a new government would be formed within the course of the day (the 6th). At six o'clock that evening, handbills were passed out on the street telling of a government headed by Groza. Of the seventeen Cabinet members, thirteen belonged to the groups whom Groza could command. The Cabinet was sworn in at seven that evening. Later the King received Vishinsky and Marshal Malinowski who had come to Bucharest from his field headquarters.

The next day Molotov concluded his answer to Harriman's accumulated protests by observing, "At the same time, I presume that the question raised in your letter has lost its keenness inasmuch as the government crisis in Rumania brought on by the terroristic policy of Radescu which was incompatible with the principles of democracy has been overcome by the formation of the new government." It was, in truth, easier to find reasons why Radescu and some of those associated with his government ought to have been discharged than it was to find reasons why Groza was qualified to govern Romania.

The Soviet government hastened to solidify the position of the Groza regime by doing at once what it had refused to do before; that is, it announced that it would return to Romania, in accordance with the armistice agreement of September 12, 1944, the northern Province of Transylvania. The American government reserved its right to continue to resist by announcing on the 16th of March that it had asked the Soviet Union and Great Britain to resume consultations regarding political conditions in Romania. The State Department firmly stated that it considered the Groza government under the control of the National Democratic Front to be a minority government which did not represent all the democratic elements in the country. Molotov was not affected by these protests. Nor was he short of arguments in rebuttal which we will not repeat again.

To foretell, the American and British governments thought it expedient to allow their representatives to stay in Romania. But they refused to recognize the new government. This became a great delaying difficulty in working out a peace treaty with Romania, and the cause of long dissension.

These events in Romania were in some measure paralleled by what was occurring in Bulgaria and what was threatened in Hungary; and all were overshadowed by the grave dispute as to who was to govern Poland.

In Bulgaria the coalition Fatherland Front government enjoyed popular approval since it had thrown out the cruel and hated regime which had placed the people and country under Germany. The greatest number of its supporters were peasants, but the real power was exercised by Communist political leaders, closely connected with Moscow.

The American and British governments directed their efforts toward assuring that when elections were held they would be Western not Soviet style, so that the government chosen would be "responsive to the will of the people." To that end they proposed to the Soviet government that, as the three sponsors of the Declaration on Liberated Europe, they agree on the rules to be observed in the elections and jointly see to it that the Bulgarian government followed them. But Molotov indignantly repulsed the proposal, saying that the Soviet government saw no need or reason for such outside and foreign interference. The mistrust shown, he added, was all the more offensive because of the help which Bulgarian troops were giving the Red Army in its fight against the common enemy.

In the Control Commission the Soviet Chairman ruled. The American and British members generally learned of actions only after they were taken. They were waiting for the war against Germany to end to put forward their claim for equal share in the making of policy and control of the execution of the armistice terms.

In much of Hungary great battles were still not yet over, and military needs and purposes remained predominant.

The Allied Control Commission was set up without trouble. American and British political representatives were admitted. Both groups were treated with consideration by Marshal Voroshilov, who was both Soviet Commanding Officer and Soviet Chairman of the Control Commission. But while frank and cordial, he did not abide by the statutes of the Commission (agreed on at Moscow on January 20th), which, according to the American understanding, provided that the American and British members were to be informed about policy directives before they were issued to the Hungarian government, and were to get copies of all important papers. Protests were disregarded. The American and British governments were forced to wait until the war against Germany ended, to press further for equal status on the Commission and a reduction in its authority.

The Soviet government tolerated, and in some ways upheld, the coalition government under Miklos with its Communist component. It discouraged local Communist agitation and warned that it would not allow civil strife. But it hurried to exact the reparations due under the armistice accord, and it was insistent that Hungary provide food not only for the Russian troops in that country but also for those on other fronts. Although at first it opposed a swift and drastic program of land reform, at the end of March this was demanded and the government issued a decree putting it into effect at once; it aimed to win support in those areas already freed and possibly also to attract those Hungarian soldiers who were still opposing the Red Army. The American and British observers thought it probable that the Communists were merely giving other elements a respite, while war booty was being removed and food being taken from the farmers, and while they extended their control over all channels of public information.

During this same period a new government for Czechoslovakia was formed and installed. Benes, the President, together with leading members of the London government-in-exile, went to Moscow during the second half of March. There they worked out a basis for the reorganization of the government with the Slovak National Council and the Czech Communist leaders who had been living in Moscow.

Benes was not wholly satisfied with the outcome. "It might have been worse," was his comment to Harriman. He was pushed into granting the Communists and their associates a greater number of posts in the government than he had wished or expected. Of the twenty-five Ministries, seven were to be headed by Communists. Fierlinger, the Czech Ambassador in Moscow and a close co-worker with the Soviet authorities, was to be Prime Minister. Benes thought he would not be too troublesome, since he was a career diplomat without political following. He also thought that since the Communists and more radical Socialists (he was a Moderate Socialist himself) would be in a minority, they could be controlled.

According to Benes, neither Stalin nor Molotov—who at this time were thwarting all efforts to bring about a genuinely representative meeting of Poles—had interfered in the arrangement for the coalition or the selection of individuals. They had, furthermore, during his second visit to Moscow, reaffirmed their promise not to meddle in the Czechoslovakian social system or political affairs. At the dinner he gave Benes, Stalin had offered two toasts. In the first he repudiated any idea of Pan-Slavism. In the second he referred to the suspicion that the Soviet Union wanted to Bolshevize Europe. "You were justified in sharing this opinion," he said, turning to Benes. But no longer, since Soviet policy has been reoriented. The various Communist parties would become nationalist parties, absorbed in the interests of their own countries. In private talk with Benes he had gone even further, saying that as the Czechoslovak Communist leaders had been in Moscow five years, he, Benes, should try to broaden their outlook, since, although they were good patriotic men, they wore "blinkers." Stalin had also promised to provide equipment for the Czechoslovak Army in return for the supplies which the Russians were requisitioning; to furnish the means of starting the wheels of production; to return the Danube River boats and grant the use of the Port of Galatz leading to the Black Sea. And, perhaps, of more commanding interest, he promised that the Soviet government would lend support to deportation from Czechoslovakia of some two million Germans and half a million Hungarians—the minorities who had torn the Czechoslovak state apart and had been responsible for Munich. Toward patching up the quarrel over Poland, Benes could do nothing.

Benes and part of his official following hurried from Moscow to the temporary capital at Kosice in Slovakia behind the Red Army lines. The new government was announced and was allowed to begin to take over the civil administration in liberated sections of the country. But almost at once signs appeared that the Communist elements were not going to accept a subordinate role calmly. Still Benes and his colleagues continued to trust the assurances given them in Moscow. They made a declaration of the foreign policy they were going to pursue: this was pro-Soviet and Slav-oriented, but did not shut out the West.

Finland was not occupied by Soviet forces—the only Axis member east of Germany not to be. Although the Soviet government kept most close watch, the Finns were allowed to work out their own political changeover without constant coercion. The Soviet chairman of the Control Council did not use his authority under the armistice terms to confer marked favor on the local Communists, nor to destroy the conservative government which had taken over after surrender.

Several reasons may be found for this moderate course. The Finns had shown that they were a tough people to subdue; they were not likely to be anybody's puppets. A stable government was needed while fighting went on against remnants of the German Army that were still in the north of the country. Reparations were wanted. The Finns were in the main carrying out their armistice obligations in a way that seemed to satisfy Moscow. Territorial adjustments were smoothly accomplished.

Then in March 1945 elections were held in a way which American observers found quiet, orderly, and validly democratic. There was a substantial swing to the left, which portended extensive social and economic changes. But in contrast to what was happening elsewhere, both the West and the Soviet government accepted the outcome as right, resting on a good and fair balance between the various elements in Finland.

Observing the maxim that the annals of the good are short, we may note that amid the dissension over political developments elsewhere, the Finnish example was a healthy one. In the spreading gloom, it encouraged the hope that, with patience, the same reconciling outcome might yet follow elsewhere.

60. The Incurable Troubles over Poland

It was the division over Poland, not genuinely mended at Yalta, that revealed most clearly the Soviet intent. No subject engaged Allied diplomacy more at this time. None has left behind as immense a record of notes and memos written, of words spoken. But as the same essential differences appeared over and over, and as the state of the matter was the same at the end as at the start, a summary will tell the story.

At Yalta it had been agreed that Molotov and the American and British Ambassadors at Moscow should meet as a group to bring about a "reorganization" of the existing Provisional Polish government. The assigned purpose was to agree upon the way to form a new one which all three Allied governments would be willing to recognize. It was understood that as soon as practicable this reformed government would hold free elections, in which all qualified parties could participate, to determine the more permanent political structure. But how was this Commission of three to proceed with their consultations with Poles from inside and outside Poland? Must all three consent to invitations, or could each invite those whom he thought ought to be heard? Must the Warsaw (former Lublin) group be consulted first, before spokesmen for other Polish groups? Must it be asked about other selections; and, if so, must its objections be heeded? And more basic than these and other questions of procedure, how thorough a reorganization was the Commission, under the ambiguous Yalta formula, to aim to bring about? Must the existing Provisional Government recognized by Moscow be accepted as the "basis," the "nucleus," the "kernel" of the new government, to which some few others were merely to be added, and in which they were to be absorbed? [3] Or was there to be a much larger redistribution of offices and authority as between the elements in this Provisional Government and other Polish political parties and groups?

[3] All three terms are used in one or other of the American or British translations of statements made by Stalin and Molotov, or in the paraphrase of messages reporting these statements.

571

Who now would want to follow, in the retelling, the tight and twisting arguments over each of these questions that went on in and out of the Commission? Events did not wait upon their outcome; the Red Armies were marching deeper into Germany and turning over to the Provisional Government administration of the areas which Moscow wished it to have.

Molotov was his most stiff and cunning self. Churchill and Clark-Kerr were aroused by their failure to make the Soviet government appreciate how deeply disturbed the British people were by the prospect that the Poles would not be masters in their own house. Churchill had told the House of Commons on his return from Yalta: "The agreement provides for consultations, with a view to the establishment in Poland of a *new* [my italics] Polish Provisional Government of National Unity. . . . His Majesty's Government intend to do all in their power to ensure that . . . representative Poles of all democratic parties are given full freedom to come and make their views known." [4]

The House of Commons was not inclined to condone failure in this matter. Harriman, in touch with the President, was more disposed to acknowledge that the Yalta agreement contemplated that the Warsaw group would have the leading part both in the consultations and in the reformed government. But the Americans too came to feel that Moscow was distorting the Yalta compromise; that it would not allow any new government to be formed that was not securely subject to its will; that in reality it wanted Poland to be merely a protective and obedient projection of Soviet power. To assure this, the Soviet government seemed ready to ignore opinion in the West, risk the rupture of the arrangements for joint control of Germany, and even, perhaps, to disassociate itself from the new collective system that was to be formed of the United Nations. The Americans were dismayed and depressed.

It will be enough to illustrate the basic issues by a few points on which the argument centered; and to illustrate the states of mind by a few extracts from the correspondence.

The Commission (Molotov, Clark-Kerr, and Harriman) could not even agree, after many hours of talk that started on February 23rd, upon what Poles should be invited to come to Moscow for consultation. Molotov insisted that the Poles connected with the Provisional Government recognized by Moscow should be consulted before the others. He also demanded in effect that all nominations of other Poles from within and outside Poland must be approved by this Warsaw group as well as by the Soviet government. They did not regard anyone outside their

[4] *Triumph and Tragedy*, page 400.

circle and orbit as really democratic unless they were senescent or political nonentities. Harriman and Clark-Kerr futilely contended that "The Commission must be free to choose whomever it thinks fit, and in exchange it would not wish to stand in the way of any nomination on the part of Mr. Bierut, President of the Provisional Government, which seems proper." Molotov did not directly deny that the Commission was entitled to that freedom, but proved by his arguments that the freedom meant nothing. He and the Warsaw group had to be pleased!

Wrangles over nominations for invitations to individual Poles from outside and inside Poland to come for consultation went on for weeks. The British and American governments accepted, while regretting, the fact that most of the Poles still connected with the government-in-exile in London after Mikolajczyk's resignation had disqualified themselves. So had the brave commanders who had led the Poles in the war, such as General Anders; for they had spoken out bitterly against all features of the Yalta accord on Poland, and they made no secret of their intense distrust of the Soviet Union. But the British and Americans thought it essential as well as fair that certain former members of the Polish government-in-exile, leaders of democratic political parties, be called into consultation. Mikolajczyk's presence, in particular, they thought desirable because of the regard in which he was held by the Polish soldiers who had fought in the war, by other Poles abroad, and by British and American public opinion. But the Warsaw group objected to having Mikolajczyk come even for consultation, on the score that he had spoken out against the Yalta accord.

One of the chief causes of British and American complaint as this controversy went on was that they had so little information as to what was going on in Poland, and what the Polish people in Poland really wanted. Up to then the Soviet government, on the score that this was an active military area, had refused to allow them to send in either military or civilian representatives. At the second meeting of the Commission (on February 27th) Molotov took heed of this complaint. To the surprise of the Ambassadors he suggested they might send observers in to investigate and report.

When, two days later (March 1st), Clark-Kerr told Molotov that his government had informed him that it was eager to send observers to Moscow, he found the offer was a dodge to get the British and American governments to ask this as a favor of the Warsaw government. Of course Molotov did not use these words; he said that the Commission would have to consider the self-respect of the Poles and take up the

573

proposal with them, as they were bosses in their own country. And then, when the project was again presented, Molotov's answer on March 22nd to Harriman and Clark-Kerr was more indignant still, saying that the proposal ". . . could sting the national pride of the Poles to the quick," and adding that in any event the American and British governments should address themselves directly to the Polish government in Warsaw.

The President and Churchill next tried to get Stalin's assent to having the American and British members of the Commission, or their staffs, visit Poland. Churchill in his messages to Stalin protested the veil of secrecy being drawn over the Polish scene. Stalin's answer was that the Poles in Warsaw thought this an insult to their national dignity. Besides, he added, they thought the British government unfriendly; representatives of better-disposed governments, such as the Czech and Yugoslav, were being allowed in.

In a message of March 13th to Roosevelt, Churchill had concluded that they were in the presence ". . . of a great failure and an utter breakdown of what was settled at Yalta. . . ." [5] His fears of Russian intentions were sharpened by what had so lately occurred in Romania. He urged Roosevelt to join him in a message which would cause Stalin to recognize how serious a view they took of what was occurring.

Roosevelt had been loath to engage himself still more deeply in the Polish question by taking it up personally with Stalin, so in the answer that he made to Churchill on March 16th he had advised greater patience and more ingenuity in getting the negotiations in Moscow moving. Even up to then, I think, the President still thought his most useful role was that of mediator between the Soviet and British governments.

While Roosevelt was still hesitating over Churchill's suggestion that they address themselves jointly to Stalin, he learned that Molotov was not going to be sent to the San Francisco Conference. He had at once (March 24th) asked Stalin to try to find a way to let him come, if only for the vital opening sessions. He was afraid, the President said, that the whole world would construe his absence as protest or dissent. Stalin had answered (March 27th) only that it was absolutely necessary that Molotov be in Moscow in April for other official business. The President, he remarked, would understand that fear of the inference that might be drawn from his absence could not determine decisions. This show of aloofness had worried the President, all the more so since, during these same last days of March, as will be told elsewhere, Stalin was almost making mock of what the Americans and British were tell-

[5] *Ibid.*, page 426.

ing him of secret talks in Switzerland about a possible German surrender in Italy, and accusing them of deception.[6]

So at last, at the end of the month (March 29th), he conceded wearily that the time had come to take up directly with Stalin the broader aspects of the Soviet attitude, with particular reference to Poland, and he submitted to Churchill the text of a message which he was thinking of sending to Stalin. In elucidation of the basis of his thought, he told Churchill:

"You will recall that agreement on Poland at Yalta was a compromise between the Soviet position that the Lublin government should merely be 'enlarged' and our contention that we should start with a clean slate and assist in the formation of an entirely new Polish government. The wording of the resulting agreement reflects this compromise but if we attempt to evade the fact that we placed, as clearly shown in the agreement, somewhat more emphasis on the Lublin Poles than on the other two groups from which the new government is to be drawn, I feel we will expose ourselves to the charge that we are attempting to go back on the Crimea decision. It by no means follows, however, and on this we must be adamant, that because of this advantage the Lublin group can in any way arrogate to itself the right to determine what Poles from the other two groups are to be brought in for consultation."

Churchill, though he did not think the proposed message to Stalin gave full expression to his views, endorsed it. Roosevelt sent it off on April 1st with some additions. This presentation and Churchill's concurrent one to Stalin started an exchange that lasted until Roosevelt died, and was then taken up by Truman, and then went on past the German surrender, without bringing agreement one pace nearer.

In his message to Stalin, the President said in sum that as he understood it, the reorganization of the Lublin government was to be done in such a way as to bring into being a new government, in which the members of the Lublin government would play a prominent role. But, he added, any arrangement which resulted in a thinly-disguised continuation of the existing Warsaw regime would be entirely unacceptable and would cause the American people to regard the Yalta agreement as having failed. This statement he had followed up with proposals which would have allowed the Commission in Moscow to get on with its work, without having to get passes from both Warsaw and Moscow before it could make a move.

On the next day, April the 2nd, the Commission met again. On returning to the Embassy, Harriman grimly reported to Washington the fact that "No agreement was reached on any point. Molotov," he added,

[6] See Part 61.

"was much more firm than ever tonight in his opposition to Miko-lajczyk and more and more open in his insistence that our guiding influence should be the opinion of the Warsaw Poles as it was their government which was to be reorganized 'in accordance with the Crimea decision.'" We were, the Ambassador thought, at the breaking point unless Stalin's answers to the President and Prime Minister opened some new route. Perhaps his hope that it might was encouraged by the fact that, on this same day, Stalin showed much satisfaction with the campaign plans in the West about which, as will be told in another place, Eisenhower was consulting him.

Stalin's answer (April 7th) to Roosevelt started with a flat assertion, which no one could contradict: "Matters on the Polish question have really reached a dead end." The reason, he argued, was that the British and Americans were departing from the principles of the Yalta accord. This, he asserted, had provided that the existing Polish Provisional Government should be the "kernel" of the new one; the Ambassadors were trying, however, to liquidate it and form an entirely new one. This general statement Stalin had followed by proposals which in substance were the same as those which Molotov had been making. But in concluding he interjected a new specific suggestion: "As regards the numerical correlation of old and new ministers in the composition of the Polish government of National Unity, there could be established approximately a similar correlation to that realized in respect to the government of Yugoslavia." Of the twenty-seven top places in the new government of Yugoslavia besides Tito, twenty-one were held by his adherents and only six by men from other groups and parties. This minority were finding themselves without influence or power to protect their supporters.

As a tribute to Roosevelt after his death, Stalin agreed to Harriman's request that he send Molotov to San Francisco, thereby ceasing to use the threat of not joining in the United Nations as a means of having his way about Poland. He agreed also that while in the United States Molotov might discuss the Polish impasse.

Churchill had been urging Roosevelt to join with him in a public statement about their difficulties with the Russians—especially over Poland. The new President was confronted with this idea on his second day in office. This, as matters stood, could only have been an announcement of failure, placing blame upon the Soviet authorities. Truman feared the Soviet reaction might well do harm to the prospects of the San Francisco Conference and upset the going military collaboration. So (on the 13th) he informed Churchill that, although mindful of the danger that delay would serve to consolidate the Lublin group, he felt that they should explore to the full every possibility before taking this drastic step. He proposed that they might jointly put up to Stalin a definite program for Poland. A draft, over which the State Department had worked hard in an earnest wish to find a solution, was sent to the Prime Minister for consideration.

While the text was being amended to meet Eden's opinion that the American proposal yielded too much to Stalin, Churchill moved fast to clear up one of Stalin's objections. He prevailed upon Mikolajczyk to make a declaration that he accepted the Crimea decision in regard to the future of Poland, and that he considered close and lasting friendship with Russia essential. Upon having this called to his attention, Stalin hailed it as a "great step forward," but added that he would be glad to have Mikolajczyk make clear whether he "also accepts that part of the decisions of the Crimea Conference which deals with the eastern frontiers of Poland." [7] Mikolajczyk confirmed that he did—his ultimate and vain capitulation—and Churchill hurried to let Stalin and Truman know of it.

The joint message (presented on April 18th) was a most earnest effort to correct Stalin's "completely erroneous" view of American and British position. They, Churchill and Truman, assured Stalin that they were not seeking to ignore the Warsaw government in any way nor to deny it a prominent part in the new government to be formed, but they could not admit its right to veto candidates from other Polish groups for consultation. Their sole purpose was to bring a more full and truly representative government into existence. They were eager to have the Commission progress in its work, and they proposed a detailed plan by which it might at last do so. Then, presumably since Stalin had so often construed silence for consent, they said they could not, before the consultations with the Polish leaders, pledge themselves in regard to the composition of the new government; and in any case they did not think the Yugoslav arrangement was suitable for Poland.

The plea and the proposal did not produce any new inclination to compromise. Instead, confirmatory reports were received of what Vishinsky had intimated to Harriman a few days before—that the Soviet government was about to conclude a treaty of mutual assistance with the Warsaw group. Harriman had warned him that the action would be taken as a sign that Russia did not intend to carry out the Yalta agreement. The State Department instructed the American Embassy in Moscow to protest and to ask that decision be deferred until the subject could be discussed with Molotov, who was due to arrive in the

[7] *Triumph and Tragedy,* page 489.

United States within a few days. The British Foreign Office sent a similar instruction. The protests were unheeded. While Molotov was on his way, the Treaty was signed; it was published the day he arrived in the United States (the 22nd). President Truman, in telling of this episode in his Memoirs, reports that ". . . I made up my mind I would lay it on the line with Molotov." [8]

Molotov was the same man on the American side of the Atlantic as he had been on the other. In his long talks with Stettinius and Eden on April 22nd and 23rd he made no apologies, and defended every bastion and outpost of the Soviet interpretation of the Yalta accord. In answer to the complaint that the Soviet government, without consultation, had just signed a mutual aid treaty with the Polish Provisional Government, he averred that it was natural and necessary to forward the war against Germany. It was absurd, he added, to think that any reorganized government would reject the treaty. He also maintained that the Warsaw government was justified in their attitude about consultation with other Poles.

President Truman then tried to move the unmovable. But the only enjoyment he could have derived from his talk with Molotov was that of blunt speech. At the end of an exchange in which Molotov argued that the only obstacle to a smooth agreement about Poland was that we would not accept the Yugoslav formula, the President, according to his subsequent account, said, ". . . that an agreement had been reached on Poland and that it only required to be carried out by the Soviet Government." [9] He wanted, he affirmed, friendship with Russia, but also wanted it clearly understood that this could only be on a basis of mutual observance of agreements, not on the basis—as he expressed it—"of a one-way street." Molotov, if Truman's memory serves, answered only, "I have never been talked to like that in my life." Molotov's report to Stalin on this talk has not been published. Truman asked him during their talk, April 23rd, to transmit another message from him to Stalin. This asserted that the American and British governments had gone as far as they could to carry out the intent of the Yalta accord, and most seriously asked Stalin to accept the proposals which he and Churchill had jointly made some days before.

Molotov left Washington for San Francisco with the understanding that after Stalin had been heard from again the talks would be resumed. When Stalin's answer came (April 25th) it left no ground for thinking

[8] Harry S. Truman, *Year of Decisions,* Garden City, N.Y.; Doubleday & Co., Inc., 1955, copyrighted by Time Inc., page 50.
[9] *Ibid.,* page 82.

he would give in. In fact, after rebutting the British-American proposal with every assertion and accusation he had previously made, he extended the argument to broader ground, saying that although he did not know whether the governments in Greece and Belgium were "really representative," he had not interfered, for he recognized the significance of these countries to the security of Great Britain; and, by implication, he would expect the same forebearance in regard to Poland. In conclusion he asserted that the British and American governments were putting the USSR ". . . in an unbearable position trying to dictate to it their demands." He saw only one way out of this situation: "to adopt the Yugoslav example as a pattern for Poland." [10]

None of the subsequent appeals made by Churchill and Truman caused Stalin to change his position, nor did the attempts to prove to Molotov at San Francisco how much the whole cause of cooperation after the war would be served if a mutually agreeable settlement of the Polish issue could be found. Stalin was not shaken by the grave comment with which Churchill ended his last main message on the subject (April 29th): "There is not much comfort in looking into a future where you and the countries you dominate, plus the Communist Parties in many other States, are all drawn up on one side, and those who rally to the English-speaking nations and their associates or Dominions are on the other. It is quite obvious that their quarrel would tear the world to pieces and that all of us leading men on either side who had anything to do with that would be shamed before history." [11] But Stalin was not worried over that; Communist leaders, while alive, write their own history as they want it; they expect their successors to do the same.

Each day it was being made surer that the Warsaw government could not be displaced, and could not turn aside from Moscow. The Soviet High Command had turned over to it the administration not only of those lands which had been part of Poland before the war but also areas which had been German and were within the designated zone of Russian occupation, including Danzig and districts in Silesia. When first questioned about this, the Soviet government (on April 2nd) had adopted the view that this conveyance did not conflict with agreements about occupation and control of Germany ". . . as neither in the above-mentioned agreements, nor in the decisions of the Crimea Conference, is the question of administration of occupied German territory touched upon." Further, it argued that this step could not be connected or identified with that of Poland's future frontiers. That assertion was almost

[10] *Ibid.*, pages 85–86.
[11] *Triumph and Tragedy*, page 497.

certain to prove false. The Polish Prime Minister had broadcast (on March 31st) "besides Gdansk [Danzig] we have received back the Masurian lands, Lower and Upper Silesia, and the hour is not distant when the Polish frontiers will be established on the Neisse, the Oder, and the Baltic shores." The Polish press was construing the action similarly, telling of it in such headlines as "All Silesia Unites With Poland," "All Silesia Returns to the Motherland." To all intents and purposes this area, and afterwards East Prussia (except the part which the Soviet Union reserved for itself), were incorporated into Poland. The Warsaw government began to expel such Germans as were still there, to move Polish settlers in, and to distribute the great estates among small farmers.

Then also the Soviet secret police in Poland lured out of their hiding places the remaining leaders of the Polish underground army attached to the government-in-exile in London and to the political parties which had formed the London government. Despite what was thought to be a guarantee of personal safety, these sixteen men were arrested and held for weeks while the Soviet government denied knowledge of their whereabouts. When forced by insistent British and American inquiries and by the spread of rumor to reveal what had been done, the captives were charged with "diversionary acts in the rear of the Red Army," of terrorism and spying. No way was found to prevent their march to prison, where they would be no danger to the authority of Warsaw. "This," Stalin grimly told Churchill on May 5th, "is the manner in which it is necessary for the Red Army to defend its troops and its rear from diversionists and disturbers of order." [12]

Thus, when on May 7th Germany signed its formal surrender, the coalition was still harshly at odds over Poland. The American and British governments were refusing to recognize or deal with the Warsaw government behind which Moscow stood. It was one of the alienating differences which caused President Truman to send Hopkins to Moscow to find out whether previous accords with Russia still stood, whether the coalition formed for war might stay together in the making of the peace.

[12] *Ibid.,* pages 500–01.

PERIOD THIRTEEN

The Spring of 1945; Victory Close but the Common Cause Cut by Mistrust between the West and the Soviet Union

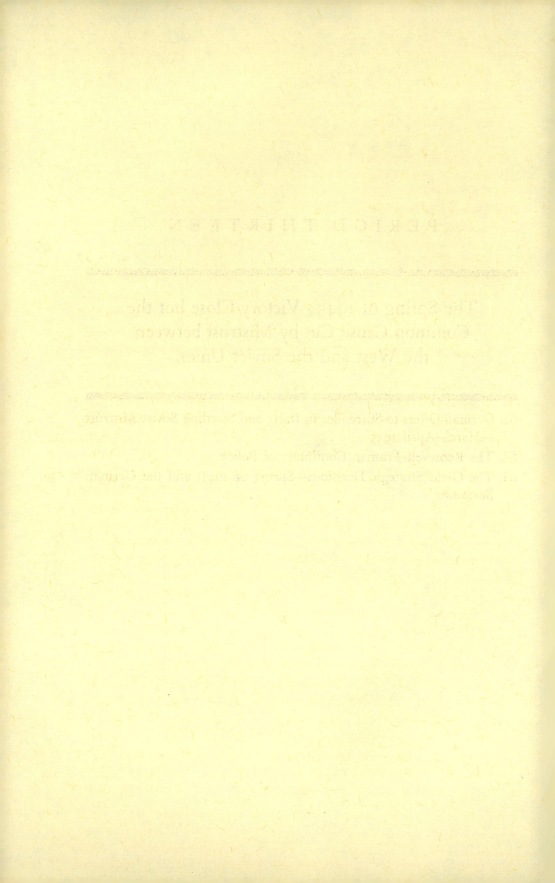

61. German Offers to Surrender in Italy; and Startling Soviet Mistrust—March–April 1945

WHILE trouble over Poland was dragging along, a startling episode was occurring in connection with soundings for the surrender of German forces in North Italy. Stalin's mistrust broke out of the thin shell formed by his wartime association. His behavior revealed how far his mind was warped by suspicion, and his language showed what a ruffian was behind his even manner.

Late in February an important Italian industrialist, Baron Luigi Parilli, had informed Gero Von Gaevernitz, a trusted member of the Office of Strategic Services in Switzerland, that several German officials, including General Karl Wolff, ranking SS officer in Italy, wanted to make contact with the Allies, with a view to ending resistance in North Italy.[1] Wolff was said to be ready to arrange to turn over North Italy to the Allies under conditions which would spare useless death and wanton destruction. After investigation, a meeting had been arranged at Lugano with one of Wolff's chief assistants and aides, who had promised to return on March 8th with credentials and definite proposals. This had been reported by Allen Dulles, the head of the OSS, to Washington, London, and Allied Force Headquarters (AFHQ) at Caserta, with the statement that unless instructed to the contrary, he would listen to what the emissaries had to say on their return. On the 8th Wolff himself turned up in Zurich and informed Dulles in substance that he was convinced of the need for immediate German surrender and would do his best to win over General Kesselring, the German Commander-in-Chief in Italy, to the plan and persuade him to come secretly to Switzerland to meet our military representatives.

An account of this talk had been immediately transmitted to AFHQ at Caserta and to the American and British Chiefs of Staff. In its messages the OSS had emphasized that it had engaged in no negotiations, that it had merely listened to Wolff's story, and advised him that we were interested only in unconditional surrender. It still considered the whole affair subject to test. But General Alexander had decided to act without waiting for definite news of Kesselring's decision. On March 11th he had informed the Combined Chiefs of Staff that he was thinking of sending his American Deputy Chief of Staff, General Lemnitzer,

---

[1] Karl Wolff was an ex-officer of the Imperial German Army who had joined Himmler's personal staff in 1932 as Sturmbannfuehrer, equivalent to Captain's rank, and had remained one of his most close associates thereafter.

583

and his British Assistant Chief of Staff (Intelligence), General Airey, to Switzerland to represent the Allies in these talks. These officers were, he explained, being instructed to tell the Germans that they must come to his headquarters at Caserta, after arranging a method of communication with Kesselring; and that the discussions at Caserta would deal with the method of unconditional surrender on a military basis only, not on a governmental or political basis. Care was needed, Alexander had remarked, because Wolff and others in his group had been associated with Himmler.

The Combined Chiefs had authorized Alexander to go ahead and send his representatives to Switzerland at once. They advised him, however, that they thought the Russians ought to be told at once what was afoot; and they stipulated that these representatives from AFHQ should not have any contact with the Germans until so instructed. Harriman and Clark-Kerr had passed Alexander's report on to Molotov by separate letters on March 12th. The Combined Chiefs, they had explained to him, had agreed to the proposal on the condition that Alexander would not send his men to Bern until the Soviet government was informed. Since they were being kept waiting, would the Soviet government be quick in its response? [1a] Molotov had given it before the clock went round. His replies to both letters were in substance the same: that the Soviet government did not object to the continuation of these "negotiations" (as he insisted on calling them); but that it would like representatives of the Soviet High Command to take part in them; and that several senior Soviet officers then in France were being authorized to do so.

Harriman had advised the State Department (on March 13th) that he saw no warrant for the Soviet request, since the Germans were merely proposing to surrender military forces on an Anglo-American front. He did not think that the Soviets would allow American officers to participate in a parallel action on the Eastern Front, and indeed he doubted whether they would even have let us know of soundings for such a surrender. In his opinion, no advantage of any sort would be gained by acceding to the Soviet wish; on the contrary, the Russians would take it as a sign of yielding and make even more unreasonable demands in the future. Further, the Ambassador thought that if Red Army officers did take part in the talks in Switzerland they might make obstructive demands. General Deane had expressed the same view

[1a] The two officers left Alexander's Headquarters by air for Lyons, France, at once—before the Soviet answer to this notice was received. But they did not cross the Swiss frontier until March 15th—after the Soviet answer was known. Wolff did not return to Switzerland until the 19th.

584

in a concurrent message to General Marshall. From a military point of view he thought that it would be neither necessary, desirable, nor useful to approve the Soviet request.

The Combined Chiefs of Staff had reached the same conclusion. They did not want Soviet officers to figure in these preliminary talks in Switzerland. But in recognition of Soviet interest in the way any surrender would be set and carried out, they were willing to have them present at any substantive talks that might follow in Italy. Accordingly their answer to Molotov's letter (March 15th), as made through the two Ambassadors, had explained that the only purpose of the meeting in Switzerland was to make contact with a view to getting German representatives to Allied Force Headquarters in Italy, where all matters concerning surrender would be discussed; that Alexander was being ordered to keep the Soviet government informed of the results of the first contacts in Switzerland, and to arrange for the presence of Soviet representatives at any subsequent talks in Italy; that "However, as the German proposal is for the surrender of a military force on the U.S.-British Front, Field Marshal Alexander, as Supreme Commander in this theatre, would alone be responsible for conducting the negotiations and for reaching decisions."

While the first notice to Molotov (that of the 12th) could have been taken to mean that the officers whom Alexander was going to send to Switzerland might enter into at least a preliminary understanding about the definite details of surrender, this second one had made firmly clear that this was not so. In effect, it had said that until the meeting in Italy the arrangements for surrender would remain open, subject to the understanding that they would have to be unconditional and would deal only with military matters.

Upon his arrival in Bern (on March 15th) General Lemnitzer had sent a message to Alexander with regard to adding a Russian officer to the group, stating: "I have now had an opportunity to observe the security measures required in getting Airey and me to Bern. Our position is considerably underground since we are in civilian clothes and are using assumed names. The introduction of a Russian officer must obviously be even more underground."

There can be little doubt that the Combined Chiefs hoped by their answer (of the 15th) to Molotov to serve two purposes. They wanted to remain free to act quickly if the German wish to arrange for a military surrender should turn out to be genuine, without having to reckon with possible hindering Soviet conditions or objections. But they also wanted to assure the Soviet government a chance to have its say before anything was settled. Their good faith is indicated by urgent requests sent by the Combined Chiefs to the American and British Military Attachés in Moscow and to Eisenhower to find out where in France those Soviet officers whom Molotov wished to have take part in the discussions were, and to tell them to be ready to start for Caserta on short notice.

But the Soviet government was not willing merely to stand by while these introductory contacts continued. Molotov's response (of the 16th), made through the two Ambassadors, had been mistrustful and rude. It said that the refusal was ". . . utterly unexpected and incomprehensible from the point of view of Allied relations between our countries." In view of this, the Soviet government could not give its agreement (consent was really meant) to any negotiations with the Germans in Bern. It wished them to be broken off at once. From then on, his letter concluded, any idea of the conduct of separate negotiations with German representatives without the participation of all three Allied powers should be ruled out.

Harriman had surveyed (in a message of the 17th) the conceivable reasons why the Russians were being so challenging. Perhaps, he surmised, they did not believe us; perhaps they thought that the method and terms of surrender would be settled in reality in Switzerland and that the later talks in Italy, to which the Soviet officers were to be admitted, would be merely to place a formal stamp on what had been already decided, and so be too late to allow effective consideration for Soviet views. Or, he had said, they might fear that other German commanders besides those in Northern Italy were planning to surrender to the West before making any similar offer to the East. Or, they might be defending their prestige; the Soviet government had been boasting that Germany was being beaten almost entirely by the Red Army, and since the further advance from the east might be slow because of the spring thaws, it wanted to be sure to appear before the world as a full participant in any major surrender in Italy that might lead to one in the west.

Alexander, before knowing of this Soviet demand that talks with the Germans be broken off, had sent (on the 16th) a message to the heads of the American and British military missions in Moscow asking them to tell the Soviet government that for security reasons he did not think it desirable that the Soviet officers who were to come to his headquarters should do so until he sent word. He had asked that the Soviet government be assured that he would give all possible advance warning so that they could arrive in ample time to participate in the talks; and that they should hold themselves ready to fly to Caserta on twenty-four hours' notice. Although Molotov's peremptory letter was in hand before this message from Alexander arrived in Moscow, General Deane and Admiral Archer (head of the British Military Mission) had passed it on to General Antonov. They had been promptly called before the Soviet General Staff, and presented by Antonov with a letter addressed to them jointly. This, after referring to Molotov's note, said that the Soviet military officers had been instructed not to go to Caserta.

Actually during this interval the circuit with the Germans had been deranged by a series of mishaps—the full recording of which I must regretfully leave to the writers of adventure tales. The summoning by Hitler of General Kesselring from Italy to take command of the Western Front was only one of them. But despite the risks of exposure, word had been gotten to Wolff that if he was ready to return to Switzerland and had a concrete plan, he would be received, and that the Allies would be in a position to consult quickly on any procedural points. He had not been informed, however, of the arrival of any officers from AFHQ. A meeting had been managed on the 19th at Ascona, a small town near the Italo-Swiss border, the Allied officers traveling in civilian clothes, with fake papers and identities.

There Wolff had reviewed in full the problem and alternative ways of proceeding. Though Generals Lemnitzer and Airey had tried to impress him with the need for hurry, he had clung to the opinion that it would be best for him to talk with Kesselring (in Berlin or France) before approaching Vietinghoff, the new Commander-in-Chief in Italy. This meeting had ended with the understanding that Wolff would set off on this errand, return to Italy, and then, if Vietinghoff could be persuaded, authorized envoys would be sent to Switzerland, and from there they would be taken under Allied auspices to Caserta to work out the military technicalities and sign the instrument of surrender.

In the face of Soviet resentment, the American and British Chiefs of Staff had stuck by their opinion that it was proper that the preliminary passage toward surrender should be conducted by the commander in the field without an outside guardian. They had repeated it firmly in the answer made to Molotov's demand that the talks be ended. This— conveyed in a letter from Harriman on the 21st—had stated that the American government was surprised at the tenor of Molotov's letter. The Soviet government, it remarked, did not seem to grasp that the only purpose of a meeting in Switzerland was to establish contact with a view to getting authorized representatives of the German command to go to Alexander's headquarters in Italy. The staff officers sent by Alexander to Switzerland, it was emphasized, had no authority to do more. Further, if and as the Germans should come to Caserta, the talks with them there would be limited to the effectuation of an unconditional military surrender on the spot of the German forces in Northern Italy, and would be conducted by Alexander. The reason why Soviet officers were being asked to be present at any such talks was to enable the Soviet government to be sure that this was all that was done. "Wherever," the answer went on, "occasions may arise for the discussion between our three powers of political as distinguished from merely military matters of surrender, it goes without saying that each of the three powers should be fully represented and participate in the discussions." The note had concluded that in view of these explanations it was intended to proceed along the lines already set, and it was hoped that Soviet officers would after all attend any meeting that might take place at Caserta. On the same day, Clark-Kerr, in a parallel letter to Molotov, extended the same reasons and assurances.

The Soviet government had valid reasons for wanting to be sure of the way in which any surrender on the Italian front was managed. They were entitled to be sure that it would not allow the Germans to transfer men or equipment from Italy to the east, or otherwise make it more possible for the Germans to sustain resistance on the Soviet Front. However, the Americans and British were fully aware of these considerations, and had not the slightest intention of allowing any harm to come to the Soviet forces as a result of what might be arranged in Italy. On the other hand, they were afraid that the Russians might, for reasons of tactics or prestige, make conditions that would cause unjustified delay. The Soviet government might actually not want a surrender in Italy to occur before the break came in the east. As commented upon by Eisenhower a few days later with reference to a possible similar development on the Western Front: "He feared that if the Russians were brought into a question of the surrender of Kesselring's forces [in the west], what could be settled by himself in an hour might be prolonged for three or four weeks, with heavy losses to our troops." [2]

But the Soviet government would take nothing on trust. Molotov's next answer (March 22nd) had revealed a blatant suspicion that a secret deal was being made, or had been made. It said, in substance, that the British and American statements were untrue. As the Soviet government viewed the matter, during the previous two weeks, behind the back of the Soviet Union, actual negotiations had been going on with representatives of the German military command. The Soviet government regarded this as completely impermissible and again insisted that the talks be stopped. "In this instance," the note stated, "the Soviet

[2] *Triumph and Tragedy*, page 443.

government sees not a misunderstanding but something worse."

At this juncture Roosevelt had taken heed. In a message to Stalin (sent on the 24th and probably delivered on the 25th) he said that perhaps the facts had not been correctly presented to the Marshal. He therefore went on to review in detail the course of events, reporting that so far the efforts to arrange a meeting with authorized German officers had met with no success but that a chance remained. It was the duty of the American government, he had emphasized, to give every help to all attempts of officers commanding Allied forces in the field who believed there was a possibility of forcing the surrender of enemy troops in their area. He had mentioned as a parallel the possibility that the Germans might send a flag of truce to the Soviet general at Konigsberg or Danzig. "There can be," he had then asserted, "in such a surrender of enemy forces in the field no violation of our agreed principle of unconditional surrender and no political implications whatever." Should any meeting be arranged, he had continued, to discuss the details of surrender by the commander of forces in the field, he would be glad to have the benefit of the experience and advice of any Soviet officers who could be present. But, his message had ended, he could not agree to suspend investigation of the possibility because of Molotov's objection for some reason completely beyond his comprehension.

Stalin's answer (March 29th) had been wholly unbelieving. He had claimed that the Germans had been using the talks in Switzerland as a smoke screen to confuse the Anglo-American Command in Italy; and that while these had been going on the Nazis had moved three divisions from Italy to the Eastern Front. "This circumstance," he had stated, "is irritating to the Soviet Command and creates ground for distrust." [3]

The Joint Chiefs of Staff had been much upset by this slur. Marshall and Leahy had put in careful work on an answer that would give as good as was got. It had been sent as a personal message from Roosevelt to Stalin. Just before this was put on his desk, Harriman, along with Clark-Kerr, had left for the Kremlin on another errand—to deliver an important message direct from Eisenhower to Stalin. This dealt with coordination of advances from the west and east, and plans for the junction of U.S.-British and Soviet armies. Of these, and of the fuss which they stirred up between the American and British governments, more will be told in another place.[4] Here it is enough to note that the

[3] The text of Stalin's answer of March 29th has not yet been located. This short description of its contents is derived from Leahy's book, *I Was There*, page 333. But its main, if not complete, substance is, I think, indicated by Roosevelt's answer, given immediately hereafter.

[4] See Part 63.

plans had greatly pleased Stalin. In reporting to the President about the session with Stalin (on the night of the 31st) centering on the Eisenhower proposals, Harriman wrote, "I regret that I did not receive until after our talk your last message regarding the Berne meeting, which I sent to Marshal Stalin by letter [April 1st]. In the mood he was in at the end of our conversation, I feel that if I had delivered your message to him personally I might have been able to get at the bottom of the Soviets' strange behavior in connection with this incident."

He was sorry, Roosevelt had said in his second communication to Stalin, that although they seemed to be in agreement on the basic principles, the preliminary investigation of willingness of the German forces in Italy to surrender was still causing mistrust. He had again gone over the facts; had again said that the Soviet representatives would be welcome at any actual negotiations for surrender; that this would have to be unconditional; and there was no thought of discussing with the Germans any terms which would allow them to transfer forces from the Italian to any other fighting front. He had denied that the lag in Allied offensive operations in Italy resulted in any way from an anticipated agreement with the Germans; the recent interruption was due mainly to the fact that Allied divisions had been transferred to the French front. Alexander was going to start a new offensive in Italy in about ten days; he would have only seventeen dependable divisions opposing twenty-four German divisions, but still everything possible would be done to prevent Germany from withdrawing any more forces from Italy. Lastly, the President had reminded Stalin that the initiative had come from a German officer reputed to be close to Himmler, and that there was a good chance that his purpose was to create suspicion and mistrust between the Allies. "There is no reason," he had concluded, "why we should permit him to succeed in that aim."

Now there took place a turn in the talks in Switzerland which may conceivably explain Stalin's next and most accusatory answer. Wolff had run into a series of dangerous difficulties in every step of the plan which had been sketched out in the talk at Ascona on the 19th. No news of how he was faring was heard until March 30th. Then the Americans learned that he had managed to get to Kesselring and had returned to Italy, but he was finding it hard to reach Vietinghoff; and that he had been warned by Himmler, and that he and his family were being kept under close watch. A message received from him had stated: "I am ready to come to a final conversation in order to arrange matters. I hope to come with . . . and either Vietinghoff or a staff officer."

April 2nd had been fixed as the day of rendezvous with Wolff, but Parilli alone had appeared at Locarno, explaining that Wolff did not dare move at the moment. But he reported that Wolff had seen Vietinghoff and secured his approval. In the course of this talk, Parilli, having probably agreed with these two German commanders that he would do so, hinted that they might like some arrangement which would allow them to withdraw their troops across the Italian frontier after giving up their arms. He had been told that such action was entirely out of the question and could not be considered. It was made clear again to all concerned that Alexander's representatives were interested only in arranging passage of any emissaries which the Germans wished to send to negotiate surrender with the proper British, Russian, and American authorities. Using the pass-word "Nurnberg," they might make their way directly through Allied lines to Alexander's headquarters at Caserta or go there via Switzerland under Allied escort.

It may be that some report of part or all of this talk was passed on to Stalin by his agents, or those he thought to be his agents, in distorted form. Stalin, as will be seen, did not hide the fact that he had his own secret conduits of information. Or, it might be that he had been checking up on Wolff's movements and had drawn wrong inferences from Wolff's trip to Kesselring's Headquarters on the Western Front and return to Italy, concluding that Wolff was acting as an emissary to surrender Kesselring's new command in the west.

His mind was probably the more open to the belief that a deception was being practiced because of the spectacular progress of various Allied forces in the west during these last days of March and first days of April. Within the circle of the Ruhr some eighty miles in diameter, the bulk of the forces in Central Germany under Field Marshal von Model was trapped.[5] South of the Ruhr, other American forces, meeting only weak resistance, had taken Frankfurt, and turning north were racing toward Kassel and Paderborn, close to the Weser River. The German army in the west was disintegrating; and within the first two weeks of April the western command was to take over half a million German soldiers as prisoners of war.

Whatever the cause, Stalin's suspicions when he wrote his answer to Roosevelt on the 3rd were even more inflamed than before. He asserted that since the President was insisting that there had not been any negotiations up to then, he must be poorly informed. "As regards my military colleagues," he had continued, "they, on the basis of data which they have on hand, do not have any doubts that the negotiations have

[5] General Walter B. Smith, *Eisenhower's Six Great Decisions,* page 169.

taken place, *and that they have ended in an agreement with the Germans* [my italics], on the basis of which the German commander on the Western Front, Marshal Kesselring, has agreed to open the front and permit the Anglo-American troops to advance to the east, and the Anglo-Americans have promised in return to ease for the Germans the peace terms. I think that my colleagues are close to the truth." [6] More insultingly still, he had averred that as a result of what had taken place, the Germans on the Western Front had stopped fighting the American-British armies while continuing to fight the Russians. This, he had concluded, could hardly serve to maintain trust between their countries, and could bring only a momentary advantage which would soon fade away.

On the very day, April 3rd, that Stalin was making these charges, Alexander's staff officers were getting ready to leave Switzerland since there seemed no prospect of the early arrival of a German plenipotentiary.[7] They had left word behind to pass on to Wolff, for transmission to Vietinghoff, that Alexander was always ready to receive authorized representatives who wanted to come to sign the surrender.

Stalin and the Soviet General Staff had been informed of this on the 4th.

Up to then Churchill had not taken a personal part in this unpleasant bout as had Roosevelt—perhaps only because neither Roosevelt nor Stalin had up to that time sent him copies of their personal exchanges; perhaps because of wish to avoid, if it could be done with honor, another clash with Stalin at the very time that they were so sharply at odds over Poland. Or, it may be because the Prime Minister—and the British Foreign Office also—was not sure that the original Soviet request ought to have been rejected. He was, as he has since recounted in *Triumph and Tragedy,* alive to the possibilities that the talks in Switzerland might go beyond arrangements for a meeting at Military Headquarters in Italy, and that discussions of surrender might develop into peace negotiations and "trench upon" political affairs.[8]

But Stalin and his advisers did not know of these British reserved thoughts. In the plot conjured out of their suspicions, they regarded the British as prime movers. Perhaps this influence was the more easily drawn because of known past efforts of Churchill to check Bolshevism; perhaps because Alexander was British; perhaps only because Church-

[6] *Triumph and Tragedy,* page 446.

[7] *The Italian Campaign, 12 December 1944 to 2nd May 1945; A Report to the Combined Chiefs of Staff by the Supreme Allied Commander Mediterranean Field-Marshal the Viscount Alexander of Tunis.* London: His Majesty's Stationery Office, 1951, page 64.

[8] *Triumph and Tragedy,* pages 445–46.

ill was not matching the President's personal disavowals. His silence may have been misconstrued in Moscow.

Roosevelt had been shocked by the fact that Stalin could believe that his American and British friends were deceiving him. He was irritated, not appeased, by Stalin's implication that he was being misinformed or fooled by his own trusted associates. General Marshall and Admiral Leahy, at his request, had prepared the next stern but still restrained answer to Stalin's expansive accusation. This had been delivered the 5th. The President said he was astonished at the allegations made by Stalin. He denied, and gave reasons for denying, any chance that they were true or any cause for believing them. He reaffirmed that Eisenhower was instructed to demand and would demand unconditional surrender of enemy troops that might be defeated on his front; and that the advances in the west were due to military action and not to any secret deal. The two concluding sentences were:

"Finally I would say this, it would be one of the great tragedies of history if at the very moment of the victory now within our grasp, such distrust, such lack of faith, should prejudice the entire undertaking after the colossal losses of life, material, and treasure involved.

"Frankly I cannot avoid a feeling of bitter resentment toward your informers, whoever they are, for such vile misrepresentations of my actions or those of my trusted subordinates."

Churchill, having been brought up to date by Roosevelt about this correspondence, at once informed him that the British government cordially associated itself with this vigorous rejoinder: "On the whole," he had observed, "I incline to think it is no more than their natural expression when vexed or jealous. For that very reason I deem it of the highest importance that a firm and blunt stand should be made at this juncture by our two countries in order that the air may be cleared and they realise that there is a point beyond which we will not tolerate insult." [9]

The Prime Minister had at once sent a correspondingly strong message to Stalin.

But Stalin still would not believe what he was being told. In the separate answers which he had sent to the President and Prime Minister on April 7th, he defended his opinions and charges. He disclaimed doubts of Roosevelt's or Churchill's integrity and trustworthiness. He asserted that that was not the real point; actually what was at issue between them, he argued, was the question of how Allies should deal with one another. Whenever, he contended, any one of them asked to participate in any discussion about surrender, it was essential that this

[9] *Ibid.*, page 512.

ally be granted the chance. Thus the Americans and British had been wrong in refusing the Russian request. "I still think," he had said, "the Russian point of view to be the only correct one, as it precludes all possibility of mutual suspicions and makes it impossible for the enemy to sow distrust between us." Then he had showed how hard it was for him to subdue his own mistrust. "It is difficult," he had said, "to admit that the lack of resistance by the Germans on the Western Front is due solely to the fact that they have been defeated." After a brief discussion about the fight being put up by the Germans on the Eastern Front, Stalin had concluded, "You will agree that such behavior on the part of the Germans is more than curious and unintelligible." [10]

As regards the credibility of his informants, Stalin had vouched for them as extremely honest and modest people, agents whose reliability had been put to a practical test. Judge for yourself, he had said: the previous February General Marshall had sent the Soviet staff information about German plans on the Eastern Front; these same secret agents had raised doubts; Marshall's reports turned out to have been wrong and theirs had turned out to have been right; and only thus was the Red Army able to avoid a catastrophe.

Whosoever Stalin's informants were—it may be interjected—they were now misleading him. The course being pursued by the Americans and British was strictly in accord with what he was being told. Wolff, after receiving the Allied messages that had been given to Parilli on April 3rd, had had several further meetings with Vietinghoff. The next report on these had been received when Parilli reappeared on the 9th. He had brought messages from Wolff reaffirming that he considered the continuation of German resistance senseless and was prepared ". . . to draw the consequences which the situation requires." But he—probably speaking for Vietinghoff as well—had sought obscure assurances that might have guarded the effects of surrender and

[10] See *ibid.*, pages 451–452, for the whole message.
The Germans were standing fast on a front running from the Baltic, east of Prague, to the mountainous northern border regions of Czechoslovakia. They were also still fighting hard in Hungary and, by holding the Bratislava Gap, standing in the way of the best route to Vienna.
It is of interest that Churchill had also been puzzled by the German strategic performance, thinking that it might portend that Hitler might be planning to retire to Southern Germany to try to prolong the fight there. In a memo asking General Ismay for the Chiefs of Staff's comment on this, he had written (on March 17th), "The strange resistance he [Hitler] made at Budapest, and is now making at Lake Balaton, and the retention of Kesselring's army in Italy so long, seem in harmony with such an intention." He then had added, however, "But of course he [Hitler] is so foolishly obstinate about everything that there may be no meaning behind these moves." *Ibid.*, page 457.

perhaps made it possible for the Germans to move troops to the east.[11] Parilli also had stated that the German commanders in Italy, on the ground that it would expedite the surrender, had joined in an urgent request that they be given the draft of capitulation which they were expected to sign.

The response made to these suspect propositions had been quite the contrary to that which Stalin was alleging. Parilli's memos and the report on his talks had been sent at once to Caserta. Alexander had been wholly in accord with the OSS Group that the request for an outline of surrender terms looked tricky, and as an attempt to draw the Allies into something akin to negotiations. AFHQ therefore had instructed the OSS to advise Wolff that the draft copy of the capitulation would be handed to the German parliamentarians only after their arrival at the appropriate Allied military headquarters; that any officers who were sent should come with absolute authority to act. This message for Wolff had been given to Parilli on the 10th. Throughout the maze of the further broken and complicated course of contact, there was no departure —not even a slight one—from either this principle or procedure.

So much for the truth of what was going on in the talks about German surrender which aroused Stalin. Churchill had been inclined just to let Stalin stew in his suspicions. Apropos of the last message he had just received from that quarter, which was milder, he had remarked to Roosevelt, "I have a feeling that this is about the best we are going to get out of them, and certainly it is as near as they can get to an apology." But Roosevelt made one last short answer to Stalin, the very last that he was to send to that other Head of State:

"Thank you for your frank explanation of the Soviet point of view of the Berne incident, which now appears to have faded into the past without having accomplished any useful purpose.

"There must not, in any event, be mutual mistrust, and minor misunderstandings of this character should not arise in the future. I feel sure that when our armies make contact in Germany and join in a fully coordinated offensive the Nazi armies will disintegrate."

Harriman, before passing on this message to Stalin, had asked the President whether he would not consider omitting the word "minor."

[11] They asked that in any official negotiations for surrender, two points be guaranteed: (1) withdrawal (*Abzug*) with military honor after the cessation of hostilities; (2) maintenance of a modest contingent of the army group as future instrument of order inside Germany. Parilli had explained that Point 1 meant only eventual return to their homes when the prisoners would be released; and that Point 2 represented a wish. But his auditors felt that the eager intermediary was attempting to explain away clearly untenable propositions.

He had said that he thought it might well be misinterpreted in Moscow and that he must confess to the President that the misunderstanding seemed to him to be "major." Roosevelt had answered that he wanted to leave the word in, as he wished to consider what had happened as a minor incident.

To Churchill, on sending a copy of this message to Stalin, he had said, on the 12th:

"I would minimize the general Soviet problem as much as possible because these problems, in one form or another, seem to arise every day, and most of them straighten out, as in the case of the Berne meeting.

"We must be firm, however, and our course thus far is correct." [12]

62. The Roosevelt-Truman Continuity of Policy

Nothing that Roosevelt ever wrote more clearly marked than this last message to Stalin the determined optimism with which he confronted the business of managing our relations with the Soviet government. He was going to continue to act on the supposition that by patience, proofs of good will and fair purpose, the mistrust of the Soviet authorities could be subdued, and they could be converted into good partners for the benefit of all mankind. To this purpose he held to the last breath. It could not have been easy in the face of the negative answers he had been getting from Stalin on so many questions. Nor, toward the end, could it have been wholly unaffected by the opinions being pressed upon him that the Soviet government was not to be led along the proper path merely by friendship or generosity, but that it had to be opposed, and dealt with on the basis of punishments and rewards. Advice of this sort was put before him by some of his most close associates. Churchill's judgment was now set that way, but this was for the British leader really only a return to the opinion he had kept in suspense for the better conduct of the war—not so of others in the President's own circle who had formerly held with him the sense of imperative need for close relations with the Soviet government for the future after the war.

The reasons seen for changing our way of dealing with the Soviet government were perhaps most clearly set down in two messages which

[12] *Triumph and Tragedy*, page 454.

Harriman had sent from Moscow to Stettinius. The first had been sent on April 4th, the day after Stalin's most accusatory message regarding the talks in Bern, but was offered in comment on American policy in the provisions of relief supplies. It had said in part and in paraphrase:

"In respect to policy, we now have ample proof that the Soviet government views all matters from the standpoint of their own selfish interests. They have publicized to their own political advantage the difficult food situation in areas liberated by our troops such as Italy, Belgium, and France. . . . The Communist Party or its associates everywhere are using economic difficulties in areas under our responsibility to undermine the influence of the Western allies and to promote Soviet concepts and policies. . . . The Soviet Union and the minority governments that the Soviets are forcing on the people of Eastern Europe have an entirely different objective. We must clearly recognize that the Soviet program is the establishment of totalitarianism, ending personal liberty and democracy as we know and respect it."

The second message (sent on the 6th) had gone further in analytical scope. It has been discernible for many months, this had said, that the Soviet government had three concurrent lines of foreign policy; (1) overall collaboration with the United States and Britain in a world security organization; (2) creation of its own security ring through domination of the border states; (3) the penetration of other countries, by abusing democratic processes through local Communist parties and by exploiting economic troubles. It had been hoped that the Soviet government would restrain its disturbing purposes for the sake of lasting collaboration. But plainly it would not; certainly it would do its utmost, regardless of what might be expected from the world peace organization, to create a security ring about the Soviet Union by control of the border states.

In that at least, the Ambassador continued, the Soviet government was now confident it could force us to acquiesce. Thus when we resist, they retaliate, as they did by refusing to send Molotov to the San Francisco Conference, knowing how much importance we attach to its success. There was much evidence that our attitude, which Harriman thought to have been generous and considerate, had been regarded by them as a sign of weakness and of our need for their cooperation. The lesson, as read in Moscow, was that we should give only as we got; that we should maintain positions that would be hard for the Soviet authorities if they maintained positions hard for us; and that we should hurt them if they hurt us. In such a course, it was thought, lay the best chance of getting together with the Soviet Union on acceptable terms. In offering this advice, the Ambassador added, he hoped he would not be misunderstood. "Up till recently the issues we have had with the Soviets have been relatively small compared with their contribution to the war, but now we should begin to establish a new relationship. I am, as you know, a most earnest advocate of the closest possible understanding with the Soviet Union so that what I am saying relates only to how best to attain such understanding." [13]

Roosevelt's inclination was not immune to the pressure of experience, nor did he have any false admiration for the ways in which the Soviet Union was seeking to achieve certain social ends to which he too was devoted. There is no record, no graph of the impulses of the mind and spirit, to tell us to what extent, during this last and most trying period of office before his death, his reluctance to be guided by such advice was connected with his own measurement of facts and problems.

The student conjecturer can discern many queries which might have caused him to pause before changing the mode in which he had dealt with the Soviet Union ever since they became common enemies of Germany. Even though Soviet purposes in Europe should prove to be as thus reported, could they be checked by measures within our reach? Could they be restrained by counterpressure unless we were willing to leave large American military armies in the center of Europe for a long time? Even if this could be done, might we not lose Russian help in bringing about the quick end of the war against Japan? In sum, was not the more practical as well as the more promising course to keep on trying to influence Soviet actions by proof of friendship and large un-

---

[13] This opinion as to the necessity of changing the basis on which we were dealing with the Soviet government had gradually grown into a firm conviction shared by Ambassador Harriman and General Deane. The Ambassador was shocked and disturbed most of all by his experience on the Commission in trying to agree upon a method for reorganizing the Polish government. In addition, his feeling and his judgments were also affected by many other Soviet actions which he thought to be unfriendly or grasping.

Items on the bill of criticism were:

1. The refusal to allow us to send contact teams into Poland to aid in the evacuation of Americans who had been prisoners of war, which he regarded as contrary to the agreement reached at Yalta.

2. That the Soviet government had closed down the airfield at Poltava on the ground that it was not being used sufficiently any longer. It justified the detention of the flyers by reference to a few acknowledged incidents in which they had helped the Polish underground and had even helped a few individuals to get out of Poland.

3. The denial of our request to send a mission to Moscow to arrange for American use of airfields near Budapest.

4. The neglect of repeated requests to improve the courier, mail, and freight service from outside to the Embassy in Moscow.

5. The unwillingness to allow American naval officers to go to Costanza to watch over the unloading of the American ships bringing UNRRA supplies.

Added to these, both Harriman and Deane had a sense that they and their staff were often being treated with an insulting edge.

derstanding of Soviet needs? And then might not many of those matters over which dissension was then most brisk—such as what the government of Poland was to be and the conduct of control commissions in other parts of Eastern Europe—turn out in the longer stretch of time to be of little importance? Was that not likely to be so if there was in the future a collective organization of all national states for peace? Was not that the greatest prize and heritage to be won out of the war?

Roosevelt was a tired man at Warm Springs, hoping to get back normal strength and vitality. His spirit was more and more absorbed by the vision of the gathering that was soon to start at San Francisco, a vision being blurred by daily happenings. What fee ought to be paid, would have to be paid, for its realization? As great a one, I am going to infer that he thought, as faith and fairness could justify. This was the vast and crucial area of decision, with its elements deranged, and in flux, that Truman found before him.

Truman made up his mind that he would not depart from Roosevelt's course or renounce his ways—until and unless they should definitely be proved futile. He abstained from acts intended merely to pay back the Soviet government for some refusal or offense. He did not resort to retaliation. And of crucial importance, he resisted counsel—so ably presented by Churchill—that the path of military action in Europe should be bent to set a limit to the expansion of Soviet influence; and that our forces should be kept in Europe as long after German defeat as might be necessary to prevent the Soviet Union from wholly having its imperious way. All that he was brought to do, while the attempt to define and moderate Soviet wishes and intentions continued, was to defer arrangements for American help in Soviet reconstruction after the war.

In sticking to this course, Truman felt faithful to the ideas and ideals of the war leader from whose shoulders he had taken over these momentous issues. He drew confidence from the fact that he was acting in accord with the judgment of Admiral Leahy, Secretary Stimson, General Marshall, and other military advisers on whom he relied.[14] They were impressed by the way in which the Russians had carried out their military engagements. They were cool about retaliatory measures or restraints that might hinder or affect Soviet cooperation in the

[14] The Joint Chiefs had considered a program of retaliation and pressure which General Deane had submitted, and had decided against it early in March. They had stood fast against similar later suggestions, even though Soviet negative response to American requests on various military matters had become more numerous and its tone of refusal more brusque.

Pacific War. As expounded by Marshall at a meeting at the White House on April 23rd, just after Stettinius had reported that his talks with Molotov about Poland were going most unsatisfactorily, ". . . he hoped for Soviet participation in the war against Japan at a time when it would be useful to us. The Russians had it in their power to delay their entry into the Far Eastern war until we had done all the dirty work . . . and he was inclined to agree that it would be a serious matter to risk a break." [15] They were chary of any military plans or engagements for "political" purposes. They wanted, before taking any steps that might arouse Soviet resentment, to test further what might be done through friendly explanations and sustained negotiations.

Thus, while the war was ending, Truman carefully carried out all the agreements which Roosevelt had entered, even those which troubled him, as did the Yalta agreement on the Far East. Although a few of his consultants, such as Harry Hopkins and Joseph Davies, were still inclined to interpret the outlook in terms of British-Russian rivalry for power, he welcomed Churchill's warm and seasoned presentations. He sought a personal meeting with Churchill and Stalin. When compelled to defer this because of tasks in Washington, he sent envoys to Moscow and London to review with those Heads of State the whole area of unsettled questions in Europe and the Far East—in preparation for their later conference. He used all the force of American desire and diplomacy to give birth at San Francisco to a charter for the new world, in which the war coalition was to be gradually dissolved.

<hr/>

63. The Great Strategic Decisions—Spring of 1945 and the German Surrender

<hr/>

After the many decisions about the strategy for the Western Front which had been reached at the summit in Malta and Yalta, it had seemed as though the course was cleared to the end. But now there ensued divergences of judgment between the Americans and British almost as disturbing as those over the second front in 1942. They lasted until the Germans laid down their arms, and then extended to the military dispositions to be made thereafter.

There were three connected fissures in the British-American views about the military program:

[15] *Forrestal Diaries,* pages 48–51.

1. Along what routes should the final assaults from the west be directed?

2. Should the advances from the west be halted along lines fixed in advance, or go as far as they could before meeting the Russians?

3. Should the postwar zonal lines of occupation be regarded as immediate military demarcation lines; or could armies stand in advanced positions for an indeterminate period, until agreement was reached separately on time and conditions of withdrawal? More specifically, should or should not such forces of the West as might go beyond lines of zonal division in Germany and Austria, or into countries bordering the Soviet Union, such as Czechoslovakia, be drawn back into their previously defined occupation zones as soon as military circumstances permitted?

The two latter questions basically resolved themselves into whether at this time military strength should be kept deployed in support of diplomacy—to constrain the onward momentum of Soviet power. Were the Western armies to stay indefinitely on the opposite side of a line of resistance, while Heads of State argued their way toward a settlement of the world after the war?

Churchill and the British War Cabinet were convinced this was right and necessary. In fact, the Prime Minister was so gravely disturbed at the failure of other methods of making an impression on Moscow that he gloomily concluded that, unless a stand of this sort were taken there and then, another great war would surely follow. The American government, civil and military, were loath either to warp (as they conceived it) military action or delay in the execution of agreements for (as they put it) political purposes. They did not despair of the result of continued exercise of diplomacy. They did not want to risk either such confrontation of the Russians or involvement of American troops in local disputes. They were eager to get on with the war against Japan without the drag of maintaining a long military watch in the center of Europe.

It is quite possible that when the U.S.-British plans for the conduct of the campaigns on the Western Front were approved at Yalta, Eisenhower had intended to let Montgomery's command keep all the elements assigned to it for the drive across the Rhine in the north, and then in full force keep going toward Berlin. If that had been the plan in mind, then several possible reasons for changing it can be found in the military analyses of the situation.[16] American Army intelligence

---

[16] Eisenhower denied that there was a real change of plan. I leave the question for the military historians. This subject is treated in Pogue's excellent study. See also

reports on March 11th placed General Zhukov's patrols only twenty-eight miles from Berlin, and that made it seem unlikely that the city could withstand the vast Russian attack for very long. If British-American troops raced to get there first, they might well lose. Other objectives were attractive. Much of Germany's plant for producing arms had been moved from the Ruhr to the interior. There was an active idea that the German army might be preparing for a last stand in the Alpine mountain area to the south, east of Munich along the Austrian border. The reports to that effect were flimsy but taken seriously enough to have led General Marshall to suggest at the end of March that the American forces head into that area.[17] Besides these possible influences on decision, there was a wish to give the troops under American command full chance. As summarized by Pogue,

"The surprise crossings of the Rhine at Remagen and Oppenheim before the main assault in the north and the rapid exploitation of this advantage in the two areas had placed General Bradley's forces in a position to play a major role in the sweep through Germany. These unexpected strokes of fortune caught the public imagination, particularly in the United States, and reinforced the 12th Army Group Commander's [Bradley's] request for a larger part in the drive to the Elbe than he had played in reaching the Rhine. It seems probable that General Eisenhower also desired to let the 12th Army Group see what it could do."[18]

Whether or not this is an adequate interpretation of his reasons, on March 28th Eisenhower had informed Montgomery that after the task immediately before them was done, the American divisions (the Ninth U.S. Army) included in Montgomery's army group would be brought south and combined with other American forces under General Bradley. He had decided, he explained, that while Montgomery's forces should push forward toward the east and north in all their re-

---

Churchill's *Triumph and Tragedy,* pages 463–67, Montgomery's *Normandy to the Baltic,* Bradley's *A Soldier's Story,* and Eisenhower's *Crusade in Europe,* pages 400–01 and *Grand Strategy,* Vol. VI, pages 131–45.

[17] General Smith's account, given in *Eisenhower's Six Great Decisions,* pages 189–90, in a rather obscure way gives the impression that the expectation that the Germans planned to make a strong last stand in this area had a reasonably credible basis, and influenced SHAEF's strategic decisions. This belief seems to have been stimulated by the fact that many government departments were quitting Berlin and setting up their offices at or near Berchtesgaden, and by intelligence and reconnaisance reports of construction of bunkers and trenches. Most of this new construction was, however, intended to house and protect government workers and not combat troops. The area was being turned into a refuge, not a stronghold.

[18] *The Supreme Command,* page 435.

maining strength, the major Allied attack would be along the axis Erfurt-Leipzig-Dresden to link up with the Russians on the Elbe well south and west of Berlin. To the south of that main advance another American army, 6th Army Group (General Devers), was to get ready to move through the Danube Valley to meet the Russians somewhere in Austria. Montgomery, who had wanted to keep the Ninth U.S. Army under his command at least until he reached the Elbe, had been hurt and disappointed. He had answered that he thought a grave mistake was being made. But Eisenhower had stood fast in his decision. By then there were three times as many American troops as British fighting on the Western Front.

Forthwith (on March 28th), possibly in order to end all chance of further argument, Eisenhower had sent a message to Stalin telling him of these plans and asking what he thought of them. This he did as far as is known, without first informing his Deputy, Air Chief Marshal Tedder, or the Combined Chiefs of Staff, or Churchill. No doubt he counted on the support of the Joint Chiefs and the President if either his plan or his authority to communicate it directly to Stalin were challenged.[19] This message in substance set forth:

[19] At Yalta the Joint Chiefs of Staff had advised the President that they thought it was becoming highly desirable that direct liaison be established between commanders in the west and the Soviet General Staff. Since it was believed that Stalin's formal approval of this was necessary ". . . a memorandum from the President to the Prime Minister enclosing a memorandum requesting Marshal Stalin to agree to the proposed method of liaison through the Military Mission in Moscow was presented to the President, signed by him and dispatched at once to the Prime Minister." (Bohlen Notes, Meeting of the President with his Advisers, February 4, 1945, 10:30 a.m., *Yalta Documents*, 564 *et seq.*) Regrettably, the compilers of the Yalta Documents were not able to find a copy of this memo to Churchill, enclosing one for Stalin (*ibid.*, page 565). Nor is Churchill's answer to Roosevelt given in this collection of documents nor in Churchill's book. That same afternoon, the President told Stalin personally that he felt the armies were getting close enough to have contact between them, and he hoped General Eisenhower could communicate directly with the Soviet General Staff. Stalin agreed, saying he thought it was very important and promising that the staffs while at Yalta would work out the details of this suggestion (*ibid.*, page 571). Then at the meeting of the Combined Chiefs of Staff on February 5th Field Marshal Sir Alan Brooke said that the British Chiefs of Staff were equally anxious to have the necessary liaison with Soviet High Command and agreed that the Military Missions already established in Moscow shouid act as the link on a high level (*ibid.*, page 603); and General Antonov concurred.

Whether the decision reached by the three military staffs at Yalta was translated into a directive to Eisenhower before he sent his message of March 28th to Stalin is not clear from the records available. The minutes of the discussions at Yalta, no doubt known to him, may have seemed sufficient basis for the step he took. Or he might have thought the point certainly settled when he was authorized to send Tedder to Moscow to deal directly with Stalin and the Soviet Chiefs of Staff. Eisenhower, in *Crusade in Europe*,

1. That the purpose of his immediate (i.e., then current) operations was to encircle the Ruhr and destroy the enemy forces that were defending it. This operation he thought would be completed by late April, if not before.

2. His next effort would be to divide enemy forces—by making a junction with the Soviet armies.

3. That the best axis on which this junction might be achieved would be an advance from the west to Erfurt-Leipzig-Dresden, this being the area into which many German government departments were moving. His main effort would be along this line.

4. But then as soon as he could, he would seek to advance by a secondary thrust to meet up with the Soviet forces also in the Regensburg-Linz (Austria) area in the south; and if this were done German resistance in any possible redoubt in South Germany could be prevented.

5. That it would seem to be of the greatest use, before he made any final decision on these plans, to coordinate them as closely as possible with the Soviet plans. Therefore, he asked Stalin to tell him what the Soviet plans were and whether the Allied plans just explained fitted in well with them.

6. He was ready to send officers to complete the field liaison between the Allied advancing forces and the Soviet advancing forces, in order to assure coordinated action.

To summarize and interpret: prospectively the forces coming from east and west would meet up with each other in three areas; Bradley's armies would be moving eastward across the Central German country in the direction of Leipzig and Dresden and meet the oncoming Russians somewhere in their course; to the south, other American forces were to be advancing through Nurnberg and Regensburg, and along the Danube Valley in Austria, where they would meet the southern segments of the Red Army; and, though not explicitly stated in this message, it soon became clear that Eisenhower also planned to have Montgomery's army in the north drive to Bremen and Hamburg and toward the Baltic Sea, meeting the Russians somewhere along their route.

---

page 399, merely says that as Commander-in-Chief he felt that he was acting within his authority to communicate with Moscow "on purely military matters" under an arrangement made in January and approved by the Combined Chiefs of Staff.

There is nothing in the discussions at Yalta to indicate that it was then contemplated that Eisenhower would address himself to Stalin *personally* and directly, although it was fully recognized that Stalin, as head of the Soviet armed forces, would dictate the answers. Surprise is indicated in the comment made by the Secretary of the British Chiefs of Staff to Churchill ". . . they [the Chiefs of Staff] have never contemplated a direct approach by SCAEF [Eisenhower] to Marshal Stalin on the subject of our major strategy, the responsibility for which lies with the Combined Chiefs of Staff and their Governments." *Grand Strategy*, Vol. VI, page 132.

The American and British Ambassadors in Moscow had gone along with General Deane and Admiral Archer when, on the evening of March 31st, they presented this message to Stalin. After reading it, Stalin had praised Eisenhower's plan, but said he would answer more definitely after he had consulted his staff. The conversation that had ensued that evening is informative. Remember that it took place a fortnight after Molotov had first (on March 16th) urged that talks in Switzerland about the surrender of German forces in Italy be broken off, and three days before Stalin was to tell Roosevelt (on April 3rd) that he was sure a secret deal was being made by which the Germans would stop fighting in the west while continuing in the east![20] Stalin had asked whether the secondary attack in the south would come from Italy or the Western Front; he was told that it would come from the Western Front. He had shown himself curious about the number of German divisions fighting on the Western Front, and had seemed much impressed by the number of German prisoners being taken there. When Harriman had asked him about his earlier worry that Red Army operations might be hindered by roads and weather at this time, Stalin had said that conditions were better than he had anticipated and that the Russians were meeting strong German resistance in the Czechoslovak mountains but were confident of overcoming it as they already had at Lake Balaton in Hungary.

The next day, April 1st, Stalin had sent Eisenhower a written answer approving the strategy that had been outlined to him, and telling of the concerted moves the Russians planned to make. Its main points have significant bearing on later events; Stalin

1. wholly agreed with the idea of making juncture of forces in the area of Erfurt-Leipzig-Dresden;

2. stated that the Soviet High Command intended to make the main blow of the Soviet armies in this direction;

3. averred that it also favored the plan of a second supplementary juncture some place in the region of Vienna, Linz or Regensburg;

4. affirmed the opinion that Berlin no longer had the strategic significance it used to have, and said that therefore only secondary Soviet forces would be assigned to the Berlin salient;

5. advised that the Soviet armies would start their principal advance about the second half of May—the other advance in the Vienna-Linz area, he added, was already underway. But he explained that this schedule might be adjusted to meet changes of circumstance; for example, if the German armies withdrew, the dates might be advanced. Much also depended on the weather;

[20] See Part 61.

6. informed that study was being given by the General Staff to improving liaison between the two armies and he would tell Eisenhower of the decision later;

7. and finally remarked that it had been established that the size of the enemy forces on the Eastern Front was being gradually increased. Three divisions had been moved from north Italy and two divisions from Norway, in addition to the Sixth Tank Army S.S.

Eisenhower had sent a copy of this message at once to the Combined Chiefs of Staff "for information." As soon as the Prime Minister learned of it he had asked the Supreme Commander about his plans. Eisenhower had on March 30th explained them to Churchill in much the same way as in his message to Stalin. Churchill had been unhappy and displeased on three scores. First, he had the sense that Eisenhower had stretched his authority in consulting Stalin directly; then he believed that in this program he was going beyond purely military matters, and while ostensibly concerned with contacts between approaching armies he was settling major strategy which had political consequences; and finally, he judged the program itself very ill-advised. The British Chiefs of Staff had been equally aggrieved, feeling they were being short-circuited, and they had asked at once that discussion with the Russians be suspended.

The American Chiefs of Staff stolidly refused to pull Eisenhower up short in this way. They had defended his strategy as sound and his action as necessary.

"The Battle of Germany," in Churchill's summary of the American reasoning, "was at a point where it was for the Field Commander to judge the measures which should be taken. To turn away deliberately from the exploitation of the enemy's weakness did not appear sound. The single objective should be quick and complete victory. While recognising that there were factors not of direct concern to the Supreme Commander, the United States Chiefs considered his strategic concept was sound and should receive full support and that he should continue to communicate freely with the Commander-in-Chief of the Soviet Army." [21]

Churchill had carried the case to the President in a message sent on the 1st of April (the same day Stalin got the message which the President had sent to assure him that the talks in Switzerland about possible surrender of the Germans in Italy were only preliminary). The heart of Churchill's contention was that the main axis of the advance from

[21] *Triumph and Tragedy*, page 462.

the west should not be shifted southward from the Elbe and Berlin. Among his reasons were two. (1) The capture of Berlin would be the "supreme signal of defeat to the German people." (2) The Russian armies almost certainly would overrun Austria and enter Vienna. If they should take Berlin as well, would they not become overbearing? His conclusion was, "I therefore consider that from a political standpoint we should march as far east into Germany as possible, and that should Berlin be in our grasp we should certainly take it." [22]

Eisenhower tried to soften the Prime Minister's opposition by explaining (in a message sent to Churchill on April 1st) that, "In order to assure the success of each of my planned efforts, I concentrate first in the centre to gain the position I need. As it looks to me now, the next move thereafter should be to have Montgomery cross the Elbe, reinforced as necessary by American troops, and reach at least a line including Lubeck on the [Baltic] coast." About Berlin he made no promises; if it remained open to capture by the West, he said, honors would be shared between American and British forces.[23]

Churchill had recognized that he had gained a little ground. In his reply to Eisenhower (of April 2nd) he had contented himself with repeating his opinion that it was highly important that the Western armies should "shake hands" with the Russians as far east as possible. To the President on the 5th he had sent amiable word that the changes in the main plan now seemed to him less than he had supposed on first reading Eisenhower's message to Stalin—and, to express his sentiment, ended with "one of my very few Latin quotations: *Amantium irae amoris integratio est.*" The War Department had translated this as "Lovers' quarrels are a part of love" and repeated it to Eisenhower. On the next day, Churchill, in a message to Stalin, backed up Roosevelt's defense of the discussions in Switzerland about possible German surrender in Italy.

But these avowals had not ended the discussion as to whether or not a special effort should be made to reach Berlin before the Russians. The Joint Chiefs had continued to resist the wrought-up British presentations. They had stood by the conclusion recorded in a memo of April 6th: "Such psychological and political advantages as would result from

[22] *Ibid.,* page 465. Churchill had found the statement of objections on military grounds which the British Chiefs of Staff had composed and hurried over to the American associates unimpressive, marked by excessive anxiety, and not adequately aware of the circumstances and outlook influencing Eisenhower's course. The reasoning of both is well analyzed in *Grand Strategy,* Vol. vi, pages 132–139.

[23] The complete message is printed in *ibid.,* pages 140–41.

the possible capture of Berlin ahead of the Russians should not override the imperative military consideration, which in our opinion is the destruction and dismemberment of the German armed forces." [24]

The Combined Chiefs of Staff had allowed the development of the action on the Western Front to rest with Eisenhower on the basis of his previous statements of plans and intentions which he reconfirmed on April 7th. Accordingly, when Montgomery had asked for ten divisions more for a main thrust toward Lubeck and Berlin, Eisenhower (on the 8th) had reminded him that his first task was to protect Bradley's assault to the south. But, he continued, if Montgomery could get to the Elbe first, so much the better; and if afterwards, with whatever American divisions could be given him, he found that he could push beyond the Elbe to Lubeck and Kiel, the quicker he got there the better.

The basic lines for the final attack from the west had thus been set. But, despite the fact that the chance to reach Berlin before the Russians was not sought, it did present itself—not to Montgomery but to the Americans—and was passed up. United States forces under General Simpson, then a part of General Bradley's army group, had reached the Elbe River near Magdeburg on April 11th and crossed the next day —the day Roosevelt died. They were only about fifty miles from Berlin. "At that time," Bradley wrote later, "we could probably have pushed on to Berlin had we been willing to take the casualties Berlin would have cost us. Zhukov had not yet crossed the Oder and Berlin now lay almost midway between our forces. However Zhukov's eastern approaches were infinitely more negotiable than the waterlogged path that confronted us in the west." [25]

Simpson asked Bradley for permission to go on to Berlin. This could hardly have been approved without seeming to depart from the prospectus of his intentions which Eisenhower had laid before Stalin, to which perhaps the plans of the Red Army were adjusted. Anyhow, "The Supreme Commander instead ordered that he [presumably Bradley, who passed down the order to Simpson] hold on the Elbe while turning his units northward in the direction of Luebeck and southward toward the National Redoubt area." [26]

Upon informing Marshall (on April 15th) of this series of decisions, Eisenhower said he thought these the more important objectives; and

[24] *The Supreme Command,* page 445. And they so reaffirmed in another rejoinder to the British Chiefs of Staff on the same day. *Grand Strategy,* Vol. vi, page 144.

[25] Omar N. Bradley, *A Soldier's Story,* page 537.

[26] *The Supreme Command,* pages 446–47.

besides to direct effort against Berlin "would be foolish in view of the relative situation of the Russians and ourselves. . . . While it is true we have seized a small bridgehead over the Elbe, it must be remembered that only our spearheads are up to that river; our center of gravity is well back of there." [27]

The Russians, after a last fortnight of savage attack and heavy artillery bombardment, forced their way into the center of Berlin on May 2nd. They had the first somber sense of triumph, the first awesome sight of the ruins, the first parades under the pall of smoke.

Even after Berlin was eliminated as prize for whoever was able to get there first, the question remained how far toward the east the American and British forces were to advance. The British Chiefs of Staff would have liked them to keep on moving. Churchill had the same wish. Early in April he had told Roosevelt he thought that full advantage should be taken of the rapid progress in the west while Soviet forces were not yet able to deliver a decisive attack on their central front; to have them "join hands with the Russian armies as far to the east as possible." . . . [28] No new orders to that effect having been in the interval issued to or by Eisenhower, Churchill on April 18th revised the basis of his proposal. In a message to Truman he suggested that the impetus of the American advance through the center of Germany—it would be within the zone set aside for Soviet occupation—should not be stopped until Stalin promised to share the food surplus of the Eastern Zone with the rest of Germany.

But the Joint Chiefs of Staff were opposed to paying a price in lives not required for military ends. Truman answered on the 21st that he regarded the question of the tactical deployment of American troops in Germany as a military one, and thought Eisenhower should be allowed latitude and discretion. Of course Churchill thought that the question was no longer a "tactical" one, but a political one. But he was not in a position to have his way. By then the Soviet forces were past the Elbe near Dresden. Eisenhower—possibly with the exposition of his intentions that he had previously sent to Stalin in mind—decided to stop his advance on the central front at the Elbe and the branch river (the Mulde) running south from it. On the 21st he told the Russians he was going to do so, while turning his armies to the north and south

[27] *Ibid.* Leahy, *I Was There,* pages 350–51, seems to attribute the decisions largely to difficulties of supplying these advance units, rather than other military ideas or physical obstacles. This may have been another hampering circumstance which influenced the decision, but I do not think it was a major one.

[28] *Triumph and Tragedy,* page 512.

609

to clear out remaining German points of resistance.[29] American forces in the center which had gone beyond the Elbe at one point were drawn back.

To the south, patrols of the Third Army under General Patton had by then crossed the frontier of Czechoslovakia. That force had the momentum and supplies to keep rolling far into that country. But Eisenhower had planned to have it drive in a southeastern direction along the Czechoslovakian frontier toward the Danube and into Austria toward Linz. Then Eisenhower considered deploying the left of Patton's forces farther east into Czechoslovakia, as far as the line Karlsbad, Pilsen, and Ceske Budejovice (Budweis). After consulting Marshall, he informed the Russians of this purpose on April 30th, and they agreed to it. At the end of April the Red Army was some seventy miles away from Prague and still meeting tough resistance.[29a]

Churchill was advocating the most vigorous and extensive advance possible into Czechoslovakia—putting forward his arguments in a message to Truman on April 30th. In this he said he thought that the liberation of Prague and much of the territory of Western Czechoslovakia by American forces might make the whole difference in the postwar situation in that country and influence events in nearby ones; while if the Western Allies played no part in its liberation Czechoslovakia would go the way of Yugoslavia. He concluded that it was highly important that these political considerations be brought to Eisenhower's attention, so that he might take advantage of any suitable chance to move into that country.

The State Department agreed, advising the White House that it thought that if American troops went as far as the Ultava River (which runs through Prague), we would be in a better position to bargain with Russia about zones in Austria and policies in Czechoslovakia. Marshall asked Eisenhower for his opinion. The Supreme Commander answered that the Soviet General Staff contemplated operations into the Ultava (Moldau) valley. His intention was, he said, to destroy any other

[29] *The Supreme Command,* page 467. Pogue adds, "It was clear that the northern forces would cross the Elbe and hit at the enemy at the base of the Jutland peninsula, and that his forces in the south would drive through the Danube valley into Austria. Eisenhower did not explain, but it was apparent that these would continue to advance until they met the Red forces."

[29a] The pertinent section in Eisenhower's message of April 30th to the Soviet General Staff read: "3. From the head waters of the Mulde River my forces will hold initially along approximately the 1937 frontiers of Czechoslovakia. Later, if the situation should so dictate, these forces may be advanced to the towns of Karlsbad, Pilsen, Budojovice. You will be informed as my operational plans develop. I note that the Soviet forces will be undertaking the cleaning out of the Eastern shores of Elbe and Ultava (Moldau) Rivers in this sector of the front. . . ." *Grand Strategy,* Vol. VI, page 158.

remaining organized German forces. Thus, "If a move into Czechoslovakia is then desirable, and if conditions here permit, our logical initial move would be on Pilsen and Karlsbad. I shall not attempt any move which I deem militarily unwise."[30] The President and Chiefs of Staff left the decision up to Eisenhower.

On May 4th he notified General Antonov that he was willing to continue to move forward after occupying the Pilsen-Karlsbad area to the region of Prague.[31] The next day, the 5th, as Patton crossed the border in force, the underground in Prague rose in rebellion and broadcast an appeal for Allied aid. But Antonov was strongly dissenting from Eisenhower's projected thrust toward Prague. He asked the Supreme Commander not to move Allied forces in Czechoslovakia east of "the originally intended line" in order to avoid a confusion of forces, and pointed significantly to the fact that the Red Army had stopped its advance to the lower Elbe (in the north of Germany) at his suggestion.[32] Eisenhower complied on the 6th with this Soviet request, and that is as far as the American troops went. So the Red Army alone entered Prague —two days after the surrender with Germany was signed. The Russians did not wish forces of any other country to share in the eyes of the Czechoslovakian people credit for the final victory or liberation.

Similarly, the American army group under General Devers which captured Munich on the 30th of April and was at Innsbruck in Austria by May 3rd, four days before the final German surrender, stopped near there. One division pushed on to the Brenner Pass to meet Alexander's troops coming up from Italy. The rest waited while junction was made with Russian forces coming from the east.

But the advance in the north of Germany was not confined either by previous understanding or Soviet objection. Eisenhower encouraged Montgomery to push on across the Elbe and sent American divisions north to enable him to hurry and to extend his operation. This army swept past Hamburg to Lubeck and Wismar on the Baltic, reaching there a day before the Russians.

South of Austria the race was against the Yugoslavs, who wanted control over the northeast provinces of Italy and the southern edge of Austria. Of this touchy contest, which for some weeks hovered on the brink of an armed clash, the separate story will be told.[33]

[30] *Triumph and Tragedy*, pages 506–07. *Year of Decisions*, pages 216–17.
[31] To the line of the Elbe (which ran east in this part of its course) and the Ultava to clear the west bank of these rivers in conjunction with the Soviet moves to clear the east banks.
[32] i.e., had stopped east of the line Wismar, Schwerin, and Doemitz. *The Supreme Command*, page 469.
[33] See Part 65.

It has since been maintained that the restraint shown by the American authorities in not taking full advantage of the military opportunity was a grave mistake. Had they done so, the contention is, the West could have induced the Soviet government to match its subsequent withdrawal to the west by a retreat to the east. Whether or not events would have turned out this way, the purpose could obviously have been served only if the American and British governments had been willing to keep their forces in place as long as necessary.

The ultimate acts of surrender were handled dexterously and with the utmost straightforwardness. The Soviet government was not given the chance to delay or interfere with the capitulations made either in Italy or on the Western Front. But all possibility that the Soviet government could again suspect trickery was averted by the answers made to the proffers of the Germans. The Nazi leaders who took over command during these last days of doom were foiled in the efforts which they made to the very end to divide their enemies.[34]

The first act in this closing drama came in Italy. After the middle of April the position of the German Army in Italy had become desperate. The Allies had started their final offensive. On the 21st they captured Bologna, and two days later began to cross the Po, after a year and a half's struggle up from the toe of Italy. On the 24th Wolff reappeared in Switzerland with a representative of Vietinghoff and said they were ready to go to Caserta to arrange a capitulation. The Combined Chiefs of Staff authorized their reception at Caserta. As will be narrated shortly, Stalin was being assured (on the 25th), in connection with a Himmler-sponsored bid for surrender on the Western Front, that the American and British governments considered the only proper policy to be unconditional surrender on all fronts. Now (on the 26th) he was informed of the renewal of contact aimed to arrange a surrender in Italy, and asked to appoint a Soviet representative to be present at any negotiations which might take place at AFHQ at Caserta. He at once designated General Kislenko, the Soviet member of the Advisory Council for Italy.

The Germans arrived at Caserta on the 28th. At the first formal meeting, Alexander's Chief of Staff gave them the terms to be imposed. These dealt only with military matters and measures, and pro-

---

[34] The German Supreme Command, up to very near the end, thought that the Western Allies, because of their fear of Communism, might very well consider a separate peace and establish a front against the Soviet armies. See *A Soldier's Record,* by General Kesselring, Supreme German Commander on the Western Front.

vided for complete surrender of all German and Italian Fascist forces on that front—with their arms and equipment.[35] The Germans signed on the 29th, and three days later the act of surrender was made effective. The more than a million Germans who were still south of the Alps put down their arms.

By then total surrender on all other fronts was very near. The Americans and Russians had met on the Elbe; the British and Russians were about to meet on the Baltic near Lubeck; the Russians were crowding against the last defenses of Berlin. On learning of Hitler's decision to remain until the last in his underground refuge in Berlin, Himmler had grasped the initiative. He had undertaken to speak in the name of the German government on the score that Hitler was no longer able to do so, being cut off, gravely ill, or perhaps already dead. He had met Count Bernadotte, head of the Swedish Red Cross, at the Swedish Consulate at Lubeck and asked that intermediary to arrange for him to meet Eisenhower in order to capitulate on the whole Western Front. Bernadotte was doubtful whether such an offer would be accepted, but he agreed to forward the request if the German troops in Norway and Denmark were included in the surrender. Himmler said he was ready to order these forces to surrender to either British, American, or Swedish commanders. When asked what he proposed to do if the Western Allies refused his offer, Himmler replied that he would take command of the Eastern Front and die in battle.[36] He evidently thought there was still a chance to cause trouble between the West and Russia, for he also said that he hoped to be able to keep on fighting in the east for some time.

The American and British Ministers in Stockholm, Herschel Johnson and Sir Victor Mallet, reported Himmler's offer to their governments. Churchill at once (April 25th) telephoned Truman.[37] They agreed that Himmler must be told that he (or any other German) would have to surrender to all three Allies at the same time, and everywhere. Whereupon, Churchill sent off at once a message to Stalin tell-

[35] The Agreement signed on April 29th was called "Instrument of Local Surrender." It applied to "German and other Forces under the Command or Control of the German Commander-in-Chief Southwest."

It provided for surrender "unconditionally." It contained only military provisions. One of its first features was a "Stay-Put Order" reading: "All formations, units and sub-units of the German Land Forces, wherever they may be, will remain in their present positions and their existing formation pending further orders from the Supreme Allied Commander." And it grounded all German aircraft.

[36] *Triumph and Tragedy*, page 535, and *The Supreme Command*, page 477.

[37] A verbatim record of this telephone conversation is given in *Year of Decisions*, pages 89–94.

ing of Himmler's proposal and then stating, "There can be no question, as far as His Majesty's Government is concerned, of anything less than unconditional surrender simultaneously to the three major Powers. We consider Himmler should be told that German forces, either as individuals or in units, should everywhere surrender themselves to the Allied troops or representatives on the spot." [38]

Truman had agreed and at once sent off a parallel message to Stalin.

Stalin had answered Churchill: "I consider your proposal to present to Himmler a demand for unconditional surrender on all fronts, including the Soviet front, the only correct one. *Knowing you, I had no doubt that you would act in this way.*" Churchill's ironical thought about this is suggested by the fact that he italicized this sentence in his retrospective account.[39] Stalin had answered Truman similarly.[40]

The American and British Ministers in Stockholm had been told (on the 26th) to pass this answer on to Himmler.[41] But he had vanished.

In the copies of Hitler's will flung out of his bunker, Admiral Doenitz had been named head of the German state and Supreme Commander of the Armed Forces. On May 3rd at Doenitz's initiative, senior German officers appeared at Montgomery's Headquarters, proposing in the name of Field Marshal Keitel, the Chief of the High Command of the Wehrmacht (OKW), that three of their armies on the Russian Front be allowed to retire west of the Elbe and that civilian refugees be allowed to pass through the British lines to Schleswig-Holstein. Montgomery refused to assent to this scheme for avoiding surrender to the Russians, and sent the German emissaries back to Keitel. On the next day (the 4th), Admiral von Friedeburg came back with authority from Doenitz and Keitel to surrender unconditionally to forces on Montgomery's front—northwest Germany, Holland, and Denmark. Montgomery accepted and the surrenders were signed, to become effective the next morning. They were regarded and handled as tactical surrenders in the field.

[38] *Triumph and Tragedy*, page 537.
[39] *Ibid.*, page 538. Churchill observed that this ". . . reply was the most cordial message I ever had from him."
[40] As printed in *Year of Decisions*, page 99, it read, "I consider your proposed reply to Himmler along the lines of unconditional surrender on all fronts, including the Soviet front, absolutely correct. I ask you to act in the spirit of your proposal, and we Russians pledge to continue our attacks against the Germans."
[41] Eisenhower sent a message to Marshall to tell him of his satisfaction with this instruction. He said that when Churchill had called him up on receiving the message from Stockholm, he, Eisenhower, had advised him strongly to take the position expressed in the instruction and that Churchill agreed that the offer looked like a last desperate effort to create a schism between the West and the Russians. "In every move we make these days," Eisenhower added, "we are trying to be meticulously careful in this regard." *Year of Decisions*, page 106.

On the same day, May 4th, Eisenhower reported to the War Department that representatives of Admiral Doenitz were coming to his headquarters at Rheims, apparently to negotiate the capitulation of the remaining German armies. He said he was informing the Russian High Command that he was going to advise the Germans to surrender all forces facing the Russians to them, and all on the Western Front, including Norway, to him; thus surrenders on both fronts would be made at the same time. The Soviet High Command approved this course. On the 5th Admiral von Friedeburg appeared at Rheims, and General Jodl joined him the next day. By agreement with the Soviet High Command, Russian officers participated in the ensuing talks. The German envoys sought to surrender to the Western Allies only. The offer was refused. They then tried to put off the formal act of surrender for a few days, so that as many as possible of the German soldiers as well as civilians might make their way out of the neighborhood of the Russians. Eisenhower cut the time short. Speaking for Eisenhower, General Smith bluntly declared that only unconditional surrender to Eastern and Western Allies was acceptable. He told them that unless the Germans speedily agreed to do this: "He [Eisenhower] would break off all negotiations and seal the Western Front, preventing by force any further westward movement of German soldiers and civilians." "I see no alternative," Jodl reported to Doenitz, "chaos or signature." He signed on the early morning of May 7th, with Soviet and French officers watching.

No use was made at this final juncture of the instrument of surrender to which so many laborious hours had been devoted in the EAC. It was discarded in favor of a much shorter Act of Military Surrender drawn up in Eisenhower's headquarters.[42] The first paragraph of this, as signed by the German envoys, read: "We, the undersigned, acting by authority of the German High Command, hereby surrender unconditionally to the Supreme Commander, Allied Expeditionary Force and simultaneously to the Soviet High Command all forces on land, sea and in the air who are at this date under German control."

Winant managed at the last moment to secure the insertion in the text of an article which stipulated: "This act of military surrender is without prejudice to, and will be superseded by any general instrument of surrender imposed by or on behalf of the United Nations and ap-

[42] The reasons remain conjectural. SHAEF had not been definitely instructed by the Combined Chiefs of Staff to use this instrument of surrender, and may have been uncertain as to whether all four governments had completed their formal approval of it. But probably more decisive was the belief that the surrender could be effected with least talk and delay by using the briefer form of military surrender. See *The Supreme Command,* pages 484–85.

plicable to Germany and the German armed forces as a whole."

This article allowed the Allies to impose the provisions of the document that had been prepared in the ECA (amended to include France).

Truman had been keeping Stalin closely advised of these steps, with a view to arranging simultaneous announcements of the triumph, as appropriate to the common effort which had brought it about. Thus, as soon as he heard from Eisenhower that the surrender was signed, he proposed a time to Stalin, all three to coordinate to 9 a.m. Washington time on May 8th. But Stalin was not to be hurried into halting the Soviet assault. He answered that the Supreme Command of the Red Army was not certain that the order of the German High Command to surrender unconditionally would be carried out by the German troops on the Eastern Front. He was afraid of a premature and misleading announcement. Thus he asked brief delay. Since this might mean needless destruction or loss of life on the Western Front, Truman and Churchill went ahead with their announcement without waiting for Stalin.

In Britain the rejoicing was most instant and deep. In the United States there was great relief and satisfaction—bordered by thoughts of the war that was still to be fought out against Japan. To the Russian people the surrender at Rheims was presented as preliminary. The Soviet press gave it only inconspicuous notice. Stalin had insisted that a formal ratification should follow in Berlin. A new German group, except for Admiral Friedeburg, went there and early on the morning of May 9th General Keitel, as head of the OKW, signed their acknowledgment of complete defeat. This time Air Marshal Tedder, Eisenhower's Deputy, signed on his behalf, Marshal Zhukov signing for the Russians. Then and only then, Stalin issued his Victory Proclamation and the Russian people gave themselves over to celebration. They included their Allies in their warm and joyful embrace.

The peoples of the coalition, out of a deeply shared experience, felt themselves friends. But even while tired soldiers gave thanks, and hats were tossing in the air, the governments of the West were worrying over what Communist Russia had in mind for Europe. Churchill was advocating that the American, British, and French forces which had won their hard way forward from the Channel and the Mediterranean should stay where they were long enough to prove that the war had been fought so that the peoples of Europe should be able to live freely and without fear in the future. Emerging from the Nazi realm of cruelty and arrogance, were they to pass into the Soviet realm of compulsion?

PERIOD FOURTEEN

May 1945; the Combat Won; the Three Wills at Odds, and the Oncoming Time Clouded

64. The Development of Policy for Germany and Austria after Yalta

NAZI GERMANY had failed to induce either of its great assailants to enter into a deal which would allow it to fight on against the other alone. But mutual mistrust within the coalition spared it from one main measure which had been contemplated. At Yalta agreement had been reached in principle that Germany was to be divided into several separate states. Provision for effecting this had been written into the terms of surrender, approved in the European Advisory Commission. But during the spring, by mutual consent, the purpose was allowed to fade out.

A special committee, consisting of Eden as chairman and Ambassadors Gusev and Winant, had been asked to design the ways and means for bringing about partition. By the time this committee first met (March 7th) all three governments had become unsure about going through with any imposed plan for partition.

Even at Yalta Churchill had been impressed by the difficulties and fearful of the consequences. The subsequent display of Soviet will to keep all countries east of Germany under its control, possibly in time to absorb them into the Soviet system, had caused him to recoil further from the idea. In words the Prime Minister used six weeks after Yalta: "I hardly like to consider dismembering Germany until my doubts about Russia's intentions have been cleared away." [1]

The Soviet government had reached the same decision, for its own reasons. The American and British armies were breaking through the German lines faster and more sweepingly than foreseen, while the Soviet forces were being held before Berlin. The Soviet leaders had assumed that the German soldiers were relaxing their resistance in the west, while continuing to fight on furiously in the east out of fear of the treatment they would get at the hands of the Russians. To these mistrustful minds it had seemed quite possible that the British and Americans might buy German surrender in the west by a secret promise not to partition—allowing the Soviet Union to remain its only proponent. Some reassuring action must have seemed advisable to soothe the German fears that were sustaining the resistance in the east. Perhaps—who is to know?—Soviet aims reached even beyond this to the idea that if Germany was allowed to remain whole, and the awful

[1] *Triumph and Tragedy,* page 443.

destruction continued, it might be easier to bring all of it under Communist domination later on.

In any case, during the last part of March and early April the tone of the Soviet press and propaganda changed perceptibly. No longer was everything German reviled. Threats of extreme revenge ceased. Soviet leaders, while not promising a kind fate for Germany, disavowed any intent of destroying the German people, and began to open the way for a less punitive approach to the German masses after the war.

This change in the Soviet position on dismemberment had been signalled by a comment made by Ambassador Gusev at a meeting of the EAC on March 26th—that the Soviet government did not regard the Yalta decision about dismemberment as obligatory but rather as a possible way of exercising pressure to make Germany harmless if other means proved insufficient. Winant had taken this to mean, and so told Washington, that the Soviet government was wavering. But later (in talking with Hopkins in Moscow in May) Stalin revealed that he had a different impression of what had happened; that the report which had come to him of this meeting was that Eden and his Foreign Office colleague, Sir William Strang, had said that the British government was against partition except as a threat to hold over the Germans' heads; and that since Winant had not spoken up in favor of this measure, although Gusev had, he, Stalin, had concluded that the American government had also given up the idea.

This was not so. But in the event, Stalin interred the idea of partition as a deliberate political action in his Victory Proclamation to the People on May 9th, just after the German surrender: "Germany has been smashed to pieces. The German troops are surrendering. The Soviet Union is celebrating victory, although it does not intend either to dismember or to destroy Germany." Neither the British nor American government sought to keep the possibility, as formerly discussed, alive. Nor did any of the three governments promise definite support to the French demand that the Rhineland, the Ruhr, and Westphalia should be separated from the rest of Germany.

However, as the war ended the prospect emerged that Germany might well be divided, not into several political states, but into separated zones of occupation, due to the tensions and rivalries among the victorious powers. These had, up to then, failed to agree on any common policy concerning the German economic structure and condition, upon the amount of reparations to be exacted, about the possible use of German prisoners of war for reconstruction work. Unless accord was reached on these vital matters, and unless persons, food, coal, and other essentials were permitted to move freely between zones, and there was a single monetary system for them all, each might become, in effect, a separate country—or, at least, the western zones might divide from the Soviet zone. Whether the members of the coalition (who in this matter had to reckon seriously with determined French desires) could reconcile their ideas and purposes sufficiently to allow the Germans to live as within a unified country, was the greatest of the questions that loomed before the Heads of State at their coming meeting.

There was dissention also over the arrangements for the occupation of Austria. The governments of the coalition had declared at Moscow in 1943 that Austria was to be reestablished eventually as a free and independent country. But there was to be joint occupation and control until a peace treaty was concluded. Within the EAC discussions had been going on for well over a year about the system and zones of occupation.

The American government had been reserved as to the part it was willing to play in the occupation of the country after the war was over. It had sought an equal place on the control commission, which, it was understood, would be set up in Vienna to direct the affairs of the country as a whole. In conjunction with that it had wanted to be in charge of one of the three (or four when France should be admitted) occupation areas into which the city of Vienna was to be divided. But the Joint Chiefs of Staff had not wished the United States to participate in the occupation of the rest of the country; Roosevelt had therefore resisted the British and Soviet offers of a zone of occupation. Then, in December 1944, Winant, the American member of EAC, had made it clear in two impressive messages to Washington that if the American government really wished to have any effective influence upon the future of the country it would have to accept responsibility for a zone. The President had thereupon consented to take one. By then it had been settled that the United States should have the southwestern zone of Germany, and the contemplated Austrian zone was to be, as regards military and supply problems, just an extension.

There was accord in the EAC about the general location of the separate zones, nothing more; the Americans to be in the northwest, the French and British in the southwest and south, the Russians in the central and northeast. Then the British had submitted a definite zoning chart, and about April 1st the Russian representative had come forward with an amended one. This the American authorities found unacceptable in both major elements: the zonal divisions for the country of Austria and the plan of allocation of sections for the city of Vienna.

The Soviet government asked that the Soviet zone should include not only Northwest Austria but also sections stretching toward the west, center, and south. Neither the British nor American governments were willing to allocate to the Soviet Union such a dominant area. The State Department, guided by the Joint Chiefs of Staff, informed Mosely (Winant's Deputy on the EAC) on April 5th that the American government would consent to placing Burgenland province (adjoining Hungary) and that part of Upper Austria northeast of the Danube under control of the Soviet government, but that it thought the extension of its authority in Styria and Carinthia unjustified. On April 9th Mosely so advised the EAC and his British colleagues spoke up correspondingly. Ultimately (that is, in June), it may be noted, the zonal divisions were established roughly along these lines.

The American Army had not wanted to race with the Red Army to see how far and fast each could go in Austria, and who should capture Vienna. But the American government had been on the alert to see to it that if Soviet forces got to this capital first, there should not be a long interval in which Austria would be run by Soviet military commanders. As early as October 1944 it had proposed to Molotov that an agreement should be made that the government whose forces might reach Vienna first should at once invite the others to send representatives to that city in order swiftly to form an Allied control council. Molotov had at the time not given any direct answer. He had merely suggested that this might be considered along with the other phases of the situation by the European Advisory Council. There it had remained hung up.

The Soviet scheme for dividing jurisdiction within the Vienna district, which was deep within the Soviet zone, was also deemed distinctly disadvantageous. It proposed a return to the boundaries of Vienna as they were before 1938; the segmentation suggested would not have accorded the American, British, and French sectors adequate space for billeting, training, and recreation. Nor would it have provided their occupying forces with adequate facilities for communication or air traffic; all five of the existing airfields would have been contained in the Soviet zone. At the April 9th meeting of the EAC, the American members argued for the adoption of wider boundaries for the Vienna district; or, if that was not acceptable, that one of the large airfields be placed under American administration and operational control. The British member proposed that one airfield in Vienna be assigned to each of the occupying powers. Furthermore they urged that the inner city (the Innere Stadt) of Vienna be regulated by the inter-Allied authority to ensure equitable use of its facilities. On the 21st the Soviet member responded with some meager counterproposals.

In the meantime it had been intimated that the beginning of preparation for joint occupation need not wait on the settlement of these matters. On April 13th, in the course of the conversation which Harriman had with Stalin after telling him of Roosevelt's death, the Marshal had referred to the need to settle the districts which each of the four Allies should have in the city of Vienna. He had suggested that the American, British, and French representatives should start at once for that city to fix the zones. By this time Soviet troops were in the city and beginning to move up the Danube toward Linz.

This word was welcomed in both Washington and London. But Stalin's invitation was soon fenced round. Perhaps this was because of intimations that if American and British missions got to Vienna soon they might try to interfere with current Soviet activities in Austria. Thus in a note which Kennan delivered to the Soviet Foreign Office (on the 20th or 21st), saying that the American representatives were ready to proceed to Vienna, the statement was made that the American government was relying on the Soviet government to instruct its forces to prevent the removal of industrial equipment or other property from Vienna, and to deter other changes which would prejudice common objectives and authority. In the note which the British Embassy in Moscow presented on the 21st, it was proposed that the representatives to be sent to Vienna should be authorized to deal with "other important political and economic questions which will arise in Austria." Whether or not because of these indications of interest in what was going on in Austria, the Soviet government thereafter began to argue, as expressed in various notes from Vishinsky between April 23rd and 30th, that Stalin's invitation meant that the Russians hoped the members of the Control Commission could reach Vienna speedily "to participate in the work of the provisional control mechanism" but not until *after* agreement had been reached in the EAC on zones of occupation for both Austria and Vienna. This seemed to offer a choice between accepting the zonal arrangements which the Russians wanted or suffering indefinite deferment.

While facing this dilemma, the American and British governments were taken aback by the sudden emergence of a provisional Austrian government. This development had been worked out in advance with Soviet knowledge and help. The American and British governments heard of it first when, on April 24th, Vishinsky informed their Ambassadors that Karl Renner, a leading Socialist of good repute (who had been former Chancellor of the Austrian Republic and the last President of the Free National Council), had presented a plan for creating a provisional Austrian government. Renner, Vishinsky explained, claimed that by virtue of his official position before the Nazis seized power, he had the legal right to take this initiative; and he planned to call together the former deputies of the Austrian Parliament who could be reached and together decide upon the composition of the new government. The note from Vishinsky telling of this concluded by remarking that, "On the assumption that the creation of a provisional Austrian government can be of substantial help to the cause of the Allies in the battle for the complete liberation of Austria from German dependence, the Soviet government considers it possible not to hinder Karl Renner and other political figures of Austria in their work of forming a provisional Austrian government."

The British and American governments answered quickly that they did not want to be rushed into a decision about this, especially since so much of Austria was still under German control. They therefore asked the Soviet government to defer recognition of the Renner or any other group.

A few days later Renner addressed himself directly to the American and British governments through the courtesy of the Russian Military Mission in Vienna. His statement began:

"Thanks to the victorious advance of the Red Army, by which Vienna and a part of Austria has been liberated from the army of the German Reich . . . and basing ourselves on the decisions of the Crimea Conference as well as of the Moscow Conference of October 1943, representatives of all political parties in the country have decided to establish an Austrian Republic as a sovereign and independent democratic State, and with this end in view have set up a Provisional Government which took up its duties today under the Presidency of Dr. Karl Renner. . . ."

The note then provided information regarding the composition of the new government and the policies it proposed to follow. The two Ministries likely to deal most directly with the Austrian people—the Ministry of the Interior and the Ministry of Education and Culture— were assigned to Communists. The American and British governments were asked not to refuse help to the new administration.

But they were not ready to commit themselves until they had a better chance to decide whether this provisional government was fairly representative of the Austrian people, whether it could and would act independently or would regard itself as compelled to please the Soviet Union first of all. They said so publicly. Then they protested in Moscow against Soviet encouragement of this initiative before consultation, as envisaged in the Declaration of Liberated Europe, and as appropriate to Allies who were still jointly engaged in the complete liberation of Austria. This went unheeded. On April 29th the Moscow radio carried the news that the Soviet Commander in Austria had recognized Renner's group as a provisional government. The American and British governments refused to follow suit.

Churchill (on the 30th) let Truman know that he was much concerned over the way the Austrian situation was going. He said that he feared that the announcement of the formation of a provisional Austrian government, together with the Soviet refusal to permit Allied missions to fly into Vienna, meant that the Russians were exploiting their chance to "organize" the country. He asked Truman if he was willing to join him in a personal objection, the text of which he submitted. This proposed message, after giving the reasons for anxiety and protest, stated the opinion that the treatment of Austria was of common concern to all four Allies who were to participate in its control. Thus, it continued, the British and American governments regarded it as essential that their representatives be allowed to proceed to Vienna at once to report on conditions there before any final settlement was reached in the EAC on matters affecting the occupation and control of the country, especially Vienna. Truman thought it best not to present the protest in the form of a joint communication. Instead, he instructed the American Embassy that same day to present a note to Stalin that was in general rapport with Churchill's message. This was done.

In answer to two letters from Kennan (sent on April 30th and May 1st) Vishinsky defended the Soviet action in recognizing the Renner government on the score that the Soviet forces operating on Austrian territory could not get along without an organization of local citizens; that the new provisional government had been formed by agreement between leaders of all the non-Fascist democratic parties in Austria; and that later on an Allied control commission would be set up to supervise the Austrian government.

The further answer received (by a letter from Vishinsky to Kennan on May 6th) was a denial of the other request also. It professed that when Stalin had agreed to allow the American and British representatives to proceed to Vienna, the Soviet government had been confident that the necessary accord concerning zones of occupation would have been concluded before they arrived there. But, it pointed out, this unfortunately had not occurred. Then, misconstruing the American thought, it went on to say that the Soviet government could not agree to having the zonal problem considered in Vienna, since it was within the competence of the EAC; and, finally, that the Soviet government found unconvincing the statement that the talks in the EAC could not be well concluded until the representatives arrived in Vienna, that the zones for Germany and Berlin were determined before Allied troops entered Germany.

Hastening the narrative, it may be foretold that Stalin did not give the required consent until ten days after the German surrender. On May 16th, after agreement had been reached on the procedure for withdrawing the troops of each ally into its assigned zones of occupation in Germany and Austria, Truman supplemented Churchill's renewed presentations to Stalin with one of his own. He could not understand, he said, the Soviet refusal to allow the British and American representatives to proceed to Vienna in order that arrangements on the occupation of Austria still pending in the EAC might be completed. Intelligent administration of the Vienna zones would be greatly helped, he contended, by examination and discussion on the spot by the military authorities who would be responsible for the smooth operation of that administration. Stalin (on the 18th) answered that he could not agree to transfer to Vienna consideration of the question about zones of occupation and other questions concerning the situation in Austria, but that he did not object to a visit by the Allied representatives to acquaint themselves with the situation and to prepare proposals for the EAC, and was so instructing the Red Army Commander in Austria. This is all that had been asked of him right along. Truman acknowledged the concession in a matter-of-fact way. And, presently, it may be added, reasonable satisfaction was given the Americans and British in the division of Vienna zones.

But I have leaped ahead of the course of other events and of coalition issues which darkened the weeks before and after the German surrender, and must now return to them.

⸎⸎⸎⸎⸎⸎⸎

65. The Dangerous Clash over Venezia Giulia

⸎⸎⸎⸎⸎⸎⸎

An attempt by Tito's partisans to establish themselves in the northeast corner of Italy—in the province of Venezia Giulia, including the port of Trieste—was another possible cause of a disturbing fracture within the coalition as the German surrender became effective.[2]

[2] An excellent description of the Italian-Yugoslav frontier line is to be found in *The Realignment of Europe*, pages 463–66, and map on page 464. The region of Venezia Giulia, as it was called under Italian rule, had before 1918 lain within the frontiers of the Austrian Empire and Kingdom of Hungary. The frontier as fixed in various agreements between 1920–1924 was based on strategic considerations. The province

Tito and his adherents were by then securing and exercising unchallenged control of the armed forces of Yugoslavia, and of the civil affairs of those regions from which the Germans had been expelled. The young King Peter, after so long a delay that Tito was on the verge of charging him with crimes and trying to bring him to trial, had agreed to the proposed appointments to the Regency Council. The Regency had been announced on March 5th, and the coalition government formed under the agreement between Tito and Subasic had officially taken office.

Early in April, Tito, accompanied by Subasic, who was serving as his Foreign Minister, had gone to Moscow. There he had signed on the 11th a mutual assistance pact similar to that of Czechoslovakia with the Soviet Union. No steps were being taken to enlarge the body which had legislative power—as recommended at Yalta. Those members of the Yugoslav government who had come from London, unable to reorganize their political groups, found themselves with little influence, and were becoming restless. The one-sided Yugoslav coalition government was on its way to dissolution.

Tito, in a talk with Alexander at the end of February, had agreed to subordinate his claim to govern the whole of the province of Venezia Giulia. He had said he would assent that the Allied military government (sometimes called by its initial, AMG, sometimes by its codename, AMGOT) might have administrative responsibility over the province, provided the local Yugoslav authorities who had already taken control in many places were allowed to remain and function. This was to be without prejudice to what was ultimately to be done about the territory.

Subsequently (March 19th) the American government informed Molotov that it favored an arrangement by which the provinces should be administered as a whole under AMG until final disposition of the area; that it feared that independent action by either of the claimants (Italy and Yugoslavia) would prejudice a fair final solution; and that it hoped that the Soviet government would take a similar view that this was the way to deal with the situation. For, the American note observed, this was not thought to be merely a boundary dispute between

---

ran from Monte Fornio on the Austrian frontier along the crest of the Julian Alps, south-southeastward across the uplands of the Carso (Karst), to within a mile of the sea at the head of Quarnero Gulf, where it turned east for a few miles to include in Italy the railroad line from Italy to Fiume and the ex-Hungarian port of Fiume itself. It included the city of Trieste and the peninsula running south known by the Austrian name as the Istrian peninsula, and various islands in the Adriatic. According to this careful source, the frontier had left some 400,000 Yugoslavs on the Italian side of the line.

Italy and Yugoslavia; it was regarded as a matter of principle, involving the peaceful settlement of territorial disputes. But Molotov had let the weeks go by without answer. Tito, after his visit to Moscow, had made it plain that he was not going to be satisfied with the arrangement which Alexander thought he had accepted.

Toward the end of April a clash became imminent as the German forces in North Italy began to give up. Tito's partisans and troops rushed toward Trieste and spread over the province of Venezia Giulia. He was directing them there in all haste, leaving until later the work of subduing the Germans who remained in the northwestern part of Yugoslavia. General Alexander was getting ready to dispatch forces into the same area as soon as the German surrender in Italy was settled.

On April 27th Churchill consulted Truman. "It seems to me vital," he stated, "to get Trieste if we can do so in the manner proposed [i.e., by Alexander], and to run the risk inherent in these political-military operations." He recalled Roosevelt's strong conviction that Trieste should be an international port, as the outlet in the Adriatic for the whole Danube River basin. And he concluded that if this possibility was to be kept open:

"The great thing is to be there before Tito's guerrillas are in occupation. Therefore it does not seem to me there is a minute to wait. The actual status of Trieste can be determined at leisure. Possession is nine points of the law. I beg you for an early decision. The plan for Anglo-American occupation of Venezia Giulia has been hanging fire in Washington for a considerable time with the result that Field Marshal Alexander is still without orders. I should be most grateful if you would give your personal attention to this." [3]

Truman, after consulting the Joint Chiefs of Staff, informed Churchill (on the 29th) that with his approval the Combined Chiefs were to accomplish what he understood Churchill's idea to be in regard to Trieste and other areas formerly under Italian rule *as a matter of military necessity*. Presumably what was in mind was the need to control the port of Trieste, the naval base at Pola, and the railway north to protect the military lines of communication with Allied forces in Austria. But the actual instruction sent by the Combined Chiefs to Alexander was a twisted skein: it would seem to have told him at one and the same time to go ahead and establish an Allied military government in

[3] Churchill prints the main portions of this message with some small omissions in *Triumph and Tragedy*, pages 551–52; and Truman in *Year of Decisions*, page 244, does the same, supplying some sentences omitted by Churchill but omitting some given by the Prime Minister, and with a different order of sentences—possibly a paraphrasing device.

these areas; to do so if he thought it required by military necessity even before Soviet and Yugoslav assent had been obtained; but to communicate with the Combined Chiefs of Staff before taking any further action if the Yugoslav forces failed to cooperate.[4]

This directive did not seem conclusive or clear enough to Churchill. On the 30th he informed Truman that the military part of this program seemed very good. But he thought the belief that the Yugoslavs, with the Soviet government behind them, would agree to this entry and assumption of control over Venezia Giulia was a delusion. They would, he predicted, try to overrun this territory and claim and occupy the ports of Trieste, Pola, and Fiume and perhaps more. The Americans and British, he stressed, had reassured Stalin in regard to the German surrender. But they had never undertaken to be limited in their advances to clear Italy, including these Adriatic areas, by the approval of the Yugoslavs or Russians, nor to report to them the military movements our commanders thought it right to make. We were, he averred, as much entitled to move freely into Trieste if we could get there as the Russians were to win their way into Vienna. "I therefore hope," he remarked, "that Alexander will be left to carry out the plan, which the Chiefs of the Combined Staffs have approved, as quickly and as secretly as possible and that above all we shall try to take possession of Trieste from the sea before informing the Russians or Yugoslavs, assuming of course that the Supreme Commander considers that it can be successfully accomplished with the amphibious and other forces at his disposal. . . ."[5]

The Prime Minister judged that this action would contribute to a United States–British–Italian harmonious combination which would split or render ineffective the Communist movement in Italy, especially in Northern Italy. It was going to be, he predicted, a shock when American armies withdrew up to a distance of one hundred and twenty miles along several hundred miles of the Western Front and Soviet advance overflowed these areas of central Germany. The shock would be the greater if at the same time the whole of the north Adriatic were occupied by the Yugoslavs. Thus he begged Truman to allow these

[4] This CCS Directive to Alexander (FAN-536) has not been published. Truman, in *Year of Decisions,* page 244, summarizes its contents without, however, mentioning the stipulation that Alexander was to communicate with the Combined Chiefs of Staff before proceeding if the Yugoslav forces refused to cooperate. This, however, is definitely recorded in a memo made by Acting Secretary of State Grew of a conversation with President Truman at the White House on April 30th; and Truman called Churchill's attention to this provision in the directive in his message of April 30th to the Prime Minister. See Joseph C. Grew, *Turbulent Era,* pages 1476–77.

[5] *Year of Decisions,* page 245.

operations within the U.S.-British accredited zone of action to proceed without any disclosure of plans; he thought, in this particular case, we were entitled to act first and explain afterward.

Truman called a meeting at the White House at once, on the 30th. Just before the discussion began it was reported that Yugoslav partisans were already in the ports of Trieste and Pola. The President was not pleased at the prospect of the Yugoslavs getting such firm control of the area that it would be hard, perhaps impossible, to shake their hold. But he was at this time as averse as Roosevelt had been to having American soldiers involved in fighting anywhere in the region. In this he reflected General Marshall's worries. Left to make policy on military grounds, Marshall and his staff might well have stayed out of the situation completely. As stated by Stimson to Grew in a telephone conversation of that date, "The Staff thought we are very likely to clash primarily with Tito, and they feel also that the Russians are backing up Tito on this matter." [6] Marshall kept reminding Truman that we wanted Soviet cooperation in the Pacific War, and that the Army did not want troops that they were planning to ship quickly to the Pacific to be tied down in the Balkans. But Stimson was ready to go along with State Department policy against the wishes of the Army staff.

Truman's answer to Churchill (prepared in the State Department and sent off on the same day, the 30th) in effect left Alexander free to proceed as far, and only as far, as he could without getting into a fight with the Yugoslavs. It conveyed no assurance of American support if Tito had to be confronted. Truman said he agreed that "in the operational phase when he [Alexander] is endeavoring to establish his lines of communication to Austria and to establish his control over Trieste and Pola, there is no need for obtaining prior Russian consent. I note . . . that before his task force enters Venezia Giulia Alexander will inform Marshal Tito of his intentions and explain to Tito that if any of his forces remain in that area they must necessarily come under Alexander's command. FAN 536 directs Alexander to communicate with the Combined Chiefs of Staff before taking further action in the area in question if the Yugoslav forces there fail to co-operate. I think this is important for I wish to avoid having American forces used to fight Yugoslav forces or being used in combat in the Balkan political arena." [7]

Alexander went ahead and ordered *British* divisions under his command to secure Trieste, the anchorage at Pola, and the lines of communication between Italy and Austria. On May 1st he told Tito of his

[6] *Turbulent Era*, page 1478.
[7] *Ibid.*, pages 1476–77.

plans, saying, "They are similar to those we discussed at Belgrade. . . . I presume that any of your forces which may be in the area affected by my operations will come under my command, as you suggested during our recent discussions in Belgrade, and that you will now issue orders to that effect." [8] At the same time he reported to Churchill that Tito's forces were fighting in Trieste and in occupation of most of the Istrian Peninsula. "I am quite certain that he will not withdraw his troops if ordered to do so unless the Russians tell him to." He added that if he were directed by the Combined Chiefs of Staff to occupy the whole of Venezia Giulia he anticipated a fight with the Yugoslav army, which would have at least the moral backing of the Russians. The import of his message was to advise care before any such order was issued to him.[9]

On May 2nd the British (New Zealand) troops met the Yugoslav forces in Trieste. They took the surrender of the German garrison which Tito had hoped to effect, and they occupied the dock area without interference. The Yugoslav partisans held the center of the city. Alexander also sent detachments into the cities of Monfalcone and Gorizia, to the north of Trieste, where Yugoslav partisans were flaunting their presence. They were conscripting Italians for forced labor, seizing banks and other properties, changing the names of the streets, paying back the Italians for what had been done to them.

On the 6th Churchill backed up Alexander's measures by telling him, "You are clearly entitled to advance as far and as fast as you can into former enemy territory until you form contact with the Russian or Yugoslav forces. . . ." [10] Tito's troops remained under orders to hold all territory up to the Isonzo River, which is ninety-five per cent of Venezia Giulia. They were even trying to establish civilian control in the adjoining part of Udine, the Italian province to the west of Venezia Giulia.

Such was the threatening situation in the region when the Germans signed their total surrender at Rheims on the early morning of the 7th. To peer again a little over the horizon of this narrative: Truman and Churchill, and their military and civil advisers, drew together in their view that Tito must not be allowed to enforce his will. On May 11th, Truman sent Churchill a message more resolute in tenor than any of his previous ones. He said that he was becoming more worried over Tito's actions in Venezia Giulia; and that he feared that if Tito succeeded, identical claims were ready for South Austria (in Carinthia and Styria), and perhaps similar designs on parts of Hungary and Greece.

[8] *Triumph and Tragedy*, page 552.
[9] *Ibid.*, page 553.
[10] *Ibid.*, page 554.

Should we, the President asked, permit our Allies to engage in "uncontrolled land-grabbing"? [10a] The minimum which the Americans and British governments should insist on, he thought, was that Alexander should obtain complete and exclusive control of Trieste and Pola, the line of communications through Gorizia and Monfalcone, and an area sufficiently east of this line to permit administrative control. As a first step he proposed that the American and British Ambassadors should submit notes to Tito, informing him that the Yugoslav government was expected to agree at once to these plans, and to instruct its forces in the region to cooperate with the Allied Commander to establish a military government in that area under his authority.

Churchill hastened to answer that he agreed with every word of Truman's message and would instruct the British Ambassador in Belgrade "to keep in step" with the American Ambassador at every stage. He did not doubt that if the forces then under Alexander's command (including seven American divisions) were placed at his disposal in the event of hostilities against the Yugoslavs, he would feel himself in a good position to carry out any policy which the two governments might order.

This situation was, in the days after the German surrender, another danger to the continuance of the coalition and the preservation of its joint plans for control of enemy territory, peace-making, and peace-keeping. It was another difficulty on which Truman was soon to consult Stalin, and test his will to cooperate; and another reason why Churchill believed that United States-British forces in Europe should be kept for the time being where they were, in main strength, and ready to fire back if fired on. That he had been advocating for several weeks.

[10a] Yugoslav partisans were occupying border regions of Austria and Tito had been seeking a share in the occupation zone in Austria. The Soviet government had been asked to discourage this claim but Vishinsky had told Clark-Kerr on April 16th that the Soviet government thought Yugoslavia had a fair right to participate in that occupation and suggested that Yugoslav troops might occupy part of the Soviet zone in Austria. The British objected on several grounds, among them because it would affect the consideration of Yugoslav claims at the peace conference. Tito then (on May 12th) proposed that Yugoslav forces be allowed to remain in Austria as part of the force under General Alexander. The American and British governments on May 16th refused to assent to this and asked Tito to withdraw his forces from Austria and to observe the 1937 frontier.

66. The Overshadowed Victory; Europe; Churchill Wants to Stand Fast against Russia

As told, Churchill, in the middle of April, had begun to urge that the advance from the west be continued as far as it could be without colliding with the Red Army. In that same message of April 18th to Truman, he had also pleaded that the American and Allied troops be kept in whatever positions they might secure until a satisfactory accord was reached with the Soviet government and we got adequate assurances about Soviet intentions toward Germany and Austria. He strove to make a distinction between "tactical" and "occupational" zones. Tactical zones he defined as those ". . . in which our troops must stand on the line they have reached unless there is agreement for a better tactical deployment against the continuing resistance of the enemy." [11] These could be arranged directly between the military authorities. The occupational zones were those to be held by the national contingents of the Allies during the period of occupation and control of Germany and had been defined in a formal agreement between the three Allies.[12] He was quite ready, the Prime Minister said, to adhere to the zonal arrangement. But he did not want Allied troops ". . . to be hustled back at any point by some crude assertion of a local Russian general." This was a matter to be managed by agreement between the governments. The movement might wait—and here the Prime Minister came to his purposeful point—until the Allied control commission for Germany had been set up, and the Russians had agreed to share the anticipated food surplus in their zone of Germany with the other zones.

A letter which Eisenhower sent to Marshall on the 23rd—after the Prime Minister had raised this question—throws light on the occasion for granting him the power to order troop withdrawals and on Churchill's anxiety. The pertinent part ran:

"I do not quite understand why the Prime Minister has been so determined to intermingle political and military considerations in attempting to establish a procedure for the conduct of our own and Russian troops when a meeting takes place. My original recommenda-

[11] *Triumph and Tragedy*, page 514.

[12] In this message, as has already been noted earlier, Churchill said that these zones were outlined "rather hastily at Quebec in September 1944, when it was not foreseen that General Eisenhower's armies would make such a mighty inroad into Germany" (*ibid*). This narrative has told how the eastern zones had in effect been settled months before and the endorsement at Quebec was only the confirming formal agreement.

633

tion submitted to the CC/S was a simple one and I thought provided a very sensible arrangement. One of my concerns in making that proposal was the possibility that the Russians might arrive in the Danish peninsula before we could fight our way across the Elbe and I wanted a formula that would take them out of that region on my request. The only area in which we will be in the Russian occupation zone is that now held by American troops. I really do not anticipate that the Russians will be arbitrary in demanding an instant withdrawal from this region. . . ." [13]

Truman, to whom the issue was new, followed the advice of the Joint Chiefs of Staff. On April 23rd he submitted to Churchill an answer prepared by that group which the two of them might send to Stalin. This proposed that our troops in Austria and Germany should retire to their respective zones as soon as the military situation permitted. It suggested a procedure to be followed by the armed forces of the three countries in occupying the assigned zones: each commander, when he felt himself prepared to occupy any portion of his proper zone that was held by other Allied troops, should inform his own government of the sector he was prepared to occupy; that government was then to consult the other two in order that the necessary instructions might be issued for the evacuation of the area involved and its occupation by the troops of the country to which it was assigned.

Churchill objected that this procedure might allow the Russians to order American and British troops back to their occupational zones at any point they might decide, not necessarily with regard to the position of the fronts as a whole. Further discussion followed, in the course of which Truman, advised by the Joint Chiefs, adopted most of the changes Churchill advocated—insisting, however, that Eisenhower was to continue to look to the Combined Chiefs of Staff and not to civilian heads of government for approval of any major adjustments. Churchill then proceeded on the 27th to submit the amended outline of procedure to Stalin, and on the same day Truman sent word to Stalin that he agreed with it. This outline proposed that while fighting continued, the boundaries between the forces of the three Allies would have to be decided by commanders in the field and be governed by operational considerations. It informed Stalin of the instructions that had been given Eisenhower as to what to do when the armies encountered one another (halt as and where they meet); and as to how his forces were to be disposed after the end of fighting in an area (in accordance with military requirements regardless of zone boundaries). Stalin was asked to issue similar instructions to the Soviet field commanders. Then, turn-

[13] *Year of Decisions*, page 215.

ing to what should be done after the fighting was over, the message stated that the next task would be to set up the Allied control commissions in Berlin and Vienna, and to redispose the forces of the Allies to take over their respective occupational zones. In the event that there was no signed instrument of surrender, and the Prime Minister remarked that it appeared that there would not be, he suggested that the governments should set up these commissions at once and entrust to them the task of making detailed arrangements for this redisposal of the forces in their zones.[14]

Stalin answered (on May 2nd) that the Soviet commanders had been instructed that when their forces met Allied forces, they should immediately come to an agreement with the American or British command on a "provisional tactical demarcation line." The rest of the proposal, denoting that the control commissions should be given the assignment of arranging for withdrawal into agreed zones, he ignored.

Two days after receiving this reply, Churchill had given full passage to his gloomy fears in a message to Eden, who was in San Francisco. This lament indicated the way in which his ideas had broadened about the range of issues with the Soviet government that ought to be settled before the American and British troops fell back to their assigned zones:

"I fear terrible things have happened during the Russian advance through Germany to the Elbe. The proposed withdrawal of the United States Army to the occupational lines which were arranged with the Russians and Americans in Quebec . . . would mean the tide of Russian domination sweeping forward 120 miles on a front of 300 or 400 miles. This would be an event which, if it occurred, would be one of the most melancholy in history." As one of the counters available which might be used to make for a peaceful settlement he reckoned, *First, the Allies ought not to retreat from their present positions to the occupational line until we are satisfied about Poland, and also about the temporary character of the Russian occupation of Germany, and the conditions to be established in the Russianized or Russian-controlled countries in the Danube Valley,* particularly Austria and Czechoslovakia, *and the Balkans.* Secondly, we may be able to please them about the exits from the Black Sea and the Baltic as part of a general settlement. All these matters can only be settled before the United States armies in Europe are weakened. . . ."[15]

Two days later, as the German envoys were on their way to Rheims

[14] The message and Stalin's answer are to be found in *Triumph and Tragedy*, pages 517–18.
[15] *Ibid.*, pages 502–03. Churchill's subsequent italics.

to sign the instrument of ultimate surrender, Churchill confronted Truman with his conclusion about the prospective redisposition of forces in most positive form. He proposed to the President that until the three heads of government met, which should be as soon as possible, ". . . *we should hold firmly to the existing position obtained or being obtained by our armies in Yugoslavia, in Austria, in Czechoslovakia, on the main central United States front, and on the British front, reaching up to Lubeck, including Denmark. . . .* Thereafter I feel that we must most earnestly consider our attitude towards the Soviets and show them how much we have to offer or withhold." [16]

This judgment he propounded several times over in succeeding days to Truman, as in his famous "iron curtain" message (of May 12th) when he concluded, "Surely it is vital now to come to an understanding with Russia, or see where we are with her, before we weaken our armies mortally or retire to the zones of occupation. This can only be done by a personal meeting. I should be most grateful for your opinion and advice. . . ." [17]

None of the decision-makers in the American government, civilian or military, were open to these importunities. None were ready to renounce past policies and intentions, in pursuance of the course advocated by Churchill, to maintain large American armies in Europe, and keep them where they were until the Soviet government satisfied our wishes and eased our anxieties. This was judged by the President and his advisers to be inadvisable, ineffective, and impractical. It was thought to be inadvisable because it might provoke a harsh dispute with the Soviet authorities, rather than lead to a good settlement. It was thought likely to turn out to be ineffective because the Soviet armies could shut us out of Berlin and Vienna and deter the operation of the control councils for these two countries, as well as forcing Soviet will on Poland and Czechoslovakia. It was regarded as impractical because American opinion expected a rapid return of veteran soldiers from Europe, and because all branches of the American military organization counted on transfers from Europe for the development of the war against Japan.

The latest (April) reports on the possibility of making atomic weapons were hopeful. On the 25th Stimson read to Truman a memo approved by General Groves, which stated, "Within four months we shall in all probability have completed the most terrible weapon ever known in human history, one bomb of which could destroy a whole city."

[16] *Ibid.*, page 501. Churchill's italics.
[17] *Ibid.*, pages 573–74.

Final proving tests were soon to be held, but the few who knew of this coming event thought it would be better to await the results of the test and let them speak for themselves; thus, if a contest of will against the Russians involving possible transit into war should prove inevitable, it would be better to have it come after we and the world knew of this new master weapon. In the meanwhile, Truman was swayed by a wish for and belief in the possibility of a satisfactory settlement through negotiations rather than by the threat of forceful opposition to Soviet impositions, with or without the new explosive weapon. This governed his response to Churchill's advice that an armed boundary be held against the Russians.

So, on May 14th, he turned aside Churchill's pleas with the mild answer that he would rather await events before adopting the course which the Prime Minister was advocating.[18] By then, the new President was becoming aware of the distressing scope of the differences with the Soviet Union. His talks with Molotov had impressed him with the stubborn will of the Soviet ruling group to have their own way. But various reasons combined to counsel restraint. The American military organization was still eager for Soviet entry in the Pacific War *in time to spare us loss and suffering*. The Secretary of State, from San Francisco, was advising him not to engage in acts of pressure or retaliation until the work of that conference was done and a charter written to hold the world together for the future. It was thought possible that Stalin was not being correctly informed by Molotov and others; that he was being led to believe that the United States and Great Britain were trying to deprive the Soviet Union of the fruits of victory.

For all these reasons and in all these circumstances Truman decided it would be reckless to risk the coalition without further effort to find out whether, in further discussion, Stalin might not make concessions as regards Polish and other issues for the sake of Western friendship. This attitude he shared with the great majority of the American people. They, like himself, were still thinking and judging in the spirit of the alliance and fellowship for war. The American authorities had done much to keep them in this mood, and little to make them realize the toughness and significance of the differences with Moscow. They were unprepared so swiftly to turn, in dealing with the Soviet Union, from the going diplomacy of friendship to the harsh diplomacy of push and power and, if need be, to a test of arms. They were quite unready to face the necessity of engaging in a prolongation of the struggle to

---

[18] On this same day Stimson fully informed Eden, who was in Washington, of the state of work on, prospects of, and plans to test the atomic bomb.

protect the freedom of European peoples, and to preserve a safe strategic position and balance of power against the Allied nation to whose survival they had contributed so much.

∞∞∞∞∞∞∞∞

67. The Overshadowed Victory; The Far East

∞∞∞∞∞∞∞∞

In the United States interest was turning to coming events in the Pacific. The American government was also becoming actively worried as to how contracts and contacts with the Soviet Union in that region, particularly concerning China, were going to turn out. Russian conduct was causing doubt as to whether we ought to pave the way for Soviet entry into the Pacific War by urging Chiang Kai-shek to concur in the Yalta conditions.

The belief was growing that even if Soviet forces did not join in the Pacific War, the losses and strain would be acceptable. The plans evolving in the papers of the Joint Chiefs of Staff were more and more impressive in their meaning of assured destruction of Japan and its last defenders—without the Russians and without the atomic bomb. The Joint Chiefs on April 24th decided that two of the particular operational advantages of Soviet entry were not necessary or worth the effort. The request for the use of bombing bases in the Maritime Provinces, so long and diligently sought, was dropped. General Deane became convinced that even with full cooperation the Soviet authorities would not be able to build and equip B-29 long-range bombing bases in the Amur River area in less than a year. Studies showed that even if the greatest effort was made to send planes, men, and supplies to these bases, the volume of explosives that could be dropped during that year on the Japanese mainland from there would be only a small fraction of what could be flown from other bases under our control. The project for opening a northern sea route of supply through the Kuriles to support the Soviet offensive from Manchuria was also suspended.[19]

But even so, Soviet help was still wanted early enough to lessen the cost in lives and shorten the ordeal. The battle for Okinawa was going on. Despite greater numbers and immense fire power, American troops were suffering heavy losses as the Japanese stood and died in the

[19] Leahy, *I Was There*, pages 352–53. General Lawrence S. Kuter, *Airman at Yalta*, pages 44–46. Deane, *The Strange Alliance*, pages 262–63.

638

trenches and caves. The Kamikaze suicide planes were a menace against which there was no sure protection, and there were visions of hundreds being sent out on their last missions as our ships came close to Japan. The Japanese Army in Manchuria was mistakenly estimated to be still formidable and capable of sustaining a long and hard fight in that region with its own resources. Connectedly, it was thought that the appearance of an overwhelming force from the north might prove to be the extra onset of adversity which would force even the Japanese military rulers to recognize that the fight was hopeless, and cause the Japanese government to accept unconditional surrender before invasion. The Joint Chiefs of Staff did not debar the possibility that the end *might* be brought about by sea and air blockade and attack, but were unwilling to base their plans upon that chance. The advance reports about an atomic explosive weapon in the making did not cause them to change their minds; despite the latest awesome descriptions, its conclusive impact was not divined. So, to repeat, the wish to have Soviet participation in the Pacific War at the earliest possible time did not lapse.

But the State Department and the Embassy at Moscow were becoming anxious over the consequences of a victory in the Far East in which the Soviet Union would so largely share. Ambassador Hurley, stopping in Moscow on the way back to his post in Chungking, had reviewed Soviet aims in the Far East with Stalin. His report had been all on the reassuring side. As summarized by him (in his message to Washington on April 17th): "The Marshal . . . wished us to know that we would have his complete support in immediate action for the unification of the armed forces of China with the full recognition of the National Government under the leadership of Chiang Kai-shek. In short, Stalin agreed unqualifiedly to America's policy in China as outlined to him during the conversation."

But Harriman, who had taken part in these talks, had not been impressed in the same way. He had flown back to Washington almost as soon as the last word was spoken, and had told Truman and the State Department that he thought Hurley was taking Stalin's assurances too trustingly. Kennan, who was in charge of the Moscow Embassy in Harriman's absence, had been even more skeptical: "It would be tragic," he observed in the message by which he followed Hurley's report, "if our natural anxiety for the support of the Soviet Union at this juncture, coupled with Stalin's use of words which mean all things to all people and his cautious affability, were to lead us into an undue reliance on Soviet aid or even Soviet acquiescence in the achievement of our long term objectives in China." His analysis amounted to an almost flat statement that the Soviet government would not be satisfied unless it secured domination in Manchuria, Mongolia, and North China.

Faced with the need to decide whether to tell T. V. Soong, the Chinese Foreign Minister who was in San Francisco, of the still secret Yalta accord, the State Department turned to the military for guidance. On May 12th Acting Secretary of State Grew, impressed by Harriman's analysis of Soviet tendencies, posed some questions to the Secretaries of War and Navy—which by this time were rather like rockets shot in the air. The first was, in substance: Is the entry of the Soviet Union into the Pacific War at the earliest possible time of such vital interest to the United States as to preclude an attempt to get Soviet agreement beforehand to certain desirable political aims in the Far East? The second was: Should the Yalta decision in regard to political desires in the Far East be reconsidered, or carried into effect in whole or in part?

Stimson and Forrestal searched their minds hard for the answers. As Stimson saw the situation, the atomic bomb project might well be the dominant factor in the tangled mass of considerations before them. But the outcome of the test would not be known for weeks, and it seemed a terrible thing to gamble such high stakes in diplomacy without having the master card securely in hand.[19a] So the answers which Stimson and Forrestal made (on the 21st) left the decision to the President and the State Department. From their measured depths, some useful but not conclusive opinions could be fished: (1) That Russia would decide whether and when to enter the war on the basis of its own reckoning, with little regard for American political action. (2) That Russia had the choice of waiting until American forces had all but destroyed the Japanese, or entering sooner and saving American lives. (3) That either way, Russia would have the military power to take what had been promised it at Yalta, except perhaps the Kurile Islands, and an American attempt to take these first would be at the direct expense of other plans and involve an unacceptable cost in American lives. (4) That on military grounds there was no objection to a review of the Yalta accord which would look to fuller understanding. (5) That it was desirable to get the commitments and clarifications of Soviet policies which the State Department wished.

[19a] The reports had been more and more confident. On April 23rd the British technical adviser to the Combined Policy Committee on atomic affairs had informed the British Minister in charge of the British part in the project that it was "as certain as such things can be" a weapon would be ready by late summer. A week later Field Marshal Wilson, who, as head of the British Joint Staff Mission in Washington was on the Policy Committee, informed London that "the Americans propose to drop a bomb sometime in August." *Grand Strategy*, Vol. vi, pages 275–76.

This consultation within the American government ended in mild conclusions: we would not try to upset the Yalta accord or to revise its terms, but before asking Chiang Kai-shek to concur we would seek to get Stalin to endorse protective principles. We would test again whether the Soviet government honestly intended to allow the Chinese National Government to exercise unimpaired sovereignty over all of China and Manchuria, and whether it would actively help us to bring about political and military unification in China.

The answers to these questions might well determine whether the final phase of the war against Japan would be carried out concordantly with the Soviet Union or turn into a competitive scramble, or possibly result in a quarrel that would smash the coalition even before peace was made in Europe and before the United Nations could gather together for the first time under their new covenant.

68. Waning of the Impulse to Aid Soviet Reconstruction

Here, in order to round out our account of the matters affecting the turn of relations between the West and the Soviet Union as the war in Europe ended, note should be made of one other element—the waning of the belief that the West would contribute much to Soviet reconstruction. A backward glance over the discussions of this subject that had taken place during the war will show how by May 1945 misunderstanding was coiled about it.

Stalin and his associates, in accord with Marxist-Leninist doctrine, believed that when the war ended capitalist societies were going to run into a crisis of adjustment and great unemployment. Hence they thought that merely to save itself the United States would be eager to send the Soviet Union its products on almost any loan terms.

Such notions would have survived the talks which Stalin and Mikoyan, the Soviet Commissar of Foreign Trade, had with visitors from the American business world. For example, when Donald Nelson, the recently retired head of the War Production Board, had been in Moscow in October 1943, he had told Stalin that the United States would have a great surplus of capital equipment and machinery of the kinds which Russia would need. When Stalin had asked him whether he thought the Soviet Union could get these on credit, Nelson had answered that he thought an arrangement could be worked out whereby the pay ments during the first postwar years would be small, and grow as the Soviet Union regained its economic strength and power to pay. Stalin had named the products which Russia would most want. Nelson had said that the United States could provide them. He had promised Stalin that after his return to the United States he would advise the President to appoint a group of American businessmen to meet with Soviet representatives to work out a plan for trade and exchange with the Soviet Union. Stalin had almost beamed.

But Hull had at that time thought that before discussing possible credits with the Soviet government we ought to get assurances that it would cooperate in his world-wide program for the expansion of trade. Talks about the ways and means of setting about to do this had been going on with the British before the Conference at Moscow. The Soviet government had been invited to join in them, but it had not responded. Hull, while in Moscow, had in long discourses tried to win Stalin and Molotov over to the program he had in mind for the world. Toward his effort Molotov had showed polite but unhelpful admiration. He had seemed impressed with Hull's idealistic zeal and genuinely perplexed as to how Hull's doctrines of freer trade could be harmonized with the Communist trade methods. This failure had distressed the Secretary of State. Of all objects of his policy he was most tenacious about this one, and most alert to use all diplomatic chances to serve it. Thus he had thought that the Russians might make more of an effort to find ways of cooperating with his trade program if their chances of obtaining American loans depended upon it.

While Roosevelt was at Teheran, he and Hopkins had talked over with Harriman how the subject had best be pursued. The Ambassador had allowed it to rest until, on the last day of December 1943, Molotov had asked him whether he had anything new to say on the subject of economic aid after the war. His prepared answer had been that under the Lend-Lease Act the American government could provide supplies only for the prosecution of the war, and so other ways would have to be found to take care of Soviet reconstruction needs. It might, he went on to say, be advisable for the Soviet government to establish a credit in the United States; to make a list of what it would most urgently need, so that plans could be made in advance to produce them as soon as war demands allowed; and also to invite American technical experts to come into the Soviet Union to study Soviet needs, so that on their return to the United States they could help to satisfy them. The spirit of these suggestions was in accord with that sense of firm partnership in which the Allies had quit Teheran. Molotov had said that the Soviet government was greatly interested in these possibilities and that its needs would be enormous.

Harriman had soon thereafter sought to find out through Harry Hopkins what kind of credit might be arranged. He had thought that it ought to be relatively small to start, and expansible—something on the order of half a billion dollars at first, at low interest. He had suggested that the Soviet government ought to be asked to submit applications for the use of any such credit, item by item, thereby giving the American government a chance to decide whether the goods could be provided. He had thought it would be possible, if these discussions about a credit were held in Moscow, to get the Soviet government to provide more information in support of its *other* current requests under the Lend-Lease agreement for materials in short supply, such as aluminum, nickel, and Diesel engines. He had wanted to end the privileged Soviet position in this respect and also to assure that the Soviet requests were for legitimate war purposes, not to be hoarded for use after the war. Beyond that, he had wished to be able to use the prospect of American aid as a tool of diplomacy, and also to stimulate response to various unanswered American requests for military cooperation.

Hopkins had at this time fallen ill. The State Department had told Harriman that in general it agreed with his ideas but that it needed time to formulate definite instructions. It had been willing to have discussions about the possible credit carried on in Moscow. But other agencies of the government—the Munitions Assignment Board, the War Production Board, the War Department, the Lend-Lease Administration—had all thought this impractical. It is probable also that Hopkins was not sympathetic with the idea of making the Soviet government prove its needs one by one in view of its reluctance to impart what it considered secret information of military importance.

The subsequent talks had been taken over from Molotov by Mikoyan. The Soviet government had accepted without demur the idea that materials intended for reconstruction should be provided under a repayable credit; and it had said that since some of the requests it was just about to make would be for reconstruction, it thought it desirable that a credit arrangement be completed soon. On the 1st of February 1944, Mikoyan had proposed that this original credit might be about one billion dollars, at one-half per cent interest. After reporting this to Washington, Harriman had been told, however, that the American government was now puzzled by the legal restrictions (the Johnson Act) on its existing powers to extend any credit at all to the Soviet Union, and for that reason he had better limit himself for the time being to generalities. A message from Hopkins a few days later had been more helpful. It had suggested a basis on which Soviet orders placed while the war was on for such things as industrial equipment, oil refineries, power plants, which might have a dual use—that is, both during the war and after the war—could be handled under one of the provisions of the Lend-Lease Act. Thereby the Soviet government would be required to agree to pay for any dual-purpose equipment which had not been delivered by the end of the war on terms later to be settled. In this way Hopkins thought that the equipment most urgently wanted for postwar reconstruction and ordered in advance could be provided without having to ask Congress in haste to authorize a special credit for the Soviet Union; that could then be further considered at such time as more was known about what the Soviet Union needed and what the United States could provide. This proposed procedure had left the question of any general credit in limbo, as had the instructions to Harriman which followed from Washington.

Harriman had conformed to this line of transitional aid in his discussions with Soviet officials in the spring of 1944. The American offer was, in effect, (1) to be as flexible as possible in the administration of the Lend-Lease Act, so that the Soviet Union might get some products that might be needed or used only after the war was over, in return for a promise to pay for them later; (2) to seek legislation that would enable the government to grant a credit for other reconstruction projects, when the American political situation was favorable. In April the Soviet government had fallen in with this program as the best obtainable for the time being, and had soon started to make requests and place orders for some equipment which probably could not be produced and installed until after the war against Germany had ended. But both governments had regarded this as a makeshift until it was possible to work out a larger and more open long-term loan.

Light on what Stalin thought about the American contribution to Soviet reconstruction is to be had from some of the remarks he had made when talking with Eric Johnston later in June 1944. Johnston had described to him the wish of American industry to do business with the Soviet Union. Stalin had taken up the theme by predicting that the American government would be confronted with the task of preventing unemployment, helping the returning soldiers to find work, and so avoid depression; and he had said he wanted to know what Soviet orders could be placed in the United States to obviate such impending troubles. When Johnston ventured the opinion that the period of unemployment after the war would be short, Stalin said, on the contrary, he thought it would be quite long.

That Stalin was more fully cognizant of how much the United States had contributed to Soviet productivity than he had ever publicly acknowledged, is shown by what he said to Johnston in the course of their last conversation. Johnston was telling him how interested he was in learning about Russian production. Stalin had deprecated it as compared with American production, and then said ". . . that the United States had greatly assisted Soviet industry—perhaps two-thirds of all the large plants in the Soviet Union had been constructed with American help or experience. . . ." He was referring, it may be presumed, to the pre-war record.

However no such compulsion—based on fear of postwar business depression—as may have seemed to Stalin and his associates to throb through American business thought had governed our official dealings during the remaining year of war. The government had continued to meet any and all Soviet requests for equipment that could be construed as needed for its war effort on a Lend-Lease basis. It had begun to pool through an international organization (the United Nations Relief and Rehabilitation Administration, known as UNRRA) the far greater amount of supplies which the United States was going to contribute to the relief of all war-stricken countries, with the smaller amounts other countries could give; and it had welcomed full Soviet participation in the execution of this program. Still the American government had wanted to be reasonably assured that any credit granted to the Soviet Union would be of advantage to ourselves and the rest of the world as well as to that country. It was not driven by fear of future economic difficulties.

But American official policy had also been afflicted by a misjudgment. It was thought that Russia would find it very hard to manage after the war without the raw materials, chemicals, electrical and railway equipment that the United States could provide; and that the wish to secure these would induce it to want to keep American good will. This belief turned out to be mistaken. The Soviet government had not given signs that it would be conciliatory in order to get more goods in trade or credit from the United States.

In January 1945—with the Yalta Conference in view—the Soviet government had made its first formal request for a postwar credit. Explaining to Harriman (on January 3rd) that Soviet-American relations must have certain vistas before it, and rest on a solid economic basis, Molotov had given the Ambassador a memo defining the Soviet ideas. Its theme was, "Having in mind the repeated statements of American public figures concerning the desirability of receiving extensive large Soviet orders for the postwar and transition period, the Soviet government considers it possible to place orders on the basis of long-term credits to the amount of six billion dollars." The proposed loan should be for thirty years, payment to start after nine years, and the interest rate to be two and one-quarter per cent.

Harriman's advice to Washington had been that we ought to do everything we could to assist the Soviet Union to develop a sound economy by credits. For he explained that he was convinced ". . . that the sooner the Soviet Union can develop a decent life for its people the more tolerant they will become." But he stated again that it was his strong and earnest opinion that the question of the credit ought to be tied into our diplomatic dealings with the Soviet Union and that the Russians ". . . should be given to understand that our willingness to cooperate wholeheartedly with them in their vast reconstruction problems will depend upon their behavior in international matters."

This Soviet initiative had evoked different responses from the several departments of the American government. The Treasury had rushed in to propose that we loan ten billion dollars at two per cent, to be paid in strategic raw materials if we wished.[20] Secretary Morgenthau had contended that such an action would disperse any suspicions the Soviet authorities might have about our future intentions. The Foreign Economic Administrator, Crowley, had wanted to be vague until and unless the Soviet government met our terms of payment for long-life dual-use industrial equipment that had been or was to be delivered under Lend-Lease—a matter still unsettled after months of bargaining. The Assistant Secretary of State for Economic Affairs, Clayton, had thought that even if a credit was given, the Treasury's plan was too generous; and he agreed with Harriman that we should use any large credit to bargain with the Soviet Union. The amiable Secretary of State, Stettinius, had wanted to suit them all and the Russians besides. But he had been given pause, as had Roosevelt, by the need to get the approval of Congress. It had been decided to let the matter rest pending discussions with Stalin and other Soviet officials at Yalta.

But there it had been given only passing attention. On the second day of the Conference (February 5th), in telling Stettinius and Eden of the Russian wish to get reparations from Germany, Molotov had gone on to say that he hoped the United States would grant long-term

[20] This may have been prepared and submitted to the President before the Harriman-Molotov talk of January 3rd, but probably not.

credits to the Soviet Union. Stettinius had said that he was ready to discuss this possibility with Molotov either at Yalta or at Moscow, where he was going after the Conference. But neither Molotov nor Stalin had reverted to the subject.

During the last few months of the war, generous resort to the transitional arrangements covered by Lend-Lease was against the flow of American-Soviet relations, and not enough to turn the tide in that flow. And as that grew more troubling, American officials began to waver in their desire to aid Soviet recovery. They were not willing to be guided by Churchill's advice that we stand fast and retaliate. But they wanted to regain confidence in the ultimate intentions of the Soviet Union before exerting themselves in its behalf. And they were still hoping that even in their time of triumph the Soviet rulers would be deterred by our reserve, and tempted by the rewards of moderation.

Besides this atmospheric restraint upon loan plans, the American government was accumulating grievances about what it deemed certain sharp Soviet practices. During the spring of 1945 the Soviet government was found to be transferring goods secured from the United States under Lend-Lease, such as trucks and radio equipment, to other countries without seeking our consent. Then in March and April official disapprobation had been aroused by the highhanded way in which Soviet forces dealt with the oil properties and shipping which came under their control in Romania and Hungary. Moreover, Washington got the impression that Moscow was going to deal with all European problems of relief and recovery with no regard for anyone else's needs but its own.

Joined with the broader movement of events, these grievances and impressions pinched the impulse to ease the lot of the Russian people and marked the demise of the sense that, because of its part in the war, the Soviet Union deserved priority or special consideration. Still, there was probably no special intent to penalize the Soviet Union in the general order issued on May 8th which stopped Lend-Lease shipments so abruptly. This imperceptive step seems rather to have been prompted by a strict interpretation of the Lend-Lease Act and a wish to avoid criticism in Congress.[21] The action, soon amended, fell most heavily on

[21] It was then contended that the Executive had no choice under the express terms of the Act, the repeated assurances given Congress that it would be used only for war purposes, and the plain manifestation of the intention and wish of Congress shown in the amendment which it made in the Act when on April 10, 1945 it extended it for one year. The new stipulation read in part, *"Provided, however:* That nothing in section 3 (c) shall be construed to authorize the President to enter into or carry out any contract or agreement with a foreign government for post-war relief, post-war rehabilita-

Britain. Churchill and his colleagues took it with a distressed sigh as an imperative subject for discussion. But Stalin took it as a direct blow aimed to weaken the Soviet stand on other issues. The American government went on to complete all the provisions it had undertaken to make for the Soviet Union—under earlier Lend-Lease accords and arrangements—for Soviet entry into the Pacific War. But the spirit of sympathetic generosity, natural to partners in war and peace, had dried up. The prospect of a large loan and mutual economic aid was no longer an emollient for the fraying nerves of the coalition.

69. Testing the Possibilities of Continuing Cooperation with the Soviet Union, May 1945

As the victorious members of the coalition came into control over Germany, a personal meeting of the Heads of State seemed to be the only possible way of finding a path through or around the blocked lanes of negotiations. A few hours before the surrender at Rheims, Churchill, with Stalin's latest domineering message about Poland in mind, had remarked to Truman, "It seems to me that matters can hardly be carried further by correspondence, and that as soon as possible there should be a meeting of the three heads of Governments." [22] The Prime Minister, in several following messages in early May, pressed the idea of inviting Stalin to meet them at some "unshattered" town in Germany.

---

tion or post-war reconstruction; . . ." The opening sentence of the report from the Senate Committee on Foreign Relations submitted on April 5th to accompany this bill read, "The purpose of the Amendment to the Lend-Lease Act adopted by the House was to assure that lend-lease agreements would not be used for postwar relief, postwar rehabilitation, or postwar reconstruction purposes."

The total amount of Lend-Lease Aid extended from the time the law was enacted (March 11, 1941) to June 30, 1945, was (in terms of billions of dollars) as follows:

United Kingdom	13.5
USSR	9.1
Africa, Middle East & Mediterranean	3.3
China and India	2.2
Australia and New Zealand	1.3
Latin-America	0.2
Other Countries	1.5
Total	31.4

[22] *Triumph and Tragedy*, page 501.

Truman was willing. But domestic duties, such as the budget message, required his attention. Moreover, he felt the need for more time to study and make up his mind about the disputed issues. Probably he was on guard against being pushed too far and fast by Churchill. Added to these reasons for deliberation was his lack of enthusiasm for Germany as the meeting-place; now that the war was over, he thought Stalin should come west, perhaps to Alaska. So he answered Churchill that he would like to have the initiative come from Stalin and that it would not be convenient for him to leave Washington before July.

When on May 15th Harriman, who was about to start back from Washington for Moscow via London, expressed the opinion that the sooner the meeting the better the chance of good outcome, the President said he was not sure. But at the end of this talk he said he would attend, perhaps even in early June, if Churchill actively wanted the conference then. He did not wish to appear anxious about it, lest Stalin conclude that we thought Soviet cooperation on any terms indispensable. So he was going to let Churchill take the active part in bringing about the meeting, and wait to hear about Stalin's response before deciding.

Truman was at the same time slightly embarrassed because Churchill was reviving an invitation which Roosevelt had not lived to accept—that he visit Great Britain first, and that they might then go on to meet Stalin together. Heeding the same advisers as Roosevelt—particularly Hopkins and Marshall—he thought this would not be wise. Using the same phrase that Roosevelt used before Yalta, he told Churchill that if the meeting was arranged he thought they ought to go separately, so as not to seem to be "ganging up."

In the meanwhile, as the attempts at long range to adjust quarrelsome situations in Europe and the Far East failed, Truman decided to ask Harry Hopkins, who had been very sick, to go to Moscow as soon as he could. There he was to make clear to Stalin that we were greatly disturbed about the differences which had arisen between ourselves and the Soviet government over situations in Europe (especially Poland) and in the Far East (especially China). He was to explain our views and intentions. If and as Stalin's statements were reassuring, and seemed to provide ground for agreement, he was to work out the plans for a meeting of the three Heads of State.

On May 19th Truman sent word to Stalin saying that he was sure that the Marshal was aware, as he was, of the difficulties of dealing by correspondence with the complicated and important questions with which they were faced. Thus, pending the possibility of a meeting, he was sending Hopkins with Harriman to Moscow so that they might talk these matters over with the Marshal; then Hopkins would return to Washington at once to report personally to him.

Hopkins set off for this momentous series of talks with Stalin on May 23rd while almost every message going back and forth to Moscow was tingling with tension. He was determined to see whether the spirit of cooperation with the Soviet Union which had brought victory could not be revived. He thought that if Churchill was at this time allowed to take the lead, relations might become even more roughened because of the challenging measures which Churchill had been urging. As recorded in an entry in Forrestal's Diary after a talk in which Hopkins explained what he would try to accomplish at Moscow: "Harry said that he was skeptical about Churchill, at least in the particular of Anglo-American-Russian relationship; that he thought it to be of vital importance that we be not manoeuvered into a position where Great Britain had us lined up with them as a bloc against Russia to implement England's European policy." [23]

This anxiety was one of the reasons why Truman decided to send another special envoy at the same time to review the same troubled field with Churchill. He asked Joseph Davies to take on the job. The agent for this assignment was a provocative one. His flattering account, in book and moving picture, of life in the Soviet Union and of the Soviet official regime, had caused more experienced observers to wonder. But the main, moving purpose was creditable: to preserve a basis of cooperation with the Soviet Union for the tasks of peace making. Churchill was to be cautioned that he, Truman, intended scrupulously to support every agreement made by Roosevelt; if there were differences of opinion as to their meaning they should be cleared up; and if new decisions were needed for continued unity, their terms ought to be clear; the American government would then fulfill these obligations, and would confidently expect the same from associated governments. In effect, Davies was to bring the ardent Prime Minister to realize that the American government would not adopt the measures he was urging nor give way to mistrust and criticism of Russia, and to dispose the British government to be patient and conciliatory.

Churchill understood Davies to suggest that Truman wanted first to talk to Stalin alone somewhere in Europe before the meeting of the three. [24] In his memoirs, however, Truman has averred that he never

[23] Entry, May 20, 1945.
[24] As expressed in *Triumph and Tragedy*, page 577. "The crux of what he had to propose was that the President should meet Stalin first somewhere in Europe before he saw me."

had any thought of having prolonged discussions of official affairs with Stalin from which the Prime Minister would be excluded. His idea, according to this later account, was merely to have a brief chance to exchange impressions with Stalin before the three-cornered negotiations started. In his recollection: "Of course, since I was not personally acquainted with either Stalin or Churchill, I had intended that when we arrived at our meeting place I would have an opportunity to see each separately. In this way I would become better acquainted with them and be able to size them up, and they too would get a chance to size me up." [25]

But due possibly to the fact that Truman was not explicit in his instructions to Davies on this point, or possibly to the way in which Davies explained Truman's thought, the proposal surprised and hurt the Prime Minister.[26] Just a few days before (May 21st) he had again sent word to the President that he thought there was a very great need for a triple meeting at the earliest possible moment, and had asked: "Could you give me any idea of the date and place which would be suitable, so that we can make our several requests to Stalin. I fear he may play for time in order to remain all powerful in Europe when our forces have melted. . . ." [27]

It would have been hard anyway for the Prime Minister, who was spending himself on warnings that Russia might become the new oppressor of Europe, to listen to Davies' interpretation of his judgments and activity. As recorded by Davies in the written report he made after his return to Washington:

"I said that frankly, as I had listened to him [Churchill] inveigh so

[25] *Year of Decisions,* page 260.

[26] In *Year of Decisions,* page 261, Truman wrote that Davies represented his position and the policy of the United States with accuracy, carrying out his instructions with exceptional skill.

The report which Davies submitted after his return recorded that he (Davies) explained to Churchill Truman's wish to dispel Soviet suspicion that Britain and the United States along with the United Nations were "ganging up" against them; that such suspicion was in fact unjustified and ought to be dispelled; that this required the establishment of confidence in the good faith and reliability of the parties, which came only through frank discussions and the opportunity to know and estimate each other. On that score the President was at a disadvantage in contrast to that which the Prime Minister and Stalin enjoyed. Churchill and Eden both had had the benefit of frequent contacts and friendly association with Marshal Stalin and Commissar Molotov. "It was the President's desire therefore, in view of the responsibility which he must assume, to have a similar opportunity to know the Marshal and to have the Marshal come to know him. . . . The President therefore desires an opportunity to meet the Marshal immediately before the scheduled forthcoming meeting. He felt certain that the Prime Minister would appreciate the reasonableness of his position and facilitate such arrangements."

[27] *Triumph and Tragedy,* page 559.

violently against the threat of Soviet domination and the spread of Communism in Europe, and disclose such a lack of confidence in the professions of good faith in Soviet leadership, I had wondered whether he, the Prime Minister, was now willing to declare to the world that he and Britain had made a mistake in not supporting Hitler, for as I understood him, he was now expressing the doctrine which Hitler and Goebbels had been proclaiming and reiterating for the past four years in an effort to break up Allied unity and 'divide and conquer.' Exactly the same conditions which he described and the same deductions were drawn from them as he now appeared to assert."

Churchill had not appreciated how deeply his proposals had disturbed those civilian members of the American government who had sponsored the Yalta accords, and by whom continued cooperation with Russia was deemed essential for future peace; nor how much they had worried the military members, who were still intent on bringing the war against Japan to the quickest possible end. He had set out to shake them, and in doing so had alarmed them. In his turn he was shocked to learn that while he was sure that the United States and Great Britain were united on the basic issues, important American officials did not think so, and were apparently causing the new President to be on guard. For it may be assumed that he sensed the conclusion that Davies wrote in his report and passed out upon his return to Leahy and others. "The Prime Minister," Davies summed up, "is a very great man, but there is no doubt that he is 'first, last, and all the time' a great Englishman. I could not escape the impression that he was basically more concerned over preserving England's position in Europe than in preserving Peace. In any event, he had convinced himself that by serving England he was best serving Peace." About this, Leahy's comment is pertinent: "This was consistent with our staff estimate of Churchill's attitude throughout the war." [28]

The sense of affront left by Davies' suggestion and lecture was repressed in the brief message which Churchill sent Truman (on the 31st) after his talks with Davies ended: "I had agreeable talks with Mr. Davies which he will report to you when he returns. I must say however at once that I should not be prepared to attend a meeting which was a continuation of a conference between you and Marshal Stalin. I consider that at this victory meeting, at which subjects of the gravest consequences are to be discussed, we three should meet simultaneously and on equal terms." [29] This statement settled the matter.

[28] *I Was There*, page 380.

[29] In *Year of Decisions*, page 260, Truman gives a paraphrase of this message. Curiously, Churchill does not in his account of the episode refer to it.

Churchill had given freer expression to his indignation in a three-page note which

Stalin had a few days before told Churchill that he would be glad to meet with him and Truman in Berlin "in the very near future."

Churchill suggested that they arrange to get together on June 15th. Truman asked for more time. He said that he did not think he ought to leave the United States before July. He may have had several fresh reasons for wanting to wait, among them perhaps to give time to the men who were going to test the atomic weapon, and to remain close by as long as the Conference of the United Nations that was still going on in San Francisco might be in session.

For that is the direction toward which most Americans were looking for the peace they wanted, rather than toward another bout of wits between Heads of State. They were eager for principles, in place of bargains or force. For their aim—durable peace—they still thought principles and trust the better means. They believed that if, before the next meeting of the Heads of State to deal with the great unsettled problems of the peace, the Charter for the United Nations was adopted with Soviet participation, it would be easier to deal with all disputes.

The Conference at San Francisco had opened on April 25th, the day that the American and Russian troops met at the Elbe. The whole organized chorus of radio and press and preacher and paid publicity men, come from the world over, led on by the government, was pouring forth variations and comment on the statements that came out of conference rooms.

At Dumbarton Oaks the main lines of an organization had been designed. All countries, including the Soviet Union, had seemed pleased. But many had expressed a desire for some changes. And agreement had still to be reached in regard to the basic weight of the organization and the balance among nations within it. The smaller powers were seeking greater place and influence. The other American Republics

---

he had dictated on May 27th after his first talk with Davies and which he, according to his later recollection, gave to Davies. In regard to the proposed meeting with Stalin the Prime Minister wrote in this note, *"It must be understood that the representatives of His Majesty's Government would not be able to attend any meeting except as equal partners from its opening. This would be undoubtedly regrettable. The Prime Minister does not see that there is any need to raise an issue so wounding to Britain, to the British Empire and Commonwealth of Nations."* In printing the text of this note in *Triumph and Tragedy,* pages 578–80, Churchill italicized this passage.

Churchill, *ibid.,* page 581, states that the President "received this note in a kindly and understanding spirit, and replied on May 29th that he was considering possible dates for the Triple Conference." But Davies in his report to the President does not mention either receiving this note from Churchill or sending it on to the President. He records that after a change of mind it was decided not to exchange Aides-Memoires. Truman, in *Year of Decisions,* does not allude to the receipt of any such note from Davies, nor to any acknowledgment of it. In fact he states (page 260) that Davies did not cable him any details of his talks with Churchill.

looked to the United States to effectuate that wish. The British Dominions, which had fought the war as hard as any of the great powers, felt they were entitled to an adequate part, and looked to the British government to see that they were granted it. But by the Soviet government any extension of authority, mainly among countries attached to the West, was regarded as a threat, a danger that the Soviet Union might be outvoted or overborne. Before the Conference had met at San Francisco, the Soviet government had signalled that unless sufficiently protected against this possibility it might still decide to keep aloof. Molotov's talks with Truman in Washington and encounters with the American delegation at San Francisco were stubborn and reserved, and he was going home.

In short, under the fanfare at San Francisco during these weeks of May, there were still claims to be reconciled and differences in conception to be overcome. To the Americans who spoke for their government it seemed imperative that this should be done. Unless it were, not only might the war coalition dissolve in dispute, but the United States might even again step away from the affairs of Europe.

Thus, while Hopkins in Moscow was trying to find out whether Stalin was going to be cooperative and true to his word, and while Davies was trying to calm Churchill's fears of Soviet intentions, Stettinius remained in San Francisco to see whether fair word could be fused into fairer deed. President Truman waited to learn the result of all these efforts. So did Churchill, with sight more filled, however, by the day-by-day signs of the spread of Soviet influence over Central Europe. Stalin was directing that. He was ready to give Hopkins the answers he wanted, cleverly phrased to leave room for future divagations. He was, no doubt, observant of the fact that Americans were already clamoring to leave Europe and to turn their weapons against Japan.

This is as far along the bank of history as I have traveled. The narrative thus must rest here for the time being—with regret, for there is still so much ahead to see and to recount. The next segment of the story would go on to examine the outcome of the Conference at San Francisco and the joyous satisfaction that followed the creation of the United Nations Organization. Simultaneously, it would take heed of the course of the long talks between Hopkins and Stalin at Moscow, which also briefly seemed to augur well for the possibility that the association formed for war might be lasting. Quickly thereafter it would accompany the Heads of State to and through their disorderly conference at Potsdam, where they sought to complete the arrangements for Europe after the war, and to plan for the continuation of the war against Japan. It would tell how, while that conference was still going on, word came of the successful test of the atomic bomb in New Mexico; of the ultimatum to Japan, of its rejection and the subsequent awesome atomization of Hiroshima and Nagasaki; and of the Russian entry into the Pacific War just before Japan bowed to the demand for unconditional surrender. Following on, it would note the evidences of the fast-fraying of the accords between the West and the Soviet Union, and the struggle for the control of China. Hardest of all to tell, and wearisome and discouraging to read, would be the next succession of dreary conferences (in Moscow, London, Paris, and Berlin) that failed to stop the dissolution of the coalition, and the gradual regression into separate national wills which left the world dangerously divided. All this and much more awaits another opportunity, other narrators and other interpreters, and a freer and fuller disclosure of the records.

Roosevelt and his colleagues were right: the nations needed moral law and freedom. Churchill was right: the nations needed magnanimity and balance of power. Stalin was sullying a right: the Russian people were entitled to the fullest equality and protection against another assault upon them. But under Stalin they were trying not only to extend their boundaries and their control over neighboring states but also beginning to revert to their revolutionary effort throughout the world. Within the next few years this was to break the coalition and, along with the spread of nationalist passion in hitherto passive parts of the world, create the turbulence in which we are all now living.

APPENDIX I

Note about Origins and Nature of the So-called Curzon Line

THE so-called Curzon Line was derived from two separate decisions of the Paris Peace Conference, each made under different circumstances and for different purposes. The Supreme Council of the Allied Powers on December 8, 1919, in a *Declaration Relating to the Provisional Eastern Frontiers of Poland* had approved a boundary for the northern section of the eastern frontier of the resurrected state of Poland. This ran down from the east Prussian frontier to the Galician boundary, upstream on the River Bug near Krilov. The line was not drawn farther south in this declaration because the Council was thinking of constituting the area or areas south and east (the eastern part of Galicia, one of the fragments of the Austro-Hungarian Empire which was being broken up), into a separate state. Consistently with this general idea, on November 21, 1919, it had adopted a *Statute of Eastern Galicia* which provided for a twenty-five-year Polish mandate under the League of Nations, at the end of which the future status of the area was to be determined by the Council of the League. This specified the western boundary of the proposed mandate—which was to be the southern section of the eastern boundary of Poland proper. That designated line ran from Belzec on the former frontier between Austria-Hungary and Russia southwestward, passing west of Rawa Ruska and east of Przymysl (leaving the city and province of Lwow within the mandate), and thence to the Czecho-Slovak border.

Neither of these proposals had been accepted by either the Polish or Soviet governments. The Polish government ignored the declaration defining the northern section of its frontier and opposed the suggested mandate so vehemently that the Council suspended the execution of the Statute of Eastern Galicia a month later. Resentment at not having been accorded outright possession of Lwow was one of the main reasons why the Poles rejected the mandate.

The fighting between the Poles and Bolshevists had continued. In July 1920, after the Polish expedition against Kiev was defeated, the Polish government sought Allied help. Its armies were still 125 miles east of the December 8, 1919 frontier line and still in control of the whole of Galicia, but in growing danger of being routed by the Bolshevists unless aided. The Polish Prime Minister, Wladislaw Grabski, presented his request for intervention to the Supreme Council meeting at that time at Spa. On July 10 the British Prime Minister, Lloyd George, bluntly told him that such support would be available only if the Polish Army retreated to its "legitimate frontier." (Harold

Nicolson, *Curzon, The Last Phase, 1919–1925,* page 204.) Grabski acceded. An accord, approved by representatives of the Allied Associated Powers, was immediately drawn up and signed by him.

Thereunder the Polish government agreed (according to text given in article by W. Sworakowski, in *Journal of Central European Affairs,* April 1944, called, *"An error regarding Eastern Galicia in Curzon's note to the Soviet Government of July 11, 1930."* It does not seem to be published in any official collection of documents):

"a. That an armistice shall be signed without delay, and the Polish Army withdrawn to the line provisionally laid down by the Peace Conference of December 8, 1919, as the Eastern boundary within which Poland was entitled to establish a Polish administration whereas the Soviet armies shall stand at a distance of 50 kilometres eastwards of that line.

". . . In eastern Galicia both armies shall stand on the line fixed at the date of the signature of the armistice, after which each army shall withdraw 10 kilometres in order to create a neutral zone.

"b. That as soon as possible thereafter a conference sitting under the auspices of the Peace Conference should assemble in London to be attended by representatives of Soviet Russia, Poland, Lithuania, Latvia and Finland, with the object of negotiating a final peace between Russia and its neighboring states; representatives of Eastern Galicia would also be invited to London to state their case for the purpose of this conference.

"c. To the acceptance of the decision of the Supreme Council regarding . . . the settlement of the question of Eastern Galicia . . .

"In the event of Poland's acceptance of the above terms the British Government shall immediately send a similar proposal to Soviet Russia, and should she refuse an armistice the Allies shall give Poland all aid, particularly in war material as far as would be possible in view of their own exhaustion and heavy obligation elsewhere. . . ."

Lloyd George had at once instructed the Foreign Office in London to convey this proposal to the Soviet government. The Foreign Office did so in the form of a note signed by Lord Curzon, the British Secretary of State for Foreign Affairs, and hence the line defined therein became known as the Curzon Line. This proposed:

"a. That an immediate armistice be signed between Poland and Soviet Russia whereby hostilities shall be suspended. The terms of this armistice shall provide on the one hand that the Polish Army shall immediately withdraw to the line provisionally laid down last year by the Peace Conference as the Eastern boundary within which Poland was entitled to establish a Polish Administration. This line runs approximately as follows: Grodno, Vapovka, Nemirov, Brest-Litovsk, Dorogusk, Ustilug, east of Grubeshov, Krilov [the last town north of the Galician border], *and thence west of Rawa Ruska, east of Przemysl to the Carpathians* [my italics].

". . . On the other hand, the armistice should provide that the armies of Soviet Russia should stand at a distance of 50 kilometres to the east of this line. In Eastern Galicia each army will stand on the line which they occupy at the date of the signature of the armistice. . . .

"The British government would be glad of an immediate reply to this telegram, for the Polish government has asked for the intervention of the Allies. . . . Further, while the British government has bound itself to give no assistance to Poland for any purpose hostile to Russia . . . it is also bound under the Covenant of the League of Nations to defend the integrity and independence of Poland *within its legitimate ethnographic frontiers"* [my italics].

The American government was not represented on the Supreme Council and did not have an observer or liaison officer at the Spa Conference. At the time it did not take any open notice of Lord Curzon's note. But on August 21, 1920, when events were going well for Poland, it suggested to the Polish government that it ". . . might well . . . declare its intention to abstain from any aggressions against Russian territorial integrity . . . and that pending a direct agreement as to its Eastern frontier, Poland will remain within the boundary indicated by the Peace Conference" (i.e. the December 8, 1919 line).

There are at least three puzzles about this Curzon note. (1) The Declaration of December 8, 1919 had not carried the line south of Krilov, and that part of its definition which I have italicized corresponds to that laid down in the Statute of Eastern Galicia to mark the division between Poland proper and the mandate for Eastern Galicia. It was this extension of the December 8 line that brought the Curzon Line into dispute. For in effect it awarded Eastern Galicia to Russia, or at least provided a basis which the Russians could and did assert justified their claim. (2) In Eastern Galicia the Curzon note seems to propose that the armies stand at two lines, several hundred miles apart, at the same time. (3) The Declaration of December 8, 1919 stated that ". . . the rights that Poland may be able to establish over the territories to the east of the said line are expressly reserved." But the Curzon note to the Soviet government does not make that clear; and it is hard to tell whether the British government intended the line therein drawn regarded merely as a demarcation line or as an enduring boundary. Some parts of the Curzon note seem to mean the one, and some parts seem to mean the other. It is quite possible that there was some difference of intention between the British and the other Allied governments in this matter.

I must leave these obscure though interesting questions to the specialist or to those who can devote adequate space to them. They were not raised at the time, since the Soviet government rejected the Allied proposal on July 18th. It followed this up by a broadcast to the world, calling British action "hostile mediation." It asked the Poles to appeal to Moscow directly, promising frontiers to the east of those marked out by the imperialists in London and Paris. This was signed by Lenin, Trotsky, and Chicherin, among others. On July 24th Russian troops crossed the Curzon Line and kept on going. But subsequently the tide again turned and the Russians failed to reach Warsaw. The Soviet government was forced to compromise and to agree in the Polish-Soviet Treaty of Riga, signed in March 1921, to the establishment of

Polish frontiers well east of the Curzon Line. But when during World War II the coalition again confronted the task of settling a boundary between Poland and the Soviet Union, Stalin effectively defended his demands by reference to British sponsorship of the line designated in the Curzon note of July 11, 1920.

APPENDIX II

⚜⚜⚜⚜⚜⚜⚜

The Three Who Led

⚜⚜⚜⚜⚜⚜⚜

CORRESPONDENCE BETWEEN THE CHAIRMAN OF THE COUNCIL OF MINISTERS OF THE U.S.S.R. AND THE PRESIDENTS OF THE U.S.A. AND THE PRIME MINISTERS OF GREAT BRITAIN DURING THE GREAT PATRIOTIC WAR OF 1941-1945. Moscow: Foreign Languages Publishing House, 1957, 2 v. in English. (American source for purchases, Chicago Council of American-Soviet Friendship, Inc.)*

NOTE the title of these volumes! Throughout the Western world the recent struggle is known as the "Second World War." But in the Soviet glossary it is called "The Great Patriotic War."

This project of publication was first conceived, I am informed, while Stalin, sender and recipient of these missives, still held sway over the Soviet Union. It was suspended during the period when Khrushchev was repudiating the course and conduct of his predecessor. But when Khrushchev recanted, or found it prudent again to show respect for the memory of Stalin, the decision was made to release this full record of his correspondence with the Presidents of the United States and the Prime Ministers of Great Britain.

In the foreword a reason for doing so is avowed. "Tendentiously selected parts of this correspondence were published outside the Soviet Union at different times resulting in a distorted picture of the Soviet attitude during the war years. This publication is to help restore historical truth." The sponsors of this publication do not explain or particularize their accusation. And the contents do not contain evidence which justifies it. We may rejoice that the Soviet authorities, who have without any scruple rewritten and fabricated history whenever it suited them, have now developed a devotion to "historic truth." But still we may regret that it was left to the Soviet Government to appear to espouse that worthy cause by being the first to present in systematic form the complete collection of the written communications between the three leaders of the great war coalition.

Why did neither the American nor British Governments do so? In search for an answer the historian is compelled to wander among surmises; those who really know are not apt to explain. Except when defending themselves, governments abstain from competition and rivalry in priority in the publication of recent historical records; they usually see no reason for hurry and many reasons for taking their own time. The latter are variable. The

---

* Originally published as an article in the January, 1959 issue of *Foreign Affairs*, "The Three Who Led," by Herbert Feis, is reprinted here, by permission, as an appendix to the 1967 edition of this volume.

archivists of all countries in whose custody such documents as these repose are more comfortable when recent records are locked up in their files than when they are released to roam in this predatory world. They may be criticized (or even lose their promotion or jobs) for permitting some revelation which an influential official or member of a legislature may judge unpatriotic or distasteful. A similar sense of caution constrains Foreign Offices —watchful lest some useful source of information should be stilled thereafter, worried about possibly providing some unfriendly foreign commentator with material that could be used to disadvantage, inclined to regard themselves as the custodian of national security, and mindful of the sensibilities of friendly foreign governments. Even more deeply ingrained is the caution of the military authorities (few more so than the American and British Chiefs of Staff) who resist all entry of outsiders into their records.

But perhaps no less pertinent in explaining this particular occurrence is a substantial professional reason. The historical sections of the American and British Governments who are responsible for the editing and publication of volumes of public documents appreciate that no collection of correspondence such as this can, *by itself*, convey an adequate or reliable version of the events and policies discussed. Important as the messages exchanged between heads of governments in wartime may have been in shaping the decisions and influencing relations of their countries, even these do not stand *by themselves* as historical records. For balanced knowledge of what was done and why, there is need to know much more; to have in hand at the same time the notes and documents which were the sills on which the top-level correspondence rested, the internal records of the decision-makers in each of the several governments, the memos of talks between diplomatic and military representatives and the messages exchanged between lesser government officials. All these crossbeams and uprights are properly deemed essential by the students of documents to arrive at a balanced knowledge of the structure of historical truth, and for critical judgment. This professional conception has determined the ordinary pattern and schedule of publication of the American and British diplomatic correspondence.

Historians are trained to defer to the expectation that historical realities are to be known in their fullness only long after they were current actualities. But in this instance I do not think it would have been imprudent, and it would have been more pleasing, had the first issuance of these documents borne an American or British imprint.

Taken by and in themselves, the volumes are reputable as a source. The collection is complete except for a few items of minor interest. There has been no tampering with the text nor any other sort of deformation of the originals. Nor, I have been informed, are there any distortions in translation of those which were written in the Russian language.

The Soviet authorities have not found it necessary to chaperon the correspondence by interpretive commentary. The footnotes which are clustered in the rear of each volume are short, factual and pertinent; they aid in identifying events, places, dates or persons referred to in the published messages. The treatment of the record, as well as the natural use of the English language displayed in the foreword and in the footnotes, suggests that the publication may have been edited or supervised by a person or persons trained in American or British universities or in their governmental departments. Could it be that a Burgess or MacLean lent his talents to the task?

II

How much do these volumes add to what is known by historians and informed officials of the West? Of important information, little—just some interesting filaments of detail about turns of relationship within the coalition and some elucidation of the causes of the growth of mutual dissatisfaction. Their character and range can be indicated by a few selections.

There is confirmation in one of the earlier messages from Stalin to Churchill (July 18, 1941) that despite the well-authenticated warnings which both the American and British Governments had passed on to him long before the event, Stalin did not believe that Hitler was going to turn against the Soviet Union.

It may not be out of place [he wrote the Prime Minister a month after the assault began] to inform you that the position of the Soviet troops at the front remains strained. The results of Hitler's *unexpected* violation of the Non-Aggression Pact and the *sudden* attack on the Soviet Union, which have placed the German troops at an advantage, are still affecting the position of the Soviet armies.

The two words which I have italicized sustain the surmise that the reason the Soviet authorities did not defend their frontier regions effectively was not because of deliberate policy of strategic retreat but because they had failed in necessary preparations.

Another of the newly published messages similarly aids understanding of a British error in judgment—the ready acquiescence of Churchill and his colleagues in the summer and autumn of 1944 in the location of the boundary between the zones of occupation in Germany allocated to the Soviet Union and those assigned to the West. The accepted line runs well west of Berlin and of the areas reached by the American and British forces before the war ended, and later the Prime Minister sought intently to alter it. His comments on the progress of combat, such as those in the message sent to Stalin on July 1, 1944, clearly evidence that at this time the Prime Minister's unalloyed desire was to have the Red army continue to crush the German armies everywhere, and his anticipation that they would reach Berlin before the Western armies. He wrote:

This is the moment for me to tell you how immensely we are all here impressed with the magnificent advances of the Russian armies which seem, as they grow in momentum, to be pulverising the German armies which stand between you and Warsaw, and afterwards Berlin. Every victory that you gain is watched with eager attention here.

By then the cross-Channel invasion was well under way. But Stalin had shown himself equally eager the summer before to have the Western Allies land in France and fight their way eastward into Germany as far as possible. This is vividly shown by the reproaches and rejoinders that passed between Stalin, Churchill and Roosevelt during that summer before the final decision to venture on the postponed cross-Channel invasion. In these volumes there is printed for the first time the texts of the aggrieved messages which Stalin sent to Churchill and Roosevelt. The full force of them can be suggested by extracts from one sent from Moscow on June 24, 1943. After reciting his version of what had gone before, Stalin went on to say:

> It follows that the conditions for opening a second front in Western Europe during 1943, far from deteriorating, have, indeed, greatly improved.
> That being so, the Soviet Government could not have imagined that the British and U.S. Governments would revise the decision to invade Western Europe, which they had adopted early this year. In fact, the Soviet Government was fully entitled to expect that the Anglo-American decision would be carried out, that appropriate preparations were under way and that the second front in Western Europe would at last be opened in 1943 . . . .
> I shall not enlarge on the fact that this responsible decision, revoking your previous decisions on the invasion of Western Europe, was reached by you and the President without Soviet participation and without inviting its representatives to the Washington conference, although you cannot but be aware that the Soviet Union's role in the war against Germany and its interest in the problems of the second front are great enough.
> There is no need to say that the Soviet Government cannot become reconciled to this disregard of vital Soviet interests in the war against the common enemy . . . .
> I must tell you that the point here is not just the disappointment of the Soviet Government, but the preservation of its confidence in the Allies, a confidence which is being subjected to severe stress.

It was left to Churchill to correct Stalin's review of the record and repel his unjust assertions. Roosevelt did not pursue the argument. Perhaps he was mindful of the Washington press release which he had authorized after his talks with Molotov in the spring of 1942—a public statement that had the surface of a promise—or perhaps just because he saw nothing to be gained by doing so. The nature of Churchill's indignant, but restrained, response is conveyed in the answer that he sent to Stalin on June 27, 1943:

> I am sorry to receive your message of the 24th. At every stage the information I have given you as to our future intentions has been based upon recorded advice of the British and American Staffs, and I have at all times been sincere in my relations with you. Although until June 22nd, 1941, we British were left alone to face the worst that Nazi Germany could do to us, I instantly began aiding Soviet Russia to the best of our limited means from the moment that she was herself attacked by Hitler. I am satisfied that I have done everything in human power to help you. Therefore the reproaches which you now cast upon your Western Allies leave me unmoved . . . .

Thus not only on the one hand have the difficulties of a cross-Channel attack continually seemed greater to us and the resources have not been forthcoming, but a more hopeful and fruitful policy has been opened to us in another theatre, and we have the right and duty to act in accordance with our convictions informing you at every stage of the changes in our views imposed by the vast movement of the war.

What, now that we have the complete survey of arguments back and forth, can be said about this generating cause of friction? The assurances given Stalin that the Western Allies were going to attempt some sort of cross-Channel operation in 1942 were vague and conditioned on further measurement of available means, probable results and competing combat demands and opportunities. But he was given more reason for believing that the operation would be launched in 1943, though still only provisional warrant for this anticipation. It was made easy for him to mistake expressions of desire and intent for promises or military forecasts. However, he was experienced and wise enough not to have done so. His protests no doubt expressed genuine disappointment; but it is probable that they were also inspired by the thought that by putting the Western Allies in the wrong the Soviet Union might gain advantage, somewhere at some time. Certainly Stalin was willfully unfair in his efforts to get the responsible British and American authorities to disregard or underestimate the difficulties, obstacles and risks that properly had to be taken into account. And he was also unfair in failing to accord due recognition to the efforts which the Western Allies were devoting to other operations against the Axis during the time which they judged themselves unready and unable wisely to attempt the cross-Channel operation. He did not recognize the heroic battle to retain the use of the sea lanes to Europe; the compressing campaigns which resulted in securing control of the whole of North Africa, gradually bringing France back as a competent ally and driving Italy out of the war; the crescending air assault on Germany; and, above all, the vast grappling and bloody struggles in which American forces confined Japan in the Pacific.

Stalin during this same period did not feel called upon to justify to his allies the Soviet decision to be neutral in the war against Japan; his own view of Soviet capabilities and tasks seemed enough. Just so, Western commentators will not, now that they have the fuller record, find reasons in it for inferring that Great Britain and the United States allowed their Soviet ally to bear more than its necessary share of the agony of the war either by intention or because of their heedless preference for other and more manageable operations.

The Russians, by entering into the Ribbentrop-Molotov Pact, had unleashed the Germans towards the West. But when, despite the grovelling Soviet efforts to mollify Hitler, the Panzers turned toward the East, the Russians demanded as a matter of right that the Allies ward them off, no matter what the consequences. What fools we and the British would have been to venture on the cross-Channel invasion until the military chances were acceptable!

<h1 style="text-align:center">III</h1>

Let me turn from these selections which concern military matters to those which add to our knowledge of the perplexing questions of what happened to an interesting political proposal made by Stalin. During the summer and autumn of 1943 he became aggrieved and aroused because he believed that the American-British combination was denying the Soviet Union a merited right to be fully informed about the policies being pursued in North Africa and Italy, and the chance to share in determining them. Thus, in connection with his complaints over the way in which negotiations for Italian surrender had been conducted, he informed Roosevelt and Churchill that he thought

> the time is ripe for us to set up a military-political commission of representatives of the three countries—the U.S.A., Great Britain and the U.S.S.R.—for consideration of problems related to negotiations with various Governments falling away from Germany . . . . I propose setting up the commission and making Sicily its seat for the time being.

Neither the President nor the Prime Minister repelled the proposal; rather the contrary. But the President stayed on guard. In contrast to his (and Secretary Hull's) later support for the principle that the policies pursued toward and in the defeated Allies of Germany should be determined jointly, at this juncture he preferred to retain flexibility. The purposeful interest which the Soviet Government and the French Communists had shown in North Africa had troubled him. And now Eisenhower and the American and British commanders under him who were fighting the campaign in Italy were worried about possible Soviet interference in their operations and policies. So Roosevelt tried to sheer away from immediate decision by proposing instead that the Soviet Government send an officer to Eisenhower's headquarters to join in the discussion of a settlement with the Italians.

The Prime Minister was no more ready than the President to grant the Soviet Government a veto right over the conduct of operations or the direction of political or social affairs in Italy. But he assented to Stalin's proposal—if it could be made to mean what he thought it ought to mean. It would have been understood, he explained in his response to Stalin, that the commission would not have the power to make final decisions; that would remain with the governments. It would have to be agreed that the commission would not interfere with the military functions of the Allied Commander-in-Chief. It would seem advisable that the commission should, in the first instance, handle the Italian question only; and when other cases arose, experience would have shown whether this or some other organ would be the best medium for arriving at joint views and plans.

Here the further trail of discussion of this consequential proposal cannot be followed through the rather dense forest of diplomatic foliage. But messages in this collection make it easier to follow it up to the Conference of Foreign Ministers (Hull, Eden, Molotov) in Moscow in October; for the terminal stage, however, the student will have to consult records of that Conference and the correspondence about the Advisory Commission for Italy.

In the outcome the President and the Prime Minister had their way. The commission that was constituted was authorized only to advise, not to determine, what was done in, for and to Italy. And later on, Stalin was wont to defend his refusal to accord the Western Allies an effective voice in the control of Bulgaria, Hungary and Rumania on the score that similar Soviet claims in regard to Italy had been rejected. When another commission was later established in London (the European Advisory Commission) to consider policies to be adopted for surrender and control of Germany's other satellites, it also was authorized only to propose, not to dispose. Through it the procedure for joint consultation was regularized; and by it many of the main accords regarding treatment of the Axis members were developed. But fortunes of war, relative military power, national and political purposes and geography—rather than principle—determined the measure of influence exercised by each of the three main Allies in each separate situation. Roosevelt and Hull never reconciled themselves to the rule of such realities. Churchill however did so. A year later he entered into an understanding with Stalin about the measure of their respective influence or "responsibilities" in the smaller countries of Eastern and Central Europe except Poland.

It is, then, for providing more or less new information about such matters that these volumes will be valued by the historian. But the interest of others will circle rather about the general impressions of the nature and views of the three correspondents which linger in their lines.

IV

Of the literary style and mode of expression of the signatories of these messages, those who lived through the period will find only familiar repetitions. Even the most routine of those sent off by Churchill were zestful, fluid and sparkling with the dew of his personality. Those bearing the name of Roosevelt were usually flat and friendly—the phraseology being the standard usage of diplomacy when the original draft was prepared in the State Department, stiffly lucid when it was produced in the Pentagon. Those of Stalin are dun-colored, purposeful, not wasteful of a word; even those conveying congratulations read as though they were taken out of a manual used by the authors of greeting cards.

Roosevelt and Churchill often expounded the aspirations and principles of democracy. Stalin rarely made similar attempts to secure approval of Marxist-Leninist doctrine.

All three men deeply felt that they and the nations for whom they spoke were engaged in a noble struggle against evil and base cruelty; none had twinges of doubt that the agony of the war was well endured for the sake of preserving a conception of decency in human life and affairs.

This vital sense of good purpose ought not to be erased from memory by later regrets, in the way that some old frescos done by great Renaissance artists were covered over in duller times by duller tones.

Despite this common bond of detestation of the enemy, the only period when Stalin and his associates might have been induced to curb their aggressive temper and circumscribe their aims out of deference for their allies was in 1941-42, when the Soviet Union was in dire need of Western support and coöperation. Then, greatly suffering, on the verge of being forced to yield, the Soviet Government might have restrained its desire to extend its control far beyond its boundaries. Did not Stalin urge Churchill in 1941 to come with all available force into the Balkans? And did he not tell Sikorski that he would be content with only small changes in the Soviet-Polish boundaries as they had been before Germany and the Soviet Union had divided Poland between them? But after the Soviet rulers became reassured of their power to survive the German assault, and as the paths for expansion became cleared, diplomacy, no matter how skilled, could not, I believe, have induced them to restrain themselves. Their later course shows the revival of their determination to regain everything they had obtained as a result of their deal with Hitler; and to strive to get those further extensions to which Hitler had refused assent, such as the establishment of military bases within range of the Dardanelles. The change in the expectations of Stalin and his associates of what they could secure by the exercise of Soviet power is reflected in the change in tone of Stalin's messages—from amiability—to reserve—to bluntness—to bold rudeness.

The flow of these communications confirms the opinion that after the American Government had sent combat forces to Europe it could not, unless it had reached a definite understanding with the Soviet Union about war aims, have exercised a determining influence upon the course of most postwar developments in Europe. But it supports the belief that it might have done so in the Far East. For in that region we had by far the strongest and most flexible military force, and the conformation of the war in the Pacific enabled us to have our way in matters both of strategy and diplomacy. But we wasted our opportunity—most of all by clinging to the formula of unconditional surrender for Japan, and by publicly proclaiming our intent not only to expel Japan from the mainland of Asia but also to deprive it of all the rest of its empire, before we could know whether China and Russia would be permanent friends. If Roosevelt and Hopkins had had a more real and correct understanding of Stalin's nature and techniques, and if Marshall, MacArthur and Stimson had not attached undue importance to Soviet participation in the Pacific war, the whole scene in that region might be far more satisfactory today.

Now with our retrospective knowledge and chance to reëxamine the whole past, the prevailing American optimism regarding the possibility of dealing with Stalin on friendly and frank terms in a spirit of good faith and in a belief in his moderation is amazing. How did Roosevelt, how did most of the American nation, fail to grasp, or ignore, or overlook the traits which had enabled Stalin to get and hold supreme power in the Soviet Union? Among the variety of explanations that have been attempted for this fault of judgment, I believe one is of more importance than is usually recognized: it was that our perceptions were blurred by the more intense glare of Hitler's evil light. But considering again in our own day the inner history of Stalin's career, as known to many Bolshevik associates whom he mastered, how clearly the dominant traits appear: opportunist, sly, malevolent, persistent, most skilled in the graduation of pressures, ablest of all dissemblers, a person about whose every statement his familiars were apt to ask: what skein is he going to wind around that bobbin?

Churchill, of course, had a more caustic feeling about the nature of the Soviet régime and a more real grasp of the nature of the men who controlled it. But he failed to bring about a correction in the American view. This was partly his fault—partly ours. Roosevelt and those who shared his feelings and purposes were determined not to allow their hopeful belief in the possibility of coöperation with the Soviet Union to be destroyed; for unless this could be made to come true, they foresaw only grim disorder in the world. This devotion to a great political purpose inclined them to attribute prejudiced and nationally selfish motives to the advice of the British Prime Minister when he advocated bolder resistance to Soviet claims or actions. But Churchill's effectiveness in persuasion may also have been reduced by American memory of the effort he had made after the 1917 Revolution to bring about intervention in Soviet affairs, an effort which for many years had deterred any tendency toward reconciliation between the West and the Soviet Union; the Americans were afraid of being led into a repetition of this failure. Then also his reactions to Soviet actions and to Stalin's personality were deemed at times intemperate. They fluctuated over a wide arc of feeling and judgment. His rejoicing over Soviet military achievements inspired messages to Stalin of unqualified admiration. His satisfaction when some quarrel was adjusted found expression in messages which seem brimful of trust. But many more were devoted to contesting some Soviet action or tensely conveying his fears and criticisms.

As for Stalin, he was always measuring Roosevelt and Churchill. He never became so absorbed in his relations with them as to be distracted from essential Soviet purposes. He remains on every one of these pages a member of the Politburo.

It is permissible to imagine that these volumes might be reissued, say 25 years from now, under another title, "The Correspondence of the Three Men Who Presided over the Great Upheaval." By then, while the details of the correspondence will have diminished in interest, the significance of the events to which they relate will have grown. During this war period the dissolution of the British and French empires was hastened, the way was opened for the vast expansion of the realm of Communist control and power, the energy within the atom was released for weapons of destruction and for tasks of production; and the nations sought with a moving sense of longing to create a new and livable basis of association with each other in the United Nations. It is becoming that the mind should indulge in the prayerful hope that in that later time the upheaval will have subsided into a reliable state of stability.

Index

INDEX

Cetnik bands in Yugoslavia, 201–203, 332
Chamberlain, Neville, British Prime Minister, 4, 239; speech on Polish independence, 29
Charles, Sir Noel, British diplomat ("Direct representative to Italian government"), 328
Chennault, Claire L., U.S. Air Force General in China, 248
Cherbourg, 50, 262n.
Cherwell, Lord, Adviser to Churchill, 370
Chiang Kai-shek, Chinese Generalissimo, 151, 401; requests of, 45; and decisions at Casablanca Conference about, 107; projected meeting with Roosevelt, 242, 243; and Cairo meeting, 245–252, 256; and Cairo Declaration, 251, 252, 252n., 253; and decisions at Second Quebec Conference about, 397; and General Stilwell, 246, 397–398; and Stalin's view of his leadership, 407; and Chinese Communists, 253, 398, 407, 408, 507–508, 510; and Vice-President Wallace, 408, 508; and Chou En-lai, 507; and question of informing him of secret Yalta agreement, 512, 514, 515, 515n., 641; concurrence in Yalta secret treaty, 638; and Sino-Soviet accord foreshadowed at Yalta, 508
Chicago Tribune, Dec. 4, 1941, Text of ABC-1, 25
China, under National government (Kuomintang), 506–509, 641; and military plans for, 124, 129, 151, 186; Eden and Roosevelt's talks on (March 1943), 121, 124; and Four-Nation Declaration, 210–212, 253; economic conditions in, 247, 506; and Cairo Declaration, 251, 252, 253, 505; and Teheran Conference, 256–257, 270; as one of the "Four Policemen," 253; and Second Quebec Conference, 387–401; versus Communist government, 253, 398, 407–409, 506–508; place on Security Council of U.N., 431; and Dumbarton Oaks Conference, 436; discussed at Malta, 495–496; discussed at Yalta, 506–509, 515–516; and Sino-Soviet Treaty foreshadowed at Yalta, 508, 516
China-Burma-India Theater, 45, 246, 248, 495
China-India air route (the Hump), 39, 151, 251, 397, 401; air bases in, 151; military prospects reviewed at Malta about, 495–496
Chou En-lai, Chinese Communist leader, 507
Chunking, 397, 495, 507, 508
Churchill, Randolph, 266, 333
Churchill, Sarah, 497
Churchill, Winston Spencer, Prime Minister of Great Britain, and prospective Nazi assaults on Soviet Union, 6; and British

aid for Soviet Union, 7–8; and answer to first Soviet demand for Second Front, 8–9; and proposal to send supply mission to Moscow, 14; and repulse of Soviet complaints about aid received, 15–16; and composition of Atlantic Charter at Argentia Bay, 20–22; and first Eden visit to Moscow (Dec., 1941), 24–26; and Soviet effort to secure satisfaction of territorial desires in connection with Anglo-Soviet Treaty, 26–28; and discussion with Roosevelt on strategy (Washington, end of 1941), 47–48; first message to War Cabinet about North African operation, 47–48; and question of cross-Channel invasion or North Africa in 1942, 48–50, 52, 57; and remarks to Molotov about Second Front, 51–52, 64; and renewed Soviet demands for satisfaction about frontiers (Mar.–May, 1942), 58–64; decision (July, 1942) to go to see Stalin, 72–73; talks with Stalin in Moscow (Aug., 1942), 74–78; and explanation of TORCH to Stalin, 75–76, and what he may have said to Stalin about cross-Channel invasion in 1943, 94n.; and offer of British and American aid for Caucasus, front, 81–82, 84–85; and termination of plans for Caucasus, 97; and suspension of Northern convoys (1942), 82–84, 85, 86, 87; and perplexity over Soviet attitude (Autumn, 1942), 86; and development of trans-Iranian route, 87–88; comments on El Alamein, 90; and deal with Darlan, 90; and anticipation of what might follow TORCH, 93–94; and indecision about cross-Channel invasion (Dec., 1942) 94n., and ideas about Mediterranean operations after TORCH, 96, 97; and invitation to Stalin to meet at Casablanca, 99–101; and wish to have Eden at Casablanca, 101; and plans for Mediterranean advance at Casablanca Conference, 106; and "unconditional surrender" policy at Casablanca, 110–111; and interpretation of unconditional surrender after Casablanca, 113; reports to Stalin and Chiang Kai-shek on Casablanca decisions, 114; explanation to Stalin of delay in North African operations, 115; continued resistance to Stalin's pressure for Second Front after Casablanca, 116–117; and second suspension of Northern convoys, 118; and idea of joint U.S.-British bases after the war, 125; and visit to Washington (May, 1943 TRIDENT), 126; and plans for operations in Mediterranean (May, 1943), 126–127; approval of strategic plans made at TRIDENT, 128–129; and plans for Mediterranean after TRIDENT, 129: trip with Marshall to confer with

Churchill, Winston Spencer (*continued*)
Eisenhower about Mediterranean plan, 130–131; message to Stalin on TRIDENT decisions, 134; harsh argument with Stalin about postponement of Second Front (June, 1943), 134; attitude toward de Gaulle, Spring, 1943, 137–140, 142; message to Stalin about de Gaulle's pretensions (June, 1943), 142; and further ideas about Italian campaign, 149; discussion with Stimson about strategic issues (July, 1943), 149–150; and strategic issues at QUADRANT Conference (Aug, 1943), 148–149; message to Stalin about QUADRANT decisions, 151; and ideas about further action in Mediterranean, 152–153; and formulation of terms for Italian surrender, 153, 154, 156, 157, 158, 159, 178–179; question of Italian King and Badoglio government, 157–158, 181–182; and announcement of Italian surrender, 165; and resentment of Stalin's complaints about Italian surrender arrangements, 172, 173; and ideas about Mediterranean operations after Italian surrender, 177; and Roosevelt directive to Eisenhower about presentation of armistice terms for Italy (Sept., 1943), 178–179; acceptance of Italy as co-belligerent, 182; and arrangements for control of Italy, 183–184; and efforts to prevent rupture between Polish government-in-exile and Soviet government, 193; and support for Yugoslav guerrillas, 202–203; and early attempts to bring order and unity to Greece, 205; instruction to Eden on military matters (Oct., 1943), 225; and effort to bring Turkey into the war, 228–231; further argument with Stalin over suspension of Northern convoys, 231–233; and praise of results of Foreign Ministers' Conference, 238; assent to going to Teheran, 241–242; dissatisfaction over plan to meet Chiang Kai-shek, 244–245; discussion with Chinese at First Cairo Conference about Far Eastern military matters, 246–248; and argument with Roosevelt about amphibious operations south of Burma, 251–253; discussion with Stalin at Teheran about Soviet desires in Far East, 254–256; and discussions at Teheran about strategy for Europe, 258–265; decision at Teheran for cross-Channel invasion in May, 1944, 263–265; and proposal at Teheran to invade Southern France, 263–265; and discussion at Teheran of Turkish entry into the war, 265–266; and declaration regarding Iran, 267–268; and discussion at Teheran of exit of Finland from the war, 268–269; and expression of ideas at Teheran on

European territorial settlements, 272; and discussion at Teheran about treatment of Germany, 272–275; and discussion at Teheran about partition of Germany, 274–275; and relations with two other Heads of State at Teheran, 276; and sense of achievement at Teheran, 276–278; and appeals for support (before Teheran) of Polish government-in-exile, 283; and discussion at Teheran about Polish frontiers and political questions, 284–287; attempts (after Teheran) to persuade Polish government-in-exile to accept Stalin's terms, 287–291, 292–295; attempt to get Stalin to be more conciliatory about Poland (Feb., 1944), 297–298; desperation over failure to adjust Soviet-Polish quarrel, 298–301; and renewed advocacy for extension of operations in Italy (Anzio), 302–303, 305–306; and rebuff by President Inonu of Turkey, 204; and opposition to ANVIL, 305, 315; confirmation (April, 1944) to Stalin of intention to carry out cross-Channel operation, 309; enthusiasm about OVERLORD, 309–310; and relations before and after OVERLORD with de Gaulle and French National Committee of Liberation, 313–322; and further argument about King of Italy and reform of Badoglio government (early 1944), 329–331; and attempts to bring unity for Yugoslavia (early 1944), 322–334; and initiative in situation in Greece, (early 1944), 334–336; and idea of dividing responsibility for control of smaller countries in Central and Eastern Europe (Spring, 1944), 339–343; and renewed opposition to ANVIL, 344–346, 348; advocacy of crossing to Istria and through Ljubljana Gap, 244–246; and proposals to Tito regarding administration of Northern Italy and Istrian regions, 347; views on interpretation of unconditional surrender policy toward Germany and German satellites, (Dec., 1943 to May 1944), 350–354, 355, (Sept., 1944 to Feb., 1945), 356–357, statement at Yalta about, 357–358; and proposals for treatment of Germany approved at Second Quebec Conference (Sept., 1944), 356; and British proposals for zonal divisions of Germany, 360–364; agreement with Roosevelt at Second Quebec Conference to effectuate Morganthau plan for treatment of Germany, 266–371; retreat from Morganthau plan, 371–373; attempt to sustain Polish government-in-exile (July, 1944), 376–377; advice to Mikolajczyk to go to see Stalin, 377; attempt to aid Polish uprising in Warsaw, (Aug.–Oct., 1944), 378–390; and arrangement for meeting with Roose-

Churchill, Winston Spencer (*continued*)
velt, Second Quebec Conference (Sept., 1944), 393–394; decision to press on with all priority on the Western Front (Sept., 1944), 399–400; and approval (at Second Quebec Conference, Sept., 1944) of plan to invade Japan, 400–401; and approval (at Second Quebec Conference · Sept., 1944) for next operation in the Pacific and Burma, 401; message to Stalin on decisions made at Quebec Conference, 401–402; and further attempt (June–Oct., 1944) to secure unity in Yugoslavia, 421–424; and further initiatives in Greek affairs (July–Sept., 1944), 424–425; agreement with Roosevelt about developments in Italian policy, 425–426; view of results of Dumbarton Oaks Conference, 437; and arrangement to visit Moscow (Sept.–Oct., 1944), 441–443; wish to have Harriman accompany him to Moscow, 442–443; and exchange of military information with Stalin during Moscow meeting, 444–447; and plans and prospects for operations in the Mediterranean and Adriatic areas, 445–446; agreement with Stalin for division of spheres of responsibility for Southeastern Europe (Oct., 1944), 447–451; and agreement with Stalin to invite Mikolajczyk to Moscow again, 453; and discussions with Mikolajczyk, Polish Committee of National Liberation and Stalin (Moscow, 1944), 454–459; talks with Stalin about Soviet entry into Pacific war (Oct., 1944), 460–462; informed by Stalin about Soviet political conditions for entering Pacific war (Oct., 1944), 465–466; estimate of outcome of talks with Stalin, 468–469; surge of anxiety over trends of Soviet policy (Jan., 1945), 468; and recognition of French Committee of National Liberation as provisional government of France, 469–471; on prospect of American troops staying in Europe after German defeat, 472; visit to Paris on Armistice Day, 1944, 472; messages to Roosevelt and Stalin about Franco-Soviet Pact, 474–475; asks Stalin to discuss military coordination with representative of Allied headquarters in the West (Dec., 1944), 480–481; asks Stalin urgently for information about major offensive (Jan., 1945), 481; uneasiness over delay in another meeting of three Heads of State, 487; and discussions preceding meeting of Heads of State at Malta and Yalta, 489–491; impression of Roosevelt's appearance on arrival at Yalta, 497; and agreement at Yalta for coordination of Eastern and Western offensives, 499–500; and arrangements for consultation between military staffs, 500–

501; reaffirmation at Yalta of plan to invade Japan, 502–503; reaffirmation at Yalta of wish to have Soviet Union in the Pacific war, 502–503; and secret accord at Yalta about Soviet desires in the Far East, 515–516; statement to Mikolajczyk of views on Polish issues before Yalta, 518–519; and Mikolajczyk's resignation, 520; discussion with Stalin and Roosevelt at Yalta about Polish issues —especially frontiers and future government, 521–529; and discussion at Yalta on German zone of occupation for France, 531–532; and discussions at Yalta on German economic treatment and reparations, 533–538; and discussion at Yalta on partition of Germany, 538–539; and initiative in Greek affairs before and after Yalta, 541–543; and initiative in affairs of Yugoslavia at Yalta, 543–545; and discussion of UNO at Yalta, 550–556; and American proposals at Yalta on UNO voting procedure, 553–554; and Soviet wish for multiple membership in UNO at Yalta, 554–555; on questions of trusteeship at Yalta, 555–556; and end of Yalta Conference, 557–558; and anxiety after Yalta about extension of Soviet control, 563–564, 565; and efforts to get satisfactory execution of Yalta agreement on Poland, 573, 574–579; correspondence with Stalin about negotiations for surrender of German forces in Italy, 592–596; and wish to maintain firm stand against Soviet Union, Spring, 1945, 600–601; and dissatisfaction (Mar.–Apr., 1945) over Stalin-Eisenhower correspondence about plans for final assaults on Germany and junction between Western and Red armies, 603–606; and wish to have U.S.-British armies continue advances in Germany, Czechoslovakia and Austria (Apr., 1945), 609–610; message to Stalin about Himmler's offer to surrender in West, 613–614; and agreement with Truman to reject Himmlers offer, 613–614; and wish (May, 1945) for Western forces to remain in place pending settlement with Soviet Union, 616, 633–638; and renunciation of idea of partitioning Germany, 619; and anxiety (Apr.–May, 1945) over Soviet policy toward Austria and Vienna, 625–626; and clash with Tito over Venezia Guilia (Apr.–May, 1945), 628–632; and famous "Iron Curtain" message (May 12, 1945), 636; and termination of Lend-Lease aid, 648; and sense of necessity (May, 1945) for meeting with Stalin and Truman (the Potsdam Conference), 648–649; and visit of Davies (May, 1945), 650–653

Ciechanowski, Jan, Polish Ambassador to the United States, 33n.

Clark, Mark, U.S. General in Italy, 303, 345, 444

Clark-Kerr, Archibald, British Ambassador to USSR, 71, 169, 170, 171, 173, 244, 253, 405, 413–417, 418, 421, 425, 429, 547–548, 584, 588, 589, 632n.; and Polish questions, 290, 292–298, 384, 385, 386, 454, 572–574; and service on commission for Poland, 529

Clay, Lucius D., U.S. General, later Commander-in-Chief of American zone in Germany, 365n.

Clayton, William L., Assistant Secretary of State, and aid for Soviet reconstruction, 646

Clemenceau, Georges, Prime Minister of France, World War I, 522–523

Colville, John Rupert, Private secretary to Churchill, 7

Combined (U.S.-British) Chiefs of Staff, directive on TORCH prepared by, 90; report at TRIDENT of, 128–129; strategic decisions at QUADRANT of, 150; and Italian surrender terms, 151, 158, 162, 163, 168, 186, 187; and Turkey's entry into the war, 229, and Teheran Conference, 264–265; and Cairo Conference, 244, 250n., 251; and postponement of ANVIL, 306; ANVIL revived as DRAGOON by, 344, 348; new directive for Italian campaign by, 306–307; directive for OVERLORD given by, 309; and military coordination with Soviet Union, 313; and de Gaulle, 319–320, 477; and German surrender terms, 356, 357, 358; and German zones of occupation, 365; and Second Quebec Conference, 365, 398, 399, 400, 425; and plan to invade Japan, 400–401, 405; and military strategy on Western Front, 446, 480, 484–485, at Malta and Yalta, 486, 491–496, 498, Spring of 1945, 493, 601–612; and information on Soviet operations, 501–505; and Mediterranean fronts at Malta and Yalta, 494–495; and Far Eastern theaters of war at Malta and Yalta, 495–496; and Eisenhower's liaison with Soviet military authorities, 500–501; views on invasion of Japan, at Yalta, 502–503, 502n.; and surrender of Germany, 612–615; and Venezia Giulia, 628–631; and drawing back of armies on Western front, 634

Committee on Dismemberment of Germany, see European Advisory Committee

Committee for National Liberation, see French Committee for National Liberation

Communist International Organization (Comintern), dissolution of, 133

Connally Resolution, 238, 428n.

Connolly, Donald H., American Army engineer, and trans-Iranian Railway, 88

Control Commission for Italy, see Italy, Control Commission for

Control Council for Germany, see Germany, Control Council for

Convoys, northern route for, 64, 72, 80, 82–84; temporary suspension during preparation for TORCH of, 72, 82, 86, 87; Stalin's response to suspension of, 86; second suspension of, 118–119, 232; resumption of, 231–233

Corsica, 150, 316, 345

COSSAC (Combined Command and Planning Organization in London) set up by Casablanca Conference, 106; work of, 129

Cotentin Peninsula, Landing on D-Day on, 304n., 305n.

Council of National Unity, Polish, 297

Cripps, Sir Stafford, British Ambassador to Soviet Union, 7, 8

Croce, Benedetto, Italian historian and statesman, 331

Cross-Channel invasion, 41–44, 43n., 47–52, 54–57, 64–68, 69–72, 79, 81, 83, 134–135, 223–230; discussed at Casablanca, 105–106; after Casablanca, 114–117; discussed at TRIDENT, 127–129; after Sicily, planned at QUADRANT, 147–151, 173; delay in, 56–57, 72, 74; decision at Teheran to start, 259–264, effected, 307, 309, 319

Crowley, Leo T., U.S. Foreign Economic Administrator, 646

Cunningham, Sir Andrew, British Admiral, 130

Curzon Line, 26, 31, 31n., 122, 285, 286, 286n., 287, 293n., 294, 300, 374, 379, 382, 454, 455, 456, 457, 458, 458n., 460n., 522, 522n., 523, 525; origin and history of 26n., see Appendix, 657–660

Czechoslovakia, 123, 197, 262; government-in-exile in London of, 197, 199; Soviet-Czech Treaty signed, 200, 290; supplement to Treaty signed, May 8, 1944, 290n.; new government formed, 1945, 569–570; end of American advance in, 611; question of Soviet domination in, 569–570; and withdrawal of Western armies in, 363n., 635–636

Czech-Soviet Treaty, see Soviet-Czech Treaty

Dairen (see also Manchurian ports), 255, 510; Soviet rights in, discussed at Yalta, 512, 513

D'Ajeta, Marchese, Italian Counsellor of Legation, 160

Dakar, 91, 121, 139, 271, 317

Damaskinos, Archbishop of Athens, 334; becomes Regent and installed, 542

Danzig, 283, 455–456, 484, 523, 523n., 561, 579

Darlan, Jean Françoise, French (Vichy) Admiral and Vice-Premier Vichy government, deal with, 90–92; Roosevelt's statement on, 90, 91; Stalin's approval of deal with, 92; assassination of, 92; reference to deal with, 110, 141, 319

Davies, Joseph E., Former U.S. Ambassador in Moscow, 600; mission to Moscow (May, 1943) to arrange for a Roosevelt-Stalin meeting, 131–134; and mission to London (May, 1945) to see Churchill, 650–652, 653n., 654

Davis, Norman, former U.S. Ambassador-at-Large, Chairman Subcommittee on Security Problems, 108–109, 121

D-Day (Normandy invasion) June 6, 1944, Landing on Cotentin Peninsula, 305n., 306, 309

Deane, John R., General, Head of U.S. Military Mission in Moscow, 224–227, 258n., 312, 404–406, 443–444, 447, 460, 462, 463, 465, 466, 479, 482–483, 509, 584–585, 587, 598n., 599n., 605, 638

Debrecen, 452; Hungarian Provisional government established at, 547

Declaration of United Nations, see United Nations, Declaration of

Declaration on Liberated Europe, conception at Moscow Conference of, 214, discussed at Yalta, 549–550; discussed after Yalta, 565, 624

Declaration regarding Italy, at Moscow Conference of Foreign Ministers (Oct. 1943), 187–188

Declaration regarding Non-Self-Governing Territories, 215n.

de Gaulle, Charles, General, Head of the Fighting French, plans, claims and responses thereto, 92, 136–140, 215, 315; at Casablanca, 110; and Soviet Union, 140–142, 315; and the invading armies of France, 313, 319; not asked to confer on Italian armistice, 315; and Roosevelt, 316, 317, 321; and Churchill, 314, 319–320, 472–473; and French Communists, 314, 315, 317; and OVERLORD, 319; asked by Churchill and Roosevelt to come to London before D-Day, 319–320; and broadcast on D-Day, 321; and address to Consultative Assembly at Algiers, 321–322; triumphal entry into Paris (Aug. 25) of, 322; becomes head of Provisional Government, 469–471; visit to Moscow (Dec., 1944), 473–477; negotiation of Franco-Soviet Pact, 473–476; refuses recognition of Lublin government, 475–476; wish to attend Yalta Conference, 477, 532; accorded occupation zone in Germany, 532

Dependent peoples, Treatment of, 125; proposed declaration on, 214–215

Devers, Jacob L., U.S. General, 485, 603, 611

Dodecanese islands, 127, 250

Doenitz, Karl, German Admiral, 614, 615

DRAGOON, code name for invasion of Southern France, to replace ANVIL, 344, 345, 346; results of, 349

Drohobycz, 374, 460n.

Dulles, Allen W., Head of the O.S.S. (Office of Strategic Services), 356n., 583

Dumbarton Oaks Conference (Sept., 1944), 427–437; statement of issues at end of, 215n., 436–437, 550

Dutch East Indies, see Netherlands East Indies

EAC, see European Advisory Commission

Eaker, Ira Clarence, U.S. General, Allied Air Commander-in-Chief in the Mediterranean, 308, 308n.

EAM (Greek Communist Rebel Group), 424, 448, 542

East Prussia, question of cession to Poland and Soviet Russia of, 26, 122, 124, 192, 222, 271, 283, 287, 297, 367, 374, 378, 382, 447, 454, 455, 460n., 484, 498, 523, 523n.

Eastern Front, situation at end of 1944 on, 478, 478n., 479; situation at time of Yalta on, 484, 498; situation after Yalta on, 561–562; strategy on, 481–482

Economic aid for Soviet reconstruction, 642–647

Eden, Anthony, British Secretary of State for Foreign Affairs, 6–7, 24, 111, 142, 143, 147, 172, 300, 635; visit to Moscow (Dec., 1941), 25–28; and British-Soviet Treaty, 26–28, 62–63, 69n.; and Soviet frontiers, 26–27, 58, 62–63, 284; question of going to Casablanca, 101–102; visit to Washington (March, 1943), 120–125, 192, 219; and ideas about United Nations, 121, 270; and prospective Soviet territorial claims, 122–124; and trusteeships, 120; and Germany, 6; and China, 121, 124; and Italian armistice terms, 161; and USSR on Italian surrender, 167–169; at Conference of Foreign Ministers at Moscow, (Oct., 1943), 186–188, 196–234; and Declaration regarding Italy, 188; and Molotov, 204; and Italian affairs, 205, and Polish affairs, 31–32, 192, 195–197; after Teheran, 287–288, 294, 519–520, 577; and Czechoslovakia, 198; and Yugoslavia, 204; and Greece, 339, 542; and Four-Nation Declaration, 207–217; signed by 207; and military matters at Moscow Conference, 211, 223–234; and Turkey, 229–231, 265; and Northern convoys,

Eden, Anthony (*continued*)
231–233; and Soviet entry into Pacific
War, 234; and Teheran Conference, 262,
271, 350n.; and Benes, 198–199, 291,
292; and de Gaulle, 314; and French
Committee of National Liberation, 267;
and unconditional surrender, 352; and the
Morganthau proposal, 371; with Churchill at Moscow (Oct., 1944), 441–443, 448,
449, 450, 451, 453, 455, 457, 465, 466,
468; and Malta Conference, 491; and
Yalta Conference, 516, 535, 545, 555;
and Yalta secret agreement on Far East,
517; and Committee on Dismemberment
of Germany, 539, 619; informed of
atomic bomb, 637n.
EDES (Greek Resistance Group), 204
Egypt, 75, 85; battle in, 97
Ehrenbourg, Ilya, Russian journalist, 167
Eisenhower, Dwight D., U.S. General, Supreme Commander Allied Expeditionary
Force in Western Europe (at SHAEF),
as Assistant Chief of Staff on strategy,
40–41, 48–49; selected as Commander-in-
Chief of Allied Forces in North Africa,
90; and cross-Channel invasion, 48–49;
and landing in North Africa, 90; and
deal with Darlan, 90–91; notes cost of
TORCH as affecting ROUNDUP, 93–94;
announces end of Tunis resistance, 126;
dealings with French in North Africa,
137n., 139; directive for invasion of Italy
to, 128–129; and Salerno (AVA-
LANCHE) landing, 158; and Italian surrender terms, 158–160, 162–166, 170;
repudiates Badoglio's postponement of
armistice, 165; broadcasts armistice accord, 165–166; authorized to sign Italian
surrender for USSR, 173, 174; receives
full power in Italy, 174; recommendations
for Italy as co-belligerents, 176; Roosevelt's directive on Italian policy to, 177–
178; letter to Badoglio on terms, 180,
180n.; urges Italy to declare war on Germany, 180, 182; and Control Commission for Italy, 178, 182–183, 186, 187;
and Ljubljana Gap project, 260n.; and
Churchill on Italian strategy, 302–303;
belief in Stalin's word at Teheran, 264;
to command OVERLORD, 264, 302, 309;
postponement of OVERLORD to June,
1944, 304, 304n.; directive about OVER-
LORD, 309; and liaison with Red Army
Staff, 312; and French affairs, 316, 318,
319, 321–322, 470, 472, 477; and ANVIL
(DRAGOON), 345, 348; commands Allied armies in France, 394; and strategy
on Western Front, 1944, 304–305, 349,
394–396, 399, 399n., 484–485, Spring,
1945, 493, 601–602, 610n.; and differences with Montgomery, Spring, 1945,

602–603; and wish to influence Germany
to surrender, 354–357; and German zones
of occupation, 363; and surrender of
German forces in Italy, 586, 588, 593,
612, 613; and German proposals to surrender, 612, 615; surrender signed
(April, 29) at Caserta, 613; at Rheims
(May, 7), 615; and Soviet operations
(Dec., 1944 and Jan., 1945), 479–481,
482–485; and strategic plans for Europe
at Malta, 491–493, 493n.; and liaison with
Soviet military authorities, 500–501; liaison with Stalin, 501, 603n., 604n.; message to Stalin on strategy, March 1945,
589–590, 603–605; difficulty with Churchill over message to Stalin, 606; and drawing back of armies on Western Front,
633–634
ELAM-ELAS (Greek Communist Resistance Groups), 204
Embick, Stanley, U.S. General, 436
Estonia, 5, 60
European Advisory Commission (EAC)
emergence of, 213, 214, 221; first formal
meeting of (Jan. 14, 1944), 360; and
Europe after the war, 275, 420, 615–616;
Stalin's complaint of leaks in, 312; and
French Committee for National Liberation, 318; and Provisional Government
of France, 471, 474; and French civil administration, 318; and Hungary, 420,
421; and Germany, 351, 354–356, 358–
365, 533; and Committee on Dismemberment of Germany, 221, 619; and Austrian
zones of occupation, 612–623, 625–626;
and Vienna's zones of occupation, 621,
622–623, 625–626

FAN, 536, 629n., as directive for Venezia
Giulia, 630
Fierlinger, Zdenek, Prime Minister of
Czechoslovakia, 569
Finland, 5, 23, 24, 27, 58, 60; air bases in,
26; Churchill critical of Stalin's demands
in, 269; Roosevelt and Eden discuss borders of, 123; and USSR, 268–269, 446–
447, 570; and unconditional surrender of,
239n., surrender terms softened, 352–354;
discussed at Teheran Conference, 265,
268–269; Soviet terms for, 268, 271; asks
for armistice, 396; U.S. breaks relations
with, 412; armistice Sept., 1944, 412, 413;
developments after armistice, 570–571;
Allied Control Commission for, 570
FIREBRAND, code name for capture of
Corsica, 177
Flynn, Edward, leader of Democratic organization in New York, 555
Foo Ping-sheung, Chinese diplomat, Four-
Nation Declaration signed by, 207
Foreign Ministers' Conference in Moscow

Harriman, W. Averell (*continued*)
visit in Moscow (Oct., 1944), 442–443,
447, 449, 450–451, 454, 456, 458n., 460,
462, 464, 466, 505, 509; and Molotov's
statement of Roosevelt's views on Polish
frontiers at Teheran, 455, 459; and
Bidault and de Gaulle, 474–476; and
Stalin's political conditions and territorial
desires, 510–511; and talks with Stalin
about Soviet operations (Dec., 1944), 478n.,
479–480, 481, March, 1945, 561, 605;
and service on Commission for Poland,
529, 572–576, 598n.; at Yalta, 255, 511,
512, 513, 516; and Far Eastern accords at
Yalta, 511–514, 515, 516n.; and UNO,
429, 433–436, 551, 551n., 552; after
Roosevelt's death requests Stalin to send
Molotov to San Francisco Conference, 576;
and surrender of German forces in Italy,
584, 586, 587, 589–590, 595–596; and
Eisenhower message to Stalin on strategy,
589–590; and report to Truman on
Hurley-Stalin talk, 639–640; and zones
of occupation for Vienna, 623; and aid
for Soviet reconstruction, 642–646; return to Moscow with Hopkins (May,
1945) of, 650
Henderson, Loy, U.S. Chargé d'Affaires in
Moscow, 91
Hepburn, A. J., U.S. Admiral, Navy member
of Sub-Committee Problems, 108
Hess, Rudolf, flight to Scotland of, 91
Himmler, Heinrich, Nazi Chief of SS, 584,
590, 612–614
Hiss, Alger, State Department official, notes
of Yalta meeting cited, 524n., 536n.
Hitler, Adolf, German Fuehrer, 3–8, 10n.,
12, 16–18, 19, 28–29, 47, 48, 57, 65, 74,
80, 95, 111, 119, 133, 175, 176, 244, 268,
310, 479, 530, 564, 594n.; rejection of
strategic plan of his generals, 25n., and
Czechoslovakia, 28; and withdrawal from
Caucasus, 100; and defection of Italy,
156–157; Italian assurances to, 154, and
Romanian negotiations, 336; movement
inside German Army to overthrow, 354,
356n.; and Kesselring, 587; final days
of, 613–614
Hoare, Sir Samuel, British Ambassador in
Madrid, 161–162
Hong Kong, 248, 496, 512, 516, 556
Hopkins, Harry, American official and diplomat, 49, 65, 69, 132, 349, 393, 442, 477,
620; in London, 11; in Moscow, 12–13,
15; idea of joint meeting at Moscow, 13–
14; urges special clause in Atlantic Charter, 21; in London with Marshall (April,
1942), 41, 49–50, 57–58, 61 (July, 1942),
42–44, 43n., 54–56, 55n.; in Casablanca,
102, 109–110, 110n.; talks with Eden
in Washington, (March, 1943), 120–125;

views on Badoglio government, 181; and
Cairo Declaration, 252; and Teheran
Conference, 257, 260n., 271, 284; and
DRAGOON, 348; and Germany, 366;
and Harriman, 405; at Malta and Yalta,
491, 537; sent by Truman to Moscow
(May, 1945), 580, 600, 620, 649–650,
654; views on Churchill policy, 650; and
aid for Soviet reconstruction, 642–644
Horthy de Nagybanya, Nicolas V., Regent
of Hungary, 419, 420, 421, 452; abdication of, 452
Hull, Cordell, U.S. Secretary of State, 7n.,
9, 19n., 143, 193; and principles in
Atlantic Charter, 20, 22, 59, 60, 62; and
Eden on Soviet frontier terms, 25, 58,
62–64; and Eden in Washington (March,
1943); on France and trusteeships, 120,
137, 137n., 314–315; on Germany, 124;
on China, 124; summarizes talks with
Litvinov, 125; not invited to Casablanca,
102; agreed on need for Roosevelt-Stalin
meeting, 132–133, 240–241; attitude
toward de Gaulle, 102, 137, 314, 321;
and Italian surrender terms, 153; and
USSR on Italian surrender, 167–169; and
MPC, 172; views on Italian affairs, 181,
329, 426; and Polish affairs, 195, 196,
283, 294, 296, 299, 299n., 375; and
Benes, 198; and pursuit of political principles, 206–217; and Foreign Ministers'
Conference at Moscow (Oct., 1943), 186–
188, 197, 204, 205, 206–222, 223–238,
267: and Declaration regarding Italy, 188;
on military strategy at, 211, 224–228, 230,
and sense of outcome of Conference, 217,
234, 237–238, and Four-Nation Declaration, 197, 207, 237–238, Declaration
signed by, 207; and Soviet entry into
Pacific War, 233–234; and French Committee for National Liberation, 314, 318–
319; and spheres of influence (separate
responsibility), 212, 339–343; and unconditional surrender, 218–220, 351–355;
and German zones of occupation, 362–
363; and German reparations, 366, 368–
373: and economic treatment of Germany
after war, 368–373; and creation of UNO,
427–429; and Stalin-Churchill talks at
Moscow (Oct., 1944), 443; and economic
aid for Soviet Union, 642
Humbert, Crown Prince of Italy (Prince of
Piedmont), transfer of powers of Italian
Throne to, 329–331, made Lieut.-General
of Realm, 330, 331
Hump, The (air route India to China, passing over Burma), 39, 129, 151, 251, 397,
401
Hungary, 121, 152, 161, 262, 337, 568–569;
and USSR, 24, 123, 311, 425, 445, 452;
proposal to invade from the South,

Hungary (*continued*)

260; Red Army nears, 419, 447; and proposed armistice for, 352–354, 420, 452, 547, 548; spheres of influence for, 349, 448, 449, 451–453, 547n.; Regent Horthy and, 419, 420, 421, 452; abdication of, 452; Control Commission for, 450, 452, 547, 547n., 548, 548n., 568; Provisional Government formed at Debrecen in, 547; armistice accepted by, 548

Hurley, Patrick J., General, Presidential representative in China, 267, 398, 408, 507, 509, 515, 639

HUSKY, code name for Sicilian campaign, *see* Sicily

Iceland, taken over by American troops, 9; and combat resources for, 40; projected meeting place for Stalin and Roosevelt, 79, 132; convoys from, 83

India, air route to China (Hump) from, 39, 129, 151, 251, 397, 401; bases in, 39; U.S. air resources to be increased in, 403

Indo-China, 19, 251, 322, 496; possible trusteeship for, 317

Inonu, Ismet, General, President of Turkey, 120, 266, 304

Iran, Harriman visit to, 87, 88; Connolly flown to, 88; discussed at Teheran Conference, 265, 266–267; declaration about, 267, 278

Ireland, 40

"Iron Curtain," phrase used by Churchill (May 12, 1945), 636

Ismay, Sir Hastings Lionel, British General, 172, 224–227, 250n., 251, 261, 594n.

Istrian Peninsula, 631; proposal to land on, 260, 260n., 261n., 344, 346, 346n., 347, 347n., 400, 422, 444, 445, 446; proposal renounced, 446; struggle for control of, Spring, 1945, 626–632

Italy, projected invasion of Sicily, 96, 114, 126–128, 134–135; and unconditional surrender, 111, 153; decision to invade, 151; armistice announced, 152, 166; surrender (armistice) terms, 151, 153–154, 157–164; and Badoglio government in, 149, 154, 159–164; and defection from Hitler, 149, 160; and secret surrender negotiations, 160–164; landing in, 152, 158, 164; surrender terms signed by, 164; Gen. Smith's letter supplementary to, 164–165; and Stalin on surrender terms, 151, 170–171, 173–174; accepted as co-belligerent, 182; Control Commission for 178, 182–183, 184, 185, 325, 328, 416, 541; Eisenhower to head Commission, 178, 183, 325; Roosevelt's directive to Eisenhower for, 177–178, 325; suggested change in

government in, 181–182; declared war on Germany (Oct. 13, 1943), 181, 182; Advisory Council for, formed at Foreign Ministers' Conference at Moscow, 185–187, 315, 325; difficulties with USSR and Italy about Council, 186–188, 326–328; Declaration regarding, made at Foreign Ministers' Conference, 187–188; King signs decree appointing son Lt.-General of Realm, 330, 331; Anzio beach landing in, 302–303; new directive for campaign in, 306–307; and Allied Control Commission renamed Allied Commission, 425; U.S. government resumes diplomatic relations with (Oct. 26, 1944), 426; Bonomi forms new government in, 330, 541; spheres of influence in, 339, 562–563; Italy-Yugoslav frontiers discussed at Yalta, 545–546; Venezia Giulia, province of, 545–546, 626–632

Japan, 18–10, 70–71; and Tripartite Pact, 1940, 18; proposed agreement between U.S. and, 18–19, 24; and strategy toward, 37–42, 129, 150, 248, 249, 251, 256; and unconditional surrender, 109, 111, 113, 639; and Cairo Declaration, 252; offensive against decided on, 129; QUADRANT (Quebec) decisions about, 150; decisions at Teheran on, 254, 256; decisions at Second Quebec Conference on, 397, 399, 400–401; question of invasion of, 400–401, 467, 502–503, 502n.; Soviet entry into Pacific war against, 117, 233–234, 254, 277, 400, 402, 441, 460–469, 503–504, 638–639; USSR and fishing rights agreement with, 403; and cession of Sakhalin Island to USSR, 254, 255, 403; plans for advance against approved at Yalta, 501–503; U.S. and war against, 636; atom bomb used against, 655

Jassy, 413

Jodl, Alfred, German General, 615; signed German surrender, 615

Johnson, Herschel, American Minister in Stockholm, 613

Johnston, Eric, American business man, 644–645

Joint Chiefs of Staff *see* U.S. Joint Chiefs of Staff

Joyce, Kenyon A., U.S. General, Deputy President and Operating Head of Control Commission for Italy, 326

Kalgan, 464, 466

Kalinin, 17

Kamchatka, as air base, 403, 463, 464

Karelia, 269, 412, *see* Viupuri

Kassel, 484, 494, 591

Katyn massacres, 192–193, 195, 376, 388

Maisky, Ivan (*continued*)
    proposal to send Bogomolov to Algiers, 142–143; recall of from London, July 1943, 167; and Czechoslovakia, 199; and Yalta, 536

Malaya, 39, 151; peninsula of, 461

Malinowski, Rodion Y., Soviet Marshal, 418, 567

Mallet, Sir Victor, British Minister in Stockholm, 613

Malta Conference (Jan. 30, 1945), preliminaries to, 490; Combined Chiefs of Staff at, 491; strategic plans for Europe at, 491–495; strategic plans for Far East at, 495–496; unconditional surrender of Germany at, 491; and Japan at, 491

Manchuria, 251, 252, 254, 408, 463, 463n., 464–466, 468, 503, 505, 510–511, 557, 639, 640

Manchurian ports, discussed at Teheran Conference, 254–255; at Yalta, 510–513; *see also* Dairen and Port Arthur

Manchurian railways, discussed at Teheran Conference, 255, 256; at Yalta Conference, 510–513

Manhattan Project, name for secret atomic weapon project, 501

Maribor, 347

Maritime Provinces of Soviet Union, 39, 70, 71, 256, 463, 464–465, 483, 495, 503, 504, 638

Marrakech, Churchill in, 291, 303

Marshall, George Catlin, General, Chief of Staff, U.S. Army, 25n., 39, 43n., 49, 251; Marshall-Stark memo to Roosevelt, 38; in London with Hopkins (April, 1942), 41, 49–50, 57–58, 61; in London with King and Hopkins (July, 1942), 43, 54–56, 55n.; Marshall-King memo, (July, 1942), 42–43; Marshall Memorandum, 49; reports to Stimson, 50; argues against North African landing, 48, 53–56; and Caucasian front, 82; and trans-Iranian railway, 88; and Second Front in 1942, 65–66; in 1943, 93, 98, 105, 128, in 1944, 134; and OVERLORD, 250n., 266, 344; Roosevelt opposes his going to England, 100; Roosevelt wishes him to go to Moscow, 101; at Casablanca, 105–113; and Churchill in Algiers, 129–131; helps Churchill redraft message to Stalin on TRIDENT, 134; and Italian surrender terms, 159; and Chinese strategy, 246–247, 250n., 495n.; and ANVIL, 311, 344–345, 348; on Eisenhower's French problem, 321; and Eisenhower (Jan., 1945), 481; at Malta and Yalta, 478n., 494, 499, 500; and atom bomb, 501–502; and surrender of German forces in Italy, 585, 589, 593; and Truman, 599, 600, 649; and strategy on Western Front, Spring,

1945, 602, 609, 610; and Venezia Giulia, 630; and Himmler surrender proposals, 614n.; and drawing back of armies on Western Front, 638

Massigli, René, French statesman, and French Committee of National Liberation, 138; and de Gaulle's going to London before D-Day, 320

Matthews, H. Freeman, State Department official, notes of Yalta meeting cited, 522n., 524n., 525n., 527n., 536n.

McIntire, Ross T., Rear Admiral, Roosevelt's physician, 242

McNarney, Joseph, U.S. General, 56

Mediterranean Council, preliminary name for Advisory Council for Italy, 185

Melitopol, 18

Michael, King of Romania, 337, 413, 414n.

Mihailovich, Draja, General, leader of Cetniks in Yugoslavia, 201–204, 332–333, 422

Miklos, Bela, Hungarian Prime Minister, 568

Mikolajczyk, Stanislaw, Prime Minister of Poland (July 14, 1943), 194; on frontiers and territorial claims, 196, 294–295, 297, 373–374, 382, 453, 454–456, 457, 523n.; and Polish government-in-exile, 283, 292, 294–295, 297–298, 377, 389–390, 454; and Benes, 291, 292; and Churchill, 294–295, 297, 377, 453–459, 519; and Roosevelt, 295, 298–300; in Washington (June, 1944), 373–374, 377, 460, 519; and Stalin, 298, 376, 382, 384, 385n., 386, 454–455, 457, 458; and Committee of National Liberation (Lublin), 377, 382, 383–384, 454, 455, 520; first journey to Moscow (July–Aug., 1944), 377, 379, 380, 382; second journey to Moscow (Oct., 1944), 453–460; and Bierut's proposals, 383–384; and General Bor, 379, 379n.; plans to reorganize government-in-exile, 389, 454, 458; discussed at Yalta, 521; resignation of, 520, 573; Warsaw regime refuses consultation with, 573, 576; acceptance of Yalta decision by, 577

Mikoyan, Anasthasias I., Soviet Commissar of Foreign Trade, 641, 643

Military coordination of Eastern and Western Fronts, 312, 402–406, 484, 562

Military Political Commission (MPC) to consult about all defeated associates of Germany, proposed by Stalin, 172, 173, 174, 182, 213, 214; organization and development of, 178, 182–184; misunderstanding with Stalin over, 184–186; postponement of meeting of, 185; discussed at Foreign Ministers' meeting in Moscow, 186–187

Model, Walther von, German Field-Marshal, 591

Molotov, Vyacheslav, People's Commissar for Foreign Affairs, 5–6, 16, 26; in London

Molotov, Vyacheslav (*continued*)

and Washington about Second Front, 51–52, 61–67, 69–71, 76; and Eden, 62–63, 125, 204; pact with Ribbentrop, 60; Molotov-Ribbentrop line for dividing Poland, 29, 29n., 286, 286n.; and frontiers, 26, 62, 67–68, and North Africa, 91–92; and Italian surrender terms, 168–171, 173; and MPC and Control Commission for Italy, 184–185, 326, 327; and Declaration regarding Italy, 188; and Czechoslovakia, 198–200, 290, 291, 569; and Polish-Soviet relations, 196–197, 200, 292, 295, 299, 301, 375, 386, 577; and Mikolajczyk, 197, 380–382, 576; at Foreign Ministers' Conference in Moscow (Oct., 1943) 186–188, 207–217, 218–223, 224–231, 233–234, 237, 267, and Four-Nation Declaration, 207–217, Declaration signed by, 207; and Germany, 5, 218, 221–222; and Northern convoys, 64, 232–233; and Soviet entry into Pacific war, 233, 403, 406; and question of attendance at Cairo Conference, 244, 245; and Teheran Conference, 253–254, 258, 258n., 262, 265, 266, 271, 275, 286; and Advisory Council for Italy, 185, 186–187; and Chinese affairs, 210–211, 408–409, 509; and Churchill-Stalin meeting at Moscow (Oct., 1944), 443, 448, 450, 451, 452, 455, 457; reference to Roosevelt on Polish frontiers at Teheran, 285, 455, 459; and Hurley and Nelson, 408; and U.S. shuttle bases, 307, 308, 308n.; and Soviet offensive toward Poland, 378; and Romania, 337, 413–416, 565–567; and Finland, 412; and Bulgaria, 418; and Hungary, 420, 421, 452, 547–548; and Allied joint planning, 402–403; and de Gaulle, 141, 476, and French civil affairs, 319, 470; as suggested substitute for Stalin at Yalta, 489; at Yalta Conference, 511–514, 523, 525, 527, 531, 536–538, 544, 547; and UNO, 552–555; and service on Commission for Poland, 529, 571, 571n., 572–577; talks with Truman (Apr., 1945), 578–579, 637; at San Francisco Conference, 574, 576, 578, 654; and Stettinius, 600; and surrender of German forces in Italy, 584–589, 605; and Allied Control Council for Vienna, 622; and Venezia Guilia, 627–628; question of misinforming Stalin, 637; and American trade policy, 642–643; and proposal for American loan, 645–647

Molotov-Ribbentrop Treaty, *see* Ribbentrop-Molotov Pact

Monnet, Jean, and French Committee of National Liberation, 138

Montgomery, Sir Bernard, British Field Marshal, 118–119, 130, 602, 604, 607, 609, 611; ideas of strategy on Western

Front, 396, 399, 399n., 484, 485, 492–494, 561, 601, 602, 614; wish to drive on to Berlin, Spring, 1945, 603; German surrender proposals to, and accepted by, 614

Moran, Lord, Churchill's doctor, 497

Morgan, Sir Frederick E., British General, 259, 319

Morganthau, Henry, Jr., U.S. Secretary of the Treasury, 366–372, 646, and aid for Soviet reconstruction, 646; proposal for economic treatment of Germany, 367, 367n., 368, 368n., 372, 533; initialed by Roosevelt and Churchill at Quebec, Sept., 1944, 369, 370; Roosevelt and Churchill retreat from, 372–373

Moscow Meeting of Foreign Ministers, *see* Foreign Ministers' Conference

Mosely, Philip, Deputy to Winant on EAC, 365n., 622

Mountbatten, Lord Louis, Commander-in-Chief, Southeast Asia Theater, 66, 496

Munich, agreement, 4; capture of, 611; after, 28, 196, 197, 239

Muraviev, Constantine, Bulgarian Prime Minister, 417; government overthrown, 418

Murmansk, 18; convoys to, 72, 82, 83, 84

Murphy, Robert D., Consul-General in Algiers and U.S. Political Adviser in North Africa, 137n., 139n., 140, 178, 180, 315, 330, 365n.

MUSKET, code name for landing on heel of Italy, 177

Mussolini, Benito, Italian dictator, 8, 148, 149, 154, 156, 157, 159, 161, 167

Naples, 175, 176

Neisse rivers, *see* Oder-Neisse

Nelson, Donald M., American official, 408, 641–642

Netherlands, The, government of, 9, 27

Netherlands East Indies, 39, 41n., 127, 151, 461, 496

Neutrality Act, 1937, decision not to invoke against USSR, 10

New Caledonia, 39, 317

New Zealand, 41

Nimitz, Chester W., U.S. Admiral, 397

Nomura, Kichisaburo, Japanese Ambassador in Washington, 9

North Africa, landing in (TORCH): proposed, 42; discussed, 44, 47–48, 51, 57; preparation for, 75, 80, 81, 85, 88; U.S.–British differences about, 47, 57, 88–90; final plan, 56, 72–73, 89–90; directive for, 90; execution of, 90, 95; results of, 93; campaign in, 105, 115–117, 137, slowing down of, 97, 114, 117; Stalin's comment on, 96; civil administration in, 137–143

Portal, Sir Charles F. A., British Air Chief Marshal, 66

Potemkin, Vladimir P., aide to Molotov, 29–30

Potsdam Conference, projected, 654

Prague, seizure of, 4, liberation of, 610, Russians enter, 611

Provisional Austrian Government, *see* Austria

Prunas, Renauo, Secretary-General of Italian Foreign Office, 327n.

Przemysl, 286, 657, 658

QUADRANT, *see* Quebec Conference, First

Quebec Conference, First (QUADRANT) Aug., 1943, 149–151, decisions on strategy at, 149–151; and Italian surrender plans, 151, 161–165, 173–174

Quebec Conference, Second, Sept., 1944, 393–402; and Germany, 356, 363; and adoption of Morganthau proposal, 369–370; and strategy for Europe, 393–396, 399–400; and strategy for Far East, 397–399, 400–401, 405; approval of plan for landing in Greece at, 425; report to Stalin on decisions at, 151, 401, 405, 425

Quincy, U.S.S., 490, 557

Rabaul, 107

Raczkiewiez, Wladislaw, President of Polish government-in-exile, 376, 380n.

Radescu, Nicolai, Romanian Premier, 564–567

Rangoon, *see* Burma

RASHNESS, code name for Chinese overland march to coast to control Canton-Hong Kong area, 495

Renner, Dr. Karl, Austrian Socialist, President Provisional Government, 623–625

Reparation Commission for Germany *see* Germany, Reparations and Commission for

Rhenish-Westphalian Province, 473, 474

Rhodes, Island of, 230, 230n., 302

Ribbentrop, Joachim von, German Foreign Minister, and meeting with Italian envoys at Tarviso, 161, 170; Molotov Pact, 30, 60, 143, 300; line for dividing Poland, 286, 286n.; visited Finland, 412

Rola-Zymierski, Michel, General, Commander-in-Chief of Polish formation in Russia, 383

Romania, 5, 23, 152, 213, 261, 311; air bases in, 26, 27; and USSR, 26, 29, 62, 336–337, 387n., 425; after-war frontiers of, 123, 336–337; and early overtures for peace; 218, 336; and Hitler, 336; and Soviet armistice terms, 337, 414, 417; and surrender terms, 337, 352–354; accepts armistice (Aug. 1944), 413, 414; signs armistice, (Sept. 1944), 415; Allied Control Commission for, 416–417, 546–547, 564–567; war declared on Germany by, 415; Radescu government in, 564–566; King of, 337, 413, 414n., 546, 564, 566–567; Groza government, 566–567; and Communist influence in, 448, 546, 564–565

Rome, campaign for, 147, 163, 164, 165, 166, 175, 260, 263, 303, 305, 306, 331; captured, 307, 309, 313, 331, 332, 344

Romer, Tadeusz, Polish Foreign Minister, 382, 457, 458n., 526

Rommel, Erwin, German General, 48, 81; retreat of, 88, 119, 148n.

Roosevelt, Franklin D., President of the United States, and aid for the Soviet Union, 7, 9–11, 15; and first Hopkins mission to Moscow, 11–12; and proposal to send supply mission to Moscow, 14; and composition of Atlantic Charter at Argentia Bay, 20–22; and early American strategic plans, 38–42; and proposed change to Pacific first strategy, 42–43; and instructions to Marshall and Hopkins for London conference (July, 1942), 43; and question of cross-Channel invasion or North Africa in 1942, 48–50, 52–57; and premature (Apr., 1942) note to Stalin about Second Front, 51–58; and remarks to Molotov about Second Front, 51, 65–66; and renewed Soviet demands for satisfaction about frontiers (March–May, 1942), 58–64; and invitation to Molotov to visit Washington (May–June, 1942), 65–66; and exposition to Molotov about international organization, 67–68; and statement to Molotov about trusteeships, 68; message to Stalin (June, 1942) about Japanese attack on Siberia, 70–71; and authorization to Harriman to accompany Churchill to Moscow (Aug. 1942), 73–74; eagerness to meet with Stalin, 79–80, and offer of British and American aid on Caucasus front, 81–82, 84, 85; termination of plans for Caucasus, 97; and suspension of Northern convoys (1942), 82–84, 85, 87; and anxiety about Soviet situation and intentions, 84–85; and development of trans-Iranian route, 87–88; and plan for TORCH, 89; and deal with Darlan, 90; and ideas about Mediterranean operations after TORCH, 96, 97; and invitation to Stalin to meet at Casablanca, 99–101; and wish not to have Hull and Eden at Casablanca, 102; and preliminary consideration of unconditional surrender policy, 108–109; and announcement of "unconditional surrender" policy at Casablanca, 109–110; and meaning he attached to unconditional surrender policy, 111–113; reports to Stalin and Chiang

Roosevelt, Franklin D. (*continued*)
Kai-shek about Casablanca decisions, 114; explanation to Stalin of delay in North African operations, 115; and attempt to satisfy Stalin's wish for a Second Front, after Casablanca, 116–117; talks with Eden (Mar., 1943) concerning permanent organization, prospective Soviet territorial claims, Poland, Germany and Far Eastern questions, 120–124; approval of strategic plans made at TRIDENT, 128–129; and change of American Ambassador in Moscow, 131; and Davies mission to Moscow (May, 1943), 131; revived wish to talk with Stalin, 131–132; message to Stalin on TRIDENT decisions, 134; and attitude towards de Gaulle (Spring, 1943), 137–140, 142; and strategic issues at QUADRANT Conference (Aug., 1943), 148–149; message to Stalin about QUADRANT decisions, 151; and formulation of terms for Italian surrender, 153, 154, 156, 157, 158, 159, 178, 179; and question of Italian King and Badoglio government, 157–158, 181–182; and announcement of Italian surrender, 165; resentment of Stalin's complaints about Italian surrender arrangements, 172, 173; and continuing wish to meet with Stalin (Autumn, 1943), 174–175; and directive to Eisenhower about presentation of armistice terms for Italy (Sept., 1943), 177–178; acceptance of Italy as co-belligerent, 182; and arrangements for control of Italy, 183–184; and evolution of thought regarding international organization, 216; reception of news of Soviet intention to enter Pacific War, 233–234; praises results of Foreign Ministers' Conference, 238; reluctance to go as far as Teheran to meet Stalin, 239–243; final assent to going to Teheran, 242–243; and plan to meet Chiang Kai-shek (at Cairo), 242–245; and discussion with Chinese at First Cairo Conference about Far Eastern military matters, 246–248; and argument with Churchill about amphibious operations south of Burma, 248–251; and the Cairo Declaration, 251–253; discussion with Stalin at Teheran about Soviet desires in Far East, 254–256; memo to Stalin about air bases in Soviet Maritime provinces, 256; memo to Stalin about advance planning for naval cooperation in the Northwest Pacific, 256; and discussions at Teheran about strategy for Europe, 258–265; decision at Teheran for cross-Channel invasion in May, 1944, 263–265; and proposal at Teheran to invade Southern France, 263–265; and discussion at Teheran of Turkish entry into

the war, 265–266; and declaration at Teheran regarding Iran, 267–268; and discussion at Teheran of exit of Finland from the war, 268–269; exposition at Teheran of ideas regarding international organization ("the Four Policemen"), 269–271; and discussion at Teheran about treatment of Germany, 272–275; and discussion at Teheran about partition of Germany, 274–275; and relations with two other Heads of State at Teheran, 276; and sense of achievement at Teheran, 276–278; and appeals for support (before Teheran) of Polish government-in-exile, 283; and discussion at Teheran of Polish frontiers and political questions, 284–287; reluctance to get involved with Soviet-Polish quarrel after Teheran, 294–295, 296, 299; message to Stalin (May, 1944) about Polish frontiers and Mikolajczyk's visit to Washington, 300–301; and consent to Anzio operation, 303; and rebuff by President Inonu of Turkey, 304; and wish for American shuttle bombing bases in Soviet Union, 307; confirmation (Apr., 1944) to Stalin of intention to carry out cross-Channel operation, 309; and wish to concert military planning with Soviet Union, 311–312; and relations before and after OVERLORD with de Gaulle and French National Committee of Liberation, 313–322; and de Gaulle's visit to Washington (July, 1944), 321–322; and further argument about King of Italy and reform of Badoglio government (early 1944), 329–331; grants Churchill lead in Greek matters, 335; and Churchill's idea of dividing responsibility for control of smaller countries of Central and Eastern Europe (Spring, 1944), 339–343; and rejection (June, 1944) of Churchill's proposals regarding Istria and Ljubljana, 346; and final support of ANVIL (July, 1944), 348; and views on interpretation of unconditional surrender policy toward Germany (Dec., 1943 to May, 1944), 350–354, 355, (Sept., 1944 to Feb., 1945), 356–357, statement at Yalta about, 357–358; and proposals for treatment of Germany approved at Second Quebec Conference (Sept., 1944), 356; first counter-suggestion for zonal division of Germany by, 360; differences with Churchill over zonal division of Germany, 361–363; agreement with British on plan of zonal division of Germany (Second Quebec Conference, Sept., 1944), 363–364; agreement with Churchill at Second Quebec Conference to effectuate Morganthau plan for treatment of Germany, 366–371; retreat from Morganthau plan, 371–373; talks with

Roosevelt, Franklin D. (*continued*)

Mikolajczyk in Washington (June, 1944), 373–374; request to Stalin to receive Mikolajczyk, 374; instruction to Harriman for presentation of Polish matters to Stalin (June, 1944), 374–375; advice to Mikolajczyk to go to see Stalin, 377; and the Polish uprising in Warsaw, 378–390; and arrangement for meeting with Churchill, Second Quebec Conference (Sept., 1944), 393–394; and crisis in Chinese military relations (Sept., 1944), 397–398; and decision to press on with all priority on the Western Front (Sept., 1944), 399–400; approval (at Second Quebec Conference, Sept., 1944) of plan to invade Japan, 400–401; and approval (at Second Quebec Conference, Sept., 1944) for next operations in the Pacific and Burma, 401; message to Stalin on decisions made at Quebec Conference, 401–402; and further attempts (March–Sept., 1944) to induce Stalin to begin joint planning for naval and air operations in the Pacific, 402–406; assurance to Stalin of wish to have Soviet Union enter Pacific war, 406; attempts (June–Aug., 1944) to secure Soviet aid for Chinese unification, 407–408; approval of Churchill's plans for Greece (Sept. 1944), 425; agreement with Churchill about developments in Italian policy, 425–426; further evolution of ideas about international organization, 429–430; and question of voting procedure at Dumbarton Oaks Conference, 432–434, 436; view of results of Dumbarton Oaks Conference, 437; relation to Churchill-Stalin meeting (Oct., 1944), 442; authorizes Harriman to accompany Churchill to Moscow, 442–443; attitude toward Churchill-Stalin accord on spheres of responsibility for Southeastern Europe, 449–451; and the question of what he had said about Polish-Soviet boundaries, 459–460; enthusiasm over Soviet operational plans against Japan (Oct., 1944), 465; informed by Harriman of Soviet political conditions for entering Pacific war (Oct., 1944), 466; and outcome of Churchill-Stalin talks, 469; and recognition of French Committee of National Liberation as provisional government of France, 469–471; on need, as viewed in November, 1944, to keep American forces in Europe after German defeat, 472; and reequipment of French army, 472; messages to Churchill and Stalin about Franco-Soviet Pact, 474–475; asks Stalin to discuss military coordination with representative of Allied headquarters in the West (Dec., 1944),

480–481; message to Stalin (Jan., 1945) about Stalin's talks with Air Marshal Tedder, 482; and discussions preceding meeting of Heads of State at Malta and Yalta, 489–491; and U.S.-British discussion of military plans at Malta, 491–496; Churchill's impression of, on arrival at Yalta, 497; and agreement at Yalta for coordination of Eastern and Western offensive, 499–500; and arrangements for consultation between military staffs, 500–501; and knowledge of atomic bomb development at time of Yalta, 501; reaffirmation at Yalta of plan to invade Japan, 502–503; reaffirmation at Yalta of wish to have Soviet Union in the Pacific war, 502–513; renewal at Yalta of request for air bases in the Maritime provinces, 504; and Harriman's report (Dec., 1944) of Stalin's statement of Soviet wishes in the Far East, 511; negotiations at Yalta with Stalin of secret accord about Soviet conditions for entering Pacific war, 505–517; and Chiang Kai-shek's wish to have him act as mediator between China and the Soviet Union, 508–509; message to Chiang Kai-shek (Nov., 1944) intimating Russian intentions, 509; and question of informing Chiang Kai-shek of secret agreement with Stalin, 515–516; and trusteeship for Korea discussed at Yalta, 518; and statement to Mikolajczyk of views on Polish issues before Yalta, 518–519; appeal to Stalin (Dec., 1944) to desist from recognizing the Lublin group as provisional government, 520–521; and discussion with Churchill and Stalin at Yalta about Polish issues—particularly frontiers and future government, 521–529; and discussion at Yalta on German zone of occupation for France, 531–532; and discussions at Yalta on German economic treatment and reparations, 533–538; and discussion at Yalta on partition of Germany, 538–539; and assent to Churchill-Stalin agreement at Yalta about Yugoslavia, 545; and discussion of UNO at Yalta, 550–556; and proposals at Yalta on UNO voting procedure, 551–554; and Soviet wish for multiple membership in UNO at Yalta, 554–555; on questions of trusteeship at Yalta, 555–556; and end of Yalta Conference, 557–558; and efforts to get satisfactory execution of Yalta agreement on Poland, 574–578; references to death of, 576, 608; correspondence with Stalin about negotiations for surrender of German forces in Italy, 589–596; last message to Stalin, 595–596; and determination till end of his life to try to work with Soviet Union, 596–599; Truman continuation of policy,

Stalin, Josef V. (*continued*)
382–384, 389–390; response to Roosevelt's proposals (March–Sept., 1944) to begin joint planning for naval and air operations in the Pacific, 402–406; query (Sept., 1944) as to U.S.-British for Soviet Union to enter Pacific war, 405–406; and Tito's visit to Moscow (Sept., 1944), 423–424; approval of Churchill's plans for Greece (Sept., 1944), 425; and question of voting procedure at Dumbarton Oaks Conference, 433, 434–435; exchange of military information with Churchill during Moscow visit, 444–447; proposes to Churchill Allied military operations in Istria headed toward Vienna, 444–445; agreement with Churchill for division of spheres of responsibility for Southeastern Europe (Oct., 1944), 447–451; agreement with Churchill to invite Mikolajczyk to Moscow again, 453; and discussions with Mikolajczyk, Polish Committee on National Liberation and Churchill (Moscow, 1944), 454–459; statement about Soviet plans to enter Pacific war (Oct., 1944), 460–462; explanation of Soviet operational plans against Japan (Oct., 1944), 462–465; explanation to Churchill of political conditions for entering Pacific war, 465–466; estimate of outcome of talks with Churchill, 468–469; and recognition of French Committee of National Liberation as provisional government of France, 469–471; agrees to de Gaulle visit to Moscow, 473; messages to Churchill and Roosevelt about de Gaulle visit, 473–474; and course of talks with de Gaulle, 473–477; and consummation of Franco-Soviet Pact, 476; explanation to Harriman (Dec., 1944) about Soviet plans for operations on Eastern Front, 479–480; informs Churchill of immediate plans for offensive (Jan., 1945), 481; talks with Air Marshal Tedder, 481–482; renews suggestion (Dec., 1944) that Allies cross Adriatic to meet Russians in Austria, 485; and discussions preceding meeting of Heads of State at Malta and Yalta, 489–491; and exposition at Yalta of situation on Eastern Front, 498; and agreement at Yalta for coordination of Eastern and Western offensives, 499–500; and arrangements for consultation between military staffs, 500–501; confirmation at Yalta of date of Soviet entry into Pacific war, 503–504; and American requests at Yalta for air bases in the Maritime provinces, 504; and statement to Harriman (Dec., 1944) of Soviet wishes in Far East, 510–511; negotiations at Yalta of secret accord about Soviet conditions for entering Pacific war,

505–517; comment to Roosevelt about situation in China, 507–508; agreement to receive Soong early in 1945, 509; and question of informing Chiang Kai-shek of secret agreement with Roosevelt, 515–516; and trusteeship for Korea discussed at Yalta, 518; rejection of Roosevelt's plea (Dec., 1944) to desist from recognizing the Lublin group as provisional government, 520–521; discussion with Churchill and Roosevelt at Yalta about Polish issues —particularly frontiers and future government, 521–529; and discussion at Yalta on German zones of occupation for France, 531–532; and discussion at Yalta on German economic treatment and reparations, 533–538; and discussion at Yalta on partition of Germany, 538–539; and interest in Greek affairs shown at Yalta, 542; and agreement at Yalta about Yugoslavian affairs, 543–545; and discussion of UNO at Yalta, 550–556; and American proposals at Yalta on UNO voting procedure, 553–554; and Soviet wish for multiple membership in UNO at Yalta, 554–555; on questions of trusteeship at Yalta, 555–556; and end of Yalta Conference, 557–558; and indifference toward Yalta accord on military consultation, 562; refusal to compromise with Churchill and Roosevelt about Poland after Yalta, 574–579; agrees to send Molotov to San Francisco Conference, 576; and use of Lublin government to administer liberated parts of Poland, 579–580; and arrest of leaders of Polish underground army, 580; and correspondence with Roosevelt and Churchill about negotiations for surrender of German forces in Italy, 589–596; and correspondence with Eisenhower (Mar., 1945) about plans for final assaults on Germany and junction between Western and Red armies, 603–606; assured of Soviet part in surrender of German forces in Italy, 612; informed by Churchill and Truman of Himmler's attempt to surrender in West, and approval of their answers, 613–614; and insistance on separate German surrender ceremonies at Moscow, 616; and renunciation of idea of partitioning Germany, 620–621; and question of zones of occupation for Vienna, 623, 626; and admission of Allied representatives to Austria, 626; and question of withdrawal of troops into occupational zones (Apr.–May, 1945), 634, 637; and expectation of depression in capitalist countries after the war, 641–644; talk with Nelson about American postwar credits, 641–642; talk with Johnston about postwar dealings with U.S., 644–645; and termination of

Truk, 107

Truman, Harry S., President of the United States, and Polish questions, 575–580; and San Francisco Conference prospects, 600, continuation of Roosevelt's policies, 599–600; meeting with Molotov, 578–579, 637; sends Hopkins to Moscow, 580, 600, 620, 649–650; and Churchill, 599–600, 609, 613, 649; and strategy on Western Front, Spring, 1945, 609, 610; and surrender negotiations on Western Front, 612–614; announces surrender, 616; arrangements for personal meeting with Churchill and Stalin, Spring, 1945, 648–649; and Austrian affairs, 625–626; and clash over Venezia Giulia, 628–632, 629n.; and drawing back of armies on Western Front, 634–637; and anxiety over prospects, Spring, 1945, 637, 649–650; and atomic bomb, 636–637; and Far Eastern affairs, 639; and Davies mission to London, 650–652

Trusteeships, International, discussed by Roosevelt and Molotov, 68; discussed by Hull and Eden (March 1943), 120, 124; discussed at Moscow (Oct. 1943), 214–215; discussed at Teheran, 274, 317; discussed at Yalta, 555–556

Tunis, 56; battle of, 91, 115, 116, 118–119

Tunisia, advance in, 91, 118–119; resistance ended in, 97n.; as a "strong point" after the war, 121

Turkey, 111, 152, 337; and entrance into the war, 96, 120, 225, 228–231, 260, 263–266, 304; asked to help hold the Aegean islands, 231, 260; discussed at Teheran, 265–266; at Cairo, 304; discussed at Churchill-Stalin meeting at Moscow (Oct., 1944), 449

Tuscaloosa, S.S., 83

Ukraine, 65, 285, 293, 293n., 430, 455, 456, 554

"Unconditional surrender," formula announced at Casablanca Conference, 108–111, 109n.; principle, 153–154, 158, 350–358; at Foreign Ministers' Conference at Moscow, 218, 220; at Teheran Conference, 273, 350, 350n., 351n.

"Union of Polish Patriots in the USSR," 192, 194, 293, 380

United Nations, Declaration of (Jan. 1, 1942), 3, 22, 23

United Nations Organization, first conception of, 21–22; discussed by Roosevelt and Molotov (1942), 68; discussed by Roosevelt and Eden (March, 1943), 121; conception at Foreign Ministers' Conference at Moscow of, 207–208, 215–216; discussed at Teheran Conference, 253, 258, 269–271, 429; plans at Dumbarton Oaks

Conference for, 427–437, 653; discussed at Yalta, 550–558, creation at San Francisco Conference of, 653–654; initial membership in: discussed at Dumbarton Oaks, 430, discussed at Yalta, 551; multiple membership, Soviet claim for: at Dumbarton Oaks, 430, at Yalta, 554–555; Security Council in: at Dumbarton Oaks, 430–431, at Yalta, 550–552; question of representation in: at Dumbarton Oaks, 430, at Yalta, 551–552; territorial trusteeships, at Yalta, 551, 555–556; voting procedure in: at Dumbarton Oaks, 431–436, at Yalta, 550–554, discussed by Churchill and Roosevelt thereafter, 434

UNRRA (United Nations Relief and Rehabilitation), 645

U.S. government, general policies, 9–19, 13; search for political principles, 19–23, 206–217; and military strategy, 37–57, 126–129, 147–148, 149–153, 225–226, 393–401, 460–468, 478–479; and spheres of influence, 212–213, 301n., 339–343, 447, 448–451; and Yalta Conference, 497–558; Declaration on Liberated Europe, 549; and Venezia Giulia, 545–546, 627–629, 632; and Austria, 223, member of Control Commission for, 621, and Vienna zones of occupation in, 621–623; and provisional Austrian government, 623–625; and Bulgaria, 417–419, 547, 567–568; and China, 245–254, 407–409, 450; and Czechoslovakia, 197–200; and Finland, 352–353, 411, 412; and France, 137–143, 315, 469–471, 477, recognition of Provisional Government of, by, 315, 426n.; and Germany, 220–222, dismemberment of, 124, 126, 174, 221–223, 274–275, 359, zones of occupation in, 318, 340, 360–365, 620–621, reparations, 359, 365–373; and Great Britain concerning Atlantic Charter, 25, difference over strategy on Western Front, Spring, 1945, 600, 601–612; and Greece, 424; and Hungary, 420, 568–569; and Italy, attitude toward, 147–148, 153, 156–159, 161, 181–182, 328–330, 425–426, resumes diplomatic relations with, 426, at Yalta, 541; and Japan, 18–19, 38; and The Netherlands, 18, 41n.; and Poland, 30–34, 195, 390, 519, 525–526, 572–573; and Romania, 336–337, 415–417, 547, 565–567; and USSR about Italy, 326–328, about Poland, 572–580; after Yalta, suspicions and policies, 562–563; and question of reassurance about Yalta agreement on Far East, 640–641, and economic aid for Soviet reconstruction, 401, 642–647

U.S. Joint Chiefs of Staff, 38, 39, 41, 42, 44, 44n., 49, 54, 93, 99–100; ideas of strategy after TORCH of, 96–98, at Casablanca

PART II. PRINTED SOURCES CITED

Ageton, Arthur A., with William H. Standley, *Admiral Ambassador to Russia,* 135 n.

Alexander, Sir Harold, *Report on Campaign in Italy,* 592n.

Anders, Wladyslaw, *An Army in Exile,* 380n.

Badoglio, Pietro, *Italy in the Second World War,* 180n., 326n., 327n., 328n.

Benes, Eduard, *Memoirs of Dr. Eduard Benes,* 200n., 290n., 291n.

Bonnet, Georges, *Defense de la Paix:* II, Fin d'une Europe, 29n.

Bor-Komorowski, Tadeusz, *The Secret Army,* 379n., 380n., 381n.

Bradley, Omar N., *A Soldier's Story,* 602n., 608n.

Bryant, Arthur, *The Turn of the Tide 1939–1943,* 50n., 55n., 94n., 147n.

Bundy, McGeorge, and Henry L. Stimson, *On Active Service in Peace and War,* 150n., 251n., 321n., 368n., 369n.

Butcher, Harry Cecil, *My Three Years with Eisenhower,* 130n., 149n.

Churchill, Winston S., *Closing the Ring,* 130n., 139n., 147n., 152n., 156n., 157n., 158n., 159n., 169n., 170n., 175n., 184n., 202n., 203n., 205n., 222n., 228n., 229n., 230n., 232n., 242n., 245n., 248n., 249n., 251n., 261n., 262n., 263n., 266n., 270n., 273n., 278n., 284n., 286n., 288n., 291n., 302n., 306n., 307n., 314n., 320n., 329n., 330n., 332n., 333n., 335n., 339n.

———, *The Grand Alliance,* 6n., 7n., 8n., 15n., 21n., 27n., 32n., 38n., 39n., 47n., 48n., 58n.

———, *The Hinge of Fate,* 43n., 51n., 52n., 54n., 64n., 69n., 72n., 73n., 74n., 75n., 76n., 77n., 81n., 83n., 84n., 85n., 86n., 90n., 93n., 96n., 97n., 99n., 100n., 111n., 114n., 115n., 116n., 118n., 120n., 126n., 129n., 130n., 131n., 134n., 211n., 351n.

——— *Onward to Victory,* Speeches of the Right Honorable Winston S. Churchill, 113n.

———, *Triumph and Tragedy,* 261n., 310n., 340n., 341n., 342n., 346n., 361n., 363n., 371n., 373n., 387n., 388n., 389n., 396n., 399n., 400n., 422n., 437n., 441n., 442n., 444n., 446n., 448n., 449n., 450n., 456n., 458n., 459n., 461n., 467n., 468n., 469n., 471n., 481n., 490n., 516n., 517n., 523n., 528n., 529n., 540n., 541n., 553n., 557n., 564n., 565n., 572n., 574n., 577n., 579n., 580n., 588n., 592n., 593n., 594n., 596n., 602n., 606n., 607n., 609n., 611n., 613n., 614n., 619n., 628n., 631n., 648n., 650n., 651n., 653n.

———, *The Unrelenting Struggle,* 23n., 24n.

Clark, Mark, *Calculated Risk,* 303n., 345n.

Clay, Lucius D., *Decision in Germany,* 365n.

Cline, Ray S., *Washington Command Post:* The Operations Division, 401n.

Clissold, Stephen, *Whirlwind,* An Account of Marshal Tito's Rise to Power, 422n.

Craven, W. F. and Cate, J. L., *The Army Air Forces in World War II,* Vol. II, 44 n.

Deane, John R., *The Strange Alliance,* 638n.

Dedijer, Vladimir, *Tito,* 422n.

De Gaulle, Charles, *The Call to Honour,* 140n., 141

Dulles, Allen, *Germany's Underground,* 356n.

Standley, William H., and Arthur A. Ageton, *Admiral Ambassador to Russia*, 135n.

State Department Bulletin, Nov. 21, 1942, Statement by President on North and West Africa, 90n.

Stettinius, Edward R., Jr., *Lend-Lease Weapon for Victory*, 78n.

———, *Roosevelt and the Russians*, 517n.

Stimson, Henry L., and McGeorge Bundy, *On Active Service in Peace and War*, 150n., 251n., 321n., 368n., 369n.

Sworakowski, W., article in *Journal of Central European Affairs*, April, 1944, 658

Times (London), Jan. 27, 1942, 111n.

Times (New York), June 25, 1941, 10n.; Jan. 27, 1942, 111n.

Truman, Harry S., *Year of Decisions*, 578n., 579n., 611n., 613n., 614n., 628n., 629n., 634n., 651n., 652n., 653n.

USSR, Embassy in Washington of, *Information Bulletin*, 70n.

Watson, Mark S., *Chief of Staff: Pre-War Plans and Preparations*, 15n., 37n.

Welles, Sumner, *Seven Decisions that Shaped History*, 60n.

Whitehill, W. M., and Ernest J. King, *Fleet Admiral King*, 107n.

Wilmot, Chester, *The Struggle for Europe*, 356n., 478n., 479n.

Wilson, Sir Henry Maitland, *Eight Years Overseas*, 347n., 418n., 423n.

Yalta Documents, 364n., 369n., 442n., 443n., 468n., 472n., 477n., 478n., 491n., 494n., 495n., 496n., 501n., 503n., 508n., 511n., 512n., 515n., 516n., 522n., 523n., 524n., 525n., 527n., 532n., 536n., 537n., 543n., 551n., 553n., 603n.